Interactive
Programming
Environments

Interactive Programming Environments

EDITORS

David R. Barstow

Schlumberger-Doll Research
Ridgefield, Connecticut

Howard E. Shrobe

Massachusetts Institute of Technology
Cambridge, Massachusetts

Erik Sandewall

Linköping University
Linköping, Sweden

McGRAW-HILL BOOK COMPANY

New York   St. Louis   San Francisco   Auckland   Bogotá
Hamburg   Johannesburg   London   Madrid   Mexico
Montreal   New Delhi   Panama   Paris   São Paulo
Singapore   Sydney   Tokyo   Toronto

Library of Congress Cataloging in Publication Data
Main entry under title:

Interactive programming environments.

Includes index.
1. Electronic digital computers—Programming.
I. Barstow, David R.   II. Shrobe, Howard E.
III. Sandewall, Erik.
QA76.6.I525   1984   001.64'2   83-13572
ISBN 0-07-003885-6

34567890   KGP/KGP   898765

ISBN 0-07-003885-6

*The editors for this book were Stephen G. Guty and Margaret Lamb,
the designer was Naomi Auerbach, and the production supervisor
was Thomas G. Kowalczyk. It was set in Century Schoolbook
by Waldman Graphics.*

Printed and bound by The Kingsport Press.

Contents

v

26. Rationale for Stoneman   535

John N. Buxton
University of Warwick
Coventry, England

Larry E. Druffel
Defense Advanced Research Projects Agency
Arlington, Virginia

27. The Spice Project   546

Scott E. Fahlman, Samuel P. Harbison
Carnegie-Mellon University
Pittsburgh, Pennsylvania

28. From Interactive to Intelligent Programming Environments   558

David R. Barstow
Schlumberger-Doll Research
Ridgefield, Connecticut

Howard E. Shrobe
Massachusetts Institute of Technology
Cambridge, Massachusetts

Preface

One of the more important advances in computer science has been the development of software tools to assist in the programming process itself. The earliest tools were text editors and compilers. Later, interactive environments including interpreters and debuggers were developed. Recently, these interactive environments have been expanded to include tools like editors that are sensitive to the syntax of the language, special printing programs that reformat a program to increase readability, and file systems that coordinate all the files that make up a single program. Currently, tools and environments which exploit the high-resolution graphics capabilities of personal workstations are being developed. The more elaborate sets of tools are generally referred to as "programming environments," and are viewed by some as the next major step in software engineering, following the advances made by high-level programming languages and by programming methodologies. Unfortunately, the term "programming environments" has different meanings for different people, often corresponding to different conceptions about the programming process. Perhaps the best definition is simply "computer-aided design systems for software."

In this book we have chosen to focus primarily on *interactive* programming environments. We have chosen this focus because of the rapidly increasing importance of interactivity in programming environments (as well as in other forms of computer usage). Interactive programming environments can be generally characterized by four observations. First, within a unified framework, they provide a large set of tools, most of which are specific to a particular programming language. Second, they take advantage of the fact that programs have an underlying structure that is more than a string of characters, using this structure as an organizational tool. Third, they support incremental program development, in both the design and maintenance activities. Finally, they are highly interactive in nature, promoting and exploiting a fairly high bandwidth of communication between the user and the environment.

Interactive programming environments are related to several traditional areas of computer science: *software engineering,* since well-designed environments could have a major impact on software development and since it is important to consider the entire software development process when designing an environment; *programming languages,* since many parts of an environment are language-specific and interactive environments will have a major impact on future programming languages; and *artificial intelligence,* since some of the most innovative programming environments have been built in artificial intelligence centers and since future programming environments are certain to have "intelligent tools" of some kind. The papers collected together in this book reflect this diversity. In selecting these papers we have tried to cover the major technical developments of the last decade. We could not, of course, include every paper on the subject nor could we cover every topic. We have no doubt overlooked some papers or topics that should have been included. We hope, however, that the set is sufficiently broad and representative in its coverage to be useful both to those learning about interactive programming environments and to those designing future environments.

We have divided the papers into five sections. The first section includes papers which describe the motivations and characteristics of interactive programming. The second section includes papers dealing with specific environments for particular languages and situations. The third section is concerned with specific issues which arise in many different environments. The fourth section includes descriptions of experimental systems which test the role of artificial intelligence in interactive programming environments. The final section includes papers concerned with the future of interactive programming environments.

In addition to the reference lists for each paper, a comprehensive reference list is included at the end of the book. Citations within the papers have been changed to refer to the comprehensive list. In a few cases, this has resulted in unusual citations (e.g., a reference to [1978b] when no [1978a] is included in the paper's reference list). We trust that the value of the comprehensive list outweighs the few inconveniences which occur as the result of it.

The development of programming environments is inherently experimental: it is impossible to design an environment from scratch and get it right. We hope that this book presents a clear picture of the experiments performed in the 1970s, so that future interactive programming environments may benefit from these experiences.

David R. Barstow
Howard E. Shrobe
Erik Sandewall

Interactive
Programming
Environments

Perspectives on Interactive Programming Environments

This section includes three papers describing some motivations for and some observations about interactive programming environments. Winograd's paper, written before there had been widespread use of interactive programming environments, was quite prophetic. He cited the now more widely recognized problem of complexity in large software systems and suggested that the barrier could best be broken by building large programming support systems, what we now call programming environments. Among the characteristics he felt would be important are:

- Since such systems may require the user to do some extra work (e.g., describe the motivation for some decision), the systems must also do a great deal for the user; the user must feel that his/her efforts are worth it in the end.
- Such systems should be coherent and integrated; systems consisting simply of several tools pasted together would prove insufficient.
- Such systems should be capable of maintaining higher level descriptions of the program; simply remembering the program at the code level is insufficient.
- Such systems would need to "know" a great deal of specific knowledge about the process of programming.

The first characteristic is a clear warning about the importance of keeping the ultimate user in mind. The second and third are themes which will be repeated throughout this volume. The final characteristic is one that has not yet been realized; the papers in the section of the book about artificial intelligence address this problem, but such work has not proceeded beyond the research stage.

Sheil focuses on a programming methodology which he calls "exploratory programming." The central points of his discussion are:

- Many computer applications are not well enough understood to permit complete software specification. Exploratory programming is appropriate in those cases because it leads to more flexible designs than can be achieved through conventional programming methodologies.

- Interactive programming environments for building "real" programs through exploratory programming must include tools for both contracting the code and for monitoring its performance.

- Personal workstations, with their high-resolution displays, permit very powerful programming environments in support of exploratory programming.

The first point is especially important, since such applications are becoming increasingly common. Since these applications are (obviously) intended for real users, the second point must be kept in mind during the development process. Finally, the third point addresses what is probably the single most important influence on interactive programming environments today—the relatively inexpensive availablility of personal workstations which provide both significant computing power and alternative styles of interaction.

Sandewall draws on his experiences with two particular programming environments (INTERLISP and MACLISP) to make observations not only about those two environments but also about the characteristics which are important outside the LISP context. In the process he makes several observations:

- When considering different implementation languages for software systems, it is important to consider the complete programming environment as an interactive system, rather than just the language itself.

- The traditional paradigm of the "edit, compile, run" cycle is based on certain divisions of activities (e.g., parsing, code generation) which may be inappropriate in an interactive programming environment.

- An important feature of several advanced programming environments is that they provide a multitude of "hooks" for the user, ways that the user may insert his/her own code to affect behavior of the system.

- This feature is valuable in a programming methodology which he calls "structured growth". It involves first solving a simplified version of the problem and then repeatedly expanding its capabilities.

The first observation is one of the underlying motivations for this book. The second is another theme which is repeated frequently throughout the book. The third and fourth are also characteristic of many of the efforts discussed in this book, but they are rarely stated explicitly.

Thus, these three papers set the stage for the experiences which will be described in the rest of the book.

1 Breaking the Complexity Barrier (Again)

TERRY WINOGRAD

Stanford University
Stanford, Caliornia

This paper does not describe an existing programming system. It is intended to bring together a bunch of ideas about what future programming systems might be like, and what it is necessary to do if we want to build them. Most of the stuff in it is based on ideas which come from a variety of sources—in fact from almost any computer system you know of. In particular, a lot of them are embedded in LISP (INTERLISP and MACLISP in particular), DDT, MULTICS, LOGO, ITS, PLANNER, CONNIVER, Hewitt's work on intentions and actors, Goldstein's work on program understanding, and various LISP facilities like LISP LOGO and GRIND, Sussman's HACKER, Winston's INDEX program, Teitelman's DWIM and CLISP, and many many others. I am aware that many similar facilities exist in a number of other programming environments, but for this paper, I will refer to those with which I am most familiar. The bibliography contains references to many of them, mostly at the Artificial Intelligence Lab at M.I.T. It is not necessary to understand details of these facilities in order to get the basic thrust of the paper. What is important is the basic ideas they represent. I will not attempt to credit them properly, instead concentrating on putting them together. It is pleasing to think that ideas which are so much "in the air" must be at least headed in the right direction.

1. WHY?

1.1   The Complexity Barrier

A number of people have suggested to me that large programs like the SHRDLU program for understanding natural language [Winograd 1972] represent a kind of dead end in AI programming. Complex interactions between its components give the program much of its power, but at the same time they present a formidable obstacle to understanding and extending it. In order to grasp any part, it is necessary to understand how it fits with other parts, and even with a fair quantity of comments, the code presents a dense mass, with no easy footholds. Even having written the program, I find it near the limit of what I can keep in mind at once. After being away from it for a few months, it is quite difficult to answer questions about specific parts of it, or to anticipate the effects of suggested changes. The problem of complexity is of course not unique to AI. Other programs, such as large operating systems, face many of the same sorts of difficulties.

There are two basic lines of attack suggested for dealing with complexity. The first aims for uniformity of knowledge and strong modularity. The complexity must be controlled, the argument goes, by finding a few simple uniform ways of representing the knowledge. These should be handled by automatic procedures which are not directly controlled by the programmer, and the complexities will be handled automatically by a kind of "symbol crunching" power. In the area of natural language, the obvious candidates for such representation are context free grammars and logical notations like the predicate calculus. There are various ways of showing that, perhaps with a few special tricks, all of the facts can be represented in such a way. The question of efficiency is to be tackled abstractly through better parsers and theorem provers. The clarity of such an approach comes from two kinds of separatism—the process is divided into separate phases, such as parsing, semantic analysis, and deduction, on the assumption that interactions between them can be handled in a standard limited way. In addition, there is a kind of independence of the pieces of knowledge, in which one axiom or rule can be understood, modified, or added in a way which is more or less independent of just how it will be fit in with the others. To the degree this is successful, it is of great benefit in being able to understand and work with the program, since such a program really is in some meaningful sense no more than the linear sum of its small parts.

The second basic reaction to growing complexity is a more mystical hope that programs can somehow learn things we do not know how to tell them. The dream is that we can start with a minimum of structure, then provide masses of data and expect the program to build its own complexities. The plans are usually vague, but seem to depend on the same kind of assumption of local independence described above. The facts are in a way like a large, generally unstructured table, and all that is necessary for handling wide areas (such as a natural language) is to have enough entries. In the learning approach it is assumed that these can be added automatically, so the programmer does not have the burden of worrying about all the specific knowledge the program must have.

I agree that both of these lines would be desirable *if they would work*. However, there is no reason to assume that things are simple in the ways we would like them to be. Neither knowledge of human neurophysiology, nor experience in fields like linguistics, gives hope that the human mind is based on such neat principles. Clearly a person learns from experience, and a truly intelligent program must be able to do the same. This does not imply that learning happens through a simple process of adding axioms or productions to a stock, or that the bootstrapping begins with a particularly straightforward and transparent device. Learning is a complex process of integrating new knowledge into a structure of what is already known—a kind of debugging. The ultimate goal of writing learning programs can only be achieved through first having an understanding of the structures which must be built and changed, and the ways in which they interact.

Our immediate problem, then, is to find some way of breaking the "complexity barrier". We must be able to write and understand programs an order of magnitude larger than the ones now existing, without straitjacketing them into rigid, inadequate formalisms. Anyone acquainted with the history of computing will see this as an old familiar problem, which has been solved in many forms before. Symbolic assemblers, higher level languages, and symbol-manipulation languages have each in turn pushed back the barrier. Schoolchildren today write LOGO programs which perform functions more complex than the efforts of the finest programmers working with the early computer systems. I believe the time is ripe for another major step in this progression. I do not believe it will come directly from such ideas as backtracking and multiple process capabilities such as those being built into "new languages" such as PLANNER, CONNIVER, QA4, LISP70, etc. [Hewitt 1972] [McDermott and Sussman 1972]. Although these provide additional sorts of power, they often make programs even more difficult to understand. I also do not think that the concepts of structured programming are sufficient. Careful attention to abstractions of structure and local modularity will be an important ingredient of any system, but like the more advanced control structures, they are only one ingredient.

The key to future programming lies in *systems which understand what they are doing.* Just as SHRDLU has a model of the BLOCKS world, our new system (let's call it **A** for the time being) must be based on an explicit model of the programming world. It must have concepts for all of the basic ideas used in programming—the knowledge that turns an intelligent person into a competent programmer. Onto this it must be able to add a detailed model of each program that is written in it. If our application program works with "description nets" or "object semantic structures" the model must have information about how such objects are created, changed, and used, what kinds of things they contain, what properties can be expected of them, and what role they play in the general structure of the program.

A must be built around a general reasoning system more powerful than those of existing problem solvers, and must be able to make use of deductions to help with every phase of the programming process. We can think of it as a kind of assistant, and the model should allow us to express to it any comment which we would make in explaining the program to another person. It must be highly incremental, not insisting on "full information" but accepting new information as it is given, and integrating it into the already existing model.

A is not meant to be an "automatic programmer" which knows enough to write programs from general specifications, to learn how to program, or to understand programs from their code. These represent a more advanced level of development, which will share many of its capabilities. Neither is it a program checker, which guarantees the correctness of programs we write, or an efficiency expert which improves the code. We can better think of it as a moderately stupid assistant, to whom we give all the information we possibly can, and who in turn relieves us of much of the burden of memory, tedious checking, and drawing more-or-less straightforward conclusions.

1.2 Four Ways of Helping

It will probably not be obvious just what things **A** might do would be most useful, until people begin working with such a system. In this section we will look at some obvious examples.

1.2.1 Error checking A vast number of the errors in any program (particularly one by a sloppy programmer like me) do not represent interesting conceptual problems. They are misspelled words, mischosen variables, wrong arguments to a function, and a plethora of other minor annoying lapses. A moderately stupid assistant watching carefully over my shoulder could pick up almost all of them, saying things like "Didn't you want to add that item to the new list, not the old one?" Current systems do a lot of this sort of checking at a syntactic level. Compilers catch errors like the wrong number (or types) of arguments, and systems like INTERLISP try to catch misspellings and correct them on the basis of local context. By using the semantic model of the program, **A** could catch these plus many others before the program is ever run.

1.2.2 Question answering One of the hardest parts of programming is trying to understand the effects of a change. If I am about to change a subroutine, I must have answers to questions like "Who calls this?", "What sorts of arguments will it get?" (note that this is semantic—it may be obvious from its syntax that it gets a list, but I need to know whether it will be a list of semantic markers, or English words, or data-base assertions or...) "Is it ever called with a negative argument?" "Do any of the things it calls make use of the global variable TIME?", etc. etc. etc.

The answers to many such questions are straightforward and contained in a good cross-reference listing like those done by the MACLISP INDEX program [McDonald 1974].To be useful in a large program, this information must be available in a form where questions can be asked interactively, and can be answered on the basis of simple deductions. The addition of a semantic model of the program (what this function is supposed to do, what this variable is being used for...) allows new levels of information to be available, at a level of abstraction far removed from the mechanics of calling functions and accessing variables.

The question answering doesn't have to be in English (although that would be a pretty kind of bootstrapping if the system were used for natural language understanding programs). The internal model should be natural and straightforward enough that the questions can be formulated directly within its formalisms, just as Charniak's story understander [Charniak 1972] uses a semantic representation instead of English as its input.

A will be building up a model of the program as it is being written, so questions from the user can be important in the initial creation of a program, as well as the later stages of debugging and modification. This question-answering ability is one of the basic keys to answering the question "How can anyone but the author ever understand and modify a big program?"

1.2.3 Trivia Often, a programmer really doesn't want to bother knowing the answer to a question. If he has a variable named ITEM which is to be added to LIST, he must worry about whether ITEM is the item itself, or a singleton list containing the item, and whether the list is ordered, or does not contain duplicate items, etc. Rather than asking for all this information, he would rather say to his moderately stupid assistant, "Write the appropriate call to add ITEM to LIST." The assistant could do the checking, and decide whether to use a CONS, APPEND, MERGE, or whatever. Note again that he needs more than syntactic information. He must work with a model which describes how the list is created, how it will be used, what types of items are reasonable to find in it.

Clearly we can expect this much of **A**. We can write (ADD ITEM to LIST), and let the system expand it. Here again many of the ideas are already around. Structured programs which contain loops in terms of UNTIL and FOREACH are expanded into sets of instructions with the necessary tests and jumps. Symbolic access functions can be compiled or macro-expanded into particular data structure accessing functions suited to the occasion. Here also, the addition of knowledge about what things are for, and what conditions they can be expected to meet, opens possibilities for a much wider range of such structured constructions, which remove a tremendous load of trivia from the programmer's mind.

1.2.4 Debugging A really intelligent assistant would go ahead and debug programs for us once we had sketched them out. Maybe someday that will be a reality, but even our moderately stupid assistant can be of great help, as long as he is also patient. It would often be tremendously useful to ask "Which subroutine set that variable to NIL?" when the resulting error comes up later in the processing. A patient moderately stupid assistant could simply turn on a complete trace of all subroutines, checking the value of the variable before and after each call. **A** could easily do this and much more. We will go into this more fully in Part 2. It is in debugging that capabilities such as backtracking and multiple procedures will be necessary. We can start one program running, while starting another which watches it, and can back it up if necessary to look for trouble sources. Many systems (most LISPs for example) have a variety of interactive debugging features—traces, breakpoints, error interrupts, stack examiners—and some like INTERLISP have backtracking features specfically for debugging. The next step must be to put these under the control of a program with deductive capacity, and access to a detailed model of the program being run.

1.3 What For?

My interest in building **A** is primarily to continue research in artificial intelligence. As we try to deal with larger areas of human knowledge and competence, it will be absolutely vital to have tools for handling the kinds of size and complexity which naturally arise. However, I think it is wrong to see this as a specifically AI problem. Practical programs, such as those for algebraic manipulation and automatic programming clearly face all of the same problems, and need new power just as badly. But many AI techniques (like list processing) have found their way into the most mundane byways of programming, and there is no reason that the same would not happen for the kind of ideas represented in **A**.

It is not unrealistic to foresee the costs of computation and memory plummeting by orders of magnitude, while the cost of human programmers increases. It will be cost effective to use large systems like **A** for every kind of programming, as long as they can provide significant increases in programmer power. Just as compilers have found their way into every application over the past twenty years, intelligent program-understanding systems may become a part of every reasonable computational environment in the next twenty.

An interesting question is raised by the prospect of such systems being used in writing the complex programs which will play an ever-increasing role in our society. Many observers ([Weizenbaum 1972] is a good example) have noted the dangers of having programs which are so large and complex that they cannot be understood even by their programmers, while at the same time they are so vital to continued functioning of our society that we cannot afford to mistrust them. This paper proposes the idea of building programs around a problem-solving system which has an extended model of the program at many levels of abstraction. It knows just what each part is for, how it works, how it is used. This knowledge is organized in a form which can be communicated and explained to a human user. Interacting with such a model may allow a kind of understanding which keeps us from reaching the point where it is impossible to question, change, or disagree with our programs. Earlier, I raised the question of whether we can count on "self-organizing" systems to learn any complex aspect of behavior. Even if they could, it may well be a wise decision to work instead towards programs organized around concepts and abstractions which we have explicitly constructed. At least then we can always expect our computers to tell us what they are thinking.

2. WHAT

This section explores what our imaginary **A** might be like to use in programming. It will concentrate on a user's point of view, leaving separable questions of implementation for Section 3.

2.1 The Form of the System

First, it is important to realize why **A** is a system, not a language. To achieve the goals outlined in Part 1, it must combine the powers of a compiler, an interpreter, an editor, a debugging system, a documentation system, and a problem-solver. To interact properly, these must form a single closely integrated system, not a collection of independent facilities. The user can intermix writing a program, editing it, running pieces of it, asking questions about it, stating new information, increasing the store of abstract concepts for describing it, and debugging, all without switching between systems, writing and loading files, and the rest of the mechanics that usually go with working on a program. All of the parts must communicate with each other—information in the model is vital to the compiler and debugger; the editor must recognize when changes call for modifications to the model; the debugger must know a lot about the exact forms used by the compiler and interpreter; and so on throughout the system.

A user sits down and begins writing a program by first giving general information about its organization. He should give the same type of information about program structures, data structures, and purposes as he would give to a human assistant who asked "OK, what is basically going into this program?" The system must be reactive, asking for information which is vital, but not trying to fill out some large amount of information by bothering the user with too many questions. **A** should be highly incremental, asking for knowledge when it is actually needed, and accepting bits and pieces in any order. It must also be able to make reasonable assumptions about many aspects of the program which are not explicitly specified.

Following the initial description, the user could begin entering the program, with **A** "watching over his shoulder". An example of what **A** would be doing is the cross-referencing of functions. If we type a call to a function FROG with a single argument, and no such subroutine exists, **A** should note that it needs to be written, and not bother asking any questions. If further on we create a call to FROG with two arguments, **A** might query which was intended (being ready to accept the fact that FROG has a variable number of arguments). By using the semantic information in the model, arguments should be checked to see if they are of the same semantic type. On request, **A** would type out a list of "subroutines called but not yet defined", and could answer questions about where and how they had been used. If the code calling one of them was run before the subroutine was defined, the error system would stop and describe the situation, letting the user define it or put in some kind of a dummy function (which would be labelled as such in the model).

Any programmer familiar with highly interactive systems can picture the process which follows. Pieces of the program are entered, run, debugged, and edited in succession. The important difference is that much of the interaction will be in providing and requesting declarative information about what is there, what is to be done, and what is going on.

2.2   The Form of Programs

So far, we have talked a lot about writing programs in **A**, without mentioning what language they will be written in. In fact it isn't at all critical to the ideas involved. The language could look something very much like LISP, ALGOL, PL1 or whatever you prefer. The critical element is that the code be in machine manipulable form, and that the system have a careful conceptual model of just what forms the language uses, and what its constructs do. Since I am most familiar with LISP, I will use a LISP-like format, but the reader can easily perform a mental translation to DO's or BEGIN and END's or numbered lines, or whatever seems comfortable. In giving examples of a specific program, I will use things from SHRDLU, but again this is only as an example.

The critical elements of programs written with **A** will include their comments, structuring, and semantic-oriented data structure use.

2.2.1   Comments   The key to the whole approach of **A** is that the system must know as much about what the program is trying to do as would a human assistant. This is not the same as the approach taken in program verification—the programmer does not have to be able to give airtight logical statements about just what conditions should be true at each point in the code. Instead, he should be able to state a variety of information at different levels of abstraction. He should be able to attach a comment to any "chunk" of the program, whether it be a subroutine, a function call, a block, or even a specific access of a single variable.

2.2.1.1.   Types of comments   As examples of comments we might use, let us take conditions, assertions, purposes, and English.

1. *Conditions.*   Conditions are akin to intentions [Hewitt 1972] and the logical statements of program verifiers. They fall into two obvious categories—preconditions and postconditions. A precondition is a statement which should be true before the chunk is done, a postcondition afterwards. They might be things like "The list should be empty here.", "X should be a syntactic node whose feature list contains no time reference." These conditions are not executed as a matter of course when the program is run, but are used for compiling and debugging purposes. They can be monitored and take part in deductions designed to figure out what is going on when the program is running, or to make decisions about how to compile some segment of code.

2. *Assertions.*   Assertions are statements associated with a piece of code,

stating things like "This structure is now completed." or "Do not clobber this data structure internally while using it as an argument." or "At least one syntax node should eventually point to the same place in the sentence as this one." They are not things which can be checked at the point in the program when the corresponding code is run, but rather are statements which will be used by deductions elsewhere (for example in other condition comments). In debugging, they are asserted as the program passes them (in some sort of context structure). We can assert things which are to be true during the running of the chunk, and things which will be true afterwards. In a way, the declaration statements of ordinary computer languages are akin to these assertions. However, **A** must accept a much wider range of information.

3. *Purposes*. Purposes provide an abstract description of what pieces of the program are doing. For example, "This part checks for cases in which the sentence contains a particle separated from the verb." or "This function converts the semantic relation list into an equivalent piece of PLANNER code." To make such statements into explicit testable conditions would involve reduplicating their entire contents. These comments are vital to question answering. In answer to "What was the program doing when it bombed out?" or "What part uses the function FROG?" an answer like "the part which converts relations to PLANNER code" is a much better answer than "the function ELEPHANT." As higher level problem solving processes are added to the compiler and debugger, these comments can allow **A** to take higher and higher level descriptions of what the code should do, and convert them directly into programs.

4. *English*. All of the comments in the other 3 categories have been stated here in English to make them understandable to the reader. In fact, they would be in a semantic language looking more like:

```
(CONDITION (NOT (EMPTY X)))
(ASSERTION (COMPLETE X SEMANTIC-STRUCTURE))
(PURPOSE (CONVERT (RELATIONS NODE) (PLANNERCODE NODE)))
```

The need to clearly delineate the set of concepts used in the program should be an aid to writing clear and well-organized programs. In addition, there will always be a residue of things we want to say about the program, which cannot be stated within the constraints of the model. These can be tacked on in ordinary English, to be used by human readers of the program. Of course, in the ultimate **A**, all of the comments could be in English, and the language-understander would analyze them and convert them into the appropriate internal forms when possible.

2.2.1.2 How do they get there?   Readers familiar with real programmers will already have made a mental note that the system will never work, since programmers are notoriously bad at actually including comments. The obvious reason for such laziness is that nothing is immediately gained by putting them in. In the course of writing a moderate size program, it is easier to remember things than write them down, and it is not very compelling to think about other people who may work with the program later. If the system really makes use of the comments in a helpful way, intelligent users will quickly be conditioned to put in more and more information. There is a threshold effect—unless the program does a lot of useful things with comments, they will never get put in, so it won't even be able to do a few useful things. This is an important reason for thinking of **A** as an integrated system, not a bunch of ideas which can be added piecemeal to existing systems.

Many comments can be entered by **A**. For example, when it first sees a call to a new function, it can annotate the function according to the arguments it was given (e.g. FROG takes a semantic marker list), and information about the environment in which it was called. It needs to remember which comments are annotations, since violation of a user-supplied comment calls for interaction, while violation of an annotation might simply cause an assumption to be dropped (e.g. FROG really takes any list of atoms). The most obvious set of annotations is the cross-referencing of the use of functions and free variables. Such a listing not only supplies answers to user questions, but allows the editor and compiler to be smart about changes. If a function is edited to take different arguments, the compiler can use the information to find all of the previous calls and change them. If a new assertion is made about what some variable is used for, **A** can check and see if it is consistent with all of the current uses. As with other areas, the degree of annotation will grow as **A** is given more knowledge. It could expand into a more complete program-understander which analyzes the program structure to understand what is intended and how it will actually function.

2.2.2 Program structure Programs written using **A** should be highly structured around semantic purposes. For example, a program might contain a loop which goes through a list, picking out all of the elements fitting some particular criterion (say not being "funny"), then for each successful item generates a set of items to be added to some list of results. This sequence is a coherent "chunk" of the program, and should be represented as such. There should be a whole set of concepts for operations found in programs, and macros which allow them to be written directly and expanded by the system. The chunk described above might be written as:

```
(CREATELIST    CALLED: RESULTLIST
               MAPPING: ONE-MANY
               FROM: OLDLIST
               CONDITION: (NOT (FUNNY ITEM))
               GENERATOR: INTERPGEN    )
```

In this example, RESULTLIST and OLDLIST are the names of already known variables, FUNNY is a predicate, INTERPGEN a generator function, and the rest of the words are specially known to the program which expands the CREATELIST macro. The macros must be smart, having sensible defaults for information not specified, the ability to create temporary variables and special control structures when needed, and to use context and semantic information in deciding what is being said in a particular bit of information (for example whether an atom represents a variable to be accessed or a function to be called). Part of the defaults may be related to natural language, like constructions involving simple pronoun reference and noise words. Some users may want to be able to write things like:

```
(IF ((THE DETERMINER) OF (THE NODE) IS EVERY)
    (ADD (THE NODE) TO NEWLIST)
    (OTHERWISE (ADD (THE DETERMINER) TO DETLIST)
               (PUT IT AS DETERMINER ON NEWNODE)))
```

A bit more cleverness could provide a simple parser, which makes it unnecessary to put the parentheses in such simple structures. All this could be written using the system and added bit by bit. The idea is to make the macros as flexible and forgiving as possible. They have all of the information in the model available to decide exactly what the user means, and since they are expanded only once when a call is entered or changed, there is no appreciable efficiency loss caused by making them hairy. There is a tradeoff between wanting to accept vaguely specified things, while not creating unnecessary bugs due to giving the system too much rein. Exactly where the crossover occurs will depend on the individual user, and should be variable.

With good structuring, programs will almost form their own comments, and the system can make use of this as well in building the model. In the ultimate future, the user would write only "comments" and let **A** do the programming. The mechanisms proposed here are a first straightforward step in that direction.

2.2.3   Semantic-oriented data structure use

In any large program, a single syntactic data type is used in a variety of ways. An atom (with its property list) might be an English word, a semantic marker, a node of a parsing tree, or a semantic structure. In writing a program, the user should not need to be continually concerned with the exact form of the structures being used. This is not to say that he should not be allowed to choose, but once some initial specifications are made, the details should become invisible. The program should always refer to the "feature list of the parsing node" whether it happens to be the 4th item in a vector, the CADDAR, an item on the property list or association list, or whatever. The system should have standard ways of setting, changing, and accessing structures, and should expand them into the necessary low level calls. This demands use of the model, since a call like (CHANGE FEATURELIST OF X TO NEWLIST) might have a variety of expansions depending on just what the variable X is being used for at the moment.

2.3   Running Programs

By this point, hard-core computer hackers may have given up in disgust at the gross inefficiency which seems to be implied by all of the above. Programming has always been plagued by the need to trade off flexibility for efficiency, and we cannot wish the problem away by just asserting "Well, computation is getting faster and cheaper every day." There is a Parkinson's law of program complexity which leaves us always in the same bind. As power goes up, so does the desire to build bigger and more complex programs, and at every level there will be limitations imposed by processing capability.

In **A** we want to get around this—we want to have our cake and eat it too. It seems that within an integrated moderately intelligent system this can be achieved through "multi-level redundancy." Our slogan might be "A job worth doing is worth doing several different ways." In the rest of this paper I will discuss a number of examples of multi-level redundancy. The basic idea is that we need not choose a single tradeoff between flexibility and efficiency. We can have several different resources for the same job, each of which has a different set of priorities. The system must orchestrate these, using the appropriate one for any job.

An example of multi-level redundancy in already existing systems is the co-existence of compiled and interpreted programs in many interactive LISP systems. Parts of the code which are undergoing change and debugging are run interpretively to provide easy editing and extensive dynamic information about what is going on. Parts which are considered sound are compiled so that they are more efficient, at the cost of having their inner workings become invisible to the programmer. There are even distinctions between different levels of compiled code (such as block-compiling in INTERLISP, or the NO-

UUO option in MACLISP), buying still more efficiency at the cost of burying information about what is happening, and making more kinds of changes impossible.

A needs to have at least three levels of program running capability, which we will call *compiled, interpreted*, and *cogitated*. The first two levels correspond generally to compiled and interpreted code in current systems. With the full use of a model and problem-solving system, the compiler should be able to tailor very efficient code. As it is working on any piece, it has information available about the entire program—how the piece will be called and used, what types of data it will be given, etc. The input to the compiler will be the higher-level macro calls described in section 2.2, opening the possibility for more "smart" compiling suited to special cases.

The interpreter is designed to handle code which looks approximately like current LISP. The macros are expanded into the COND's and MAP's and CADAR's which can be interpreted directly and efficiently as the program is run. The comments and structured calls are left around to be used and edited, but in such a way that they are invisible to the interpreter and don't get in the way to slow things down. The interpreter should maintain well disciplined stacks, variable-bindings, etc. which must be easily useable by the debugging parts of the system.

The cogitator is a smart, careful interpreter. As it interprets each piece of code, it looks at the comments, checks to see that conditions are met, maintains a structure of data contexts and assertions about what is going on, may call sophisticated programs to decide whether the expansion of a macro is right, and interacts with all of the debugging aids in following the program, checking for things to happen, filtering out information to show the user, etc.

At any moment the program will be using a combination of all three levels. Some tried and true parts will be running compiled. Others will be "sort of OK" running interpretively, and those under active debugging and change will be cogitated. Each level provides a different mix of facilities. The internal variables and function call nesting are not available for compiled code (which may have made special use of machine registers and jump instructions to gain efficiency). They are available on demand for interpreted code. If the program stops in progress, the user (or debugging programs) can look at the state of the stack, including variable bindings, etc. In cogitated mode, everything can be monitored. For example, the program might be stopped when a certain condition is met, such as a particular variable being accessed, or a function called with some peculiar configuration of arguments.

Of course it would be hopeless if the user had to worry explicitly about the interactions between these different levels. Almost everything must be handled automatically. When he asks for certain kinds of debugging information, the system should automatically shift from one level to another. All of the levels of code must be kept simultaneously in the system. If the user wants to edit a function which is currently running compiled, the system should provide him with the original version to edit, then re-expand it into interpretive code, and let it run that way. At some later point when the user specifies or after some default time interval, **A** should recompile it, and use the new compiled version unless requested not to. This kind of switching back and forth depends heavily on having lots of information around. If other code has compiled specially designed calls to a "well-established" subroutine, the user changes it only at the pain of having to recompile these. This does not imply the cost of having to be conscious of them, since the system maintains the necessary information to make the changes automatically. All this hair will cause implementation problems, which are discussed in Part 3.

2.4   Input-Output

Another area where multi-level redundancy is needed is in the reading and printing of information. Systems like LISP are built with a uniform simple way of representing data structures in print, and interpreting character strings which are input. They buy efficiency and simplicity by making the assumption that there is a unique print-name or print-form for every structure. Anyone who tries to write complex programs discovers the need to augment this basic capability with a variety of specialized read and write functions. GRINDEF (prettyprint) is an obvious example of a better way to print certain data (especially LISP programs). In SHRDLU there are separate special print functions for English sentences, syntax trees, semantic structures, and specialized data-base information. There are three separate readers (in addition to the standard LISP one) for English, top-level commands, and responses to certain kinds of queries. Goldstein's LISP-LOGO has its own parser for input, and a special function for printing programs in the LOGO format.

What is needed in a system is the flexibility to program input-output functions explicitly. Things like "readtable," "system character status," "character read macros," and so forth are designed to meet this need, but are far too low-level. There should be special parts of the system designed to help the user with the kind of facilities he wants to create. The programmable GRINDEF [Goldstein 1973] is a step in this direction, and should be matched by a general programmable parser using a kind of procedural grammar. There would be defaults and standard built-in functions for handling much of the material.

The general input-output philosophy should be opposed to the idea that there is a unique print form for any structure. In SHRDLU, many structures are in the form of atoms with property lists. The atom print-name for these is totally unenlightening, but we may not want to see the entire property list, since it may contain both irrelevant information and items which print badly (like multiple pointers into the same list, or pointers into long lists, or even circular structures). Printing and reading must be context-dependent acts. When asked to print something, **A** must decide what kind of thing it is, and just what print form is appropriate for what is being done. An obvious example is programs. If we are editing a function call, we may not want to see the internal structure of all of its arguments in their full depth, but rather some skeleton version. At times we may want to see the program with comments, at other times without, and at other times we may want the print form to include the cross-referencing information collected about it. This must be explicitly controllable, but have good defaults to avoid making the user be worried about print form every time he looks at or enters something.

The smart print and read will coexist with a more straightforward efficient one like those now existing. This would be used for things like transferring programs to other systems, or storing them away on back-up files. Note that this does not include reading files in and out for using the system. As far as the user is concerned, the system simply contains all of the information and program as a whole. How it actually allocates space between storage media should be an invisible detail of system implementation.

2.5   Block Structure

It may seem wrong at first glance to say that "The system simply contains all of the information and program as a whole." Clearly there is a conceptual structure dividing up what is there, and these are usually embodied in a file-structured system. If there are no separate files, how can you deal with separate parts of the system and programs, get listings, or do any of a number of other things requiring segmentation? The answer in **A** is to have a concept of segmentation, but one which is much more general than a list or tree of files. One type of abstraction the user can work with is a "block" of programs, which can be given a name, and have various program pieces and sub-blocks associated with it. These do not, however, form a simple tree-structure. A particular program or sub-block may be in the intersection of several larger blocks, and the block divisions may occur along several dimensions. We may want to divide things up according to when in the processing they are called, but also according to what types of data structures they work with, or even which programmer wrote them.

There are a variety of uses for this block information, in addition to any good things it may do to programmers to be asked to think about how their program is organized. It can be used for a kind of context-dependent recognition of things typed in. There might be two different functions of the same name, but no conflict since they are in different blocks (or by different programmers) and the system can decide on which to use by keeping track of where it is.

In asking for a listing, current file systems always seem to give too much or too little information. **A** should be able to honor requests (stated in an appropriate language) like "Give me an alphabetical listing of all of the functions I wrote which are concerned with generating English answers, and make calls to Micro-Planner, complete with comments and macro expansions, but no cross-references." Again, all of the parts of the system must be integrated and must keep a complete program model for this to be successful. This must be combined with careful attention to standard defaults, so the user is not subjected to having to remember all the details, or to an endless routine of choosing among alternatives.

3. HOW

Most of the discussion in parts 1 and 2 concentrated on what **A** should do, rather than how it could do it. We have intentionally put off questions of practicality and implementation for this section. There are a variety of important issues concerning problems of size and complexity, both in running the system and in getting it written.

3.1 Implementation Problems

The first issue which comes to mind is "Where do we start?" Is it necessary to start from scratch, or is it possible to build **A** in some existing high level system? There are a number of simple matters which can be dealt with directly. First, any host system must obviously be highly interactive. It would be ludicrous to think of implementing **A** in an environment of batch-like processing. Second, the host must have primitives for dealing efficiently with a full variety of basic data types, including lists, arbitrary length vectors, character strings, and numbers of various flavors. In addition, it must be cleanly structured so that, for example, its stacks are informative and easily interpretable. It must have primitives which allow direct "hands on" access to things such as input and output character strings and interrupts, machine instructions in compiled code, etc.

It is not obvious that any existing system has the necessary combination of these, although it seems reasonable that they might be so modified without major disruption. There are, however, more basic issues which raise substantial problems. These are primarily related to problems of size and the consequent problems of running efficiency.

In Part 1, the need for **A** was explained on the grounds of wanting to build programs an order of magnitude larger than the largest current systems. This led to the paradoxical solution of handling bigger programs by greatly expanding the amount of information stored about each part of them. By including different levels of program (compiled, interpreted, and cogitated) plus comments, a detailed model, and cross-reference information, we expand the space occupied by a program at least an order of magnitude. In addition, the system itself is going to be extremely large, incorporating the functions of interpreter, editor, smart compiler, question answerer, deductive system, plus a model of programming in general which is significantly larger than current models like the BLOCKS world.

Including all of this, we would expect programs to be at least a hundred times as large as the largest ones today. We are already pushing the limit of 2^{18} words on the PDP-10, so we will need memory sizes on the order of 2^{25} words (2^{30} bits), perhaps even more. Since there is no likelihood of physical memories of that size being practically cheap in the near future, it is clear that we will use some sort of multiple level virtual memory system.

It is not clear what available systems are suitably large and efficient. First there is the problem of address space. If the size were caused simply by the proliferation of facilities (editor + debugger + question-answerer + ...) it might be possible to use some clever system of "forks" or overlays. However the majority of storage will contain information intimately associated with the pieces of the program, and it is not apparent that a scheme of large disjoint memory segments will be workable.

Address space is only part of the problem. Even if the virtual space is big enough, we must deal directly with the problem of excessive paging. If the working set at any point gets much larger than the size of fast memory, things will grind to a halt. Current systems either make no attempt (MACLISP) or only a small one (INTERLISP, by putting CONSes on the same page as their CDR) to control memory usage. To make **A** possible, we need much more explicit control. A program being read in, for example, will contain information which has very different uses. The code itself will be run (or parts of it expanded into code to be run), many of the comments will be used only when cogitating, and the English comments only for listings and providing information. If these are stored together as they come in, the working set will be multiplied by a significant factor. We need to store different kinds of things in different places. Some pages will have compiled code, other pages interpretive code, other pages machine-useable comments, other pages English comments, etc. In addition, unless page size is very small (not true of most existing systems) some attention should be paid to the block structure assigned to the program, to group together things which are likely to be used together.

This storage control must be integrated into every part of the system—structure being read by the reader must be properly assigned, the compiler must worry about linkages between different types of structure (for example, quoted list structures occurring in compiled code), the editor must worry about making program changes in a way which doesn't cause proliferation of a single piece over many pages, etc. To achieve this, each of these must be a smart system, and the underlying system must have primitives for memory storage manipulations.

The greatest interaction (and problem) comes in garbage collection. In doing a typical sweep phase, a system needs to look at every page of active storage—not just once, but as many times as there are references to it on other pages. Most systems avoid collecting areas such as system code and compiled code, but in **A** most of the space will be filled with changeable-structure material (such as lists) which must be garbage collectable. The entire area of program, comments, data base, etc. must be changeable at any time. The cost of garbage collecting this area would be tremendous. Even the current SHRDLU can take several minutes for a garbage collection when the time sharing system is heavily loaded.

What is needed is a multi-level garbage collector. Some of the storage is highly volatile, like the area in which data structures are being built by the programs as they run in doing a job like analyzing a sentence. Other areas are less volatile, like programs in the process of being debugged, or areas of long term storage being used by active programs (for example a memory of past events). Others are still more stable, like compiled user programs, and finally there is the system itself, much of which would be written in the same way as user programs, and which, although relatively unchanging, can be worked on and modified within the normal functioning of the debugger, editor, and compiler. When the system runs out of working space, or finds that it is spread across too many pages, it should garbage collect only the active working space, assuming that any space which could be gained in more stable areas is unimportant at the moment. At regular intervals it should collect a wider circle of space, including the programs which have been modified. Finally, occasionally it should go around and look over everything, doing a "spring housecleaning". Successfully implementing this scheme is complicated, since there will be pointers from one area to another which need to be handled specially, and extra problems raised by the relocation of some types of storage such as compiled programs and vectors. Note that this is crucial, since we are not looking at a system which is "loaded" each time it is to be run. An old superseded compilation of a program will sit there forever occupying a piece of some page unless there is some way to garbage collect it and move something else into the space. It seems reasonable in a virtual memory system to have all garbage collection be compacting, since there are very fast algorithms for relocation if a clean set of pages is available.

Much of the problem of doing the memory allocation could be taken over by a smart garbage collector. Again multi-level redundancy is needed. The collector which clears out working space every time it is needed should be as efficient as possible, sacrificing flexibility if necessary. The periodic collector could choose a different tradeoff, taking lots of time to do useful work. By using the information available in various parts of the system, it could make sophisticated decisions on just where to store things. We could include a kind of sleep mode, where **A** runs some sample cases based on previous experiences, collecting and evaluating statistics on storage usage to improve the allocation of areas. A smart collector could even let us make major mind changes. If a particular data structure is originally a fixed-length vector, and we discover it should really be a list, the situation is hopeless unless we can go back and change all of the already existing ones, as well as places in the program where use of these structures has been compiled. The garbage collector has the ability to sweep through the entire memory, and if given enough information (and time) could make the necessary changes. This means that the smartest garbage collector should be user-programmable, just like the smartest read and print.

3.2 Building the System

This presentation of **A** raises the paradox of fighting size with more size. The power to handle large programs comes from increasing the amount of information we store about them. Similarly we are battling complexity with complexity. The initial section presented the argument that current systems are inadequate for building large, highly integrated programs. It proposes to solve that problem by building **A**, which itself is larger and more complex than any existing AI program. Since it will not spring full-blown from the head of Zeus, we must worry about how it will get written.

This is not an easy problem. Many of the suggestions for **A**'s organization will create tremendous problems of debugging. Multi-level redundancy may be of great utility once it is working, but there may be a nightmare of bugs caused by having three different interpreters which do not exactly coincide on how they run a piece of program. An intelligent garbage collector opens all sorts of possibilities for overcoming problems of size, but also creates possibilities for bugs of the worst kind. The kind of programming and debugging tools needed to cope with this are precisely those which will not exist until **A** exists.

Clearly bootstrapping must be used as much as possible. Parts of the program can be written, then used to write and debug others. There is no need for a compiler in order to get an interpreter running, even though all of the concepts of how it will work and interact with other components should be worked out ahead. The actual compiler can be written within **A**, and compile itself into a more efficient version. Similarly, almost all of the editing and debugging tools can be written directly in the language, then turned on themselves.

A central core must first exist, with a simple evaluator, primitives for manipulating built-in data structures, and the stupid versions of the garbage collector, reader, and printer. These can in turn be used to build the more advanced parts of compiler, editor, cogitator, debugger, garbage collector, etc. If it is possible to build the system within an already existing language system, this core may already exist. However, there may well be no system with enough flexibility in such central aspects as address space, memory management, control structure, and garbage collection. In that case things would have to be built from scratch, with the advantage that this would allow more total and integrated planning of every aspect of the system.

Finding a compatible base is only one step. An even more critical one is the construction of a deductive program capable of doing the kind of problem solving needed to do all the things described above. Current systems are only a first step, and **A** seems like a chance to combine work on useable systems with basic research in problem solving. Hopefully both will profit from the meeting.

REFERENCES

[Charniak 1972] E. Charniak. *Toward a model of children's story comprehension.* Massachusetts Institute of Technology, MIT-AI-266, 1972.

[Goldstein 1973] I.P. Goldstein. Pretty-printing, converting list to linear structure. Massachusetts Institute of Technology, MIT-AI-279, 1973.

[Hewitt 1972] C. Hewitt. *Description and theoretical analysis (using schemata) of PLAN-NER: a language for proving theorems and manipulating models in a robot.* Massachusetts Institute of Technology, MIT-AI-TR-258, April 1972; see also C. Hewitt. *PLANNER: A language for manipulating models and proving theorems in a robot,* Massachusetts Institute of Technology, memo 168.

[McDermott and Sussman 1972] D.V. McDermott, G.J. Sussman. *The CONNIVER Reference Manual.* Massachusetts Institute of Technology, Artificial Intelligence Laboratory Memo 259, May 1972.

[McDonald 1974] D. McDonald. The LISP indexer. Massachusetts Institute of Technology, Artificial Intelligence Laboratory, May 1974.

[Weizenbaum 1972] On the impact of the computer in society. *Science,* 176 (1972), 609-614.

[Winograd 1972] T. Winograd. *Understanding Natural Language.* Academic Press, 1972.

2 Power Tools for Programmers

B. A. SHEIL

XEROX Palo Alto Research Center
Palo Alto, California

An oil company needs a system to monitor and control the increasingly complex and frequently changing equipment used to operate an oil well. An electronic circuit designer plans to augment a circuit layout program to incorporate a variety of vaguely stated design rules. A newspaper wants a page layout system to assist editors in balancing the interlocking constraints that govern the placement of stories and advertisements. A government agency envisions a personal workstation that would provide a single integrated interface to a variety of large, evolving database systems.

Applications like these are forcing the commercial deployment of a radically new kind of programming system. First developed to support research in artificial intelligence and interactive graphics, these new tools and techniques are based on the notion of exploratory programming, the conscious intertwining of system design and implementation. Fueled by dramatic changes in the cost of computing, such exploratory programming environments have become a commercial reality virtually overnight. No fewer than four such systems were displayed at NCC '82 and their numbers are likely to increase rapidly as their power and range of application become more widely appreciated.

Despite the diversity of subject matter, a common thread runs through our example applications. They are, of course, all large, complex programs whose implementations will require significant resources. Their more interesting similarity, however, is that it is extremely difficult to give complete specifications for any of them. The reasons range from sheer complexity (the circuit designer can't anticipate all the ways in which his design rules will interact), through continually changing requirements (the equipment in the oil rig changes, as do the information bases that the government department is required to consult), to the subtle human factors issues that determine the effectiveness of an interactive graphics interface.

Whatever the cause, a large programming project with uncertain or changing specifications is a particularly deadly combination for conventional programming techniques. Virtually all modern programming methodology is predicated on the assumption that a programming project is fundamentally a problem of implementation, rather than design. The design is supposed to be decided on first, based on specifications provided by the client; the implementation follows. The dichotomy is so important that it is standard practice to recognize that a client may have only a partial understanding of his needs, so that extensive consultations may be required to ensure a complete specification with which the client will remain happy. This dialog guarantees a fixed specification that will form a stable base for an implementation.

The vast bulk of existing programming practice and technology, such as structured design methodology, is designed to ensure that the implementation does, in fact, follow the specification in a controlled fashion, rather than wander off in some unpredictable direction. And for good reason. Modern programming methodology is a significant achievement that has played a major role in preventing the kind of implementation disasters that often befell large programming projects in the 1960s.

The implementation disasters of the 1960s, however, are slowly being succeeded by the design disasters of the 1980s. The projects described above simply will not yield to conventional methods. Any attempt to obtain an exact specification from the client is bound to fail because, as we have seen, the client does not know and cannot anticipate exactly what is required. Indeed, the most striking thing about these examples is that the clients' statements of their problems are really aspirations, rather than specifications. And since the client has no experience on which to ground these aspirations, it is only by exploring the properties of some putative solutions that the client will find out what is really needed. No amount of interrogation of the client or paper exercises will answer these questions; one just has to try some designs to see what works.

The consequences of approaching problems like these as routine implementation exercises are dramatic. First, the implementation team begins by pushing for an exact specification. How long the client resists this coercion depends on how well he really understands the limits of his own grasp of the problem. Sooner or later, however, with more or less ill-feeling, the client accepts a specification and the implementation team goes to work.

The implementors take the specification, partition it, define a module structure that reflects this partitioning, freeze the interfaces between them, and repeat this process until the problem has been divided into a large number of small, easily understandable, and easily implementable pieces. Control over the implementation process is achieved by the imposition of structure, which is then enforced by a variety of management practices and programming tools.

1. USE OF INTERNAL RIGIDITY

Since the specification and therefore the module structuring, is considered fixed, one of the most effective methods for enforcing it is the use of redundant descriptions and consistency checking. Hence the importance of techniques such as interface descriptions and static type checking, which require that multiple statements of various aspects of the design be included in the program text. These statements allow mechanical checks that ensure that each piece of the system remains consistent with the rest. In a well-executed conventional implementation project, a great deal of internal rigidity is built into the system, ensuring its orderly development.

The problems usually emerge at system acceptance time, when the client requests not just superficial, but radical changes, either as a result of examining the system or for some completely exogenous reason. From the point of view of conventional programming practice, this indicates a failure at specification time. The software engineer should have been more persistent in obtaining a fuller description of the problem, in involving all the affected parties, etc. This is often true. Many ordinary implementation exercises are brought to ruin because the consequences of the specification were never fully agreed upon. But that's not the problem here. The oil company couldn't anticipate the addition of a piece of equipment quite different from the device on which the specification was based. No one knew that the layout editors would complain that it doesn't "feel right" now that they can no longer physically handle the copy (even in retrospect, it's unclear why they feel that way and what to do about it), etc., etc., etc. Nor would any amount of speculation by either client or software engineer have helped. Rather, it would have just prompted an already nervous client to demand whole dimensions of flexibility that would not in fact be needed, leaving the system just as unprepared for the ones that eventually turned out to matter.

Whatever the cause, the implementation team has to rework the system to satisfy a new, and significantly different, specification. That puts them in a situation that conventional programming methodology simply refuses to acknowledge—except as something to avoid. As a result, their programming tools and methods are suddenly of limited effectiveness. The redundant descriptions and imposed structure that were so effective in constraining the program to follow the old specification have lost none of their efficacy—they still constrain the program to follow the old specification. And they're difficult to change. The whole point of redundancy is to protect the design from a single unintentional change. But it's equally well protected against a single intentional change. Thus, all the changes have to be made everywhere. (Since this should never happen, there's no methodology to guide or programming tools to assist this process.) Of course, if the change is small (as it "should" be), there is no particular problem. But if it is large enough to cut across the module structure, the implementation team finds that it has to fight its way out of its previous design.

Still no major problem, if that's the end of the matter. But it rarely is. The new system will suggest yet another change. And so on. After a few iterations of this, not only are the client and the implementation team not on speaking terms, but the repeated assaults on the module structure have likely left it looking like spaghetti. It still gets in the way (fire walls are just as impenetrable if laid out at random as they are when laid out straight), but has long ceased to be of any use to anyone except to remind them of the project's sorry history. Increasingly, it is actively subverted (enter LOOPHOLES, UNSPECS, etc.) by programmers whose patience is running thin. Even if the design were suddenly to stabilize (unlikely in the present atmosphere), all the seeds have now been sown for an implementation disaster as well.

2. EXPLORE DESIGN PROBLEMS

The alternative to this kind of predictable disaster is not to abandon structured design for programming projects that are, or can be made to be, well defined. That would be a tremendous step backwards. Instead, we should recognize that some applications are best thought of as design problems, rather than implementation projects. These problems require programming systems that allow the design to emerge from experimentation with the program, so that design and program develop together. Environments in which this is possible were first developed in artificial intelligence and computer graphics, two research areas that are particularly prone to specification instability.

At first sight, artificial intelligence might seem an unlikely source of programming methodology. But constructing programs, in particular programs that carry out some intelligent activity, is central to artificial intelligence. Since almost any intelligent activity is likely to be poorly understood (once a program becomes well understood we usually cease to consider it "intelligent"), the artificial intelligence programmer invariably has to restructure his program many, many times before it becomes reasonably proficient. In addition, since the intelligent activities are complex, the programs tend to be very large, yet they are invariably built by very small teams, often a single researcher. Consequently, they are usually at or beyond the manageable limits of complexity for their implementors. In response, a variety of programming environments based on the Lisp programming language have evolved to aid in the development of these large, rapidly changing systems.

The rapidly developing area of interactive graphics has encountered similar problems. Fueled by the swift drop in the cost of computers capable of supporting interactive graphics, there has been an equally swift development of applications that make heavy use of interactive graphics in their user interfaces. Not only was the design of such interfaces almost completely virgin territory as recently as 10 years ago, but even now, when there are a variety of known techniques (menus, windows, etc.) for exploiting this power, it is still very difficult to determine how easy it will be to use a proposed user interface and how well it will match the user's needs and expectations in particular situations. Consequently, complex interactive interfaces usually require extensive empirical testing to determine whether they are really effective and considerable redesign to make them so.

While interface design has always required some amount of tuning, the vastly increased range of possibilities available in a full graphics system has made the design space unmanageably large to explore without extensive experimentation. In response, a variety of systems, of which Smalltalk is the best known, have been developed to facilitate this experimentation by providing a wide range of built-in graphical abstractions and methods of modifying and combining them together into new forms.

In contrast to conventional programming technology, which restrains the programmer in the interests of orderly development, exploratory programming systems must amplify the programmer in the interests of maximizing his effectiveness. Exploration in the realm of programming can require small numbers of programmers to make essentially arbitrary transformations to very large amounts of code. Such programmers need programming power tools of considerable capacity or they will simply be buried in detail. So, like an amplifier, their programming system must magnify their necessarily limited energy and minimize extraneous activities that would otherwise compete for their attention.

3. SOURCES OF DESIGN POWER

One source of such power is the use of interactive graphics. Exploratory programming systems have capitalized on recent developments in personal computing with extraordinary speed. The Xerox 1108 Interlisp-D system, for example, uses a large format display and a "mouse" pointing device to allow very high bandwidth communication with the user. Designers of exploratory programming environments have been quick to seize on the power of this combination to provide novel programming tools, as we shall see.

In addition to programming tools, these personal machine environments allow the standard features of a professional workstation, such as text editing, file management, and electronic mail, to be provided within the programming environment itself. Not only are these facilities just as effective in enhancing the productivity of programmers as they are for other professionals, but their integration into the programming environment allows them to be used at any time during programming. Thus, a programmer who has encountered a bug can send a message reporting it while remaining within the debugger, perhaps including in the message some information, like a back-trace, obtained from the dynamic context.

Another source of power is to build the important abstract operations and objects of some given application area directly into the exploratory environment. All programming systems do this to a certain extent; some have remarkably rich structures for certain domains, (e.g., the graphics abstractions embedded within Smalltalk). If the abstractions are well chosen, this approach can yield a powerful environment for exploration within the chosen area, because the programmer can operate entirely in substantively meaningful abstractions, taking advantage of the considerable amount of implementation and design effort that they represent.

The limitations of this approach, however, are clear. Substantive abstractions are necessarily effective only within a particular topic area. Even for a given area, there is generally more than one productive way to partition it. Embedding one set of abstractions into the programming system encourages developments that fit within that view of the world at the expense of others. Further, if one enlarges one's area of activity even slightly, a set of abstractions that was once very effective may become much less so. In that situation, unless there are effective mechanisms for reshaping the built-in abstractions to suit the changed domain, users are apt to persist with them, at the cost of distorting their programs. Embedded abstractions, useful though they are, by themselves enable only exploration in the small, confined within the safe borders where the abstractions are known to be effective. For exploration in the large, a more general source of programming power is needed.

Of course, the exact mechanisms that different exploratory systems propose as essential sources of programming power vary widely, and these differences are hotly debated within their respective communities. Nevertheless, despite strong surface differences, these systems share some unusual characteristics at both the language and environment level.

4. THE LANGUAGE LEVEL

The key property of the programming languages used in exploratory programming systems is their emphasis on minimizing and deferring the constraints placed on the programmer, in the interests of minimizing and deferring the cost of making large-scale program changes. Thus, not only are the conventional structuring mechanisms based on redundancy not used, but the languages make extensive use of late binding, i.e., allowing the programmer to defer commitments for as long as possible.

The clearest example is that exploratory environments invariably provide dynamic storage allocation with automatic reclamation (garbage collection). To do otherwise imposes an intolerable burden on the programmer to keep track of all the paths through his program that might access a particular piece of storage to ensure that none of them access or release it prematurely (and that someone does release it eventually!). This can only be done by careful isolation of storage management or with considerable administrative effort. Both are incompatible with rapid, unplanned development, so neither is acceptable. Storage management must be provided by the environment itself.

Other examples of late binding include the dynamic typing of variables (associating data type information with a variable at run-time, rather than in the program text) and the dynamic binding of procedures. The freedom to defer deciding the type of a value until run-time is important because it allows the programmer to experiment with the type structure itself. Usually, the first few drafts of an exploratory program implement most data structures using general, inefficient structures such as linked lists discriminated (when necessary) on the basis of their contents. As experience with the application evolves, the critical distinctions that determine the type structure are themselves determined by experimentation, and may be among the last, rather than the first, decisions to evolve. Dynamic typing makes it easy for the programmer to write code that keeps these decisions as tacit as possible.

The dynamic binding of procedures entails more than simply linking them at load-time. It allows the programmer to change dynamically the subprocedures invoked by a given piece of code, simply by changing the run-time context. The simplest form of this is to allow procedures to be used as arguments or as the value of variables. More sophisticated mechanisms allow procedure values to be computed or even encapsulated inside the data values on which they are to operate. This packaging of data and procedures into a single object, known as object-oriented programming, is a very powerful technique. For example, it provides an elegant, modular solution to the problem of generic procedures (i.e., every data object can be thought of as providing its own definition for common actions, such as printing, which can be invoked in a standard way by other procedures). For these reasons, object-oriented programming is a widely used exploratory programming technique and actually forms the basic programming construct of the Smalltalk language.

The dynamic binding of procedures can be taken one step further when procedures are represented as data structures that can be effectively manipulated by other programs. While this is of course possible to a limited extent by reading and writing the text of program source files, it is of much greater significance in systems that define an explicit representation for programs as syntax trees or their equivalent. This, coupled with the interpreter or incremental compiler provided by most exploratory programming systems, is an extraordinarily powerful tool. Its most dramatic application is in programs that construct other programs, which they later invoke. This technique is often used in artificial intelligence in situations where the range of possible behaviors is too large to encode efficiently as data structures but can easily be expressed as combinations of procedure fragments. An example might be a system that "understands" instructions given in natural language by analyzing each input as it is received, building a program that captures its meaning, and then evaluating that program to achieve the requested effect.

5. A BASIC TECHNIQUE EXPANDED

Aside from such specialized applications, effective methods for mechanically manipulating procedures enable two other significant developments. The first is the technique of program development by writing interpreters for special purpose languages. Once again, this is a basic technique of artificial intelligence that has much wider applicability. The key idea is that one develops an application by designing a special language in which the application is relatively easy to state. Like any notation, such a language provides a concise representation that suppresses common or uninteresting features in favor of whatever the designer decides is more important.

A simple example is the use of notations like context-free grammars (BNF) to "metaprogram" the parsers for programming languages. Similar techniques can be used to describe, among other things, user interfaces, transaction sequences, and data transformations. Application development in this framework is a dialectic process of designing the application language and developing an interpreter for it, since both the language and the interpreter will evolve during development. The simplest way of doing this is to evolve the application language out of the base provided by the development language. Simply by allowing the application language interpreter to call the development language interpreter, expressions from the development language can be used wherever the application language currently has insufficient power. As one's understanding of the problem develops, the application language becomes increasingly powerful and the need to escape into the development language becomes less important.

The other result of having procedures that are easily manipulated by other procedures is that it becomes easy to write program manipulation subsystems. This in turn has two key consequences. First, the exploratory programming language itself can grow. The remarkable longevity of Lisp in the artificial intelligence community is in large part due to the language having been repeatedly extended to include modern programming language syntax and constructions. The vast majority of these extensions were accomplished by defining source-to-source transformations that converted new constructions into more conventional Lisp. The ease with which this can be done allows each user, and even each project, to extend the language to capture the idioms that are found to be locally useful.

Second, the accessibility of procedures to mechanical manipulation facilitates the development of programming support tools. All exploratory programming environments boast a dazzling profusion of programming tools. To some extent, this is a virtue of necessity, as the flexibility necessary for exploration has been gained at considerable sacrifice in the ability to impose structure. That loss of structure could easily result in a commensurate loss of control by the programmer. The programming tools of the exploratory environment enable the programmer to reimpose the control that would be provided by structure in conventional practice.

Programming tools achieve their effectiveness in two quite different ways. Some tools are simply effective viewers into the user's program and its state. Such tools permit one to find information quickly, display it effectively, and modify it easily. A wide variety of tools of this form can be seen in the two Interlisp-D screen images (see pp. 26–27), including data value inspectors (which allow a user to look at and modify the internal structure of an object), editors for code and data objects, and a variety of break and tracing packages. Especially when coupled with a high bandwidth display, such viewers are very effective programming tools.

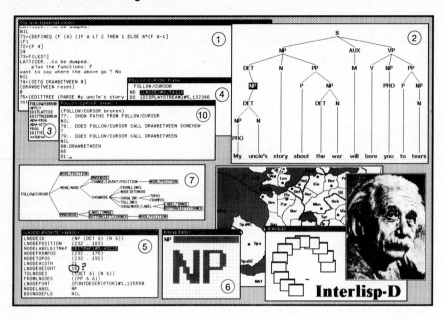

These two screen images show some of the exploratory programming tools provided in the Xerox Interlisp-D programming environment. The screen is divided into a series of rectangular areas or windows, each of which provides a view onto some data or process, and which can be reshaped and repositioned at will by the user. When they overlap, the occluded portion of the lower window is automatically saved, so that it can be restored when the overlapping window is removed. Since the display is bit-mapped, each window can contain an arbitrary mixture of text, lines, curves, and pictures composed of half-tones or solids. The image of Einstein, for instance, was produced by scanning a photograph and storing it digitally.

In the typescript window (labeled 1), the user has defined a program F (factorial) and has then immediately run it, giving an input of 4 and getting a result of 24. Next, in the same window, he queries the state of his files, finding that one file (LATTICER) has already been changed and one function (F) has been defined but not associated with any file yet. The user sets the value of DRAWBETWEEN to 0 in command 74, and the system notes that this is a change and adds DRAWBETWEEN to the set of "changed objects" that might need to be saved.

Then, the user runs the program EDITTREE, giving it a parse tree for the sentence "My uncle's story about the war will bore you to tears." This opens up the big window (2) on the right in which the sentence diagram is drawn. Using the mouse, the user starts to move the NP node on the left (which is inverted to show that it is being moved).

While the move is taking place, the user interrupts the tree editor, which suspends the computation and causes three "break" windows to appear on top of the lower edge of the typescript. The smallest window (3) shows the dynamic state of the computation, which has been broken inside a subprogram called FOLLOW/CURSOR. The "FOLLOW/CURSOR Frame" window (4) to the right shows the value of the local variables bound by FOLLOW/CURSOR. One of them has been selected (and so appears inverted) and in response, its value has been shown in more detail in the window (5) at the lower left of the screen. The user has marked one of the component values as suspicious by circling it using the mouse. In addition, he has asked to examine the contents of the BITMAP component, which has opened up a bitmap edit window (6) to the right. This shows an

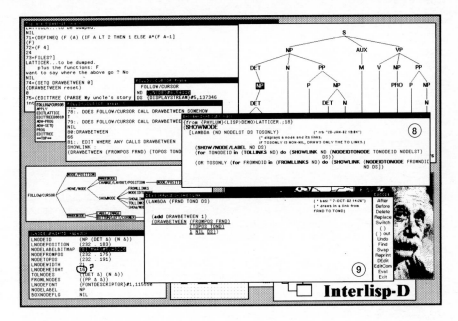

enlarged copy of the actual NP image that is being moved by the tree editor. Then, inside the largest of the three break windows (10) the user has asked some questions about the FOLLOW/CURSOR subprogram that was running when he interrupted, and queried the value of DRAWBETWEEN (now 66). The SHOW PATHS command brought up the horizontal tree diagram on the left (7), which shows which subprograms call each other, starting at FOLLOW/CURSOR.

Each node in the call tree produced by the SHOW PATHS command is an active element that will respond to the user's selecting it with the mouse. In the second image, the user has selected the SHOWNODE subprogram, which has caused its source code to be retrieved from the file (<LISP>DEMO>LATTICER) on remote file server (PHYLUM) where it was stored, and displayed in the "Browser printout window" (8) which has been opened at middle right. User functions and extended Lisp forms (like *for* and *do*) are highlighted by system-generated font changes.

By selecting nodes in the SHOW PATHS window, the user could also have edited the code or obtained a summary description of any of its subprograms.

Instead, the user has asked (in the break typescript window (10)) to edit wherever anybody calls the DRAWBETWEEN system primitive (which draws lines between two specified points). This request causes the system to consult its dynamically maintained database of information about user programs, wherein it finds that the subprogram SHOWLINK calls DRAWBETWEEN. It therefore loads the code for SHOWLINK into an edit window (9) that appears under the "Browser printout window." The system then automatically finds and underlines the first (and only) call on DRAWBETWEEN. Note that on the previous line DRAWBETWEEN is used as a variable (the same variable the user set and interrogated earlier). The system, however, knows that this is not a subprogram call, so it has been skipped over. If the user were to make any change to this subprogram in the editor, not only would the change take effect immediately, but SHOWLINK would be marked as needing to be updated in its file and the information about it in the subprogram database would be updated. This, in turn, would cause the SHOW PATHS window to be repainted, as its display might no longer be valid.

6. A WIDE VARIETY OF TOOLS

The other type of programming tool is knowledge based. Viewer-based tools, such as a program text editor, can operate effectively with a very limited understanding of the material with which they deal. By contrast, knowledge-based tools must know a significant amount about the content of a user's program and the context in which it operates. Even a very shallow analysis of a set of programs (e.g., which programs call which other ones) can support a variety of effective programming tools. A program browser allows a programmer to track the various dependencies between different parts of a program by presenting easy to read summaries that can be further expanded interactively.

Deeper analysis allows more sophisticated facilities. The Interlisp program analyzer (Masterscope) has a sufficiently detailed knowledge of Lisp programs that it can provide a complete static analysis of an arbitrary Lisp program. A wide variety of tools have been constructed that use the database provided by this analysis to answer complex queries (which may require significant reasoning, such as computing the transitive closure of some property), to make systematic changes under program control (such as making some transformation wherever a specified set of properties hold), or to check for a variety of inconsistent usage errors.

Finally, integrated tools provide yet another level of power. The Interlisp system notices whenever a program fragment is changed (by the editor or by redefinition). The program analyzer is then informed that any existing analysis is invalid, so that incorrect answers are not given on the basis of old information. The same mechanism is used to notify the program management subsystem (and eventually the user, at session end) that the corresponding file needs to be updated. In addition, the system will remember the previous state of the program, so that at any subsequent time the programmer can undo the change and retreat (in which case, of course, all the dependent changes and notifications will also be undone). This level of cooperation between tools not only provides immense power to the programmer, but relieves him of detail that he would otherwise have to manage himself. The result is that more attention can be paid to exploring the design.

A key, but often neglected, component of an exploratory programming system is a set of facilities for program contraction. The development of a true exploratory program is design limited, so that is where the effort has to go. Consequently, the program is often both inefficient and inelegant when it first achieves functional acceptability. If the exploration were an end in itself, this might be of limited concern. However, it is more often the case that a program developed in an exploratory fashion must eventually be used in some real situation. Sometimes, the time required to reimplement (using the prototype program as a specification) is prohibitive. Other times, the choice of an exploratory system was made to allow for expected future upheaval, so it is essential to preserve design flexibility. In either event, it is necessary to be able to take the functionally adequate program and transform it into one whose efficiency is comparable to the best program one could have written, in any language, had only one known what one was doing at the outset.

The importance of being able to make this post hoc optimization cannot be overemphasized. Without it, one's exploratory programs will always be considered toys; the pressure to abandon the exploratory environment and start implementing in a real one will be overwhelming; and, once that move is made (and it is always made too soon), exploration will come to an end. The requirement for efficient implementation places two burdens on an exploratory programming system. First, the architecture must allow an efficient implementation. For example, the obligatory automatic storage allocation mechanism must either be so efficient that its overhead is negligible, or it must permit the user to circumvent it (e.g., to allocate storage statically) when and where the design has stabilized enough to make this optimization possible.

Second, as the performance engineering of a large system is almost as difficult as its initial construction, the environment must provide performance engineering tools, just as it provides design tools. These include good instrumentation, a first-class optimizing compiler, program manipulation tools (including, at the very least, full functionality compiler macros), and the ability to add declarative information where necessary to guide the program transformation. Note that, usually, performance engineering takes place not as a single "post-functionality optimization phase," but as a continuous activity throughout the development, as different parts of the system reach design stability and are observed to be performance critical. This is the method of progressive constraint, the incremental addition of constraints as and when they are discovered and found important, and is a key methodology for exploratory development.

Both of these concerns can be most clearly seen in the various Lisp-based systems. While, like all exploratory environments, they are often used to write code very quickly without any concern for efficiency, they are also used to write artificial intelligence programs whose applications to real problems are very large computations. Thus, the ability to make these programs efficient has long been of concern, because without it they would never be run on any interesting problems.

More recently, the architectures of the new, personal Lisp machines like the 1108 have enabled fast techniques for many of the operations that are relatively slow in a traditional implementation. Systems like Interlisp-D, which is implemented entirely in Lisp, including all of the performance-critical system code such as the operating system, display software, device handlers, etc., show the level of efficiency that is now possible within an exploratory language.

The increasing importance of applications that are very poorly understood, both by their clients and by their would-be implementors, will make exploratory development a key technique for the 1980s. Radical changes in the cost of computing power have already made such systems cost-effective vehicles for the delivery of application systems in many areas. As recently as five years ago, the tools and language features we have discussed required the computational power of a large mainframe costing about $500,000. Two years ago, equivalent facilities became available on a personal machine for about $100,000, and a year later, about $50,000. Now, a full-scale exploratory development system can be had for about $25,000. For many applications, the incremental cost has become so small over that required to support conventional technology that the benefits of exploratory development (and redevelopment!) are now decisive.

One consequence of this revolutionary change in the cost-effectiveness of exploratory systems is that our idea of exploratory problems is going to change. Exploratory programming was developed originally in contexts where change was the dominant factor.

There is, however, clearly a spectrum of specification instability. Traditionally, the cost of exploratory programming systems, both in terms of the computing power required and the run-time inefficiencies incurred, confined their use to only the most volatile applications. Thus, the spectrum was arbitrarily dichotomized into exploratory (very few) and standard (the vast majority).

Unfortunately, the reality is that unexpected change is far more common in standard applications than we have been willing to admit. Conventional programming techniques strive to preserve a stability that is only too often a fiction. Since exploratory programming systems provide tools that are better adapted to this uncertainty, many applications that are now being treated as standard but which in fact seem to require moderate levels of ongoing experimentation may turn out to be more effectively developed in an exploratory environment.

We can also expect to see a slow infusion of exploratory development techniques into conventional practice. Many of the programming tools of an exploratory programming system (in particular, the information gathering and viewing tools) do not depend on the more exploratory attributes of either language or environment and could thus be adapted to support programming in conventional languages like FORTRAN and COBOL. Along with these tools will come the seeds of the exploratory perspective on language and system design, which will gradually be incorporated into existing programming languages and systems, loosening some of the bonds with which these systems so needlessly restrict the programmer.

To those accustomed to the precise, structured methods of conventional system development, exploratory development techniques may seem messy, inelegant, and unsatisfying. But it's a question of congruence: precision and inflexibility may be just as disfunctional in novel, uncertain situations as sloppiness and vacillation are in familiar, well-defined ones. Those who admire the massive, rigid bone structures of dinosaurs should remember that jellyfish still enjoy their very secure ecological niche.

3 Programming in an Interactive Environment: The LISP Experience

ERIK SANDEWALL

Linköping University
Linköping, Sweden

LISP systems have been used for highly interactive programming for more than a decade. During that time, special properties of the LISP language (such as program/data equivalence) have enabled a certain style of interactive programming to develop, characterized by powerful interactive support for the programmer, nonstandard program structures, and nonstandard program development methods. The paper summarizes the LISP style of interactive programming for readers outside the LISP community, describes those properties of LISP systems that were essential for the development of this style, and discusses some current and not yet resolved issues.

© 1978, Association for Computing Machinery, Inc. Reprinted by permission from *ACM Computing Surveys*, 10:1 (March 1978), pp. 35-71.

1. INTRODUCTION

Why do some programming systems have to be large and complex?

In recent years there has been a trend towards simple designs in computer science research. The widespread revulsion against OS/360 in the academic community led to a quest for primitive concepts in operating systems and for very simple systems, which have been successfully developed by, for example, Brinch Hansen [Brinch-Hansen 1976]. Similarly, reaction against large and messy programming languages encouraged the development and adoption of languages that minimized the number of facilities and features, notably PASCAL [Wirth 1971b]. I believe that the great attraction of very simple programming languages such as BASIC and very simple database systems such as MUMPS [MUMPS 1976] in the world of practical computing are other examples of the same trend towards simplicity.

Despite the above, the present paper is concerned with programming systems which by necessity have to be large and complex and which are very hard to structure well because we know so little about their design. Such systems are of interest for a combination of two reasons.

First, there is a long list of things that one wants a programming system, particularly if it is interactive, to do for the programmer. ("Programming system"), is used to mean an integrated piece of software which is used to support program development including but not restricted to a compiler. The reader can easily generate his own list of functions, but here are some possibilities:

1. Administration of program modules and of different generations of the same module (when errors are corrected and/or the scope of the program is extended);

2. Administration of test examples and their correct results (including side effects), so that the relevant tests are performed automatically or semi-automatically when sections of the program are changed, and a report is made to the user if a discrepancy has been observed;

3. Administration of formal and informal documentation of program segments, and automatic generation of formal documentation from programs;

4. Interdialect translation;

5. Checking of compatibility between parts of programs;

6. Translation from general-purpose or specialized higher-level languages to the chosen base language ("preprocessors"), with appropriate support for compile-time and run-time error diagnostics in the base language, comments, etc.;

7. Support for a given programming methodology. For example, if top-down programming is to be encouraged, then it is natural to let the interactive programming system maintain successive decomposition steps, and mutual references between an abstract step and its decomposition;

8. Support of the interactive session. For example, a *history facility* [Teitelman 1978] allows the user to refer back to previous commands to the system, edit them, and re-execute them. An *undo facility* [Teitelman 1978] allows the programmer to back up and undo effects of previously performed incorrect commands, thus salvaging the data-structure environment that was interactively created during the interactive debugging session;

9. Specialized editing, performed with an editor that understands at least the syntax of the chosen programming language, and which therefore allows the user to refer to natural entities in this language and to give fairly high-level instructions as to where additions to the program are to be inserted;

10. Optimizing programs which transform a program into an equivalent but more efficient one;

11. Uniform insertion programs, which in a given program systematically insert additional statements, for example, for producing trace printouts or for counting how often locations in the program are visited during execution.

Second, and this is the crucial point, if these functions are performed by separate and independent programs, a considerable duplication of effort will result. Syntax analysis has to be performed not only by a compiler or interpreter, but also by specialized editors, optimizing programs, uniform insertion programs, documentation generators (such as cross-indexers), and so on. Analysis of the relationships between modules (calling structure, data-flow structure, etc.) is needed for generation of documentation, administration of test examples, compatibility controls, and program optimization. Since the results of an execution count may be used to tell an optimizer where it should spend its efforts, programs for these two tasks should be able to communicate. Also, some of the above facilities, such as the *undo facility*, are only possible if they are integrated into the programming system. For these reasons, it is natural to try to integrate facilities such as the above into one coherent programming system, which is capable of performing them all in an economic and systematic fashion.

I believe that the development of integrated, interactive programming systems, and the methodology for such systems, is the major research issue for programming systems and programming methodology today. It is significant for programming methodology, since every detailed recommendation on how to write programs is also a recommendation on how to design an interactive programming system that supports the methodology. In the area of research on programming systems, this is relatively unexplored territory waiting to be considered now that other problems, such as compiler design for conventional languages, seem to be fairly well understood.

The task of designing interactive programming systems is hard because there is no way to avoid complexity in such systems. Because of all the dependencies between different parts of an interactive programming system, it is hard to break up the design into distinct subproblems. The only applicable research method is to accumulate experience by implementing a system, synthesize the experience, think for a while, and start over.

Such systems have been built and used for the programming language LISP. I believe that the time is now ripe for a synthesis and discussion of the experience that has accumulated in this context. The present paper is intended to serve such a purpose.

1.1 Background

Requirements on a programming language for integrated, interactive programming systems   In a research project to design and build an integrated, interactive programming system as an implementation experiment, one early decision must be which programming language the system will support. This language must satisfy minimal criteria, as follows.

• *Bootstrapping.*   An obvious choice is to implement the system itself in the language it supports; then one needs to work only with a single language, and the system supports its own development.

• *Incrementality.*   To achieve real interaction, the basic cycle of the programming system should be to read an expression from the user, execute it, and print out the result while preserving global side effects in its database. The expression may, of course, contain such things as calls to procedures.

• *Procedure-orientation.*   For obvious reasons, the language chosen should be procedure-oriented.

• *Internal representation of programs.*   Since most of the operations listed in the previous section are operations on programs, the language should make it as easy as possible to operate on programs. Therefore, there should be a predefined, system-wide internal representation of programs which reflects their structure in as pure a form as possible, for example, as a tree structure. This structure should be a data structure *in* the programming language, so that user-written programs may inspect the structure and generate new programs. As a consequence, the kernel of the programming system must contain the following programs:

1. a *parser* which transforms the user's programs to the internal representation;
2. a *program-printer* that performs the reverse operation;
3. a *compiler* that transforms the internal data-structure representation to machine language for the host machine.

Notice that the tasks performed by a compiler for a conventional language are divided among the parser and the compiler in this architecture.

• *Full checking capability.*   All possible input from the programmer/user must result in rational responses from the system.

• *Declaration-free kernel.*   The contents and use of declarations is one of the important issues that one wants to experiment with in a research system, and therefore should not be frozen in the system kernel. Instead, the internal form of programs should be declaration-free, and one of the services of the developing programming system should be to account for declarations as input by the user.

• *Data structures and database.*   The system must minimally have data structures that are able to represent programs as tree structures, and a database facility where one can conveniently store and retrieve properties of items that appear in the program or in descriptions of the program. (Variable names and procedure names are simple examples of such items.) A relational database where program items are allowed to appear as arguments of relations, so that facts about them can be stored, is one way to satisfy the database requirement.

In addition to these minimally necessary data structures, the system will, of course, contain additional data-structuring facilities which may be desirable for the intended experimental applications of the system.

• *Defined input/output for data structures.*   In order to test a procedure interactively, one wants to be able to type in a call to the procedure and obtain back the value. Since the arguments and/or the value may be data structures, I/O for data structures must be defined in the system. Since programs are internally stored as data structures, this I/O may also be used as parser and program-printer.

• *Handles and interactive control.*   The actions taken by the system in specific situations should be controllable by the user in such a way that a user-defined procedure (a "handle") can be inserted instead of the original procedure provided by the system. For example, such handles are useful for the operation applied to expressions input by the user, and reactions to errors and exceptional conditions during the execution of a procedure.

Also, the system must allow for an assortment of different control signals that may be typed-in by the user at arbitrary times to control the ongoing computation. The "killer" interrupt, which terminates the interactive session and returns to the operating system, is exactly what the user does *not* want. The response to control signals should also be user-controllable through handles.

Additional properties may, of course, be required or desired, but the above list will do for our purpose. A quick check of existing languages against this list shows that:

- Most conventional languages (FORTRAN, PL/I, SIMULA, PASCAL, etc.) have insufficient data structure facilities (especially I/O), are not incremental, have no internal representation as above;
- BASIC has no data structures;
- LISP, SNOBOL, and APL satisfy the requirements, in different ways with respect to data structures and internal representation of programs.

At least for LISP (and I believe also for SNOBOL and APL), the match to the requirements is quite accidental: the language was developed for other purposes, and most texts about the language describe it in a different way. It is not my intention here to argue that LISP should necessarily be chosen; a project to build an integrated programming system might also choose a less-known language, or design its own. My purpose is simply to explain the experience accumulated in the LISP community with integrated, interactive programming systems.

1.2   The LISP Users' Community

Before a discussion of the accumulated experience from implementation and use of LISP systems, a few observations about the community of LISP users are in order. The following account is simplified and slightly caricatured to make its point as concisely as possible.

LISP is used almost entirely as a research tool. It is the dominant language for artificial intelligence research, and a major implementation language for formula manipulation systems. Typical applications are semantic understanding systems, program analysis and generation, and theorem proving. The average LISP user writes a program as a programming experiment, i.e., in order to develop the understanding of some task, rather than in expectation of production use of the program. The act of developing the program, not the act of running it (even for test data), constitutes the experiment. As a consequence, the program is likely to be large and complex, to undergo drastic revisions while it is being developed, and to be thrown away before it has been "completed" by conventional programming standards since it will already have served its purpose before then.

The environment in which the program is written is specialized for this style of research. The programmer works in a large group with relatively good computing facilities. He expects to have a terminal at his desk and to be able to use it continuously as a tool. More importantly, his group will have been one of the first to be able to use computers in this fashion.

One consequence of this scenario (which as I said is simplified and to some extent exaggerated) is that a considerable experience with interactive programming has developed in the LISP community, both with respect to programming style and program structure. Another consequence is that this know-how about interactive programming has not been properly exposed: the researchers have tended to consider the principles embodied in the program as the principal result of their work, and the craft of programming as a trivial aspect. They have probably been less motivated to discuss programming methodology than average progammers are, since the style is one of throw-away programming. To the extent that attention has focused on programming systems and programming methodology, these have been viewed as potential applications of artificial intelligence techniques. The emphasis has therefore been on longer-range goals and relatively utopian systems. One example is provided by Winograd [Winograd 1973].

An additional reason for the reluctance in the LISP community to discuss programming style may be a reaction to the debate about **goto**, which raged in the community in the early sixties. Programs without **goto** are written in LISP using recursive procedures and/or standard procedures with open procedural arguments, and a so-called "PROG feature" enables a restricted form of **goto** locally in a block. The controversy was resolved by a general agreement that the matter was not as important as it first seemed; this has discouraged subsequent discussion of other aspects of programming style.

1.3   Current Dialects and Implementations

Most implementations of LISP systems were accomplished in a research group that wanted to use the system, with strong feedback from users to implementors. As a consequence, the language has changed over time to satisfy new user needs, and several dialects have appeared.

The original variant of LISP was called LISP 1.5 and is described in the *LISP 1.5 Programmer's Manual* [McCarthy et al. 1962], a document which is still a standard reference but has long since become obsolete. Besides the original implementation for IBM 7090, there have been implementations for CDC 3600, IBM 360/370, and the UNIVAC 1100 series. There is also an implementation written in FORTRAN [Nordström1970].

The LISP 1.6 dialect has been developed for DEC-10 under TOPS-10 (the manufacturer-provided operating system). This dialect again split into two branches, one at Stanford that preserves the name LISP 1.6, and one at MIT called MACLISP. The latter exists both under TOPS-10 and under the local operating system, ITS (Incompatible Timesharing System).

The INTERLISP dialect was originally developed at Bolt, Beranek and Newman, Inc. (BBN) under the name BBN-LISP. After a part of the implementing group moved to Xerox Palo Alto Research Center and the responsibility for the system became shared, it changed to the new and more neutral name. The original implementation for INTERLISP was for DEC-10 under the TENEX operating system, also developed by BBN. It has been adapted for use under the TOPS-20 operating system. Additional implementations exist for IBM 360 and 370, and are being developed for other computers.

These three dialects differ in several important ways:

• Mechanisms for variable binding are different. All LISP systems use late binding, also called dynamic binding, but the three major types of systems use different mechanisms for storing the variable-value binding pairs. This is a fairly technical issue and not of interest here, but it is one of the more important points of incompatibility between programs in different dialects.

• Mechanisms for nontrivial input/output, file handling, etc. are different in the different dialects.

• INTERLISP has a very large repertoire of facilities that support the user in his work with his own program: MACLISP has fewer such facilities and organizes them differently, namely, as separate programs rather than as part of an integrated programming system. This will be discussed further below.

Additional dialects and implementations exist, although a complete listing does not seem to be available. LISP for CDC 6600 builds on LISP 1.5 but has a number of special facilities, such as three-pointer cells. Variants of LISP 1.5 have been implemented on 16-bit PDP machines. The implementation of IN-TERLISP for IBM 360 has been transferred to computers from other manufacturers (Siemens, ICL) with compatible instruction sets.

The INTERLISP variant relies heavily on the special facilities provided by the TENEX and TOPS-20 operating systems. For the benefit of DEC-10 users running TOPS-10, the LISP 1.6 system has been modified and extended with a subset of INTERLISP's user support facilities. The work was done by a group at the University of California at Irvine, and the resulting system is called UCI-LISP.

Special-purpose processors running single-user LISP systems have been developed at Xerox Palo Alto Research Center, at the MIT Artificial Intelligence Laboratory, and at Bolt, Beranek, and Newman, Inc. (BBN). All of these are experimental systems, and documentation is scant or entirely unavailable. The BBN machine is described in [Ash et al. 1977]. [*Editors note*: See also the Lisp Machine article in this book.]

It is quite easy to write a simple LISP interpreter, and a large number of more or less complete systems have been developed, including multiple implementations for the same computer series. The list given here is therefore by no means complete. It is intended to give some idea of the range of existing implementations, and to characterize the two systems that will be used in the discussion that follows, namely, MACLISP and INTERLISP.

1.4 A Simple LISP Application

The present paper is intended to discuss issues and principles of interactive programming systems that arose in the experience with LISP systems, rather than the details of LISP itself; it should be possible to read the paper without previous knowledge of the programming language LISP. For concreteness, however, the paper also presents specific LISP programs or sessions which illustrate some of the issues. These examples will be helpful for readers who have previously learned the LISP language, for example, from one of the current textbooks [Weissman 1967] [Haraldson 1975] [Allen 1978] [Winston and Horn 1981], but may be skipped by readers who do not know LISP. These examples are printed in smaller type than the rest of the text. The examples use the INTERLISP dialect, but should be equally intelligible to readers who are used to other dialects. (Of course, another dialect would have served as well for the examples.)

The following simple application will be used for all the examples. It has been chosen to illustrate some of the points in the section on requirements above. The task is to write a system which administers the calendars of meetings, appointments, etc. for a number of users. It should provide services such as the following:

- update and print-out each user's personal calendar;
- determine a suitable time for a meeting between two people, or a meeting of a committee, send a message to the intended participants, and update their calendars.

Later extensions might include these services:

- allow a user who receives a "computer mail" message about a seminar or other open meeting to transfer the message to the appropriate position in the calendar;

• reschedule appointments when a higher-priority or less easily movable appointment is suggested.

The set of services should be extensible in response to suggestions from the users. I will attempt to illustrate how the problem may be approached and the first stage of the program development, but certainly not the full solution.

In working out this application, we bypass the problem of how the system can be made to communicate with several users at once, and assume that all calendars go into the same database. Obviously our program will emphasize simplicity rather than economy of operation. It will be referred to in the balance of the paper as the *demo program*.

In the first step of program development, the programmer selects a representation of data in the database and makes a first guess about which procedures he will need to write. These decisions are, of course, based on the given list of required or suggested facilities in the final system. The creative activity of making those decisions will also by bypassed here. Once the data structure has been chosen, the writing of the procedures is usually a straightforward task.

In the chosen data structure for the demo program, each user is represented as an atom, e.g., LARSON. The user's calendar is represented as a property called CALEND, which might look as follows:

```
(((MON JAN 12)
 ((9 15) (10 00) SEE ANDERSON)
 ((10 45) (11 00) SEE LUNDSTROM)
 ((13 00) (15 00) ATTEND X-COMMITTEE-MEETING))
((TUE JAN 13)
 ((10 30) (11 30) ATTEND (INFORMATION ABOUT NEW PRODUCTS)))
 ...)
 ...)
```

In general, it is a list of day-plans, where each day-plan consists of a date followed by a list of appointments. Each date is a list of day-of-week, month, and day. Each appointment is a list of starting time, ending time, verb, and object. Each starting time and ending time is a list of hour (on a 24-hour clock, for simplicity) and minute.

For convenience, we define selector functions which retrieve the components of some of these structures, e.g.,

```
(DEFINEQ
(HOURS
  [LAMBDA (TIME)
    (CAR TIME)])
(MINUTES
  [LAMBDA (TIME)
    (CADR TIME)])
(FROM
  [LAMBDA (APP)
    (CAR APP)])
(TO
  [LAMBDA (APP)
    (CADR APP)]));¹
```

---

[1] Procedure definitions are reproduced here as printed by INTERLISP's indentation printing program, pp. A left square bracket is equivalent to a left parenthesis. A right square bracket is equivalent to one or more right parentheses, sufficiently many to match back to the corresponding left bracket or to the beginning of the expression.

We also define some other elementary functions, such as the obvious next-day function:

```
(DEFINEQ
(NEXTDAY
   [LAMBDA (DATE)
      (CONS (GETPROP (CAR DATE)
                     (QUOTE NEXTWEEKDAY))
            (COND
               ((EQ (CADDR DATE)
                    (GETPROP (CADR DATE)
                             (QUOTE NRDAYS)))
                   (LIST (GETPROP (CADR DATE)
                                  (QUOTE NEXTMONTH))
                      1))
               (T (LIST (CADR DATE)
                        (ADD1 (CADDR DATE]))
```

This definition assumes that the standard data about the succession of months and weekdays, and the length of months, are stored as properties. This information is input interactively by typing in:

```
(PUTPROP 'JAN 'NEXTMONTH 'FEB)
(PUTPROP 'FEB 'NEXTMONTH 'MAR)
...
(PUTPROP 'JAN 'NRDAYS 31)
...
(PUTPROP 'MON 'NEXTWEEKDAY 'TUE)
...
```

When we have done this in our interactive session, we can check out the procedure definition by typing in, for example,

```
(NEXTDAY '(MON JAN 10))
```

and getting back

```
(TUE JAN 11)
```

To check the exception case in the conditional, we type in

```
(NEXTDAY '(MON JAN 31))
```

and get back

```
(TUE FEB 1)
```

We are then fairly satisfied with the procedure.

A procedure to determine a shared free time period for a new appointment should run down successive days and for each day seek a time that is available for all participants. This may be done by first forming the set of free slots or "holes" for each person, and then forming intersections (in the obvious sense) of such sets of holes for different people. The set of holes is formed by the function *holesin (st, apl, et)*, where *st* is the starting time (e.g., (9 00) = 9 a.m.), *apl* is a list of appointments during the day, and *et* is the ending time (e.g., (17 00) = 5 p.m.). The definition is obvious:

```
(DEFINEQ
(HOLESIN
  [LAMBDA (ST APL ET)
    (COND
      ((NULL APL)
        (LIST (LIST ST ET)))
      (T (CONS (LIST ST (FROM (CAR APL)))
               (HOLESIN (TO (CAR APL))
                 (CDR APL)
                 ET]))
```

Thus, the value is a list of free slots, each indicated as a list of starting time and ending time. The given definition will include zero-length periods in the list, and might be trimmed to avoid that.

The procedure is immediately tested with an example. We set the global variable *apl1* to an appointment list, which we intend to use for testing purposes:

```
12__(SETQ APL1 '(
      ((9 15) (10 0) SEE ANDERSON)
      ((10 45) (11 0) SEE LUNDSTROM)
      ((13 0) (15 0) ATTEND
         X-COMMITTEE-MEETING)
      ))
(((9 15) (10 0) SEE ANDERSON)
((10 45) (11 0) SEE LUNDSTROM)
((13 0) (15 0) ATTEND X-COMMITTEE-MEETING))
```

Here "12__" is typed out by the system and serves to number the interaction (for future reference), as well as for a prompt. Then follows the expression we type in, and the value that the system returned. We then use *apl1* in a test of *holesin*:

```
13__(HOLESIN '(9 0) APL1 '(17 0))
(((9 0) (9 15)) ((10 0) (10 45)) ((11 0) (13 0))
((15 0) (17 0)))
```

Thus, there are free slots from 9:00 to 9:15, from 10:00 to 10:45, etc.

Next, to form the list of common holes in two such lists, we define

```
(DEFINEQ
(COMMONHOLES
  [LAMBDA (L M)
    (COND
      ((NULL L)
        NIL)
      ((NULL M)
        NIL)
      ((BEFORETIME (FROM (CAR M))
                   (FROM (CAR L)))
        (COMMONHOLES M L))
      ((BEFORETIME (TO (CAR L))
                   (FROM (CAR M)))
        (COMMONHOLES (CDR L)
          M))
      [(BEFORETIME (TO (CAR M))
                   (TO (CAR L)))
        (CONS (CAR M)
          (COMMONHOLES L (CDR M]
      (T (CONS (LIST (FROM (CAR M))
                     (TO (CAR L)))
               (COMMONHOLES (CDR L)
                 M]))
```

The definition is obvious. It arranges that the first hole in l will start before the first hole in m, and then checks the three possible cases: the first element in m entirely after the first element in l, entirely included, or partially included. It proceeds appropriately for each case.

The definition of *commonholes* assumes a "<" predicate on time specifications, with the obvious definition

```
(DEFINEQ
(BEFORETIME
  [LAMBDA (V U)
   (OR (LESSP (HOURS V)
            (HOURS U))
      (AND (EQ (HOURS V)
            (HOURS U))
          (LESSP (MINUTES V)
               (MINUTES U]))
```

Again the definition is immediately tested:

```
36—(SETQ H1 (HOLESIN '(9 0) APL1 '(17 0)))
(((9 0) (9 15)) ((10 0) (10 45)) ((11 0) (13 0))
((15 0) (17 0)))

37—(SETQ H2 '(
    ((8 45) (10 30))
    ((10 40) (11 30))
    ((11 50) (12 20))
    ((12 40) (15 30)) ))
  (((8 45) (10 30)) ((10 40) (11 30)) ((11 50) (12 20))
    ((12 40) (15 30)))
```

Finally, to find which periods of duration $\geq$ d minutes are free for both persons *p1* and *p2* on day *date*, we define (using the iterative statement of INTER-LISP):

```
(DEFINEQ
(COMMONTIME
  [LAMBDA (P1 P2 DATE D)
   (for V in (COMMONHOLES
        (HOLESIN STARTDAY
           [CDR (SASSOC DATE
               (GETPROP P1
                  (QUOTE CALEND]
           ENDDAY)
        (HOLESIN STARTDAY
           [CDR (SASSOC DATE
               (GETPROP P2
                  (QUOTE CALEND]
           ENDDAY))
           collect V when (GREATERP
           (DURATION V) D]))
```

This definition looks up the calendars for the given date, determines the remaining free time for each, combines them using *commonholes*, and selects a subset of the resulting list, consisting of those elements which have the required duration. The definition uses two auxiliary functions. The function *sassoc* is like the standard LISP *assoc*, but does the comparison with *equal* rather than *eq* and is defined with INTERLISP's iterative statement as

```
(DEFINEQ (SASSOC
  [LAMBDA (X L)
   (for V in L do (RETURN V)
      when (EQUAL X (CAR V]))
```

The function *duration* which converts a time-interval into a number of minutes is defined as

```
(DEFINEQ
(DURATION
  [LAMBDA (P)
    (PLUS [TIMES 60 (DIFFERENCE
             (HOURS (TO P)) (HOURS (FROM P]
          (DIFFERENCE (MINUTES (TO P))
             (MINUTES (FROM P]))
```

Both of these are, of course, trivial.

The global variables *startday* and *endday*, intended to specify the beginning and the end of the working day, are defined through:

```
45_(SETQ STARTDAY '(9 0))
(9 0)
46_(SETQ ENDDAY '(17 0))
(17 0)
```

To test *commontime*, we design simple calendars as CALEND properties of LARSSON and SVENSSON, and then find a common time for them. We also make simple tests of *duration* and *sassoc*:

```
48_(DURATION '((8 45) (9 15)))
30
49_(DURATION ' ((10 30) (12 50)))
140

50_(PUTPROP 'LARSSON 'CALEND
     (LIST (CONS '(MON JAN 10) APL1)))
(((MON JAN 10) ((9 15) (10 0) SEE ANDERSON)
((10 45) (11 0) SEE LUNDSTROM)
((13 0) (15 0) ATTEND X-COMMITTEE-MEETING)))

51_(PUTPROP 'SVENSSON 'CALEND
   '(((FRI JAN 7)
     ((10 30) (11 30) SEE GUSTAFSSON)
     ((14 15) (16 15) ATTEND (INFORMATION
   ABOUT NEW CAR-POOL RULES)))
     ((MON JAN 10)
     ((9 0) (10 30) SEE PERSSON)
     ((13 30) (14 45) VISIT LIBRARY))))
(printout of value omitted)

64_(SASSOC '(A B) '((A AA) (B BB) ((A B) AABB)
    (C D)))
((A B) AABB)

77_(COMMONTIME 'LARSSON 'SVENSSON
   '(MON JAN 10) 90)
(((11 0) (13 0)) ((15 0) (17 0)))
```

Thus, among the common free slots for Larsson and Svensson on January 10, only those between 11:00 and 13:00, and between 15:00 and 17:00, were 90 minutes or longer.

In this fashion the program development continues. The example may raise questions regarding the notational aspects of the programming language, and regarding the programming methodology. These issues will be treated at length later on in the paper, with reference to this example. Let us simply note here that the example has illustrated some key characteristics of the language:

- There are two unusual data structures in LISP, namely the properties of atoms which allow one to store binary relations in the database, and the list structures which allow one to form composite expressions, such as, in the example, the calendar for a number of days.
- The database (stored on property-lists) is used not only for the data of the program, but also for constants of the program such as the NEXT-MONTH and similar properties.
- LISP atoms are different from named scalars in PASCAL since they are dynamic. New atoms are created all the time during the interactive session. (In PASCAL, scalars have to be declared in the program, and I/O of named scalars is not defined in the standard language.)
- Each procedure definition is a list structure. It can therefore be processed like any other data in the system. The question of readability and syntactic sweetening in programs will be discussed later in this paper.
- To define a procedure in the system, one uses a procedure-defining procedure (*defineq* in our example) which takes as argument a list of a procedure name and its intended definition. Procedure-defining procedures have all the properties of other procedures; in particular, they may be called from other procedures, which is the basic requirement for a program-generation facility.
- The normal routine in program development is to first structure one's data, then write the corresponding procedures (which are often obvious when the data structure is given), and then immediately to run a number of test examples for the procedure. This routine is possible because list structures have a textual representation in terms of sequences of characters, as well as an implementation in terms of records and pointers in the programming system. Therefore, I/O for them is defined.
- The argument/value relationship ("input-output characteristics") is more useful for describing what a procedure does than comments at arbitrary places in the program.

2. RESIDENTIAL AND SOURCE-FILE SYSTEMS

The description of the demo program omitted a discussion of debugging and program correction. The approach to this issue is different in different LISP systems. We will discuss it here with special reference to two systems, IN-TERLISP and MACLISP.

Interactive program development consists alternatingly of *tests* of procedures (or other program parts) and *editing* to correct errors discovered during the tests and/or to extend the program. INTERLISP systems, unlike many other interactive programming systems, support both of these operations. The user talks exclusively to the INTERLISP system during the interactive session. Procedures are stored in internal form as data structures in the system, and editing of procedures is done by rearranging those data structures. We shall refer to this architecture as a *residential* interactive system, since the primary copy of the program (the copy that is changed during editing operations) resides in the programming system itself. The executing system (containing procedures in internal form, test data, etc.) can also be preserved *between* runs as a dump of the virtual memory, and will be referred to as an *incarnation* of the system.

The MACLISP implementation, on the other hand, assumes the existence of a separate text editor. Programs are maintained as text files, which can be read ("loaded") by the LISP system. When a program is to be changed, the user leaves the LISP system, uses a text editor that operates on the program file, returns to the LISP system, and reloads that file. We refer to this as a *source-file system*. This is, of course, also the standard way of implementing and using languages other than LISP.

The LISP 1.6 implementation represents an intermediate stage. It contains a resident editor ("ALVINE"), but one which is not as well-developed as the one in INTERLISP, and many users prefer to use a general-purpose text editor, thus running in source-file mode.

The primary source for an evaluation of residential vs. source-file systems should, of course, be user reaction. Unfortunately, this source of verdicts is not particularly reliable: as usual, users of the various systems tend to prefer the one with which they are familiar. Also, it is hard to isolate the issue of source-file vs. residential systems from the many marginal circumstances that influence the convenience of the respective systems. The purpose of the present section is to discuss those circumstances.

2.1   Parallel Jobs

When a source-file system is used, the user must be able to maintain the programming system and the editor as parallel jobs, and to switch between them using a minimal number of keystrokes. Such service is provided by MACLISP through ITS and at Stanford through their terminal system, but is not available to users at other locations who run LISP 1.6 or MACLISP under TOPS-10.

2.2   Use of Text Files in a Residential System

INTERLISP contains a facility (makefile) whereby procedure definitions in internal form can be printed on a text file in an input-compatible format, i.e., those files can be read into the system again.

Example   In the demo example, if the user decides to name the file CALEND, he might define the contents of the file through

```
(SETQ CALENDCOMS '(
   (FNS HOURS MINUTES FROM TO
       NEXTDAY HOLESIN COMMONHOLES
       BEFORETIME COMMONTIME SASSOC
       DURATION)
   (PROP (NEXTMONTH NRDAYS) JAN
       FEB ...)
   (PROP (NEXTWEEKDAY) MON TUE ...)
   ))
```

Here the global value of the variable *calendComs* is set to a list of three commands, the first of which specifies which procedure definitions are to be included in the file. The second command specifies a number of objects, namely the "names" of months, whose NEXTMONTH and NRDAYS properties are to be printed on the file, and similarly for the third command. Then doing

```
(MAKEFILE 'CALEND)
```

will cause the file to be created. Similarly, to store the calendars of a number of persons according to the storage conventions of the demo program, one might type

```
(SETQ CURCALENDCOMS '(
  (PROP (CALEND) LARSSON SVENSSON ...)
  ))
```

(remember that the calendar was stored as the CALEND property of the owner) followed by

```
(MAKEFILE 'CURCALEND)
```

The contents of these files are loaded back by typing

```
(LOAD 'CALEND)
(LOAD 'CURCALEND)
```

The *makefile* facility might seem redundant, since the philosophy of residential systems implies that one should be able to use the same incarnation during the entire lifetime of the program, but is useful for several reasons:

1. *Transfer of programs.* An auxiliary program that has been developed in one environment might be needed in another. A text file of procedure definitions can be printed from one incarnation and loaded into the other.

2. *Back-up.* A system incarnation is relatively vulnerable to system failures and to mistakes by the user. Text files of all procedures (and related data) are useful as a back-up.

3. *Complete garbage collection.* Printing out all procedures and all necessary data as text files and reloading them into a fresh incarnation serves as a strict form of garbage collection.

4. *Copy for the user.* Some work with a program is best done by having a paper copy of the whole program to read and annotate. Saved text files can be listed and used for this purpose.

The usefulness of the second and third features depends in each instance on the reliability of the system, in the broad sense, and on the thoroughness of the garbage collector. The fourth feature has been debated: several INTER-LISP users feel that copy for the user should be produced by a printout program which is separate from the file generator. This would make it possible to make the printout nicer-looking (since the reloadability restriction would no longer apply), and would also permit more compact reloadable text files, since legibility for users could be ignored almost entirely in such files.

The file generated by *makefile* merely contains a sequence of forms, i.e., expressions of the same kind as those that are input interactively by the user. The function *load* reads the file using the same routine used for reading user input (except that some interactive features are suppressed). Corresponding to the FNS command in *calendcoms*, the file will contain calls to the procedure-defining procedure *defineq*; corresponding to PROP commands, it will also contain calls to a procedure that stores property values given as arguments. Using other commands, one can cause the file to contain calls to an arbitrary set of other procedures, for example, for doing a computation to initialize global variables or the database. Such files are widely used in LISP programming regardless of dialect.

2.3   Size of Text Files

A large LISP program consists of a large number of procedures. It is common practice to organize it as a small number of text files, with many procedure definitions or other operations in the same file. For every file, there may be a parallel file containing the compiled versions of the same procedures. An alternative method would be to let every procedure definition be an individual file.

The usual practice has several disadvantages.

1. In residential systems it is a cause of inefficiency: if one or a few procedures have been changed, then the whole file containing those definitions must be regenerated. The operation of "pretty-printing" a file of procedure definitions (i.e., printing with meaningful indentation) is fairly expensive in processor time. Similarly, the whole file may have to be recompiled after an edit, even if compilation is done independently for each procedure, which again is a waste.

These have been major problems in the INTERLISP environment. The attempted solution has been to add extra intelligence (= a kludge?) to the pretty-printer, so that it will copy the old pretty-printed file character-by-character into a new file, and only substitute freshly generated output for those procedures where a change has been made. A similar addition has been made to the compiler. While these improvements on the INTERLISP system level provide the illusion that each actual file consists of many small files, it would clearly be more elegant and economical to design this facility into the operating system in the first place (particularly since very small files are potentially very useful for other purposes as well, e.g., for the user's archive of computer mail).

2. In source-file systems, the recommended routine of text-editing the source file and reloading it into the programming system does not work well. For example, if the file also contains initialization operations as discussed under "nontrivial use of text files" above, they may cancel the test data that have been laboriously built up during the interactive session. Also, if some of the other procedures in the file have been temporarily changed in their internal versions, for example, to obtain trace printouts, the changes will be overwritten. In such cases, one would like to reload just one procedure definition, rather than the whole file.

In MACLISP, a facility has recently been introduced which attempts to solve the problem through a LISP procedure for editing procedures, which pretty-prints its argument as a temporary file, calls the text-editor and causes it to operate on that file, allows the user to edit, returns to the LISP system, and reloads the temporary file, all automatically. This, however, is a sensitive and error-prone process since the source files also have to be maintained, and does not seem to be in widespread use yet. Again, the problem would be resolved if each procedure definition were its own text file.

The ability to handle a large number of very small files is a nontrivial requirement on future operating systems (or to be precise, file management systems) intended for use in interactive program development. This requirement has several implications:

• There must be economical storage and representation of such small files. In LISP an average procedure definition may be a few hundred characters, and definitions of less than a hundred characters occur for many programs (as exemplified by the demo program).

• File catalogs must have enough space and the right organization to handle the resulting very large number of files.

• File naming conventions must enable the user to operate conveniently with large numbers of files. It is no longer sufficient to let each file have one single name, even if it is mnemonic. Instead, tree-structured or property-oriented naming is necessary, together with utility functions that operate on groups of files.

• Since several programs in a residential programming system need to maintain and make use of knowledge *about* procedures, the interface between the file catalog and the database maintained by the programming system becomes critical. User-written programs must be able to retrieve information, and even store their own information in the catalog, which then generalizes into a "system database," and/or enable user programs to maintain their own "shadow catalogs" whose contents are a superset of the system catalog. Even in the second case, the supporting program that maintains the shadow catalog must be able to inspect the main system-supported catalog, and in some way keep up to date with it.

2.4   Handling of Comments

Different LISP implementations have developed different conventions for comments. In source-file systems, comments are ignored by the read routine, and exist only in the text files. In residential systems, comments must clearly be preserved in the internal representation of procedures, so that they will be available when definitions are printed out to the user or on a file. Thus, if comments are a significant percentage of the total text, they become a memory problem. Even if virtual memory is used, they contribute to fragmentation if they are stored in the same pages as surrounding code (assuming, of course, that the code is executed much more often than it is edited). On the other hand, if comments are located on separate pages, one may have to make "comment text" a separate data type, and/or treat it separately in the general-purpose I/O for data structures to make it possible to use it for procedure definitions.

Many users prefer to have one relatively large main comment for each procedure which specifies the intended purpose and typical behavior of the procedure, and only very sparse additional comments. It is not at all clear that such comments should be integrated into the program code, since one may often want to print out those descriptive comments together with other documentation (such as cross-reference information) but without the code. Internally, it would be better to store the definition and the main comment of a procedure in two separate locations in the database, although, of course, one should be able to move easily from one to the other. In the text-file representation, it would be tempting to store the definition and the main comment as two separate files, if small files, as discussed, are made available.

2.5   Current Editing Methods

The question of residential versus source-file systems is strongly interrelated with the question of editors. Existing LISP programming environments offer a range of different types.

MACLISP under ITS (the local operating system at MIT) coexists with an editor (a variant of the standard DEC text-editor, TECO) which permits display editing ("the real-time feature"), i.e., the user who runs from a display

terminal may display the text that is being edited, and use single-keystroke
control codes to move a cursor around the screen and perform changes (insertions, deletions) one character at a time. This is an extremely convenient and
natural form of editing, but as noted above, it is not easy to integrate such an
editor into the programming system. [*Editors note*: see article by Stallman in
this book.]

The INTERLISP editor, which is part of the INTERLISP system and, therefore, written in LISP, is a procedure for editing arbitrary list structures (=
tree structures), but, of course, primarily intended for list structures that
represent programs. The central routine is called with a list structure as argument, and receives user commands that operate on this tree. Elementary
commands move a cursor up and down the tree, perform simple changes, and
print out the "current" part of the tree (from the cursor and a few levels down).
A wide repertoire of higher-level commands is available, for example, commands for searching occurrences of certain patterns and for substitution by
pattern, all the time in terms of tree structures rather than text. This editor
was developed for an environment of hard-copy terminals, and although it can
obviously be used on display terminals as well, it does not make full use of
their possibilities. [*Editors' note*: see article by Barstow in this volume].

Example of the INTERLISP editor   In the demo program, suppose we want to
correct the procedure *holesin* so that it suppresses zero-length periods in the
list that it returns as value. This is easily done by introducing two additional
branches in the conditional expression in the definition of *holesin*, so that the
expression comes to read:

```
(COND
   ((EQUAL ST ET) NIL)
   ((NULL APL) ... )
   ((EQUAL ST (FROM (CAR APL)))
    (HOLESIN (TO (CAR APL)) (CDR APL) ET))
   (T ... ))
```

where the dots indicate the two old branches in the conditional. This update
would be performed using the following edit commands (commands in capital
letters, comments in small letters):

```
(EDITF 'HOLESIN)
F COND
(-3 ((EQUAL ST (FROM (CAR APL)))
   (HOLESIN (TO (CAR APL)) (CDR APL) ET]
      insert new element before the third
      element of the current expression
(-2 ((EQUAL ST ET) NIL]
      insert new element before the second
      element of the current expression
PP
      pretty-print the current expression
      to check that it came out right
      (optional)
OK
      return from the editor
```

Both of these editors have higher-level capabilities, for example, for defining
and using macros. The INTERLISP editor may also call arbitrary LISP programs, which is a very powerful feature. Even if the language for writing

Table 1. Possible Choices of Editing Capabilities

Issue	Choice A	Choice B
Objects on which the editor operates	Text	List structures
Preferred medium	Hard copy (i.e., a 'print' command is used to display the current state of the edited item)	Screen (i.e., editor dynamically maintains a picture of the item that is being edited)
Size of increment in communication between editor and rest of programming system	File (i.e., editor is used to edit a file, which is then loaded into the programming system)	Single edit operation (i.e., each individual edit command is available to the rest of the programming system) (this corresponds to a residential editor)

macros in TECO has the power of a programming language, it is an advantage to be able to communicate between code that is executed in the editor and the database that the integrated programming system maintains for describing the program under development.

The choice between the residential INTERLISP editor and the display-oriented editing used in the MACLISP environment (as well as by some INTERLISP users) differs for different people, even after careful discussion and comparison of the alternatives, and may, therefore, be explained as a matter of personal taste. However, these two alternatives do not exhaust the full range of possible choices. We can distinguish three dimensions of choice, as detailed in Table 1.

For each of these dimensions, Choice B is clearly better than Choice A, all other things being equal. A list-structure editor communicates with the user in terms of the real structures of interest, rather than their incidental textual representation. Also, everybody who has used a screen-oriented editor will agree to its superiority.

For the third dimension, size of increment, there is a possible intermediate case, namely, the procedure-level edit in which the main programming system "knows" that a certain procedure is being edited, but does not know the details of how it is changed. The new MACLISP editor described above is on this level. Choice B is superior to this intermediate choice, which again is superior to Choice A, with respect to the possibilities they offer for bookkeeping when a procedure has been edited. For example, if the edit is intended to be definite rather than temporary, then information which has previously been computed from the old definition becomes obsolete and must be deleted and possibly replaced at once. If the procedure had been compiled, it now has to be recompiled. If the procedure-call structure or other similar formal documentation had been extracted from the program, that analysis must be reperformed or, better still, amended in those parts which need to be changed. If code had been temporarily inserted in the old definition, for example for trace printouts or statistics gathering, that code should probably be added to the edited procedure as well. (Editing should sometimes be done on a clean version where these temporary changes have been made, so that the edit is retained when the insertion is removed, and so that program files will be correct when they are generated.) The list could be continued; the general observation is that the editor is a crucial part of a residential programming system and has to communicate with almost everything else. It is, therefore, very important to organize the total system so that such communication is helped rather than hindered. Both in principle and in practice, this is done much better when the programming system has access to more details of the editor's operations, i.e., the increments are small.

The trivial form of an editor is the one represented by the left-hand column, i.e., a hard-copy-oriented text editor that is applied to program files. The INTERLISP editor and the editing facilities of the MACLISP environment represent improvements in different dimensions. For the future, one would, of course, want a system that implements the advanced, Choice B facilities in all three dimensions.

Theoretically, the simplest way of accomplishing that is to write the entire screen-oriented editor, including input and output of individual characters, in LISP. Unfortunately, this does not seem to be realistic, except in a personal-computer environment, because the run-time characteristics of a large LISP system makes it hard to implement low-level routines for continuously updating a screen. The dedicated single-user LISP machine at MIT, described above, however, has a screen editor written in LISP. [*Editors' note*: see the article on the Lisp Machine in this volume].

2.6   Procedure-Level Awareness of Editing

A possible compromise is to maintain the display editor as a separate program, but enable the LISP system to call it after having stored a procedure definition as an intermediate file. This approach could be used in a residential system. It would be easier to do there than it was in the source-file MACLISP environment, since the automatic maintenance of source files would no longer be necessary. This approach represents Choice B along the dimension of the medium, and the intermediate choice along the awareness-level dimension. Some disadvantages remain: this approach enables the programming system to know *which* procedures have been edited, but not easily *which parts* of procedures have been edited. It does not apply for certain types of data structures that do not print well, such as common sublists and circular structures. Nor does it apply when one is really interested in editing the contents of the "relational" database (property-list information), rather than list structures. Finally, the powerful ability to call arbitrary LISP code from editor commands is likely to be lost.

A variation of the same idea is to locate the display-oriented editor in the terminal communication interface of the operating system, and to let it operate on a buffer containing the immediately past history of the conversation between user and computer.[2] Besides trivial uses, for example for scrolling back to the previous interaction, the buffer would be used for editing of procedures in a residential system as follows: when the user asks to edit the definition of a certain procedure, the system prints out the definition on the user terminal. The user edits it, changes its status from "output" to "input", and sends it back to the computing system as a new definition of the procedure. This solution has the same disadvantages as the previous variation, but has the

---

[2] Such a facility has been proposed at the Stanford Artificial Intelligence Project (the "page editor").

possible advantage that the editor in the terminal communication interface can be used for a number of other purposes as well.

2.7   Screen Supervisor

Another possible approach is to let the structure editor itself be integrated in the LISP system, but to let it communicate with a screen supervisor routine which is responsible for receiving commands (including cursor movements in some sense) and for updating the screen, and which is set up so that it can provide sufficiently fast response. One may want to locate it in a processor other than the one that runs the LISP system. In this architecture, the resident LISP editor and the screen supervisor routine have to communicate for each edit operation made by the user. One would expect systems of this kind to consume a lot of processor time, which, however, should not be a big problem in the future. But some hard design problems must also be solved for this approach, and it should be regarded as an interesting research topic and not a simple implementation job. An experimental system has recently been presented by Teitelman [Teitelman 1977].

Among these alternative implementation strategies, the approach using a screen supervisor routine implies structure editing, whereas the approach of using a display editor which communicates with the LISP system in increments of one procedure at a time can be implemented more straightforwardly if one assumes text editing rather than structure editing. However, the use of a text editor enables one to use the same editor for several programming languages and for ordinary text, as opposed to having a separate editor for each purpose. In some computing environments, this is a significant advantage.

2.8   Efficiency Considerations

Since a residential system may be expected to provide more services to the user, one would presumably be willing to pay for this by a certain increase in resource requirements, namely processor time and/or memory requirements. Even if one figures on computer costs only, a system which makes it possible to develop the same program in a smaller number of terminal hours because it has better debugging facilities may clearly be acceptable even if its costs per terminal hour are higher.

It is, however, very hard to quantify the variables in this tradeoff. There is considerable controversy regarding the relative resource consumption of MACLISP and INTERLISP for the DEC-10. Also, these systems differ in ways which are significant for resource consumption, or measurements of resource consumption, but which are not directly related to the issue of residential versus source-file systems; for example, INTERLISP is more complete in its checking of possible user errors. Some other difficulties are related to the issue at hand, but would go away if the system were built right. As noted earlier, printing text files of program definitions is quite costly; this problem would be greatly reduced if each procedure were its own file, as proposed above. Additional considerations are introduced by system facilities that are expensive in resources (time or space) and unwanted by many users, but hard to remove from the integrated system. With all these incidental circumstances, it is very hard to tell how costly the residential design as such has to be. Furthermore, if the present optimistic expectations about the advent of personal computers for LISP materialize, the question might lose its interest as the residential design becomes affordable.

2.9   Complexity Considerations

A related problem in residential systems is their complexity. There are so many things that one would like to do in a residential system with an integrated set of facilities for the user, and which in principle one could clearly do. Unfortunately, too many of these features interrelate in too many ways, and it becomes very hard to control the resulting complexity. This leads to unpredictability, unreliability, unhabitability, undocumentability, and other unpleasant properties. As always, the user, who was the intended beneficiary of the system, instead becomes the victim.

2.10   Summary

The residential system design offers many possibilities to the system designer, and should in principle allow very attractive systems. But in designing such systems, one must be careful not to sacrifice objectives which are of basic importance to users, such as an editing regime which is as convenient as possible; convenient handling of text files; convenient storage of comments; efficiency; and control of complexity.

3.   SUPERIMPOSED LANGUAGES

One of the consequences of the program/data equivalence in LISP is that it is useful as a high-level implementation language for new languages that the user invents in the course of his work. This is clearly a useful property in experiments with programming systems. It has been used in a number of different ways.

3.1   Providing a Surface Language

The usual syntax for writing LISP programs as parenthesized expressions ("S-expressions") was illustrated in the demo example. It is widely known and sometimes abhorred by people that do not use the language. This notation came up in the first place as a corollary of two basic design choices in LISP, namely, that 1) programs should be represented as data structures; and 2) I/O for all data structures should be defined.

Thus, in the basic programming system, one does not have to implement a special program for reading source programs and convert them to internal representation as list structures: it is possible to rely on the general-purpose I/O, and it is clearly advantageous to do so in a minimal implementation. However, if one should prefer some other notation for programs, one may, of course, implement an alternative read program which converts that notation to the internal representation.

Example   Suppose we want to use an ALGOL-like notation, with the following infix operators for list structures:

```
l.hd              the head (first element of) the list l
l.tl              the tail of the list l, i.e., the remainder after the
                  head has been removed
l o m             the list obtained from the list m by adding one
                  element, l, at the front
<l₁, l₂, ... lₘ>  the list with the <lᵢ> as successive elements
```

Then the procedure *holesin* in the demo program would be written as

```
holesin (st, apl, et) = =
if apl = NIL then <<st,et>>
else <st, from (apl.hd)> o holesin (to (apl.hd),apl.tl,et)
```

instead of the S-expression representation:

```
(HOLESIN
  [LAMBDA (ST APL ET)
    (COND
      ((NULL APL)
       (LIST (LIST ST ET)))
      (T (CONS (LIST ST (FROM (CAR APL)))
              (HOLESIN (TO (CAR APL))
                      (CDR APL)
                   ET])))
```

A LISP program for reading the ALGOL-like notation would rely on low-level input primitives: the LISP system kernel contains procedures both for low-level I/O (which read or write one character or one atom at a time) and high-level I/O (which read or write a list structure as a parenthesized expression in one single stroke). The program reader itself must, of course, be entered into the system in S-expression form, as in the second example above.

Notice, then, that such a program is *not* a translator from the ALGOL-like notation to the S-expression representation above. There are three representations involved: the list structure (tree structure) used inside the computer, the textual S-expression representation, and the textual ALGOL-like representation. The general-purpose input routine translates from the second to the first representation; the alternative input routine for programs, from the third to the first representation.

We shall use the term *surface language* for a notation for programs that has to be read by a special program reader, e.g., the ALGOL-like notation in the example. The issue of such surface languages is bound to come up whenever one organizes a programming system according to the criteria in the section on requirements above, and it may, therefore, be worthwhile to summarize the LISP experience with them.

In the early stages of LISP's history, everyone seems to have assumed that surface languages would appear. After all, John McCarthy, who originated LISP, was also a member of the committee that defined ALGOL 60. The name LISP 1.5 seems to indicate that it was an intermediate solution to be used until LISP 2 (which would use such a surface language) appeared. The LISP 2 project started out ambitiously, but reportedly caught the PL/I disease (proliferation of features) and did not enjoy the PL/I antidote (money), and, therefore, was never completed.

Since that time, a considerable number of readers for surface languages with the same intended purpose have been written [Henneman 1964] [Smith 1970] [Hearn 1968]. Users have been reluctant to adopt these systems; most users of LISP systems prefer not to use them. Some reasons are:

• The representation obtained from standard high-level I/O, although forbidding at first, is quite easy to work with when one gets used to it.
• The major problem when writing S-expressions, namely, matching of parentheses, has been solved with the introduction of "super-parentheses", such as the right bracket in the example above.
• The legibility problem has been solved by systematic indentation ("pretty-

printing") to indicate depth of parentheses, equivalent to depth in the tree structure.

• It is very difficult to write a good surface-language system. Writing the translator itself is the trivial part; what is harder is to make sure that error diagnoses and other communications with the user will come out right. One must allow mixed representations, such as those needed to support program-generating programs.

• In integrated systems, these problems become much harder: one must arrange for correct printout of the surface language from the internal representation, which means that either the transformation must be reversible or the source form must be preserved. One must also modify the editor to allow the user to edit in the surface representation. It turns out that the surface language processor tends to interrelate with almost every part of the integrated programming system, i.e., there is a serious structuring problem.

The moral of the story is that if a surface language is to be used, then it should be designed into the system from the start. ECL [Wegbreit et al. 1972] has taken this approach; it is only described to the users in terms of its surface language, although the internal structure of its programming system is very similar to a LISP system. But one should also be aware that the decision to use a surface language will place a heavy burden on all other facilities that one wants to build into the system. Further, it isolates the user from the internal representation of programs, and discourages him from using it for his own purposes.

3.2 Viewing Control Primitives as Procedures

If one decides not to have a special reader for procedure definitions, one must look into other ways of improving the local readability of procedure definitions. Let us discuss first the issue of control primitives, where several approaches have been tried.

In its original conception [McCarthy et al. 1962], LISP was a very simple programming language with conditional expressions, and function calls allowing recursion as the only control primitives. While these primitives are theoretically sufficient, they force the programmer to introduce and name a new procedure almost every time a loop is to be performed. This is clearly inconvenient. However, other control primitives can easily be accommodated within the syntax of LISP's standard input/output, i.e., nested tuples.

The obvious notation for an iteration statement and for local *goto's* in a block are exemplified by the following two equivalent procedures for printing n and n^2 where n ranges from 1 to m:

```
(DEFINEQ
[PRINTSQUARES1 (LAMBDA (M)
  (FOR N FROM 1 TO M DO (PROGN
      (PRIN1 N)
      (TAB 10)
      (PRINT (TIMES N N]
[PRINTSQUARES2 (LAMBDA (M) (PROG (N)
      (SETQ N 0)
LOP   (SETQ N (ADD1 N))
      (COND ((GREATERP N M) (RETURN)))
      (PRIN1 N)
      (TAB 10)
      (PRINT (TIMES N N))
      (GO LOP])
```

The *for* expression and *prog* expression in these examples satisfy the data-structure syntax, and also satisfy a basic assumption of the LISP interpreter, namely, that in every list which is to be evaluated (every "form"), the first element must be a function name or operator which specifies how the rest of the form is to be treated. (Infix operators are harder to handle and will be discussed below.) The *prog* primitive was implemented on the machine-code level in early stages of LISP's development, which established a *de facto* standard. The *for* primitive was not standardized. One can guess that the following reasons contributed:

1. It is easy for each user to define a *for* primitive similar to the one above, using the existing primitives of the languages.

2. Many variations of *for* statements are possible, for example, involving loops over the members of a list, and there are different ways of collecting a value of the expression—one may form a list of the value returned in each cycle of the loop, add those values if they are numbers, form their union if they are sets, or perform almost any other binary operation.

3. The prevailing ethics of LISP programming in its early days encouraged the use of so-called mapping functions. For the example above, one would define a mapping function that might be called *mapint*, and use it as follows:

```
(DEFINEQ
(PRINTSQUARES3 (LAMBDA (M)
  (MAPINT 1 M (FUNCTION (LAMBDA (N) (PROGN
       (PRIN1 N)
       (TAB 10)
       (PRINT (TIMES N N]
```

Here *mapint* would be defined as (in LISP 1.5):

```
(DEFINEQ
(MAPINT (LAMBDA (FROM TO FN)
      (COND ((GREATERP FROM TO) NIL)
            (T (PROG2 (FN FROM)
                  (MAPINT (ADD1 FROM)
                      TO FN]
```

which means it calls the procedural argument *fn* for integer arguments ranging from *from* to *to* in steps of 1. Mapping functions are nice and pure in theory but not so convenient in practice, since each user tends to build up a wildly growing fauna of different mapping functions. In a *for* operator, it is easier to accommodate different facilities through different choices of keywords, such as *from* and *to* in the example. INTERLISP [Teitelman 1978] contains a rich *for* statement in its program library; it allows one to write, for example, the following expression for forming a list of those members of a given list k whose position number is a member of a given list p:

```
(FOR X IN K AS I FROM 1 COLLECT X WHEN
    (MEMBER I P))
```

where x and i are the two iteration variables and run in parallel.

Mapping functions and the *for* operator have one thing in common: they are higher-level constructs which allow the user to express program control conveniently, and which have been defined from other and more basic primitives in the LISP system. Additional control structures such as a *case* construct (called *selectq* in INTERLISP) have also been developed in some LISP systems and by individual users. This development can be understood by viewing LISP as a very-high-level implementation language, and as an extensible language with facilities for defining new control structures.

If interpretation of the LISP program is sufficient, then the implementation of constructs such as *for* and *selectq* only requires system primitives which exist in LISP 1.5 and all subsequent systems, namely, the so-called FEXPR's (or NLAMBDA's) and also the *prog* facility. In order to compile them as well, one needs either a macro facility or handles on the compiler. (Handles will be described in a later section.) In fact, a macro facility may be viewed simply as a handle on the compiler. Current LISP systems are usually equipped with a macro facility for exactly this purpose.

3.3   Infix Operations

Perhaps the most striking difference between the basic LISP notation and conventional programming languages is the absence of infix operators. The interpreter assumes as input a data structure where the procedure name or operator is the first element of every sublist. Such data structures print as shown in the following example: $a*b + c - d$ become

```
(PLUS (TIMES A B) (DIFFERENCE C D))
```

Several methods are possible for allowing the user a more natural notation:

1. Introduce a special operator that indicates infix expressions, so that one would write the above example as

```
(| A TIMES B PLUS C MINUS D)
```

The | operator would then be defined in the same way as *for* and *selectq*, discussed in the previous section.

2. Modify the LISP interpreter to allow, for example,

```
(A TIMES B PLUS C MINUS D)
```

3. Modify the I/O conventions so that the printed expressions are infix, but the internal representation as data structures is prefix like before.

4. Rely on the exception handling mechanism in the interpreter. The user is allowed to type, for example,

```
A*B + C − D
```

which is read as one single atom by the input routines. When the interpreter encounters this "variable", an error occurs because the "variable" does not have a value. The error machinery will then inspect the name of the "variable", reconstruct its intended meaning, and convert to the basic LISP notation.

The first method does not look as well as the others, but is easy to implement and use and can be implemented by any user who wants an infix-notation facility. The second approach has been used in QLISP [Griss 1976], but not in LISP for several reasons including compatibility. The third approach would very likely cause confusion for users, if provided as an add-on feature. However, Tholerus [Tholerus 1975] has developed this idea in a systematic way; his proposal should be considered seriously in designing future systems. The fourth method is used by the CLISP facility in INTERLISP [Teitelman 1978].

It has several advantages, such as allowing a natural notation and being transparent to users who do not use the facility (at least theoretically). However, the CLISP facility which in its entirety contains several other mechanisms besides this one, is controversial among INTERLISP users: some like it, some do not. It is an open question whether this is due to remaining initial difficulties in the current implementation, or whether it is inappropriate to locate the infix/prefix transformation in the exception-handling machinery.

Since numerical computations are usually of minor importance in LISP applications, the availability of infix operators for arithmetic functions is not very important. Infixes for Boolean connectives and for common operations on lists, such as *cons, append, member, union,* and many similar functions are more significant. However, a possible objection is that infixes seem to do best in relatively small expressions, and may do more harm than good in complex expressions with many levels of application of functions, which are common in LISP. Consider for example the following translation into CLISP (in the INTERLISP system) of the function *next-day* as defined in our calendar application:

```
(NEXTDAY
  [LAMBDA (DATE)
    <(GETPROP DATE:1 'NEXTWEEKDAY)!
         (if DATE:3=(GETPROP DATE:2
                        'NRDAYS)
             then <(GETPROP DATE:2
                            'NEXTMONTH)
                   1>
             else (LIST DATE:2 DATE:3+1))>])
```

Here the exclamation sign is used as an infix operator for *cons.* It is not at all clear that readability has increased compared to the original definition.

3.4 Declarations

The term "declarations" is used here for information about entities in a program (variables, procedure names, etc.) which is stated once and then used during the execution of the program and/or in an analysis of the program, such as a compiler. With this definition, declarations in an incremental system often take on a different appearance than in a conventional compiling system. In the conventional system, declarations are always statements in the program that is fed to the compiler. In an incremental system, where one has a database which may be updated and used by successive expressions that are evaluated by the system, it is possible to input declarations separately, to store them in the database, and to use them either statically when procedures are input or compiled, or dynamically when they are interpreted. This approach also makes it possible to extend the use of the declarations gradually, and, thus, obtain a more and more complete description of the program.

The first use of declarations in conventional languages such as ALGOL was to distinguish integer, real, and Boolean variables. This usage is not necessary in interpreted LISP, since the distinction is made in the data and determined dynamically during execution. The first use of declarations in LISP was instead to provide the compiler with information about free variables, i.e., variables that are declared in one procedure and used in another procedure deeper in recursion.

When LISP is to be compiled on today's conventional computers with typeless data, however, the compiler can make good use of typing information for numerical data (integer, real, etc.). Most LISP systems do this in the same fashion as assembler languages, i.e., by having a separate real plus, integer plus, etc., in addition to the general-purpose plus. The specialized functions are recommended for frequently executed parts of the program. Surface-language systems such as REDUCE [Hearn 1968] also allow conventional, ALGOL-like type declarations for variables, and do the same type checking, type conversion, and selection of operation as a conventional compiler.

The approach used by the current LISP systems in this area may seem shockingly primitive, but one must remember that numerical calculations play a very minor part in the artificial intelligence applications in which the systems are most used. REDUCE, on the other hand, is used mainly for formula manipulation, where heavy calculations do occur and where there is a fairly broad assortment of numerical or pseudonumerical types: real, integer, complex, rational, polynomial, etc.

Especially for artificial intelligence applications of LISP, declarations of data structures are potentially more useful. Relatively little has been done to implement such facilities, and some users argue that they are not needed.

Example   Let us first illustrate with an example what data structure can do in the LISP context. The data structure for the personal calendar in the demo program could be described as per Display 1, according to a design proposal for an extension to REDUCE [Griss 1976].

The definition should be self-explanatory since the data structure has been defined informally above. The final LIST in the definition of TIME is a constructor function which is defined by default in the other declarations. With these definitions, the user can declare variables to have one of these types, for example

```
DECLARE FR:FROM;
```

and to select and change their components using a functional notation, for example

```
HOURS(FR).
```

```
                        DISPLAY 1
RECORD CALENDAR = LISTOF DAYPLAN;
RECORD DAYPLAN = STRUCT(DATE:DATELIST, APPS:LISTOF APPOINTMENT);
RECORD DATELIST =
   STRUCT(DAYOFWEEK:DAYNAME, MONTH:MONTHNAME, DAY:INTEGER);
RECORD DAYNAME = (MON, TUE, WED, THU, FRI, SAT, SUN);
RECORD MONTHNAME = analogous
RECORD APPOINTMENT =
   STRUCT(FROM:TIME, TO:TIME, VERB:ATOM, OBJECT:SYMBOLIC);
RECORD TIME = STRUCT(HOURS:INTEGER, MINUTES:INTEGER):LIST;
```

This machinery obviously serves two major purposes, namely, to make programs more easily legible and to make type checking possible. Since REDUCE is a surface language to LISP's interpretable data structures, the type checking and choice of operation for each selector is done when a procedure is read into the system. The checking is done individually for each procedure that is input, and global declarations may be stored permanently in the database.

The arguments for such a use of declarations are the same as in other languages, and are well known. However, some LISP users oppose it on the same grounds as they resist separate readers for programs, namely, that declarations used in this way interact unfavorably with other parts of the programming system and tend to insulate the program from the programmer. It is then often argued that 1) The kinds of bugs which can be diagnosed by type checks can also be quickly found and corrected in interactive program development; 2) Bugs in symbol-processing programs have more visible effects, and are therefore easier to find, than bugs in programs for, let us say, numerical computation or simulation; and 3) The obligation to declare the data type of variables in conformity with one of the proposed systems does more harm than good because it restrains the programmer.

These statements are, of course, contested, but their validity may be a matter of personal programming style.

Even if one does not need declarations for type checking, there is still the question of program legibility. Many LISP programmers solve this problem in the manner indicated in the demo program, i.e., by defining low-level procedures such as *hours* and *from* which select components of structures, and then use them rather than the elementary combinations of *car* and *cdr*. This practice can obviously be automated. This has been done in the so-called record package in INTERLISP, where some of the declarations in the above example for REDUCE could be written as

```
(RECORD DAYPLAN (DATE APPOINTMENTLIST))
(RECORD DATE (DAYOFWEEK MONTH DAY))
(RECORD APPOINTMENT (FROM TO VERB OBJECT))
(RECORD TIME (HOURS MINUTES))
```

The facility in INTERLISP does not do any type checking, and only serves the purposes of legibility and data independence. It is weaker than the proposed facility in REDUCE in some ways; for example, it does not allow one to declare APPOINTMENTLIST to be a list of APPOINTMENTs in the example. It is stronger in some other ways, particularly since it allows records to be implemented in various ways such as lists, arrays, hash-arrays, property-lists, etc., and, therefore, achieves data independence over a wider range of realizations.

Still other uses of declarations are for documentation purposes and as support for utility programs that perform service operations on parts of the database, e.g., data entry, tabular presentation, and merges of structured data from different sources. The design of such facilities has been treated in [Sandewall 1975] and [Hewitt 1972].

These different experiments with the use of declarations in LISP systems have one thing in common, namely, that they all work by extensions to the basic LISP system. The approach is similar to the one used for control primitives, as discussed above: the basic system is used as an implementation tool and for its extensibility. It does not contain the desired facilities, but it makes it easy to implement the facilities of one's choice, and to experiment with changes in these facilities. In the case of declarations, the program/data equivalence and the database during the interactive session are the significant properties of the language that make this approach possible.

The extensibility properties which make it possible to implement subsystems for control structures and high-level data structures are also generally available for the users of these subsystems. For example, the *for* construct in INTERLISP allows the user to add more keywords to the existing ones (*do, collect, while,* etc.) and to define how the new keywords are to be used. Similarly, the proposed new type facility in REDUCE stores coercion rules as properties of data-type names or, more abstractly, as a network with names of data types as nodes. This network is available to the user, who can extend it dynamically.

The language extensions mentioned here, such as REDUCE and the CLISP facility in INTERLISP, are by no means the only ones. Because of the ease of implementing simple facilities of this kind, many LISP users implement and use their own.

A conclusion from this experience is that extensibility in programming languages may not be particularly interesting as a goal in itself. If the language is designed on certain basic premises, such as incrementality and program/data equivalence, extensibility is obtained automatically.

3.5   Very-High-Level Languages

The period 1970-75 saw a number of attempts to create very-high-level languages based on LISP. PLANNER [Hewitt 1972], QA4 [Rulifson et al. 1972], CONNIVER [McDermott and Sussman 1972], QLISP [Sacerdoti et al. 1976], and POPLER [Davies 1973] are the best known ones. An early forerunner was LISP A [Sandewall 1968]. These systems have been reviewed in [Bobrow and Raphael 1974].

The basic feature of these systems is that they integrate a number of ideas and facilities which could be described and discussed separately, but which enhance each other and therefore should be implemented together. They include:

• A common mechanism for invocation of programs and data. A procedure call and an instruction to check for the existence of a relationship in the database should use the same syntax and should be interchangeable.

• Pattern-directed invocation. Each invocation should be an expression containing constants and variables, which calls for the values of the variables to be computed through access to the database to find entries that match the pattern, and/or through calls to procedures whose "names" or description indicate that they can be useful for filling in blanks in such patterns.

• Nondeterminism, meaning that the computation may split in such a fashion that it continues independently in each of the branches. Pattern-directed invocation may result in nondeterminism, since one pattern may be matched in several ways and since several procedures or data items may be relevant for the same pattern.

The implementation of at least some of these systems was quite modular. It consisted of a pattern-matcher, a database handler, a nondeterministic executive, etc., with common conventions and mutual procedure calls as the common glue. In retrospect, it appears that the glue was not as strong as it first seemed.

Each of the modules could be built in many different ways, and the particular combination of choices implicit in any one system found very few satisfied users. Also, the resulting systems were big and clumsy, and users were reluctant to pay the price in computer resources of using the entire systems. Except for a few striking early demonstrations, for example, by Winograd [Winograd 1971], these systems do not seem to have been used much. The present trend is to make use of, and continue to develop, each module separately, and to use them as individual tools for various applications.

Higher-level languages of still another type built on the LISP system, namely, embedded languages, are closely related to questions of program structure, and are discussed separately further on.

4. PROGRAMMING METHODOLOGY

The LISP community has barely participated at all in the last few years' debate on structured programming and other aspects of programming methodology. However, some program development methods are explicitly encouraged by properties which are now classical in the LISP language and existing LISP systems.

For bottom-up program development, it is desirable to be able to test procedures as they are developed. LISP systems support this practice through the incremental implementation and the predefined I/O for data structures. This was illustrated in the demo program.

The complementary method of top-down programming (usually carried out through stepwise refinement) also suggests some reasonable properties for interactive programming systems, for example:

- If the definition of the procedure P contains a call to the procedure Q, but Q is not actually called for a certain argument vector $\mathbf{x}$ to P, then the programming system should be able to operate and to compute P ($\mathbf{x}$) even if Q has not yet been defined.
- If P calls Q as in the previous case and Q is undefined, but computation of P ($\mathbf{y}$) actually leads to a call to Q, then the programming system should make a "soft landing." In other words, it should not print an error message and abort, but rather preserve the current environment and allow the programmer to inspect the situation, decide on a suitable value that Q could have returned, type it into the programming system, and make the computation continue.

The first of these possibilities is, of course, available in LISP, as in most interpretive systems. My own experience as well as reports from other programmers indicates that this method is standard practice.

The second method, i.e., interaction as a substitute for an undefined procedure, is supported by INTERLISP systems (and also, but not as smoothly) by MACLISP.

Example The following sample console session illustrates what happens in our calendar application if the function *beforetime* (which is intended to check whether one hour-minute combination precedes another one) has not been defined when the function *commonholes* is tested. User input is in italics.

```
34_(COMMONHOLES H1 H2)
u.d.f.
(BEFORETIME broken)
35: IN?
COMMONHOLES:(BEFORETIME (FROM (CAR M)) (FROM (CAR L)))
35: (FROM (CAR M))
(3 45)
36: (FROM (CAR L))
(9 0)
37: RETURN T
BEFORETIME = T
```

The system has typed out *u.d.f.* (for "undefined function") and the name of the offending function. The user typed the command IN? to find out where the problem occurred. He then typed in the arguments of the function in the offending position, to find out their current values. With this, he decided the value that the offending expressions should have, and allowed the computation to continue.

The next time the problem occurs, he decides that he had better define *beforetime* after all. He does so in the ordinary way, and then proceeds as follows:

```
41:GO
  BEFORETIME = NIL
(((9 0) (9 15)) ((10 0) (10 30))
((10 40) (10 45)) ((11 0) (11 30))
((11 50) (12 20)) (12 40) (13 0))
((15 0) (15 30)))
```

The computation proceeds to the final answer.

The example is slightly artificial, since normally INTERLISP would not bother with an interaction when the error occurs at such a shallow level of recursion.

The common programming practice, however, is not to leave procedures undefined intentionally, but instead to make a simple definition at first, and later substitute a more elaborate one. The original definition may be a real dummy, for example, it may simply return a constant value, but more often it is a viable, although simplified, case of the intended definite procedure. For example, input/output of object data is often done in the form of S-expressions (i.e., using high-level kernel I/O) in early stages of program development, and nicer-looking I/O is substituted later on. This enables the programmer to focus first on the essential aspects of the problem.

Example   This practice was illustrated in the calendar example, where we showed how calendars were output using the standard I/O for data structures. The resulting notation is obviously not acceptable for the final user, but is acceptable for small test cases during program development. As a first step towards improved readability, one could try the system's standard pretty-printer (for printing using indentation), which would print Svensson's calendar in the example above as

```
(((FRI JAN 7)
  ((10 30)
   (11 30)
   SEE GUSTAFSSON)
  ((14 15)
   (16 15)
   ATTEND
   (INFORMATION ABOUT NEW CAR-POOL RULES)))
 ((MON JAN 10)
  ((9 0)
   (10 30)
   SEE PERSSON)
  ((13 30)
   (14 45)
   VISIT LIBRARY)))
```

As this clearly did not work very well, one could define a special printing function for calendars as

```
(DEFINEQ
 (PRINCAL
  [LAMBDA (P)
   (for DAY in (GETPROP P (QUOTE CALEND))
        do (PROGN (PRINT (CAR DAY))
                  (for ENTRY in (CDR DAY)
                       do (PROG2 (TAB 6) (PRINT ENTRY)))
                  (TERPRI]))
```

This results in the output shown by Display 2.

DISPLAY 2

```
95_(PRINCAL 'SVENSSON)
(FRI JAN 7)
    ((10 30) (11 30) SEE GUSTAFSSON)
    ((14 15) (16 15) ŒATTEND (INFORMATION ABOUT NEW CAR-POOL RULES))
(MON JAN 10)
    ((9 0) (10 30) SEE PERSSON)
    ((13 30) (14 45) VISIT LIBRARY)
```

This example serves to illustrate two different principles. First, we notice that a few lines of programming produced a reasonably legible printout, and infer that 15 or 20 more lines of straightforward code should be sufficient for producing a listing that is entirely satisfactory to the final user, with 10:30 instead of (10 30) etc. The programmer can therefore confidently assign low priority to communication of data from the program: it is something which almost takes care of itself, with just a little help. An analogous situation holds for input of data to the program. In a conventional programming language, the programmer would have to write and debug input/output routines for data before even starting to test and debug any other code.

The example also illustrates a method of program development which may be characterized as *structured growth*: an initial program with a pure and simple structure is written, tested, and then allowed to grow by increasing the ambition of its modules. The process continues recursively as each module is rewritten. The principle applies not only to input/output routines, but also to the flexibility of the data handled by the program, the sophistication of deduction, the number and versatility of the services provided by the system, etc. The growth can occur both "horizontally," through the addition of more facilities, and "vertically" through a deepening of existing facilities and making them more powerful in some sense.

That LISP users tend to prefer structured growth rather than stepwise refinement is not an effect of the programming system, since both methods are supported. I believe, however, that it is a natural consequence of the interactive development method, since programs in early stages of growth can be executed and programs in early stages of refinement cannot. Nor has there been much discussion about the matter, at least not in terms of abstract programming methodology. (The term structured growth has not been used before.) Structured growth seems to be simply a technique that people tend to use spontaneously if they are given a free choice in an open environment.

An obvious objection to this programming method is that it may encourage "featurism," i.e., large programs with many different facilities, rather than concise programs that embody a small number of powerful principles. A possible answer is that a computer program that approximates an aspect of intelligent human behavior very often has to account specifically for many different kinds of situations, and, thus, that one really needs a programming technique for building feature-rich systems, whereas attempts to find simple principles are doomed anyway. Incidentally, the techniques for obtaining feature-rich systems may also be important for designing programs with which untrained humans find it comfortable to interact.

From the moralistic view of programming methodology, one might, of course, still argue that the method of structured growth is a bad habit, since it encourages one to make changes in programs, and changes are a known source of errors. The answer would be that even if some kinds of program changes are dangerous and/or bad, that does not prove that all of them are.

Stepwise refinement and structured growth are both variants of top-down programming, since they encourage one to decide on the overall structure of the program first, and then proceed to decisions about its parts. Much could be done in the programming system to further support top-down work in addition to what is done by current LISP systems, for example:

- Keep track of "open statements" or "expansion points." When users type in a piece of code which they know has to be refined or rewritten later, it should be possible to tell this to the system and ask later what work remains to be done.
- Distinguish different types of edit operations. Given an initial approximation to a program, some changes will be made to correct bugs, and some to extend the program. It would be desirable to treat these two kinds of changes separately, so that several layers of refinement or growth could be maintained in parallel. It is a common observation that early versions of a program are useful introductions to later, full-grown versions. Similarly, the value of (idealized) early-refinement steps as documentation has been emphasized in [Berry 1975]. The problem, of course, is that the distinction between the different types of edits is not as clear-cut as one would wish.

5. PROGRAM STRUCTURE

The debate about structured programming in the world of conventional programming languages has been very much concerned with the proper syntax and semantics for control primitives, such as iteration statements (*for* loops), selection statements (*case* statements), and others. In one sense these questions are about the local structure in the program text. However, they also affect the global structure of programs because of the principle of hierarchical design of programs: the top-level structure of a program is a procedure or block which refers to subprocedures and/or subblocks recursively, but all entities on all levels are constructed in the same language. This view has been expressed by, for example, Dahl [Dahl and Hoare 1972].

The feeling about these issues in the LISP community is quite different. Local smoothness of notation is often considered uninteresting, for example when the S-expression notation is used for programs, or when mapping functions are used rather than a *for* operator (see the section on superimposed languages above).

This attitude combines with a nonhierarchical view of program structure. Many LISP programmers seem to have a two-level model of their programs: on the higher level, a program is a collection of procedures, which are related through their invocation structure (procedure-call structure); on the lower level, each procedure has a definition. The higher-level structure is the important one for understanding a program: it is supported by documentation which specifies the behavior of each procedure on its data, by documentation tools for automatic extraction of the invocation structure, by the advice facility (see below), etc. Questions of control primitives clearly do not arise on this level. While they do arise when one descends into the interior of the black box that is a procedure, one tries to stay away from this as much as possible, and when one does work with the definition of a procedure one fully expects to face difficulties of many kinds, all trivial and uninteresting. Incidentally, the same two-level view of programs seems to be common among users of APL.

Program structure in LISP programs does not end with the procedure-call model, however. The following are some other principles of program structure that are prevalent in the programming practices of the community.

5.1   Programmable Systems

It is common practice in computer science to think of "elementary algorithms," i.e., subroutines which can be specified, analyzed, and programmed in closed form, and then serve as building blocks for larger programs. This concept may have been inherited from numerical analysis or from engineering. Knuth's works [Knuth 1968a] are a systematic exposition of such algorithms.

In LISP programming, such algorithms often serve as mainframes rather than building-blocks for programs. The algorithm is written in open-ended form, i.e., some of its operations are marked as "user-defined" or as "handles." When the algorithm is to be used for a specific application, appropriate code is attached to each handle.

From a formal programming-language point of view, one might argue that such use of elementary algorithms does not alter their status as procedures since the handles may be easily implemented as procedural arguments. But the real issue is a different one: the view of the algorithm in the program structure is changed. Instead of being a small building block, which for many purposes can be viewed as a black box, it becomes a major way of determining the structure of the program. There are also other consequences. Conventional analyses of mathematical properties of algorithms become irrelevant, because of the arbitrary code that is attached to the handles. Also, in the practice of LISP programming, it is often more convenient to store the attached procedures in the database of the programming system, and let the general algorithm look them up as needed, rather than use a large number of procedural arguments. This matter is discussed in detail in [Sandewall 1977].

A few examples of programmable systems involve:

Parsing of a programming language whose syntax can be described by a context-free grammar (if the borderline between syntax and semantics is chosen so as to make this possible). This is a classic problem, and a number of algorithms for this task have been developed and studied extensively. In a LISP-style language, it is more natural to write a parser which, for each reserved word and infix operator, looks up an associated piece of code and executes it. In practice, it is natural to separate priority degrees as passive parameters outside the procedures, and let them determine when and how the operator-associated procedures are to be called. Thus, handles may contain both passive data (parameters) and active data (procedures). Systems of this kind have been proposed independently by Pratt [Pratt 1973] and Tholerus [Nordström and Tholerus 1974].

Static analysis ("compile-time analysis") of conventional programming languages. Knuth [Knuth 1968b] has proposed a scheme for such analysis that uses attributes associated with nodes in the syntactic parse tree. Nordström [Nordström 1976] has modified the method and allowed arbitrary procedures to be associated with productions and called in a more selective way, and thereby made systematic use of the handles on the basic algorithm. The resulting program structuring method is reminiscent of one proposed by Hoare [Hoare 1973] and results in a very well-structured program.

Analysis of natural language. Woods's Augmented Transitional Network Parser [Woods 1970] is a widely used program that makes systematic use of programmability. Its kernel algorithm is that of a finite-state automaton, which has been made programmable by allowing handles in every state transformation. This also eliminates the restriction on the power of finite-state acceptors.

The LISP interpreter itself, like other routines in most modern LISP systems, is highly programmable and has a large number of handles. Thus, for example:

- The three steps in the system's *basic loop* (read—evaluate—print) are just initial assignments to handles, and may be changed as the user desires;
- *Exception conditions*, for example for undefined variables, cause a call to a procedure that the user may define;
- *Pretty-printers* are usually programmable so that they can be fitted to the user's needs.

5.2 Procedural Embedding

The classical view of a computer program, i.e., that a program is composed of a number of elementary algorithms and operates on a body of data, has failed in the LISP-using community not only through the emergence of programmable systems, but also through the doctrine of procedural embedding of knowledge. A short review of history may be in order here.

In the middle 1960's, it was suggested that certain artificial intelligence systems should be organized as theorem provers that would contain most of their knowledge as "data," i.e., as expressions in a logical calculus. The system would also contain a theorem-proving program which would make deductions from the available data, answer questions, etc. The advent of the resolution method in 1965 as well as some demonstrations of its use increased the enthusiasm for this view.

Strong objections to this view surfaced around 1970. It was argued that a logical calculus was not an appropriate vehicle for the kind of information that has to reside in an artificial intelligence system, and that major parts of the information in the computing system must be represented procedurally, i.e., as executable code, rather than as inert data. While it is not possible to portray this long controversy here, let us note that the current fashion among the remaining theorem-prover enthusiasts is to view a theorem-prover as an interpreter for a very-high-level language, which in a sense marks the triumph of the procedural school.

The rejection of theorem-proving represents the rejection of an algorithm, which for a while seemed to be of basic importance, and even a rejection of the use of closed algorithms as the top level of a system. With resolution, one could make a mathematical analysis of variants of the resolution algorithm and hope to learn something about the behavior of the system being constructed. With the procedural approach, one is encouraged to think of large systems simply as programs, where closed algorithms appear only at the lowest levels. Mathematical analysis of the algorithms can then at best say something about the limits of its competence.

One might have expected this development to focus attention on issues of program structure and programming methodology, but, in fact, the questions of design of very-high-level programming languages came to dominate instead.

5.3 Embedded Languages

Another practice of program structuring, also related to programmable systems, is to organize the program around a highly specialized "language" that describes the application. For example, the INTERLISP *makefile* facility, which is used to generate text-format files of procedure definitions and initialization data, is organized as an executive which interprets a file descriptor for the desired file. The file descriptor contains information about which procedures are to be printed on the file, in which format they are to be printed, what other operations are to be performed when the file is generated and when it is loaded, and so on. This has already been illustrated in the example in the section on Residential and Source-File Systems above. The descriptor may initially have been a catalog or a parameter, but as the *makefile* package underwent structured growth, the descriptor acquired all the characteristics of a programming language.

The point lies not in the significance of this particular example, but in the general observation that the programming language has encouraged the use of such embedded languages. They are, of course, internally represented as data structures (making them easy to interpret) and externally as standard printouts of those data structures (which makes them sufficiently easy to read, and which makes I/O of expressions in the embedded language trivial). Since programs and data are interchangeable, it is possible for an expression in the embedded language, which, of course, is data to its interpreter and therefore to the LISP system, to contain calls to procedures that are written in LISP.

The programming method of using embedded languages is very widespread among LISP users, although many such languages are so small that they are not advertised as such. If one wants to enable programmers to mold the programming system to fit their needs, then use of embedded languages in this sense is probably a more viable approach than use of extensible languages.

The use of specialized languages for specific tasks in a class of applications represents a nonconventional method of decomposing complex problems. Instead of hierarchical decomposition, where a large problem is decomposed into small problems of the same kind as the top-level problem (for example, all subproblems are subprograms), we instead decompose the problem into two parts: 1) design an appropriate language for expressing solutions to problems similar to the given one; and 2) express the solution to the problem in that language. This method of decomposition has a definite advantage in situations where the given task may be redefined at a later stage. However, for implementing such specialized languages in a convenient fashion, one needs a very-high-level implementation language. When it allows the implementation of embedded languages, LISP serves exactly this purpose.

5.4   Production Systems

Embedded languages that started out as simple auxiliary devices sometimes grow into full-fledged systems. The very-high-level languages, as discussed above, may have followed this path. Another example is production systems, which have recently attracted attention as a nice way of structuring many types of problems (see, for example, [Gibbons 1976]). Production systems have been used successfully in the MYCIN project [Shortliffe 1973].

5.5   Data-Driven Systems

There is one underlying method that makes possible programmable systems, embedded languages, and several other practices, namely what we have called *data-driven programming* [Sandewall 1975] [Sandewall 1977]. It is similar to indirect jumps in machine language, and can be described as follows: in conventional high-level languages, each procedure has a name, and one procedure calls another if the definition of the former explicitly contains the name of the latter. A data-driven call is one where the calling procedure accepts "input" data (for example, input from the user, or arguments to the procedure), looks up a procedure which in the database of the programming system has been associated with these data, and calls that procedure. This is not possible in conventional high-level languages, but is possible in LISP because of the program/data equivalence.

Example   In the domain of the demo program, suppose we want to define a procedure *nextweekday* which is a refinement of *nextday*. Remember that *nextday* computes the next day in the calendar after a given day, e.g., *nextday* of (FRI JAN 14) will be (SAT JAN 15). The new procedure *nextweekday* will skip Saturdays, Sundays, holidays, etc. Because of the variety of different reasons why a certain day may not be a working day ("weekday"), we decide to associate with each day-of-week (such as SAT) a procedure which takes a day as argument, and returns T if this day is an acceptable weekday as far as it knows, and NIL otherwise. We proceed similarly for the names of the months. In both cases, these procedures that implement local expertise are stored on the property-list of the day-of-week and the month, under the indicator OK-AS-WEEKDAY. Then *nextweekday* can be defined as shown in Display 3.

DISPLAY 3

```
(DEFINEQ
(NEXTWEEKDAY
  [LAMBDA (DATE)
    (FOR D__(NEXTDAY DATE) BY (NEXTDAY D)
      DO (IF (AND (APPLY* (GETPROP (CAR D) 'OK-AS-WEEKDAY)
                          D)
                  (APPLY* (GETPROP (CADR D) 'OK-AS-WEEKDAY)
                          D))
          THEN (RETURN D]))
```

In this case, using INTERLISP's iteration statement, *d* will range over *nextday (date), nextday (nextday(date))*, etc., until a *d* is found which satisfies the two criteria. Then the knowledge that Saturdays are never acceptable weekdays can be embedded as

```
(PUTPROP 'SAT 'OK-AS-WEEKDAY
  '(LAMBDA (D) NIL))
```

The knowledge that Mondays are acceptable except in August is embedded as

```
(PUTPROP 'MON 'OK-AS-WEEKDAY
  '(LAMBDA (D) (NOT (EQ (CADR D) 'AUG]
```

The knowledge that Christmas day is the only nonacceptable day in December except the ones accounted for by the days of week is represented as

```
(PUTPROP 'DEC 'OK-AS-WEEKDAY
  '(LAMBDA (D) (NOT (EQ (CADDR D) 25]
```

In general, the method described through this example makes it possible to organize knowledge as many small procedural chunks, and to associate these chunks of knowledge with *data items* (namely names of months and names of days of week) which occur in the application and which are therefore automatically understood by the programmer. This turns out to be a very common programming technique in the LISP community. One somewhat larger example is analyzed in detail in [Hewitt 1972]. This technique strongly facilitates the writing of interpreters for embedded languages, and in programmable systems is an often preferred alternative to having procedural arguments. Also, an indirect or data-driven procedure call is equivalent to a case statement (at least for single-step indirectness and a static database), but is much more convenient to work with interactively since it is particularly easy to add additional case branches by adding more entries to the database (see the discussion above about structured growth), and since the database of data-driven procedures may be presented in different ways to the user at different times. Nordström's method for organizing a program according to a syntax for the data structures of its application differs from Hoare's method discussed above in exactly this respect.

Although the LISP system kernel makes data-driven programming possible, the higher-level mechanisms in current LISP systems do not encourage it. One consequence of data-driven programming is that procedures are often not characterized by a single mnemonic name, but instead by the position in the database where they are located. However, many user-supporting programs in the INTERLISP system which operate on procedures assume that each procedure has an individual name (an atom) which is used for storing additional information about the procedure. This assumption is used in so many places that it is probably too late to change it in the present system.

One way of using data-driven programming is described by Aiello [Aiello et al. 1976].

5.6   Low-Level Program Generation

All programmers, in any programming language, sometimes run into situations where they have to prepare nontrivial amounts of program in a routine fashion. Procedures and macros are well-known devices for handling such situations. The program/data equivalence in LISP makes possible another and more powerful method to handle such situations, namely, the use of procedure generators.

Usually, the concept of a program-generating program is surrounded by a mystique and a feeling that it is something that may arrive in the distant future. This is certainly appropriate with respect to programs that generate a whole program from its specifications. But a more pragmatic approach to program generation is evident in the LISP community, namely the approach where the programmer identifies regularities in the structure of the program that he/she is writing or going to write, and immediately writes a small program generator that handles that regularity. Winograd mentions this technique in [Winograd 1974].

Example   In the implementation of *nextweekday* described in the previous example, we may wish to generate the procedure definitions for some of the months automatically. Suppose many months are characterized by a number of fixed dates during the month which are not acceptable weeks, i.e., their OK-AS-WEEKDAY properties have the form

```
(LAMBDA (DATE) (NOT (MEMB (CADDR DATE)
  '( ... )]
```

where ... indicates a list of integers. We could then define a procedure *ok-month (m,l)* where m is the name of the month, and l is the list of integers, in either of the two ways, shown in Display 4 and Display 5 respectively.

DISPLAY 4

```
(DEFINEQ
(OK-MONTH (M L) (PUTPROP M 'OK-AS-WEEKDAY
  (FUNCTION (LAMBDA (DATE) (NOT (MEMB (CADDR DATE) L])
```

DISPLAY 5

```
(DEFINEQ
(OK-MONTH (M L) (PUTPROP M 'OK-AS-WEEKDAY
  (SUBST L 'L '(LAMBDA (DATE) (NOT (MEMB (CADDR DATE) (QUOTE L])
```

The first variant is the most elegant one, but assumes that the operator *function* returns a closure where the current value of *l* is preserved. Such closures or "funarg-expressions" were defined in the original LISP 1.5, were ignored in some later implementations, but have gradually found their way back into the language. The second variant constructs the appropriate definition for each case by performing a substitution in a schema for the definition.

This procedure may then be called as, for example,

```
(OK-MONTH 'JAN '(1))
```

assuming that New Year's day is the only nonstandard holiday in January.

5.7   Advising and Insertive Programming

When low-level program generation is performed, one often wants to arrange matters so that several expressions or commands (usually input by the user) will make successive amendments to the definition of a procedure, for example, so that each expression adds one more branch to a *selectq* (= *case*) statement. This is, of course, easy if the definitions are so regular that the program generator can correctly determine the correct place in which to make the amendment. This practice of insertive programming is discussed and illustrated in [Sandewall 1977].

Example   In the data-driven OK-AS-WEEKDAY procedures used in the previous example, every such procedure will contain certain criteria for days that are not allowed. If we standardize the form of the procedures to be

```
(LAMBDA (DATE) (NOT (OR.........)))
```

then it is easy to write a procedure *holidayrule (m,x)* which takes a month or day-of-week *m* and and expression *x*, where *x* is supposed to be the criterion for a holiday, and which adds *x* to the OK-AS-WEEKDAY property of *m*. The definition would go as shown in Display 6. It can then be called as, for example,

```
(HOLIDAYRULE 'JAN '(EQ (CADDR DATE) 1))
```

or (to declare the third Friday in September a holiday):

```
(HOLIDAYRULE 'SEP
    '(AND (EQ (CAR DATE) 'FRI)
          (BETWEEN 15 (CADDR DATE) 21)))
```

Here *between* is defined so that it is true here when $15 \leq caddr(date) \leq 21$. In this fashion, separate holiday rules can be input independently, to gradually build up a procedure.

DISPLAY 6

```
(DEFINEQ
(HOLIDAYRULE (LAMBDA (M X) (PROG (D)
  (SETQ D (GETPROP M 'OK-AS-WEEKDAY))
  (COND [(NULL D) (PUTPROP M 'OK-AS-WEEKDAY
                     (SUBST X 'X '(LAMBDA (DATE) (NOT (OR X]
          (T (NCONC1 (CADR (CADDR D)) X]
```

A similar, although more complex facility is *advising*, which is meant to allow the user to make changes to existing programs without knowing their exact structure. In the simplest case, the user-programmers are supposed to know the system as a procedure-call structure, i.e., they know the names, intended purpose, and procedure-call structure of the procedures but these remain black boxes, and the users have no knowledge of the "inside" of the procedures. The advise facility in INTERLISP then allows the user to reroute outgoing or incoming procedure calls for a procedure, and to associate additional (side) effects with them.

In practice, advising is implemented through insertive programming, since every advised procedure is wrapped into an extra, outermost **begin-end** block ("PROG expression") whose structure is known to the advising routine. Of course, this machinery is supposedly invisible to the user.

Example We wish to "tell" the procedure *nextday* in the demo application about the rule for February 29 during leap years and ordinary years. Assuming that the NRDAYS property of FEB is 29, we can do this by advising *nextday* to step to March 1 if its proposed value is February 29, and the current year is not a leap year. This is done in INTERLISP as:

```
(ADVISE 'NEXTDAY 'AFTER
  '(IF (AND (EQ (CADR !VALUE) 'FEB)
            (EQ (CADDR !VALUE) 29)
            (NOT (LEAPYEAR)))
       THEN (SETQ !VALUE (LIST (CAR !VALUE)
         'MAR 1]
```

Technically, the advising scheme is very elegant. Jim Goodwin has suggested[3] that (like data-driven procedures) it is an example of a machine-code-level facility that has been made available in a high-level form: advising is high-level patching. The crucial question about its usefulness is whether the user's actual request, the thing that really is to be done, can be translated into the right operation on the procedure-call structure (or whatever other model of the program the advising package supports). This is partly a question of how the program has been organized, and partly of how it has been documented.

In summary, the LISP programming culture offers a variety of unorthodox programming methods and program structures. Some, such as the structured-growth method of program development, are really consequences of the inter-activity and incrementality in the system. Others, such as data-driven programming, program generation, and the use of embedded languages, are consequences of the equivalence between programs and data, which LISP at present shares with only a few other research-oriented languages.

---

[3] Personal communication.

6. SESSION SUPPORT

One of the significant improvements in residential programming systems involves the possibility of letting the system support the interactive session, for example "remember" what the user has done before, and enable him/her to redo or undo those actions by convenient commands. This line of research has been pioneered by Teitelman in the INTERLISP system [Teitelman 1969]. [*Editors' note:* See articles by Teitelman in this volume.] I shall only add here a few short notes on some nontrivial issues that arise in this context.

6.1 History—Structure or Text?

The INTERLISP system preserves the recent session history, i.e., a sequence of input expressions and corresponding output, in internal (list-structure) form. Some simple uses of this history are for scrolling and the REDO command, whereby the user can reexecute a previously entered command, possibly after having edited it.

An alternative way of approaching the same objective might be to use a display-oriented editor in the terminal communication interface, as described in the section on alternative editing methods above. In addition to its previously described uses, such an editor could also copy previous input to a later place in the conversation buffer, edit it, and send it as fresh input to the programming system. The potential advantage to the user would be that one could manage with a smaller repertoire of commands, since the ordinary editing commands would also be sufficient for redoing and similar operations. On the other hand, there is the disadvantage, particularly for sophisticated users, that the preservation and use of history interfaces less well with the programming system per se.

In choosing between these two approaches, one must also decide whether one prefers to regard the session history as a structure (in which case the INTERLISP approach is better) or as a text file (in which case the new approach would seem more appropriate). [*Editors' note:* see the article on the LISP Machine in this volume.]

Why choose between structure history and text history, why not have both? This suggestion is likely to be resisted by programming-language purists, who wish to have a minimal number of orthogonal features in a programming system, and to be welcomed by systems engineers who wish to give the user everything that can possibly be of use. The only way to resolve that issue is to define what operations are to be performed by the structure history and the text history, respectively.

6.2 Cancellation of Features

One of the most impressive features in the INTERLISP system is the DWIM (Do-What-I-Mean) facility, which is invoked when the basic system detects an error and which attempts to guess what the user might have intended. When this facility is presented to new users, it is not uncommon for them to use it for a trivial typing error that could easily be corrected using the character-delete key. However, the user relies on DWIM for the correction, which at periods of peak computer load may take considerable time. Moreover, a user who does not know how the DWIM facility works might be reluctant to hit an interrupt key for fear of making things even worse. For this reason, the actual DWIM program has been set up so that supposedly it can be safely interrupted at any point. The information on how to interrupt it is an essential part of the instructions to the user.

Two general morals may be drawn from this example:

1. When you provide users with luxurious features, always make sure that they are able to, and know how to, cancel them at times when they cannot afford their use;

2. This affects decisions on the budget for computer equipment. As computer systems become more and more heavily loaded, more of the advanced features in interactive programming systems are canceled. If the intended purpose of the research was to develop and make experimental use of those facilities, then the real productivity of the research decreases rapidly.

6.3   Program Changes

Many of the advanced features in residential programming systems become changed, temporarily or permanently, in the users' procedures. More often than not, the old definition has to be stored so that it can be reinstated if the user so desires.

In this situation, the relationship between the different changes becomes precarious. If the user first performs operation A, then performs operation B, and then undoes A, should then the original definition (before A was performed) be reinstated, or should B be performed on it also? There is no simple answer—what would be better depends on the choice of A and B. But in the existing INTERLISP system, where each program-changing operation has its own recovery mechanism, there have been amusing examples of unintended and counter-intuitive results as the different recovery operations interacted with each other. Perhaps the conclusion is that a uniform system for maintenance of old versions and updates of procedures that can be used by all definition-changing utilities should be introduced early in the design of the system.

These examples of open issues in the design of session-support systems show that, although impressive systems already exist, there is room for additional work—not merely to extend or rewrite existing software, but also to reconsider and analyze questions that involve principles.

7. POTENTIAL APPLICATIONS

As described in this paper, programming in LISP is characterized by the peculiar architecture of the programming system and the programming techniques made possible by that architecture. At present, LISP is mostly used for two types of applications:

1. Experimental programming in artificial intelligence research, where programs are developed for the purpose of better understanding certain complex programming tasks;

2. Implementation of formula manipulation systems.

I believe that the same technology would also be useful for a number of other applications, particularly:

• For pilot implementation of data processing applications. A pilot system may be used to give the end user a hands-on impression of possible facilities in a proposed new data processing system. The pilot implementation does not need to run efficiently or handle large volumes of data, but it requires a programming language in which it can be implemented quickly and modified easily to accommodate changes proposed by the end user when he tries the system. The interactive character and the database facilities in LISP systems meet these requirements.

• For personal databases, i.e., for databases which are used in an office-system or word-processing environment, and which are constructed and used by one or a few individuals for their personal use.

• In computer science research on programming languages and databases. LISP used as a very-high-level implementation language may make it possible to experiment with proposed new concepts in languages and database systems, instead of just thinking about them.

In all three cases, the suggestion is that one should use a programming system which incorporates the significant properties of LISP systems, as discussed in this paper. It is, of course, immaterial whether one uses a dialect of LISP itself or a newly invented language.

8. CONCLUSION

This paper has given an overview of existing programming methodology in the LISP user's environment, emphasizing methods for interactive program development. The major conclusions are:

1. The "residential" design of programming systems, whereby all facilities for the user are integrated into one system with which the user communicates during the entire interactive session, offers great possibilities for user convenience. At the same time, a number of basic user demands may conflict with the attempt to build such a residential system.

2. The design of a residential interactive programming system is interrelated with the design of the *surrounding runtime environment* in at least two important respects: the role of the file system (especially the requirement for a very large number of very small files, and a file directory which can serve as or communicate with a database for user-written programs), and the proper place of text editing and other terminal support in the overall system architecture (inside the programming system, or as a separate module).

3. A residential interactive programming system will need to contain a large number of modules that support various facilities. These modules interact in many ways, which causes the design of the programming system to be a *very hard structuring problem*. Two modules have been identified which tend to interact with almost everything else, namely, the editor and the surface-language analyzer (the latter being optional).

4. The observed behavior of LISP users indicates that top-down programming can be done not only using stepwise refinement, but often in a better way, through what has been called here *structured growth*, which is a relatively disciplined way of *changing* one's programs.

5. Several programming methods in a LISP environment can be summarized as involving the use of *superimposed languages*, be they ALGOL-like surface languages, very-high-level languages, or embedded languages for very specialized purposes. Of these, embedded languages are believed to be the most viable.

6. A technique which is useful in several ways is what we have called here *data-driven procedure calls*, which resembles indirect jumps in machine languages; they are possible in LISP but are incompletely supported by higher-level facilities in current LISP systems. Nevertheless, the technique is frequently used in practice and has become accepted habit because of its power.

The experience and practices of the LISP programming community may contribute new and unorthodox input to the general discussion about programming systems and programming methodology.

ACKNOWLEDGMENTS

This paper is based on discussions with a large number of devoted LISP programmers; their contribution is appreciated. Successive generations of the manuscript have been enhanced by valuable comments and suggestions from Jim Goodwin, Warren Teitelman, Peter Denning, and an anonymous reviewer, for which I am very grateful.

9. APPENDIX: A DIFFERENT VIEW OF THE IMPORTANCE OF STRUCTURE EDITORS

[*Editors' note*: Sandewall's article attempts to draw some distinctions between the structure editor of Interlisp and the text editor approach used in MacLisp. Unfortunately, most of these impressions were based on using early and primitive versions of the MacLisp tools. This appendix contains a reply by Richard Stallman, implementor of the EMACS editor (see the article on EMACS in *Interactive Programming Environments*) which presents a different analysis of this issue].[4]

9.1   Stallman's Letter

I disagree with Dr. Sandewall's conclusions regarding the relative desirability of text editing versus list-structure editing interactive systems. I want to correct a misimpression that his article may inadvertently have given: that everyone agrees that MacLisp's file-based text editing approach is inferior, and the new Lisp Machine of MIT's Artificial Intelligence Laboratory will be an opportunity to switch. We at MIT actually believe that editing text in files is better for the user, and our Lisp Machine editor works that way. The advantages cited by Dr. Sandewall for close coupling of the editor to the rest of the LISP system are not lost by the text-based approach. In fact, the Lisp Machine editor which is the best editor we know, is fully compatible with our latest PDP-10 editor which is the best editor for LISP we know. Now that the MIT PDP-10 editor EMACS is being exported, some Interlisp users are using it.

Our current PDP-10 system organization was just in its exploratory stages when Dr. Sandewall was here. Since that stage (as described in section 2 of his paper), the system has changed completely. Here is how we now use it: a user has a LISP job and an editor job, which communicate. The editor operates on text files. The list structure (or compiled code) is kept in the LISP environment. When the user has a change to make, he gives LISP a command to switch to the editor. In the editor, he can ask to find and change particular functions (the editor knows which file contains each function). When he says he is done, the text files are updated on disk, and the changed functions are sent to LISP to be read in and redefined. Only the text files are kept permanently. Information passes only from the text files to the LISP job, so that the

---

[4] © 1978, Association for Computing Machinery, Inc. Reprinted by permission from *ACM Computing Surveys*, 10:4 (December 1978), pp. 505-508.

user's choice of formatting is never overridden by a LISP pretty-printer. Reading just the changed functions is very fast.

The two real issues are whether to edit text or list structure, and whether to edit the program in the same environment in which it is tested. On the MIT Lisp Machine, editing is done on text, in the same LISP environment as the program is tested, but not on the same list structure.

Dr. Sandewall considers also whether to save programs as text files or LISP environments. It is worth asking which option should be used primarily in a system that provides both. The article lists some reasons why text files are "necessary even in a residential system," or, from a neutral point of view, some advantages text files have over saved environments. These include robustness, house-cleaning, and ease of loading several programs together. Text files are also essential for operating on programs with tools not written in LISP, or with tools written in LISP but not part of the standard system. A saved environment has only one advantage: if it contains precisely what you want, it is faster to load. MacLisp users generally save an environment only for a tool or system which is to be loaded frequently. These environments usually contain compiled code, the uncompiled code being stored in text files.

The advantages of editing and testing the program in the same environment is the close coupling cited by Dr. Sandewall. The disadvantage is that the erroneous program being tested can alter its definition, or simply mess up the whole LISP environment. The only known remedy is to save the text on disk often.

Here are the advantages of editing text rather than list structure.

1. The user can specify any style of indentation and the system will never override it. The editor supplies standard indentation as a default.

2. Comments are easily stored and formatted as the user likes them.

3. The user can create unbalanced parentheses while editing a function. This causes no trouble as long as the function is not redefined from the text at such times. The user can also move, delete, or copy blocks of syntactically unbalanced text. In a list-structure editor, these operations are impossible or require peculiar and unintuitive commands.

4. The editor can provide commands to move over balanced objects or delete them. The commands work by parsing the expressions (forward or backward).

5. A text editor can support extended syntax. Extensibility, as Dr. Sandewall points out, is one of the strong points of LISP. In MacLisp and Interlisp, the syntactic "macro character" escapes at parsing time to a user-supplied function, allowing arbitrary syntax extensions. For example, " ' " is normally a macro character: 'FOO is equivalent to (QUOTE FOO). Extensions destroy the one-to-one relationship between internal and printed forms. With a text editor, the user automatically edits the representation he chose to type in. A structure editor cannot come close to this without being told fully about each new extension. Text editors also need to be told about syntax extensions if expression-parsing commands are to work on them, but the instructions are simple (e.g., "treat commas like single quotes").

6. A text editor can be used for languages other than LISP (including English and alternate LISP syntaxes) with no change. The LISP-specific commands amount to only a small fraction of the whole editor.

7. With a structure editor, temporary semantic bugs can be dangerous. In editing a function which is a vital part of the system or the editor, one cannot introduce a bug one moment and fix it the next without risking a crash. But in editing text, changes take no effect until the user gives the command.

8. The editing commands most natural for use on a display terminal are those whose meaning is obvious in terms of the displayed text. A data struc-

ture of text is natural for them, but implementing them in a structure editor would be very difficult. There are few screen-oriented structure editors.

The commands which our editors provide for LISP programs include moving over and deleting S-expressions, moving to the beginning or end of the current function definition, automatic indentation of new lines or old ones, automatic indentation of new or old comments, and finding quickly (without searching) the definition of a named function. Further information is available in the MIT Artificial Intelligence Laboratory memo, "An introduction to EMACS".

In closing, I note that LISP 1.6 was an improvement of an early MacLisp, but the current export version of MacLisp has superseded it. It is not true that our PDP-10 editor is a "variant of the standard DEC text-editor, TECO." In fact, DEC's editor is a variant of an early and quite primitive version of MIT's editor, TECO, which has since become a language for writing the editors.

9.2 Sandewall's reply

Two current LISP systems, MacLisp and Interlisp, represent different approaches to editing and maintenance of program; the relative merits of these approaches has been debated intensively for a long time. In the paper, I tried to summarize the pros and cons of both approaches, although clearly there was not space to review all the arguments of each side. Mr. Stallman's letter states the case of MacLisp on this issue and is more explicit than my paper, although many of Mr. Stallman's observations had already been made in the paper. It seems that we agree on the major issues, and that any differences of opinion consists of weighing pros and cons differently. The following remarks to some of Mr. Stallman's points are therefore relatively marginal.

The description of the current system organization for MacLisp at MIT is in the paper although it is remarked that this facility "does not seem to be in widespread use yet." This was based on information given by R. Greenblatt at MIT in August 1977. Evidently the same facility is now in widespread use.

I do not believe that "advantages text files have over saved environments" represents a "neutral" view. Text files are needed in all LISP systems for certain purposes (house-cleaning, etc.), but that is in itself no reason why they should also be used as a basis for editing.

Should a program be edited in the environment where it is tested, or in another environment? I am skeptical of Mr. Stallman's argument that the program may destroy itself, or may destroy its environment so badly that saving is impossible. This would seem to be a real danger only in low-level systems work, and then should not influence the design of the whole system too much. After all, the system is built for the real users, not for the systems hackers. Also, when this danger is present, it can always be overcome in a residential environment by a simple safety measure: after you have typed in a substantial amount of text, and before you start testing, save the program in a text file.

However, a permanent problem when discussing these issues is that several different design decisions are usually intertwined and affect each consideration. In this case, the robustness of the programming system itself is significant. It is sometimes argued (at least by the Interlisp faction) that the MacLisp system does less dynamic checking, of course, in order to gain efficiency. Similarly, the UNDO facility in Interlisp provides additional robustness and is useful when debugging systems which tend to destroy themselves. Less checking and lack of an UNDO in MacLisp may account for Mr. Stallman's different experience in this respect.

Mr. Stallman cites eight reasons for editing text rather than list structure, numbers 1 through 8. Of these, 2, 4, 6, and 8 are also in the paper, and they indeed represent advantages for the text editing approach. In particular, we agree about the intrinsic difficulty to perform screen editing (using cursor movements) in a structure-editing environment, although it has in fact been done (see [Teitelman 1977]). [*Editors' note:* see also the paper by Barstow in *Interactive Programming Environments.*]

Allowing a variable style of indentation (1) is probably the kind of facility which is appreciated by those who have it, and not missed by those who have never had it—again a recurrent phenomenon in programming languages. The same applies for the use of unsyntactic expressions as intermediate states during editing (3). I have personally never felt that need except when correcting typos made on initial type-in of large procedure definitions.

Accounting for syntax extensions (5) is simpler in a text editor as long as you stay with the simple extensions such as macro characters. However, if a structure editor is to contain syntactic competence as described in (4), then it is non-trivial to account for a surface syntax such as CGOL; both the programming system (LISP system) and the editor must then contain a CGOL parser.

When central system functions such as parts of the editor have to be edited themselves in a residential system, one will of course edit another copy than the one that is presently used. This does not lose the advantages of having the definition (in this case, both copies) as list structures in the residential environment. In practice, one does not even need to create a separate copy for this purpose, since central system facilities normally run compiled: one would simply edit the "source" list-structure version which is often present for reference purposes together with the compiled code, but keep the compiled version of the old definition as the one which is actually used by the system. During debugging, one can then easily switch back and forth between the proven, compiled version, and the new, interpreted version that is to be tested.

In summary, text-based editing has a number of specific advantages, not the least one being that this approach can be made to work with a considerably less complex system. The other side of the coin—the advantages of structure editors—shall not be reviewed again here. However, item 4 in Mr. Stallman's letter should not be read to say that a text editor can easily be set up to have all the facilities of a structure editor. There are a number of other services which can only be implemented in a structure-editor environment, such as the ability to edit the program when it has been interrupted for an error, and continue execution of the edited program.

I apologize for possible errors or misunderstandings in the account of the systems' family tree. In particular, I was not aware that "X is a variant of Y" is not a symmetric relation in English. Natural language is sometimes even more evasive than programming languages.

REFERENCES

[Aiello et al. 1976] L. Aiello et al. Recursive data types in LISP: A case study in type driven programming. *Proceedings of the Second International Symposium on Programming*, Institut de programmation, Paris, 1976.

[Allen 1978] Allen, J. *The Anatomy of LISP.* McGraw-Hill, 1978.

[Ash et al. 1977] W. Ash et al. *Intelligent on-line assistant and tutor system.* Bolt, Beranek and Newman, Report No. 3607, Cambridge, Massachusetts, 1977.

[Berry 1975] D. Berry. Structured documentation. *SIGPLAN Newsletter* (November 1975).

[Bobrow and Raphael 1974] D.G. Bobrow, R. Bertram. New programming languages for AI research. *ACM Computing Surveys* 6:3 (September 1974).

[Brinch-Hansen 1976] P. Brinch-Hansen. The Solo operating system. *Software Practice and Experience*, 6:2 (1976), 141-206.

[Dahl and Hoare 1972] O.-J. Dahl, C.A.R. Hoare. Hierarchical program structures. In O.-J. Dahl, E.W. Dijkstra, C.A.R. Hoare. *Structured programming*. Academic Press, 1972.

[Davies 1973] D. Davies et al. *Popler 1.5 Reference Manual*. University of Edinburgh, Scotland, 1973.

[Gibbons 1976] Gibbons, G. Letter in ACM Forum. *Communications of the ACM*, 19:2 (1976), 105-106.

[Griss 1976] M. Griss. The definition and use of data-structures in REDUCE. *Proceedings of the ACM Symposium on Symbolic and Algebraic Computation*, (R.D. Jenks, ed.), 1976, 53-59.

[Haraldson 1975] A. Haraldson. *LISP - details*. Uppsala University, Computer Sciences Department, 1975.

[Hearn 1968] A. Hearn. *REDUCE User's Manual*. Stanford University, Stanford Artificial Intelligence Laboratory, Memo 50, 1968.

[Henneman 1964] W. Henneman. An auxiliary language for more natural expression. In E.C. Berkely, D.G. Bobrow (eds.) *The programming language LISP, its operation and applications*. MIT Press, Cambridge, Massachusetts, 1964.

[Hewitt 1972] C. Hewitt. *Description and theoretical analysis (using schemata) of PLANNER: a language for proving theorems and manipulating models in a robot*. Massachusetts Institute of Technology, MIT-AI-TR-258, April 1972; see also C. Hewitt. *PLANNER: A language for manipulating models and proving theorems in a robot*, Massachusetts Institute of Technology, memo 168.

[Hoare 1973] C.A.R. Hoare. *Recursive data structures*. Stanford University, Computer Science Department, STAN-CS-73-400, 1973.

[Knuth 1968a] D.E. Knuth. *The Art of Computer Programming, Vols. 1-3*. Addison-Wesley, Reading, Massachusetts, 1968,1969,1973.

[Knuth 1968b] D.E. Knuth. Semantics of context-free languages. *Mathematical System Theory Journal*, 1968, 127-145.

[McCarthy et al. 1962] J. McCarthy, P. Abrahams, D. Edwards, T. Hart, M. Levin. *LISP 1.5 Programmer's Manual*, MIT Press, Cambridge, Massachusetts, 1962.

[McDermott and Sussman 1972] D.V. McDermott, G.J. Sussman. *The CONNIVER Reference Manual*. Massachusetts Institute of Technology, Artificial Intelligence Laboratory Memo 259, May 1972.

[MUMPS 1976] *Introduction to MUMPS-11 Language*. Digital Equipment Corporation, Maynard, Massachusetts, DEC-11-MMLTA-C-D, 1976.

[Nordström 1970] M. Nordström et al. *LISP F1-a FORTRAN implementation of LISP 1.5*, Computer Sciences Department, Uppsala University, Sweden, 1970.

[Nordström 1976] M. Nordström. A method for defining formal semantics of programming languages applied to Simula. Uppsala University, doctoral dissertation, 1976.

[Nordström and Tholerus 1974] M. Nordström, T. Tholerus. *A parsing technique applied to the programming language REDUCE*, Computer Sciences Department, Uppsala University, Sweden, 1974.

[Pratt 1973] V. Pratt. Top down operator precedence. *ACM Symposium on the Principles of Programming Languages*, Association for Computing Machinery, 1973.

[Rulifson et al. 1972] J.F. Rulifson et al. *QA4, a procedural calculus for intuitive reasoning*, Stanford Research Institute, Menlo Park, California, 1972.

[Sacerdoti et al. 1976] E. Sacerdoti. *QLISP: a language for the interactive development of complex systems*. Stanford Research Institute, Menlo Park, California, 1976.

[Sandewall 1968] E. Sandewall. LISP A: a LISP-like system for incremental computing. *Proceedings of the Spring Joint Computer Conference*, AFIP Proceedings Vol. 32 (1968), 375-384.

[Sandewall 1975] E. Sandewall. Ideas about management of LISP data bases. *Advance Papers of the Fourth International Joint Conference on Artificial Intelligence*, Tbilisi, U.S.S.R. September 1975, 585-592.

[Sandewall 1977] E. Sandewall. Some observations on conceptual programming. In E.W. Elcock, D. Michie (eds.) *Machine Intelligence 8*, John Wiley & Sons, N.Y, 1977.

[Shortliffe 1973] E.H. Shortliffe. An artificial intelligence program to advise physicians regarding anti-microbial therapy. *Computers and Biomedical Research*, 6 (1973), 544-560.

[Smith 1970] D.C. Smith. *MLISP*. Stanford Artificial Intelligence Laboratory, Stanford, California, 1970.

[Teitelman 1969] W. Teitelman. Toward a programming laboratory. *International Joint Conference on Artificial Intelligence*, Washington, May 1969, 1-8.

[Teitelman 1977] W. Teitelman. A display-oriented programmer's assistant. CSL 77-3, XEROX PARC, 1977; reprinted in *Interactive Programming Environments*; see also *Proceedings of the Fifth International Joint Conference on Artificial Intelligence*, Cambridge, Massachusetts, August 1977, 905-915.

[Teitelman 1978] W. Teitelman. *INTERLISP Reference Manual*. Xerox Palo Alto Research Center, Palo Alto, California, December 1978.

[Tholerus 1975] T. Tholerus. *REC - a recursive programming language with visible control stack*. Computer Sciences Department, Uppsala University, 1975.

[Wegbreit et al. 1972] B. Wegbreit et al. *ECL Programmer's Manual*. Harvard University, 1972.

[Weissman 1967] C. Weissman. *LISP 1.5 primer*. Dickenson Publishing Co., Belmont, California, 1967.

[Winograd 1971] T. Winograd. *Procedures as a representation for data in a computer program for understanding natural language*. Massachusetts Institute of Technology, Artificial Intelligence Laboratory, doctoral dissertation, 1971.

[Winograd 1973] T. Winograd. Breaking the complexity barrier (again). *Proceedings of the ACM SIGIR-SIGPLAN Interface Meeting*, November 1973; reprinted in *Interactive Programming Environments*.

[Winograd 1974] T. Winograd. *Five lectures on artificial intelligence*. Computer Science Department, Stanford University, STAN-CS-459, 1974.

[Winston and Horn 1981] P.H. Winston, B.K. Horn. *LISP*. Addison-Wesley, 1981.

[Wirth 1971b] N. Wirth. The programming language PASCAL. *Acta Informatica*, 1 (1971), 25-68.

[Woods 1970] W. Woods. Transition network grammars for natural language analysis. *Communications of the ACM*, 13:10 (October 1970), 591-606.

Modern Interactive Programming Environments

This section includes descriptions of several interactive programming environments that have been developed over the last decade. The first five cover several different approaches and involve several different programming languages. Teitelman and Masinter describe INTERLISP, perhaps the most well known of the LISP environments. Teitelbaum and Reps describe the Cornell Program Synthesizer, a recently developed environment for PL/C which is now in routine educational use at Cornell. Wilander describes PATHCAL, an environment for PASCAL which was built by embedding PASCAL within INTERLISP, thus providing many of the INTERLISP facilities in the context of PASCAL. Donzeau-Gouge et al. describe MENTOR, another environment for PASCAL, built essentially from scratch. Goldberg describes the SMALLTALK environment, one of the earliest to take advantage of the high-resolution graphics provided by personal workstations. These five environments are illustrative of a large class of interactive programming environments, but certainly do not cover the field completely. Two other environments which have been developed recently are IBM's Program Development Tool [Alberga et al. 1981] and the incremental programming environment [Medina-Mora and Feiler 1981] developed as part of the GANDALF project [Habermann 1979].

Kernighan and Mashey describe UNIX , another widely known programming environment. UNIX is similar to LISP environments in many ways: it has a single unifying way of combining computations (pipes where LISP has function calls); this provides hooks for the user to control or change the computation; the underlying simplicity contributes greatly to a friendly user interface. Perhaps the most interesting distinction is that all of these facilities are provided in the command structure of the UNIX shell, rather than with respect to a particular language. One might even say that UNIX provides facilities which allow "structured growth" of command procedures. That is, UNIX is a programming environment for command procedures rather than for programs. Indeed, much programming by UNIX users is done at the command level, a fact noted by Kernighan and Mashey.

Cheatham et al. discuss the Program Development System, a programming environment aimed at a different problem: maintaining large systems that run on several different machines. The heart of their solution is to keep a record of the development history of the system, enabling it to be replayed to reflect changes at high levels. The idea of a "design history" is an important one which we may expect future programming environments to incorporate to a much greater extent than they do now.

4 The Interlisp Programming Environment

WARREN TEITELMAN, LARRY MASINTER

XEROX Palo Alto Research Center
Palo Alto, California

Interlisp is a programming environment based on the LISP programming language [Charniak et al. 1980] [Friedman 1974]. In widespread use in the artificial intelligence community, Interlisp has an extensive set of user facilities, including syntax extension, uniform error handling, automatic error correction, an integrated structure-based editor, a sophisticated debugger, a compiler, and a filing system. Its most popular implementation is Interlisp-10, which runs under both the Tenex and Tops-20 operating systems for the DEC PDP-10 family. Interlisp-10 now has approximately 300 users at 20 different sites (mostly universities) in the US and abroad. It is an extremely well documented and maintained system.

Interlisp has been used to develop and implement a wide variety of large application systems. Examples include the Mycin system for infectious disease diagnosis [Shortliffe 1976], the Boyer-Moore theorem prover [Boyer and Moore 1979], and the BBN speech understanding system [Wolf and Woods 1980].

This article describes the Interlisp environment, the facilities available in it, and some of the reasons why Interlisp developed as it has.

© 1981 IEEE. Reprinted with permission from *Computer*, 14:4 (April 1981), pp. 25-34.

1. OVERVIEW

From its inception the focus of the Interlisp project has been not so much on the programming language as on the programming environment. An early paper on Interlisp states, "In normal usage, the word 'environment' refers to the aggregate of social and cultural conditions that influence the life of an individual. The programmer's environment influences, and to a large extent determines, what sort of problems he can (and will want to) tackle, how far he can go, and how fast. If the environment is cooperative and helpful (the anthromorphism is deliberate), the programmer can be more ambitious and productive. If not, he will spend most of his time and energy fighting a system that at times seems bent on frustrating his best efforts" [Teitelman 1969].

The environmental considerations were greatly influenced by the perceived user community and the style of programming in that community: first, typical LISP users were engaged in experimental rather than production programming; second, they were willing to expend computer resources to improve human productivity; third, we believed users would prefer sophisticated tools, even at the expense of simplicity.

1.1   Experimental Programming and Structured Growth

The original architects of the Interlisp system were interested in large artificial intelligence applications programs. Examples of such programs are theorem provers, sophisticated game-playing programs, and speech and other pattern recognition systems. These programs are characterized by the fact that they often cannot be completely specified in advance because the problems—to say nothing of their solutions—are simply not well enough understood. Instead, a program must evolve as a series of experiments, in which the results of each step suggest the direction of the next. During the course of its evolution, a program may undergo drastic revisions as the problem is better understood. One goal of Interlisp was to support this style of program development, which Erik Sandewall[1] has termed structured growth: "An initial program with a pure and simple structure is written, tested, and then allowed to grow by increasing the ambition of its modules. The process continues recursively as each module is rewritten. The principle applies not only to input/output routines but also to the flexibility of the data handled by the program, sophistication of deduction, the number and versatility of the services provided by the system, etc. The growth can occur both 'horizontally' through the addition of more facilities, and 'vertically' through a deepening of existing facilities and making them more powerful in some sense" [Sandewall 1978].

1.2   Computer Costs vs. People Costs

The second major influence in Interlisp's development was a willingness to "let the machine do it." The developers were willing to expend computer resources to save people resources because computer costs were expected to con-

---

[1]Sandewall's excellent survey article [Sandewall 1978] [*Editors' note*: included in *Interactive Programming Environments*] gives an overview of existing programming methodology in the LISP user's environment, emphasizing methods for interactive program development. It includes a comprehensive description and analysis of current LISP programming environments in general, and Interlisp and MacLisp in particular.

tinue to drop. This perspective sometimes led to tools which were ahead of their time in respect to the available computer resources.

The Advanced Research Projects Administration of the Department of Defense sponsored much of this effort. As a result, we had a fair amount of freedom in the development of Interlisp, i.e., we did not have to justify the cost-effectiveness of our research to a profit-oriented management. ARPA's willingness to make Interlisp available at a number of sites on the Arpanet justified and motivated the extra effort it took to turn a research project into a real system. These Arpanet sites also provided an active and creative user community from which we obtained many valuable suggestions and much-needed feedback.

1.3   Interlisp Is for Experts

The incremental, evolutionary way in which Interlisp developed was not especially conducive to simple interfaces. It was inappropriate to spend a lot of time and effort trying to design the right interface to a new, experimental capability whose utility had not yet been proven. Would the users like automatic error correction? Was the programmer's assistant really a good idea? The inherent complexity of the interactions among some of the more sophisticated tools, such as Masterscope, DWIM, and the programmer's assistant, made it very difficult to provide simple interfaces. In many cases, unification and simplification came only after considerable experience.

Further complexity stemmed from the commitment to accommodate a wide variety of programming styles and to enable the tools to be tailored for many applications. Given the choice of sophistication and generality of tools or simplicity of design, we chose the former, under the assumption that the system was primarily for expert programmers. As a result, mastery of all of the tools and facilities of Interlisp has become quite difficult and initial learning time fairly long. We accept this as part of the price for the system's power and productivity.

2.   BACKGROUND

Programming environments have been built for a number of languages, on top of a number of operating systems, and for a variety of user communities. Each of these factors can influence the path taken in the development of a programming environment. In the case of Interlisp, the LISP language itself and the sociological factors in effect during its early development were both important.

2.1   The LISP Language

The LISP language is conducive to the development of sophisticated programming tools because it is easy to write programs that manipulate other programs. The core syntax for the LISP language is simple, and LISP programs are naturally represented in simple LISP data structures in a way that reflects the structure of the program. Since LISP requires no declarations, programs can be built up incrementally; this is more difficult in declarative languages. This means that LISP supports the structured growth style of program building.

2.2   Early Sociology of Interlisp

One unusual historical aspect of the development of Interlisp is that from the very beginning those interested in programming environments were in a position to strongly influence the development of the language system. We were not constrained to live within the language and operating system we were given, as is usually the case. Most of the additions or extensions to the underlying LISP language performed under the Interlisp project were in response to perceived environmental needs. For example, Interlisp permits accessing the control stack at an unusually detailed level. Capabilities such as this were added to Interlisp to enable development of sophisticated and intelligent debugging facilities. Similarly, uniform error handling was added to the LISP base in order to permit experimentation with automatic error correction.

3. SOME REPRESENTATIVE INTERLISP FACILITIES

3.1 File Package

Interactive program development consists alternately of testing of program parts and editing to correct errors discovered during the tests and/or to extend the program. Interlisp, unlike many other interactive programming systems, supports both the testing and editing operations. The user talks exclusively to the Interlisp system during the interactive session. During this process, the primary copy of the program (the copy that is changed during editing operations) resides in the programming system as a data structure; editing is performed by modifying this data structure. For this reason, Interlisp is called a residential system [Sandewall 1978].

In a residential system, it is important to be able to take procedures represented by data structures and print them on text files in an input-compatible format for use as backup, to transport programs from one environment to another, and to provide hard-copy listings. In Interlisp, the file package is a set of functions, conventions, and interfaces with other system packages. The role of the file package is to automate the bookkeeping necessary for a large system consisting of many source files and their compiled counterparts. The file package removes from the user the burden of keeping track of where things are and what things have changed. For example, the file package keeps track of which file contains a particular datum, e.g., a function definition or record declaration. In many cases, it automatically retrieves the necessary datum, if it is not already in the user's working environment. The file package also keeps track of which files have been in some way modified and need to be dumped, which files have been dumped but still need to be recompiled, etc. [Teitelman 1978].

Once the user agrees to operate in the residential mode, it becomes possible to design and implement such powerful tools as DWIM and Masterscope to assist in program development. The file package makes this mode attractive to the user.

The history of the file package is instructive, as it is a paradigm for the development of user facilities that has frequently been followed in Interlisp. The file package was *not* designed in a coherent, integrated way; nobody sat down and said "We need a file package." Instead, it evolved gradually. Originally, there was only a very limited facility for symbolically saving the state at the end of a session in a form that could be loaded into a LISP system to restore that state: the PrettyDef function. This took as its arguments a list of function names, a list of variable names, and a file name. PrettyDef wrote ("prettyprinted") the definitions of the named functions and the values of the named variables onto the indicated file. PrettyDef was soon extended to take a set of commands, which could indicate not only the functions and variables to be saved, but properties on property lists, values in arrays, definitions of new editor commands, and record declarations, among others. Finally, PrettyDef was extended to allow the user to augment this simple command language by defining his own filing commands (usually in terms of existing ones).

Concurrently, as the contents of source files became more complicated, the ability to interrogate files as to their contents (e.g., which file contained a particular datum and what functions were contained in a particular file) became more important. This required the system to be able to enumerate all of the user's source files, which was accomplished by adding the file to a global list so it would be noticed when it was first loaded or dumped.

The significant breakthrough occurred with the emergence of the idea (probably through some user saying, "Wouldn't it be nice if the system...") of having the system notice when a datum was changed, e.g., defined for the first time, edited, redefined, or reset, and associate this fact with the file containing the datum. This enhancement was relatively straightforward since the ability to decompose and interpret the commands that described the contents of a particular file was already available. It was implemented by a function that took the name of a datum and its type (function, variable, record definition, etc.) and marked the datum as changed and therefore in need of dumping. This function, MarkAsChanged, operated by discovering which file(s) contained the datum and associated with each such file the name of the object that had changed. Calls to MarkAsChanged were then inserted in all of the parts of the Interlisp system that changed objects—the editor, the DEFINE function, the facility for (re)declaring records, and DWIM (which can modify a function when it performs a spelling correction or some other transformation inside the function).

With this change, the file package assumed a degree of autonomy, often operating automatically and behind the scenes. Furthermore, since it was no longer a function that the user called, but included "tendrils" into many parts of the system, we began to think of it as a package. In this light, a number of extensions became apparent. For example, the "Cleanup" function provided the capability to enumerate all of the user's files and write out those that contain data that had changed. Next, an automatic warning was added to Cleanup, in case an object not associated with any file changed or was newly defined. Then a filing capability was added, which enabled the user to add a datum to a file by automatically modifying the commands for that file. Finally, Cleanup was extended to prompt the user about unfiled objects and to allow the user to specify the destinations of these objects.

By this point, the Interlisp user did not have to worry about maintaining his source files, save for occasionally calling Cleanup. The file package had become smart with respect to its built-in commands, but if a user defined a new type of command, the file package would not necessarily be able to support operations such as adding an object of that type to a file, deleting or renaming an object, or obtaining the "definition" of an object of a particular type from a file. The user was placed in the position of having to choose between using an automatic facility that did just what he wanted—provided he stuck to a predefined class of file objects—or extending this facility to print out his own types of file objects, which meant returning to manual bookkeeping of symbolic files.

Thus, the next extension to the file package identified and exposed its primitive operations and allowed the user to define or change these operations. This resulted in a more complicated interface to the file package than that used by most, but it enabled builders of systems within Interlisp to enjoy the same privileges of defining file package operations that the original implementors enjoyed. In fact, we were able to express the semantics of all of the built-in file package commands and types in terms of the above interface. We thus eliminated all distinction between built-in operations and those defined by the user (a good test of the completeness of this lower-level interface) and permitted the user to redefine the way these operations are performed.

The file package supports the abstraction that the user is truly manipulating his program as data and that the file is merely one particular external representation of a collection of program pieces. During the session, the user manipulates the pieces with a variety of tools, occasionally saving what he has done by calling the Cleanup function. The user can also operate in a mode where programs are treated as residing in a data base, i.e., the external file system, with a variety of sophisticated retrieval tools at his disposal.

Note the evolution of the file package. It started as an isolated facility that was explicitly invoked by the user to perform a particular and limited action. More and more capabilities were added, increasing the range of applicability of the tool. At the same time, the tool was integrated into the system to produce a semi-autonomous configuration in which the tool is invoked automatically in a number of contexts. Finally, the utility of the tool became so great that a form of user extensibility, to adapt the tool to accommodate unforeseen situations, became imperative.

The file package also illustrates one of the principal design criteria of the Interlisp system, the accommodation of a wide range of styles and applications. The user is not forced to choose among using a facility that is powerful and attractive but forces adherence to its prescribed conventions, abandoning the tool, or even creating a personal, renegade version whenever he needs a capability the tool does not provide. In other words, if a particular tool handles 95 percent of the user's applications correctly, he should be able to extend the tool in a prescribed and "blessed" manner to accommodate the remaining five percent without undue effort.

3.2   Masterscope

As the size of systems built within Interlisp grew larger and larger, it became increasingly difficult for a user to predict the effect of a proposed change. It was also growing difficult to effect a pervasive change, for example, to change the calling convention of a low-level procedure and be sure that all of the relevant places in programs would be found and modified. Masterscope is an interactive program for analyzing and cross-referencing user programs that addresses this problem. It contains facilities for analyzing user programs to determine which functions are called, how and where variables are bound, set, or referenced, which functions use particular record declarations, etc.

Masterscope maintains a data base of the results of the analyses it performs. The user can interrogate the data base explicitly (e.g., WHO USES FOO FREELY), or have Masterscope call the editor on all functions that contain expressions that satisfy certain relations (EDIT WHERE ANY FUNCTION USES THE RECORD DICTENTRY).

Masterscope, like the file package, has its roots in an extremely simple program. Called PrintStructure, this program analyzed function definitions and printed out the tree structure of their calls. It was first extended to include the names of the arguments for each function it analyzed, and then to include more information about variable usage within each function. However, as PrintStructure presented more and more information about larger and more complicated program configurations, it became increasingly difficult for the user to extract particular information from this massive output. It became clear that the user wanted access to specific information rather than a complete listing. This led to the idea of separating the analysis of the program from the interrogation of the data base.

The next stage was integration with the other parts of the system. As in the case of the file package, the utility of Masterscope increased greatly when the burden of remembering what had changed, and therefore needed re-analysis, was lifted from the user and carried out automatically behind the scenes. The next phase of the evolution of Masterscope was to permit the user to extend Masterscope's built-in information on analysis of special LISP forms, such as PROG, SETQ, and LAMBDA expressions. This was accomplished through the use of Masterscope "templates," which are essentially patterns for evaluation of functions. Finally, all built-in information was removed from Masterscope and replaced by templates, both to test the completeness of the interface and to expose this information to users so they could change it.

3.3 DWIM

According to Sandewall, "One of the most impressive features in the Interlisp system is the DWIM (Do What I Mean) facility, which is invoked when the basic system detects an error and which attempts to guess what the user might have intended." [Sandewall 1978]

The most visible part of DWIM [Teitelman 1972a] is the spelling corrector, which is invoked from many places in the system, including the file package, LISP editor, and the LISP interpreter itself. When an unrecognized file package command, edit command, LISP function, etc., is encountered, the spelling corrector is invoked. The spelling corrector attempts to find the closest match within a list of relevant items. If an edit command is misspelled, for example, the list of valid edit commands is searched; if the name of a function is misspelled, the corrector scans a list of the functions the user has recently been working with. If the spelling correction is successful, the cause of the error is also repaired, so subsequent corrections will not be necessary. For example, when DWIM corrects a user's misspelled function name in one of his programs, it actually modifies the user's program to contain the correct spelling (and notifies the file package of the change).

Although most users think of DWIM as a single identifiable package, it embodies a pervasive philosophy of user interface design: at the user interface level, system facilities should make reasonable interpretations when given unrecognized input. Spelling correction is only one example of such an interpretation. Depending on how far off the input is, a facility might make the transformation silently and automatically, without seeking user approval. For example, a function expecting a list of items will normally interpret an argument that is a single atom as a list made up of that single atom. In this case, the package in question probably would not even indicate to the user that it had made this correction, and in fact the user might view the package as expecting either a list or an atom. Similarly, the style of interface used throughout Interlisp allows the user to omit various parameters and have these default to reasonable values, such as "the last thing this package operated upon."

DWIM is an embodiment of the idea that the user is interacting with an agent who attempts to interpret the user's request for contextual information. Since we want the user to feel that he is conversing with the system, he should not be stopped and forced to correct himself or give additional information in situations where the correction or information is obvious.

3.4　The Iterative Expression

The various forms of the Interlisp iterative expression permit the user to specify complicated loops in a straightforward and visible manner. In one sense, the iterative expression represents a language extension, but by its design, implementation, and in particular its extensibility, it more naturally falls into the same category as other Interlisp tools.

An iterative expression in Interlisp consists of a sequence of operators, indicated by keywords, followed by one or more operands; many different operators can be combined in the same iterative statement. For example, (for X in L sum X) iterates the variable X over the elements of the list L, returning the sum of each value seen. The iterative expression could be further embellished by including "when (GREATERP X 30)" to only sum elements greater than 30, or "while (LESSP $VAL 50)" to terminate the iteration when the sum exceeds 50. Other operators can be used to specify different ranges. For example, iteration can take place over a range of numbers instead of over the elements of a list: (for I from 1 to 10 ...). Operators can also specify the value returned by the iterative expression. For example, (for X in L collect (ADD1 X)) would return a new list, consisting of the elements in L, each incremented by 1.

The iterative expression currently understands approximately two dozen operators. Furthermore, new iterative operators can be defined simply. One group, experimenting with a relational data base system, provided access to that data base merely by defining a new iterative operator called "matching." This matching operator can be used in conjunction with all of the other iterative constructs, as in "(for Records matching (PAYMENT (> 30) *) sum Record:3)," which would find all payment records in the data base and sum their third component. Such language extensions are quite difficult in most programming languages.

3.5　Programmer's Assistant

The central idea of the programmer's assistant is that the user is not talking to a passive executive that merely responds to each input and waits for the next, but is addressing an active intermediary. [Teitelman 1972b] The programmer's assistant records, in a data structure called the history list, the user's input, a description of the side effects of the operation, [Teitelman 1978] and the result of the operation.

The programmer's assistant also responds to commands that manipulate the history list. For example, the REDO command allows the user to repeat a particular operation or sequence of operations; the FIX command allows the user to invoke the Interlisp editor on the specified events and then to re-execute the modified operations; the USE command performs a substitution before re-executing a specified event (e.g., USE PRINT FOR READ); the UNDO command cancels the effect of the specified operations. In addition to the obvious use of recovering information lost through typing errors, UNDO is often used to selectively flip back and forth between two states. For example, the user might make some changes to his program and/or data structures, run an experiment, undo the changes, rerun the experiment, undo the undo, and so on.

The various replay commands, such as REDO and FIX, permit the user to construct complex console operations out of simpler ones, in much the same fashion as programs are constructed. That is, simple operations can be first checked and then combined into large ones. The system always remembers what the programmer has typed, so that keyboard input can be reused in response to an afterthought.

The programmer's assistant has been implemented for use in contexts besides the handling of inputs to the LISP "listen" loop. For example, the Interlisp editor also uses the programmer's assistant for storing operations on the history list and thereby provides all the history commands for use in an editing session. Similarly, user programs can take advantage of the history facility. A system for natural language queries of a data base of lunar rock samples provides one example of how this facility can be used. After a complicated query regarding the percentage of cobalt in a sample, a user could say USE MANAGANESE FOR COBALT to repeat the query with a different parameter.

4. WHAT MAKES INTERLISP UNIQUE?

The Interlisp programming environment has been characterized as friendly, cooperative, and forgiving. While these qualities are desirable, they are not unique to Interlisp. The two attributes that set it apart are the degree to which the system is integrated and the degree to which facilities in the environment can be tailored, modified, or extended.

4.2 Integration

Interlisp is not merely a collection of independent programming tools, but an integrated system. By integration, we mean that there need not be any explicit context switch when switching between tasks or programming tools, in switching, for example, from debugging to editing to interrogating Masterscope about the program. Thus, having called the editor from inside the debugger, the user can examine the current run-time state from within the editor or ask Masterscope a question without losing the context of the editing session. Also, the various facilities themselves can use each other in important ways, since they all coexist in the same address space. For example, the editor can directly invoke DWIM, or Masterscope commands can be used to drive the editor. The integration of facilities increases their power.

Integrated programming tools such as these are not feasible without a large virtual address space. Where the size of the programming environment is constrained, it is unreasonable to have a large variety of resident tools that can all interact with the user's run-time environment and with each other. Interlisp-10's large virtual address space of 256K 36-bit words (large, at least for the early 1970's) made it possible to add new features to the programming environment without trying to squeeze them into a small amount of space or worrying about leaving enough space for the user.

4.2 Extensibility

Most programming environments, even when they provide a variety of tools, support only a narrow range of programming styles. In the development of Interlisp, we have tried to accommodate a variety of programming styles.

The most straightforward way of allowing users to modify or tailor system tools to their own applications is simply to make sources available and allow the users to edit and modify tools as they wish. A benefit of this approach is that it absolves the system designers of responsibility for unforeseen bugs or incompatibilities. ("The manufacturer's warranty is void if this panel is removed.") Of course, this kind of extensibility isn't really defensible, as it discourages all but the most intrepid of users. If a creative user does manage to extend a system capability, he must then worry about tracking improvements and bug fixes in this tool and be constantly aware of changes to the system, which could introduce incompatibilities with respect to his modifications.

Extensions and modifications were provided in a variety of ways. Capabilities that have associated command languages lend themselves quite naturally to extensibility, because new commands can be defined in terms of existing ones. Almost all Interlisp packages (e.g., the file package, the editor, the debugger and programmer's assistant) support such extensions via substitution macros, which associate a template (composed of existing commands) with the new command. The arguments to the new command are then substituted for those of the template's as appropriate. In addition, most facilities support computed macros. A computed macro is basically a LISP expression, evaluated to produce a new list of operators/ commands/ expressions. For example, a computed edit macro produces a list of edit commands, and a computed file package command produces a list of file package commands.

However, many extensions are not expressible in terms of macros because they are triggered not by the appearance of a particular token, but by the existence of a more general condition. Interlisp provides for such extensions by allowing the user to specify a function to be called upon any object/expression/command that the particular facility does not recognize. This function is responsible for selecting from among the various conditions that might pertain and deciding whether or not it recognizes a particular case. If it does, it takes the appropriate action. Typical applications of such functions are implementation of infix edit commands and specification of the compilation of a class of expressions, such as the iterative expression.

For example, the DWIM facility, which corrects spelling errors encountered while running, is implemented via an extension to the LISP interpreter of this form, called FaultEval. Whenever the Interlisp interpreter encounters an expression for which it is going to generate an error, such as an undefined function or variable, the interpreter instead calls FaultEval. Originally, FaultEval merely printed an error message. DWIM was implemented by redefining FaultEval to try to correct the spelling of the undefined function or variable, according to names defined in the context in which the error occurred.

One might suppose that a facility as basic as correction of program errors would have been implemented by modifiying the LISP interpreter—especially since a fair amount of knowledge about the interpreter's state was required in order to be able to continue a computation after an error correction. The fact that this is not the case illustrates a basic tenet of the Interlisp design philosophy, which holds that the implementation of enabling capabilities is a top priority. When DWIM was first being implemented, the interpreter did not call FaultEval, and there was no way to trap all DWIM errors. Instead of trying to implement DWIM directly, we tried to find the enabling capability that would make it possible for a *user* to implement DWIM. This capability was provided by having the interpreter call FaultEval, which was then used to implement DWIM.

The enabling capability was then available for other applications, as well. It has allowed users to experiment with building their own tools and extending system capabilities in ways we did not foresee. For example, one application program redefined FaultEval to send error messages not to the user but instead to the implementor of the application, via computer mail.

Finally, because we realized that some users just might not like a particular facility, we made it easy for them to "turn off" any automatic facility in the system. This made the use of the programming tool a deliberate choice of the user and provided a powerful force for quality control: if the feature didn't help as much as it got in the way, people would turn it off.

The support of a wide variety of programming styles and settings of parameters has some drawbacks. Interlisp has an overabundance of user-setable parameters, to the point where new users are sometimes overwhelmed by their number of choices. In addition, it is necessary to ensure that the system will work correctly for every possible setting of the various system parameters. For example, the Masterscope facility normally relies on DWIM to perform some of its transformations, so we had to take care that Masterscope would continue to work, even if the user disabled DWIM.

5. A BRIEF HISTORY OF INTERLISP

Interlisp began with an implementation of the LISP programming language for the PDP-1 at Bolt, Beranek and Newman in 1966, followed in 1967 by 940 LISP, an upward compatible implementation for the SDS-940 computer. 940 LISP was the first LISP system to demonstrate the feasibility of using software paging techniques and a large virtual memory in conjunction with a list-processing system [Bobrow and Murphy 1967]. 940 LISP was patterned after the LISP 1.5 implementation for CTSS at MIT, with several new facilities added to take advantage of its timeshared, on-line environment.

The SDS-940 computer was soon outgrown, and in 1970 BBN-Lisp, an upward compatible version of the system for the PDP-10, was implemented for the Tenex operating system. With the hardware paging and 256K of virtual memory provided by Tenex, it was practical to provide more extensive and sophisticated user support facilities, and a library of such facilities began to evolve. In 1972, the name of the system was changed to Interlisp, and its development became a joint effort of the Xerox Palo Alto Research Center and Bolt, Beranek and Newman. The next few years saw a period of rapid growth and development at the language and system levels and at user support facilities, notably in the record package, the file package, and Masterscope. This growth was paralleled by the increase in the size and diversity of the Interlisp user community.

In 1974, Interlisp was implemented for the Xerox Alto, an experimental microprogrammed minicomputer [Thacker et al. 1979]. AltoLisp introduced the idea of providing a microcoded target language for LISP compilations, which modeled the basic operations of LISP more closely than could a general-purpose instruction set [Deutsch 1973a]. AltoLisp also served as a model and departure point for Interlisp-D, [Burton et al. 1980] [Burton 1980] and for the implementation of Interlisp for the Dolphin and Dorado Xerox personal computers [Lampson and Pier 1980], the successors to the Alto. Interlisp-D now supports a user community within Xerox Palo Alto Research Center.

5.1   Evolution of Interlisp

The origins of Interlisp at Bolt, Beranek and Newman were fortuitous. There was neither an existing LISP implementation for the available hardware nor a user community, so it was necessary to start from scratch. Along with the necessity of starting from scratch came the freedom to develop the environment. We were free to experiment with various ideas and facilities, discard those that did not work out, and learn from mistakes in the process. We approached the problem of building the programming environment with the same paradigm with which we approached the programs being developed in that environment—as an ongoing research problem, not something that had to be right the first time or even finished at all. New capabilities were often introduced without a thorough design or a complete understanding of the underlying abstractions. Furthermore, "hooks" into the system were provided at many different levels in order to encourage users to augment system packages or experiment with their own. Many of the now-permanent facilities of the Interlisp system evolved from tools designed by individual users to augment their own working environments.

The result was a somewhat chaotic growth pattern and a style sometimes characterized as baroque. Interlisp was not designed, it evolved—but this was the right approach. As Sandewall [Sandewall 1978] points out, "The task of designing interactive programming systems is hard because there is no way to avoid complexity in such systems.... The only applicable research method is to accumulate experience by implementing a system, synthesize the experience, think for a while, and start over." Had we been required to convince a disinterested third party of the need for certain enabling facilities in the language or operating system in order to perform experiments—whose exact shape and ultimate payoff were unknown—many of the more successful innovations would not exist. The value of a number of these innovations, including history, UNDO, and spelling correction, is now well recognized and accepted, and many new programming environments are being built with these facilities in mind.

The ability of individual users to augment system tools at a variety of levels, as well as quick responses to suggestions for extensions that users could not perform themselves, contributed greatly to the enthusiasm and energy of the Interlisp community. These factors played a large part in the growth and success of the system over the last decade.

Of course, as Interlisp matured and the user community grew, we were occasionally restricted in some areas of experimentation by a concern for backwards compatibility and the fact that the system was being used to get "real work" done. But enough flexibility had been built in to permit experimentation without performing major low-level changes. Furthermore, Interlisp attracted users who appreciated its flexibility and enjoyed experimentation with avant-garde facilities. Thus, when planned evolution led to some incompatibilities and consequent retrofitting, our user community was understanding and supportive.

6. FUTURE DIRECTIONS

6.1   Interlisp and The Personal Computing Environment

Interlisp evolved in a timeshared, hard-copy terminal world, and vestiges of this heritage have carried over into implementation for personal computers. In the future, we expect to see increasing exploitation of the personal nature of the computing environment. For example, there is a significant difference between performing an Interlisp-10 operation on a lightly loaded timeshared system and one that is heavily loaded. If the former takes 50 milliseconds, the latter might take as long as five seconds of real time, especially if the computation involves a large working set, as is often the case with the more sophisticated facilities of Interlisp. This makes the probability high that portions of the working set will be swapped out before the computation completes, and therefore must be swapped back in again, adding to the delay.

This real-time difference is especially relevant when dealing with interactive tools. A system can afford to spend 50 milliseconds trying to find out what a user means, because the extra 50 milliseconds is insignificant compared to the overhead of interacting with the user. But a system that spends five seconds to perform a spelling correction is often not acceptable, because in most situations the user would prefer to retype the correct input rather than wait. In such a case, the tool not only fails to add to the interactive quality of the system for this particular user, but since the user is competing with others for the same resource, namely machine cycles, its very attempt to be helpful causes response time—and hence the interactive quality of the system—to degrade for other users. To quote Sandewall, "When this facility [DWIM] is presented to new users, it is not uncommon for them to use it for a trivial typing error that could easily be corrected using the character-delete key. However, the user relies on DWIM for the correction, which at periods of peak computer load may take considerable time.... As computer systems become more and more heavily loaded, more of the advanced features in interactive programming systems are canceled [Sandewall 1978].

The entire situation changes in the personal computing environment. It is no longer necessary to justify the use of a particular tool by a single user in terms of the overall productivity of the community, since there is no longer any competition for cycles. It even becomes reasonable to devise tools that operate continually in a background mode while the user is thinking, such as an incremental garbage collector, a program that updates a Masterscope data base, or one that performs compilations. Personal computing thus causes a qualitative change in the programming environment, because the machine can be working continually for a single user.

6.2   Integration of the Display

A significant addition to Interlisp in the new generation of personal computers, such as Interlisp-D, is the availability and integration of very high-resolution and high-bandwidth displays. Because of the high-output bandwidth of the display and the increased input bandwidth arising from the use of pointing devices, a number of trade-offs change significantly. The capabilities affect, for example, something as elementary as how much information to present to the user when an error occurs; the utility of on-line documentation assistance also increases. Complicated sequences of commands for specifying location, down to a particular frame on the stack, a particular expression in a program, etc., are obviated by the ability to display the data structure and have the user point at the appropriate place. Similarly, the choice between short, easily typed, but esoteric command or function names as opposed to those that are longer, more self-explanatory, but more difficult to type becomes academic when operations can be invoked via menus.

These are examples of how a high-resolution display can facilitate essentially the same operations found in the hard-copy domain. Perhaps more interesting are the modes of operation enabled by the display that are unlike those of the hard-copy world. DLisp is an experimental system that explores some of these techniques [Teitelman 1977]. In DLisp, the user sees his programming environment through a collection of display windows, each of which corresponds to a different task or context. The user can manipulate the windows, or the contents of a particular window, by a combination of keyboard inputs and pointing operations. The technique of using different windows for different tasks makes it easy for the user to manage several simultaneous tasks and contexts, e.g., defining programs, testing programs, editing, asking the system for assistance, and sending and receiving messages. It also facilitates switching back and forth between these tasks.

Finally, we have not really begun to explore the use of graphics—textures, line drawings, scanned images, even color—as a tool for program development. For example, the system might present storage in a continually adjusting bargraph, or display a complicated data structure as a network of nodes and directed arcs, perhaps even allowing the user to edit this representation directly. This is a rich area for development in the future.

REFERENCES

[Bobrow and Murphy 1967] D.G. Bobrow, D.L. Murphy. The structure of a LISP system using two level storage. *Communications of the ACM*, 10:3 (March 1967), 155-159.

[Boyer and Moore 1979] R.S. Boyer, J.S. Moore. *A Computational Logic*. Academic Press, New York, 1979.

[Burton 1980] R.R. Burton. Interlisp-D display facilities. In *Papers on Interlisp-D*, Xerox Palo Alto Research Center, Report No. SSL-80-4, Palo Alto, Calif. 1980, 33-46.

[Burton et al. 1980] R.R. Burton et al. Interlisp-D: overview and status. In *Papers on Interlisp-D*, Xerox Palo Alto Research Center, Report No. SSL-80-4, Palo Alto, Calif. 1980, 1-10.

[Charniak et al. 1980] E. Charniak, C. Riesbeck, D. McDermott. *Artificial Intelligence Programming*. Lawrence Erlbaum Associates, Hillsdale, N.J., 1980.

[Deutsch 1973a] L.P. Deutsch. A LISP machine with very compact programs. *International Joint Conference on Artificial Intelligence*, Stanford, California, August 1973, 697-703.

[Friedman 1974] D. Friedman. *The Little LISPer*. SRA Publications, Menlo Park, California, 1974.

[Lampson and Pier 1980] B.W. Lampson, K.A. Pier. A processor for a high-performance personal computer. *Seventh International Symposium on Computer Architecture*, La Baule, France, May 1980.

[Sandewall 1978] E. Sandewall. Programming in the interactive environment: the LISP experience. *Communications of the ACM*, 10:1 (March 1978), 35-71; reprinted in *Interactive Programming Environments*.

[Shortliffe 1976] E.H. Shortliffe. *Computer-Based Medical Consultations*. American Elsevier, New York, 1976.

[Teitelman 1969] W. Teitelman. Toward a programming laboratory. *International Joint Conference on Artificial Intelligence*, Washington, May 1969, 1-8.

[Teitelman 1972a] W. Teitelman. Do What I Mean. *Computers and Automation*, April 1972.

[Teitelman 1972b] W. Teitelman. Automated programmering—the programmer's assistant. *Proceedings of the Fall Joint Computer Conference*, AFIPS Proceedings (1972), 917-922; reprinted in *Interactive Programming Environments*.

[Teitelman 1977] W. Teitelman. A display-oriented programmer's assistant. CSL 77-3, XEROX PARC, 1977; reprinted in *Interactive Programming Environments*; see also *Proceedings of the Fifth International Joint Conference on Artificial Intelligence*, Cambridge, Massachusetts, August 1977, 905-915.

[Teitelman 1978] W. Teitelman. *INTERLISP Reference Manual*. Xerox Palo Alto Research Center, Palo Alto, California, December 1978.

[Thacker et al. 1979] C. Thacker, E. McCreight, B. Lampson, R. Sproull, D. Boggs. *Alto: a personal computer*. Xerox Palo Alto Research Center Technical Report CSL-79-11, August 1979.

[Wolf and Woods 1980] J. Wolf, W.A. Woods. The HWIM speech understanding system. in *Trends in Speech Recognition*, Prentice-Hall, Englewood Cliffs, New Jersey, 1980.

5 The Cornell Program Synthesizer: A Syntax-Directed Programming Environment

TIM TEITELBAUM, THOMAS REPS

Cornell University
Ithaca, New York

Programs are not text; they are hierarchical compositions of computational structures and should be edited, executed, and debugged in an environment that consistently acknowledges and reinforces this viewpoint. The Cornell Program Synthesizer demands a structural perspective at all stages of program development. Its separate features are unified by a common foundation: a grammar for the programming language. Its full-screen derivation-tree editor and syntax-directed diagnostic interpreter combine to make the Synthesizer a powerful and responsive interactive programming tool.

© 1981, Association for Computing Machinery, Inc. Reprinted by permission from *Communications of the ACM*, 24:9 (September 1981), pp. 563-573.

1. INTRODUCTION

The Cornell Program Synthesizer is an interactive programming environment with integrated facilities to create, edit, execute, and debug programs. Our goal was to develop a unified programming environment that stimulates program conception at a high level of abstraction, promotes programming by stepwise refinement, spares the user from mundane and frustrating syntactic details while editing programs, and provides extensive diagnostic facilities during program execution.

We attained these goals by making the Synthesizer syntax-directed: both editing and execution are guided by the syntactic structure of the programming language.

The grammar of the programming language is embodied in a collection of *templates* predefined for all but the simplest statement types. Programs are created top-down by inserting new statements and expressions at a cursor position within the skeleton of previously entered templates. In general, the editing cursor can only be moved from one template to another and from one template to its constituents, and not simply from one line of text to another. Templates reinforce the view that a program is a hierarchical composition of syntactic objects, rather than a sequence of characters.

Runtime diagnostic facilities are likewise syntax-directed. Discrete computational units of execution correspond exactly to the syntactic units of the editor. When *tracing*, the screen cursor indicates the location of the instruction pointer in the source code as the program executes. When *single-stepping*, the user controls execution with respect to the hierarchical template structure of the program. The Synthesizer consistently demands a structural perspective.

The Synthesizer's editor is a hybrid between a tree editor and a text editor. Templates are generated by command, but expressions and assignment statements are typed one character at a time. It is impossible to make errors in templates because they are predefined. Errors in user-typed text are detected immediately because the parser is invoked by the editor on a phrase-by-phrase basis. By precluding the creation of syntactically incorrect files, the Synthesizer lets the user focus on the intellectually challenging aspects of programming.

Because code is generated each time a template or phrase is inserted, execution can follow editing without delay. Execution is suspended when a missing program element is encountered, but can be immediately resumed after the required code has been inserted. Thus, incomplete programs are executable; program development and testing can be conveniently and rapidly interleaved.

The design and implementation of the Program Synthesizer began in May 1978, and demonstrable prototype versions were operational under UNIX as well as on Terak (LSI-11) microcomputers by December 1978 [Teitelbaum 1979] [Teitelbaum 1980].The Synthesizer, first used in classes at Cornell in June 1979, currently serves about 1500 of our introductory programming students a year. The Synthesizer has also been adopted for elementary programming instruction at Rutgers University, Princeton University, and Hamilton College.

The first language implemented for the Synthesizer was PL/CS, an instructional dialect of PL/I [Conway and Constable 1976]. PL/CS had previously been defined to serve as a vehicle for research on batch-oriented, error-correcting compilers [Conway 1978] as well as for program verification [Constable and O'Donnell 1978]. We are currently developing a version of the Synthesizer for Pascal.

Certain individual features of the Synthesizer have appeared in previous systems:

- immediate phrase-by-phrase syntax analysis in BASIC [Kurtz 1978],
- syntax-directed, program generation in EMILY [Hansen 1971a] and the Fortran Language Anticipation and Prompting System [Pinc and Schweppe 1973],
- full-screen editing in the RAND editor, the Berkeley display editor EX[Joy 1977], and GED[Skinner],
- tree-editing in INTERLISP [Teitelman 1978] and MENTOR [Donzeau-Gouge et al. 1975],
- selective hierarchical file display at SRI [Engelbart and English 1968],
- windowing in the Programmer's Assistant [Teitelman 1977],
- screen-oriented execution monitoring in CAPS [Wilcox 1976], and
- reverse execution in EXDAMS [Balzer 1969], PL/C [Zelkowitz 1971] and BIDOPS [Hodgson and Porter 1980].

The combination of these facilities in the Synthesizer has made it a powerful and responsive programming tool.

Related work in progress on language-specific programming environments include LISPEDIT [Alberga et al. 1981] and PL1L-EDIT [Mikellsons and Wegman 1980] at IBM, Gandalf at CMU [Feiler and Medina-Mora 1981] [Habermann 1979], ALBE at Yale [Lewis and Porges 1979], and COPE at Cornell [Archer et al. 1980].

2. PROGRAM EDITING

Programs are edited by inserting and deleting at the cursor position in a screen of text. The body of text expands either horizontally or vertically, as necessary, to accommodate insertions; it contracts when characters or lines are deleted. The screen serves as a window into a file. Whenever the cursor moves to a location in the file not contained on the screen, the file shifts automatically to include the new cursor position within the window. All screen modifications are essentially instantaneous on a high speed video terminal.

2.1   Files, Templates, Phrases, and the Cursor

A Synthesizer file is an object with hierarchical structure, not just a sequence of characters and lines. Files are composed of two kinds of elements: templates and phrases.

A *template* is a predefined, formatted pattern of characters and punctuation marks. The keywords, punctuation, and indenting format of a template cannot be altered. The template provides an immutable framework for the insertion of additional program units. *Placeholders* identify the locations where these insertions are permitted. Each placeholder designates the syntactic class of permissible insertions. For example, the template for a conditional statement is:

```
IF (condition)
   THEN statement
   ELSE statement
```

where *condition* and *statement* are placeholders.

A *phrase* is an arbitrary sequence of typed symbols. For example, each of the following lines is a phrase:

```
k>0
'not positive'
```

Both phrases and templates can be inserted into other templates at locations designated by placeholders, replacing the given placeholder. This nesting of templates, one within another, can occur to any depth.

All modifications of program text occur relative to the current position of the *editing cursor*. Although the cursor can be moved anywhere within a phrase, it can only be positioned at the leftmost symbol of a template or placeholder. The upper leftmost symbol of a template denotes the entire template including its constituents. The cursor never appears within the keywords and punctuation marks of a template or in the margins. In general, the editing cursor is advanced from one template to another and from one template to its constituents. It is possible to position the cursor only where insertions and deletions are allowed.

Thus, the Synthesizer views the following partially developed file segment as a hierarchical composition of nested templates and phrases rather than three independent lines of text. The cursor, indicated by □, is positioned at the *statement placeholder*.

```
IF ( k>0 )
   THEN Ⓢtatement
   ELSE PUT SKIP LIST ('not positive' );
```

The cursor control keys move the cursor forward and backward through the program. For want of better names, we refer to the keys as **left**,[1] **right**, **up** and **down**. Despite this nomenclature, the effect of the control keys is defined with respect to the one-dimensional reading order of a program, not the two-dimensional coordinate system of its display. Thus, both **right** and **down** move the cursor forward through the program; **left** and **up** move it backwards. Because much of the program text is immutable, the cursor jumps in logical increments, not character by character. Although **right** and **down** both move the cursor forward, their units of increment differ.

Up and **down** move the cursor one program element at a time, stopping only once per template, phrase, or placeholder. The following file segment shows with underlines all the possible stopping points for the cursor when the **up** and **down** keys are used:

```
IF ( k>0 )
   THEN statement
   ELSE PUT SKIP LIST ('not positive');
```

Left and **right** differ from **up** and **down** by also moving the cursor to every character within a phrase:

```
IF (k>0)
   THEN statement
   ELSE PUT SKIP LIST ('notpositive');
```

---

[1] Boldface words such as **left** denote single keys of the terminal.

Other commands move the cursor in logical increments greater than **up** and **down** according to the nesting structure of the templates. The two key sequence **long down** advances the cursor to the next element at the same structural level; the sequence **long up** moves backward similarly. The **diagonal** key moves the cursor to the immediately enclosing program element. The sequence **long diagonal** moves the cursor to the top of the program.

2.2 Insertions

Files are created top-down by inserting templates and phrases into existing templates, where they are instantly displayed on the screen. Templates are not typed, they are generated by command. Each insertion occurs at the position of the editing cursor. Insertions can be made in any order, but only when the cursor is located at a placeholder. In order to insert the template

```
PUT SKIP LIST (list-of-expressions);
```

into

```
IF ( k>0 )
   THEN ⌊s⌋tatement
   ELSE PUT SKIP LIST ('not positive' );
```

the user types the command ".**p**", and then strikes **return**. The insertion is instantly displayed on the screen, with the cursor automatically advanced to the placeholder, *list-of-expressions*:

```
IF ( k>0 )
   THEN PUT SKIP LIST ( ⌊l⌋ist-of-expressions );
   ELSE PUT SKIP LIST ('not positive' );
```

A template inserted by command is always syntactically correct for two reasons:

1. The command is validated to guarantee that it inserts a template permitted at the current cursor position. (For example, typing the command ".**p**" with the cursor positioned at *list-of-expressions* is an error.)
2. The template is a predefined unit. Because it is not typed, it contains no typographical errors.

Phrases, unlike templates, are explicitly typed at the position of the editing cursor. As the first character of a phrase is typed, the placeholder disappears. The phrase's right context shifts correspondingly, one character at a time, to accommodate the insertion. In the example above, ");" is the right context of *list-of-expressions*. It shifts one character at a time to the right as a phrase is typed at *list-of-expressions*. Phrases and their right contexts are automatically continued on consecutive lines, as necessary:

```
IF ( k>0 )
   THEN PUT SKIP LIST ( the number k is strictly g
          reater than zer⌊o⌋));
   ELSE PUT SKIP LIST ('not positive' );
```

Because phrases are typed by the user, their syntactic correctness must be validated. Typed text is parsed as soon as the cursor is directed away from the phrase. Thus, the moment the user strikes **return** in the example above, the missing quote is detected, an error message is printed on the top line of the screen, and the editing cursor is positioned as close to the site of error as possible. The display would then appear:

```
IF ( k>0 )
    THEN PUT SKIP LIST ( [t]he number k is strictly g
            reater than zero' );
    ELSE PUT SKIP LIST ('not positive' );
```

In this case, because the error detection mechanism properly positions the cursor, the required quotation mark can be inserted in a single keystroke. The phrase and its right context shifts right and down in response to this insertion:

```
IF ( k>0 )
    THEN PUT SKIP LIST ('[t]he number k is strictly
            greater than zero' );
    ELSE PUT SKIP LIST ('not positive' );
```

Directing the cursor away from the phrase invokes the parser again. Because the phrase is now syntactically correct, the cursor is positioned as directed. Phrases are prettyprinted and redisplayed after being parsed successfully.

2.3 Modifications

Structural changes to the program are accomplished by removal and insertion of whole templates and phrases. This highly disciplined mode of modification guarantees the structural integrity of the program at every step. The position of the editing cursor always denotes a whole program unit: template, phrase, or placeholder. Thus, it is not necessary to specify line limits in order to remove an entire program unit:

```
delete      (move the template or phrase to the file DELETED),
clip        (move the template or phrase to the file CLIPPED),
.mv f       (move the template or phrase to the file f).
```

After a program unit has been removed, the display is immediately redrawn and the original placeholder reappears. The editing cursor can then be repositioned and the file segment reinserted:

```
insert      (insert the contents of CLIPPED at the current cursor
            position),
.ins f      (insert the contents of file f at the current cursor
            position).
```

In the example below, because the cursor is positioned on the "IF", it denotes the whole code segment shown:

```
[I]F ( k>0 )
    THEN PUT SKIP LIST ('the number k is strictly
            greater than zero' );
    ELSE PUT SKIP LIST ('not positive' );
```

Suppose we wish to enclose this IF-statement within a WHILE-loop. In a conventional, line-oriented, text editor, the lines

```
DO WHILE ( condition );
    END;
```

would be inserted before and after the IF-statement in separate editing steps. The first of these editing steps would drastically alter the structure of the program; in fact, it would make it temporarily incorrect due to the unbalanced DO-END pair. Such modifications have been the bane of incremental compilation schemes.

By contrast, in the Synthesizer, the two lines are part of one template and are therefore inserted simultaneously. First, the IF-statement is temporarily removed from the file, leaving the cursor positioned at a {*statement*} placeholder:

```
⌂statement}
```

Next, the WHILE-loop is inserted and the cursor advanced into the body of the loop to a subordinate {*statement*} placeholder:

```
DO WHILE ( condition );
   ⌂statement}
    END;
```

Finally, the IF-statement is inserted into the body of the loop, automatically indented further to the right:

```
DO WHILE ( condition;
   I F ( k>0 )
      THEN PUT SKIP LIST ('the number k is strict
           ly greater than zero' );
      ELSE PUT SKIP LIST ('not positive' );
END;
```

The special function keys enable this manipulation to take place in a sequence of just seven keystrokes:

clip   (remove the IF-statement),
.dw **return**   (insert the WHILE-loop),
return   (move the cursor to {*statement*}),
insert   (reinsert the IF-statement within the WHILE-loop)

The reverse manipulation, extracting the IF-statement and discarding the WHILE-loop, would require only four keystrokes:

clip   (remove the IF-statement),
diagonal (move the cursor to DO),
delete   (delete the WHILE-loop),
insert   (reinsert the IF-statement).

Individual phrases are modified by first positioning the cursor anywhere within the phrase, and then modifying individual characters. As each change is typed, the context surrounding the phrase adjusts instantly. Character insertions are made simply by typing; there is no separate "insert mode." Using special function keys, it is possible to erase characters forwards or backwards either one at a time or all the way to the boundary of the phrase. Whenever modified, a phrase is checked for syntactic correctness, exactly as if it had just been introduced for the first time. If every character of a phrase is deleted, the appropriate placeholder automatically reappears.

Templates, unlike phrases, cannot be modified—they are immutable. Insertions are permitted within templates only at the positions designated by placeholders. The predefined keywords and punctuation marks of a template cannot be changed. In fact, it is not even possible to position the editing cursor within the characters of a template.

An initial and overriding goal of the Synthesizer was to guarantee that programs were completely correct at every stage of their development. Any modification that introduced an error was to be prevented. Context-sensitive constraints of the syntax forced us to retreat from that position. For example, consider the problem of changing the type of a program variable. Because a keyword such as FIXED is part of an immutable declaration template, it is necessary to delete one declaration and insert another. However, the implemented dialect of PL/I requires that all variables be declared; deleting the declaration would introduce undeclared-variable errors in every phrase referencing the variable.

Rather than having a separate mechanism to make such modifications atomic operations, the Synthesizer tolerates invalid phrases, highlighting them with the complemented character font until corrected. Thus, the moment a declaration is deleted, all phrases containing the undeclared variable are highlighted. When the new declaration is inserted, all are redisplayed in the normal font.

To illustrate this, consider deleting the declaration of the variable temp from:

```
DECLARE ( temp ) FIXED;
DECLARE ( m, n ) FLOAT;
temp= m;
m= n;
n= temp;
```

Errors introduced in the first and third assignment statements because of undeclared variables are highlighted:

```
DECLARE ( m, n ) FLOAT;
temp= m;
m= n; n= temp;
```

When temp is redeclared, uses of temp become correct and are again displayed in the normal font:

```
DECLARE ( m, n, temp ) FLOAT;
temp= m;
m= n;
n= temp;
```

Users often forget declarations until reminded by an *undeclared-variable* error message. Tolerance of invalid phrases simplifies correction of this common error. When an error is detected in a phrase, any movement of the cursor away from the phrase overrides the error prevention mechanism and highlights the invalid phrase. The proper declaration can be inserted at any time.

As an additional benefit, the ability to override the error prevention mechanism allows free-form ideas to be sketched temporarily in the file without regard to the syntax of the programming language. These informal program notes and plans remain highlighted until they are either completed correctly or deleted. Although invalid phrases are permitted in programs, the overall structural integrity of files is maintained because the correct nesting of templates is always enforced.

2.4 Syntactic Iteration and Optional Placeholder

As described thus far, creating a file in the Synthesizer is exactly analogous to deriving a sentence with respect to a context-free grammar for the given programming language. Although a nontechnical vocabulary has been adopted in the presentation, the following correspondencies should be clear:

placeholder	nonterminal symbol
template	right side of a production
command	the name of a production
insertion	derivation
file	derivation tree
cursor position	node of derivation tree
file display	sentential form

In addition, the editor incorporates the usual metasyntactic formalism for syntactic iteration:

{*placeholder*}   zero or more occurrences of *placeholder*

Conceptually, each item in such a list is preceded and followed by {*placeholder*}. However, these placeholders are only displayed when the cursor is positioned there (or when there are no occurrences in the list). In fact, **return** is the cursor motion that means:

advance the cursor to the next template, phrase, or placeholder *including iterated placeholders*.

The following sequence of display snapshots illustrates repeated use of **return** to advance the cursor:

Original screen	After 1 **return**	After 2 **returns**	After 3 **returns**
[x]= 0;	x= 0;	x= 0;	x= 0;
y= 0;	[{]*statement*}	[y]= 0;	y= 0;
	y= 0;		[{]*statement*}

When entering templates and phrases, each insertion terminated by **return** has the desired effect of advancing the cursor to the next possible placeholder for an insertion. Cursor motions other than **return** do not reveal iterated placeholders.

Optional components of templates are denoted by square brackets:

[*placeholder*]   zero or one occurrence of *placeholder*

In order to avoid excessive clutter on the screen, such optional placeholders are not normally displayed. A separate cursor motion is used to reveal them and to position the cursor there. For example, from

```
[D]O WHILE ( condition );
    {statement}
    END;
```

the move to optional component command advances the cursor to

```
□loop-name: DO WHILE ( condition );
    {statement}
    END;
```

2.5 Comment Templates

The limited number of lines displayed on video terminals hampers editing large files. *Comment templates* provide a mechanism for hiding details of a file, thereby allowing more of the program to be displayed. The comment template also provides a mechanism for controlling the speed as well as the scope of runtime diagnostic monitoring. A comment template is a single program unit expressing a program specification together with its refinement [Conway and Gries 1979]. It is the structural unit used to express computational abstractions in programs:

```
/* comment */
    {statement}
```

The two placeholders, *comment* and {*statement*}, are part of *one* template. The {*statement*} part of the template is indented to show that it is the refinement of the specification provided in the *comment* part. Thus, a comment is not an arbitrary lexical insertion into the program; rather, it is a structural unit in its own right. The *scope* of a comment is the list of statements in its refinement.

The display of the refinement of a comment can be suppressed simply by striking the **ellipsis** key. For example,

```
/* Swap m and n */
    temp= m;
    m = n;
    n= temp;
PUT SKIP LIST (m, n);
```

would be redisplayed instantly as

```
/* Swap m and n */
    □...
PUT SKIP LIST (m, n);
```

Having hidden the details of the code, more of the program fits on the screen while the comment remains displayed to specify what the hidden refinement does. The hidden code at "..." can easily be revealed by striking **ellipsis** again. Thus, comment templates provide selective display of the hierarchical structure of files. The ellipsis feature is intentionally coupled with comment templates in order to encourage program documentation.

Comment templates serve a purpose during execution as well as editing. During program execution, "..." is considered a single atomic step for the runtime flow-tracing and pacing features described in the next section. For example, suppose the execution pace were set at a half-second per step. Then, "..." would be executed in as close to half a second as possible, regardless of the complexity of the statements hidden below the "...". Thus, judicious use of "..." provides selective control of the speed and scope of diagnostic monitoring.

The ellipsis feature of comment templates provides an incentive to use comments during program development, rather than after the fact. Because it rewards a skillful, precise use of comments, this feature promotes good programming style and method.

3. EXECUTION OF PROGRAMS

Because programs are translated and maintained in interpretable form during editing, there is no compilation delay between editing and execution. Whenever execution is suspended, control returns to the editor, a printed message explains why execution was suspended, and the file cursor is positioned in the source program at the point of suspension. It is possible to run incomplete programs. Execution is suspended whenever a placeholder is encountered and can be resumed after the missing program element has been inserted. After most editing changes to a program, it is still possible to resume execution; certain changes, such as modifying a declaration, destroy the possibility of resuming execution.

The high transmission rate of a video display terminal allows the incorporation of unique runtime debugging aids. Display-oriented monitoring facilities provide a window into the computer through which one observes a running program. Their power is enhanced when combined with syntax-directed commands for controlling execution.

The flow of execution through the program can be traced using the screen cursor to indicate the location of the instruction pointer at each moment. The stopping places for the cursor during flow tracing correspond to the structural units of the editor—one cursor jump for each template and phrase. Thus, the editor and the interpreter share a unified view of program structure—separate editable units are seen as separate computational units. During flow tracing, the program display is automatically redrawn whenever control passes outside the display window or a procedure is called. Judicious use of the ellipsis feature can eliminate the trace of uninteresting sections of code and minimize undesirable redrawing of the program display.

Flow tracing at full speed provides a visible performance measure: the distribution of light intensities at the various cursor locations clearly indicates the fraction of time spent there. A *pace* feature allows the user to slow execution to any speed.

A syntax-directed *single-step* feature permits manual control of program execution. There are five ways to specify the step size of each resumption in terms of the template and phrase structure of the file:

resume   execute one step of the current program element,
long resume   execute all steps of current program element,
return   complete a list of statements,
diagonal   complete the enclosing template,
long diagonal   complete the enclosing procedure.

Consider stepping through the following program segment:

```
DO WHILE ( k<n ) ;
   I F ( k>0 )
      THEN PUT SKIP LIST ('the number k is strict
         ly greater than zero' );
      ELSE PUT SKIP LIST ('not positive' );
   k= k+1;
END;
```

resume would advance the cursor to (k>0), **long resume** would advance the cursor to (k = k + 1;) by executing the entire IF-statement, **return** would complete the statements in the body of the loop and position the cursor at k<n, **diagonal** would position the cursor at *DO* until the loop is completed, and **long diagonal** would position the cursor at the top of the procedure until control returns to the calling procedure.

In this way, the Synthesizer maintains a unified view of both static and dynamic program structure. The syntactic units of the editor are the computational units of the interpreter.

Selected variables can be monitored during execution by displaying their names and values in a separate partition of the screen. The result of each assignment to a variable immediately appears on the screen replacing the previous value displayed for that variable. Currently, only one element of an array is displayed at a time. A least-recently updated replacement strategy is used when there is not enough room to display all monitored variables.

The facilities described above allow one to observe an error as it occurs. The *pace* feature, the *step* feature, and the pause statement serve as a throttle, providing control over the rate of execution, and thus providing a better chance for seeing errors. The program can be run at top speed until reaching the vicinity of the bug, whereupon it can be paced or single-stepped until the error is observed.

It is easy to overshoot the mark, so the Synthesizer has a gear shift as well; a recently implemented reverse execution facility allows the program to run backwards a bounded number of steps. As with forward single-stepping, the step-size of each backwards step is specified in terms of the syntactic structure. Using the visual feedback provided by flow tracing and variable monitoring, and by alternating the direction of execution in the vicinity of a bug, the user is able to converge swiftly and precisely on the error. While reverse execution capabilities have been implemented by others [Balzer 1969] [Hodgson and Porter 1980] [Zelkowitz 1971], the novelty in the Synthesizer is the presence of enough immediate visual feedback to make the feature meaningful as a real-time control mechanism.

4. ADVANTAGES OF TEMPLATES

The Synthesizer's use of templates is central to achieving our design goals. The integrated behavior of templates and the cursor enforces the proper view that a program is a hierarchy of structurally nested components. Each template insertion is syntactically correct because template commands are only valid in appropriate contexts, and the templates are predefined. A program developed on the Synthesizer is always well-formed, regardless of whether it is complete or not.

Templates eliminate mundane tasks of program development. Typographical errors in structural units are impossible; indentation is automatic, both when a template is introduced and when it is moved, and errors cannot be introduced by modification because templates are immutable.

Placeholders in templates serve both as prompts and as syntactic constraints, by identifying places that can or must be refined, as well as by restricting the range of choices to legitimate insertions. The template-generated skeleton simplifies incremental compilation by bounding the extent of the program affected by modifications.

Template insertion is an economical mode of program entry with a corresponding economical implementation. Short commands insert long templates; because so few keystrokes are needed, typing mistakes are effectively minimized, and program entry is rapid. When statements are synthesized by command, there is no need for a parser to analyze the text. Thus, a template-based environment is ideal for microcomputers where space is in short supply.

Templates correspond to abstract computational units; because they are both inserted and manipulated as units, the process of programming begins and continues at a high level of abstraction; the user is never mired in syntactic detail. At runtime, templates provide a framework for the structured, single-step debugging facility. Thus, templates provide a unified view of both static and dynamic program structure.

5. INTEGRATION OF TEXT AND STRUCTURE

The Synthesizer is based on the premise that programs are not text. Although we want to promote the structural perspective, we recognize that abstract programs must be viewed and manipulated with respect to some concrete textual representation. The hybrid design of the Synthesizer seeks a pragmatic balance between the extremes of a derivation-tree editor and a text editor.

We believe we have successfully interleaved structural and textual features so that shifts between the two perspectives occur smoothly and spontaneously. Partitioning a language such as PL/I into templates and phrases seems natural and lets each construct be edited in an appropriate manner. User competence and comfort within the environment is enhanced by the persistence and uniformity of the template-phrase distinction throughout the system. The dual interpretation of the cursor as both text pointer and tree pointer seems intuitive: when the cursor is moved, it is perceived as a point stepping through program *text* in increments dictated by syntactic structure; when it stops, the cursor designates an entire *structure* that can be clipped or deleted as a unit.

Although, on the whole, we believe the Synthesizer accomplishes a harmonious integration of text and structure, occasionally, tension between the two perspectives leads to confusion and some inconvenience. One common difficulty stems from the fact that different abstract objects have identical representations as text. For example, consider trying to move the phrase (k = 0) to *statement* in the code segment below:

```
IF ( k=0 )
    THEN statement
```

Although (k = 0) is textually correct as an assignment statement[2] it cannot be moved to *statement* because it is an instance of the syntactic class *condition*. By preventing such implicit syntactic transformations, a structure editor may detect modifications with unforeseen and unintended consequences. However, when the consequences are intended, requiring a special mechanism to divorce a phrase of text from its syntactic classification is inconvenient.

A second example of tension between the textual and structural perspectives is the result of our decision to differentiate between declarations of formal parameters and local variables in the procedure template:

```
name: PROCEDURE ( parameters );
    {parameter declaration}
    {declaration}
    {statement}
    END name;
```

Although the templates for declaring parameters and local variables are distinct,

```
DECLARE ( list-of-parameters ) FIXED;
DECLARE ( list-of-variables ) FIXED;
```

---

[2] Ignoring the missing semicolon for the sake of discussion.

once expanded they appear the same, as in:

```
name: PROCEDURE ( j );
    DECLARE ( j ) FIXED;
    DECLARE ( k ) FIXED;
    {statement}
    END name;
```

Now suppose we wish to change (k) to be a parameter of the procedure. Because (k) is declared as a local variable, we cannot just add it to the parameter list on the first line, even though the resulting program would be correct *as text*. This is particularly confusing because the declaration for (k) not only looks like a parameter declaration but appears to be in the right place.

This example also illustrates an interplay in the Synthesizer between *incremental* error detection and *left-to-right* error detection. Whenever a phrase is created or modified, the Synthesizer's local incremental error detection mechanism verifies that the new phrase is consistent with the previous state of the program. Any inconsistency leads to an immediate error message. As we have seen, adding k to the parameter list is an error because, at the time the change is attempted, k is already declared to be a local variable.

However, when the user overrides the local error prevention mechanism and allows an invalid phrase to remain in the program, the Synthesizer abandons the incremental viewpoint in favor of a static, left-to-right notion of correctness. The incrementally incorrect parameter list j,k turns out to be correct, whereas the declaration of k as a local variable is invalid because k already appears as a parameter:

```
name: PROCEDURE ( j,k );
    DECLARE ( j ) FIXED;
    DECLARE ( k ) FIXED;
    {statement}
    END name;
```

The declaration for k must now be moved from the {*declaration*} part of the procedure template to the {*parameter declaration*} part. However, as in our first example, the problem is not just a question of the template being in the wrong position. The existing declaration is bound to the syntactic category {*declaration*} and cannot be moved to any other placeholder; it must be deleted and a new parameter declaration created.

A third example of inconvenience in the Synthesizer's hybrid design is a result of the immutability of templates. Modifications that change only a few characters of program text may require a significant amount of restructuring. For example, if the program were text, a WHILE-loop could be changed into an UNTIL-loop by substitution of just five characters. In the Synthesizer, this change must be accomplished by moving the constituents of the existing WHILE-template into a newly inserted UNTIL-template. Although such modifications can be made rapidly using the **clip**, **insert**, and **delete** keys, they are admittedly awkward.

To alleviate such inconveniences imposed by structural constraints, we are building mechanisms that streamline these operations, yet enforce a discipline that emphasizes the abstract computational meaning of program units. For example, template-to-template transformations allow controlled changes in a single step. Positioning the cursor at a DO WHILE and typing the command "**.du**" could transform a WHILE-template into an UNTIL-template, leaving its constituents in corresponding places. Similarly, a local variable declaration could be transformed into parameter declaration and repositioned in one step.

Besides purely syntactic transformations, a more powerful collection of semantics preserving transformations is also possible. For example, in one operation,

```
DO j= k to n by 1;
   {statement}
   END;
```

could be transformed into one of several equivalent alternative representations:

```
j= k;                      j= k;
DO WHILE ( j <= n );       IF ( j <= n )
   {statement}                THEN DO UNTIL ( j > n );
   j= j+1;                       {statement}
   END;                          j= j+1;
                                 END;
```

A similar transformation capability would allow procedures to be extracted from in-line code. The user would specify a section of program and the variables to become formal parameters. Then, in one operation,

```
/* Swap m and n */
   temp= m;
   m= n;
   n= temp;
```

would be replaced by

```
call swap(m,n);
```

with the appropriate procedure created automatically:

```
/* Swap m and n */
swap: PROCEDURE ( m, n );
   DECLARE ( m, n ) FLOAT;
   DECLARE ( temp ) FLOAT;
   temp= m;
   m= n;
   n= temp;
   END swap;
```

Such transformations will add considerable editing power but retain the disciplined viewpoint of the rest of the system.

A final example illustrates an awkwardness arising not from the structural constraints of the Synthesizer, but from the textual constraints of a language whose concrete syntax was defined to be unambiguous for parsers. Inserting the template

```
IF ( condition )
   THEN statement
```

into

```
IF ( condition )
   THEN statement
   ELSE PUT LIST ('whose else am i?' );
```

leads to an inconsistency between the explicitly derived structure (an IF-THEN within an IF-THEN-ELSE) and the structure implied by the parser-oriented concrete syntax (an IF-THEN-ELSE within an IF-THEN). Although tempted to adopt the derived interpretation (because prettyprinting easily distinguishes one interpretation from the other), we elected, instead, to maintain compatibility with PL/I. Therefore, we prevent such an insertion and require that the user provide a compound statement explicitly.

There are many possible alternative designs, among them the following four: a) the compound statement could be inserted automatically when necessary; b) a compound statement could be displayed automatically when necessary; c) the IF-THEN-ELSE template could be defined as

```
IF ( condition )
   THEN DO; {statement} END;
   ELSE DO; {statement} END;
```

d) the IF-THEN template could be eliminated thereby requiring that every conditional statement have an ELSE-clause. In this final case, the display of an empty ELSE clause could be suppressed unless necessary for disambiguation.

6. IMPLEMENTATION

6.1   File Trees

Synthesizer files are represented internally as executable derivation trees. Each template or phrase is represented in this tree by a separate node. The pointers connecting nodes are, in fact, **goto** instructions for the interpreter; the null pointer is a **halt** instruction. Nodes are variable length; each is composed of three sections:

extension	code	continuation

The *extension* identifies the node type and contains any other information needed to generate the display of the node but not necessary to execute it. The *code* section contains interpretable op-codes for executing the node. The "entry point" of the node is the first byte of the code section. The *continuation* contains a **goto** linking this node to the next op-code to be executed. The target of this **goto** is either the entry point of a sibling node or an interior op-code of a parent node.

For example, the template

```
IF ( condition )
   THEN statement
   ELSE statement
```

has the internal representation

This node is tagged in the extension as an IF-node. It contains op-codes that implement the proper control flow and three **halt** instructions that represent the unexpanded placeholders. When the template has been expanded to

```
IF ( k>0 )
   THEN statement
   ELSE PUT LIST ( list-of-expressions );
```

a link to Polish postfix code for the phrase k>0 replaces the first **halt** opcode, and a link to the node for the PUT-statement replaces the third **halt** opcode. A **halt** instruction remains for the other *statement* placeholder:

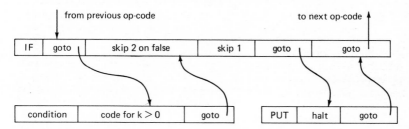

The interpreter is classical: it executes straight line code and **goto** instructions. It is completely blind to the structure of the tree and requires neither recursion nor a stack to execute a file tree. Access to variables and procedure definitions is through a symbol table.

The editor walks the tree using the same **goto** pointers as the interpreter. Each cursor position designates one of the nodes of the tree. Cursor motion is defined with respect to a preorder traversal. There are no backward pointers; thus, backward cursor motion is implemented internally by going all the way around.

6.2 Declarations

As demonstrated in Section 2.3, declarations present a special problem: modifying a declaration can simultaneously introduce errors and correct errors at other locations in the program. Internally, information about identifiers is stored in a symbol table. When a declaration is modified, the Synthesizer discards the old symbol table and traverses the tree in preorder, reparsing and redoing the semantics of every phrase. Phrases with errors are marked as invalid and are printed in the highlighted font when the screen is redrawn. Because the allocation of variables within an activation record is recomputed in the process of reconstructing the symbol table, access to the variables of a suspended activation record are lost in the process. Therefore, execution cannot be resumed after such modifications.

6.3 Displaying the Tree

The print representation of a file is generated from the tree; a text representation is not saved. The external representation of each kind of template is stored in a table. The entries of this table alternate between terminal strings and placeholder-descriptors. For example, the IF-template is encoded as:

```
''IF (''
condition-descriptor
'') \{\nTHEN ''
statement-1-descriptor
''ELSE ''
statement-2-descriptor
''\}\r''
```

The placeholder-descriptors identify the placeholders and their positions within the code section of an internal node. The terminal strings contain keywords, punctuation marks, and formatting control characters that are interpreted on output. For example,

```
\{   means   move left—margin right one unit,
\n   means   line—feed, carriage—return to current left—margin,
\}   means   move left—margin left one unit,
\r   means   carriage—return to current left—margin.
```

The print routine traverses the tree in preorder, simultaneously keeping track of position within the external representation of the appropriate template. Each terminal string encountered is printed and its formatting commands obeyed. Each phrase is translated from postfix to infix for display. (The parentheses of a phrase are saved in the extension of the node encoded one bit per operator.)

As the tree is traversed for display, a table mapping internal node addresses to external screen coordinates is updated. This table is used both for cursor motion in the editor, and at runtime for the trace feature.

6.4   Implementation of Debugging Features

The tracing, pacing, and single-step features are implemented by taking appropriate action on the interpretation of each **goto** leading to a new node.

When tracing, each **goto** uses the map from internal node addresses to screen coordinates to determine the new cursor position. If the map is not defined for a given target node, then the cursor lies outside the window and the program is redrawn with the new cursor position centered in the window. Traced programs are never permitted to run any faster than one cursor update per refresh of the video screen in order to avoid stroboscopic effects such as loops that appear to run backwards. When pacing, the interpreter waits appropriately at each **goto** before continuing execution. When stepping, the interpreter waits for a resume command before continuing.

The variable-monitoring feature is implemented in a straightforward manner: a table mapping identifiers to screen positions is maintained. Assignment to a monitored variable is detected by the interpreter whereupon the appropriate position is updated on the screen.

Reverse execution also has a straightforward implementation: the forward execution interpreter maintains a history file of the flow of control and the values destroyed by assignments to variables. The reverse execution interpreter restores values and updates the screen to give the illusion of the program executing backwards.

7.   THE SYNTHESIZER GENERATOR

Continuing research and development of the Synthesizer will increase its power, versatility, and range of application complementing the unique syntax-directed mechanisms the environment already provides. For example, global data flow analysis techniques will be used to answer queries about static program structure, as in [Masinter 1980]. The video display can be used to express static relationships between components of a program; the multiple fonts of a terminal can be exploited to highlight regions of interest. For example, the programmer might request the highlighting of all uses or all assignments to a variable X. Alternatively, the analysis can be keyed to the present location of the editing cursor. For example, the programmer might request the highlighting of all assignments to X that can account for its value at the present cursor location, or all possible uses of X that can be reached from the present cursor location.

To facilitate such further development, we are implementing a language independent system for generating Synthesizer-like systems from a grammatical specification of a given programming language. An attribute grammar will be used to define the syntax, display format, and semantics of each template and phrase. In our application, where program units are inserted and deleted in arbitrary order, semantic analysis must be both incremental and reversible. For this purpose, attribute grammars have the advantage of expressing semantics and context-sensitive constraints applicatively and on a modular basis; the arguments to each semantic function are imported explicitly from neighboring nodes in the derivation tree.

Because propagation of semantic information through the tree is implicit in the formalism, an incremental attribute evaluator can update the appropriate attribute values in conjunction with each editing operation. In particular, because the attribute dependencies are known, the evaluator can delete semantic information automatically when program units are deleted; a separate mechanism to undo semantics is not needed. We have described one such incremental attribute evaluator in [Demers et al. 1981]; more recently, we have developed an optimal-time incremental evaluator that runs in time proportional to the number of attribute values that actually must be changed [Reps 1981].

ACKNOWLEDGMENTS

Many people have participated in the development of the Synthesizer. We are deeply indebted to A. Demers for many stimulating discussions and for writing the LSI-11 operating system kernel; his insights and assistance have been invaluable. We are also extremely grateful for the generous help of J. Archer, R. Conway, M. Fingerhut, D. Gries, C. Hauser, S. Horwitz, D. Jacobs, R. Johnson, D. Krafft, S. Mahaney, and R. Olsson.

The development of the Cornell Program Synthesizer was supported in part by the National Science Foundation under Grants MCS77-08198 and MCS80-01218.

REFERENCES

[Alberga et al. 1981] C.N. Alberga, A.L. Brown, G.B. Leeman, M. Mikelsons, M.N. Wegman. A program development tool. *Conference Record of the Eighth Annual Symposium on Principles of Programming Languages*, Williamsburg, Virginia, January, 1981, 92-104.

[Archer et al. 1980] J. Archer, R. Conway, A. Shore, L. Silver. *The CORE user interface.* Cornell University, Department of Computer Science, Tech. Report No. TR80-437, September 1980.

[Balzer 1969] R.M. Balzer. EXDAMS - Extendable Debugging And Monitoring System. *Proceedings of the Spring Joint Computer Conference*, AFIPS Proceedings Vol. 34 (1969), 567-580.

[Constable and O'Donnell 1978] R. Constable, M.J. O'Donnell. *A Programming Logic.* Winthrop, 1978.

[Conway 1978] R. Conway. *Primer on Disciplined Programming Using PL/CS.* Winthrop, 1978.

[Conway and Constable 1976] R. Conway, R. Constable. *PL/CS—A disciplined subset of PL/I.* Cornell University, Department of Computer Science, Technical Report 76-293, 1976.

[Conway and Gries 1979] R. Conway, D. Gries. *An introduction to programming—a structured approach using PL/I and PL/C.* Winthrop, 1979.

[Demers et al. 1981] A. Demers, T. Reps, T. Teitelbaum. Incremental evaluation for attribute grammars with application to syntax-directed editors. *Conference Record of the Eighth ACM Symposium on Principles of Programming Languages,* January 1981.

[Donzeau-Gouge et al. 1975] V. Donzeau-Gouge, G. Huet, G. Kahn, B. Lang, J.J. Levy. A structure oriented program editor: a first step towards computer assisted programming. *International Computing Symposium,* Antibes, France, 1975; also IRIA, Rapport Laboria 114, Avril 1975.

[Engelbart and English 1968] D.C. Engelbart, W.K. English. A research center for augmenting human intellect. *Proceedings of the Fall Joint Computer Conference,* AFIPS Proceedings Vol. 33, San Francisco, December 1968. 395-410.

[Feiler and Medina-Mora 1981] P. Feiler, R. Medina-Mora. An incremental programming environment. *Proceedings of the Fifth International Conference on Software Engineering.* San Diego, California, March 1981. [*Editors' note*: see also [Medina-Mora and Feiler 1981]]

[Haberman 1979] A.N. Habermann. An overview of the Gandalf project. *Computer Science Research Review 1978-79,* Carnegie-Mellon University, 1979.

[Hansen 1971a] W.J. Hansen. *Creation of hierarchic text with a computer display.* Argonne National Laboratory ANL-7818, Argonne, Illinois, 1971; also Stanford University, Computer Science Department, doctoral dissertation, June 1971.

[Hodgson and Porter 1980] L.I. Hodgson, M. Porter. BIDOPS: a bi-directional programming system. Department of Computing Science, University of New England, Armidale, N.S.W., Australia, 1980.

[Joy 1977] B. Joy. *Ex Reference Manual.* Department of Electrical Engineering and Computer Science, University of California, Berkeley 1977.

[Kurtz 1978] T.E. Kurtz. BASIC. *SIGPLAN Notices,* August 1978.

[Lewis and Porges 1979] J.W. Lewis, D.F. Porges. *ALBE/P: a language-based editor for Pascal.* Yale University, Department of Computer Science, 1979.

[Masinter 1980] L.M. Masinter. *Global program analysis in an interactive environment.* Xerox Palo Alto Research Center, Report SSL-80-1, January 1980.

[Mikellsons and Wegman 1980] M. Mikellsons, M.N. Wegman. PDE1L: the PL1L program development environment principles of operation. IBM Watson Research Center, Research Report RC8513, Yorktown Heights, November 1980.

[Pinc and Schweppe 1973] J.H. Pinc, E.J. Schweppe. A Fortran language anticipation and prompting system. *Proceedings of the ACM National Conference,* Atlanta, Georgia, 1973.

[Reps 1981] T. Reps. *Optimal-time incremental semantic analysis for syntax-directed editors.* Cornell University, Department of Computer Science, Tech. Report No. 81-453, March 1981.

[Skinner] G. Skinner. *Ged User Documentation.* Cornell University, Department of Computer Science.

[Teitelbaum 1979] T. Teitelbaum. *The Cornell Program Synthesizer: a microcomputer implementation of PL/CS.* Cornell University, Department of Computer Science, Tech. Report No. TR79-370, June 1979.

[Teitelbaum 1980] T. Teitelbaum. *The Cornell Program Synthesizer: a tutorial introduction.* Cornell University, Department of Computer Science, Tech. Report No. TR79-381, July 1979, revised January 1980.

[Teitelman 1977] W. Teitelman. A display-oriented programmer's assistant. CSL 77-3, XEROX PARC, 1977; reprinted in *Interactive Programming Environment;* see also *Proceedings of the Fifth International Joint Conference on Artificial Intelligence,* Cambridge, Massachusetts, August 1977, 905-915.

[Teitelman 1978] W. Teitelman. *INTERLISP Reference Manual.* Xerox Palo Alto Research Center, Palo Alto, California, December 1978.

[Wilcox 1976] T.R. Wilcox, A.M. Davis, M.H. Tindall. The design and implementation of a table driven, interactive diagnostic programming system. *Communications of the ACM* 19:11 (November 1976), 609-616.

[Zelkowitz 1971] M. Zelkowitz. *Reversible execution as a diagnostic tool.* Cornell University, Department of Computer Science, doctoral dissertation, January 1971.

6 An Interactive Programming System for Pascal

JERKER WILANDER

Linköping University
Linköping, Sweden

Interactive program development tools are being increasingly recognized as helpful in the construction of programs. This paper describes an integrated incremental program development system for Pascal called Pathcal. Pathcal contains facilities for creation, editing, debugging and testing of procedures and programs. The system facilities are all Pascal procedures or variables and because of this allows the programmer to program the system in itself.

Reprinted with permission from *Behandling Information-tidskrift for Nordisk*, 20, 1980, pp. 163-174.

1. INTRODUCTION

Program development is today commonly supported by an interactive time-sharing system. A more advanced type of interactive program development tool is an incremental system. The basic programming cycle in an incremental system is not the execution of a program but rather a statement or a declaration. This property together with the ever present "database" of values and declarations constitutes an incremental system.

The incremental system is the foundation of the next generation of programming support, the "programming environment". A programming environment contains all the tools in one integrated system and it should support the terminal session (for example, by allowing editing of previously entered statements). It should provide the facilities that the operating system monitor usually provides, to allow programmability of all facilities. In a sense the programming environment could be viewed as a programming-language-oriented monitor which is incrementally extensible. The most important example of this kind of system is the INTERLISP [Teitelman 1978], but APL [APLSF 1976] has also gone a long way in this direction. For a more conventional looking language, EL1, the ECL system [ECL 1974] [Balzer 1974] could be mentioned. The IBM PL/I checkout compiler [PL/I 1976] is an example of a commercial system for a conventional language that comes close to being an incremental system. For teaching purposes in computer science, a Pascal like system called Basis has been developed [Van De Riet 1977]. The Basis language is a small subset of Pascal. In that system one is permitted to enter declarations, set variables, call procedures and edit procedures. The MENTOR system [Huet et al. 1977] contains many facilities for editing and program manipulation. That system does not contain any facilities for program execution.

This paper describes a programming system for Pascal [Jensen and Wirth 1977] called Pathcal. The Pathcal system is an attempt to provide a significant subset of the facilities provided in INTERLISP for a compiler-oriented language.

2. THE PROGRAMMING SYSTEM PATHCAL

The goal of the Pathcal project has not been to develop another programming language, but to create, within the framework of the chosen language, an interactive programming environment. The project was intended to produce experience and ideas on how to construct an interactive programming system for the Algol family of programming languages. The experiences gained are giving more knowledge about what tools are useful in interactive programming and how they should be implemented. There are more facilities in the system but these are not yet fully developed or tested and will not be described here.

A programming environment contains several subsystems such as an editor, a debug system and a prettyprinter. In Pathcal these are tightly coupled, to allow invocation of one subsystem from another. All subsystems are Pascal procedures, although some may have privileges that are not allowed in standard Pascal.

It is possible to use the Pathcal system in a manner similar to conventional programming. One may enter the program from the terminal, compile it and execute it. In addition, there is a set of facilities in Pathcal which are not normally available in conventional systems.

• *Incremental execution.* Incremental execution gives the programmer the opportunity to use statements of the language and get them executed directly. A secondary effect of this is that the system becomes fairly easy to learn. One may try most facilities in the system and the language without having to write whole programs.

• *One language system.*   Pathcal has only Pascal as command language for the subsystems. This is true except in the screen oriented text-editor, which is controlled by the cursor control keys, rubout etc. The one-language system idea is also apparent in that error messages are given in terms of the programming language. This means that it is possible to obtain the code of the incorrect statement, expression or declaration.

One advantage with this approach is that one can write loops over commands without learning an additional syntax.

• *Incremental program development.*   With Pathcal, procedures can be developed one at a time to form programs. It is thus possible to construct and test modules of the program one at a time and later combine them into a system. One may edit and test single procedures in an existing program. It is possible to test procedures that contain calls to procedures not yet defined. The program may be developed "top down", "bottom up" or the most critical portion first according to the preference of the programmer.

• *Model of the terminal session.*   Pathcal maintains a model of the terminal session and stores information about earlier interactions and their results. There are procedures in the system for re-execution and editing of previously given statements. One may also compare the results, from a test example, before and after editing of a procedure.

• *Continuation after errors.*   When an error occurs during test execution, the program will not be aborted. Instead it is interrupted, with the procedure and variable environments retained. During this interrupt, editing of procedures or use of any other Pascal statement is permitted. If a procedure is edited during an interrupt the new version will be used in the future. It is especially useful to be able to continue after an error in the case of interactive programs. One single error in the program or the type-in might then require a major effort when restarting the program, if it is not possible to repair the error and continue execution.

• *Structure editor.*   With a structure editor, program editing is performed in the terms of the programming language. One manipulates the program in terms of procedures and statements instead of lines and characters. A typical structure editor operation is the insertion of the code of one procedure into another. An advantage with a structure editor is that only those parts that really are affected by the edit are changed, which means that breakpoints and similar structure above the ordinary code may remain intact. With structure editing it is natural to include programmability of the editor.

3. AN APPLICATION OF THE PATHCAL SYSTEM

To make the system description more concrete, we will follow the development of a small Pascal procedure.

The specification of the problem is: Write a procedure HISTOGRAM that prints a histogram on the terminal. The procedure has three parameters.

1. A:MEASURE; MEASURE is an array of measurement values of type real.
2. LEN:INTEGER; LEN is the length of A (actual length).
3. WIDTH:INTEGER; This is the desired width of the histogram.

The program should find a suitable scaling factor to adjust to the width of the screen.

Before each interaction the Pathcal system prints a number followed by a prompt character. The prompt characters differ according to the situation. Greater than (>) indicates the top level (i.e. the level the user usually is connected to), colon (:) indicates a breakpoint or an error interrupt. The number is incremented after each interaction. When using procedures in Pathcal that use the session model, i.e. that refer to earlier interactions, the number is given as an argument.

The problem will be solved through three routines, which will be developed successively. The first procedure only prints one line of the histogram. The second calculates the scaling factor for the histogram and the third is the main procedure that calls the other two. The third procedure (HISTOGRAM) makes a pass through the measurement data and calls the printing routine for each item.

First declare the type of the array.

```
1> TYPE MEASUREÅRRAY [1..60] OF REAL;
   MEASURE
```

All statements have a value even in those cases when they do not have one in Pascal. Here the value is the name of the declared type.

Define the procedure that prints one line of the histogram.

```
2> PROCEDURE PRINTLINE(W:INTEGER);
     VAR I : INTEGER;
     BEGIN
       FOR I := 1 TO W DO WRITE('*');WRITELN
     END;
PRINTLINE
```

Test printline once to verify that it works. One line with 15 asterisks should get printed.

```
3> PRINTLINE(15);
***************
NIL
```

After the asterisks a NIL was written which is the value of the procedure. All procedures have a value, which is the value of the last statement executed. A statement has as value the value of the last expression executed. In this case it is a write statement, which happens to return NIL.

Define the function that calculates the maximum value in an array.

```
4> FUNCTION MAXVAL(VAR B:MEASURE;N:INTEGER):REAL;
     VAR I : INTEGER;
         MAX : REAL;
     BEGIN
       MAX := B[1];
       FOR I := 2 TO N DO
         IF MAX < B[I] THEN MAX := B[I];
       MAXVAL := MAX
     END;
MAXVAL
```

Now the function MAXVAL will be tested. One of its actual parameters is not declared, and because of this the program execution will be interrupted after an error message when the error is encountered.

```
5> MAXVAL(A,60);
   Identifier not declared.
   A
```

The primary problem in a situation like this is to find out where the execution stopped. The backtrace procedure (BT) prints the names of the currently active procedures. The list is written in calling order with the most recently called procedure first.

```
6: BT;
MAXVAL
SYSBLOCK
```

The active procedures are MAXVAL and SYSBLOCK. MAXVAL was called in interaction 5 and SYSBLOCK is the always present "procedure" that surrounds all other procedures. In more complicated cases this list is longer. The Pathcal system builds the stack frame for the procedure before checking the actual parameters. Another procedure called BTV will display all variables and their current values.

To correct the error, a declaration for A should be inserted. After that, A may be given a value. The present problem is that this declaration should be inserted in SYSBLOCK but MAXVAL has already been entered. Of course A could be declared in this position (MAXVAL) but with the disadvantage that the declaration and the value would disappear upon exit from MAXVAL.

The procedure stackset moves the execution environment to the desired position. When all necessary commands have been executed in this new environment execution may be resumed at the original point.

```
7: STACKSET(SYSBLOCK);
SYSBLOCK
```

Notice that the prompt character changes to !. This demonstrates that the execution environment has been moved from the standard environment.

```
8! VAR A:MEASURE;
   A
```

A top level declaration like this is never inserted into the program text, but only in the current execution of the procedure. To achieve the latter, the source has to be edited. In this case the procedure should not be edited because the declaration should be inserted into SYSBLOCK.

```
9! FOR I := 1 TO 60 DO A[I] := 0.5*I; (* Initialize A *)
30.0
```

This statement is not included in the program either. Instead it is executed and the array A is initialized. Correction of errors during execution can create inconsistencies. These can occur when the user changes declarations on variables whose values already have been used. This problem is in practice not very serious, because the main reason the user at all continues the execution is to find more errors. Changed declarations are indicated by the system.

Return to the original execution.

```
10! OK;
```

Resume execution at the point of error, but now with all declarations inserted. The execution should now proceed correctly.

```
11: RETTO;
30.0
```

At last, the result appears which was requested in interaction no. 5.

```
12> A[17] := 45;
45.0
```

Change input data to MAXVAL for another test.

Instead of rewriting all of the statement MAXVAL(A,60) one may refer to an earlier interaction and execute that code. This facility is useful in cases where a lot of typing has to be performed, e.g., interaction 9.

```
13> REDO(5);
45.0
```

Define the procedure HISTOGRAM.

```
14> PROCEDURE HISTOGRAM(VAR A:MEASURE;LEN,WIDTH:INTEGER);
VAR MAX:REAL;
    I : INTEGER;
  BEGIN
    MAX := MAXVAL(A,LEN);
    FOR I := 1 TO LEN DO
         PRINTLINE(ROUND(A[I]/MAX*WIDTH+0.5))
  END;
HISTOGRAM
```

Test all procedures together.

```
15> HISTOGRAM(A,5,10)
**
****
******
********
**********

NIL
```

Change input and redo the test.

```
16> A[5]:=100;
100.0
```

Re-execute interaction 16 which is two back from the current interaction.

```
17> REDO(-2);
*
*
*
*
**********

NIL
```

At this point the procedure has been tested in an elementary way and now further test data could be applied. Test data may easily be modified to construct a relatively complete test.

The HISTOGRAM module now contains three separate procedures. If this is considered inappropriate, they may be combined into a single procedure using the structure editor. The insert procedure performs this combination. The insert procedure knows about how procedures are inserted into other procedures.

```
18> INSERT(HISTOGRAM,MAXVAL);
HISTOGRAM

19> INSERT(HISTOGRAM,PRINTLINE);
HISTOGRAM
```

We now want to verify that the insertion worked as expected, and that the module has the correct structure. The prettyprint procedure gives an indented printout of the procedure text. The parts of the printout that are marked #n# where n is a number are abbreviations of the actual code in that position. They are only abbreviations in the sense that "behind" them the actual code could be found. This facility makes it easy to view the procedure at different levels of abstraction.

```
20> PP(HISTOGRAM);
    {PROCEDURE HISTOGRAM(VAR A:MEASURE;LEN,WIDTH:INTEGER);
     VAR
     MAX:REAL;
     I:INTEGER;
     FUNCTION MAXVAL(VAR B:MEASURE;N:INTEGER):REAL;
     VAR #1#
     BEGIN #2#  ;
      FOR I := 2 TO N DO #3#  ;
      #4#   END;
     PROCEDURE  PRINTLINE(W:INTEGER);
      VAR #5#
     BEGIN
      FOR I := 1 TO W DO WRITE('*');
      WRITELN
     END;
     BEGIN MAX := #6#  ;
      FOR I := 1 TO LEN DO #7#
     END;}
```

The "print depth" of the prettyprint is restricted by how deep the nesting and how long the sequence of statements and expressions are. The print level is program settable.

Redo the test to verify that the edit gave a functionally correct procedure.

```
21> REDO(15);
*
*
*
*
*********

NIL
```

Find out what happened in interaction no. 5.

```
22> HISTORY(5);
5. MAXVAL(A,60);
Value= 30.0
```

This example shows how an incremental system with the set of powerful tools found in Pathcal gives an extremely convenient programming environment.

Only simple usage of the debugging, editing, prettyprint and session support tools have been demonstrated. This relatively small set of utility functions are the most important building blocks of Pathcal. Among the things not described are breakpoints and the text editor of the system.

4. DESCRIPTION OF THE SYSTEM

Pathcal works as if one executed the program statement by statement and declaration by declaration, though with the difference that one is not required to obey a strict ordering between statements and declarations.

When declarations are entered into Pathcal they are accumulated to a special block (in the sense of Algol) called the system block. The statements entered are executed immediately. Executable statements are not accumulated to form some kind of main program. The difference between declarations and statements is less accentuated in Pathcal than in Pascal: both are executed. Statements give the result that variables get values or values get printed, and declarations that a specific procedure or variable may be used in the future. Variable values are saved on a stack, which is maintained by the system and which works in the same manner as a conventional stack for a block structured language.

In the system block there are several different declarations, including all procedures, types and variables the user has entered. It contains all subsystems needed for usage of the system, e.g., history, edit, and break procedures.

To allow smooth editing (mainly structure editing) the data-type "code" has been added to Pathcal. Code is a data type for program text in structure form. Variables of type code have as value Pascal statements, procedures, variable declarations etc. This data type makes it possible to manipulate program code from a Pascal program. One is for example allowed to move code from one procedure to another or collect code from different interactions to form new procedures.

Some of the Pathcal system procedures do not strictly obey the rules of Pascal for procedures. They sometimes allow a variable number of arguments (like READ and WRITE) and sometimes the arguments have a special status (like PP). This latter difference is similar to the procedure parameter of Pascal. Both of these changes are important, but the necessary syntactic modifications of the surface language are small.

The system block includes all user programs, procedures and other declarations. When interacting with the system one is normally connected to the system block. Interaction occurs also in other situations, primarily in the debug package (at a breakpoint or after an error). During a break it is possible, in the same manner as in the system block, to enter new declarations and to assign values etc. The main difference is that declarations are not entered into the system block but into the presently active block, which is the block of the last called procedure.

5. CONVENTIONAL TECHNIQUES
COMPARED WITH PATHCAL

In a conventional interactive programming environment there is little programming support. There is an editor, a compiler and a debugger. In this section a brief comparison with existing interactive systems, in particular the PL/I checkout compiler, will be presented.

The working cycle in conventional interactive program development is edit, compile and execute. In Pathcal the program is defined and tested piecewise. An expected working habit when using Pathcal is to build a database of procedures and later combine them into programs. The PL/I checkout compiler system does not allow partial programs to exist and does not support incremental definition of the program.

Traditional editing is performed using a text editor that knows nothing about the programming language we work with. The editor in Pathcal on the other hand recognizes Pascal symbols, statements and overall program structure.

Usually the compiler is a black box. The translator in Pathcal however stops when a syntactic error is encountered and permits the programmer to edit the source and resume the translation until another error occurs. This means that there will not be a cascade of error messages because of one single error. After each error one may correct the source of the error, and the corrected program is the object of the parser from then on. The PL/I checkout compiler uses an intermediate form between the Pathcal technique and conventional techniques. This compiler uses a technique for error correction which tries to correct misspellings and other errors. If the programmer accepts the attempted correction no further editing is needed. If an error is encountered, for which the compiler cannot suggest a correct change, one must exit from the compiler, enter the text editor and after editing restart the compiler from the beginning.

In most interactive debugging systems, values of variables can be read and set. It is however usually not possible to call procedures in the program or to enter new declarations. In Pathcal all operations are allowed in a breakpoint or error break, of course including resuming the program execution. It is possible to call any procedure, create new declarations and edit the running program. In the PL/I checkout compiler statements may be added or deleted from the code of the running program, and statements may be executed in "direct mode". No declarations may be entered or deleted in direct mode.

Support of program testing is only rarely found. Those aids that are available are mainly test-data-generators and statement frequency counting programs. Testing in Pathcal allows interactive or programmed comparison of test results. Verification of testing in Pathcal may be enhanced by special test procedures that are attached to statements in the code. These test procedures are executed when the statements, to which the specific procedure is attached, are reached. The test procedures could be viewed as a programmed precondition. This approach encourages the building of test libraries and verifiers for the programs.

There are some disadvantages with the approach used in the Pathcal system. Most of these disadvantages are considered to be manageable. The most serious difficulties are:

1. The Pathcal system assumes that the program, after development or maintenance, is to be moved into a production environment. This is also the case of the PL/I checkout compiler. This raises the issue of compatibility between the Pathcal system and its production compiler.

2. In a compute bound program efficiency might be critical even when test-

ing the program. This might be remedied partly by specialized compilers within the framework of Pathcal.

6. IMPLEMENTATION

A fundamental idea when constructing Pathcal was that all subsystems should use a single internal notation. This internal notation should be "weakly consistent" in the sense that only syntactically correct programs are stored. Semantic correctness is verified only at runtime. This limitation means that we always have well formed data structures to manipulate internally, which in itself increases the security and the simplicity of the system. The semantic checks are performed during runtime to allow a high level of incrementality. Without this restriction it is difficult to allow procedures and functions to be defined successively. Naturally one may perform full compilation of a program if it is desired but this seems unnatural in an incremental environment. The internal notation of a Pascal expression is the corresponding parse tree. Comments and break points are associated to this internal notation via hash links. The interpreter simulates the Pascal stack and variable look up mechanism by symbolic search of the stack for names.

The efficiency of the current interpreter is fairly low, partly because the symbol table and data representation has not been optimized and because the system is written in Lisp. In spite of this the Pathcal system only required approximately 75% of the cpu time required by the standard compiler [Kiscki and Nagel 1976] and editor to complete the example given above. This performance gain is due to the incremental system, which has no overhead in program startup time and requires fewer compilations. One edit and rerun of the program required 30% less time in Pathcal. A single run of the program required 30% more time with Pathcal. The loop in the HISTOGRAM procedure was approximately 25 times slower in Pathcal than with the compiled system. It is possible to construct cases where Pathcal performs worse, but the system is not intended to be used for productions runs.

7. CONCLUSIONS

Interactive and incremental program development is today only available for users of Lisp and APL. This type of program development has been described by Sandewall [Sandewall 1978].

The experiences with Pathcal show that it is both possible and reasonable to build an incremental programming system for Pascal. Most ideas included in the system are adjustments of the facilities in Interlisp. Lisp has advantages over "syntax oriented" languages in its simplicity of representation. Code and data have the same internal representation, and one never needs to use a parser after manipulation of code. In APL there is no canonical internal representation and thus it is necessary to "unparse" the function before editing it and afterwards parse it again. Lisp has fewer data types than Pascal, which allows a more efficient implementation of dynamic type checking. INTERLISP provides a set of command languages for the editor, break package, etc. Thus, the usage of a new utility system requires learning a new syntax. The command languages of INTERLISP are mostly fairly simple to learn, but as soon as one wants to perform a more complicated operation or if one wishes to combine several commands the system becomes more difficult to use. In Pathcal the command language is part of the programming language and thus it is natural to combine commands into user defined commands. The all inclusive system block, where test data and declarations are kept, has been a very successful technique. This gives convenient testing of single procedures and a good environment for the extension of the system, both by the user and by the system implementor.

ACKNOWLEDGMENTS

Kenth Ericson, Jim Goodwin, Gunilla Lönnemark and Erik Sandewall have been most helpful in preparing this report or in the construction of the system.
This work was supported by The National Swedish Board of Technical Development (STU) under contract DNR-78-4167.

REFERENCES

[APLSF 1976] *APLSF Programmer's Reference Manual*. Digital Equipment Corporation, Maynard, Massachusetts, DEC-10-LPLSA-A-D, 1976.

[Balzer 1974] R.M. Balzer. Language-independent programmer's interface. University of Southern California, Information Sciences Institute, ISI/RR-73-15, March 1974.

[ECL 1974] *ECL Programmer's Manual*. Harvard University, Center for Research in Computing Technology, TR-23-74, December 1974.

[Huet et al. 1977] G. Huet, G. Kahn, P. Maurice. *Environment de Programmation Pascal*. Manuel D'Utillisation sous SIRIS 7/8, IRIA, November 1977; [*Editors' note*: see also [Donzeau-Gouge et al]]

[Jensen and Wirth 1977] K. Jensen, N. Wirth. Pascal User Manual and report. *Springer Verlag Lecture Notes in Computer Science*, 18, 1977.

[Kiscki and Nagel 1976] E. Kiscki, H.-H. Nagel. *Pascal for the DECsystem 10*. Institut für Informatik der Universität Hamburg, Mitteilung NR. 37, IFI-HH-M-37/76, November 1976.

[PL/I 1976] *OS PL/I Checkout Compiler, CMS Users Guide*. IBM, SC33-0047/2, 1976.

[Sandewall 1978] E. Sandewall. Programming in the interactive environment: the LISP experience. *Communications of the ACM*, 10:1 (March 1978), 35-71; reprinted in *Interactive Programming Environments*.

[Teitelman 1978] W. Teitelman. *INTERLISP Reference Manual*. Xerox Palo Alto Research Center, Palo Alto, California, December 1978.

[Van De Riet 1977] R.P. Van De Riet. Basis- an interactive system for the introductory course in informatics. *International Federation of Information Processing*, 1977.

7 Programming Environments Based on Structured Editors: The MENTOR Experience

VÉRONIQUE DONZEAU-GOUGE, GÉRARD HUET, GILLES KAHN, BERNARD LANG

Institut National de Recherche en Informatique et Automatique Rocquencourt, France

We discuss in this note our experience with the MENTOR program manipulation system, from the following points of view:

- *The main design decisions we made in MENTOR;*
- *Our experience with building and using a PASCAL programming environment based on MENTOR;*
- *Our vision of a complete programming environment.*

1. A MENTOR PRIMER

MENTOR is a processor designed to manipulate structured data. This data is represented as operator-operand trees, generally called *abstract syntax trees*. MENTOR is driven by the tree manipulation language MENTOL.

1.1 Abstract Syntax

Abstract syntax trees are structured as sorted algebras; for a given language, we declare a set of *sorts*, and a set of *operators* with sorted operands. Operators may be declared with a fixed arity, or may be associative operators with a variable number of arguments, used to represent lists. We must also specify a parser which, given a sort, maps a concrete syntax string into the corresponding abstract syntax tree and some standard inverse mapping, the prettyprinting unparser.

For instance, in MENTOR-PASCAL, typical sorts are *exp, stat, varbl, ident, const, lexp, lstat*. Every meaningful PASCAL construct corresponds to an operator. Typical operators are if, ass, call, lstat, lexp, gtr, mult, index, with sorts as follows:

```
if:      exp X stat X stat → stat.
ass:     varbl X exp → stat.
call:    ident X lexp → stat.
lstat:   stat X stat X ... X stat → lstat.
lexp:    exp X exp X .. X exp → lexp.
gtr:     exp X exp → exp.
mult:    exp X exp → exp.
index:   ident X lexp → exp.
```

Also, all identifiers and constants are nullary operators, of sort respectively *ident* and *const*. Finally, our sorts are ordered; for instance, ident ⊆ varbl ⊆ exp, const ⊆ exp and lstat ⊆ stat. In any argument place of sort θ, all operators returning sort $\theta' \subseteq \theta$ are authorized.

The following PASCAL program:

```
if X>0 then P(X,A[Y,Z]) else
                begin
                Y: =Y*2;
                X: =0
                nd
```

parses into (and is the unparsing of) the following abstract syntax tree:

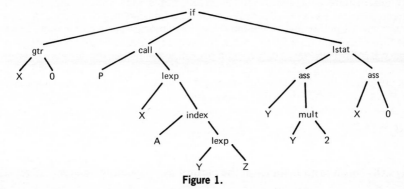

Figure 1.

1.2 MENTOL: A Tree Manipulation Language

The user communicates with MENTOR through an interpreter for a special-ized tree manipulation language, MENTOL. Values in MENTOL are abstract syntax trees (abbreviated AST from now on) and locations in these trees (abbreviated LOC). MENTOL commands are themselves ASTs in MENTOR-MENTOL. MENTOL variables, called *markers*, may be assigned LOCs. A LOC expression is obtained by composing a base marker with displacement oper-ators such as U,L,R for up,left,right, or Sn, with n an integer, for n-th son. For instance, if marker @TOP marks the top of the above PASCAL tree, @TOP S2 S1 marks the location of identifier P. The *current* marker, @K, may be abbreviated by the empty string for convenience. The MENTOL assignment statement, of the form LOC1:LOC2, is used to move around in trees, and remember places. For instance, :@TOP S2 S1 would assign the current marker to the location of P in the tree above.

The command LOC Pn prints on the console the result of unparsing the AST at LOC, down to a level of detail specified by integer n. For instance, @TOP P2 would print:

```
if # then # else ...
```

Note that list nodes are abbreviated by ..., and other nodes by #. The command @TOP P3 would give you some more detail:

```
if X>0 then P(X,A[Y,Z])
else begin
    #;#
    end
```

The standard prettyprinting effected by MENTOR puts PASCAL reserved words in lower case, identifiers in upper case, and indicates the tree structure by indentation. When the level of detail is unspecified, you get a standard abbreviation that in most cases fits on one screen. For instance, @TOP P would produce the text above in full. The reverse operation of P is &, which is an expression denoting the result of parsing a string of characters read on the input device.

An essential feature of MENTOL is pattern matching. A pattern, or *schema*, is any AST containing special terminal nodes called *metavariables*. A schema matches any tree which is an instance of the pattern, replacing metavariables by appropriate subtrees. A given metavariable may appear only once in a given pattern. Metavariables are unparsed as special identifiers, whose names start with a dollar sign. Schemas may be constructed by commands, or may be input through the parser. When the syntax tables for a given language are loaded, MENTOR constructs a set of predefined schemas, one for each operator. These elementary schemas consist of just the given operator, applied to me-tavariables; they are accessible through a marker named by the operator. For instance, in MENTOR-PASCAL, we would have:

```
?@GTR P          $EXP1>$EXP2
```

The *find* expression LOC F pat denotes the first location in the subtree marked by LOC which is an instance of the pattern pat (assuming preorder traversal).

If the subtree does not contain any such instance, the special value *fail* is returned. Another find expression, with F replaced by FF, does not limit the search to the subtree marked by LOC; that is, the search is continued in preorder beyond LOC (this is the search one ordinarily does in the listing of a program, starting from a given point). When pattern matching is successful, the markers with the same name as the metavariables of the schema are assigned to the corresponding location in the object tree. For instance, in the above example:

```
?@TOP F @GTR P
X>0
?@EXP1 P
X
```

Let us now explain briefly the main commands and control structures in MEN-TOL. When a LOC expression is used as a command, it abbreviates the operation of assigning to the base marker of LOC the result of evaluating LOC. For instance, in the example above, a more typical operation would be to use the current marker as follows:

```
?:@TOP;F@GTR;P
X>0
```

Note the sequencer semicolon. A sequence of commands is made into a command (abbreviated COM) by enclosing it between parentheses (these are not mandatory at top level). Any command may be iterated n times by postfixing it with integer n. A star means iterate until failure; for instance, U* brings the current marker to the top of the tree it was pointing into. A primitive conditional statement is provided: ?COM1, COM2 executes COM1 if the previous command succeeded, otherwise it executes COM2. The command $n exits from n levels of grouping; $-n is the same, but returns failure. There are various other control statements, such as a case statement, which we shall not discuss here. The interested reader is referred to MENTOR's manual [Donzeau-Gouge et al.]. Let us now turn to the commands that modify ASTs.

The change command, LOC1 C AST2, replaces the subtree marked by LOC1 with the tree AST2. Like in Algol 60, a form of coercion is provided: When the second argument of the change command is some location expression LOC2, it denotes a copy of the subtree marked by LOC2. Various list manipulation commands, such as insert (I) and delete (D), are provided. LOC1 X LOC2 exchanges the subtrees at LOC1 and LOC2 (provided they are disjoint). All these operations maintain the correctness of sorts. Rather than giving an exhaustive list, let us give a few examples:

```
?:@TOP
?S2 X S3
?S2 S1 I S3
?S3 C &
[STAT]:Z:=0;    %colon is prompt for parsing; note the sort reminder
?S1 X S2
ERROR: WRONG SYNTAX TYPE
?P
if X>0 then
     begin Y:=Y*2;
     P(X,A[Y,Z]);
     X:=0
     end else Z:=0
```

Let us finally explain an essential command: eval; E AST returns a copy of the tree AST, in which metavariables are instantiated according to the current environment. The eval command, together with pattern-matching, permits an easy implementation of program transformations that can be described as tree rewriting systems. For instance, assume we want to transform the operator > in the PASCAL example above into the operator > =. Assuming the current marker is initially positioned at TOP, the simplest way of doing this in MENTOL is as follows:

```
?F@GTR;CE@GEQ;P
X>=0
?@GEQ P          %This works because metavariables match
$EXP1>=$EXP2
```

We have not yet explained how we dealt with comments, and more generally with pragmats and assertions. We have designed a general mechanism that takes comments into account as a particular case of various possible annotations, meaningfully related to program constructs. The idea is to attach *attributes* to any node of an AST. These attributes are themselves ASTs in their own language. The LOC expressions are extended so as to access the various attributes of a given node and to get back from an AST to the AST node it annotates, if any. For instance, in MENTOR-PASCAL, two attributes are reserved for ordinary comments: the so-called *prefix* and *postfix* comments. These simple comments have a rather poor structure: they may be just lists of lines. We also use comments in PASCAL's abstract syntax; for instance, when we optimize some portion of a program, we keep the initial version of the construct as a comment. The system is extensible; for instance, we may declare a new abstract syntax for assertions, and annotate various constructs with them, write in MENTOL a verification condition generator that will compute from these assertions, etc.

If MENTOL consisted only of the features mentioned so far, the reader would question our calling it a programming language. What makes MENTOL a full-fledged (although not general-purpose) programming language is the possibility to write MENTOL procedures. We permit three kinds of procedure parameters:

1. LOCs passed by value;
2. LOCs passed by reference;
3. COMs passed by name.

For instance, a standard predefined procedure is FORALL, which takes two arguments: a pattern and a command. For every instance of the pattern, starting from the current marker and with a preorder tree traversal, it executes its second argument. Various utility procedures are predefined to generate new identifiers and to provide coercion mechanisms such as between identifiers, strings and comment lines. Finally, standard system procedures are provided for file manipulation, interactive help, debugging, etc.

This procedure encapsulation mechanism is essential to MENTOR. It allows the designer of a programming environment to provide the user with powerful program manipulations in terms of the logical constructs of the specific programming language manipulated. These manipulations can be heavily context dependent, and may use semantic knowledge of the programming constructs, as opposed to the purely structural context-free manipulations of the MENTOL primitives. Finally, it allows the construction of extensible systems in which the user constructs and maintains his own environment of procedures.

1.3   A PASCAL Programming Environment
Based on MENTOR

MENTOR is a general system to manipulate structured information. However, we originally intended its main application to be the realization of an interactive programming environment in which a programmer may design, implement, document, debug, test, validate, maintain and transport his programs. Furthermore, we intended this environment to be realistic enough to help in implementing large software developments and to provide a programming team with tools for specifying a design, enforcing a programming methodology and verifying interfaces. Our intention when we started the project, at the end of 1974, was to try to bridge the gap between existing programming tools such as debugging compilers and the vast amount of theoretical research on the semantics of programming languages. At the same time, we did not want to commit ourselves to any currently proposed programming methodology (top-down design, structured programming, etc.) or formalism (first-order assertions, Hoare rules, modal logic) for which a wide consensus did not exist. Rather, we wanted our system to be general enough to accommodate these various formalisms and to provide tools for implementing the proposed methodologies. We chose to implement a PASCAL environment around the MENTOR system for several reasons. Most importantly, we had chosen PASCAL as our system implementation language, and we wanted to implement first the tools we needed ourselves in our development effort. We bootstrapped as soon as the core of the system was implemented; this may be one of the most important practical decisions that forced us to focus on pragmatic issues.

The first step in this effort was the design of a structure editor for PASCAL programs, implemented in MENTOR-PASCAL. That is, we wrote a number of MENTOL procedures that are the main user commands to construct and modify PASCAL programs and their documentation. Some of these procedures are used to move in the AST of the program according to higher-level concepts. For instance, FPROC is used to move to the top of a procedure; it first asks the user the name of this procedure. VAR goes to the immediately surrounding variable declaration part, etc. Other MENTOL procedures effect simple program transformations. For instance, LABEL is used to label a statement. It requests the label name from the user, verifies that this label is neither declared nor used in the current environment, declares it, and finally labels the statement pointed to by the current marker. All these manipulations are transparent to the user as long as no error condition occurs.

We then turned our effort to implementing tools for the normalization and documentation of PASCAL programs. Normalizing programs consists of arranging them in a standard, more readable form, while preserving semantic equivalence. For instance, declarations may be rearranged so that logically related items may be declared in the same area. Various cleaning-up operations are performed to get rid of unnecessary structures (empty statements, compound statements, etc.). This is especially important when a series of program transformations have been applied mechanically, since often they are easier to program with redundant structure. Of course none of these simplifications should get rid of comments. Automatic documentation consists of generating comments automatically at various standard places in the program, generating scope structures, cross-reference tables, etc. Some of these may involve complicated computations on the program. The basic philosophy is that all generated documentation is itself structured, so that it can be used by further processes. We do not elaborate further on normalization and documentation of programs in MENTOR, and refer the interested reader to [Kahn 1978].

Another area we started to investigate was an approach to debugging by source-level program manipulation. The idea is that instead of giving you run-time debugging tools that have a more or less satisfactory user interface, we shall provide you with special versions of your source program, with user interfaces built-in. You can compile and run these special versions using your standard production compiler. For instance, a procedure PROFILE allows you to compute an execution profile of your program as a side effect of your main computation. We think this area is worthy of more research.

The effort of designing and implementing a bona fide programming environment based on MENTOR-PASCAL is still going on. Rather than listing in painstaking detail all that is available to the user in the current state of the system, let us discuss what is our idea of a satisfactory environment, and what problems we are encountering in its implementation.

The main philosophy of our programming environment is to build specialized interpreters that help the programmer by doing various computations and rearrangements on his programs. These interpreters communicate, among themselves as well as with the user, through the abstract syntax of PASCAL and its annotations. The development of a program is conceived as a multi-pass activity, each processor using as assumptions the normalization and computations effected by the previous passes. For instance, the "correction" of a piece of program may be progressively checked/debugged according to the following scenario:

- As soon as the program is input, it is correct as far as its context-free structure is concerned, and this will be enforced by MENTOR's typing mechanism during any further transformation.
- Then a "scoper" processes the program, checking for existence of declarations for the various identifiers used in the program. This pass may be described as "computing the lambda-calculus skeleton" of the program.

When all names are linked to their proper declaration, it is easy to write a typechecker that will check for the correct typing of all the programming language operations. This step is conceptually, and indeed in our scenario implemented as, a non-standard interpretation of the programming language constructs. A complete set of MENTOL procedures for PASCAL scope and type checking has been developed, and used to develop type-preserving manipulations in MENTOR-PASCAL [Melese 1980].

- At this stage it is natural to check for run-time errors, termination, and aliases. Here we need much more semantic information. Most of the checks mentioned are undecidable in general, but easy sufficient conditions are reasonable to implement. These checks can be realized by the combination of specialized data-flow analysis routines and a general symbolic interpreter. A set of MENTOL procedures that checks aliasing in PASCAL and its application to proving sufficient conditions for a procedure to be free of side effects is described in [Morcos-Oury 1979].
- The hardest part of program verification remains: checking that the program actually corresponds to what the programmer expected. The traditional approach would be to implement a debugging interpreter, which would execute directly from the abstract syntax and various other structures (symbol tables) constructed by the above processes. A more formal approach would request that the user state formal specifications, such as first-order assertions, and would check the adequacy of the program with respect to its specifications. For instance, verification conditions may be generated through symbolic execution, and then input to a theorem prover. The formulae generated, as well as the proof trees, would of course be in turn AST's manipulable by MENTOR;

the user could therefore monitor the proof with the same tools he is using for manipulating his programs. This semi-automated approach would alleviate the difficulty of having to implement a completely automatic theorem prover, a task which is still beyond the state of the art. Another rigorous approach would be to process in MENTOR a complete description of the semantics of the programming language used and to limit the proofs to identities between mathematically well-understood concepts. Such a grandiose meta-system could be conceived as essentially combining the capabilities of the SIS [Mosses 1979] and LCF [Gordon et al. 1977] systems within MENTOR.

A similar scenario can easily be designed for program optimization: local optimizations are performed by program transformations, then more global optimizations are effected at the source level after doing the necessary computations by MENTOL procedures. The program is then compiled in an object code which has its own abstract syntax. Final optimizations are performed by transformations on the object code.

The general strategy behind a programming environment as sketched above is to effect successive refinements on the original program by going from the simpler, better understood tasks, to the more sophisticated and costly verifications. However, only a small fraction of the above ambitious plan has been actually implemented in MENTOR-PASCAL. There are two primary reasons for this, which are actually complementary aspects of the same phenomenon:

1. Even the easiest and most natural program transformations are hard to implement in a totally safe way in the current state of baroqueness of programming languages. For instance, it is impossible in PASCAL to separate scope-checking from type-checking because of the WITH construct. The lack of orthogonality of the language makes it a complex and costly process to do anything but the most trivial program transformations. For instance, replacing tail recursions by gotos in recursive procedures with call-by-value arguments represents about 200 lines of MENTOL procedures. Again, the assumption must be made (and checked) that no WITH statement occurs.

2. The more mundane transformations have proved to be challenging and interesting research problems. Their careful implementation is often crucial, since many computations involved turn out to be very time consuming. An especially interesting area of applications is the transport of programs. Our largest application so far was to transport MENTOR from its original IRIS 80 implementation to its PDP 10 version. This is performed in a completely mechanical manner by a set of MENTOR procedures. This way any new release of MENTOR can be followed (after a few hours of computation) by a release of a totally compatible PDP 10 release.

The conclusion we can draw from this state of affairs is that no really satisfactory programming environment will exist for ugly languages. On the other hand, it is clear that purely applicative languages are not about to be widely accepted; in the real world of programming, complex data structures with sharing and complex control structures and parameter passing mechanisms are the rule rather than the exception. We are not arguing in favor of simplistic toy-programming languages; the point is rather that the study of program transformations provides interesting guidelines for the design of future programming languages. As might be expected, these design criteria are closely related to those based on semantic considerations [Tennent 1977]. We have hope that the state of affairs will improve with the advent of new programming languages whose designs will have benefited from programming languages semantics research and experience gained with systems such as MENTOR. A positive step in this direction has been taken with the ADA language development, since the design of the language included a formal semantics definition. It is interesting to note that this formal semantics is based on a MENTOR-compatible abstract syntax definition.

2. THE MAIN DESIGN DECISIONS IN MENTOR

2.1   The Abstract Syntax

The notion of abstract syntax is familiar to any compiler writer. It is a tree-like representation of the structure of programs. Operators of the abstract syntax are the basic building blocks of the language. We want to strongly emphasize that abstract syntax is *not* parse trees. It is indeed very different conceptually, although our trees can be obtained by collapsing and normalizing parse trees. Here are a few important differences:

1. Lists are represented as one list node, not as binary trees.
2. The reserved words of the language occur as node labels, not as leaves.
3. Non-terminals of the grammar do not generate nodes. Certain ones correspond to sorts, others do not appear at all. For instance, an identifier may occur directly as an expression, the intermediate levels of parsing such as simpleexp, factor, term being collapsed.
4. Parentheses are *not* part of the structure; they are generated optionally by the unparser if the context requires it (e.g. because of precedence reasons).

Point 3 is particularly important: every node of the abstract syntax leaves a concretely visible mark in the print-out, and this is a big help for the use going up and down the tree. This makes MENTOR significantly different from previous structured editors such as Hansen's, where the user moved around in his program with the help of grammar menus.

Point 4 is important too. For the MENTOR user an exp is an exp. Precedence relations are left for the unparser to worry about. For instance, with the example above:

```
?@TOP F@MULT;S1C&
[EXP]:Y+1;
?U;P
Y:=(Y+1)*2
```

Similarly, the problem of PASCAL's dangling else completely vanishes:

```
?@TOP S2 C&             %we change the then part of an if
[STAT]:IF Y<X THEN X:=Y;   %into a conditional statement
?@TOP P
if X>0 then
     if Y<X then S:=Y else   %note the extra else generated
else Z:=0
```

MENTOR trees are not LISP trees either. Even for the LISP language, the coding of programs as binary trees with atom leaves is rather remote from the abstract structure of the program. Also points 1 and 2 above apply. Our structure is much richer; for instance, in MENTOR-PASCAL, we have about 100 operators, whereas LISP structures have only one (cons). For these reasons, we consider MENTOR significantly different from, say, the INTERLISP editor.

So much for the choice of the general formalism of abstract syntax. Of course for each particular language there is a certain degree of freedom in the design of the particular operators and sorts. As we mentioned above, it is crucial that almost every operator add some concrete representation to the unparsing of a piece of program. An important, but not mandatory, requirement is that the unparsing of an operator should not depend too much on the context in which it occurs. This requirement is met by most operators in MENTOR-PASCAL, except that certain nodes are sometimes surrounded by parentheses according to the context. There are two primary occurrences of this phenomenon:

1. Parentheses surrounding list nodes may change with the context. For instance, an lstat is usually unparsed as a compound begin ... end, except when appearing as the loop of a repeat.

2. Parentheses may be needed for precedence, or dangling structures such as shown above for the else. Our unparser always generates the minimum number of parentheses needed for a correct parsing. This is the only normalization (besides indentation of course) that is completely automatic and over which the user has no control.

When designing an abstract syntax for a specific language, the following trade-off occurs. Various constructs of the language may be represented by the same concrete strings. Now there is a choice as to whether you want to separate these two constructs as two distinct operators, or if you want to merge them into one. The maximum discrimination has the advantage that your structure will have a finer grain; for instance, you will catch by the find command instances of one construct independently from instances of the other. On the other hand, certain program transformations will be harder, and the user has more constructs to learn. For instance, should parameter declarations use the same construct as variable declarations? As might be expected, referential transparency and orthogonality are important properties for a programming language to possess for a completely satisfactory design of it abstract syntax.

We feel that allowing arbitrary annotations of nodes by abstract syntax trees in specialized languages was an important design decision. This makes our system open ended to various developments, without interfering with the tools already designed: a given interpreter may have access to certain annotations, the others being invisible. For instance, certain annotations are comments for the user to see. Others may be pragmats for the compiler, specifications in some formal language for use by a verifier, data structures for control flow analysis, original code commenting some optimized sections, example runs, assertions for run-time checks, etc. It is important that these various structures do not interfere with one another and with the program itself.

It may be appropriate to discuss here why we decided to stick to trees, and not go to more complicated graph structures, such as (shared) dags or control flow graphs. The main reason is that we know how to keep the integrity of these context-free structures in an incremental way. For instance, we could imagine keeping the programs correct according to full PASCAL syntax, including type checking for instance. But, aside from the fact that it would be a lot more costly to maintain all the information needed for checking this correctness during the editing of the program, this would have the additional (and in our opinion insuperable) drawback that it would preclude the development of programs except in the most awkward fashion.

2.2 MENTOL

MENTOL is our tree-manipulation language. The above description of its main commands gives a flavor of MENTOL programming. The salient features of the language are:

1. It is an interactive language, used for editing; but it may also be used to program lengthy batch computations.

2. It is not applicative; MENTOL constructs divide into expressions, that are simply evaluated for their result, and commands, which have various side effects.

3. It is a specialized language, for manipulating trees; it has no pretense of being general-purpose, although it has rudimentary arithmetic capabilities.

4. It has reasonably good user interaction facilities: there are various debugging aids such as a trace package, an interrupt facility, and the user may execute in coroutine with programs, a very handy feature for "controlled" program manipulation.

5. MENTOL has its own abstract syntax. It is therefore possible to edit and develop MENTOL programs under MENTOR. Actually a standard facility exists to go back and forth between a PASCAL editing session and a MENTOL editing environment, in which the (advanced) user may modify his PASCAL manipulation programs.

6. File manipulation primitives are provided. Several formats of files are known to MENTOR: standard text files, that may be input (through parsing) and output (through unparsing). Tree files, that keep ASTs from one session to the next without the need to reparse. MENTOL files, containing MENTOL procedures, and a special case of which is used as the initialisation file, loading a specific user's structure editing prelude.

Pattern matching deserves a little discussion. As we have already remarked, pattern matching is a fundamental operation in MENTOL. The user may construct any tree pattern, i.e., any AST with metavariables occurring anywhere. However, metavariables may occur in only one occurrence. This condition is required because of the side effects on the corresponding markers. Note that this is not really a restriction, since a primitive is provided for testing equality of trees. No list metavariables are provided at the moment, because associative pattern matching is a complicated operation (a tree may match a pattern in more than one way if such list variables are allowed), and because it was never strongly felt to be desirable, except probably for orthogonality. But we want to stress the considerable pattern matching capability we have in MENTOR, as opposed say to string searching in a more conventional editor. Anybody who tries to trace uses of an identifier I in his program (as opposed to all occurrences of the character I, in other identifiers, reserved words, strings and comments!) will understand this point. Furthermore the MENTOL pattern matching is fast, because types are used to focus the search on the relevant part of the trees. For instance, MENTOR knows that in PASCAL, statements are disjoint from declarations, and may not occur in expressions. It will therefore focus the search for a statement on a narrow region in the program tree (and of course comments will not get in the way either). We may therefore argue that tree pattern matching is faster than string pattern matching. We believe this is one of the main arguments for having typed rather than untyped structures.

It is clear that MENTOL is not the last word in tree-manipulation languages. However, we wanted to acquire a reasonable amount of experience with writing program transformations in MENTOL before drawing definite conclusions about such languages. All in all, MENTOL has well served its purpose: it is easy to learn, it is fairly easy to debug, it is fast enough for editing. However, long MENTOL procedures are hard to read, and a compiler is clearly needed for complicated transformations done in batch mode.

2.3 A Special Word for Screen Editor Fans

One of the most commonly heard criticisms of MENTOR is that it should be possible to edit programs on your screen in the same way as for instance with the EMACS editor. We do not believe that this would be an easy task, and we do not even think that such a facility is really desirable.

The first point concerns portability. In the initial MENTOR design, we had planned to define a screen as partitioned between several areas, and to have the text under the current marker represented specially on the screen. We went as far as implementing these displays, but then changed our minds, mostly because it was very hard to distribute our system. We reverted to teletype-compatible output. MENTOR can be transported to any machine with any interactive operating system (modulo the PASCAL transport problems, of course). No special terminals are needed, but of course the system will be more pleasant to use if the rate of transmission is higher, so that it is not too costly to have the current marker expression printed often.

The second point concerns the difficulty to maintain two separate representations. Remember, the text printed on your screen is nowhere kept; it is just computed on demand by the prettyprinter. The ability to manipulate screen images would force us to keep the printed text internally, and to try and link it to the corresponding AST. After a modification has been effected on the screen, the parser would have to be called in action to validate the changes before updating the tree accordingly. The difficulties may not be insurmountable, but it is not clear that the end result would be worth the effort.

Finally, a major drawback of mixing structure editing and display editing is that the user would have to learn how to use two command languages instead of one. We believe that most users would stick to either mode, but would not like mixing them.

3. CONCLUSIONS

MENTOR has been used for most of its own development and maintenance. Various groups at INRIA use MENTOR as their main programming tool for developing PASCAL programs. MENTOR has been distributed in various research and teaching institutions. In particular, it is being used at Universite de Toulouse for teaching programming in PASCAL. Using MENTOR requires some training. It seems that on the average a PASCAL programmer needs about a week to get accustomed to this new world of trees. Past this period, few return to the standard tools.

It is our thesis that using an abstract manipulation system as the core of a programming environment is a good paradigm. However, it is very important that the user may correspond to the system through the concrete syntax he is used to: he should be able to visualize his trees with unparsing, and conversely input his program text with parsing. The abstract syntax manipulation language should have a powerful procedure abstraction mechanism, permitting extension of the system at will with complicated semantic checking, such as data flow analysis and ultimately formal proofs. It is important to be able to manipulate structured annotations, linked to the structure of the program, but conceived as separate entities and not as extensions of the user's programming language syntax. In our opinion, a satisfactory programming environment should unify under a common set of tools the whole range of a programming team's activity: design, development, documentation, debugging, maintenance and transport. The long range goal of software reliability will be attainable only when new programming languages, designed along sound semantic principles, are available.

ACKNOWLEDGMENTS

MENTOR was designed and implemented at IRIA by the authors of this paper. Various other people have been involved occasionally in the MENTOR project: V. Chari, J.J. Levy, B. Melese, E. Morcos-Oury, Y. Sugito.

REFERENCES

[Donzeau-Gouge et al.] V. Donzeau-Gouge, G. Huet, G. Kahn, B. Lang. *The MENTOR User's Manual*. Available from INRIA, Rocquencourt, France.

[Gordon et al. 1977] M. Gordon, R. Milner, C. Wadsworth. *Edinburgh LCF*. Edinburgh University, Computer Science Department, Report CSR-11-77, 1977.

[Kahn 1978] G. Kahn. Normalisation et documentation des programmes. Note technique, IRIA, Mai 1978.

[Melese 1980] B. Melese. *Manipulation des programmes Pascal au niveau concepts du langage*. Universite d'Orsay, These de 3eme cycle, Juin 1980.

[Morcos-Oury 1979] E. Morcos-Oury. Etude des effets de bord des appels de procedure et de fonctions dans le langage PASCAL. Universite Paris XI, These de 3eme cycle, Octobre 1979.

[Mosses 1979] P. Mosses. *SIS - semantics implementation system. Reference Manual and User Guide*. Report DAIMI MD-30, Computer Science Department, Aarhus University, August 1979.

[Tennent 1977] R.D. Tennent. Language design methods based on semantic principles. *Acta Informatica*, 8 (1977), 97-112.

8 The Influence of an Object-Oriented Language on the Programming Environment

ADELE GOLDBERG

XEROX *Palo Alto Research Center*
Palo Alto, California

This is an extended version of a paper which was published in *Proceedings of the 1983 ACM Computer Science Conference,* February 1983, Orlando, Florida, pp. 35–54.

1. INTRODUCTION

There exists a buzzword in the user interface research community that symbolizes how the user should feel about a computer-based environment in which productive work can be carried out. The buzzword is "friendly." It is a strange choice of word in that it seems to imply the existence of personal support for the user by a friend, who happens not to be made of flesh and blood, but of metal and electricity. Friends help us. Friends help us learn, help us develop positive situations, help us understand and get out of negative situations. We like to be around them. The problem of creating a "friendly" programming environment centers on the kind of help the system provides, and the ease with which we can cause the effects we wish to cause. To support program development, help takes the form of methods for finding information about existing functionality, methods for accessing that functionality, methods for describing new programs, and methods for discovering and fixing any faults in those programs. Ideas about the kinds of help needed specify some of the system functionality that ought to exist. In particular, the system should be able to help the user find out what went right, find out what went wrong, find out what can be done next, and find out something about any system component.

Another way to think about the word "friendly" is that it is a measure of the distance between the things the user thinks about doing and the things the user actually can do in the system. There are several places in which this measurement can be taken in a programming environment. One is at the interface between the user's conceptualization of the actual world he wishes to represent and the programming language in which the user must describe this world so that the computer can simulate it. Another place for measurement is at the interface betweening the programming language and the visual presentation of the language to the user. A third place is at the interface between the visual presentation of the language and the way the user must physically indicate what actions should take place. These interfaces are illustrated in Figure 1.

The purpose of this paper is to summarize the ways in which the choice of an object-oriented programming language influences the various places at which we can measure the "friendliness" of the programming environment for that language. The particular system chosen to illustrate such influences is the Smalltalk-80^{tm} programming environment.

2. THE SMALLTALK-80 PROGRAMMING LANGUAGE

The Smalltalk-80 system is documented in a number of articles and books [*Byte* (August 1981), Goldberg 1983, Goldberg and Robson 1983, Krasner 1983]. The language is based on a uniform use of *objects* and *messages*. An object is a uniform representation of information that is an abstraction of the capabilities of a computer to store information. An object has the capacity to store information; we say that an object has *private memory*. An object also has the capacity to manipulate its stored information or to carry out some activity. These are called the *operations* of an object. The set of operations is referred to as the object's *interface*. A crucial property of an object is that its private memory can only be manipulated by the operations in the object's interface.

An object represents an encapsulation of all operations within a single data type. In the Smalltalk-80 language, object is the *only* structuring mechanism. Objects that share a common description of their private memory and that

Figure 1 Three interfaces: (1) real train to simulated train; (2) user interface to computer; (3) simulation described in computer.

share a common set of operations can be grouped together. A group of objects related in this way is called a *class*. Objects in a group are called *instances* of the class. This terminology follows that of the Simula programming language. Programming in the Smalltalk-80 system consists of creating new classes, creating instances of classes, and specifying a sequence of operations on these instances.

An object carries out one of its operations when another object sends it a message to do so. Each object knows the messages it can understand; associated with each such message is a procedure or *method* that describes how the object should answer the message. Message-passing represents a uniform form of control in the Smalltalk-80 system. It is similar to procedure calls, but differs in that the referent of a message name that is part of an algorithm's expressions is bound to an actual procedure at runtime, not at load time. The same name can be used by several different classes of objects. The message receiver is determined at runtime. The message name is then specified as the one found in the receiver's class description. By convention only, the name is used to refer to a generic action, such as **print** or **display**. However, since each class of objects can associate its own method with the name, the details of the action to be taken may differ greatly. For example, each object may respond to the message **print** by displaying different information about itself. The programmer, therefore, does not commit completely to the type of the message receiver nor to the procedural arguments at design time. A weak form of type exists in that the receiver is presumed to be able to respond to the literally-named message. Type inferencing techniques have been devised for this system; for more information about type inferencing, see the explanations by Borning and Ingalls [1982a] and Suzuki [1981].

Refining existing class descriptions is a powerful way in which to approach Smalltalk-80 programming. Such refinement is supported by the ability to create a *subclass* of an existing class. As in Simula, a Smalltalk-80 subclass describes a group of objects that inherit information from an already existing class. A subclass can add new functionality or private memory, and can modify or prohibit existing functionality. The basic form of subclassing in the system supports a linear hierarchy of classes. Inheriting from multiple classes has also been explored, and is provided in the 1983 version 2 release of the Smalltalk-80 system. For a description of the particular multiple inheritance mechanism provided in this version of the system, see Borning and Ingalls [1982b].

The ability to create subclasses means that it is beneficial to specify a class that embodies *default* behavior. The user, after working with the defaults, can then choose to refine this behavior by creating a subclass. The original class continues to work correctly even though the user's modifications are incompletely tested. The basic idea, then, is that the user should be able to write programs in such a way that only specifies how they differ from some previously existing programs. The ability to inherit functionality and default descriptions, and to incrementally modify this inherited capability, reduces the time and the chances for error in the programming process. The ability to create subclasses also means that much of the code in the system is reusable; several subclasses can rely on a common superclass's implementation of a method.

3. A "FRIENDLY" LANGUAGE
OF DESCRIPTION

What are the advantages of the Smalltalk-80 object-oriented form of programming? First, the information known privately to an object is protected: it can only be accessed directly by the methods of the object itself. This means that the representation of information of an individual kind of object can be changed without affecting its interactions with other kinds of objects. This ensures that there is a structure or discipline by which objects interact and that a user can make incremental changes to very complex systems. Complexity in the system is reduced by minimizing interdependencies. As long as an object can respond to a well-defined set of messages, other objects can rely on their ability to successfully access that object's capabilities. Complexity is further reduced by grouping together similar parts of the system, as achieved by the class structure.

Classes are the chief mechanism for extension in the system. In the Smalltalk-80 system, classes represent numbers, text strings, dictionaries, spatial locations, areas, text editors, processes, compilers, debuggers, and so on. The process of creating an application in Smalltalk-80 draws on the programmer's abilities to synthesize from existing capability. Subclasses support the ability to factor the system in order to avoid repetitions of the same concepts in many different places. Classes and subclasses provide a framework for organizing information in such a way that software modification and maintenance is facilitated. It is possible to start with an existing, running system, and incrementally modify it to create a new result. Thus prototyping and redesign are made easier.

What are the advantages of the Smalltalk-80 object-oriented form of programming in terms of measuring the distance between the user's conceptualization of what to do and the programming language in which he must do it?

The design of user-defined simulations or applications starts with an itemization of the kinds of things that must be accounted for in the computerized system. The questions typically asked in this design phase are questions such as what kinds of information must be represented? what is the relationship among the various kinds of information? and what kinds of functionality must exist for operating on this information?

They are answered in the Smalltalk-80 sense by identifying the kinds of information to be represented, seeing if a match exists in the system-supplied data structures and, if not, having the user define a class that represents the desired data structure. Ordered collections are defined in the Smalltalk-80 system. A user can represent a circular list of items with an ordered collection, where the user's programs handle the link between the last and the first item in the list. If the user wishes to represent information as a circular list of items, but feels that it is inappropriate to implement that list as an ordered collection, then the user is not forced to use the system's ordered collection. Rather, the user can create a class that specifically describes circular lists. The operations on a circular list are then defined in terms of messages and their associated methods. The ability to extend the system with user-defined data structures (and with user-defined control structures) means that it is possible to write programs in terms of concept-oriented rather than implementation-oriented data objects and control. For further examples of data-structure and control-structure extensibility in the Smalltalk-80 language, see Althoff, [1981] and Deutsch [1981].

As another example, suppose the user wishes to simulate the operation of a cafeteria. The information that must be represented might include the washer, the cook, the servers, the people who buy the food, and the queues into which the buyers line up. After some consideration, the user might notice that all of the people share some functionality—all of them are people with a task to do in the simulation. Some are workers who give service; some are customers who get service. A representation of the cafeteria might be handled by describing a class of objects that represent people with tasks to do, people who can enter into a queue and wait until called to do their tasks. In addition, a queue is needed into which objects, such as the people, can be entered and removed. The user can create the simulation in a very direct way—by defining a class that represents people with tasks to do and by defining two subclasses, one representing workers and the other representing customers. There must also be a class that represents a waiting queue, although in this case an ordered collection might suffice. Another class representing the cafeteria would also be needed. It would refer to the collection of workers and a waiting queue of customers. Operations on the cafeteria would schedule the workers to do their tasks, such as seeing if there are customers waiting to be served.

The full generality (all the existing objects) might not be relevant to the user at any one time. The set of messages of each class description represents a special purpose sublanguage. A user might only need the functionality of one class and would therefore concentrate on learning the set of messages of that class. For example, the user might wish to concentrate on line-drawing, only sending messages to instances of the system class **Pen.**

A set of class descriptions (one or more), chosen because they interact in a way that forms a concise applications package, forms a subsystem. This subsystem shares all of the support of the general system, but confines itself to one domain of applicability. An example of a subsystem, taken as an extension of the previous example, is one consisting of objects representing simulations, simulation objects, and simulation resources. With such a subsystem, the user can program in the sense of creating subclasses of the classes that describe simulations or simulation objects in general, specifying particular resources, arrival schedules, service times, and tasks to do. The simulation subclasses inherit scheduling capability so that they can be run and so that data on their behavior (such as bottlenecks in the queues or average waiting times) can be collected. A subsystem is an easier world to work in simply because there is quantitatively less information with which to deal. But the operation of the subsystem is precisely like that of the more general system, so that the user can gradually grow in expertise. (The example of a simulation subsystem is specified in Part Three of the Smalltalk-80 book by Goldberg and Robson [1983].)

Subsystems or applications packages abound in the Smalltalk-80 system, which includes

• *Text creation and editing:* Objects representing text, formatted text (paragraphs), and editors for formatted text.
• *Graphics or "painting":* objects representing bitmapped images, and editors for creating forms using freehand drawing techniques, as well as structured methods for rotation, scaling, and translating.
• *Document creation:* objects representing documents that contain both text and images, and editors for galley-layout.
• *Programming:* objects representing class descriptions and an organization of the classes, objects for retrieving and editing class descriptions, compiler, decompiler, formatting assistance, debugger, inspector, and the ability to give explanations of syntactic tokens.

The language structure matches a way the user can organize information and access a subpart for purposes of easier introduction to the system. All source program information about all of the objects in the system are made available to the user. Moreover, program development is incremental. The user can define a class and some of its messages, then test the methods associated with these messages, then add more messages, and continue to test. User packages are "first-class citizens" so that all accessing, testing, and documenting capabilities afforded the system programmer are available to any user. Of course, this is accomplished in the Smalltalk-80 language at the expense of not having a static type structure.

4. VISUAL MANIFESTATIONS OF OBJECTS AND MESSAGES

The programming environment for an object-oriented language focuses on providing visual access to each object in the language. The program development tools that make up part of the environment are each represented as objects themselves that are visually presented. A consequence of this representation of the tools as objects is that their description is itself accessible to the user, who can modify them, adding functionality or simply issuing personal preferences for their aesthetic presentation.

A bitmapped display screen is used in the Smalltalk-80 programming environment to present graphical and textual views of the information about objects to the user. Menus and views are the primary ways objects are visually presented. This section contains a summary of the key kinds of views in the system.

4.1 Menus

Any object has both an external view and an internal view. A possible external view is a view of the messages that the object can receive. These are typically

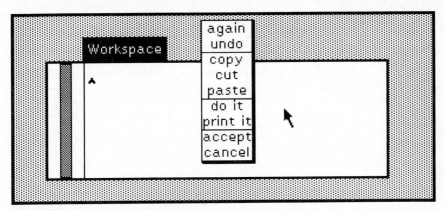

Figure 2

presented to the user in the form of *menus* on the screen. Items in a menu can be textual or graphical. For example, the external view of a text editor might consist of the textual menu shown in Figure 2; this menu appears in a text workspace when the user presses a special function key or button on a pointing device.

The external view of a graphics editor might consist of icons denoting messages for changing the tools with which black and white dots are "brushed" onto the screen. The Smalltalk-80 graphics editor uses the iconic menu shown in Figure 3; this menu appears fixed along the bottom of a graphics workspace (or "canvas") in which the user creates pictures.

In each case, it is possible for the user to locate the class description for the

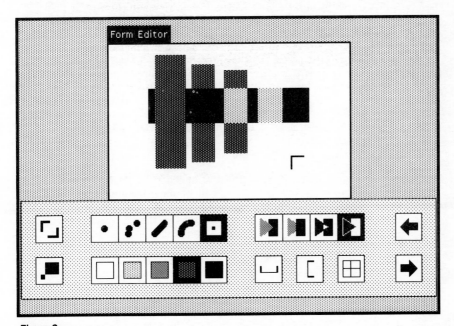

Figure 3

object being viewed, for example, the text or graphics editor, and further locate the message and method corresponding to the menu item. The menu itself is an object that can be modified if the user wishes to add or remove functionality accessible by selection from the menu.

Menus may be fixed on the display screen alongside a view in which other aspects of the object are displayed (as is done in the graphics editor), or they may "pop-up" on the screen in response to the user's pressing a function key (typical for the text editor). They serve the purpose of reminding the user what actions can be successfully carried out next.

4.2   Inspector View

The internal view of an object is a view of the information that the object stores. We refer to this information as the object's *private memory*. Access to the private memory is often necessary for debugging purposes, to check out the current state of an object, or to patch the state of an object in order to continue testing some functionality.

An inspector view in the Smalltalk-80 system consists of two parts. One part provides a textual menu of the names of the variables in the object's private memory; the other part is an area in which values can be displayed and expressions can be evaluated. An example inspector for an **Array** of elements, each of which is a character, is shown in the images of Figure 4. The names of the variables of an **Array** are the indices to the elements of the **Array** (Figure 4a). The textual menu of an inspector includes the pseudo-variable **self**, which is a reference to the inspected object.

The user can choose one of the names in order to see its current value (Figures 4b and 4d). If the user chooses **self**, a description of the inspected object displays (Figure 4c). The user can specify a new value for a variable by typing an expression in the text area of the inspector, and then choosing a command (**accept**) from a special inspector pop-up menu (Figure 4e and 4f).

Every object in the system responds to the message **inspect** to create an inspector view of itself. Similarly, every object responds to the message **print** to provide some printed description of itself. These two messages are specified in the superclass of all objects, class **Object**. Subclasses can re-implement the message **inspect** or **print** to provide special inspectors or print descriptions. In the Smalltalk-80 system, instances of class **Dictionary** create an inspector view in which the menu of variable names is a menu of the dictionary keys, and the text area displays the dictionary values associated with the selected keys. An example inspector for a **Dictionary** is shown in Figure 5.

4.3   Browser Views

A browser is a view made up of subviews, at least one of which contains a menu. The content of a subview is dependent on selections made in other subviews or on commands chosen from pop-up menus associated with the subview. A system browser is a view of the classes in the Smalltalk-80 system. The description of a class consists of the name of its superclass, a declaration of the variables representing the private memory of its instances, and the set of messages with their associated methods. Existing classes are examined and changed using a browser. New classes are added to the system using a browser.

A system browser consists of five rectangular subviews. Along the top are four subviews showing textual menus. The first (leftmost subview) is a list of the categories of classes in the system; the second is a list of the classes in the selected category. The third subview displays the categories of messages for

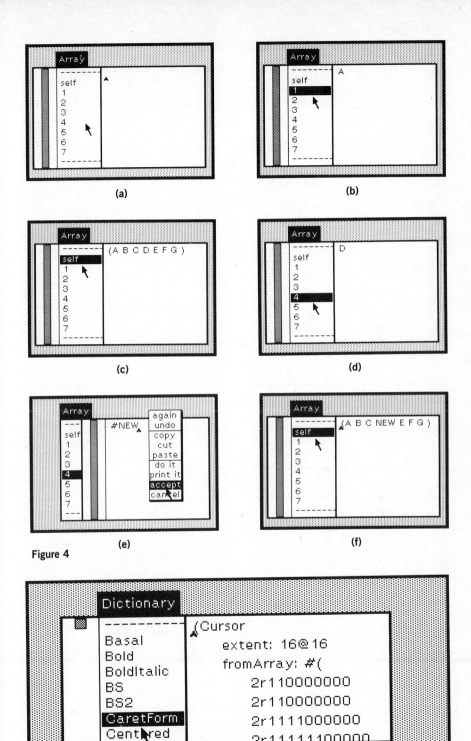

(a)

(b)

(c)

(d)

(e)

(f)

Figure 4

Figure 5

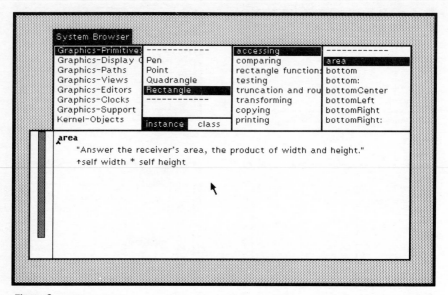

Figure 6

the selected class; and the fourth (rightmost subview) is a list of the message selectors in the selected category. The selected item in each menu is shown in reverse video. The contents of the menu cannot be edited through the view, only selected. The categorization of classes and messages in the system is a form of on-line documentation to assist the user in finding information; it is orthogonal to the semantics of the language. A system browser provides a

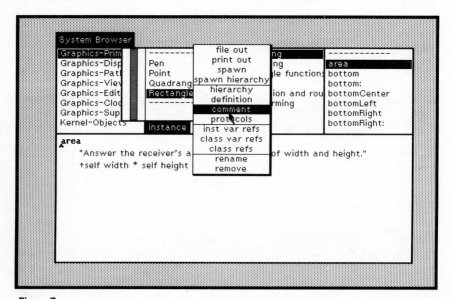

Figure 7

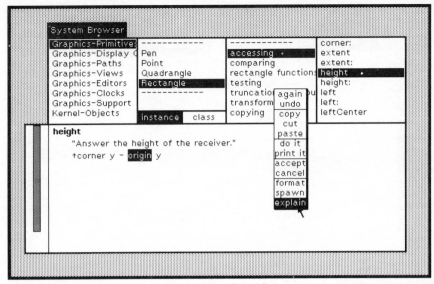

(a)

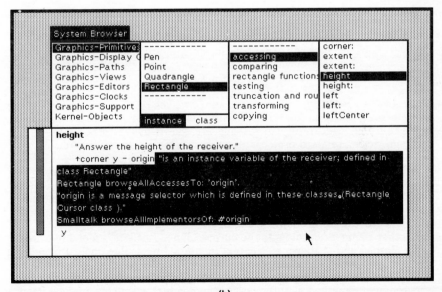

(b)

Figure 8

hierarchical indexing approach to information storage and retrieval, where the categories serve as the search indexes.

Below the four menu subviews is a subview showing some text. That subview is a text workspace in which the text can be edited. The selections in the four menus determine what text is visible in the lower subview; usually, this

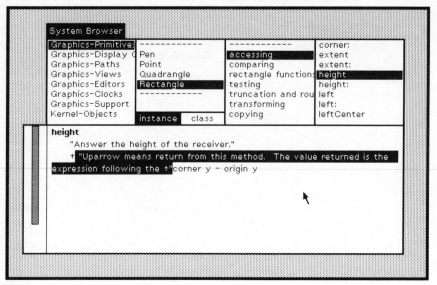

Figure 9

text is a Smalltalk-80 method associated with the selected message of the selected class. Because classes and messages are organized into categories, two selections are needed to identify the class and message category as well.

The system browser shown in Figure 6 shows the method used by instances of class **Rectangle** to respond to the message **area.** The leftmost subview shows that the selected class category is **Graphics-Primitive**; all classes in this category are shown in the second subview. The third subview shows that the selected message protocol is **accessing**. The protocols of messages to which an instance of **Rectangle** can respond are shown in the third subview; all messages in the selected protocol are shown in the rightmost subview.

4.3.1 On-line documentation   Two forms of documentation are accessible about classes. One is a comment about the purpose of the class itself. This is obtained by selecting a menu item **comment** associated with the second subview of a browser, the one in which class names are listed. A comment about the class **Rectangle** is shown in Figure 7.

Another comment documents the purpose of a method. It is found by choosing a method and is shown as the text (delimited by double quotes) included at the beginning of the method definition. As an example, see the comment in Figure 6 for the **Rectangle** message **area.** Programmers can also document the design of a method by interspersing quoted text within the method itself.

4.3.2 Explanations   Suppose a programmer seeks to understand an existing method. One form of explanation could be explanation about the tokens that appear in a method. In the Smalltalk-80 system, the programmer can select any token and then choose the item **explain** from the pop-up menu associated with the subview (Figure 8a). A short explanation of the role of that token is inserted near the token (Figure 8b). The explanation, as shown in the example, can include expressions that can be evaluated in order to create a kind of browser that helps the user examine all the places in the system where the variable is mentioned.

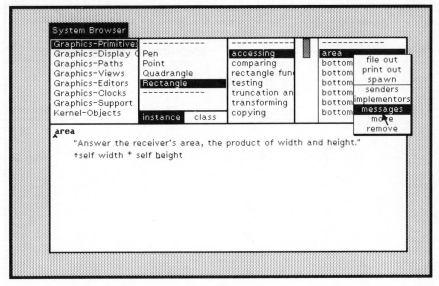

(a)

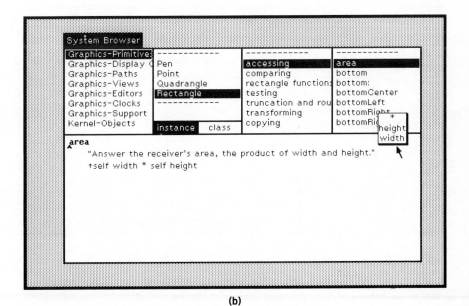

(b)

Figure 10

The token selected for explanation might be a variable name that the programmer could not identify, which is the example given in Figure 8*b*; or it might be a syntactic element, such as uparrow (↑) as shown in Figure 9; or it might be a message selector or class name.

4.3.3 Examples Many classes in the system include the message category **examples**. In this category are messages that a user can execute to see ex-

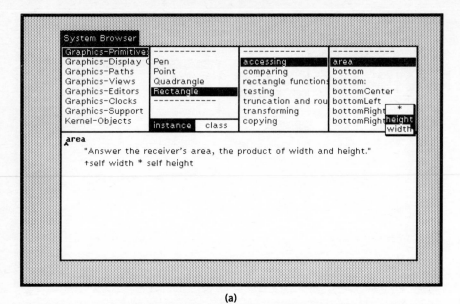

(a)

Implementors of height

DisplayObject height
Paragraph height
PopUpMenu height
Rectangle height

height
    "Answer the number that represents the
height of the receiver's bounding box."
        ↑self boundingBox height

(b)

Figure 11

ample uses of the class. The example methods can be read to learn how to create instances of the class and how to sequence messages to the instances.

4.3.4 Message-set browsers   Because of the class and message structure of the system, it is possible to provide various explanations of the structure of the system. For example, the programmer can ask which messages are sent in a particular method. The request is made by choosing an item from a pop-up menu associated with the rightmost subview of the browser, the subview in which message selectors are listed (Figure 10a). The answer is given as a menu of the message selectors used in the selected method. The menu shown in the rightmost view of the browser in Figure 10b contains the messages in the method for accessing the area of a **Rectangle**.

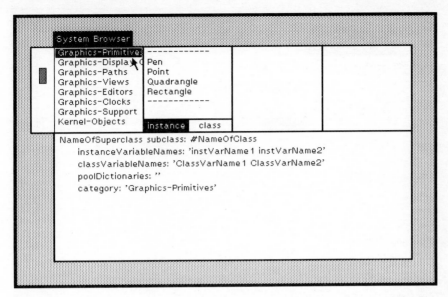

Figure 12

If the programmer selects one of the names in the menu (Figure 11*a*), a new kind of browser is created called a message-set browser (Figure 11*b*). The top view of this new browser is a menu of items that refer to all the methods with which the selected message is implemented. By choosing one of these menu items, the method associated with the message can be viewed and, if desired, edited and recompiled. The explanation mechanism for tokens in the method is also available.

Another item in the pop-up menu associated with the rightmost subview of the system browser allows the user to ask about all the classes in which the selected message is implemented. The response to such an inquiry is a message-set browser on the methods associated with the selected message in each of these classes so that the implementations can be viewed. Or the user can ask about all the methods in the system from which the selected message is sent. Again, the result is a message-set browser on the methods that include the use of the message. These queries about classes and messages support the programmer in learning about the system and how it is structured.

4.3.5 Templates Whenever the system "knows" something about the form in which information should be provided, a template is displayed. The user edits the template, replacing descriptive words with the actual language and syntax. For example, if the user wishes to add a new class to the system and the new class should be categorized in **Graphics-Primitives**, then the user chooses this class category in the system browser. If none of the classes in the second subview are selected, then the lower subview contains a template describing the various parts of a class description (Figure 12). This template is in the form of a message to an existing class requesting that a subclass be created.

The user changes words like **NameOfSuperclass**, **NameOfClass**, **instVarNames**, and **ClassVarNames** in order to describe the new class. In Figure 13, the template has been edited so that a new class representing **Polygons** is specified. The superclass of **Polygon** is **Object**. Its private memory consists

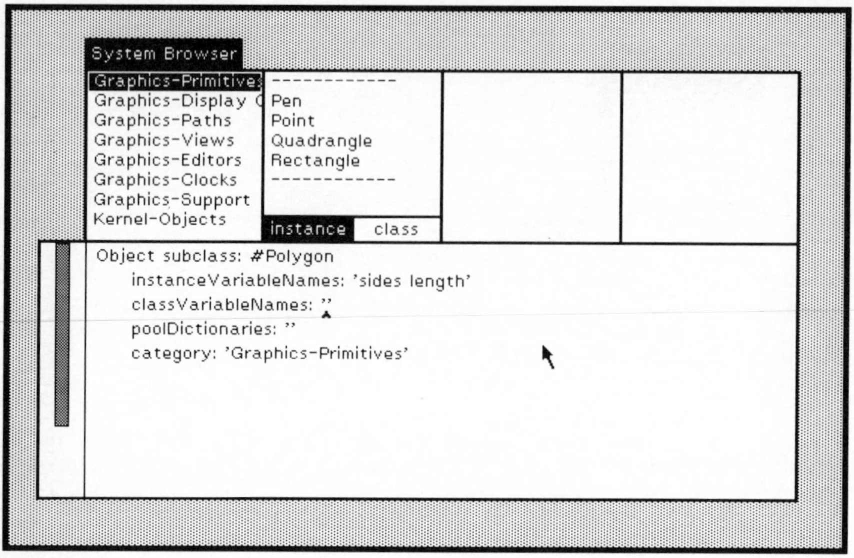

Figure 13

of two variables representing the number (**sides**) and length of the sides (**length**) of a polygon.

From a pop-up menu representing messages to the code editor, the item **accept** (meaning "compile") is chosen (Figure 14). When the new class is successfully defined, its name is displayed in the menu in the second subview (Figure 15). In this way, user-defined classes can be examined and modified in the same way as system classes.

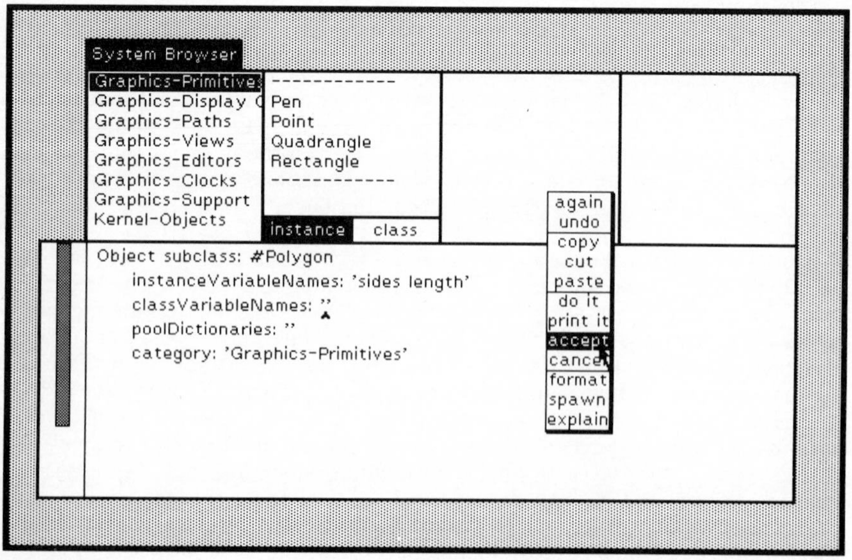

Figure 14

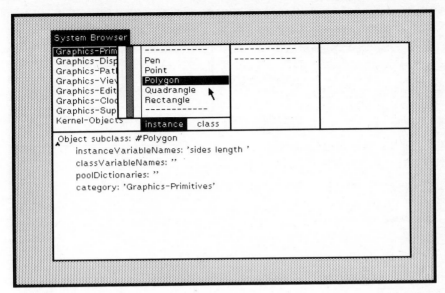

Figure 15

Similarly, a template for defining new methods is provided whenever a message protocol is selected but no messages are selected. To define a new method, a message protocol is first specified by selecting the menu command **add protocol** (Figure 16a). A prompter appears in which the protocol name is typed (Figure 16b). The new protocol is selected and the method template appears (Figure 16c). This template is edited to specify the three parts of a

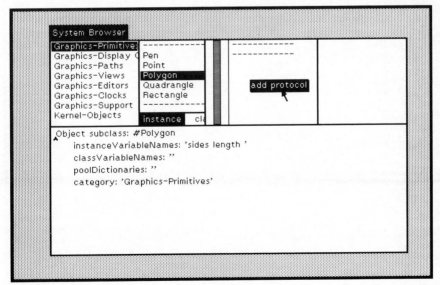

(a)

Figure 16

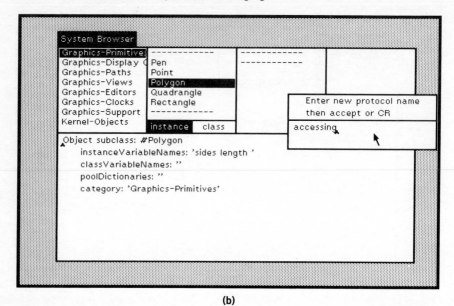

(b)

Figure 16 *(continued)*   **(c)**

method: the message pattern, comment about intended role of the message, and statements that implement the behavior of the message. By choosing the pop-up menu item **accept**, the method is compiled (Figure 16*d*). The Smalltalk-80 system uses an incremental compilation approach to the development of class descriptions. When the new message is successfully compiled, its name is displayed in the rightmost subview of message selectors (Figure 16*e*).

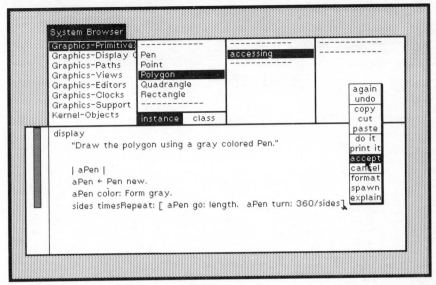

(d)

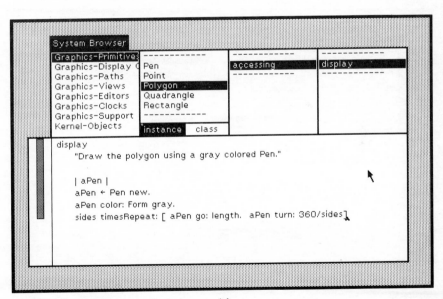

Figure 16 *(continued)*   **(e)**

4.4 Notification and Handling of Errors

4.4.1 Syntax errors If there is a syntax error when a method is compiled, the error is displayed in reverse video adjacent to the point at which the error was found. The user can then edit the text in order to make a correction. The method shown in Figure 17a has a syntax error in that an argument to the message **at:put:** is omitted. The attempt to compile this method causes an

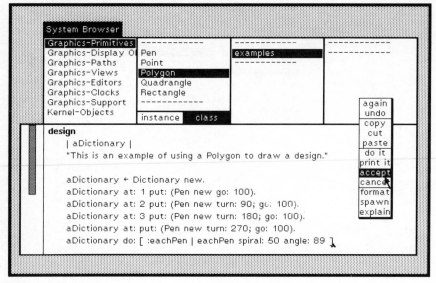

(a)

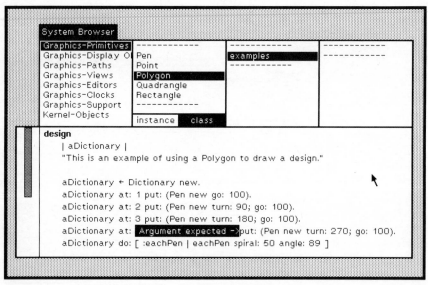

Figure 17   (b)

appropriate notification to be inserted in the text after the keyword **at:**, as shown in Figure 17b.

4.4.2 Spelling correction   A reason why a method might not compile correctly is that a message selector is not recognized or an undeclared variable name is used. The reason for the error might be that that user mistyped a keyword or a variable name. The Smalltalk-80 system includes a spelling

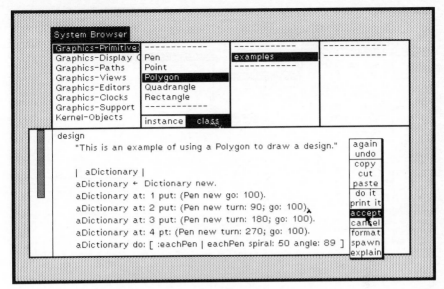

(a)

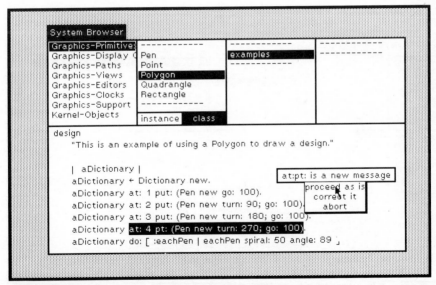

Figure 18   **(b)**

corrector that is capable of assisting the user in determining correct spellings. The method shown in Figure 18*a* includes the message **at:pt:** which was not recognized. When the user tries to compile this method, a pop-up menu appears (Figure 18*b*). This menu informs the user that there is an incorrect message selector in the method.

The user can choose to proceed as is (because the message will be defined later), to abort so that the text editor can be used to make a correction, or to

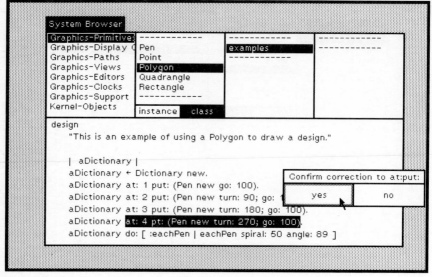

(c)

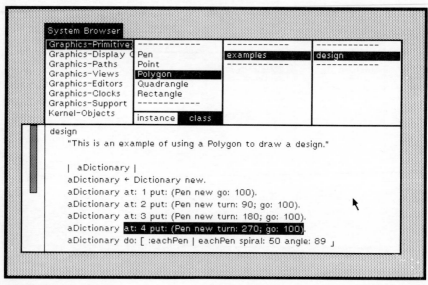

Figure 18 *(continued)*   **(d)**

get help from the system to correct the error. The system guesses a correct message selector and proposes it to the user (Figure 18*c*). The proposed correction is presented in a "binary-choice menu" (these menus are also called "confirmers"). If the user chooses the item **yes** in this menu, the text of the method is changed by the system and the attempt to compile the method proceeds (Figure 18*d*).

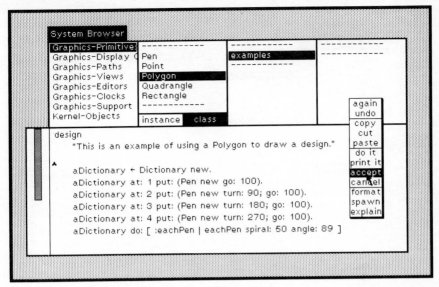

(a)

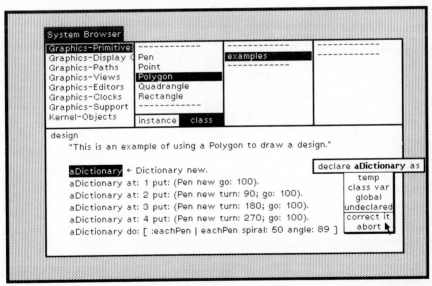

Figure 19   **(b)**

If the method includes an undeclared variable (Figure 19*a*), a menu appears (Figure 19*b*). This menu asks the user to declare the variable as either a variable known only to the method (a temporary variable), known only to instances of the class (an instance variable), known to all instances of the class (a class variable), or known to all objects (a global variable). The user can choose to abort in order to use the text editor to correct the error. Or the

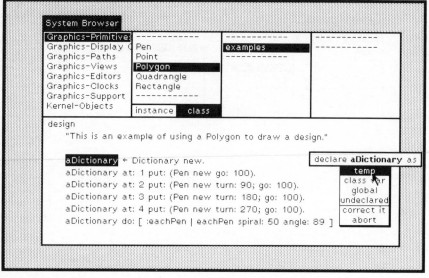

(c)

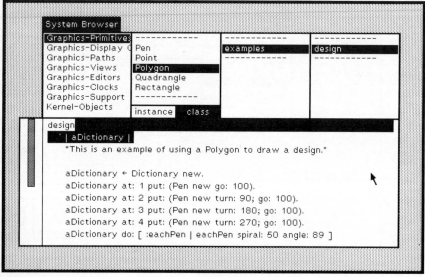

Figure 19   (*continued*)   (d)

user can choose to get help from the system to correct the error; the system checks to see if the variable name is like any variables within the context of the method and then proposes a change, if it can. In the example, the undeclared variable should be declared as a temporary variable of the method. By choosing the menu item **temp** (Figure 19*c*), the declaration is automatically inserted into the method and the method is successfully compiled (Figure 19*d*).

4.4.3 Runtime errors The syntax of the Smalltalk-80 programming language is very simple. Errors found at runtime typically take the form of a message being sent to an object, but the message is not in the protocol of that object. When an error is encountered, the process in which the error occurred is suspended and a view of that process is created. A process in the Smalltalk-80 system is itself an object whose internal state can be inspected. Suspended processes can be viewed in two ways, with *notifiers* and with *debuggers*. A notifier provides a simple description of the process at the time of the error. A debugger provides a more detailed view in which it is possible to change the state of the suspended process before resuming it.

Suppose an instance of the new class **Polygon** is sent the message **display**. And further suppose that the method associated with the message **display** consists of sending messages to a gray colored line-drawing object (an instance of a **Pen**). The example method is shown in Figure 20. (Note that this method differs from that of Figure 14.)

In this example, sending the message **display** to an instance of **Polygon** results in an error. The process representing the sending of the message (a "message-send") is suspended and viewed with a notifier. This notifier is shown in Figure 21.

The cause of the error is shown at the top of the notifier view. Within the view are several lines indicating the sequence of messages that were sent (initiated) before the error occurred, but which were not completed. These lines indicate part of the state of the suspended process. From the notifier, it is possible for the Smalltalk-80 programmer to see that an instance of class **Form** was sent the message **grey**, which **Forms** do not understand.

4.4.4 Debugging A debugger is a view of a suspended process that reveals more detail than provided by a notifier. The user can select the menu item **debug** in a menu associated with the notifier. The notifier is then replaced

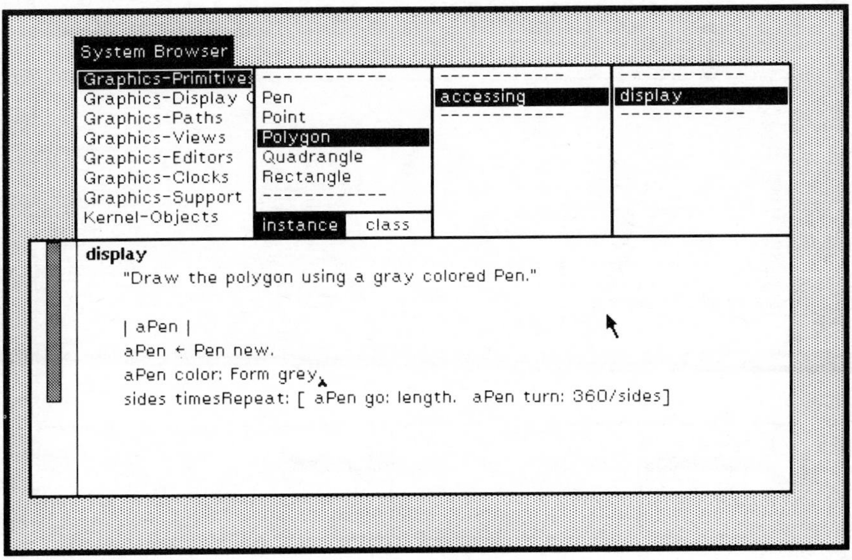

Figure 20

Figure 21

with a debugger. The debugger for the error shown in Figure 21 is presented in Figure 22.

The debugger has six subviews. The top subview is a list of each message that was sent, but whose response was not yet completed before the error interrupt occurred. By choosing one of these messages, the corresponding method can be viewed in the next subview. This view is the same as the one available in the text subview of a system browser. The text can be edited and the method recompiled. When a method is displayed, the last message sent before the

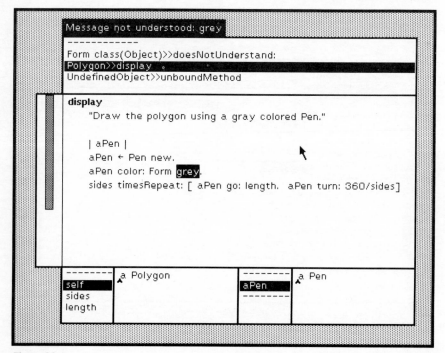

Figure 22

process was suspended is shown in reverse video. This focuses the programmer's attention directly at the location of the problem. The programmer can choose each message, in sequence, in order to explore the context of each previous message.

The lower four subviews of the debugger are used to examine the values of the variables used in the method. They function like two inspector views. The leftmost two subviews make up an inspector for the message receiver of the currently selected, interrupted message. The rightmost two subviews make up an inspector for the interrupted process. Its menu displays the message argument names and the variables declared as part of the method (that is, the temporary variables that only exist for the purposes of executing the method).

When the source of the runtime error is determined, the method can be edited and recompiled within the debugger subview. It is not necessary to return to a system browser and locate the method to be modified. Each kind of view provides a different way of accessing the same class descriptions. In addition, the debugger supports single-stepping through the messages so that the programmer can trace the behavior of a process in the system.

In the case of the example, the source of the error is the spelling of the message **grey**—which should be **gray**. The text edit can be made in the debugger text subview, and then a request to compile the method can be made. After successful compilation, the message **display** to **Polygon** is placed at the top of the menu of message-sends, and it is selected. The programmer can then choose a command to resend the selected message.

4.5 Other Browser Queries and Other Browsers

The previous examples illustrated the ways in which objects can be viewed and examined. The object- and message-orientation of the Smalltalk-80 system suggested these viewing possibilities. The kinds of queries that can be made are basically the ones a programmer must be able to make to determine the structure of the system. The system browser as the program editing interface provides the framework for both the incremental development of class descriptions as well as the context for accessing information about classes. In addition to the capabilities already shown, it is possible to modify the class and message organizations, to determine the inherited variables of a class, to file out or to pretty print all or part of a class description, to see a formatted list of a class's position in the class hierarchy (as shown in Figure 23a and b), and to obtain a browser for the classes in the hierarchy of a particular class (as shown in Figure 24a and b).

Each new class added to the system by the programmer is accessible via a browser and can be queried in the same way as all system-provided classes. In addition, the system classes include those representing views and techniques for interacting with views (controllers). Using instances of these classes, the programmer can create new kinds of browsers that present only a subset of the available system. This provides a way to concentrate attention on a particular set of classes or a way to filter information. Also, as shown by the several ways in which a method can be accessed for editing and recompilation purposes, the system supports linking several views to the same information, and handling the problem of maintaining updates to all views when the information is edited in one of them.

4.5.1 File list view Browsers are used in a variety of other ways in the Smalltalk-80 system. For example, a browser is used to access an external file

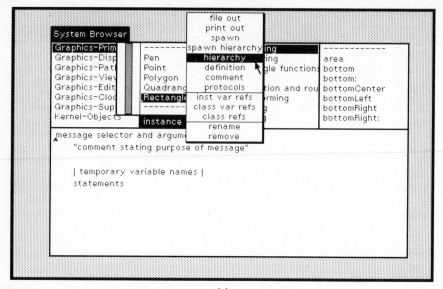

(a)

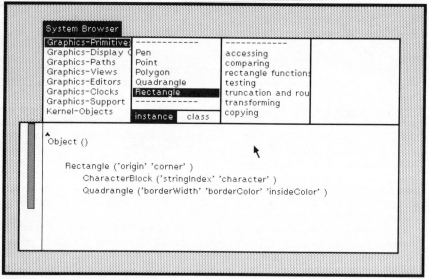

Figure 23   **(b)**

system. This kind of browser is illustrated in Figure 25. It consists of three subviews. In the top view, the user types a pattern for the file names (* means match anything). Upon issuing the command **accept** found in a pop-up menu associated with the top view, the second view displays a menu of the file names that matched the pattern. If a file name is selected, its contents can be read and edited in the bottom view. Files located on either local or remote file servers can be accessed in this way.

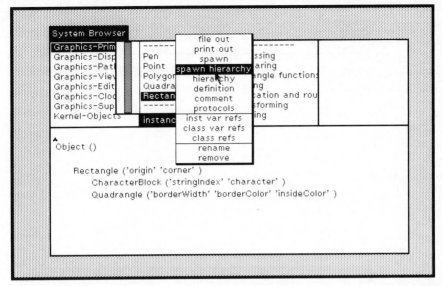

(a)

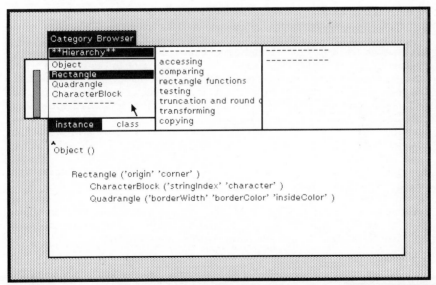

Figure 24   (b)

Applications packages developed in the Smalltalk-80 system make use of browsers, for example, to browse electronic mail. Various studies have been carried out to browse an on-line policy manual, a telephone directory, a database of publication abstracts, and a database about product information. In this last study, we used a product database that was market-oriented; one of the purposes of the browser was to help the user learn how to relate product features to customer needs. Another example, of browsing a history textbook, can be found in [Weyer, 1982].

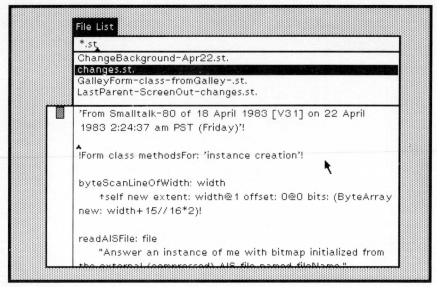

Figure 25

4.5.2　Change management　The actions taken by the user of the Smalltalk-80 system are saved in two ways: in an internally-maintained set of references to class and method changes, and on an external file containing descriptions of each change and each evaluation. The user can refer to the internal set of changes to determine the additions that have been made to the system since the beginning of a work session. This set can be used for identifying class and method descriptions to be saved on an external file to be shared with other Smalltalk-80 programmers. A browser for viewing the set of changes looks just like, and provides the same functionality as, a message-set browser. The external change file is used primarily to recover from system crashes. The file is an ordered audit trail. The user can create a browser on the file. Commands in pop-up menus associated with this browser allow the user to explore the changes file and to selectively (re-)evaluate expressions and definitions. Multiple changes files can be viewed using the browser, so that the work of several people can be viewed and combined. The browser also supports the ability to analyze whether the definitions being viewed conflict in the sense that there are several different definitions of the same class or method.

4.5.3　Version management　The interface to the Smalltalk-80 system version handler is also handled using browsers [Putz, 1983]. The central feature of the Smalltalk-80 development support is a network-based database containing information about past and proposed changes to the system, as well as bug reports and an informal library of application subsystems. This database supports documentation of system changes and system release versions, documentation of known bugs and other problems, and cross referencing between related entries in the database (for example, bug reports and their corresponding bug fixes). A browser is used to explore, add to, and edit the database.

　There are actually three different browsers that filter information from the database: version browser, new feature browser, and bug report browser. An example version browser is shown in Figure 26. It consists of two subviews.

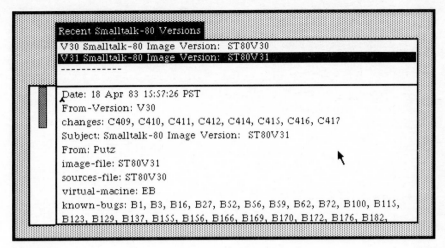

Figure 26

The top subview is a menu of dated versions. When a version is selected, the bottom subview displays a message indicating the date, originator, references to changes (for example, C409) that were added to a previous version, reference to the "parent" version, references to bugs still in the version (for example, B1), and the names of the external files needed to access the version. The version browser supports the user in examining the changes introduced in the currently selected version of the system, the changes submitted but not included (referred to as "goodies"), remaining known bugs, and the known bugs for which fixes can be retrieved but are not as yet incorporated into the system. Each of these options is presented in a menu associated with the top subview of the version browser; each results in a different browser that presents the requested information. Bug fixes might conflict in the sense that they change the same methods; the system includes a mechanism for checking a set of fixes for conflicts, leaving it up to the programmer to resolve the differences. Using the browser, the programmer can select the version of the system with which he or she prefers to work.

The browser in Figure 27 was created by asking to see all the known bugs in the version of the system currently being used. The numbers in the top subview correspond to those cross-referenced in the version browser.

The browser in Figure 28 is for "goodies"—new ideas for the system contributed by anyone with access to the electronic mail network. If the user likes the description of the goodie and wants to try it, then choosing a command from a pop-up menu associated with the top subview requests that the appropriate class descriptions and new methods be brought into the system. The programmer of the goodie and the name of the source file for obtaining the necessary information is listed in the text subview of this browser.

Different browsers are used for submitting bug reports or fixes or goodies, and for composing a new version of the system. The bug report and bug fix browser is a modification of an electronic mail retrieval browser. The user can browse for a reported bug and then fill out a form that documents the proposed bug fix. The bug fix is added to the database when the user selects a command from the pop-up menu associated with the browser. Cross referencing to the bug report is done automatically. If there is no bug report selected, then there will be no cross reference.

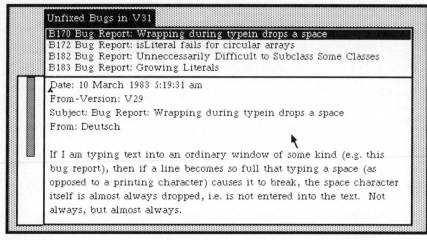

Figure 27

New versions are created by selecting from a menu of submitted system changes (bug fixes or goodies) in order to compose a list of changes. These changes can be analyzed to see if there are any conflicts. We have chosen to design the release system so that there is a set of versions and "interim" versions so that any programmer can create a proposed version for people to try out. This is useful especially when a major user interface idea is to be tested before official distribution.

5. A "FRIENDLY" LANGUAGE OF INTERACTION

The particular style of a programming environment and the choice of tools provided in the environment depend somewhat on the number of programmers to be supported in the system. The focus of the Smalltalk-80 programming

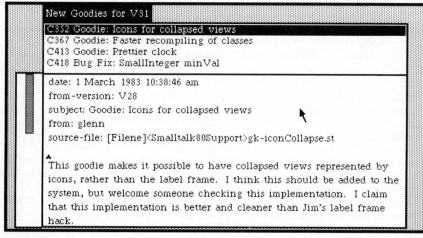

Figure 28

environment is to support a single person's efforts. There is an emphasis on programming by plugging together instances of existing classes or by refining existing classes. Each of these are ways of giving the single person the benefit of the efforts of many programmers. The long-term, anticipated use of a Smalltalk-like system is that a novice will be able to get started easily and be able to develop simple things right away. Hence there is an emphasis on developing a simple-to-learn user interface that is uniform across functionality, so that it is not necessary to learn many different ways of doing similar things. The modularity of the object-oriented system facilitates shared use of functionality. For example, the same text editor is used wherever text editing is available. And most editors feature the availability of *undo* mechanisms or user confirmation before carrying out destructive requests. Because novices and even experts tend to forget explicit backup of their work, the system automatically maintains an audit trail of messages sent; it is possible to re-send these messages in order to recover user actions that took place up to the point of any crash. As noted earlier, there is also an emphasis on documentation for each class and each method.

The user and the Smalltalk-80 programming environment interact through a bitmapped display screen, a keyboard, and a pointing device. As stated earlier, the display is used to present graphical and textual views of information to the user. The keyboard is used to present textual information to the system. The pointing device is used to select information on the display screen. The Smalltalk-80 system uses a pointing device called a *mouse*. A *cursor* on the screen shows the location currently being pointed by by the mouse. The cursor is moved by moving the mouse over a flat surface. The mouse has buttons on it which are used to make different kinds of selections and to obtain pop-up menus.

The user interface, as described in previous sections, is based on an information storage and retrieval model, where the information is uniformly represented as objects. Actions to be taken are indicated by selecting from menus of items denoting messages to objects. Selection is done by placing the cursor over the desired menu item and pressing a button on the mouse. Alternatively, the menu is obtained by pressing a button on the mouse; the cursor is moved to the desired item without releasing the button; and then the button is released in order to indicate selection is complete. The basic idea is to let the user point to a visible menu item, rather than have to remember a command that must be typed on the keyboard.

Most editors in the Smalltalk-80 system are designed to be non-preemptive. That is, the user points to an area where something should happen, selects that area, and then chooses an operation from a menu. Simply by pointing to another area, the user can signal a change of mind about what actions to take. This non-preemptive form of moving about the system, issuing commands (that is, sending messages), is typical of the user's interactions with the system. For example, a user can change the view to be worked with simply by moving the cursor to a new view and pressing a mouse button to select the new view.

The cursor can take on a variety of shapes in order to provide additional visual feedback to the user. Generally the cursor has an arrow shape. Whenever the system must preempt the user, perhaps because it takes significant time to respond to the user's request, the cursor takes on the shape of an arrow with a star or the shape of a timer to indicate that the user must wait.

The user interface concepts of pointing to make a selection and non-preemptive control are two ways in which the Smalltalk-80 system attempts to provide a supportive interface between the visual presentation of the language and the way the user must physically indicate what actions should take place.

REFERENCES

[Althoff 1981] J. Althoff. Building data structures in the Smalltalk-80 system. *Byte.* (August 1981), 230–278.

[Borning and Ingalls 1982a] A. Borning, D. Ingalls. A type declaration and inference system for Smalltalk. *Proceedings of the Ninth Annual ACM Principles of Programming Languages Symposium,* Albuquerque, New Mexico, January 1982.

[Borning and Ingalls 1982b] A. Borning, D. Ingalls. Multiple inheritance in Smalltalk-80. *Proceedings of the National Conference on Artificial Intelligence,* Pittsburgh, Pennsylvania, August 1982.

[Deutsch 1981] P. Deutsch. Building control structures in the Smalltalk-80 system. *Byte.* (August 1981), 322–346.

[Goldberg. 1983] A. Goldberg. *Smalltalk-80: The Interactive Programming Environment,* Addison-Wesley, 1983.

[Goldberg and Robson 1983] A. Goldberg, D. Robson. *Smalltalk-80: The Language and Its Implementation,* Addison-Wesley, 1983.

[Krasner 1983] G. Krasner (ed.) *Smalltalk-80: Bits of History, Words of Advice,* Addison-Wesley, 1983.

[Putz 1983] S. Putz. Managing the evolution of Smalltalk. In G. Krasner (ed.) *Smalltalk-80: Bits of History, Words of Advice,* Addison-Wesley, 1983.

[Suzuki 1981] N. Suzuki. Inferring types in Smalltalk. *Proceedings of the Eighth Annual ACM Principles of Programming Languages Symposium,* Williamsburg, Virginia, January 1981.

[Weyer 1982] S. Weyer. *Searching for information in a dynamic book.* Xerox Palo Alto Research Center, Report No. SCG-82-1, Palo Alto, California, February 1982.

9 The UNIX Programming Environment

BRIAN W. KERNIGHAN

Bell Laboratories
Murray Hill, New Jersey

JOHN R. MASHEY

Bell Laboratories
Whippany, New Jersey

The UNIX* operating system provides an especially congenial programming environment, in which it is not only possible, but actually natural, to write programs quickly and well.

Several characteristics of the UNIX system contribute to this desirable state of affairs. Files have no type or internal structure, so data produced by one program can be used by another without impediment. The basic system interface for input and output provides homogeneous treatment of files, I/O devices and programs, so programs need not care where their data comes from or goes to. The command interpreter makes it convenient to connect programs, by arranging for data communications.

Complex procedures are created not by writing large programs from scratch, but by interconnecting relatively small components. These programs are small and concentrate on single functions, and therefore are easy to build, understand, describe, and maintain. They form a high level toolkit whose existence causes programmers to view their work as the use and creation of tools, a viewpoint that encourages growth in place of reinvention.

Tools interact in a limited number of ways, but can be used in many different combinations. Thus, an addition to the toolkit tends to improve the programming power of the user faster than it

---

© 1981 IEEE. Reprinted with permission from *Computer*, 14:4 (April 1981), pp. 25-34. Adapted from a paper originally published in *Software—Practice and Experience*, 9:1 (January 1979), reproduced by permission from John Wiley & Sons.

*UNIX is a trademark of Bell Laboratories.

increases the complexity of interconnection and maintenance. Finally, tools are connected at a very high level by a powerful command languager interpreter. The error-prone and expensive process of program writing can often be avoided in favor of program-using.

In this paper we will present a variety of examples to illustrate this methodology, focusing on those aspects of the system and supporting software which make it possible.

1. INTRODUCTION

Software stands between the user and the machine.
—HARLAN D. MILLS

There is more than a grain of truth in this remark. Many operating systems do some things well, but seem to spend a substantial fraction of their resources interfering with their users. They are often clumsy and awkward, presenting major obstacles to getting a job done.

Things needn't be that way. For over eight years, we have used the UNIX operating system and have found it helpful, productive, and a pleasure to use.

We are not the only ones who feel this way. Although the basic UNIX system was literally developed in a year by two people working in an attic, and has, until recently, been available only as an unsupported package, the benefits it provides are so compelling that over 3000 UNIX systems are now in place around the world. At Bell Laboratories, UNIX systems provide more time-sharing ports than all other systems combined. These ports are accessed by thousands of people; many use them on a daily basis. UNIX has spawned a host of offshoots—at least six companies[1] offer or plan to offer systems derived from or compatible with the UNIX system, for processors ranging from microprocessors to large mainframes.

In this article we describe what appears to be a new way of computing. We emphasize those things that are unique, particularly well done, or especially good for productivity. We also discuss aspects of the system that have changed our view of the programming process itself and draw some lessons that may be valuable to future implementors of operating systems.

Neither of us was involved with the development of the UNIX system, although we have contributed applications software. We describe the system from the user's viewpoint, based on our own experiences and those of the large community of users with whom we have been involved. This is a valid perspective because good systems have many more users than developers. (A developer's retrospective can be found in [Ritchie 1978].)

2. FILE SYSTEM AND INPUT/OUTPUT

File system structure As any operating system should, UNIX provides facilities for running programs and a file system for managing information. The basic structure of the file system is fairly conventional—there is a rooted tree in which each interior node is a directory (that is, a list of files and directories),

---

[1] Cromemco, Onyx, Yourdon, Whitesmiths, Amdahl, and Wollongong Group.

and each leaf is either a file or a directory (see Figure 1). Any file can be accessed by its name, either relative to the current directory or by a full path name that specifies its absolute position in the hierarchy. Users can change their current directory to any position in the hierarchy. A protection mechanism prevents unauthorized access to files.

Several design choices increase the uniformity of the file system by minimizing irrelevant distinctions and arbitrary special cases. These choices permit programs that access the file system to be substantially simpler and smaller than they would be if this regularity were absent.

First, *directories are files*. The only distinction between a directory and an ordinary file is that the system reserves to itself the right to alter the contents of a directory. This is necessary because directories contain information about the physical structure of the file system. Since directories are files, they can be read (subject to the normal permission mechanism) just as ordinary files can. This implies that programs such as the directory lister are in no sense special. They read information that has a particular format, but they are not system programs.

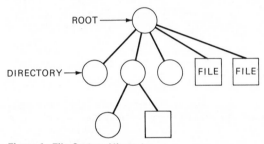

Figure 1. File System Hierarchy.

In many systems, programs like directory listers are believed to be (and often are) part of the operating system. In the UNIX system, they are not. One of the distinguishing characteristics of UNIX is the degree to which this and similar "system" functions are implemented as ordinary user programs. This approach has significant benefits: it reduces the number of programs that must be maintained by system programmers, it makes modification easier and safer, and it increases the probability that a dissatisfied user will rewrite (and perhaps improve) the program.

The next aspect of the file system is critical: *a file is just a sequence of bytes*. As far as the file system is concerned, a file has no internal structure; it is a featureless, contiguous array of bytes. In fact, a file is better described by the attributes it lacks.

• There are no tracks or cylinders; the system conceals the physical characteristics of devices instead of flaunting them.

• There are no physical or logical records or associated counts; the only bytes in a file are the ones put there by the user.

• Since there are no records, there is no fixed/variable length distinction and no blocking.

• There is no preallocation of file space; a file is as big as it needs to be. If another byte is written at the end of a file, the file is one byte bigger.

• There is no distinction between random and sequential access; the bytes of a file are accessible in any order.

- There are neither file types for different kinds of data nor any access methods; all files are identical in form.
- There is no user-controlled buffering; the system buffers all I/O itself.

Although these may seem like grave deficiencies, in fact, they are major contributions to the effectiveness of the system. The file system strives to hide the idiosyncrasies of particular devices upon which files reside, so all files can look alike.

It should not be inferred from the foregoing that files do not have structure. Certain programs do write data in particular forms for the benefit of people or other programs. For example, the assembler creates object files in the form expected by the loader, the system itself uses a well-defined layout for the contents of a directory, and most programs that manipulate textual information treat it as a stream of characters with each line terminated by a newline character. But these structures are imposed by the programs, not by the operating system.

Programming interface   Seven functions comprise the programmer's primary interface to the file system: OPEN, CREATE, READ, WRITE, SEEK, CLOSE, and UNLINK. These functions are direct entries into the operating system.

To access a file, OPEN or CREATE must be used:

```
FD = OPEN(FILENAME, MODE)

FD = CREATE(FILENAME, MODE)
```

OPEN opens FILENAME for reading, writing, or both, depending on mode. FILENAME is simply the name of the file in the file system—a string of characters. CREATE also opens a file, but truncates it to zero length for rewriting, in case it already exists. It does not complain if the file already exists.

Both OPEN and CREATE return a file descriptor, a small positive integer that serves thereafter as the connection between the file and I/O calls in the program. (A negative return indicates an error of some sort.) The file descriptor is the only connection; there are no data control blocks in the user's address space.

Actual input and output are done with READ and WRITE.

```
N_RECEIVED = READ(FD, BUF, N)

N_WRITTEN = WRITE(FD, BUF, N)
```

Both calls request the transfer of N bytes to or from the buffer BUF in the user's program from or to the file specified by FD; N can have any positive value.

Both READ and WRITE return the number of bytes actually transferred. This can be less than N, when, for example, the system reads a file whose size is not a multiple of N bytes. A return of zero on reading signals the end of file.

As far as a user program is concerned, input and output are synchronous and take place in chunks of whatever size is requested. The system handles buffering and blocking into proper sizes for physical devices. Not only does this simplify user programs, it converts the haphazard suboptimizations of individual user programs into global optimization across the entire set of active programs. For example, the system handles queues of disk requests so that disk head motion and rotational delays are minimized. In many applications, this approach actually improves disk performance, which is often more critical than CPU performance. Such global optimization aids adaptation to both changes in disk configuration and the increasingly common use of larger, but fewer, disks per system.

I/O is normally sequential, that is, each command continues where the preceding one left off. This default may be changed by the call SEEK.

```
SEEK(FD, POSITION, RELATIVE_TO)
```

This requests that the pointer for the next read or write be set to the byte specified by POSITION, relative to the beginning, current position, or end as specified by RELATIVE_TO. Thus, SEEK provides a convenient random access capability.

Finally, the function CLOSE(FD) breaks the connection between a file descriptor and an open file; UNLINK(NAME) removes the file from the file system.

Given this interface, many programs become simple indeed. For example, here is the executable part of a program COPY that copies one file to another, written in the C programming language [Ritchie et al. 1978] [Kernighan and Ritchie 1978].

```
FIN = OPEN(NAME1, READMODE);

FOUT = CREATE(NAME2, WRITEMODE);

WHILE((N = READ(FIN, BUF, SIZEOF BUF))>0)
        WRITE(FOUT, BUF, N);
```

The buffer BUF may be of any convenient size. The file names NAME1 and NAME2 are character strings, typically set from the command line when the program is executed. Another half-dozen lines of declarations make this into a complete program that will copy any file to any other file.

Input/output devices   The interface described above applies to all files. This goes further than might be expected, for all peripheral devices are also files in the file system. Disks, tapes, terminals, communications links, the memory, and the telephone system all have entries in the file system. When a program tries to open one, however, the system brings into execution the proper driver for the device, and subsequent I/O goes through that driver. The I/O device files all reside in one directory for convenient administration, and they can be distinguished from ordinary files by the rare programs that need to do so. In general, however, considerations specific to particular devices are pushed out into the device drivers where they belong, and user programs need know nothing about them. The file system conceals the physical peculiarities of devices instead of making them visible.

From the programmer's standpoint, the homogeneity of files and peripheral devices is a considerable simplification. For example, the file copy program COPY that we wrote in the previous section could be invoked as

```
COPY FILE1 FILE2
```

to copy the contents of FILE1 to FILE2. But the files can be devices, so

```
COPY DEVICE/TAPE DEVICE/PRINTER
```

copies the magnetic tape onto the printer, and

```
COPY DEVICE/PHONE DEVICE/TERMINAL
```

reads data from the telephone onto a user's terminal. The program copy is in all cases identical to the four lines of C we wrote above. The COPY program need not concern itself with any special characteristics of files, tape drives, printers, terminals, or telephones, for these are all concealed by the system. COPY only has to copy data, and accordingly is much simpler than it would be if it had to cope with a host of different devices and file types. It is also much simpler to have one COPY program instead of a host of different "utility" programs corresponding to the host of different possible copying operations.

As another instance of the value of integrating I/O devices into the file system, interuser communication by the WRITE command is trivial. Since a user's terminal is a file, no special mechanism is needed to write on it. Unwanted messages can be prevented merely by changing the permissions on the terminal, to make it impossible for others to write on it.

Simplicity is achieved by the elimination of special cases, such as discrimination between devices and files.

3. THE USER INTERFACE

Running programs   When a user logs into a UNIX system, a command interpreter called the shell [Thompson 1975] [Bourne 1978b] accepts commands from the terminal and interprets them as requests to run programs. The form is as suggested above: a progam name, perhaps followed by a list of blank-separated arguments that are made available to the program. For example, the command

```
DATE
```

prints

```
WED OCT 28 09:45:24 EST 1981
```

The program name is simply the name of a file in the file system; if the file exists and is executable, it is loaded as a program. There is no distinction between a "system" program like DATE and one written by an ordinary user for private use, except that system programs reside in a known place for administrative convenience. Commonly used programs such as DATE are kept in one or two directories, and the shell searches these directories if it fails to find the program in the user's own directory. (It is even possible to replace the shell's default search path with one's own.) Installing a new program requires only copying it into this directory:

```
COPY COPY COMMAND/COPY
```

installs COPY from the current directory as the new system version in /COMMAND.

Filename shorthand   A typical UNIX system lives and breathes with file system activity. Most users tend to have a large number of small files; the Bell Labs system used for computing science research, for example, has about 45,000 files for about 50 active users. The average file size is about 10,000 bytes, but the median is much smaller.

Most programs accept a list of file names as parameters; lists are often quite long. For example, here is a listing of a directory.

```
ADDSET.C        TEMP1
COMMON          TEMP2
DODASH.C        TEMP3
ESC.C           TEMP4
FILSET.C        TEMP5
GETCODE         TRANSLIT.C
MAKSET.C        XINDEX.C
TEMP            XLATE.A
```

The names that end in .C are C source programs (a convention, not a requirement of the operating system). To print all these files with the command PR, one could say

```
PR ADDSET.C DODASH.C ESC.C FILSET. MAKSET.C TRANSLIT.C XINDEX.C
```

but this is obviously a nuisance and impossible to get right the first time. The shell, however, provides a shorthand. In the command

```
PR *.C
```

the character * is interpreted by the shell as "match anything." The current directory is searched for names that (in this case) end in .C, and the expanded list of names is handed to PR; PR is unaware of the expansion.

The shell also recognizes other pattern-matching characters, less frequently used than *. For example,

```
RM TEMP[1-5]
```

removes TEMP1 through TEMP5 but does not touch TEMP.

Filename shorthand is invaluable. It greatly reduces the number of errors in which a long list is botched or a name omitted, it encourages systematic naming of files, and it makes it possible to process sets of files as easily as single ones. Incorporating the mechanism into the shell is more efficient than duplicating it everywhere and ensures that it is available to all programs in a uniform way.

Input/output redirection   As we mentioned earlier, the user's terminal is just another file in the file system. Terminal I/O is so common, however, that by convention the command interpreter opens file descriptors 0 and 1 for reading and writing the user's terminal before executing a program. In this way, a program that intends only to read and write the terminal need not use OPEN or CLOSE.

The command interpreter can also be instructed to change the assignment of input or output to a file before executing a program.

```
PROGRAM <IN >OUT
```

instructs the shell to arrange that PROGRAM take its input from IN and place its output on OUT; PROGRAM itself is unaware of the change.

The program LS produces a listing of files in the current directory, redirecting the output with

```
LS >FILELIST
```

which collects the list in a file. The program WHO prints a list of currently logged-on users, one per line.

```
WHO >USERLIST
```

produces the same list in the file USERLIST. If the file named after > exists, it is overwritten, but it is also possible to append instead of replace:

```
WHO >>USERLIST
```

appends the new information to the end of USERLIST.
    The text editor is called E;

```
E <SCRIPT
```

runs it from a script of previously prepared editing commands.
    These examples have been chosen advisedly. On many systems, this set of operations is impossible because in each case the corresponding program firmly believes that it should read or write the terminal, and there is no way to alter this assumption. On other systems, it is possible, but difficult, to perform the redirection. It is not enough, however, for a procedure to be just barely possible; it must be easy. The < and > notation is easy and natural.
    Again, observe that the facility is provided by the command interpreter, not by individual programs. In this way, it is universally available without prearrangement.

Tools   One of the most productive aspects of the UNIX environment is its provision of a rich set of small, generally useful programs—tools—for helping with day-to-day computing tasks. The programs shown below are among the more useful. We will use them to illustrate other points in later sections of the article.

```
WC FILES ...
 Count lines, words, and characters in files.
PR FILES ...
 Print files with headings, multiple columns, etc.
LPR FILES ...
 Spool files onto line printer.
GREP PATTERN FILES ...
 Print all lines containing pattern.
```

Much of any programmer's work is merely running these and related programs. For example,

```
WC *.C
```

counts a set of C source files;

```
GREP GOTO *.C
```

finds all the GOTOs.

Program connection   Suppose we want to count the number of file names produced by the LS command. Rather than counting by hand or modifying LS to produce a count, we can use two existing programs in combination.

```
LS >FILELIST

WC <FILELIST
```

LS produces one line per file; WC counts the lines.

As another example, consider preparing a multi-column list of the file names on the on-line printer. We use the multi-column capabilities of the PR command and the spooling provided by LPR.

```
LS >FILELIST

PR -4 <FILELIST >TEMP

LPR <TEMP
```

This is an example of separation of function, one of the most characteristic features of UNIX usage. Rather than combining things into one big program that does everything (and probably not too well), one uses separate programs, temporarily connected as needed.

Each program is specialized to one task and accordingly is simpler than it would be if it attempted more. It is unlikely that a directory-listing program could print in multiple columns, and to ask it to also spool for a line printer would be preposterous. Yet the combination of operations is obviously useful, and the natural way to achieve it is by a series connection of three programs.

Pipes   It seems silly to have to use temporary files just to capture the output of one program and direct it into the input of another. The UNIX pipe facility performs exactly this series connection without any need for a temporary file. The pipeline

```
LS | PR -4 | LPR
```

is a command line that performs the same task as the example above. The symbol | tells the shell to create a pipe that connects the standard output of the program on the left to the standard input of the program on the right. Programs connected by a pipe run concurrently, with the system taking care of buffering and synchronization. The programs themselves are oblivious to the I/O redirection. The syntax is again concise and natural; pipes are readily taught to nonprogramming users.

In principle, the pipe notation could be merely a shorthand for the longer form with temporaries. There are, however, significant advantages in running the processes concurrently, with hidden buffers instead of files serving as the data channels. A pipe is not limited to a maximum file size and therefore can cope with an arbitrary amount of data. Also, output from the last command can reach the terminal before the first command receives all of its input—a valuable property when the first command is an interactive program like a desk calculator or editor.

As a rule, most programs neither know nor care that their input or output is associated with a terminal, a file, or a pipe. Commands can be written in the simplest possible way, yet used in a variety of contexts without prearrangement. This would be must less possible if files did not share a common format.

As an example of a production use of program connection, a major application on many UNIX systems is document preparation. Three or four separate programs are used to prepare typical documents: TROFF, the basic formatting program that drives a typesetter; EQN, a preprocessor for TROFF that deals solely with describing mathematical expressions; TBL, a table-formatting program that acts as a preprocessor for both EQN and TROFF; REFER, a program that converts brief citations to complete ones by searching a data base of bibliographic references; PIC, a program that translates a language into commands for drawing simple figures; and a number of postprocesors for TROFF that produce output on various devices. Placing all of these facilities into one typesetting language and program not only would create an absolutely unworkable monster, it would not fit into the limited address space of the PDP-11. As it is, however, each piece is independent enough to be documented and maintained entirely separately. Each is independent of the internal characteristics of the others. Testing and debugging such a sequence of programs is immensely easier than it would be if they were all one, simply because the intermediate states are clearly visible and can be materialized in files at any time.

Since programs can interact, novel interactions spring up. Consider three programs: WHO, which lists the currently logged-on users, one per line; GREP, which searches its input for all occurrences of lines containing a particular pattern; and WC, which counts the lines, words, and characters in its input. Taken individually, each is a useful tool. But consider some combinations:

```
WHO | GREP JOE
```

tells whether JOE is presently logged in,

```
WHO | WC
```

tells how many people are logged in, and

```
WHO | GREP JOE | WC
```

tells how many times JOE is logged in. None of these services requires any programming, just the combination of existing parts.

The knowledge that a program might be a component in a pipeline enforces a certain discipline on its properties. Most programs read and write the standard input and output if it is at all sensible to do so; accordingly, it is easy to investigate their properties by typing at them and watching their responses. Programs tend to have few encrustations and features (WHO will not count its users, or tell you that JOE is logged on). Instead, they concentrate on doing one thing well, and they are designed to interact with other programs; the system provides an easy and elegant way to make the connection. The interconnections are limited not by preconceptions built into the system, but by the users' imaginations.

In this environment, people begin to search for ways to use existing tools instead of laboriously making new ones from scratch. As a trivial example, a colleague needed a rhyming dictionary, sorted so that words ending in "a" come before those ending in "b", and so on. Instead of writing a special SORT or modifying the existing one, he wrote the trivial program REV, which reverses each line of its input. Then

```
REV <DICT | SORT | REV >RHYMINGDICT
```

does the job. Note that REV need only read and write the standard input and output.

Placing a sorting program in a pipeline illustrates another element of design. The pipe notation is so natural that it is well worthwhile to package programs as pipeline elements ("filters") even when, like SORT, they can't actually produce any output until all their input is processed. Recall the uses of GREP: it has appeared as the source for a pipeline, as the sink, and in the middle.

The existence of pipes encourages new designs as well as new connections. For example, a derivative of the editor, called a stream editor, is often used in pipelines, and the shell may well read a stream of dynamically generated commands from a pipe.

Program sizes   The fact that so many tasks can be performed by assemblages of existing progams, perhaps augmented by simple new ones, has led to an interesting phenomenon—the average UNIX program is rather small, measured in lines of source code.

Figure 2 demonstrates this vividly. The number of lines of source in 106 programs, including most of the commonly used commands, but excluding compilers, was counted with WC. The counts have been sorted into increasing order of number of source lines with SORT, converted into a graph with GRAPH, then converted into TROFF commands. The x axis is the number of lines; the y axis is simply the ordinal number of the program.

The median program here is about 250 lines long; the 90th percentile is about 1200 lines. That is, 90 percent of these programs have less than 1200 lines of source code (about 20 pages). Clearly, it is much easier to deal with a 20-page program than a 100-page program.

The programs are written in C, as are essentially all UNIX programs that yield executable code, including the operating system itself. We feel that C itself is another source of high productivity—it is an expressive and versatile

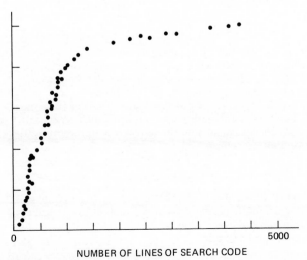

NUMBER OF LINES OF SEARCH CODE

Figure 2. Program Sizes on UNIX.

language, yet efficient enough that there is no compulsion to write assembly language for even the most critical applications.

C is available on a wide variety of machines, and with only modest effort it is possible to write C programs that are *portable*, programs that will compile and run without change on other machines. It is now routine in our environment for programs developed for the UNIX system to be exported unchanged to other systems. There is obviously a considerable gain in productivity in not having to rewrite the same program for each new machine.

Since the operating system itself and all of its software is written in C, it too is portable. The UNIX system itself has been moved from the PDP-11 to, among others, the Interdata 7/32 and 8/32, DEC VAX 11/780, Univac 1100, Amdahl 470/V7, and IBM S/370. From the user's standpoint, these systems are indistinguishable to the point that a command called WHERE, which identifies the current machine, has become widely popular. The original porting of UNIX to the Interdata 8/32 is described by Johnson and Ritchie [Johnson and Ritchie 1978]. Miller describes transporting UNIX to the Interdata 7/32 in an independent experiment [Miller 1978]. There are also UNIX look-alike systems on a variety of microcomputers.

4. AVOIDING PROGRAMMING

The command language   We have already mentioned the basic capabilities of the UNIX shell, which serves as the command interpreter. The critical point is that it is an ordinary user program, not a part of the system [Thompson 1975]. This has several implications: the shell can readily evolve to meet changing requirements and can be replaced by special versions for special purposes on a per-user basis. Perhaps most important, it can be made quite powerful without consuming valuable system space.

Much of the use of the shell is simply to avoid programming. The shell is an ordinary program, so its input can be redirected with <. Thus, if a set of commands are placed in a file, they can be executed just as if they had been typed. The command to do so is

```
SH <CMDFILE
```

(SH is the name of the shell). The file CMDFILE has no special properties or format—it is merely whatever would have been typed on the terminal, but placed in a file instead. Thus, a "catalogued procedure" facility is not a special case, but a natural by-product of the standard I/O mechanism.

This is such a useful capability that several steps have been taken to make it even more valuable. The first is the addition of a limited macro capability. If there are arguments on the command line that invoke the procedure, they are available within the shell procedure.

```
SH CMDFILE ARG1 ARG2 ...
```

It is manifestly a nuisance to have to type SH to run such a sequence of commands; it also creates an artificial distinction between different kinds of programs. Thus, if a file is marked executable but contains text, it is assumed to be a shell procedure and can be run by

```
CMDFILE ARG1 ARG2 ...
```

In this way, CMDFILE becomes indistinguishable from a program written in a conventional language; syntactically and semantically, the user sees no difference whatsoever between a program that has been written in hard code and one that is shell procedure. This is desirable not only for ease of use, but because the implementation of a given command can be changed without affecting anyone.

As a simple example, consider the shell program TEL, which uses GREP to search an ordinary text file, /USR/LIB/TEL, for telephone numbers, names, etc. In its entirety, the procedure is

```
GREP $1 /USR/LIB/TEL
```

$1 stands for the first argument when the command is called; the command

```
TEL BWK
```

produces

```
BRIAN KERNIGHAN (BWK) 6021
```

Since TEL uses the general-purpose pattern finder GREP, not a special program that knows only about telephone directories, the commands TEL 6021, TEL BRIAN, and TEL KERN all produce the same entry.

The shell is actually substantially more powerful than might be inferred from simple examples like TEL. It is a programming language in its own right, with variables, control flow, subroutines (calling other programs), and even interrupt handling. In fact, as the shell has become more powerful and provided more facilities, there has been a steady trend toward writing complicated processes in the shell instead of in C. However, it has remained true that the shell is just an ordinary user program; its input is ordinary text; and a user cannot, by running a program, determine whether or not it is a shell process.

Although the shell resembles a typical procedural language, it has rather different qualities. Most important, in certain ways it is a very high-level language, and as such is far easier to learn, use, and understand than lower-level languages. Shell programs are inherently easier to understand and modify than conventional programs because they are small (usually a handful of lines) and use familiar high-level building blocks.

The shell language is rapidly extensible—users can create new commands on the spur of the moment, and it can be adapted to meet performance requirements without disturbing its user interface. The elements of its language are generally quite independent, that is, changes to most pieces can be made without affecting the others. The shell provides most of the interconnection among programs—the complexity of interaction is linear (or less) because components are so independent of one another. As a result, it is difficult, even for a beginner, to write unmodular shell procedures. Modularity is inherent in the language and occurs without effort or careful planning. The fact that the language has no GOTO statement probably helps.

Usage statistics   The ease with which command language programs can be written has led to a steady growth in their use. This is illustrated by usage figures for a representative system, one of the nine that in 1977 made up the original Programmer's Workbench (PWB/UNIX) installation [Dolotta and Mashey 1976] [Ivie] [Dolotta et al. 1978]. The system served about 350 users, who owned a total of 39,000 files and 2850 directories. The mean file size was about 3700 bytes; the mean number of files per directory was 14. A majority of the people using this system worked on programs to be run on IBM S/370 computers; some worked on software to run on a UNIX system; everyone used the system for documentation and project management activities. Project sizes ranged from one person to about 50.

By 1980, this system had grown to more than 20 machines, including PDP-11s, VAXs, and a part of a Univac 1100, serving a user population of well over 1000.

In 1977, we surveyed command language usage by running a program that searches for shell procedures, records their size distribution, and prints them for visual inspection. We found 2200 shell procedures and only 500 compiled programs; the former is a conservative count, because the search program necessarily misses some files that actually are shell procedures. The shell procedures counted were fairly small, averaging a little over 700 bytes apiece. Examining the distribution of lines per procedure, we found a mean of 29 lines, a median of 12, and a mode of one. In fact, 11.7 percent of all procedures consisted of but a single line. About 45-50 percent of the procedures contained some conditional logic; about half of these (or 20-25 percent of the total) included loops, primarily to perform the same operation on each file in an argument list.

Spot checks in 1980 indicate that programming usage increased since 1977, as it had between 1975 and 1977 [Mashey 1976] [Dolotta and Mashey 1980]. The proportion of shell programs is higher in the more recent period, though the characteristics of individual programs are much the same. One new wrinkle is that it has become common for each user to have a collection of personal commands, a result of the fact that the shell permits users to alter the default search path for finding commands. These personal commands are almost invariably shell programs.

Several conclusions can be drawn. First, people make significant use of shell procedures to customize the general environment to their particular needs, if only to abbreviate straight-line sequences of commands. For example, most one-line procedures consist of a single command (like TEL) or pipeline and are often used to provide fixed argument values to commands that cannot reasonably know correct default values. Thus, commands need not be complicated by special default rules, but can still be quickly customized for local needs. Second, programming goals are accomplished by writing shell procedures rather than compiled programs. Examples include small data-base management packages, procedures to generate complex job control language for other systems, and project management procedures for configuration control, system regeneration, project scheduling, data dictionary management, and interuser communciation. Third, as people become accustomed to this methodology, its use increases with time.

Current programming methodology An unusual programming methodology grows from the combination of a good toolkit of reliable programs that work together, a command language with strong programming features, and the need to manage constant change at reasonable cost.

First, it is often possible to avoid programming completely because some combination of parts from the toolkit can do the job. A spectrum of cooperating utilities like GREP, SORT, and WC goes a long way toward handling many of the simple tasks that occur every programming day. In addition, we are seeing the development of general-purpose data transformers that can convert data from a file or program into some different form for another program. One notable example is SED, the stream-oriented version of the text editor.

Second, if a program is necessary, the initial version can often be written as a shell procedure instead of as a C program. This approach permits a prototype to be built quickly, with minimal investment of time and effort. If it is used a few times and thrown away, no great effort has been expended. Even if a C program is needed, it may well be tiny, performing some simple transformation like the REV program.

Third, almost any program must be continually modified to meet changing requirements, and no amount of initial design work is a complete substitute for actual use. In fact, too much design without experience can lead to a first-class solution to the wrong problem. A program may require a period of rapid and drastic evolution before stabilizing. Modification of a shell procedure is both cheap and reliable, since it is a small object built of generally reliable parts and exists only as a file of editable text. No compilation is necessary, and there are no object modules to maintain and update.

Fourth, once a procedure evolves to an effective, more-or-less stable state, it can be left alone—if it is fast enough for its intended uses, which are by then well known. If it is too slow, it can be entirely rewritten in C, or at least some small, crucial section can be recoded, with the existing version providing a proven functional specification. Deferral of efficiency considerations until the design and the usage patterns have stabilized usually prevents the all too common error of premature optimization.

Capabilities are improved in several ways. A task that recurs frequently may show the clear need for a general-purpose tool; by the time it is written, its requirements are fairly well defined. An existing tool can be upgraded as it is recognized that some change would enhance its usability or performance. Finally, new ways of combining programs can be added to the shell.

The effect of this methodology is to substitute reliable, low-cost programming for unreliable or expensive programmming. The effort required to produce both reliability and efficiency is reserved for code that really requires these attributes. Effort is applied efficiently because accurate requirements are known by the time the code is written.

Although this approach is hardly applicable to all problems, it fits some quite well; serious production systems have been successfully created in this way.

Usage in development projects   Shell programming has been used for years to support programming projects. As one example, one of the authors manages a team of software people, systems engineers, and psychologists in producing a management decision support system now being deployed in the Bell System. Shell procedures are used extensively to help manage the project. The result is a cohesive, integrated, heavily automated environment, used not only by programmers, but by everyone involved in the project, including managers, planners, and end users. Simple procedures exist to control the product, regenerate it from the source code, and even deliver it electronically to remote machines, all without much manual effort. Other procedures are used to avoid repetitive coding by converting skeleton programs or lists of data items into complete C or PL/I programs. Some programs are transformed to become documents, and vice versa, so that people tend to view the system as an integrated data base of project information and procedures, in which the line between software and documentation is quite fuzzy.

Heavily integrated programming environments are proposed often, but few are actually built; fewer still are successful. An irony of the environment described above is that its outward appearance is of a comprehensive, integrated system. In fact, it is made up of just the opposite—small shell procedures and UNIX commands.

This project also illustrates the use of shell procedures in the delivered product. A hybrid mainframe-minicomputer product, it contains about 15K lines of PL/I, 10K lines of C, 30K lines of documentation, and 16K lines of shell. Shell procedures provide most of the user-visible functions. This project's success has often depended on the ability to write something quickly using the shell, obtain user feedback, and adapt it rapidly to fit real needs discovered in the field. In numerous cases, the first version of a program was written quickly and then discarded just as quickly—not because it was slow, but because requirements changed as soon as end users saw the results of those requirements.

5.   UNIX AND MODERN PROGRAMMING METHODOLOGIES

Even though at its birth a system may be clean and easy to use, the natural increase of entropy tends to cause it to grow ugly and unpleasant. Like any other system, UNIX is vulnerable to this process, although so far it has aged gracefully. Fortunately, its creators have always favored taste, restraint, and minimality of construct [Thompson 1975] [Ritchie 1979] [Ritchie 1978] They have maintained a steady pressure to reduce the number of system calls, subroutines, and commands by judicious generalization or by combination of similar constructs.

In some environments, every new construct is hailed as an advance—an expression of the philosophy that more is always better. UNIX developers view additional constructs with suspicion, while greeting with pleasure proof that several existing constructs can be combined and simplified as a result of some new insight. Anything new must prove that it truly deserves a niche in the scheme of things, and it must then hold its place against competition. In the long run, any given niche really has room for but one occupant, so people continually attempt to identify distinct niches and fill them with the fittest competitors.

The capacities of human beings to comprehend, document, and maintain computer software have limits, which must be respected; therefore, redundant and overlapping software must be avoided. It is especially important to maintain simplicity in constructs that are central to everyone's use. No feature is truly free; each has costs as well as benefits, which must be weighed carefully before the feature is included in central progams like the UNIX kernel, the C compiler, the shell, or the text editor.

System evolution   The current UNIX system has evolved through a process resembling Darwinian selection. In the first stage of the cycle (mutation), the "standard" version of the system is used by many people, who inevitably customize it for their local needs. They usually lobby to have their favorite features included in the next standard version. In the second stage (selection and cross-breeding), the next standard version is created and often includes features from the strongest mutants. Meanwhile, the weaker mutants die out, since people tire of supporting unnecessary differences. Although the UNIX system has grown more complex in this process, features usually have been validated in more than one project before inclusion in the standard version.

Programming methodologies can also be selected by first encouraging experimentation, then eliminating the least competitive approaches. No one can afford to swallow the entire deluge of available methodologies, for each addition seems to produce fewer results than its predecessor. Thus, one should pick and choose with care. Although there is no panacea for programming ills,

UNIX usage seems to solve many common problems without bother or new methodologies. There are two reasons for this.

First, the UNIX system supports many approaches in such a natural and pervasive way that people apply them without great effort, often without awareness of the published literature. Second, other approaches are made unnecessary by using the UNIX system in the first place. Some examples follow.

Structured coding is taken for granted, since modern control-flow constructs are provided by C, the shell, and most other language processors used on UNIX systems. The code that people see, adapt, and imitate is usually well structured. People learn to code well in the same way that they learn to speak their native language well, by imitation and immediate feedback.

Formal walk-throughs are used only occasionally on UNIX systems, because people often look at each other's code, comment on it in person and through interuser communication facilities, and take pieces of it for their own use. The ideas of programming teams and egoless programming fit into the UNIX environment well, since they encourage sharing rather than isolation. Although some programs have always been "owned" by one or two people, many others have been passed around so much that it is difficult to tell exactly who wrote them. Programming groups of widely varying personalities exist happily in the UNIX environment; neither chief programmers nor truly egoless ones are common.

Design techniques such as data flow diagrams, pseudo-code, and structure charts are seldom necessary, especially in light of the ease of writing a few short shell procedures to provide the code and documentation for the highest levels of control. For example, Yourdon and Constantine [Yourdon and Constantine 1978] say "...it is definitely true that many UNIX designers (the authors included) do nothing more than program the bubbles in a data flow graph, without the intermediate step of converting it into a structure chart." Certain aspects of the *Jackson Design Methodology* [Jackson 1975], such as program inversion and resolution of structure clashes, seem unnecessary in a system that provides pipes, allows the use of small programs, and eliminates logical and physical records.

The idea of a development support library is justifiably popular [Baker 1975] The UNIX system performs the services required of such a library efficiently and conveniently, especially when compared to packages grafted onto existing batch systems. Since the latter were originally built for different purposes, their communication and file systems are often not oriented to interactive work.

Baker [Baker 1975] has observed that the exact role of the program librarian in an interactive development environment "remained to be determined." In the presence of a UNIX system the role seems to be minimal, especially in the original sense of providing control and eliminating drudgery. Programs, documents, test data, and test output are stored in the UNIX file system and protected either by the usual file access mechanism or by more elaborate software, such as the Source Code Control System [Rochkind 1975] [Glasser 1978].Much of the drudgery found in other systems is simply bypassed by UNIX; it has always been fit for human beings to use. Tools have been built to automate many common programming tasks [S. Feldman 1979] and project control procedures are easily written as shell procedures. Many of our programming groups have experimented with the librarian concept and concluded that, given a decent environment, there is little need for a program librarian.

None of this should necessarily be taken as a criticism of these techniques, which can be useful in some situations. We simply prefer to minimize the number of techniques we must use to get a job done, and we observe that UNIX service is the last one we would give up.

6. ATTRIBUTES OF PROGRAMMING ENVIRONMENTS

Programming environments resemble programming languages. Most people use only a few, prefer either their first or their current one above all others, and argue the merits of one versus another. And yet, there are few truly objective metrics for comparison. In this section, we suggest some important attributes by which to classify programming environments and analyze the design tradeoffs found in them. The UNIX system is evaluated in these terms.

Group size, organization, and sociology Programming environments usually reflect the size, organization, and sociology of the groups that create them. At one extreme is the loosely coupled set of individuals, each with his own computer or isolated virtual machine. Examples include personal computers, the Xerox Alto/Ethernet architecture, and perhaps IBM's VM370/CMS. At the other extreme, some systems are built specifically to handle the problems of large programming teams. ICL's CADES [Pearson 1979], which supported a 200-person project, is an example of a successful system of this type.

UNIX systems typically lie between the two extremes. Through 1974, UNIX best supported a single, cooperative, tightly coupled group of people on each machine. By 1975, PWB/UNIX began offering better support for larger groups and multiple groups per machine. Over the years, the mechanisms needed to support this variety have evolved and been included in the standard system. Although some large projects (of more than 200 people) are successfully supported on networks of UNIX machines, most people who work together prefer to use the same machine so they can easily share procedures and data bases.

System adaptability This attribute measures the ease of adapting a system to change its capabilities. Systems at one extreme have many capabilities, but every capability is fixed, unchangeable by the user. At the other extreme, the system provides few features and is easy to change; or else provides a good toolkit, but requires that tools be combined to do the job. The first extreme offers a system optimized for some job; the second offers flexibility, but at the cost of modifying a system or assembling some tools. The first is often easier for the beginner; experts tend to favor the second.

The UNIX system favors a minimum of built-in constructs and maximum ease of adaptability. Ease of change is sometimes a disadvantage. Because it is easy to change the operating system, variants proliferate—often for no good reason. A second disadvantage is that new users can be overpowered by the toolkit provided. They know there is a way to do a job, but there are so many tools that it is difficult to find the right one.

Level of expertise Systems often aim at different levels of expertise and at different mixtures of expertise level. Early UNIX systems were used and supported by expert programmers. Later versions have tended to add more facilities for less-experienced people. Often, a programming group contains a single "guru", who customizes the general environment to support the specific needs of people less skilled in the use of UNIX tools.

Life cycle Assume that a software product's life cycle consists of requirements analysis, design, code, test, and deployment, with maintenance considered to be repeated cycles of the previous steps. Different programming environments support these phases unequally. For example, PSL/PSA [Teichroew and Hershey 1977] and similar systems emphasize requirements analysis. Many systems emphasize coding or testing aids. UNIX systems seldom support ambitious packages for requirements analysis and design, but do support these activities in general ways, e.g., by providing good text-processing tools and file organizations that are convenient for managing data bases of requirements and design information. PWB/UNIX was somewhat unusual for its time, in emphasizing deployment, support, and maintenance tools and in specifically attacking time-consuming programming drudgery.

Integration of facilities   At one extreme—found all too often—system features are independent to the extent that they are difficult to use together, even when it is necessary to do so. At the other extreme, a few systems offer tight integration of as many facilities as possible, so that the system displays a comprehensive, uniform interface to the user. Good examples are Interlisp [Teitelman 1978] [Teitelman 1977] and Smalltalk [Kay and Goldberg 1976]. The UNIX toolkit approach lies somewhere in the middle. Most tools are specifically written to be modular and independent, even if the result is a set of tools rather than a single large command that could be used in their place. This approach has some disadvantages that strongly integrated systems do not. Sometimes commands use unnecessarily different calling conventions, simply because they are contributed by different people. In cases where commands are often used together or interact in peculiar ways, users would prefer to have more integrated combinations. For example, there are circumstances in which the one-way flow of information in a pipe is just not adequate. This is particularly evident in complicated text-processing applications, in which preprocessors need better communication with TROFF than a pipe can provide.

Specialization   Systems differ radically in their views of specialization, not only for attributes mentioned above, but for others such as language, methodology, and target computer. At one extreme is a system that supports one choice very well and others not at all. As examples, one finds "single-language" systems and program development systems that not only support but enforce a single choice of methodology. At the other extreme lie those systems that would support all choices in a fairly equal fashion.

UNIX systems lie in the middle. Although they support a number of languages, C and the shell are usually supported significantly better than anything else. UNIX systems are fairly impartial with regard to methodology, and they support the production of code for many different target execution environments. The best-supported target is the UNIX system itself. Next best are those non-UNIX systems, including most microprocessors, that are dominated by their supporting UNIX systems and therefore often use interfaces built for development convenience. Next are those machines for which UNIX-based support software has been written, but which dominate the attached UNIX systems so that interfaces may well be less convenient than desired. Examples include special-purpose computers (switching machines) and large, non-UNIX mainframes that enforce their own interfaces. Finally, some targets are not supported at all, and thus require the writing of new interfaces.

Failure and success   Winners and losers can seldom be distinguished solely by studying the published literature, which contains proposals for systems never built, glowing accounts that outshine the actual user manuals, and descriptions of systems that work but have not spread beyond their original environments. People seldom write retrospectives on failures; when written, they often go unpublished. In this section, we propose a success scale for programming environments and place UNIX on that scale.

Extreme failure is represented by a system that is never built at all, or by a paper system whose ideas are never taken up by any successful system.

Medium failure is represented by a system that is built but soon abandoned, even by its immediate inventors. If a system is used only by its inventors and would vanish upon their departure, it probably falls into this category.

Many programming environments enjoy minor success. They are used by people other than the original inventors and are recognized further afield, but obtain only a small slice of the potential market.

Extreme success has several attributes. A truly successful system's use spreads far beyond its original inventors. It is used enthusiastically by many people and quickly occupies niches from which it is difficult to dislodge. People build new systems using its ideas or even parts of its software. Finally, people assume the system is so well known that they mention it without citation.

Given its exponential growth rate and widespread impact, it is not surprising that the UNIX system rates quite high on this scale. One can trace the spread of many software tools from the UNIX system through a book [Kernighan and Plauger 1976] into various other environments [Hall et al. 1980] [Snow 1978] [Enslow 1979]. Much of the current research on secure systems is UNIX-based [Woodward 1979] [Popek 1979] [McCauley and Drongowski 1979], many industry and government groups have chosen UNIX as the basis for inclusion in their own programming environment systems [McCauley et al. 1979] [Risenberg 1980] [Stockenberg and Taffs 1979] [Allshouse et al. 1979] [Wegner 1980] [Robinson and Krzysiak 1980], and numerous vendors offer UNIX-related products.

Reasons for success   To be successful, any programming environment must score well on at least some technical attributes. However, technical quality is not enough for success—many high-quality systems have fallen by the wayside. At least part of the UNIX system's success must come from its adaptability and nonspecialization, which allow it to thrive in many different niches.

Success or failure often depends on nontechnical factors, whose importance often goes unrecognized by those who evaluate systems on purely technical terms. For example, a system is seldom widely successful if it is based on "orphan" hardware, i.e., hardware that is out of production or produced only in small numbers. UNIX popularity was certainly not harmed by the initial choice of hardware, the DEC PDP-11.

Another impediment to success is a high rating on what we call the "gulp factor." Suppose that an organiztion must swallow a new system in a giant gulp because it requires a greal deal of time or money, demands massive changes in programming techniques, or requires abandoning much existing code. Such a system is much harder to spread than is a system like UNIX, which is relatively cheap, can be integrated slowly into the existing environment, and can help with the maintenance of old code. Small UNIX systems have often opened doors for later, larger machines—the original Programmer's Workbench/UNIX installation started as a single PDP-11/45 in 1973 and currently contains over 20 PDP-11/70s and VAX-11/780s. Some of that expansion depended on the ability to pick up existing code (Cobol, for example) and assist in its maintenance. The decreasing ratio of new development to maintenance indicates that any programming environment faces an uphill battle if it insists that all existing code be discarded and that all work be done from the very beginning of the project life cycle.

Finally, it is a nontechnical plus for a system to be fun to use. This factor alone can make up for many other deficiencies.

7. CONCLUSIONS

We have found the UNIX environment to be an especially productive one. This is largely because it presents a clean and systematic interface to programs that run on it, it has a wealth of small, well-designed programs that can serve as building blocks in larger processes, and it provides mechanisms by which these programs can be quickly and effectively combined. The programmable command language itself is the single most important such program, for it provides the means by which most other programs cooperate.

These facilities are used for a wide range of applications. Design, coding, and debugging are all made easier by the use of combinations of existing, small, reliable components instead of the construction of new, large, unreliable ones. Finally, the UNIX system goes a long way toward solving people's programming problems without requiring a host of additional tools and methodologies.

The UNIX system is exceptionally successful—we hope this article helps to explain why and how this success came about.

ACKNOWLEDGMENTS

Ken Thompson and Dennis Ritchie are the creators of the UNIX system; without their insight and good taste, none of this would be possible. We are also indebted to the many people who have built on the UNIX base.

REFERENCES

[Allshouse et al. 1979] R.A. Allshouse, D.T. McClellan, G.E. Prine, C.P. Rolla. CSDP as an Ada environment. *Proceedings of the ADA Environment Workshop*, DoD High Order Language Working Group, San Diego, November 1979, 113-125.

[Baker 1975] F.T. Baker. Structured programming in a production programming environment. *Proceedings of the International Conference on Reliable Software*, 1975, 172-185.

[Bourne 1978b] S.R. Bourne. An Introduction to the UNIX shell. *The Bell System Technical Journal*, 57:6 (October 1978), 2797-2822.

[Dolotta and Mashey 1976] T.A. Dolotta, J.R. Mashey. An Introduction to the Programmer's Workbench. *Proceedings of the Second International Conference on Software Engineering*, San Francisco, California, October 1976, 164-168; [*Editors' note:* see also [Dolotta et al. 1978]]

[Dolotta et al. 1978] T.A. Dolotta, R.C. Haight, J.R. Mashey. The Programmer's Workbench. *The Bell System Technical Journal*, 57:6 (July-August 1978), 2177-2200; reprinted in *Interactive Programming Environments*.

[Enslow 1979] P.H. Enslow, Jr. *Portability of large COBOL programs: the COBOL programmer's workbench*. Georgia Institute of Technology, Sept. 1979.

[Glasser 1978] A.L. Glasser. The evolution of a source code control system. In S. Jackson, J. Lockett (eds.). *Proceedings of the Software Quality and Assurance Workshop*, ACM, (1978), 122-125; also in *SICSOFT*, 3:5 (November 1978), 121-125.

[Hall et al. 1980] D.E. Hall, D.K. Scherrer, J.S. Sventek. A virtual operating system. *Communications of the ACM*, 23:9 (September 1980), 495-502.

[Ivie 1977] E.L. Ivie. Programmers Workbench—a machine for software development. *Communications of the ACM*, 20:10 (October 1977), 746-753. [*Editors' note:* see also [Dolotta et al. 1978]]

[Jackson 1975] M.A. Jackson. *Principles of Program Design*. Academic Press, London, 1975.

[Johnson and Ritchie 1978] S.C. Johnson, D.M. Ritchie. Portability of C programs and the UNIX system. *The Bell System Technical Journal*, 57:6 (July-August 1978), 2021-2048.

[Kay and Goldberg 1976] A. Kay, A. Goldberg. *Personal dynamic media*. Learning Research Group, Xerox Palo Alto Research Center, 1976; excerpts published in *IEEE Computer Magazine*, March 1977, 31-41.

[Kernighan and Plauger 1976] B.W. Kernighan, P.J. Plauger. *Software Tools*. Addison-Wesley, Reading, Massachusetts, 1976.

[Kernighan and Ritchie 1978] B.W. Kernighan, D.M. Ritchie. *The C Programming Language*. Prentice-Hall, Englewood Cliffs, New Jersey, 1978.

[Mashey 1976] J.R. Mashey. Using a command language as a high-level programming language. *Proceedings of the Second International Conference on Software Engineering*, San Francisco, California, October 1976, 169-176.

[McCauley and Drongowski 1979] E.J. McCauley, P.J. Drongowski. KSOS—the design of a secure operating system. *Proceedings of the National Computer Conference*, AFIPS Proceedings (June 1979), 345-353.

[McCauley et al. 1979] E.J. McCauley, G.L. Barksdale, J. Holden. Software development using a development support machine. *Proceedings of the ADA Environment Workshop*, DoD High Order Language Working Group, San Diego, November 1979, 1-9.

[Miller 1978] R. Miller. UNIX—a portable operating system? *Operating Systems Review*, 12:3 (July 1978), 32-37.

[Pearson 1979] D.J. Pearson. The use and abuse of a software engineering system. *Proceedings of the National Computer Conference*, AFIPS Proceedings (June 1979), 1029-1035.

[Popek 1979] G.J. Popek et al. UCLA secure UNIX. *Proceedings of the National Computer Conference*, AFIPS Proceedings (June 1979), 355-364.

[Risenberg 1980] M. Risenberg. Software costs can be tamed, developers told. *Computerworld*, Jan. 29, 1980, 1-8.

[Ritchie 1978] D.M. Ritchie. UNIX time-sharing system: a retrospective. *The Bell System Technical Journal*, 57:6 (July-August 1978), 1947-1969.

[Ritchie 1979] D.M. Ritchie. The evolution of the UNIX time-sharing system. *Proceedings of the Symposium on Language Design and Programming Methodology*, Sydney, Australia, 1979.

[Ritchie et al. 1978] D.M. Ritchie, S.C. Johnson, M.E. Lesk, B.W. Kernighan. The C programming language. *The Bell System Technical Journal*, 57:6 (July-August 1978), 1991-2019.

[Robinson and Krzysiak 1980] R.A. Robinson, E.A. Krzysiak. An integrated support software network using NSW technology. *Proceedings of the National Computer Conference*, AFIPS Proceedings (1980), 671-676.

[Rochkind 1975] M.J. Rochkind. The source code control system. *IEEE Transactions on Software Engineering*, SE-1:4 (December 1975), 364-370.

[S. Feldman 1979] S.I. Feldman. MAKE—a program for maintaining computer programs. *UNIX Programmer's Manual*, 9 (April 1979), 225-265.

[Snow 1978] C.R. Snow. The Software Tools Project. *Software—Practice and Experience*, 8:5 (September-October 1978).

[Stockenberg and Taffs 1979] J.E. Stockenberg, D. Taffs. Software test bed support under PWB/UNIX. *Proceedings of the ADA Environment Workshop*, DoD High Order Language Working Group, San Diego, November 1979, 10-26.

[Teichroew and Hershey 1977] D. Teichroew, E.A. Hershey III. PSL/PSA: a computer-aided technique for structured documentation and analysis of information processing systems. *IEEE Transactions on Software Engineering*, SE-3:1 (January 1977), 42-48.

[Teitelman 1977] W. Teitelman. A display-oriented programmer's assistant. CSL 77-3, XEROX PARC, 1977; reprinted in *Interactive Programming Environments;* see also *Proceedings of the Fifth International Joint Conference on Artificial Intelligence*, Cambridge, Massachusetts, August 1977, 905-915.

[Teitelman 1978] W. Teitelman. *INTERLISP Reference Manual*. Xerox Palo Alto Research Center, Palo Alto, California, December 1978.

[Thompson 1975] K. Thompson. The UNIX command language. in *Structured programming - Infotech state of the art report*. Infotech International Ltd., Berkshire, England, March 1975, 375-384.

[Wegner 1980] P. Wegner. The ADA language and environment. *Proceedings of Electro/ 80*, Western Periodicals Co., North Hollywood, California, May 1980.

[Woodward 1979] J.P.L. Woodward. Applications for multilevel secure operating systems. *Proceedings of the National Computer Conference*, AFIPS Proceedings (June 1979), 319-328.

[Yourdon and Constantine 1978] E. Yourdon, L.L. Constantine. *Structured Design*, Yourdon Press, New York, 1978.

10 A System for Program Refinement

**THOMAS CHEATHAM, JUDY TOWNLEY,
GLENN HOLLOWAY**

Center for Research in Computing Technology
Harvard University
Cambridge, Massachusetts

*The Program Development System (PDS) is a programming
environment, an integrated collection of interactive tools that support
the process of program definition, testing, and maintenance. The
PDS is intended to aid the development of large programs, especially
program families whose members must be maintained in synchrony.
The system facilitates implementation by stepwise refinement, and it
maintains a refinement history that allows program modifications
made at a high level of abstraction to be reflected efficiently and
automatically in the corresponding low level code. Analysis tools are
used both to support program validation and to guide program
refinement.*

*We describe the PDS and the tools incorporated in it, and we
conclude with an example of its use.*

1. INTRODUCTION

The difficulty and cost of developing and maintaining large software systems has been widely recognized. This has led to the realization that we need better programming tools. A good language alone is not enough though: it cannot cope with the complexities of integrating and maintaining large systems of programs. What is needed is a computer-based facility that can support the entire process of program definition, testing, and maintenance. We have been developing such a facility as an extension to the ECL programming system [ECL 1974]. It provides a programming environment consisting of an integrated collection of tools. The tools are designed to address the problems that arise in the construction of large systems that may take several months to a few years to develop, may be written by more than one person, and are likely to be modified. Such systems are often program families [Boyle] [Parnas 1975]. (The different versions of an operating system generated for different machine configurations, for example, comprise a family of programs; the specializations of general purpose mathematical software for particular numerical domains also form a family, as do the programs that handle the protocols of a network, providing identical functionality on a variety of host systems.)

We have been using the tools—called the Program Development System (PDS)—in the development and maintenance of our software. In the following sections we describe the components of the PDS and give an example in the appendix illustrating its use. Before proceeding, however, we should remark that the PDS is a programming environment; it does not define or enforce a particular programming discipline. We only hope by providing good tools to encourage good programming practices.

2. OVERVIEW OF THE PDS

Programming problems are generally divided into subproblems that we call *modules*. The collection of modules that solve a particular problem is called a *program*. A module consists of *entities*—procedural expressions, data definitions, documentation, and so on—and *interface specifications*. The interface specifications describe the entities that the module assumes are provided by other modules—called its *imports*—as well as those entities that it provides, its *exports*. The implementation of entities within a module usually depends upon these assumptions, and the integrity of a module depends on the consistency of them. The PDS checks that the modules comprising a program are consistent with respect to their interface specifications and that proposed changes to a module do not violate those assumptions.

A module may have several descendants, reflecting a subdivision of the problem, a more precise definition of it, or diverse specializations of it. All are considered *refinements*. That is, a particular module may define a task too complex to be conveniently thought of as a unit; we would then divide the module into sub-modules that are conceptually simpler. All, and only, the entities of the parent module are in some descendant. On the other hand, the refinement might involve a commitment to a specific implementation of certain entities within the module. Or, thirdly, the descendants of the module might represent the various implementations of it for different run-time environments, a situation arising in the derivation of program families. The phrase, refinement process, encompasses all three activities.

We thus view a program as being defined at several levels—a view commonly held by structured programming adherents. The highest or most *abstract* level may be English text describing what is to be accomplished. The lowest or most *concrete* level is the machine instructions to be executed by a particular computer and operating system. The intermediate levels represent the gradual refinement of the program from the abstract to the concrete; at any particular level, the implementation of certain aspects may be specified more precisely than others. In a family of programs, the higher levels emphasize the properties shared by several members of the family.

The creation of the various levels is not necessarily from top to bottom. Seldom is our understanding of a problem sufficient to permit such an orderly evolution. The *representation* of the refinement, however, can be from the most abstract and readable to the most precise.

Conventional programming systems provide little support for this view of the programming process. Higher level versions, if they exist at all, are seldom maintained: most systems do not have facilities that help the programmer keep them up-to-date. A fundamental goal of the PDS is to support this multi-level view of a program: it provides the structure and means for moving easily among the levels and helps the user maintain the program at all levels.

The PDS constructs and uses a *data base* of facts about a program and its constituents, the modules and entities. The data base includes, for example, a representation of the interdependence among the modules and a history of their refinement. The *executive* of the PDS provides an interactive interface to the user. It accepts commands, directs the commands to particular components of the PDS for execution, and records their effects on the program data base. The other components of the PDS are the *tools* available to the programmer. We divide them roughly into three categories:

1. Specification tools for defining, editing, and refining modules,
2. Analysis tools that check the integrity of the modules and derive facts that assist refinement, and
3. Execution tools that establish a run-time environment for a program and monitor its execution.

The internal form of any program, module, or entity is not a text string but a computation tree, represented in list structure. Such a representation is easy to manipulate and interpret. The commonality of this representation, plus the fact that the tools share a data base and that their actions are coordinated by the executive, all contribute to making the PDS a smooth, coherent facility.

3. SPECIFICATION TOOLS

3.1   Defining a Module

A module in the PDS has a name, a refinement history, a derivation number, and an arbitrary number of other attributes. The history specifies the set of refinements that were applied to the parent module to derive the current module. Derivation numbers augment module names to facilitate the identification of modules derived from the same parent. Other attributes typically associated with a module are its time of creation, initialization instructions, and its imports and exports. Still others may be defined by the user or by a PDS tool. Attributes thus provide a general mechanism for communication among parts of the PDS and facilitate the integration of new tools.

To define a module M, the user may issue the command to the PDS executive,

```
CreateModule M
```

after which the user may interactively specify the components of the module. Alternatively, if the user has already created a file F of procedures, data definitions, and so on, he may request the contents be made into a module:

```
MakeModule M From F
```

After the PDS constructs a module or program, it has the responsibility for maintaining the representation of it in both primary and secondary storage. The user need no longer be concerned with the contents of various files; the PDS keeps a record of where the modules and programs are stored and performs the necessary file handling operations.

3.2   Defining Entities

As mentioned above, a module is a collection of entities, such as procedures, modes, data definitions, and notations. Like modules, entities have attributes. Attributes permit the *incremental* definition of procedures, modes, and other data. A procedure P, for example, may be initially defined by the expression

```
P IsA Procedure()
        —'this is text describing what P will do';
```

The user may subsequently provide the names and modes of the arguments of P, using the command

```
P Has FormalParameters(X:INT, B:BOOL)
```

FormalParameters is an attribute and its value is a list of pairs of argument descriptors - in this case, one for integer X and one for Boolean B. The user may eventually specify the mode of the result of P

```
P Has ResultType(REAL)
```

and its body

```
P Has Body(...)
```

These particular attributes permit the incremental definition of a procedure. The PDS can construct the explicit procedure—its *value-binding*—from these attributes. Alternatively, of course, the user may directly define the explicit procedure. The PDS includes similar commands for incrementally defining mode and data entities. Incremental definition of entities is important to our style of program development; it permits the implementer to avoid overspecification of entities at higher levels and avoid redundant definition of entity attributes when refining them at lower levels.

The ability to define new notation is also important in program development. A programming problem is more easily understood and solved using a notation that is appropriate and natural for it. Thus the PDS includes facilities for maintaining user-defined notations. A user may specify new operators, giving each a certain infix, prefix, or matchfix[1] priority and an associativity

---

[1] A matchfix operator is the first of a pair of operators that together behave like parentheses; the matchfix operator is applied to the arguments between the pair. Thus, for example, {x,y} is interpreted as the function { applied to the arguments x and y.

rule. The PDS associates the definitions with the module and the parser and unparser (a pretty-printer) use them to read and print the module. The user may also define new phrases, involving distributed operators, by analogy with known phrases. For example, he might produce a new syntactic format for iterations over a set by making

```
For E in S DO ... END
```

analogous to the built-in iterator

```
FOR E FROM S REPEAT ... END
```

Like other entities, notations may be exported and imported across module boundaries.

The user ascribes meaning to the notation either in the conventional way, by associating a *routine* with an operator name, or by giving a pattern-replacement rule whose pattern part matches a phrase in the extended syntax. As will be described below, the PDS treats such rules as generalized procedure definitions.

Entities may be grouped to facilitate their identification in commands to the executive. The attributes of an entity specify the groups to which it belongs. For example, a user may specify that an entity E belongs to the group of exports by assigning it the appropriate attribute.

```
E Has Group(Exports)
```

Various tools in the PDS reference the attributes, as will be noted when we describe the tools.

3.3   Editing

The PDS includes various editing facilities. The executive handles commands for moving around the parts of a module, adding attributes to a module, adding or changing entities, adding attributes to existing entities, and so on. The user may also call on a list structure editor, via the executive, to alter the value-bindings of entities. A new *version* of a module is created as a result of altering the value-bindings. The old version is retained as a backup, but the commands used to change it are not recorded.

The executive maintains a directory that relates the versions and derivations of each module to files on secondary storage. The directory includes file addresses and sites of individual entities so that incremental updates can be performed efficiently.

The PDS uses its knowledge about the structure of modules and entities to insure that only syntactically valid statements are entered and that certain obvious conflicts are avoided. For example, if P is a procedure in a module, then the executive will not permit the user to define a mode-valued entity named P in the same module.

3.4   Refinement

The refinement of a module or entity is the process by which we go from a more abstract definition to a more concrete. This process may proceed in stages, resulting in several levels of refinement. Refinement, in general, involves making certain design decisions, such as choosing a low-level data representation and tailoring an algorithm to make effective use of the representation. A new *derivation* of a module is created as a result of refinement; the commands used to derive it become part of its history. The executive hosts both interactive refinement and the application of a batch of commands that have been collected in a refinement module.

One way to specify the refinement of an entity or module is via the incremental definition or redefinition of its attributes. Two other tools that aid in this process are the rewrite facility and the history mechanism.

3.4.1 The Rewrite Facility
The rewrite facility enables the user to specify program transformations in the form of parameterized pattern-replacement rules. This facility serves two purposes. First, the rewriting rules may be used as generalized procedure definitions, designated by pattern rather than by simple name and substituted in-line rather than called. Second, the rewrite facility may be used to optimize entities during refinement, e.g., to tailor code in accordance with representation choices.

As an example of the use of a rewriting rule, suppose we have defined the notation

```
For s in S DO ... END
```

to describe an iteration over the elements s of a set S. We may later decide to represent S as an array and wish to refine the iteration to reflect this decision; we may do so by providing a rewriting rule:

```
For $x in $X DO ... END <->
  FOR I FROM 1 TO LENGTH($X)
    REPEAT
      DECL $x:ElementType SHARED $X[I];
      ...;
  END
```

The symbol <-> separates the pattern

```
For $x in $X DO ... END
```

from the replacement (the expression to its right). The $ preceding an identifier indicates that the identifier is a parameter of the pattern; a parameter may match an arbitrary expression. The ellipsis "..." denotes a nameless parameter that matches an arbitrary sequence of statements.

To apply a rewriting rule R to an entity E, the pattern matcher looks for occurrences of the pattern-part of R in E, making a consistent correspondence between parameters in the pattern and expressions in E. If successful, the appropriate substitutions are made for parameters in the replacement part of R and the result is substituted for the matched expression in E. The pattern matcher repeatedly processes the entity until no rules apply.

The user may associate a predicate with a rewriting rule:

```
pattern WHERE predicate <-> replacement
```

The predicate is any Boolean expression and may involve the parameters of the pattern. To apply such a rule, we first match the pattern-part and then test the predicate, after making the appropriate substitutions for any parameters that occur in the predicate. A typical use of the WHERE clause is to restrict the applicability of a rule to a particular class of data. The data type information used by the pattern matcher is derived by an analyzer described in section 4.2.

Rewriting rules, like other entities, are stored and updated by the executive; they may be exported and imported, and they may be grouped, for export or to permit selective application. That is, a group of rewriting rules may be applied to a group of entities.

One of the purposes of the rewrite facility is to enable in-line substitution of (non-recursive) procedures. An attribute of a procedure entity indicates whether it is to be expanded in line or left closed when its module is readied for execution.[2] This attribute may be added or changed at any stage in the refinement process.

A complete description of the rewrite facility is available in [Conrad 1976b].

3.4.2 History Mechanism Refinement is, in general, a process of trial and error. The PDS helps the user keep track of the process by maintaining a *history* of the derivation of a module. The PDS retains with each module a record of how the module was derived. A module is either a *base* module (the abstract representation) or a *derived* module (the result of some refinement). A derived module M1 is obtained from a module M2 by applying a set of refinement commands to M1. The refinements may include rewrite commands, attribute specifications, requests to the compiler, and so on. The history is the record of these transactions.

The history is also a repository in which the user can record the reasons for each refinement and its implications for the rest of the implementation. After making a series of refinements, the user is able, using the history, to return to a more abstract level of representation of a module, examine the module and its assumptions at that level, and in that context propose modifications of it.

The PDS then uses the history to rederive the more concrete representations. Those aspects of the earlier derivation that are unaffected by the change are incorporated in the new modules without reprocessing. Other parts of the derivation may have to be replayed to take the modifications into account.

A similar concept is used in Moriconi's system [Moriconi 1978] for developing and maintaining the incremental verification of programs. We do not use any heuristics, however, to determine which refinements must be reapplied.

For example, if we add a rewriting rule to a group, we reapply all the transformations in the group to the designated source entities. Similarly, if we change the body of a procedure, we reapply all, but only, the rewriting rules associated with that procedure. We do not attempt to determine whether the change alters the applicability of the rewriting rules but we also do not reapply the transformations associated with other groups.

4. ANALYSIS TOOLS

We currently have a small repertoire of analysis tools, ranging from very simple to quite powerful. We hope to devote a major part of our effort during the next year to enhancing these analyzers and their use by other tools in the PDS.

---

[2] In-line substitution is facilitated by the semantics of procedures in EL1, which permits replacement of a procedure call by an equivalent block without renaming of variables.

4.1   Simple Integrity Checking

At some stage in the refinement process, the user may wish to know if the interface specifications are consistent and what entities have yet to be fully defined. Given a module or program, we can derive such information. To validate interface specifications, we compare the import and export groups of the modules to insure that the assumptions of all of the modules are consistent with respect to those specifications. That is, we check that the entities that one module expects to import are in fact exported by another module and that they have the expected types.

In addition, we look for undefined or incompletely defined entities within a module. We first record the names of the entities described in a module. Then, taking into account formal parameters and locally-declared variables, we scan the value-bindings of the entities, looking for uses of either undefined entities or entities that have no value-binding. We also keep a record of the number of times an entity is used by another entity. We process in this fashion both data definitions and procedures (whether defined as rewriting rules or routines). The information may be used to reorganize the contents of the modules according to usage patterns, it reveals entities that are never referenced, and it provides an indication of all the places that might be affected by a proposed change.

4.2   Mode and Value Propagation

We have developed two other analyzers: one called the expression analyzer [Holloway 1976] that propagates manifest constants and mode information, and the other, a symbolic evaluator [Cheatham et al. 1979a] [Ploedereder 1979] that propagates mode and value information represented as symbolic expressions.

Good programmer support depends upon a spectrum of good analyzers. The expression analyzer is at one end of that spectrum; it is a practical tool, ready to be incorporated into the PDS. It can be used by the rewrite facility to permit full exploitation of the semantic applicability criteria.

The symbolic evaluator is more powerful than the expression analyzer. It takes into account sharing patterns among variables, it uses symbolic expressions to represent the uncertainty that arises from branches in the control flow, and it develops and attempts to solve recurrence relations to describe the effects of loops. The symbolic evaluator does not handle all of EL1, however, and is not yet efficient enough for general use.

We hope eventually to use the symbolic evaluator to do consistency checking of EL1 programs—to check that the arguments in a procedure call are valid in mode and number, that the subscripts in a selection expression are in range, that the value of a pointer being dereferenced is not NIL, and so on [Townley 1978]. We are also developing other tools that will use its results, including a source-to-source optimizer (much like those proposed in [Darlington and Burstall 1976], [Loveman 1977], and [Standish et al. 1976]) and a verifier [Ploedereder 1979].

Both analyzers operate only on concrete EL1. We recognize the importance of having an analyzer that can handle the abstract versions of a module and can deal gracefully with incompletely specified entities. Syntactic analogies have been useful in specifying extended notations; we are experimenting with semantic analogies for such notations as well. A semantic analogy is a pattern-invoked rule that gives a sketch of the meaning of an abstract notation in lower level terms. It is not an implementation, but provides details about scope, modes, and evaluation order that permit analyzers to deal with abstract programs before the implementation of every abstraction has been given.

Also, because our system emphasizes program transformations, we need to be able to keep the analysis data base up-to-date efficiently as refinement proceeds. Most transformations are valid precisely because they cause little change in the underlying meaning of a program. We are studying incremental analysis methods that exploit this fact and that minimize reanalysis by preanalyzing transformations.

5. EXECUTION TOOLS

When a collection of modules constituting a program is ready to be executed, the PDS gathers the relevant modules, hides (by appropriate renaming) the names of entities not exported, applies non-exported rewriting rules, and makes available to other modules (by further renaming, if necessary) those entities that are exported. It then applies all imported rewriting rules to the appropriate entities. The PDS will turn to the user, if necessary, to provide missing information or to disambiguate the interpretation of entities or commands. The final result is a program containing the value-bindings of all the entities from all the modules, ready for execution.[3]

Several monitoring facilities are available to assist the user in tracing the execution of the program [Conrad 1976a] [Conrad 1976c]. The user can attach probes to routines that record the number of times each routine is called, the amount of time required by each call (optionally broken down by caller-callee pairs), the frequencies of individual statement executions, or the results of other user-provided measurement expressions planted throughout the routine. We also have tracing facilities that permit the user to inspect the computation state before and/or after the call of a routine.

The user is able to correct errors that occur during execution and continue the computation. Alternatively, he may return to the executive of the PDS, make the change at the appropriate level of refinement, and permit the system to rederive the executable form. Certain changes can be incorporated quickly. For those that cannot, the user may fix the executable representation and the system will make a record of the changes and update the refinement history at the conclusion of the debugging session.

As we gain experience with the PDS, we hope to build better debugging aids. For example, using the representation of the refinement history of the various entities, we would like to report errors in terms of higher level concepts. This is, in general, very difficult, but the PDS gives us a good framework for addressing the problem.

6. CONCLUSIONS

We have been using various facilities of the PDS for several years on projects ranging in size from a few pages of code to large systems consisting of several modules and many thousands of lines of code.

---

[3] ECL has both an interpreter and a compiler; we generally use the interpreter while debugging a program and compile modules only after they become stable.

For all but the smallest programs, we tend to invent new notation for each problem. Our modules are coded, printed, and read in terms of the extended notation. The refinement of the notation is often deferred for some time and may change, sometimes radically, as our approach to the problem evolves.

We tend to debug at the abstract level. Once an error is encountered and we identify the procedure in which the error occurs, we look at the abstract representation of the procedures involved to find and correct the error. We use the abstract descriptions of a program to study the effects of a proposed modification. The final executable representations can often be rederived automatically, and we seldom look at them.

We have used the PDS in the development of the symbolic evaluator mentioned in section 4.2, for example, and are using it in the development of two program families.

The first of these is a family of interpreters for EL1, the programming language in the ECL system. The goal is to have an abstract model, providing a semantic definition of EL1, and to derive, through refinement, interpreters that run on two different machines. The interpreter family, in addition to facilitating the portability of EL1, is designed to permit the transfer of an ongoing computation from one machine to another, without doing any recomputation.

The other example is the development of a family of MSG programs [Holloway et al. 1978]. MSG is the interprocess communication handler of the National Software Works. Again, we are developing first an abstract model and then deriving by refinement the implementations. In this case, the two implementations—one for the UNIX operating system and one for TENEX— will differ significantly.

As the examples illustrate, the PDS is not oriented to any particular application area. Rather, it is a collection of simple, but flexible, tools that have assisted us in the development and maintenance of software.

APPENDIX: AN EXAMPLE OF PROGRAMMING BY REFINEMENT

We present an example that illustrates the decomposition of a program into modules and the derivation of concrete modules from an abstract version. Though this example is necessarily small, we reiterate that these techniques have been used in a number of medium- and large-scale systems programming applications.

Consider a module named Graphs that defines a number of graph algorithms. Among them is a function that derives a spanning tree for a graph. The tree T is represented as a subset of the edges of the graph G. The algorithm begins by constructing a partition of the vertices of G, placing every vertex into a distinct equivalence class. Then the edges (v,w) of G are considered in turn. If vertices v and w are in separate classes, (v,w) is added to T and the classes are merged. The algorithm terminates when the vertices are all in the same class or when the edges are exhausted. (See [Aho et al. 1974] for additional discussion.)

Relevant portions of the Graphs module are shown in Figure 1.

```
Module Graphs;
  Uses(Sets);
  Imports(union:PROC(AnySet, AnySet; AnySet),
          "{":PROC(FORM LISTED; AnySet),
          Size:PROC(AnySet; INT));
  LocalSyntax(EquatePhrase('V1 equals V2 under P',
                           'V1   -   V2   -   P'),
              EquatePhrase('Equate V1 with V2 under P',
                           '  -   V1  -   V2  -   P'),
              EquatePhrase('of', '-'));
  Graph Is Structure(V:VertexSet, E:EdgeSet);
  Vertex IsA MODE;
  VertexSet IsA MODE;
  Edge Is Structure(head:Vertex, tail:Vertex);
  EdgeSet IsA MODE;
  VertexPartition IsA MODE;
  .
  .
  SpanningTree Is
    EXPR(G:Graph; EdgeSet)
      BEGIN
        DECL T:EdgeSet;
        DECL P:VertexPartition of G.V;
        For v in G.V DO P <- P union {{v}} END;
        For e in G.E
          DO
            Size(P) LE 1 => -'terminate early';
            NOT(e.head equals e.tail under P) ->
              BEGIN
                Equate e.head with e.tail under P;
                T <- T union {e};
              END;
          END;
        T;
      END;
  .
  .
  .
```

Figure 1.

Graphs imports several entities from a module called Sets, a general purpose package defining mathematical sets. Module Sets is outlined in Figure 2. It exports many of the notations used in SpanningTree and provides definitions for the corresponding operators. The set iterator, For ... in ... DO ... END, is defined in Sets, as are the operators Union and Size and the set former, {...}. Module Graphs defines the additional notation for dealing with partitions.

The LocalSyntax attribute of a module defines notations used in the text of the module. EquatePhrase(New, Old) causes the lexemes of the phrase New to be made synonymous for purposes of parsing with the corresponding lexemes of Old. In this example, we will not implement the symbols "Equate", "with", and so on, as individual operators. Instead, the phrase "Equate v with w under P" will be implemented as a single operation, that which merges the equivalence classes of v and w under partition P. Similarly, "v equals w under P" is treated as a single operation, namely the test whether v and w are in the same class in P. Such notational extensions promote clarity without compromising efficiency.

```
Module Sets;
   ExportedSyntax(MATCHFIX(''{'',''}''),
                 EquatePhrase('For E in S DO ... END',
                              'FOR E FROM S REPEAT ... END'),
                 EquatePhrase('union', '+'),
                 EquatePhrase('less', '-'),
                 INFIX(''member''),
                       .
                     . );
   Set     Is EXPR(ElementType:MODE; MODE) ...;
   AnySet IsA MODE-'the union of all set modes';

             .
             .
   union  Is EXPR(L:AnySet, R:AnySet; AnySet) ...;
   less   Is EXPR(L:AnySet, R:AnySet; AnySet) ...;
   Size   Is EXPR(S:AnySet; INT) ...;
   member Is EXPR(E:ANY, S:AnySet; BOOL) ...;
   {      Is EXPR(Members:FORM LISTED; AnySet) ...;
             .
             .
```

Figure 2.

The ExportedSyntax attribute of module Sets defines notations that may be required by other modules making use of Sets. MATCHFIX("{","}") produces a new way of bracketing lists of expressions, e.g.

```
{A+B,{ }, 2, {X}}
```

INFIX("member") declares member to be an infix operator.

Module Graphs declares several modes. Two of these, Edge and Graph, have definitions at the abstract level; the rest remain unspecified pending refinement.

Given an understanding of the EL1 language and the definitions in the module Sets, the procedure SpanningTree is a readable encoding of the algorithm sketched above. In EL1, the infix operator " => " terminates a loop when its left operand has value TRUE. In that case, the value of the right operand becomes the value of the loop. The value of a BEGIN block is normally the value of its last statement. Thus the result of SpanningTree is the set T. Comments are included as infix or prefix expressions using the operator—:

```
expression-'a comment';
```

or

```
-'a comment';
```

The phrase "of G.V" in this example is a pragmatic comment. The program is complete without it, but it is useful in the refinement of vertex partitions.

We will create a small program family from Graphs by giving two different refinements of it, one for simulation and another for use in production. The first simply fills in the parts of the module left unspecified in the abstract version by taking further advantage of the facilities provided by Sets. This may not be very efficient, but it is a quick way to test the abstract algorithms on sample data, and perhaps to make measurements that will guide a more efficient realization. The second refinement of Graphs will use efficient representations for some of the sets involved. It could be extended so that all dependence on the general purpose set package is eliminated.

In order to know what entities remain partially or totally undefined in the abstract module Graphs, the implementer may invoke the integrity checker, described in section 4.1. This tool lists the names of the modes (such as Vector and EdgeSet) that have no bindings and the keywords (such as "equals" and "of") that have syntactic but not semantic specifications. The user then designs refinements to fill in these missing pieces and to modifiy abstract entities if necessary.

Figure 3 shows the first refinement, called Simulate. Graph vertices are represented by integers, so the mode Vertex is bound to INT. To produce the various types of sets, a data type generator called Set, one of the exports of module Sets, is applied to the element types. (Mode-valued procedures can be defined by the programmer in EL1.)

In this refinement, the pragmatic comment operator, "of", is identified with the actual comment operator, so that "VertexPartition of G.V" has the value VertexPartition.

The partition operations, equals and Equate, are defined in terms of a local function, Find, which produces the equivalence class of a given vertex. (By giving Find the attribute "local", the implementer insures that its name will not be exported, i.e., not exposed to other modules using the graph package.)

```
Module Simulate;
    Uses(Sets, Graphs);
    Imports(Set:PROC(MODE; MODE),
            union:PROC(AnySet, AnySet; AnySet),
            ''{'':PROC(FORM LISTED; AnySet),
            member:PROC(ANY, AnySet; BOOL),
            less:PROC(AnySet, AnySet; AnySet));

    Vertex Is INT;
    VertexSet Is Set(Vertex);
    EdgeSet Is Set(Edge);
    VertexPartition Is Set(VertexSet);

of Is-;

    $vl equals $v2 under $P <->
      $vl member Find($v2, $P);

    Equate $vl with $v2 under $P <->
      BEGIN
        DECL Cl:VertexSet LIKE Find($vl, $P);
        DECL C2:VertexSet LIKE Find($v2, $P);
        $P <- ($P less Cl less C2) union {Cl union C2};
      END;

    Find IsLocal
      EXPR(v:Vertex, P:VertexPartition; VertexSet)
        For C in P DO v member C => C END;
```

Figure 3.

To apply the refinement module Simulate to module Graphs, the user issues the command

```
Merge Simulate Into Graphs
```

The PDS produces a derived module (also called Graphs, but with a new derivation number) containing the original entities plus the completions and additions from Simulate. (In general, other transformations of the abstract entities could be performed at this point as well.) Next, to put Graphs into a form that can either be executed interpretively or compiled, the user says

```
MakeProgram Graphs
```

(The system interprets "Graphs" as meaning the most recent derivation.) MakeProgram expands all procedures marked for in-line substitution and renames variables as necessary to enforce module scope rules. To run the program, the user may say

```
LoadProgram Graphs
```

in response to which, the PDS loads the final derivations of Graphs and the modules it uses (in this case, just Sets) into an ECL execution environment, performing any initialization that may have been specified.

The user may instrument the program, if he wishes, and test it on sample data. In general, this will lead to changes in the abstract version or in the refinements. The system assists with these changes and efficiently rederives a new executable instance, keeping records so that the implementer can revert to an old version if necessary.

As a result of the experience gained by simulation, the user may wish to make tentative refinements that enhance performance. For instance, he might choose to implement VertexPartition using the Fisher-Galler method for managing equivalence classes [Knuth 1968a]. Figure 4 shows a refinement module called FisherGaller that incorporates this decision. First, since no sets of vertices will need explicit representation outside the partition, a VertexSet can be represented by a simple integer giving the number of vertices in the graph. That is, the graph G will have G.V vertices, labeled 1 ... G.V. The iterator over vertex sets can thus be replaced by a counting loop. Recall that we may augment a pattern in a rewriting rule by a predicate. In this case we add the constraint

```
WHERE $V HasMode VertexSet
```

to specify that the expression bound to $V must have the mode VertexSet.

In the Fisher-Galler algorithm, a set partition is represented by a table having an entry per set element, or in this case, per vertex. Each entry includes the name of the class that contains it and a link to the next entry for its class. A class name is the name of a representative vertex in the class. The test for equivalence of two vertices can be performed simply by comparing the names of their classes. Two classes C1 and C2 can be merged by setting the names of all C1's entries to the name of C2 and then appending the membership list of C2 to that of C1. A size field is also maintained in the partition table to keep track of the number of equivalence classes. It is incremented when a class is added, and decremented when two classes are merged.

Figure 4 gives a straightforward realization of this method. Note that the pragmatic comment "of G.V", relating the partition variable P to the set that it partitions, is used in this refinement to specify the length of the partition table.

After FisherGaller has been used to refine the abstract module Graphs, the only remaining dependence on module Sets is through the mode EdgeSet and

```
Module FisherGaller;
   Uses(Sets, Graphs);
   Imports(Set:PROC(MODE; MODE));
   Vertex Is INT;
   VertexSet Is INT;
   EdgeSet Is Set(Edge);

   For $v in $V DO ... END
      WHERE $V HasMode VertexSet <->
      FOR $v FROM 1 TO $V REPEAT ... END;

   VertexPartition of $V <->
      STRUCT(size:INT, items:VECTOR($V, ClassItem));
   ClassItem Is STRUCT(name:Vertex, next:INT);

   $P <- $P union { {$v} }
      WHERE $P HasMode VertexPartition <->
      BEGIN
         $P.items[$v].name <- $v;
         $P.items[$v].next <- 0;
         $P.size <- $P.size + 1;
      END;

   Size($P) WHERE $P HasMode VertexPartition <->
      $P.size;

   $v equals $w under $P <->
      $P.items[$v].name = $P.items[$w].name;

   Equate $v with $w under $P <->
      BEGIN
         DECL v:Vertex BYVAL $v;
         REPEAT
            DECL Item:ClassItem SHARED $P.items[v];
            Item.name <- $P.items[$w].name;
            v <- Item.next;
            v = 0 => Item.next <- $w;
         END;
         $P.size <- $P.size - 1;
      END;
         .
         .
         .
```

Figure 4.

operations over edge sets. The implementer has the choice of leaving in this dependence or of picking his own concrete representation for edge sets. He might use a connection matrix, for instance, or a linked list, or a hybrid of the two. He might develop several alternative edge set representations, corresponding to different applications for the graph module. The facilities for segregating design decisions and for maintaining the refinement history of a program family enable a user to explore such options conveniently and efficiently.

ACKNOWLEDGMENTS

This work was supported in part by the Department of the Navy, Naval Electronic Systems Command, under contract N00039-78-G-0020.

REFERENCES

[Aho et al. 1974] A.V. Aho, J.E. Hopcroft, J.D. Ullman, *The Design and Analysis of Computer Algorithms*, Addison-Wesley, 1974.

[Boyle] J.M. Boyle. An introduction to the transformation-assisted multiple program realization (TAMPR) system. Argonne National Laboratory, Applied Mathematics Division (undated).

[Cheatham et al. 1979a] T.E. Cheatham, Jr., G.H. Holloway, J.A. Townley. Symbolic evaluation and the analysis of programs. *IEEE Transactions on Software Engineering*, SE-5:4, July 1979.

[Conrad 1976a] W.R. Conrad. *PROBE User's Guide*. Harvard University, Center for Research in Computing Technology, June 1976.

[Conrad 1976b] W.R. Conrad. *Rewrite User's Guide*. Harvard University, Center for Research in Computing Technology, August 1976.

[Conrad 1976c] W.R. Conrad. COST User's Guide. Harvard University, Center for Research in Computing Technology, November 1976.

[Darlington and Burstall 1976] J. Darlington, R.M. Burstall. A system which automatically improves programs. *Acta Informatica*, 6, 1976.

[ECL 1974] *ECL Programmer's Manual*. Harvard University, Center for Research in Computing Technology, TR-23-74, December 1974.

[Holloway 1976] G.H. Holloway. *User's guide to the expression analyzer and query facility*. Harvard University, Center for Research in Computing Technology, May 1976.

[Holloway et al. 1978] G.H. Holloway, W.R. Bush, G.H. Mealy. Abstract model of MSG—first phase of an experiment in software development. Harvard University, Center for Research in Computing Technology, TR-25-78, October 1978.

[Knuth 1968a] D.E. Knuth. *The Art of Computer Programming, Vols. 1-3*. Addison-Wesley, Reading, Massachusetts, 1968,1969,1973.

[Loveman 1977] D. Loveman. Program improvement by source-to-source transformation. *Journal of the ACM*, 24:1 (January 1977).

[Moriconi 1978] M.S. Moriconi. A designer/verifier's assistant. SRI International, Computer Science Laboratory, Technical Report CSL-80, October 1978.

[Parnas 1975] D.L. Parnas. *On the design and development of program families*. Fachbereich Informatik, Technische Hochschule, Darmstadt, July 1975.

[Ploedereder 1979] E.O.J. Ploedereder. Pragmatic techniques for program analysis and verification. *Proceedings of the Fourth International Conference on Software Engineering*, Munich, Germany, September 1979.

[Standish et al. 1976] T.A. Standish, D. Harriman, D. Kibler, J. Neighbors. *The Irvine program transformation catalogue*. Computer Science Department, University of California at Irvine, January 1976.

[Townley 1978] J.A. Townley. Program analysis techniques for software reliability. *Proceedings of the ACM Workshop on Reliable Software*, Bonn University, September 1978.

Aspects of Interactive Programming Environments

The papers in this section each address the details of specific issues related to interactive programming environments. There are several themes which run through many of the papers:

- A program is more than just its text; there are underlying structures which can and should be exploited in programming environments. An obvious example is the syntactic structure of the program, exploited by the structure-oriented editors common in most interactive programming environments.

- Advanced graphics facilities can considerably enhance the user interface. This is reflected both in screen-oriented editors and in the high-resolution graphics devices provided by personal workstations.

- Interactive programming environments can and should provide substantial support for many facets of the programming process. This is perhaps best illustrated by INTERLISP's Programmer's Assistant.

- There is a clear willingness to allocate sufficient computational resources to enable programming environments to provide that support. The extreme case here is the personal workstation, in which an entire mini-computer is put at the disposal of a single user.

The first two papers are two of the earliest papers which address specific aspects of interactive programming environments. Hansen describes an early structure-oriented editor, together with some lessons for the human engineering side of building interactive computer systems. Those lessons are still valid today. Teitelman's initial paper on the Programmer's Assistant was the first to suggest that the environment could actively support many aspects of the interactive programming process, including the maintainance of a complete record of the session, permitting mistakes to be undone and other computations to be redone without repeating the entire command.

The next two papers describe two attempts to add display power to INTERLISP's teletype-oriented interface. Teitelman describes an implementation of the Programmer's Assistant which exploits the high-resolution graphics of a personal workstation. Barstow describes an extension of the INTERLISP editor which exploits the graphics capabilities of a character-oriented display device.

In the next paper, Stallman describes EMACS, one of the most sophisticated screen-oriented text editors. Perhaps the most interesting aspect is the fact there are a variety of special commands which understand the syntactic structure of LISP. That is, EMACS is a text editor which can deal effectively with the textual representation of the underlying LISP structures. This is only one of several approaches to the problem of combining the textual and structural representations of a program. (The technique described by Barstow in the previous paper represents the opposite approach: start with an internal structural representation and use a display to show the textual view.)

In the next paper, Greenblatt et al. describe the Lisp Machine developed at MIT. The Lisp Machine is one of several recently developed personal computer workstations. It includes a powerful processor, large memory, high-resolution display device, and a disk for file storage. All of these are made available to a single user. When combined with sophisticated tools that take advantage of these computational resources, the result is an extremely powerful interactive programming environment.

The next two papers describe programming environments related to UNIX. Dolotta et al. describe the Programmer's Workbench, a collection of tools which support the programmer in dealing with a variety of different machines. Wasserman describes work aimed at incorporating several tools into a UNIX-based environment and notes a long-term goal of providing personal workstations with such tools.

The final three papers discuss specific structural issues related to interactive programming environments. Goldstein and Bobrow describe the structures used by PIE, a personal information environment, to record the development history of software systems. Goodwin describes the need for language and environment structures which allow dynamic data types. Sandewall et al. describe an alternative view of the process of developing and distributing software: that software development consists of modifying programming environments and that software distribution consists of communication between such environments.

11 User Engineering Principles for Interactive Systems

WILFRED J. HANSEN

Carnegie-Mellon University
Pittsburgh, Pennsylvania

Reprinted with the permission of AFIPS from: *Fall Joint Computer Conference Proceedings*, 1971, AFIPS Volume 39, pp. 523-532.

1. INTRODUCTION

The "feel" of an interactive system can be compared to the impressions generated by a piece of music. Both can only be experienced over a period of time. With either, the user must abstract the structure of the system from a sequence of details. Each may have a quality of "naturalness" because successive actions follow a logically self-consistent pattern. Finally, a good composer can write a new pattern which will seem, after a few listenings, to be so natural the observer wonders why it was never done before.

Just as a composer follows a set of harmonic principles when he writes music, the system designer must follow some set of principles when he designs the sequence of give and take between man and machine. This paper reports a set of principles—called user engineering principles—which were employed while designing the Emily text editing system. These principles evolved during the course of the project, but were originally based on the author's experiences with a number of other text editing systems [McCarthy et al. 1967] [Weiher 1967] [TECO] [Wylbur 1968].

In text editing applications, the user sits at a console and creates, views, or modifies a document, be it program, speech, article or a chapter of his next book. Here the computer is a tool for the creative worker and the emphasis must be on capturing his thoughts with minimal interference. More common in commercial environments are interactive systems designed as tools to coordinate the work of many clerical workers. Examples are order entry, point-of-sale, inventory control, defense surveillance, and the like. The principles outlined below, though originally intended for creative work, are equally applicable to clerical work. Sometimes more so, because clerks may not have the commitment of the creative worker.

One restriction on a few of the principles below is that they apply to systems with display devices for output. This is essential, because a basic principle is that the system respond to the user as fast as possible. A visual display can present more information in less time than available hardcopy devices. The "economy" of the terminal device must be weighed against the cost of attention-wander-time as the user interacts with the system. Other than the terminal, cost is not a problem in the application of these user engineering principles. In general, they dictate features that are inexpensive to design into a system. They are, however, often expensive to include after implementation is under way.

Disciplines similar to user engineering have been called human engineering, human factors, and ergonomics, but these terms most often refer to analog systems like airplane cockpits where the pilot guides a process. User engineering applies to digital systems where the goal is to store or retrieve information. D. Englebart [Engelbart 1971] refers to these principles as "User Feature Design." His point is that this term emphasizes that the features are being designed for the user rather than the other way around. In fact, though, any interactive system will require retraining of the users and some systems—like Emily—may require the user to alter thinking habits of many years standing. (But let there be no mistake, the author is deeply committed to a policy of modifying the system to fit the user.) Other sets of user engineering principles have been reported by L. B. Smith [Smith 1969] and J. G. Mitchell [Mitchell 1970]. Their suggestions are compatible with those below, but less comprehensive. The reader should also read R. V. Miller's paper [Miller 1968] in which he attempts to estimate a maximum permissible response time in seventeen interactive contexts.

The user engineering principles in the third section below are illustrated by reference to the Emily text editing system. For this reason, the Emily system is sketched in the next section. More complete descriptions are available elsewhere [Hansen 1971a] [Hansen 1971b] [Hansen 1971c]. Emily has been implemented for an IBM 2250 Graphic Display Unit, model 3. The 2250 displays lines and characters on a 12″ by 12″ screen. The user can give commands to the system with a light pen, a program function keyboard, and an alphameric keyboard.

2. THE EMILY SYSTEM

Emily is primarily intended for construction and modification of computer programs written in higher level languages. Many such systems exist, but all existing systems require the programmer to enter his text as a sequence of characters. With Emily, the user constructs his text by selecting choices from the menu to replace certain symbols in the text. For example, the symbol <STMT> might be replaced by

```
DO <ARITHV>=<ARITHX> TO <ARITHX>;
   <STMT*>
END;
```

Replaceable symbols begin with "<", end with ">", and contain a name that usually has some relation to the meaning of the string generated by the symbol. Such symbols are called *non-terminal symbols* because of their role in the Backus-Naur Form (BNF) notation for describing programming languages [Backus 1959].

In BNF a syntax for a formal language has three parts—a set of *terminal symbols*, a set of *non-terminal symbols*, and a set of *syntactic rules*. The terminal symbols are those characters and strings of characters (punctuation, reserved words, identifiers, constants) that can be part of the completed text. The non-terminal symbols are a specific set of symbols introduced only to help describe the structure of the formal language. Every non-terminal symbol must be replaced by terminal symbols before the entire text is complete, but the only allowable replacements for a given non-terminal are specified by the syntactic rules. In each rule, the given non-terminal is on the left followed by a colon followed by the sequence of symbols that may replace the non-terminal. As an example, Figure 1 shows a portion of the syntax for PL/I. Figure 2 shows a DO loop generated using this syntax.

```
1     <STMT>  :  DO <ARITHV>  =  <ARITHX> TO <ARITHX>;  <STMT*> END;
2            :  <ASGN STMT>
3     <STMT*>  :  <STMT>
4     <ASGN STMT>  :  <ARITH>  =  <ARITHX>;
5     <ARITHX>  :  <ARITH>
6            :  <ARITHV>
7            :  <NUMBER>
8            :  <ARITHX>  +  <ARITHX>
9     <ARITHX*>  :  <ARITHX>
10    <ARITHV>  :  <ARITH>
11           :<ARITH>  (<ARITHX*>)
12    <ARITH>  IS AN IDENTIFIER
13    <NUMBER>  IS A CONSTANT
```

Figure 1. Portion of syntax for PL/I.Each rule specifies a possible replacement for the non-terminal to the left of the colon. If the left side is omitted, it is the same as the previous line. Rules 12 and 13 specify special classes of terminal symbols.

```
┌───────┐
│<STMT>│
└───────┘

DO  ┌─────────┐  = <ARITHX> TO <ARITHX>;                          10
    │<ARITHV>│
    └─────────┘
    <STMT*>
END;

DO  ┌────────┐  = <ARITHX> TO <ARITHX>;                            1
    │<ARITH>│
    └────────┘
    <STMT*>
END;

DO I =  ┌─────────┐  TO <ARITHX>;                                  7
        │<ARITHX>│
        └─────────┘
    <STMT*>
END;

  . . .                                                  13,7,13,3,2
DO I = 1 TO 20;                                                    4
    ┌────────────┐
    │<ASGN STMT>│
    └────────────┘
END;


  . . .                                                 12,8,5,12,6,11,
                                                          12,9,5,12
DO I = 1 TO 20;
    S = S + A(I);
END;
```

Figure 2. Steps in the generation of a DO loop. In each step, the non-terminal in the rectangle is replaced according to the rule whose number appears at the right.

It is important to note that a string generated according to a syntax is not simply a sequence of characters, but can be divided into hierarchies of substrings on the basis of the syntactic rules. Each non-terminal in the sequence of symbols for a rule generates a subsequence. The DO statement in Figure 2 can be one of a sequence of statements in some higher DO loop and can also contain a subordinate sequence of statements (generated by <STMT*>). Replacement of a non-terminal by a rule can be thought of as replacing the non-terminal with a pointer to a copy of the rule. The non-terminals in this copy can be further replaced by pointers to copies of other rules. In a diagram each syntactic rule used in the generation of the string is represented by a *node* (a rectangle). The node contains one pointer to a subordinate node for each non-terminal in the syntactic rule. The subordinate node is called a subnode or a descendant, while the pointing node is called the parent.

2.1 Emily Text Structure

Text in the Emily system is stored in a *file*, which may contain any number of *fragments*. Each fragment has a name and contains a piece of text generated by some non-terminal symbol. Generated text is physically stored in a hierarchical structure like that described above. Each node is a section of memory containing (a) the number of the syntax rule for which this node was generated, and (b) one pointer to each subnode. In a completed text, there is one descendant node for each non-terminal in the syntax rule and the pointer to a descendant is the address of the section of memory where it is stored. If no text has been generated for a non-terminal symbol, there is no subnode and the corresponding pointer is replaced by a code representing the non-terminal symbol. If a subnode of a node is an identifier, the pointer points at a copy of the identifier in a special area. All pointers at a given identifier point to the same copy in this identifier area. Other than identifiers, each node is pointed at exactly once within the text structure. This guarantees that if a node is modified, only one piece of text is affected.

Notice that punctuation and reserved words do not appear in this representation of text. Instead, they can be generated because the syntax rule number identifies the appropriate rule. Two tables in Emily contain coded forms of the syntax rules. One table, called the *abstract syntax*, controls the hierarchical structure of generated text. It specifies which syntax rules can replace a given non-terminal symbol and the sequence of non-terminal symbols on the right-hand side of each syntax rule. Another table, the *concrete syntax*, tells how to display each rule; it includes punctuation, reserved words, and formatting information like indentation and line termination.

2.2 Creating Text

The Emily user creates hierarchical text in a series of steps very similar to Figure 2. In each step the right side of a rule is substituted for a non-terminal symbol. Before the user creates any text, the fragment contains a single non-terminal symbol. In the case of Figure 2, that symbol is <STMT>. The user sees the result of each step on the 2250 display. Figure 3 shows the steps of Figure 2 as they appear on the screen.

While using the Emily system the 2250 screen appears to be divided into three areas: text, menu, and message. The text area occupies the upper two-thirds of the screen and displays the text the user is creating. The lower third of the screen is the menu where Emily displays the strings the user can substitute in the text. The bottom line of the screen is the message area, where Emily requests operands and displays status and error messages.

Non-terminal symbols[1] in the text area are underlined to make them stand out. One of the non-terminals is the *current non-terminal* and is surrounded by a rectangle. The menu normally displays all strings that can be substituted for the current non-terminal. These strings are simply the right sides of the syntax rules that have the current non-terminal on the left.

When the user points the light pen at an item in the menu Emily substitutes that item for the current non-terminal. Usually, the substitution string contains more than one non-terminal and the new current non-terminal is the first of these. The user can also change the current non-terminal by pointing the light pen at any non-terminal in the display. Emily moves the rectangle to that non-terminal and changes the menu accordingly. When the current non-terminal is an identifier, the menu displays identifiers previously entered in the required class (some of the classes for PL/I are <ARITH>, <CHAR>, and <ENTRYNM>). The user may select one of these, or he may enter a new identifier from the keyboard. Constants are also entered from the keyboard.

2.3 Viewing Text

Since text is stored hierarchically within Emily, it can be viewed with operations that take advantage of that structure. The user may wish to descend into the structure and examine the details of some minor substructure. Alternatively, he may wish to view the highest levels of the hierarchy with substructures represented by some appropriate symbol. Both of these viewing operations are possible with Emily.

---

[1] When it is displayed, a non-terminal is the end (or terminal) of a branch of the hierarchical structure. It is called a non-terminal because it must be replaced with a string of terminals before the text is complete.

Figure 3. Generation of a DO loop with Emily. These photographs show the same steps as shown in Figure 2. The menu displays all the choices available in the implemented PL/I syntax. An arrow indicates the syntax rule the user will select next. Up to twenty-two lines of

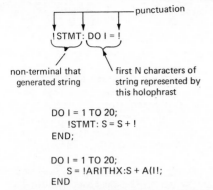

```
DO I = 1 TO 20;
    !STMT: S = S + !
END;

DO I = 1 TO 20;
    S = !ARITHX:S + A(I!;
END
```

Figure 4. Examples of holophrasts. All three examples show the DO loop, but each has been contracted differently. The user may change N, the number of characters of the substring. In the examples, N is seven.

The symbol displayed to represent a substructure is called a *holophrast*. This symbol begins and ends with an exclamation mark and contains two parts separated by a colon. The first part is the non-terminal symbol that generated the substructure and the second part is the first few characters of the represented string. Figure 4 shows three examples of holophrasts. Note that contraction to a holophrast only changes the view of the file and it does not modify the file itself. Moreover, the user never enters a holophrast from the keyboard; they are displayed only as a result of contracting text.

The user contracts a structural unit in the display by pushing a button on the program function keyboard and then pointing at some character in the text. The selected character is part of the text generated by some node in the hierarchical structure. The display of this node is replaced by a holophrast. If the user points at a holophrast, the father of the indicated node contracts to a holophrast which subsumes the earlier one. To expand a holophrast back to a string, the user returns to normal text construction mode and points the light pen at the holophrast.

The operations to ascend and descend in the text hierarchy are also invoked by program function buttons. To descend in the hierarchy the user pushes the IN button and points at a part of the text. The selected node becomes the new *display generating node*; subsequent displays show only this node and its sub-nodes. The OUT button lets the user choose among the ancestors of the display generating node and then makes the selected ancestor the new display generator.

2.4   System Environment

At Argonne National Laboratory, the 2250 is attached to an IBM 360 model 75. The 75 is under control of the MVT version of OS/360. Unit record input/output is controlled by ASP in an attached 360/50. The 360/75 has one million bytes of main core and one million bytes of a Large Capacity Storage Unit.

The Emily system itself requires 60K bytes of main core (the maximum permitted for a 2250 job at Argonne) and about 400K bytes of LCS. Emily is written in PL/I and uses the Graphic Subroutine Package to communicate with the 2250. Files for Emily are stored on a 2314 disk pack. Emily is table driven and can manipulate text in any formal language. To date, tables have been created for four languages: PL/I, GEDANKEN [Reynolds 1970], a simple hierarchy language for writing thesis outlines, and a language for creating syntax definitions.

3. USER ENGINEERING PRINCIPLES

The first principle is **Know The User**. The system designer should try to build a profile of the intended user: his education, experience, interest, how much time he has, his manual dexterity, the special requirements of his problem, his reaction to the behavior of the system, his patience. One function of such a profile is to help make specific design decisions, but the designer must be wary of assuming too much. Improper automatic actions can be an annoying system feature.

A more important function of the first principle is to remind the designer that the user is a human. He is someone to whom the designer should be considerate and for whom the designer should expend effort to provide conveniences. Furthermore, the designer must remember that human users share two common traits: they forget and they make mistakes. With any interactive system problems will arise—whether the user is a high school girl entering orders or a company president asking for a sales breakdown. The user will forget how to do what he wants, what his files contain, and even—if interrupted—what he wanted to do. Good system design must consider such foibles and try to limit their consequences. The Emily design tried to limit these consequences by explicitly including a fallible memory and a capacity for errors in the intended user profile. Other characteristics assumed are:

- curious to learn to use a new tool,
- skilled at breaking a problem into sub-problems,
- familiar with the concept of syntax and the general features of the syntax for the languages he is using,
- manually dextrous enough to use the light pen,
- not necessarily good at typing.

Throughout the following discussion, reference is made to "modularity" and "modular design." These terms refer to the structure of the program, but have important consequences for user engineering. A modular program is partitioned into subroutines with distinct functions and distinct levels of function. For instance, a high level modular subroutine implements a specific user command but modifies the data structure only by calls on lower level modules. To be useful for the general case, the lower modules must have no functions dependent on specific user commands. In the Emily system, for example, there are user commands to MOVE and COPY text and there are low level routines for the same functions. These low level routines always destroy the existing information at the destination, but the user commands are defined to move that existing information to the special fragment *DUMP*. The low level routines must be called twice (destination→*DUMP*; source→destination) to implement the user commands, but these same routines are used in several other places in the system. Designing adequate modularity into a system requires careful planning at an early stage, but pays off with a system that takes less time to implement, is easier to modify, and can be debugged with fewer problems and more confidence of success.

Specific user engineering principles to help meet the first principle can be categorized into

- minimize memorization,
- optimize operations,
- engineer for errors.

The principles are outlined in Figure 5.

```
User Engineering Principles
   First principle: Know the user
   Minimize Memorization
      Selection not entry
      Names not numbers
      Predictable behavior
      Access to system information
   Optimize Operations
      Rapid execution of common operations
      Display inertia
      Muscle memory
      Reorganize command parameters
   Engineer for Errors
      Good error messages
      Engineer out the common errors
      Reversible actions
      Redundancy
      Data structure integrity
```

Figure 5. User engineering principles.

3.1   Minimize Memorization

Because the user forgets, the computer memory must augment his memory. One important way this can be accomplished is by observing the principle **Selection Not Entry**. Rather than type a character string or operation name, the user should select the appropriate item from a list displayed by the computer. In a sense, the entire Emily system is based on this principle. The user selects syntax rules from the menu and never types text. Even when an identifier is to be entered, Emily displays previously entered identifiers, though the user must type in new identifiers. Because the system is presenting choices, the user need not remember the exact syntax of statements in the language, nor the spelling of identifiers he has declared. Moreover, each selection—a single action by the user—adds many characters to the text. Thus if the system can keep up with the user, he can build his text more quickly than by keyboard entry.

The principle of "selection not entry" is central to computer graphics and by itself constitutes a revolution in work methods. The author first saw the principle in the work of George [George 1968] and Smith [Smith 1969] but has since observed it in many systems. The fact is that a graphic display—attached to a high bandwidth channel—can display many characters in the time it would take a user to type very few. If the choices displayed cover the user's needs, he can enter information more quickly by selection. Ridsdale [Ridsdale 1971] has reported a patient note system used in a British hospital that is based on the principle of selection. In this system, selection is not by light pen but by typing the code that appears next to the desired choice in the menu.

Experience with Emily suggests that keyboard code entry is better than light pen selection because of two user frustrations. First, the menu does not provide a target for the light pen while the display is changing; and second, the delay can vary depending on system load. With keyboard codes, the user can go at full speed in making selections he is familiar with, but when he gets to unfamiliar situations he can slow down and wait for the display. Thus, his behavior can travel the spectrum from typing speed to machine paced selection.

The second principle to avoid memorization is **Names Not Numbers**. When the user is to select from a set of items he should be able to select among them by name. In too many systems, choices are made by entering a number or code which the system uses to index into a set of values. Users can and do memorize the codes for their frequent choices, though this is one more piece of information to obscure the problem at hand. But when an uncommon choice is needed, a code book must be referenced. Symbol tables are understood well enough that there is no excuse for not designing them into systems so as to replace code numbers with names. In Emily, there are names for files, fragments, display statuses, syntaxes, and non-terminals. Conceivably, the user could even supply a name to be displayed in each holophrast. In practice, though, so many holophrasts are displayed that the user would never be done making up names. For this reason, the holophrast contains the non-terminal and the first few characters of the text—a system generated "name" with a close relation to the information represented by that name.

It is also possible to forget the meaning of a name, so a system should also provide a dictionary. System names should be predefined and the user should be allowed to annotate any names he creates. The lack of a dictionary in Emily has sometimes been a nuisance while trying to remember what different text fragments contain.

The next principle, **Predictable Behavior**, is not easy to describe. The importance of such behavior is that the user can gain an "impression" of the system and understand its behavior in terms of that impression. Thus by remembering a few characteristics and a few exceptions, the user can work out for himself the details of any individual operation. In other words, the system ought to have a "Gestalt" or "personality" around which the user can organize his perception of the system. In Emily all operations on text appear to make it expand and contract. Text creation expands a non-terminal to a string and the viewing operations expand and contract between strings and holophrasts. This commonality lends the unity of predictable behavior to Emily.

Predictable behavior is also enhanced by system modularity. If the same subroutine is always used for some common interaction, the user can become accustomed to the idiosyncracies of that interaction. For instance, in Emily there is one subroutine for entering names and other text strings so that all keyboard interactions follow the same conventions.

The last memory minimization principle is **Access To System Information**. Any system is controlled by various parameters and keeps various statistics. The user should be given access to these and should be able to modify from the console any parameter that he can modify in any other way. With access to the system information, the user need not remember what he said and is not kept in the dark about what is going on. Emily provides means of setting several parameters, but fails to have any mechanism for displaying their values. This oversight is due to a failure to remember that the user might not have written the system. Another such oversight is a failure to provide error messages for many trivial user errors. Even worse, the "MULTIPLE DECLARATION" error message originally failed to say which identifier was so declared. This has been corrected, but should have been avoided by attention to the "Access to system information" principle of user engineering.

3.2   Optimize Operations

The previous section stressed the design—the logical facilities—of the set of commands available to the user. "Optimize operations" stresses the physical appearance of the system—the modes and speeds of interaction and the sequence of user actions needed to invoke specific facilities. The guiding principle is that the system should be as unobstrusive as possible, a tool that is wielded almost without conscious effort. The user should be encouraged to think not in terms of the light pen and keyboard, but in terms of how he wants to change the displayed information.

The first step in operation optimization is to design for **Rapid Execution Of Common Operations**. Because Emily text is frequently modified in terms of its syntactic organization, a data structure to represent text was chosen so as to optimize such modification. The text display is regenerated frequently, so considerable effort was expended to optimize that routine. More effort is required, though; it is still slow largely because a subroutine is called to output each symbol. Less frequent operations like file switching do not justify special optimization. Lengthy operations, however, should display occasional messages to indicate that no difficulty has occurred. For instance, while printing a file Emily displays the line number of each tenth line as it is printed.

As the system reacts to a user's request, it should observe the principle of **Display Inertia**. This means the display should change as little as necessary to carry out the request. The Emily DELETE operation replaces a holophrast (and the text it represents) with a non-terminal symbol. The size and layout of the display do not change drastically. Text cannot be deleted without first being contracted to a holophrast; thus deletion—a drastic and possibly confusing operation—does not add the disorientation of a radically changed display. The Emily display also retains inertia in that the top line changes only on explicit command. Some linear text systems always change the display so the line being operated on is in the middle of the display. Because the perspective is constantly shifting, the user is sometimes not sure where he is. The Emily automatic indentation provides additional assistance to the user. As text is created in the middle of the display, the bottom line moves down the display. Since this line is often not indented as far as the preceding line, its movement makes a readily perceptible change in the display.

One means of reducing the user's interaction effort is to design the system so the user can operate it on **Muscle Memory.** Very repetitive operations like driving a car or typing are delegated by the conscious mind to the lower part of the brain (the medulla oblongata). This part of the brain controls the body muscles and can be trained to perform operations without continual control from the conscious mind. One implication of muscle memory is that the meaning of specific interactions should have a simple relation to the state of the system. A button should not have more than a few state dependent meanings and one button should be reserved to always return the system to some basic control state. With such a button, the muscle memory can be trained to escape from any strange or unwanted state so as to transfer to a desired state. In Emily the buttons of the program function keyboard obey these principles. The NORMAL button always returns the entire system to a basic state waiting for commands. Other buttons have very limited meanings and it is almost always possible to abort one command and invoke another simply by pushing the other button (without pushing NORMAL first).

A second implication of muscle memory for system design is that the system must be prepared to accept commands in bursts exceeding ten per second. (Typing 100 words per minute is 10 characters per second. A typing burst can be faster.) It is not essential that the system react to commands at this rate, because interactive computer use is characterized by command bursts followed by pauses for new inspiration. But if command bursts are not accepted at a high rate, the muscle memory portion of the brain cannot be given full responsibility for operations. The conscious brain has to scan the system indicators waiting for GO. Command bursts from muscle memory account for the unsuitability of the light pen for rule selection as discussed under "selection not entry."

In addition to optimizing the interaction time, the system designer must be prepared to **Reorganize Command Parameters**. Observation of users in action will show that some commands are not as convenient as their frequency warrants while other commands are seldom used. Inconvenient commands can be simplified while infrequent commands can be relegated to subcommands. Such reorganization is simplified if the original system design has been adequately modularized. High level command routines can be rewritten without rewriting low level routines and the latter can be used without fear that they depend on the higher level.

A good example of command reorganization in Emily has been the evolution of the view expansion commands. In the earliest version, pointing the light pen at a holophrast expanded it one level, so that each of the subnodes of the holophrast became a new holophrast. With this mechanism, many interactions were required to view the entire structure represented by a holophrast. Very soon the system-designer/user added a system parameter called "expansion depth." This parameter dictated how many levels of a holophrast were to be expanded. To set the expansion depth, the user pushed a button (on the program function keyboard) and typed in a number (on the alphameric keyboard). It soon became obvious that users almost always set the expansion depth to either one or all. Consequently, two buttons were defined, so that the user could choose either option quickly. Later, the button for typing in the expansion depth was removed and that function placed under a general "set parameters" command. Further experience may show that only the "expand one level" button is required. It would take effect only during the next holophrast expansion. At all other times, holophrasts would always be expanded as far as possible.

3.3   Engineer for Errors

Modern computers can perform billions of operations without errors. Knowing this, system designers tend to forget that neither users nor system implementers achieve perfection. The system design must protect the user from both the system and himself. After he has learned to use a system, a serious user seldom commits a deliberate error. Usually he is forgetful, or pushes the wrong button without looking, or tries to do something entirely reasonable that never occurred to the system designer. The learner, on the other hand, has a powerful, and reasonable, curiosity to find out what happens when he does something wrong. A system must protect itself from all such errors and, as far as possible, protect the user from any serious consequences. The system should be engineered to make catastrophic errors difficult and to permit recovery from as many errors as possible.

The first principle in error engineering is to **Provide Good Error Messages**. These serve as an invaluable training aid to the learner and as a gentle reminder to the expert. With a graphic display it is possible to present error messages rapidly without wasting the user's time. Error messages should be specific, indicating the type of error and the exact location of the error in the text. Emily does not have good messages for user errors. Currently, the system blows the whistle on the 2250 and waits for the next command from the user. Each error is internally identified by a unique number, and it will not be difficult to display the appropriate message for each number.

It is not enough to simply tell the user of his errors. The system designer must also be told so he can apply the principle **Engineer Out The Common Errors**. If an error occurs frequently, it is not the fault of the user, it is a problem in the system design. Perhaps the keyboard layout is poor or commands require too much information. Perhaps consideration must be given to the organization of basic operations into higher level commands.

Emily provides several means of feedback from the user to the system designer. (Though for the most part, they have been one and the same.) A log is kept of all user interactions, user errors, and system errors. There is a command to let the user type a message to be put in the log and this message is followed by a row of asterisks. When the user is frustrated he can push a "sympathy" button. In response, Emily displays at random one of ten sympathetic messages. More importantly, frustration is noted in the log and the system designer can examine the user's preceding actions to find out where his understanding differed from the system implementation.

"Engineering errors out" does not mean to make them impossible. Rather they should be made sufficiently more difficult that the user must pause and think before he errs. In Emily, time consuming operations like file manipulation always ask the user for additional operands. If he does not want the time consuming operation he can do something else. To delete text, the user must think and contract it to a holophrast. This means that large structures cannot be cavalierly deleted.

A single erroneous deletion can inadvertently remove a very large substructure from the file. To protect the user **The System Must Provide Reversible Actions**. There ought to be one or more well understood means for undoing the effects of any system operation. In Emily, a deleted structure is moved to *DUMP*. If the user has made a mistake, he can reach into this "trash can" and retrieve the last structure he has deleted. (Deletion does destroy the old contents of *DUMP*.) A more general reversible action mechanism would be a single button that always restored the state existing before the last user interaction. Emily has no such button, but the QED system [Thompson 1968] supplies a file containing all commands issued during the console session. The user can modify this file of commands and then use it as a source of commands to modify the original text file again.

Besides helping the user escape his own mistakes, error engineering must protect the user from bugs in the system and its supporting software. Modular design is important to such protection because it minimizes the dependencies among system routines. The implementer should be able to modify and improve a routine with confidence that his changes will affect only the operation of that routine. Even if the changes introduce bugs, the user will be protected if the designer has observed the principles of redundancy and data structure integrity.

Redundancy simply means that the system provides more than one means to any given end. A powerful operation can be backed up by combinations of simpler operations. Then if the powerful operator fails, the user can still continue with his work. Such redundancy is most helpful while debugging a system, but very few systems are completely debugged and any aids to the debugger can help the user. As an adjunct of redundancy, the system must detect errors and let the user act on them, rather than simply dumping memory and terminating the run. In Emily, the PL/I ON-condition mechanism very satisfactorily catches errors. They are passed to a subroutine in Emily that tells the user that a catastrophe has occurred and names the offending module. Control then returns to the normal state of waiting for a command from the user, who has the option to continue or call for a dump.

A system should provide sufficient **Data Structure Integrity** that regard-less of system or hardware trouble some version of the user information will always be available. This principle is especially applicable to Emily where most of the information is encoded by pointers. A small error in one pointer can lose a large chunk of the file. Some effort has been spent ensuring that errors in Emily will not damage the part of the data structure kept in core during execution. But if an error abruptly terminates Emily execution (such errors are generally in the system outside Emily) the file on the disk may be in a confused state. Currently, the only protection is to copy the file before changing it, but there are file safety systems that do not rely on the user to protect himself, and one of these should be implemented for Emily.

Protection and assistance for the user are keywords in user engineering. The principles outlined in this paper are not as important as the general approach of tailoring the system to the user. Only by such an approach can Computer Science divest the computer of its image as a cold, intractable, and demanding machine. Only by such an approach can the computer be made sufficiently useful and attractive to take its place as a valuable tool for the creative worker.

ACKNOWLEDGMENTS

I am grateful to Dr. John C. Reynolds and Dr. William F. Miller. Any success of the Emily project is due to their persistent advice and encouragement.

The work reported here was supported by the U. S. Atomic Energy Commission. The text is taken from the second and fourth chapters of the author's thesis [Hansen 1971a].

REFERENCES

[Backus 1959] J.W. Backus. The syntax and semantics of the proposed international algebraic language of the Zurich ACM-GAMM conference. In *Proceedings of the International Conference on Information Processing*, UNESCO, 1959, 125-132.

[Engelbart 1971] D.C. Engelbart, Private communication, Stanford Research Institute, Menlo Park, California, 1971.

[George 1968] J.E. George. *Calgen—an interactive picture calculus generation system.* Stanford University, Computer Science Department, Report 114, 1968.

[Hansen 1971a] W.J. Hansen. *Creation of hierarchic text with a computer display.* Argonne National Laboratory ANL-7818, Argonne, Illinois, 1971; also Stanford University, Computer Science Department, doctoral dissertation, June 1971.

[Hansen 1971b] W.J. Hansen. Graphic editing of structured text. In R.D. Parslow, R.E. Green (eds.) *Advanced Computer Graphics.* Plenum Press, London, 1971.

[Hansen 1971c] W.J. Hansen. *Emily user's manual.* Argonne National Laboratory, Argonne, Illinois. 1971.

[McCarthy et al. 1967] J. McCarthy, D. Brian, G. Feldman, J. Allen. THOR—a display based time sharing system. *Proceedings of the Spring Joint Computer Conference*, AFIP Proceedings Vol. 30 (1967), 623-633.

[Miller 1968] R.B. Miller. Response times in man-computer conversational transactions. *Proceedings of the Fall Joint Computer Conference*, AFIPS Proceedings Vol. 33 (1968), 267-277.

[Mitchell 1970] J.G. Mitchell. *The design and construction of flexible and efficient interactive programming systems*, Department of Computer Science, Carnegie-Mellon University, Pittsburgh, Pennsylvania, 1970.

[Reynolds 1970] J.C. Reynolds. GEDANKEN—a simple typeless language based on the principle of completeness and the reference concept. *Communications of the ACM*, 13:5, May 1970, 308-319.

[Ridsdale 1971] B. Ridsdale. The visual display unit for data collection and retrieval. In R.D. Parslow, R.E. Green (eds.) *Advanced Computer Graphics.* Plenum Press, London, 1971.

[Smith 1969] L.B. Smith. *The use of man-machine interaction in data-fitting problems.* Stanford Linear Accelerator Center, Report 96, Stanford, California, 1969.

[TECO] *TECO Programmer's Reference Manual.* Digital Equipment Corporation, Maynard, Massachusetts, DEC-10-ETEE-D (revised from time to time); see also *PDP-6 Time Sharing TECO.* Stanford University, Stanford Artificial Intelligence Laboratory, Operating Note 34, 1967; see also P.R. Samson. *PDP-6 TECO.* Massachusetts Institute of Technology, Artificial Intelligence Laboratory, AI Memo 81, July 1965.

[Thompson 1968] K. Thompson. QED text editor. Bell Telephone Laboratories, Murray Hill, New Jersey, 1968.

[Weiher 1967] W. Weiher. Preliminary description of EDIT2. Stanford Artificial Intelligence Laboratory, Operating Note 5, Stanford, California, 1967.

[Wylbur 1968] *Wylbur Reference Manual.* Stanford University Computation Center, Campus Facility Users Manual, Appendix E, Stanford, California, 1968.

12 Automated Programmering: The Programmer's Assistant

WARREN TEITELMAN

XEROX Palo Alto Research Center
Palo Alto, California

*This paper describes a research effort and programming system
designed to facilitate the production of programs. Unlike automated
programming, which focuses on developing systems that write
programs, automated programmering involves developing systems
which automate (or at least greatly facilitate) those tasks that a
programmer performs other than writing programs: e.g., repairing
syntactical errors to get programs to run in the first place, generating
test cases, making tentative changes, retesting, undoing changes,
reconfiguring, massive edits, et al., plus repairing and recovering
from mistakes made during the above. When the system in which the
programmer is operating is cooperative and helpful with respect to
these activities, the programmer can devote more time and energy to
the task of programming itself, i.e., to conceptualizing, designing
and implementing. Consequently, he can be more ambitious, and
more productive.*

Reprinted with the permission of AFIPS from: *Fall Joint Computer Conference
Proceedings*, 1972, AFIPS Volume 41, pp. 917-921.

1. BBN-LISP

The system we will describe here is embedded in BBN-LISP. BBN-LISP, as a programming *language*, is an implementation of LISP, a language designed for list processing and symbolic manipulation [Teitelman et al. 1971]. BBN-LISP as a programming *system,* is the product of, and vehicle for, a research effort supported by ARPA for improving the programmer's environment.[1] The term "environment" is used to suggest such elusive and subjective considerations as ease and level of interaction, forgivingness of errors, human engineering, etc.

Much of BBN-LISP was designed specifically to enable construction of the type of system described in this paper. For example, BBN-LISP includes such features as complete compatibility of compiled and interpreted code, "visible" variable bindings and control information, programmable error recovery procedures, etc. Indeed, at this point the two systems, BBN-LISP and the programmer's assistant, have become so intertwined (and interdependent), that it is difficult, and somewhat artificial, to distinguish between them. We shall not attempt to do so in this paper, preferring instead to present them as one integrated system.

BBN-LISP contains many facilities for assisting the programmer in his nonprogramming activities. These include a sophisticated structure editor which can either be used interactively or as a subroutine; a debugging package for inserting conditional programmed interrupts around or inside of specified procedures; a "prettyprint" facility for producing structured symbolic output; a program analysis package which produces a tree structured representation of the flow of control between procedures, as well as a concordance listing indicating for each procedure the procedures that call it, the procedures that it calls, and the variables it references, sets, and binds, etc.

Most on-line programming systems contain similar features. However, the essential difference between the BBN-LISP system and other systems is embodied in the philosophy that the user addresses the system through an (active) intermediary agent, whose task it is to collect and save information about what the user and his programs are doing, and to utilize this information to assist the user and his programs. This intermediary is called the programmer's assistant (or p.a.).

2. THE PROGRAMMER'S ASSISTANT

For most interactions with the BBN LISP system, the programmer's assistant is an invisible interface between the user and LISP: the user types a request, for example, specifying a function to be applied to a set of arguments. The indicated operation is then performed, and a resulting value is printed. The system is then ready for the next request. However, in addition, in BBN-LISP, each input typed by the user, and the value of the corresponding operation, are automatically stored by the p.a. on a global data structure called the *history list.*

The history list contains information associated with each of the individual "events" that have occurred in the system, where an event corresponds to an individual type-in operation. Associated with each event is the input that initiated it, the value it yielded, plus other information such as side effects, messages printed by the system or by user programs, information about any

---

[1] Earlier work in this area is reported in [Teitelman 1969].

errors that may have occurred during the execution of the event, etc. As each new event occurs, the existing events on the history list are aged, with the oldest event "forgotten".[2]

The user can reference an event on the history list by a pattern which is used for searching the history list, e.g., FLAG:←$ refers to the last event in which the variable FLAG was changed by the user; by its relative event number, e.g. -1 refers to the most recent event, -2 the event before that, etc., or by an absolute event number. For example, the user can retrieve an event in order to REDO a test case after making some program changes. Or, having typed a request that contains a slight error, the user may elect to FIX it, rather than retyping the request in its entirety. The USE command provides a convenient way of specifying simultaneous substitutions for lexical units and/or character strings, e.g., USE X FOR Y AND + FOR *. This permits after-the-fact parameterization of previous events.

The p.a. recognizes such requests as REDO, FIX, and USE as being directed to *it*, not the LISP interpreter, and executes them directly. For example, when given a REDO command, the p.a. retrieves the indicated event, obtains the input from that event, and treats it exactly as though the user had typed it in directly. Similarly, the USE command directs the p.a. to perform the indicated substitutions and process the result exactly as though it had been typed in.

The p.a. currently recognizes about 15 different commands (and includes a facility enabling the user to define additional ones). The p.a. also enables the user to treat several events as a single unit (e.g. REDO 47 THRU 51), and to name an event or group of events, e.g., NAME TEST -1 and -2. All of these capabilities allow, and in fact encourage, the user to construct complex *console* operations out of simpler ones in much the same fashion as programs are constructed, i.e., simpler operations are checked out first, and then combined and rearranged into large ones. The important point to note is that the user does *not* have to prepare in advance for possible future (re-) usage of an event. He can operate straightforwardly as in other systems, yet the information saved by the p.a. enables him to implement his "after-thoughts."

3. UNDOING

Perhaps the most important after-thought operation made possible by the p.a. is that of *undoing* the side effects of a particular event or events. In most systems, if the user suspects that a disaster might result from a particular operation, e.g., an untested program running wild and chewing up a complex data structure, he would prepare for this contingency by saving the state of part or all of his environment before attempting the operation. If anything went wrong, he would then back up and start over. However, saving/dumping operations are usually expensive and time-consuming, especially compared to a short computation, and are therefore not performed that frequently. In addition, there is always the case where disaster strikes as a result of a supposedly debugged or innocuous operation. For example, suppose the user types

```
FOR X IN ELTS REMOVE PROPERTY 'MORPH FROM X
```

which removes the property MORPH from every member of the list ELTS, and then realizes that he meant to remove this property from the members of

---

[2] The storage used in its representation is then reusable.

the list ELEMENTS instead, and has thus destroyed some valuable information.

Such "accidents" happen all too often in typical console sessions, and result in the user's either having to spend a great deal of effort in reconstructing the inadvertently destroyed information, or alternatively in returning to the point of his last back-up, and then repeating all useful work performed in the interim. (Instead, using the p.a., the user can recover by simply typing UNDO, and then perform the correct operation by typing USE ELEMENTS FOR ELTS.)

The existence of UNDO frees the user from worrying about such oversights. He can be relaxed and confident in his console operations, yet still work rapidly. He can even experiment with various program and data configurations, without necessarily thinking through all the implications *in advance*. One might argue that this would promote sloppy working habits. However, the same argument can be, and has been, leveled against interactive systems in general. In fact, freeing the user from such details as having to anticipate all of the consequences of an (experimental) change usually results in his being able to pay more attention to the conceptual difficulties of the problem he is trying to solve.

Another advantage of undoing as it is implemented in the programmer's assistant is that it enables events to be undone *selectively*. Thus, in the above example, if the user had performed a number of useful modifications to his programs and data structures before noticing his mistake, he would not have to return to the environment extant when he originally typed FOR X IN ELTS REMOVE PROPERTY 'MORPH FROM X, in order to UNDO that event, i.e., he could UNDO this event without UNDOing the intervening events.[3] This means that even if we eliminated efficiency considerations and assumed the existence of a system where saving the entire state of the user's environment required insignificant resources and was automatically performed before every event, there would still be an advantage to having an undo capability such as the one described here.

Finally, since the operation of undoing an event itself produces side effects, it too is undoable. The user can often take advantage of this fact, and employ strategies that use UNDO for desired operation reversals, not simply as a means of recovery in case of trouble. For example, suppose the user wishes to interrogate a complex data structure in each of two states while successively modifying his programs. He can interrogate the data structure, change it, interrogate it again, then undo the changes, modify his programs, and then repeat the process using successive UNDOs to flip back and forth between the two states of the data structure.

4. IMPLEMENTATION OF UNDO

The UNDO capability of the programmer's assistant is implemented by making each function that is to be undoable save on the history list enough information to enable reversal of its side effects.[4] For example, when a list node is about to be changed, it and its original contents are saved; when a variable is reset, its binding (i.e., position on the stack) and its current value are saved. For each primitive operation that involves side effects, there are two separate

---

[3] Of course, he could UNDO all of the intervening events as well, e.g., by typing UNDO THRU ELTS.

[4] See [Teitelman et al. 1971, 22.39-43], for a more complete description of undoing.

functions, one which always saves this information, i.e., is always undoable, and one which does not.

Although the overhead for saving undo information is small, the user may elect to make a particular operation *not* be undoable if the cumulative effect of saving the undo information seriously degrades the overall performance of a program because the operation in question is repeated so often. The user, by his choice of function, specifies which operations are undoable. In some sense, the user's choice of function acts as a declaration about frequency of use versus need for undoing. For those cases where the user does not want certain functions undoable once his program becomes operational, but does wish to be able to undo while debugging, the p.a. provides a facility called TESTMODE. When in TESTMODE, the undoable version of each function is executed, regardless of whether the user's program specifically called that version or not.

Finally, all operation involving side effects that are *typed-in* by the user are automatically made undoable by the p.a. by substituting the corresponding undoable function name(s) in the expression before execution. This procedure is feasible because operations that are typed-in rarely involve iterations or lengthy computations *directly*, nor is efficiency usually important. However, as a precaution, if an event occurs during which more than a user-specified number of pieces of undo information are saved, the p.a. interrupts the operation to ask the user if he wants to continue having undo information saved.

5. AUTOMATIC ERROR CORRECTION: THE DWIM FACILITY

The previous discussion has described ways in which the programmer's assistant is *explicitly* invoked by the user. The programmer's assistant is also automatically invoked by the system when certain error conditions are encountered. A surprisingly large percentage of these errors, especially those occurring in type-in, are of the type that can be corrected without any knowledge about the purpose of the program or operation in question, e.g., misspellings, certain kinds of syntax errors, etc. The p.a. attempts to correct these errors, using as a guide both the context at the time of the error, and information gathered from monitoring the user's requests. This form of *implicit* assistance provided by the programmer's assistant is called the DWIM (*Do-What-I-Me*an) capability.

For example, suppose the user defines a function for computing N factorial by typing[5]

```
DEFIN[((FACT (N) IF N = 0 THEN 1
                ELSE NN * (FACT N-1)].
```

When this input is executed, an error occurs because DEFIN is not the name of a function. However, DWIM notes that DEFIN is very close to DEFINE, which is a likely candidate in this context. Since the error occurred in type-in, DWIM proceeds on this assumption, types = DEFINE to inform the user of its action, makes the correction and carries out the request. Similarly if the user then types FATC(3) to test out his function, DWIM would correct FATC to FACT.

---

[5] In BBN-LISP] automatically supplies enough right parentheses to match back to the last [.

When the function FACT is called, the evaluation of NN in NN*(FACT N-1) causes an error. Here, DWIM is able to guess that NN probably means N by using the contextual information that N is the name of the argument to the function FACT in which the error occurred. Since this correction involves a user *program*, DWIM proceeds more cautiously than for corrections to user type-in: it informs the user of the correction it is about to make by typing NN(IN FACT)→N? and then waits for approval. If the user types Y (for YES), or simply does not respond within a (user) specified time interval (for example, if the user has started the computation and left the room), DWIM makes the correction and continues the computation, exactly as though the function had originally been correct, i.e., no information is lost as a result of the error.

If the user types N (for NO), the situation is the same as when DWIM is not able to make a correction (that it is reasonably confident of). In this case, an error occurs, following which the system goes into a suspended state called a "break" from which the user can repair the problem himself and continue the computation. Note that in neither case is any information or partial results lost.

DWIM also fixes other mistakes besides misspellings, e.g., typing eight for "(" or nine for ")" (because of failure to hit the shift key). For example, if the user had defined FACT as

```
(IF N=0 THEN 1 ELSE NN*8FACT N-1),
```

DWIM would have been able to infer the correct definition.

DWIM is also used to correct other types of conditions not considered errors, but nevertheless obviously not what the user meant. For example, if the user calls the editor on a function that is not defined, rather than generating an error, the editor invokes the spelling corrector to try to find what function the user meant, giving DWIM as possible candidates a list of user defined functions. Similarly, the spelling corrector is called to correct misspelled edit commands, p.a. commands, names of files, etc. The spelling corrector can also be called by user programs.

As mentioned above, DWIM also uses information gathered by monitoring user requests. This is accomplished by having the p.a., for each user request, "notice" the functions and variables being used, and add them to appropriate spelling lists, which are then used for comparision with (potentially) misspelled units. This is how DWIM "knew" that FACT was the name of a function, and was therefore able to correct FATC to FACT.

As a result of knowing the names of user functions and variables (as well as the names of the most frequently used system functions and variables), DWIM seldom fails to correct a spelling error the user feels it should have. And, since DWIM knows about common typing errors, e.g., transpositions, doubled characters, shift mistakes, etc.,[6] DWIM almost never mistakenly corrects an error. However, if DWIM *did* make a mistake, the user could simply interrupt or abort the computation, UNDO the correction (all DWIM corrections are undoable), and repair the problem himself. Since an error had occurred, the user would have had to intervene anyway, so that DWIM's unsuccessful attempt at correction did not result in extra work for him.

---

[6] The spelling corrector also can be instructed as to specific user misspelling habits. For example, a fast typist is more apt to make transposition errors than a hunt-and-peck typist, so that DWIM is more conservative about transposition errors with the latter. See [Teitelman et al. 1971, 17.20-22] for complete description of spelling corrections.

6. STATISTICS OF USE

While monitoring user requests, the programmer's assistant keeps statistics about utilization of its various capabilities. Table 1 contains 5 statistics from 11 different sessions, where each corresponds to several individual sessions at the console, following each of which the user saved the state of his environment, and then resumed at the next console session. These sessions are from eight different users at several ARPA sites. It is important to note that with one exception (the author) the users did not know that statistics on their session would be seen by anyone, or, in most cases, that the p.a. gathered such statistics at all.

The five statistics reported here are the number of:

1. requests to executive, i.e., in LISP terms, inputs to evalquote or to a break;
2. requests to editor, i.e., number of editing commands typed in by user;
3. units of undo information saved by the p.a., e.g., changing a list node (in LISP terms, a single *rplaca* or *rplacd*) corresponds to one unit of undo information;
4. p.a. commands, e.g., REDO, USE, UNDO, etc.;
5. spelling corrections.

After these statistics were gathered, more extensive measurements were added to the p.a. These are shown for an extended session with one user (the author) in Table 2.

7. CONCLUSIONS

We see the current form of the programmer's assistant as a first step in a sequence of progressively more intelligent, and therefore more helpful, intermediary agents. By attacking the problem of representing the intent behind a user request, and incorporating such information in the p.a., we hope to enable the user to be less specific, and the p.a. to draw inferences and take more initiative.

However, even in its present relatively simplistic form, in addition to making life a lot more pleasant for users, the p.a. has had a surprising synergistic effect on user productivity that seems to be related to the *overhead that is involved when people have to switch tasks or levels.* For example, when a user types a request which contains a misspelling, having to retype it is a minor

Table 1. Statistics on Usage

Sessions	exec inputs	edit commands	undo saves	p.a. commands	spelling corrections
1.	1422	1089	3418	87	17
2.	454	791	782	44	28
3.	360	650	680	33	28
4.	1233	3149	2430	184	64
5.	302	24	558	8	0
6.	109	55	667	6	1
7.	1371	2178	2138	95	32
8.	400	311	1441	19	57
9.	294	604	653	7	30
10.	102	44	1044	1	4
11.	378	52	1818	2	2

Table 2. Further Statistics

exec inputs	3445	
undo saves	10394	
changes undone	468	
calls to editor	387	
edit commands	3027	
edit undo saves	1669	
edit changes undone	178	
p.a. commands	360	
spelling corrections	74	
calls to spelling corrector	1108	(see note 1)
# of words compared	5636	(see note 2)
time in spelling corrector (in seconds)	80.2	
CPU time (hr:min:sec)	1:49:59	
console time	21:36:48	
time in editor	5:23:53	

NOTE 1. An "error" may result in several calls to the spelling corrector, e.g., the word might be a misspelling of a break command, of a p.a. command, or of a function name, each of which entails a separate call.

NOTE 2. This number is the actual number of words considered as possible respellings. Note that for each call to the spelling corrector, on the average only five words were considered, although the spelling lists are typically 20 to 50 words long. This number is so low because frequently misspelled words are moved to the front of the spelling list, and because words are not considered that are "obviously" too long or too short, e.g., neither AND nor PRETTYPRINT would be considered as possible respellings of DEFIN.

annoyance (depending, of course, on the amount of typing required and the user's typing skill). However, if the user has mentally *already performed that task*, and is thinking ahead several steps to what he wants to do next, then having to go back and retype the operation represents a disruption of his thought processes, in addition to being a clerical annoyance. The disruption is even more severe when the user must also repair the damage caused by a faulty operation (instead of being able to simply UNDO it).

The p.a. acts to minimize these distractions and diversions, and thereby, as Bobrow puts it [Bobrow 1972]

> . . . greatly facilitates construction of complex programs because it allows the user to remain thinking about his program operation at a relatively high level without having to descend into manipulation of details.

We feel that similar capabilities should be built into low-level debugging packages such as DDT, the executive language of time sharing systems, etc., as well as other "high-level" programming languages, for they provide the user with a significant *mental mechanical advantage* in attacking problems.

REFERENCES

[Bobrow 1972] D.G. Bobrow. Requirements for advanced programming systems for list processing. *Communications of the ACM*, 15:7 (July 1972), 618–627.

[Teitelman 1969] W. Teitelman. Toward a programming laboratory. *International Joint Conference on Artificial Intelligence*, Washington, May 1969, 1-8.

[Teitelman et al. 1971] W. Teitelman, D.G. Bobrow, A.K. Hartley, D.L. Murphy. *BBN-LISP TENEX Reference Manual*. BBN Report, July 1971.

13 A Display-Oriented Programmer's Assistant

WARREN TEITELMAN

XEROX Palo Alto Research Center
Palo Alto, California

This paper continues and extends previous work by the author in developing systems which provide the user with various forms of explicit and implicit assistance, and in general cooperate with the user in the development of his programs. The system described in this paper makes extensive use of a bit map display and pointing device (a mouse) to significantly enrich the user's interactions with the system, and to provide capabilities not possible with terminals that essentially emulate hard copy devices. For example, any text that is displayed on the screen can be pointed at and treated as input, exactly as though it were typed, i.e., the user can say use this expression or that value, and then simply point. The user views his programming environment through a collection of display windows, each of which corresponds to a different task or context. The user can manipulate the windows, or the contents of a particular window, by a combination of keyboard inputs or pointing operations. The technique of using different windows for different tasks makes it easy for the user to manage several simultaneous tasks and contexts, e.g., defining programs, testing programs, editing, asking the system for assistance, sending and receiving messages, etc. and to switch back and forth between these tasks at his convenience.

1. INTRODUCTION

Lisp systems have been used for highly interactive programming for more than a decade.[1] During that period, much effort has been devoted to developing tools and techniques for providing powerful interactive support to the programmer. The Interlisp programming system [Teitelman 1978] represents one of the more successful projects aimed at developing a system which could be used by researchers in computer science for performing their day to day work, and could also serve as a testbed for introducing and evaluating new ideas and techniques for providing sophisticated forms of programmer assistance. Interlisp on the PDP-10 is currently used by programmers at over a dozen ARPA network sites for doing research and development on advanced artificial intelligence projects such as speech and language understanding, medical diagnosis, computer-aided instruction, automatic programming, etc. Implementations of Interlisp on several other machines are currently planned or in progress.

This paper describes a system written in Interlisp which extends the Interlisp user facilities to take advantage of a display.[2] The paper is not an "idea" paper in the sense that Artificial Intelligence papers usually are. Instead, this paper describes a working system which implements and *integrates* a number of ideas and techniques previously reported in the literature by several different individuals, including the author. The idea of a display composed of multiple, overlapping regions called "windows" is attributable to and an essential part of the Smalltalk programming system designed and implemented by the Learning Research Group at Xerox Research Center [Kay and Goldberg 1976]. In particular, much of the way that windows are used in the system described here was influenced by the work of Dan Ingalls on the Smalltalk user interface. The idea of using the display as a means for allowing the user to retain comprehension of complex program environments, and to monitor several simultaneous tasks, can be found in the work of Dan Swinehart [Swinehart 1974]. The use of the "mouse" as a pointing device for selecting portions of a display goes back to the early work on NLS [English et al. 1967]. Finally, the techniques used for automatic error correction and the idea of having the user interact with the system through an active intermediary which maintains a history of his session, both of which appear in this paper, are parts of the standard Interlisp system [Teitelman 1969] [Teitelman 1972b]. The work reported in this paper is of interest primarily in how the realization of these various ideas in a single, integrated, working system dramatically confirms their value.[3]

---

[1]An excellent survey of the state of the art may be found in [Sandewall 1978].

[2]See the Acknowledgments at the end of this article for others involved in the project.

[3]When I first began to work in 1969 on what was to become DWIM, the automatic error correction facility of Interlisp, by implementing a primitive spelling corrector which would automatically correct a certain class of user spelling errors, I discussed this project at length with a colleague over a period of months. One day soon after this facility was finally completed and installed in our Lisp system, this same colleague rushed to my office and in great excitement exclaimed that the system had corrected an error. I was surprised at his enthusiasm, since we had been discussing this system for months. He replied, "Yes, but it really did it!" The system described herein implements ideas that many of us have been saying would be a good thing to have. And they really are!

2. OVERVIEW OF THE SYSTEM

The system described in this paper is implemented on a version of Interlisp [Teitelman 1978] running on MAXC, a computer at the Xerox Research Center in Palo Alto. This computer emulates a PDP-10, and runs the Tenex operating system, so that from the standpoint of the user, the system he is using is Interlisp-10. The raster-scan display used by the system described in this paper is maintained by a separate 65K 16 bit word minicomputer. The minicomputer is linked to MAXC through an internal network, and implements a graphics protocol similar to the Network Graphics Protocol [Sproul and Thomas 1974], but specialized for text and raster-scan images. All of the work described in this paper deals with the "high end" of the system, i.e., the user interface, and is written entirely in Interlisp.

The user communicates with the system using a standard typewriter-like keyboard. In addition, he has available a pointing device commonly called a "mouse" [English et al. 1967] used for pointing at particular locations on the screen. For those unfamiliar with this device, the mouse is a small object (about 3" by 2" by 1") with three buttons on its top. The system gives the user continuous feedback as to where it thinks the mouse is pointing by displaying a cursor on the screen. The user slides the mouse around on his working surface (causing bearings or wheels on the bottom of the mouse to rotate), and the system moves the cursor on the display. The user indicates that the mouse has arrived at some desired location by pressing one of the three buttons on the top of the mouse. The interpretation of the buttons depends on the particular program listening to the mouse. For example, when the mouse is positioned over a piece of text, and one of its buttons pressed, the corresponding text is "selected." Such selections are indicated by inverting the text, i.e., displaying it as white characters on a black background.

The user interacts with the system either by typing on the keyboard, or by pointing at commands or expressions on the screen, or an asynchronous mixture of the two. In particular, any material that is displayed on the screen can be selected and then treated as though it were input, i.e., typed.

The ability to be able to select, i.e., point at, material currently displayed and cause it to be treated as input is extremely useful, and situations where such a facility can be used occur very often during the course of an interactive session.

Why is such a facility useful? Because most interactions with a programming system are not independent, i.e., each "event" bears some relationship to what transpired before, usually to a fairly recent event. Being able to point at (portions of) these events effectively gives the user the power of *pronoun reference*, i.e., the user can say use *this* expression or *that* value, and then simply point. This drastically reduces the amount of typing the user has to do in many situations, and results in a considerable increase in the effective "bandwidth" of the user's communication with his programming environment.

The user views his environment through a display consisting of several rectangular display "windows". Windows can be, and frequently are, overlapped on the screen. In this case, windows that are "underneath" can be brought up on top and vice versa. The resulting configuration considerably increases the user's effective working space, and also contributes to the illusion that the user is viewing a desk top containing a number of sheets of paper which the user can manipulate in various ways.

One facility provided by these windows that is not available with sheets of paper is the ability to *scroll* the window forward or backward to view material previously, but not currently, visible in the window. Thus a single window can be used to view and manipulate a body of text that would require many sheets of paper.

Each window corresponds to a different task or aspect of the user's environment. For example, there is a TYPESCRIPT window, which contains the transcript of the user's interactions with the Lisp interpreter through the programmer's assistant, a WORK AREA window which is used for editing and prettyprinting, a HISTORY window, a BACKTRACE window, a MESSAGE window, etc. Using different windows for different tasks

> ... makes it easy for the user to manage several simultaneous tasks and contexts, switching back and forth between them at his convenience.

Being able to switch back and forth between tasks results in a relaxed and easy style of operating more similar to the way people tend to work in the absence of restrictions. To use a programming metaphor, people operate somewhat like a collection of coroutines corresponding to tasks in various states of completion. These coroutines are continually being activated by internally and externally generated interrupts, and then suspended when higher priority interrupts arrive, e.g., a phone call that interrupts a meeting, a quick question by a colleague that interrupts a phone call, etc. Our previous experience with Interlisp supports the contention that it is of great value to the user to be able to switch back and forth quickly between related tasks. The system described in this paper makes this especially convenient, as is illustrated in the sample session presented in the body of the paper.

One technique heavily employed throughout the system is the use of *menus*. A menu is a type of window that causes a specified operation to be performed when a selection is made in that window. Menus serve a number of important functions. They make it easy for the user to specify an operation without having to type. They act as a prompt for the user by providing him with a repertoire of commands from which to choose. For example, often a user will not remember the name of a command, or may not even be aware of the existence of a command.

However, most importantly, *menus greatly facilitate context switching*. As with most systems, the interpretation of the user's keystrokes (with the exception of interrupt characters which usually have a globally defined effect) depends on the state of the system. For example, when addressing the Lisp interpreter, the characters that the user types are used to construct Lisp expressions which are then evaluated. When using the editor, the characters are inserted in the indicated expression, etc. The important point is that once the user starts typing, he normally has to complete the operation or abort it. However, by selecting a menu command using the mouse, even in the midst of typing, the user can temporarily suspend the operation he is performing, go off and do something else, and then return and continue with his current context. This is also illustrated in the sample session below.

3. A SAMPLE SESSION WITH THE SYSTEM

Since so much of the utility of the system described in this paper rests on visual effects, it is difficult to transmit the feel and smoothness of the system through words. Therefore, the form chosen for presenting the system in this paper is to take the reader through a sample session with the system, using frequent "snapshots" of the display as a substitute for the actual display itself. This session is divided into two parts. The first part is a "toy" session, in that the user is not performing any serious work. It is included only to introduce the salient features of the system. The second part of the session shows some more sophisticated use of these features in the context of an actual working session involving finding and fixing bugs, testing programs, sending and receiving messages, etc.

For readers not familiar with Lisp, please ignore Lisp related details (which we have tried to minimize). The important point is the way the system allows the user to switch back and forth between several tasks and contexts. Such a facility would be useful in any programming environment.

3.1   Sample Session—Part I

1. Figure 1 shows the initial configuration of the screen. Three windows are displayed: the TYPESCRIPT window, which records the user's interactions with the programmer's assistant and the Lisp interpreter; the PROMPT window, which is the black region without a caption at the top of the screen used for prompting the user; and a *menu*, which is the smaller window with caption MENUS to the right of the TYPESCRIPT window. A menu is just like any other window, except that whenever a selection is made in a menu, a specified operation is also performed. This particular menu is a menu of *menus*, hence its caption. If the user selects one of its commands, each of which is the name of a menu, the corresponding menu will be displayed at the location he indicates. He can then select, and thereby perform, commands on that menu. The crosshairs shape in the lower right hand portion of the TYPESCRIPT window is the cursor, and indicates the current position of the mouse.

In Figure 1, I have just typed in a Lisp definition for the function FACT (factorial). Lisp has given me the error message "incorrect defining form" (displayed in bold face to set it off). The system displays a blinking caret[4] to

---

[4]In these figures, the caret is always shown in its "on" position.

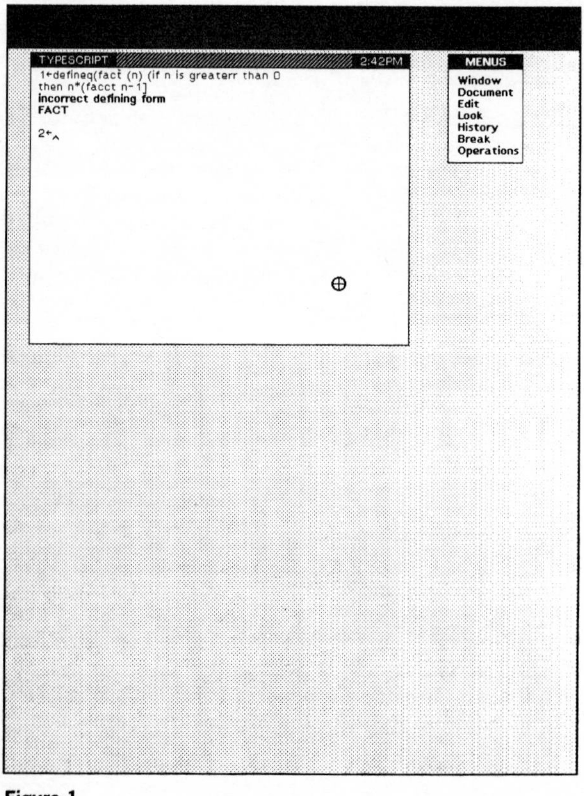

Figure 1.

indicate where the next character that I type, or the system prints, will be displayed. In Figure 1, the caret now appears immediately following the "2 ←", where 2 is the event number for my next interaction with the programmer's assistant, and ← is the "ready" character.

2. I don't understand what caused this error, so I type ? to the **P.A.** (programmer's assistant), requesting it to supply additional explanatory information. The **P.A.** looks at the previous event to determine the nature of the error. In this case, using built-in information about the arguments to DEFINEQ, the **P.A.** tells me that the problem is that DEFINEQ encountered an atom where it expected a list, i.e., a left parenthesis is missing from in front of the word "fact".[5] Since the programmer's assistant is maintaining a history of my interactions with the system, I don't have to retype the DEFINEQ expression. Instead, I can edit what I have already typed, and simply insert the missing left parenthesis. The EDIT menu will allow me to perform various editing operations using the mouse for pointing and the keyboard, where necessary, for supplying text. In Figure 2, I have already moved the mouse so that the cursor is positioned over the EDIT command on the MENUS menu, in preparation for "bringing up" the EDIT menu.

---

[5]If the **P.A.** did not know anything about this particular error, it would refer to the index of the on-line Interlisp Reference Manual and present the corresponding text associated with the error message by way of explanation. The user can also augment the built-in information that the **P.A.** has about system functions by informing the **P.A.** about the requirements of his own functions. He can then use the ? command to explain errors in his own programs.

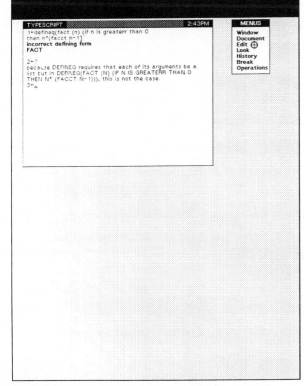

Figure 2.

3. I press a button on the mouse to select the EDIT command in the MENUS menu. The system indicates the selection by displaying EDIT as white on black. The PROMPT window tells me to use the left button on the mouse to indicate where I want the center of the (EDIT) menu to appear. The cursor is changed to an icon of a menu with a cross in its center to suggest the operation that is pending. At this point, I don't *have* to complete this operation. I can type in other expressions to the programmer's assistant, perform other menu operations, etc. The process which is waiting for me to supply the indicated information is simply a co-routine which has been suspended.[6] However, since I want to fix up the DEFINEQ expression before going on to anything else, I move the cursor to the position at which I want the EDIT menu to appear, which is below the MENUS menu and to the right of the TYPESCRIPT window, as shown in Figure 3.

---

[6]See description of the "Spaghetti Stack" facility in [Bobrow and Wegbreit 1973] and [Teitelman 1978].

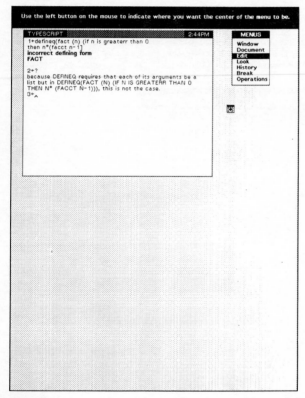

Figure 3.

4. I press the left button on the mouse, causing the EDIT menu to appear at the location of the cursor. In this position, the EDIT menu slightly overlaps both the TYPESCRIPT window and the MENUS menu, so the system automatically adjusts the EDIT menu by sliding it off these windows to its location as shown in Figure 4.[7]

---

[7]I could force the EDIT menu to overlap the TYPESCRIPT window by positioning it exactly using one of the commands on the WINDOW menu. However, since in this case I only positioned the menu approximately, the system tries to "Do What I Mean", a philosophy of system design we have tried to follow throughout the Interlisp system [Teitelman 1969].

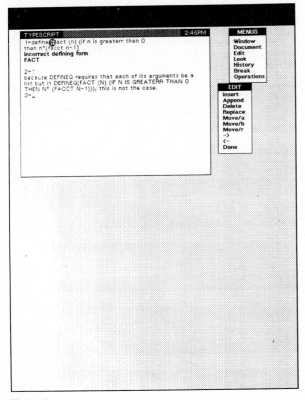

Figure 4.

5. Now I am ready to edit. I select the left parenthesis in the first line of the TYPESCRIPT window, and then select the INSERT command on the EDIT menu. The line of text in the TYPESCRIPT window is broken just before the selection (the left parenthesis), and the caret is moved to that location. The PROMPT window instructs me to input material. Anything I type will appear at the location indicated by the caret.

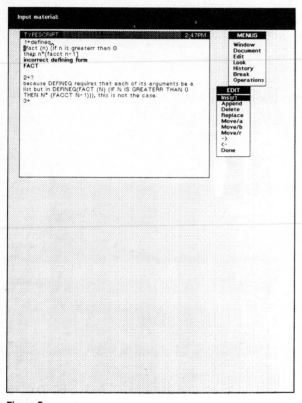

Figure 5.

6. I type in a single left parenthesis, and terminate the INSERT operation. The line of text I have been editing is rejoined, and the caret returned to the appropriate location at the end of the TYPESCRIPT window. I now want to cause the corrected text to be *re-input* in order to perform my original operation, i.e., define my function. Therefore, I select the text by first selecting the "d" in "defineq" and then extending this selection through the final "]". Then, using the same method as previously shown for bringing up the EDIT menu, I bring up the WINDOW menu in order to obtain the command for inputting selected material.

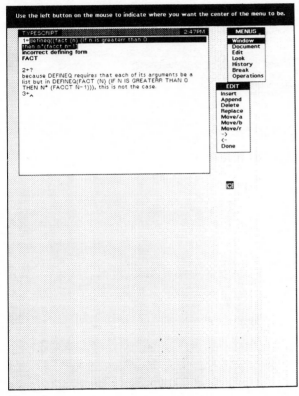

Figure 6.

7. The WINDOW menu contains the command "READ SELECTIONS" which is the command that I *think* does what I want. I therefore select this command, but instead of *clicking* the mouse button, I *hold* the mouse button down. This instructs the system to tell me what it *would* do if this operation were actually performed. Here, the PROMPT window informs me that the "READ SELECTIONS" command causes the selected material to be treated as input. Figure 7 shows the display as of this point. The cursor has been changed to an arrow to indicate that a selection is about to be made. The material that would be selected, namely the "READ SELECTIONS" command, is underscored. If I want to perform this selection, I simply release the mouse button. Otherwise, I can move the mouse to another location and release it there in order to perform a selection at the new location, or move it off of the menu entirely to abort the selection.

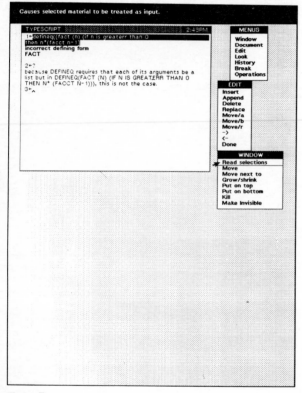

Figure 7.

8. I release the mouse button, and the selected material is treated exactly as though I had typed it, i.e., becomes event number 3 and causes the function FACT to be defined. As mentioned before, this ability of being able to select, i.e., point at, material currently displayed and cause it to be treated as input is extremely useful, and the situations where such a facility can be used occur very often during the course of an interactive session.

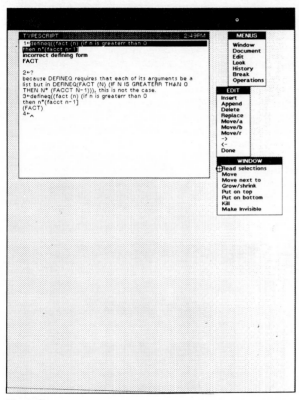

Figure 8.

9. I now try out my function by typing FACT(3). At this point, CLISP [Teitelman 1973] is invoked to translate the if-then expression in the definition of FACT into an equivalent Lisp construct. CLISP runs into a problem regarding the GREATERR, and DWIM offers a spelling correction. I type Y (the spelling corrector supplies the "es"), and the correction is made. I had also misspelled the recursive call to FACT in the body of the definition of FACT. Since the programmer's assistant "noticed" this new function, i.e., FACT, when I first defined it, DWIM is able to suggest the correction of FACCT to FACT, which I also confirm. Figure 9 shows the display after these two corrections have been made. At this point, the definition of FACT has been translated to Lisp successfully, at least from a syntactic standpoint, and an error is encountered which DWIM cannot handle. The error message NON-NUMERIC ARG NIL is printed, and Interlisp goes into a break. A menu of break commands automatically appears just below the TYPESCRIPT window.

At this point the user is once again addressing the Lisp interpreter through the programmer's assistant. However, the context of his computation has been preserved and is available so that the user can, for example, examine the values of locally bound variables, see the control structure that led to this point in the computation, etc., and if he wishes, fix or bypass the problem and continue the computation. This capability is most important for interactive debugging [Teitelman 1969]. In this particular case, the arithmetic operation MULTIPLY (as implemented by the Lisp function ITIMES) is waiting for a number, i.e., the value of the break will be used as a multiplicand. In effect, *the system has called the user as a subroutine to supply this number.*

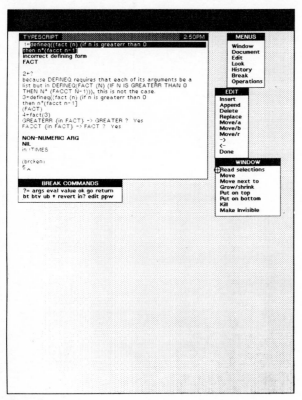

Figure 9.

10. I select the BTV command, requesting a backtrace of function names along with the names and values of the bound variables for each corresponding function call. The backtrace is printed in a separate BACKTRACE window, which is automatically displayed when the backtrace command is invoked. The backtrace window is shown at the right of the screen in Figure 10. Note that it overlaps the three menus. However, I can still perform operations using those menus by pointing at the part of the menu that is visible. I can select elements in the BACKTRACE window to focus the attention of the break package on a particular frame, e.g., to evaluate an expression in a different context, to cause the computation to revert back to that point, etc. The backtrace shows me that I am under my function FACT, and that it made three recursive calls before the error, with N being decremented by 1 each call, so it looks like FACT is recurring properly.

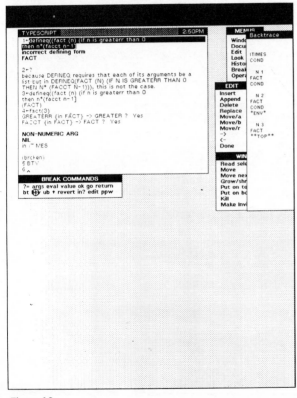

Figure 10.

11. I still don't understand why the error occurred, so I try typing the ? command again. In this case, the programmer's assistant tells me that the problem is that one of the operands to * (the MULTIPLY operator) was (FACT N-1) and that the value of (FACT N-1) is NIL when N = 1. In other words, when FACT is called with N = 0, it returns NIL. The **P.A.** is able to generate this explanation because (1) it knows that all of the arguments to * must be numbers, and (2) it can examine the state of the computation on the stack. In this case, it found that the second operand to ITIMES was NIL, which is not a number, and that the expression that produced this particular value was (FACT N − 1) in the expression (N*(FACT N − 1)) which is contained in the function FACT, and that at the time this call occurred, the value of N was 1.

I now realize that the problem is simply that I neglected to specify the value of FACT for N = 0.[8] Therefore, I prettyprint the definition of FACT in preparation for editing it. Figure 11 shows the definition of FACT prettyprinted in my WORK AREA window, which automatically appeared when prettyprint was called. Note that the definition of FACT now shows the two misspelled words, GREATERR and FACCT, spelled correctly.

---

[8] In Interlisp, if none of the predicates of an if-then expression evaluate true, the value of the expression defaults to NIL.

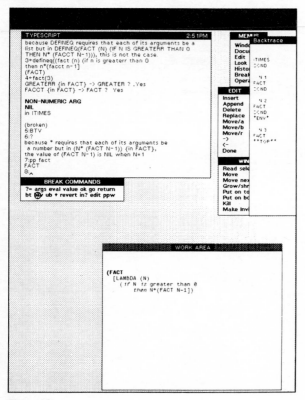

Figure 11.

12. I select the right square bracket in the definition of FACT in the WORK AREA window, and then select the INSERT command on the EDIT menu. The EDIT menu automatically moves so as to be close to the window that I am editing. I make the necessary correction by typing ") ELSE 1", i.e., if N is not greater than 0, FACT should return 1. Figure 12 shows the display just before I complete the INSERT. Note that the caret appears in the WORK AREA window where I am typing. The cursor is in the upper right hand portion of the screen at the location of the INSERT command before the EDIT menu moved to be close to the WORK AREA.

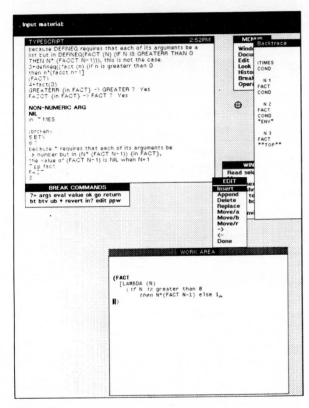

Figure 12.

13. I complete the INSERT, and then select the DONE command on the EDIT menu to indicate that I am finished editing this expression. The PROMPT window reports that the definition of FACT has been changed. Note that I did not *have* to finish editing FACT at this point: I could have typed in expressions to be evaluated, performed other menu operations, etc., even edited other expressions, before selecting the DONE command for this expression. This is another example of being able to suspend different tasks in varying states of completion and go back to them at some later point.

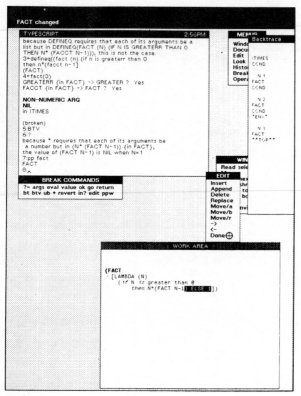

Figure 13.

14. I now test out my change by typing FACT(2), which works correctly. Now I want to *continue* with the computation. Note that I am still in the original break that followed the error. The arithmetic operation * (i.e., the Lisp function ITIMES) is still waiting for a number to be used as a multiplicand. I therefore select the RETURN command on the BREAK menu. The PROMPT window tells me to INPUT EXPRESSION and the caret moves to the PROMPT window. I type 1 as the value to be returned from this error break. Figure 14 shows the display at this point just after I type 1, which is echoed (displayed) in the PROMPT window.

Note: in actual practice, for a computation as trivial as FACT(3), I would probably simply reset (abort back to the top) and reexecute FACT(3) rather than bothering to continue the computation, since so little has been invested in getting to this point. However, *being able to continue a computation following an error is especially useful when an error occurs following a significant amount of computation, or when the computation has left things in an "unclean state" as a result of global side effects. Such a facility is also essential for good interactive debugging.*

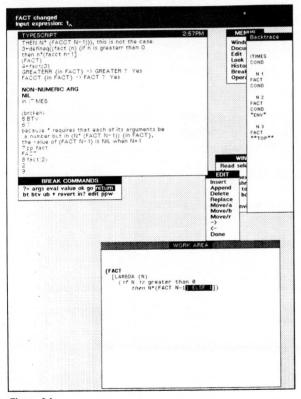

Figure 14.

15. I complete typing the expression for the RETURN command, thereby causing 1 to be returned as the value of the break, which causes (1 * 1) to be computed and returned as the value of FACT(1), which then causes (2 * 1) to be computed, etc., and finally the original computation of FACT(3) finishes and returns 6 as its value as shown in Figure 15, in the next to the bottom line of the TYPESCRIPT window. The BREAK menu has disappeared since we are no longer in a break.

I now want to try FACT on some other values, so I bring up the HISTORY menu, and select the USE command, which is a command to the programmer's assistant to reexecute a previous event, or events, with new values. The PROMPT window instructs me to select the targets and to input the objects to be substituted. I select the "3" in FACT(3) (near the top of the TYPESCRIPT window) and input "4 5 10" (echoed in the PROMPT window), i.e., I am requesting that FACT(4), FACT(5), and FACT(10) be computed.

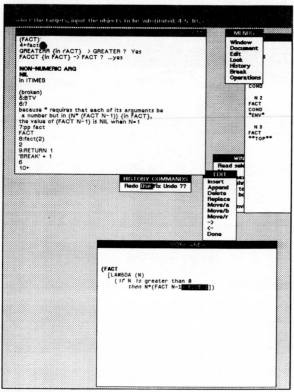

Figure 15.

16. The resulting history operation is equivalent to typing USE 4 5 10 FOR 3 IN 4,[9] which the **P.A.** prints in the TYPESCRIPT window to show me what is happening. This USE command now causes three computations to be performed, corresponding to the result of substituting 4 for 3 in FACT(3), the result of substituting 5 for 3 in FACT(3), and the result of substituting 10 for 3 in FACT(3). The values produced by these three computations, 24, 120, and 3628800, are printed in the TYPESCRIPT window, as shown in Figure 16. Finally, I ask for a replay of the history of my session, by selecting the ?? command in the HISTORY menu. The HISTORY window is brought up, and the history of my session, in reverse chronological order, is printed in this window, as shown in Figure 16.[10]

---

[9] 4 is the event number of the event corresponding to FACT(3).

[10] In addition to seeing a replay of his history, the user can also *scroll* the (contents of the) TYPESCRIPT window backwards in time to see the transcript of earlier interactions with the system. The difference between the history and the TYPESCRIPT is that the TYPESCRIPT contains a record of all characters input or output, e.g., includes messages printed by the system and by the user's programs. The history contains a subset of these characters, organized according to *events*. For example, 6, the value returned by FACT(3), actually appears 18 lines below FACT(3) in the TYPESCRIPT window, but in the HISTORY window, it would be shown as the value of event number 4, regardless of the fact that events 5 thru 9 occurred between the time that event 4 was begun and the time it completed.

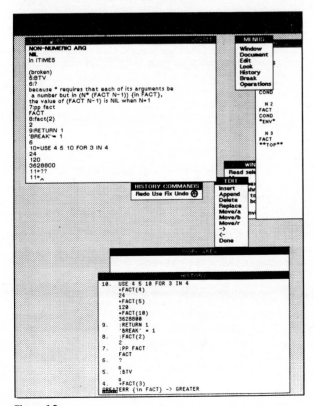

Figure 16.

This completes the "toy" session designed to illustrate some of the basic features of the system. Note that at this point the display contains nine different windows. Five of these windows are control windows (menus). The other four windows describe various processes. Note that the windows have not been a burden on the user: he does not "manage" the windows, although he could perform explicit operations on them such as changing their position, or size, or shape, or editing their contents as we have seen. The feeling to the user is that the windows more or less manage themselves, and this contributes greatly to the smoothness of the system.

3.2   Example Session—Part 2

However, to really appreciate the power of the system, one must see how the various facilities, and the user, interact in a real working situation. The following session, which is a continuation of the above session, illustrates this. In addition to the prettyprinting, editing, break, and history facilities illustrated earlier, several other important Interlisp facilities are introduced during the course of the session below, such as Helpsys, which interfaces with the on-line Interlisp Reference Manual to allow the user to ask questions and see explanatory material from the manual, and Masterscope, a sophisticated interactive program for analyzing and cross referencing user programs. Masterscope then allows the user to interrogate the resulting data base both with respect to the control structure of his programs, i.e., who calls/is called by whom, and to their data structure, i.e., where variables are bound, set, or referenced, or which functions use particular record declarations. The facilities are necessarily used in a fairly simple and straightforward fashion in the session below. However, the important point to observe is how the display together with multiple windows enables the user to call up the various packages quickly and easily and then to dismiss them when he is finished, all with minimal interference with his context, i.e., the *user's* context, not that of his program.

Receiving and sending messages from other users play an important part in this session, as they do in real life applications. The system described in this paper makes it especially easy to process messages because the reading and sending of messages is implemented *within the Interlisp system*, instead of in a separate subsystem. Thus, the user does not have to give up his context in order to process his mail. Furthermore, since the message facilities are now part of the Lisp environment and vice versa, the user can obtain material from messages that he receives and *insert it directly into his own programs* or *evaluate the corresponding expressions* by using the READ SELECTIONS command described earlier. Conversely, the user can insert material from his own environment, or from messages that he has received since they are also a part of his environment, into messages that are to be sent. Both of these facilities are extremely useful.

Note: the session presented below is "canned" in that the events described did not actually occur so fortuitously in a single session, nor in such a nice sequence for the purpose of demonstrating the system. However, the session is genuine in that the figures that accompany the text are in fact actual snapshots of the display taken in sequence through a session in which the indicated operations were performed. And, in fact, the events described were culled from actual sessions over the course of several months, i.e., I really did find the bugs, make the changes, and receive and send the messages depicted on the following pages.

17. I observe an anomaly in my history window as shown in Figure 16: a sequence of bells (displayed as little boxes) in the middle of my history. When the history was actually printed, the system paused at this point and seemed to be waiting for me to type something. I decide to ask a colleague about this. I therefore bring up the OPERATIONS menu and select the SNDMSG command. SNDMSG brings up its own window, and asks me who the message is to. I respond "Masintr" (misspelled—his name is actually Masinter). SNDMSG then asks whether I want any "carbon copies" sent to other recipients, and I simply type a carriage return, since I don't. SNDMSG then asks what the subject of the message is, and I type "bells". Figure 17 shows the display at this point. The caret is in the SNDMSG window, immediately following the word "bells".[11]

---

[11]Although this SNDMSG looks like the SNDMSG facility provided by Tenex, it is entirely a part of and written in the Interlisp system.

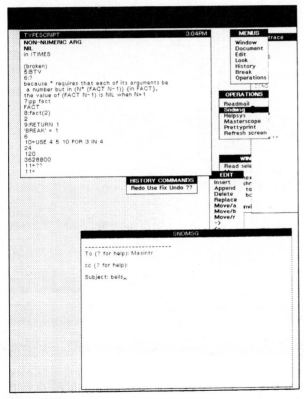

Figure 17.

18. I complete typing the message, and terminate with a control-Z to indicate that I want the message sent.[12] SNDMSG does not recognize the recipient, "Masintr", and calls the spelling corrector, which returns the correct spelling, "Masinter".[13] The message header is fixed accordingly, and the system informs me in the PROMPT window that the message has been sent.

---

[12]The Interlisp version of SNDMSG adheres to the Tenex convention for sending messages.

[13]Both SNDMSG and READMAIL are "watching" what I am doing, and build a list of those users that I exchange messages with. When I misspelled Masintr, the spelling corrector was called with this list, and was able to perform the correction. Had it failed, I would have been informed and allowed to intervene, as shown later in the session.

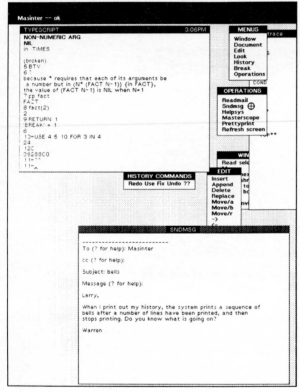

Figure 18.

19. At this point, I am informed in the TYPESCRIPT window by the programmer's assistant that there is [Mail from System], i.e. some mail has arrived for me. I had previously instructed the **P.A.** to periodically check whether any new mail had arrived, and to so inform me. Since I am not doing anything at this point except waiting for Masinter to respond to my message, I elect to see my mail, type Yes to the question "Want to see it now ?", and the message is displayed in the MESSAGES window. The message is from a user of Interlisp at the Information Sciences Institute in Los Angeles with a question about Interlisp.[14]

---

[14]Both Xerox PARC and the Information Sciences Institute are hosts on the ARPA network. The mail facilities supported by the various hosts of the network enable users at any site to exchange messages with users at any other site. Such "electronic" mail has become the preferred form of communication for questions, bug reports, suggestions, etc.

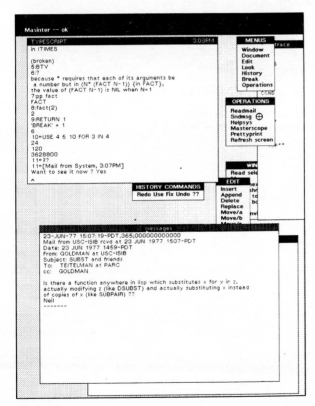

Figure 19.

20. I decide to respond to the message from Goldman right now, and select the SNDMSG command in the OPERATIONS menu. The SNDMSG window comes back on top, and I type my response. I finish the message without noticing that I had inadvertently typed the subject of the message in the cc (carbon copies) field, and the beginning of the message in the subject field. SNDMSG was unable to interpret the word "Subst" as a message recipient, and informs me in the PROMPT window that the message wasn't sent.

Figure 20.

21. Using the EDIT menu, I edit the message, and move "subst" to the subject field, and "Neil" into the body of the message. Then I select the DONE command. The PROMPT window informs me the message has been sent.[15] Note that I can send a message, change a part of it, and resend it, e.g., to different recipients, again and again.

---

[15]The operation to be performed with the DONE command is selected is specified by the program that originally prints the corresponding material. In the case of SNDMSG, the operation is to send the message. In the case of prettyprint (as illustrated in Figure 13), the operation is to redefine the corresponding function.

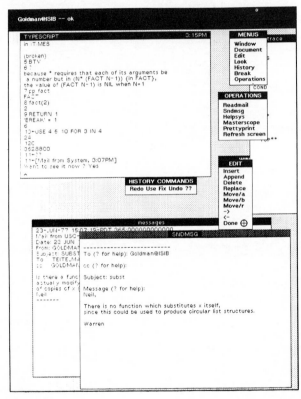

Figure 21.

22. The **P.A.** now tells me that I have more mail, which I read. It is the response from Masinter. He explains that the bells in my history window are a Tenex feature, and offers to write a Lisp function for me which will turn this Tenex feature off for my specialized application.

Figure 22.

23. Since this function will be used to set the page height, and I already have a function for setting the page *width*, I ask Masinter whether he can simply combine the two operations in a single function. I want to include the definition of the function that sets the page width in the message I send to him. So I type the first part of the message as shown, and then I select the PRETTYPRINT command of the OPERATIONS menu. The PROMPT window asks me to supply the name of the function(s) I want prettyprinted. Figure 23 shows the display as of this point. Note that the caret is in the PROMPT window.

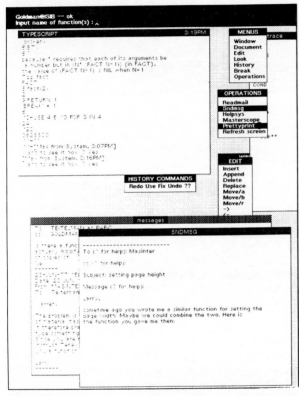

Figure 23.

24. I type in the name of my function, SETPAGEWIDTH. The WORK AREA window, which had become covered by the HISTORY, SNDMSG, and MESSAGES window, reappears on top, and the definition of SETPAGEWIDTH is prettyprinted.[16] I will include this definition in the message which I am composing by using the READ SELECTIONS command in the WINDOW menu. I select the definition, and move the mouse to the READ SELECTIONS command, as shown in Figure 24.

---

[16]In this case, the function SETPAGEWIDTH was compiled, and its symbolic definition not loaded into my system. PRETTYPRINT therefore asked the Interlisp file package where the symbolic definition for that function was located and then loaded it in. All of this happens automatically without any need for supervision.

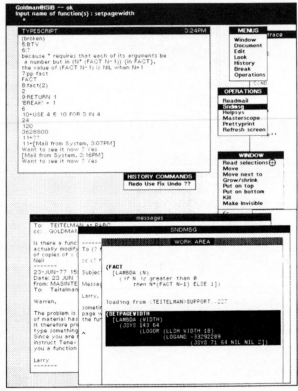

Figure 24.

25. I select the READ SELECTIONS command, and the effect is the same as though I had typed in the selected material: my SNDMSG window comes back on top, and the definition for SETPAGEWIDTH from the WORK AREA window is inserted into the message, as shown in Figure 25. I complete the message by asking Masinter about a totally different matter, which is why the mail check routine tells me I have mail from SYSTEM, rather than giving me the name of the sender.

Note: this casual exchanging of messages back and forth is an important part of the way that many of us use computers today. Twenty or so of my colleagues are using the same time sharing system as I am, not to mention the much greater number of users on other machines on the ARPA network, and we exchange messages frequently. Thus, it is of great value to me to be able to switch contexts from debugging a program to sending or receiving mail with a minimum amount of overhead. In this case, it was also particularly important to be able to point at a piece of my programming environment, i.e. the definition of a function, and insert it directly into a message. The same facility would be useful for example in reporting a bug, where I might want to include an entire sequence of interactions with the system in my message. The inverse operation, of pointing at a piece of a message I receive and then installing it in my programming environment, is also very useful, as we will see in the next interaction.

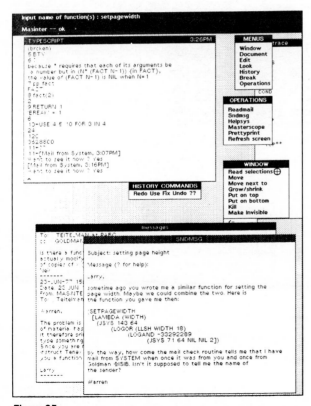

Figure 25.

26. The **P.A.** now tells me I have more mail. It is the reply from Masinter containing the definition for the function SETPAGE. I select the definition, move the mouse to the READ SELECTIONS command in the WINDOW menu, and

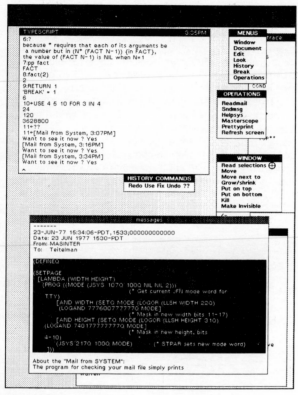

Figure 26.

27. select the READ SELECTIONS command thereby defining SETPAGE, as shown in the TYPESCRIPT window in Figure 27. I now use SETPAGE to set my page width and height both, and then select the ?? command in the HISTORY menu to see if the bells are printed. They aren't; this time the entire history is printed without any pause. (In Figure 27, the HISTORY window shows the end of the history, i.e., the beginning of the session where I defined FACT.)

Let us pause now and review the sequence of operations commencing with noticing the problem and culminating in its solution:

1. I noticed a problem,
2. sent a message,
3. received an explanation,
4. sent back a reply containing a piece of one of my programs,
5. received a message containing a program which I could use to fix the problem,
6. installed the program in my environment by pointing at it, and
7. fixed my problem.

This particular problem admittedly was a trivial one, and could easily have been ignored or tolerated by the user. The important point here is that the configuration of the system makes it *so easy for the user to attack and solve such problems that he is willing to do so.* The leverage that the system provides the user is even more valuable when the user is attacking conceptually difficult problems.

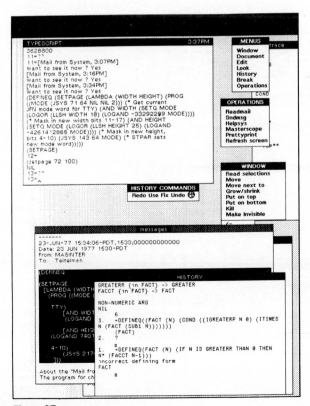

Figure 27.

28. I use the PUT ON TOP command of the WINDOW menu to bring the message window back on top to read the rest of the message from Masinter. Since the message is too long to fit in the window at one time, I *scroll* the contents of the window to see the rest of the message by placing the mouse in an imaginary bar to the left of the window and pressing the left button (for scrolling up—the right button is used for scrolling down). The line opposite the mouse is then scrolled to the top of the window. Masinter explains that the mail checker I am using simply checks the last user to write on my message file. If my message file is busy, or the mail is coming from over the ARPA network, as was the case with the message from Goldman, then the "user" that actually writes on my message file is, in fact, the system. He suggests that if I want to bother, I can find out the real name of the sender by actually looking in the message file at the message itself. Masinter says he has a function called GETMAILPOS which will return the position of the last message in the file.

I decide to make the suggested change, so I type "LOAD(" to the programmer's assistant (as shown in the TYPESCRIPT window), and then select the name of the file in the message (in order to use the READ SELECTIONS command).

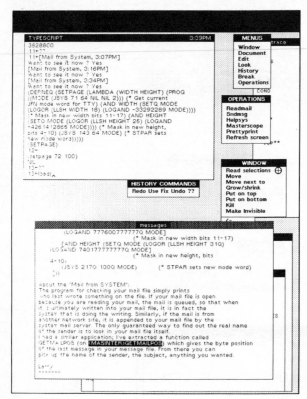

Figure 28.

29. I select the READ SELECTIONS command, and the file is loaded, thereby defining the function GETMAILPOS. Now I need to find out where to make the change to compute the real identity of the sender. I therefore use the Masterscope command on the OPERATIONS menu to call Masterscope. My interactions with Masterscope are shown in the MASTERSCOPE window at the bottom of the screen in Figure 29. I ask Masterscope the names of all of the functions called by CHECKMAIL. Masterscope obtains and analyzes the symbolic definition for CHECKMAIL. I notice the function INFORMAIL among the names of the functions called by CHECKMAIL. INFORMAIL looks like it might be the function I want. I select INFORMAIL and

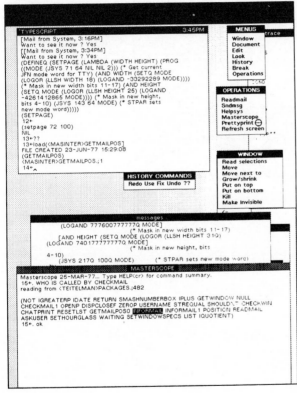

Figure 29.

30. prettyprint it, and see that INFORMAIL is indeed the function that prints the [Mail from —] message, and so is the place to make my modification. I use the INSERT command on the EDIT menu and begin making the change. Figure 30 shows the definition of INFORMAIL with the text "(FILESEARCH" inserted.

Figure 30.

31. At this point, I realize that I don't remember how to use the function FILESEARCH, so, *while in the middle of editing*, I use the OPERATIONS menu to call HELPSYS, to interrogate the on-line Interlisp Reference Manual. The interactions with HELPSYS are shown in the HELPSYS window at the bottom of the screen in Figure 31. I first ask HELPSYS about FILESEARCH, and it tells me that there is no such subject in the manual, so I try the phrase "searching files." This causes HELPSYS to give me an explanation of the function FILEPOS, which is the name of the function I want.[17]

---

[17]If that had failed, I would have asked HELPSYS about FILE$, which would have given me a list of all words or topics beginning with the letters FILE, just as though I had looked in the index of the manual itself.

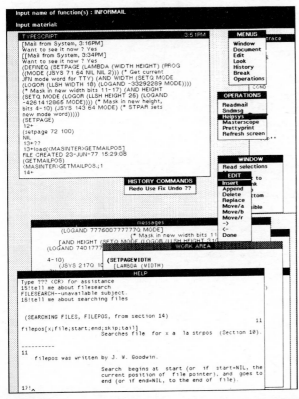

Figure 31.

32. I exit HELPSYS and the WORK AREA window comes back on top, and I am right back in the middle of my edit. I type a sufficient number of backspaces to erase the "SEARCH" in FILESEARCH, and then type POS and continue with my INSERT. The text from the manual about FILEPOS told me that its first argument is the target of the search, in my case the string "From:" in the message. To guarantee that I have the right string, I scroll the MESSAGES window backwards until the beginning of a message is visible, then select this string from an actual message, and then use the READ SELECTIONS command to insert it into my edit.

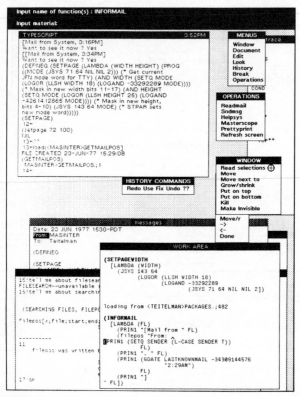

Figure 32.

33. I complete my INSERT and select the DONE command. The PROMPT window says that the function INFORMAIL has been changed. Basically, the change I made to INFORMAIL says to begin searching the mailfile as of the location specified by Masinter's function GETMAILPOS, looking for the string "From:"[18], and then to read a single word from the file and set SENDER to this word. I test out my change by typing INFORMAIL(T). The last time I got mail INFORMAIL said [Mail from System]. This time it tells me [Mail from Masinter], so the change worked.

Let us review the sequence of operations:

1. I observed some undesirable behaviour in a program I was using;
2. sent a message inquiring about the behaviour;
3. got a reply back suggesting the nature of the problem, how it might be changed, and a program which would help in making the change;
4. used Masterscope to find out what to change;
5. began making the change and then in the middle,
6. used Helpsys to tell me how to make the change,
7. completed the change, and tested it successfully.

---

[18]The extra arguments to FILEPOS specify that the search is to stop *after* the string, not at its beginning as is the default case.

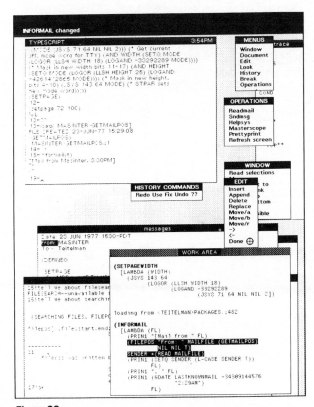

Figure 33.

34. The **P.A.** (via INFORMAIL) now tells me that I have mail from Burton, which I agree to see. However, I realize that I would have liked INFORMAIL to say I had mail from Burton at BBN-TENEXD, just as it does in the message file, rather than just Burton.

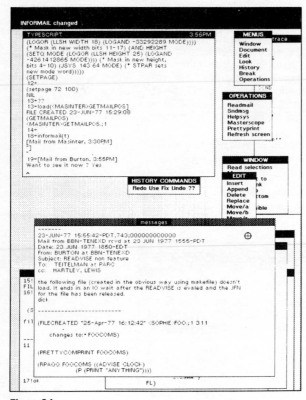

Figure 34.

35. The problem is that the Interlisp function READ, which I used in the change I made to INFORMAIL, just returns the next expression/word in the file, which in this case was simply Burton. I should have used the function RSTRING, which will read everything up to the next carriage return. Therefore, I bring my WORK AREA window back on top, and edit the definition of INFORMAIL, replacing the call to READ by an appropriate call to RSTRING. I then select the DONE command. The PROMPT window tells me that IN-FORMAIL has been changed (again). I test out the change by typing INFOR-MAIL(T). This time INFORMAIL tells me I have mail from Burton at BBN-TENEXD, exactly as I planned.

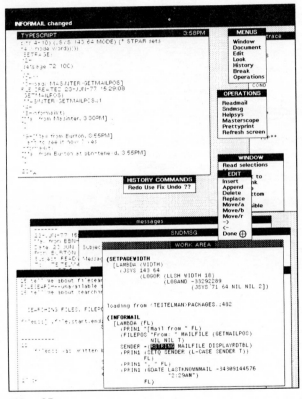

Figure 35.

36. As long as I am at it, I decide I would also like INFORMAIL to tell me the subject of the message, so I further edit INFORMAIL to search the mailfile for the string "Subject:", which I again obtain from a message itself and insert using the READ SELECTIONS command. Figure 36 shows the edit as of this point.

Figure 36.

37. I complete the edit, which basically says that if the string "Subject:" is found in the message, INFORMAIL should print it and the rest of the line that follows it. I select the DONE command, and the PROMPT window reports that INFORMAIL has been changed. I test out my change, this time by selecting the previous event in the TYPESCRIPT window and then using the REDO command on the HISTORY menu. As shown in Figure 37, INFORMAIL tells me the full name of the sender, as well as the subject.

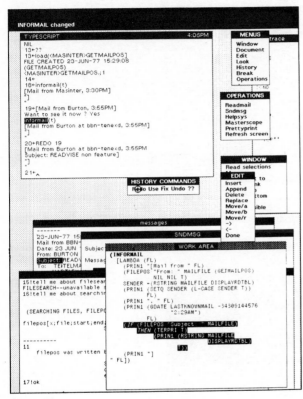

Figure 37.

38. I now read the message from Burton. It describes a short file that he says will not load correctly. In order to check this out, I need to make such a file and load it and see why it fails. I bring up the DOCUMENT menu and select the WRITE command. The PROMPT window tells me that I should select the material I want to be written onto the file, and supply the name of the file. I select the corresponding portion of my message. Figure 38 shows the display at this point.

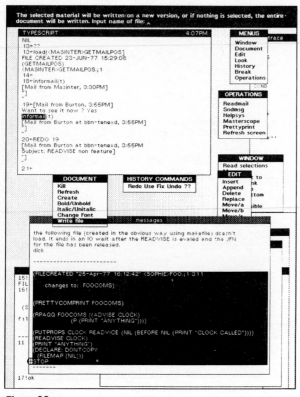

Figure 38.

39. I give the name of the file to be created, BURTON.BUG, and the PROMPT window tells me that the file has been written. At this point, the programmer's assistant tells me I have a message from Card. Since I am in the middle of something, I decide *not* to read the message now, and type No to the question "Want to see it now ?". I load the file BURTON.BUG that I just created, and the file loads successfully.

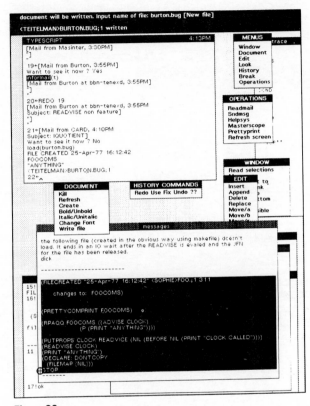

Figure 39.

40. Since the process of loading this file made some changes to my environment, namely advising the function CLOCK, I *undo* this operation by selecting the corresponding event in the TYPESCRIPT window, and then selecting the UNDO command on the HISTORY menu. I then send Burton a message asking for more details, and suggest that the problem may be due to some files having gotten smashed at BBN.

41. I now go back and select the READMAIL command on the OPERATIONS menu to read Card's message, which is a comment about the Interlisp manual, which I will respond to. However, I realize that I could easily have forgotten about Card's message and gone on to something else, so I decide I

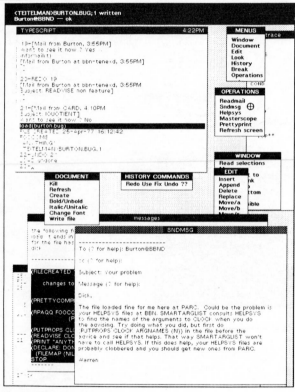

Figure 40.

would like the mail checker to remind me, by changing the caption of my message window, that I have mail waiting when I decline to read it immediately. I will perform this change by simply *advising* the Interlisp function ASKUSER[19], which is responsible for the "Want to see it now ? - Yes/No" interaction. I advise ASKUSER AFTER, i.e., the advice will be executed on the way out of the function, if its value is 'N, then to change the caption as indicated. Then I realize that this change will affect *all* calls in the system to ASKUSER, whereas I only want this to happen on calls to ASKUSER from CHECKMAIL. So I select ASKUSER in event 23, i.e., the ADVISE operation, then select the UNDO command on the HISTORY menu to undo this event. Then I select the USE command to reexecute the ADVISE operation using (ASKUSER IN CHECKMAIL) instead of ASKUSER. Figure 41 shows the display after the ADVISE operation has been reexecuted.

---

[19]Advising is an Interlisp facility which lets the user treat a function, or a particular call to a function, as a black box, and make changes that affect it on entry or exit, without having to be aware of the details of what is inside the box. It is described in [Teitelman 1969]. Advising is often used for reconfiguring system programs, and also for trying out changes to the user's programs, with minimal investment in order to see how they work, before going back and making the changes in some more permanent fashion.

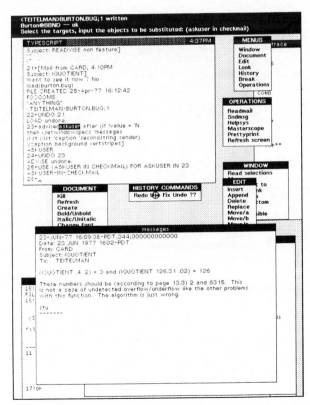

Figure 41.

42. I test out my change by sending myself a test message, and answering No when asked if I want to see it now. The caption on my MESSAGES window is changed so that the name of the sender of the message, in this case me, appears in the right hand corner of the caption, and the background of the caption is changed to vertical stripes.

4. CONCLUSIONS

The system described in this paper has been in use by actual users other than the author only a few months. However, our conjectures about the usefulness of this kind of facility were if anything conservative. The ability to suspend an operation, perform other operations, and then return without loss of context is widely appreciated. The technique of using different windows for different tasks does make this switching of contexts easy and painless. Even when the user is not switching contexts, the use of multiple windows is extremely helpful. For example, a standard complaint with conventional display terminals is that material that the user wants to refer to repeatedly, e.g., a printout of some function, or a record of some complicated interaction, is displaced by subsequent, incidental interactions with the system. In this situation when using a hard copy terminal, the user simply tears off the portion he is interested in and saves it beside his keyboard. Being able to freeze a portion of the user's interactions in a separate window, such as the WORK AREA, while

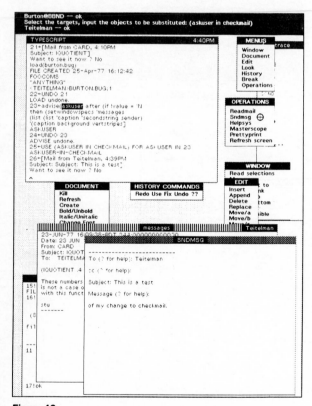

Figure 42.

allowing subsequent interactions to scroll off the screen seems to combine some of the best aspects of hard copy and display terminals.

Finally, users just seem to enjoy aesthetically the style of interacting with the system, such as using menus, the feedback via the prompt window and changing cursors, being able to scroll the windows back and forth, etc. We think this is an area that will see an increasing amount of activity in the future as the cost of bit map displays and the necessary computing power to maintain them continues to drop.

ACKNOWLEDGMENTS

The author would like to acknowledge and thank R. F. Sproull and J. Strother Moore, who designed and implemented critical support facilities without which this system would not have been possible, and whose ideas and intuitions provided extremely valuable guidance and inspiration during the development of the system. The form and capabilities of some of the display primitives in the current system were suggested by an earlier version of a display text facility for Interlisp designed by Terry Winograd. Finally, all of the work described herein depends heavily on the leverage provided by the Interlisp system itself, which is the result of the efforts of many individuals over a period of almost a decade, made possible by continuing ARPA support over that period.

REFERENCES

[Bobrow and Wegbreit 1973] D.G. Bobrow, B. Wegbreit. A model and stack implementation for multiple environments. *Communications of the ACM*, 16:10 (October 1973), 591-603.

[English et al. 1967] W.K. English, D.C. Engelbart, M.L. Berman. Display selection techniques for text manipulation. *IEEE Transactions on Human Factor in Electronics*, HFE-8:1 (March 1967).

[Kay and Goldberg 1976] A. Kay, A. Goldberg. *Personal dynamic media*. Learning Research Group, Xerox Palo Alto Research Center, 1976; excerpts published in *IEEE Computer Magazine*, March 1977, 31-41.

[Sandewall 1978] E. Sandewall. Programming in the interactive environment: the LISP experience. *Communications of the ACM*, 10:1 (March 1978), 35-71; reprinted in *Interactive Programming Environments*.

[Sproull and Thomas 1974] R.F. Sproull, E.L. Thomas. A network graphics protocol. *Computer Graphics, SIGGRAPH Quarterly*, Fall 1974.

[Swinehart 1974] D.C. Swinehart. *Copilot: a multiple process approach to interactive programming systems*. Stanford Artificial Intelligence Laboratory Memo AIM-230, Stanford University, July 1974.

[Teitelman 1969] W. Teitelman. Toward a programming laboratory. *International Joint Conference on Artificial Intelligence*, Washington, May 1969, 1-8.

[Teitelman 1972b] W. Teitelman. Automated programmering—the programmer's assistant. *Proceedings of the Fall Joint Computer Conference*, AFIPS Proceedings (1972), 917-922; reprinted in *Interactive Programming Environments*.

[Teitelman 1973] W. Teitelman. CLISP—Conversational Lisp. *Proceedings of the Third International Joint Conference on Artificial Intelligence*, Stanford, California, August 1973, 686-690.

[Teitelman 1978] W. Teitelman. *INTERLISP Reference Manual*. Xerox Palo Alto Research Center, Palo Alto, California, December 1978.

14 A Display-Oriented Editor for INTERLISP

DAVID R. BARSTOW

Schlumberger-Doll Research
Ridgefield, Connecticut

DED is a display-oriented editor that was designed to add the power and convenience of display terminals to INTERLISP's teletype-oriented structure editor. DED divides the display screen into a Prettyprint Region and an Interaction Region. The Prettyprint Region gives a prettyprinted view of the structure being edited; the Interaction Region contains the interaction between the user and INTERLISP's standard editor. DED's prettyprinter allows elision, and the user may zoom in or out to see the expression being edited with more or less detail. There are several arrow keys which allow the user to change quite easily the focus of attention in certain structural ways, as well as a menu-like facility for common command sequences. DED also allows an expression to be prettyprinted automatically while it is being typed by the user. Together, these features provide a display-facility that considerably augments INTERLISP's otherwise quite sophisticated user interface.

1. INTRODUCTION

Although programs are written in a programming language, the human process of programming often occurs within a programming environment—a set of software tools that assist in different aspects of the programming process. LISP systems are perhaps the best developed programming environments (at least, of those focusing primarily on the activity of coding). Sandewall has given a lengthy discussion of the nature of programming within such environments, focusing on INTERLISP [Teitelman 1978] and MACLISP [Moon 1974], the two most advanced LISP programming environments [Sandewall 1978]. A major feature of both environments (as well as other non-LISP environments [Teitelbaum and Reps 1980]) is a structure-oriented editor—an editor which understands the syntactic structure of the language and commands which operate on structural objects (e.g., expressions, statements) rather than on textual objects (e.g., characters, lines). Users of such editors generally find them very valuable: textual and structural errors are much less frequent and the coding process is correspondingly faster and easier.

A general issue in such editors is the problem of combining the visual representation of the program (which is primarily textual in nature) with the structural features of the language. For example, the current focus of attention might be an entire expression, rather than a single character location which is the norm for text editors. In the case of MACLISP, the solution to this problem is to start with a display-oriented text editor (EMACS [Stallman 1981]) and to add operations which correspond to the syntactic structure of LISP (e.g., a command for moving to the beginning of the next S-expression). Considerable effort has gone into developing a convenient interface between MACLISP and EMACS; the result is a sophisticated display-oriented editor within a LISP programming environment. This style of interaction has been developed considerably further in work on the Lisp Machine [Greenblatt et al. 1984].

With INTERLISP, the opposite approach was taken: the editor is totally structural in nature. All of the commands know about the structure of S-expressions and make structural modifications to in-core S-expressions rather than textual modifications to an external file. A highly sophisticated LISP editor, integrated with a powerful programming environment, has evolved from this starting point. The editor's sophistication, however, is marred by one major drawback: it is built around a teletype-style interaction. If you wish a visual presentation of the expression being edited, you must explicitly request that it be typed out on the terminal. While this made sense when INTERLISP was originally developed (the late 1960's when display terminals were rare), it is now a hindrance, since display technologies can add considerable power and comfort to a human interface. A display-oriented editor (called DED) has been built to bring some of this power and comfort to the INTERLISP environment without changing its fundamentally structural nature, and without forcing users to change their patterns of thinking. INTERLISP with DED thus represents another approach to the problem of combining the visual representation of a program with structural editing. (DLISP was another attempt to add display capabilities to INTERLISP [Teitelman 1977]. DLISP was aimed at the Programmer's Assistant, so DED and DLISP actually solve different problems.)

DED includes the following features:

- The display screen is divided into two regions: one is for the standard style of interaction with INTERLISP's editor; the other gives a prettyprinted version of the S-expression being edited.

- The prettyprinter allows elision: the most detailed parts of the prettyprinted expression are shown in abbreviated form.
- The user may zoom in or out to see the expression with more or less detail.
- There are several "arrow" keys which can be used to move the "cursor" on the prettyprinted expression (in addition to INTERLISP's usual attention-changing commands).
- A menu-like facility allows common command sequences to be entered quickly.
- An expression can be prettyprinted automatically while the user types it.

Together, these features provide a display facility which considerably augments INTERLISP's otherwise quite sophisticated user interface. Users have found it quite easy to learn and have not felt that it disrupts those aspects of INTERLISP that they already use. Thus, the original goal of DED has been achieved: much of the power of display terminals has been added to INTERLISP without losing the structural orientation of the editor and without forcing radically new patterns of behavior onto users.

2. THE USER'S VIEW

2.1   Screen Organization

The user interface to DED is a character-oriented display terminal with 24 lines of 80 characters each. (The terminal is a DEC VT100; those parts of DED which depend on VT100 features will be noted in the section below on implementation.) The 24 lines are broken into two main regions: the Prettyprint Region and the Interaction Region. The Prettyprint Region contains a prettyprinted version of the expression being edited. INTERLISP's current focus of attention is indicated within the Prettyprint Region by highlighting the enclosing parentheses. The Interaction Region contains the interaction between the user and INTERLISP's standard editor (i.e., the prompt characters, the user's typed command, and INTERLISP's response). For example, Figure 1 shows the complete definition of a function to be edited; Figure 2 shows the screen when the user starts to edit the definition of the function. The current focus of attention is shown by highlighting its matching parentheses, indicated by small boxes [(and)] in the figures. Note the menu facility in the upper right corner; this will be omitted from later figures. Note also that the definition is not printed in full detail; omitted subexpressions are shown as "&" in the Prettyprint Region.

Most editing with DED is carried out by issuing standard INTERLISP commands. Changes are reflected immediately in the displayed expression. A change

```
(LAMBDA (LST)      (* DRB: "24-Oct-80 14:35")
                   (* a test function for DED)
  (COND
    ((NULL (CDR LST))
     LST)
    ((LESS ((CAR LST)
            CADR LST))
      (CONS (CAR LST)
            (TESTFN (CDR LST))))
    (T (TESTFN (CONS (CAR LST)
                     (CDDR LST)))))))
```

Figure 1. Definition of TESTFN

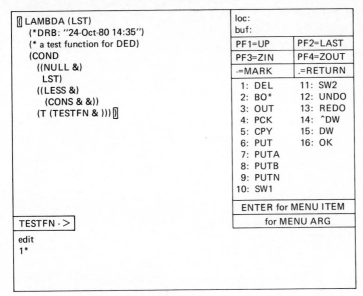

```
⟦ LAMBDA (LST)                          loc:
    (*DRB: "24-Oct-80 14:35")           buf:
    (* a test function for DED)     ┌─────────────┬─────────────┐
    (COND                           │ PF1=UP      │ PF2=LAST    │
      ((NULL &)                     ├─────────────┼─────────────┤
       LST)                         │ PF3=ZIN     │ PF4=ZOUT    │
      ((LESS &)                     ├─────────────┼─────────────┤
       (CONS & &))                  │ -=MARK      │ .=RETURN    │
      (T (TESTFN & )))⟧             ├─────────────┼─────────────┤
                                    │  1: DEL     │ 11: SW2     │
                                    │  2: BO*     │ 12: UNDO    │
                                    │  3: OUT     │ 13: REDO    │
                                    │  4: PCK     │ 14: ^DW     │
                                    │  5: CPY     │ 15: DW      │
                                    │  6: PUT     │ 16: OK      │
                                    │  7: PUTA    │             │
                                    │  8: PUTB    │             │
                                    │  9: PUTN    │             │
                                    │ 10: SW1     │             │
                                    ├─────────────┴─────────────┤
                                    │   ENTER for MENU ITEM     │
  ┌──────────────┐                  ├───────────────────────────┤
  │ TESTFN - >   │                  │      for MENU ARG         │
  └──────────────┘                  └───────────────────────────┘
  edit
  1*
```

Figure 2. Starting to edit TESTFN

in the user's focus of attention is also reflected immediately. Thus, after executing "F LESS" and "(1 ILESSP)", the screen is as shown in Figure 3.

2.2 Zooming In and Out

DED's prettyprint algorithm is controlled by two parameters which determine the depth to which prettyprinting is carried out. These are roughly equivalent to CARN and CDRN in INTERLISP's PRINTLEVEL: whenever the CDR-depth of the tail of an expression exceeds CDRN, the tail is printed as "—"; whenever the CAR-plus-CDR-depth of an expression exceeds CARN, the ele-

```
(LAMBDA (LST)
   (* DRB: "24-Oct-80 14:35")
   (* a test function for DED)
   (COND
     ((NULL &)
      LST)
     ((⟦I LESSP & ⟧)
      (CONS & &))
     (T (TESTFN &))))

┌──────────────┐
│ TESTFN -- >  │
└──────────────┘
edit
1* F LESS
2*(1 ILESSP)
3*
```

Figure 3. After a search and a modification

```
(COND
  ((NULL (CDR LST))
   LST)
  ([ILESSP (& CADR LST)]
   (CONS (CAR LST)
         (TESTFN &)))
  (T (TESTFN (CONS & &)))))



TESTFN --> LAMBDA
edit
1*F LESS
2*(1 ILESSP)
3*ZIN COND
4*
```

Figure 4. After zooming in

ment is printed as "&". The current values of CARN and CDRN are 3 and 15, respectively, and most users feel comfortable with them.

DED commands for zooming in allow the user to see specific subexpressions in more detail. When DED zooms in to a subexpression, that subexpression is shown in the Prettyprint Region. In order to indicate the location of the displayed expression within the entire expression, the CARs of the nested expressions surrounding the displayed expression are shown in the line (called the "zoom line") separating the Prettyprint Region and Interaction Region. For example, Figure 4 shows the screen after DED has zoomed in to the COND. DED automatically zooms in whenever the user's focus of attention moves to an expression too deep to be visible in the Prettyprint Region. For example, Figure 5 shows the screen after executing the search command "F CDDR". The zoom out command causes DED to redisplay the expression which was displayed prior to the most recent zoom in command. That is, DED maintains

```
(CONS
     [CDDR LST ])
     (CAR LST)




TESTFN --> LAMBDA COND T TESTFN
edit
1*F LESS
2*(1 ILESSP)
3*ZIN COND
4*F CDDR
5*
```

Figure 5. After searching to a non-visible expression

a stack of displayed expressions; zooming in corresponds to a push operation, zooming out corresponds to a pop operation.

DED always ensures that the user's focus of attention is a subexpression of the expression displayed in the Prettyprint Region. Thus, for example, if a search command shifts the focus of attention to an expression not contained in the current expression, DED zooms out (pops the stack of displayed expressions) until the displayed expression contains the new focus, and then, if necessary, zooms in to an expression such that the new focus is visible despite the elision of the prettyprinter.

2.3   Keys to Change the Focus of Attention

In order to allow the use of INTERLISP's line editor for entering standard commands, DED updates the display only after a complete line of edit commands has been executed. This has generally turned out to be quite comfortable with one exception: as commands to change the focus of attention are entered, the display does not immediately indicate the new focus of attention. To solve this problem, DED includes several single-key commands to change the focus of attention. After INTERLISP has typed the command prompt, and before the user has started typing normal edit commands, these special keys may be typed. Each corresponds to a different kind of (structural) motion, and the new focus of attention is displayed immediately.

There are six different commands, as follows:

1. **UPARROW:** Move up one level (INTERLISP's 0 command).

2. **DOWNARROW:** Move to the first element of the next level down (INTERLISP's 1 command); if there is no lower level, move to the next element at the same level.

3. **LEFTARROW:** Move to the previous element at the current level (INTERLISP's BK command); if there is no such element, move up one level.

4. **RIGHTARROW:** Move to the next element at the current level (INTERLISP's NX command); if there is no such element, move down one level.

5. **UP:** Move to the tail beginning with the current focus of attention (INTERLISP's UP command).

6. **LAST:** Move to the last element of the next level down (INTERLISP's -1 command).

None of these keys ever causes the focus of attention to move outside of the currently displayed expression.

There are also two special keys to zoom in or out and two for marking a location and returning to previously marked locations.

In addition to these special keys, DED includes a menu-like facility for special or common command sequences. (Since a VT100 does not have a mouse or other pointing device, the menu facility is used by typing a number followed by a special menu activation key.) Among the menu commands are the following:

1. **PCK:** Deletes the current expression and saves it in the "pick buffer". If preceded by <number> picks the first <number> elements of the current expression.

2. **CPY:** Copies the current expression into the pick buffer, but does not delete it. If preceded by <number>, copies the first <number> elements of the current expression.

3. **PUT:** Replaces the current expression by (a copy of) the contents of the pick buffer; if the current expression is a tail, puts the contents of the pick

```
(COND
  ((NULL (CDR LST))
    LST)
  ([[ILESSP (& CADR LST)]]
    (CONS (CAR LST)
          (TESTFN &)))
  (T (TESTFN (CONS & &))))



TESTFN --> LAMBDA
edit
1*F LESS
2*(1 ILESSP)
4*ZIN COND
4*F CDDR
5*BF ILESSP
6*
```

Figure 6. Before using special keys

buffer before the current expression. (The pick buffer is saved, so successive PUTs will put multiple copies of the same expression.)

4. **SW1:** Marks the current location as the first of a "swap pair" (see SW2).

5. **SW2:** Swaps the current expression with the expression marked by the most recent SW1.

Thus, Figure 6 and Figure 7 show the display before and after the following keys have been typed: DOWNARROW, RIGHTARROW, DOWNARROW, PCK, UP, PUT. (The "BF ILESSP" command on the previous line is a backward search.) Figure 8 shows the display after typing the following keys: UPARROW, RIGHTARROW, SW1, UPARROW, RIGHTARROW, DOWNARROW, RIGHTARROW, SW2.

2.4 Prettyprinting While Reading

The final major feature of DED is an ability to prettyprint an expression while it is being read. (In fact, this is a feature which has been added to INTERLISP's

```
(COND
  ((NULL (CDR LST))
    LST)
  ((ILESSP [[CAR LST ]]
           (CADR LST))
    (CONS (CAR LST)
          (TESTFN &)))
  (T (TESTFN (CONS & &))))


TESTFN -- > LAMBDA
edit
1*F LESS
2*(1 ILESSP)
3*ZIN COND
4*F CDDR
5*BF ILESSP
6*
```

Figure 7. After using special keys to move an expression

```
(COND
  ((NULL (CDR LST))
    LST)
  ((ILESSP (CAR LST)
          (CADR LST))
    (TESTFN (CONS & &)))
  (T ⟦ CONS (CAR LST)
          (TESTFN &)⟧))
```

```
TESTFN --> LAMBDA
```
```
edit
1*F LESS
2*(1 ILESSP)
3*ZIN COND
4*F CDDR
5*BF ILESSP
6*
```

Figure 8. After using special keys to swap two expressions

general read routine, not just the editor.) Whenever, "{" is typed, a special read routine is entered which controls all echoing. In particular, carriage-returns and tabs are inserted wherever necessary for the input to appear prettyprinted. In addition, balanced parentheses are highlighted. These two features have been found to be quite helpful when typing large expressions.

3. NOTES ON THE IMPLEMENTATION

3.1 The Display Chain

INTERLISP's editor was originally based on the concept of a "current expression": that part of the structure which is the user's current focus of attention. All INTERLISP commands are made with respect to the current expression. To this, DED adds a "display expression", the part of the structure which is displayed at a given time. DED is built so that the current expression is always within (that is, a substructure of) the display expression. If we define the "top expression" to be the entire structure being edited, then the following relation always holds:

current expression < *display expression* < *top expression*

where < denotes "is a (not necessarily proper) substructure of."

In order to keep track of the location of the current expression within the top expression, INTERLISP's editor uses a structure called an "edit chain", which is a list of expressions. The first expression is the current expression, the last expression is the top expression, and each expression on the list is either a member or a tail of the expression following it on the list. Thus, the edit chain provides a stack of nested expressions, leading from the top expression to the current expression. In a similar manner, DED maintains a "display chain," a stack of nested expressions to be displayed. Expressions are added to and removed from the display chain as the user zooms in and out.

DED ensures that the display chain is always a subsequence of the edit chain. That is, every member of the display chain must be a member of the edit chain and in the same order. As the user's edit chain is changed to reflect his/her current focus of attention, DED's display chain is also changed when necessary. This ensures that the "subexpression" constraint mentioned above is always satisfied.

There was one complication involved in implementing the display chain. Except for the automatic zooming feature, all expressions zoomed to are necessarily already on the edit chain. (E.g., the user zooms to the current focus of attention.) In one case, automatic zooming may result in zooming in to a tail which is not on the edit chain. This caused considerable complexity in the implementation until it was decided to modify the edit chain itself in such cases. The only effect on the user is that, in a few cases, a "0" command moves the focus of attention to a tail which had not previously been a focus of attention. This has not disturbed any of DED's users.

3.2   DED's Prettyprinter

INTERLISP did not have the right "hooks" to permit modifying its pretty-printer to elide expressions below a given depth. (More precisely, if it had the hooks, I was unable to find them.) Therefore, a new prettyprinter was written. The technique used was to call a special function whenever "white space" was called for. This function tests whether a single space should be printed or whether a carriage-return and indentation are required. (Note that the same function is also used to determine when to insert carriage-returns and indentations when prettyprinting while reading.) Its decision is based on the CAR and CADR of the expression being printed and on the elements before and after the "white space." This is both simpler and less flexible than INTER-LISP's prettyprinter, but functions well enough for the display editor. Elision is accomplished by keeping track of the CAR- and CDR-depth of the expression being printed; as soon as the depth limit is exceeded, expressions are no longer printed.

(At the suggestion of Steve Wesfold, I modified the elision algorithm to ensure that the current expression would be printed with at least a certain level of detail; in effect, the current expression may get more detail than the surrounding expression. This change has proved quite valuable.)

The new prettyprinter also has a facility for keeping track of the line and column number of the first and last characters of every expression being printed. Since the prettyprinter does not use brackets for super parentheses, these characters are always "(" and ")" for an expression or " " and ")" for a tail. A simple hash table (using INTERLISP's hash arrays) is used. This table is used both for indicating the current focus of attention on the displayed expression and for highlighting balanced parentheses when prettyprinting while reading.

(While I was at first worried about how to keep track of screen positions when scrolling occurred during prettyprinting while reading, this turned out to be relatively simple. The lines and columns associated with expressions being prettyprinted are all relative to the first prettyprint line. Thus, the following expression gives the display line which corresponds to prettyprint line p_1 when the current prettyprint line is p_2 and the current display line is d_2, as determined by asking the terminal to report its current position:

$$d_2 - (p_2 - p_1)$$

Note that there is no need to remember the display line when p_1 is typed. In retrospect, this is obvious; when I first looked at the problem it wasn't, although perhaps it should have been!)

3.3   PROMPTCHARFORMS

Virtually all of DED's features are handled by a single expression on PROMPTCHARFORMS. (PROMPTCHARFORMS is an INTERLISP hook which allows the user to specify arbitrary computation to be performed (i.e., expressions to be evaluated) just prior to the time that the next prompt is typed to request input from the user.) DED's expresson on PROMPTCHARFORMS calls a function which decides whether to update the display (by testing whether there have been any side effects since the previous update), tests whether to do an automatic zoom, and shows the new current focus of attention. The prompt characters are then typed on the prompt line, the special keys are checked, and finally control is returned to INTERLISP's editor.

3.4   Dealing with a Display

This was my first serious effort at making effective use of a display device; what follows are notes on doing this within INTERLISP. Unfortunately, IN-TERLISP does not provide all of the hooks that would be useful. In particular, there is no way (that I know of) to intercept every character before it is sent to the terminal. The main implication is that one cannot keep a precise model of the entire screen (unless you prevent INTERLISP from typing anything at all). This was a problem principally in dealing with the user's interaction with INTERLISP's standard editor. What happens if the user's command to IN-TERLISP causes so much to be printed that the entire screen scrolls up a few lines? One possibility would be to redisplay the entire screen whenever that happens, although detecting the occurrence of such accidental scrolling is still a problem. Fortunately, the VT100 terminal provides a simple solution: the scrolling region can be changed under program control. Whenever DED is in operation, the VT100's scrolling region is changed to be the Interaction Region.

Another vexing problem involved the carriage-returns that both INTER-LISP and TOPS-20 insert into the output stream whenever too many characters have been typed. This is helpful except when sending control sequences to the display, in which case it can cause great difficulties. INTERLISP's PRIN3 and PRIN4 are helpful here, but the final solution was to convince both INTERLISP and TOPS-20 that the linelength was infinite when entering display mode and that the character count was 0 when leaving display mode. (My sincere thanks to Bill van Melle for helping to solve this problem.)

3.5   Device-Specific Aspects of DED

As noted above, DED was built to use a DEC VT100 terminal. There are three features of the VT100 that are crucial to DED's success. First, it is possible to highlight (using reverse video) arbitrarily many portions of the screen. This is especially important for indicating the location of the current focus of attention within the displayed expression, but has been used in several other ways. Second, it is possible to request from the terminal the current cursor location. This is used in both the prettyprinting reader and in repositioning the cursor within the Interaction Region before returning control to INTER-LISP's editor. (Note that this would be less necessary if INTERLISP provided a way of maintaining a complete model of the screen by intercepting every character that is sent to the terminal.) Third, as was mentioned above, it is possible to restrict the scrolling region. Of these features, highlighting and cursor-position reporting are fairly common on other display devices.

In an attempt to gain device independence, all of DED's interactions with the display are controlled by a table describing the appropriate protocols for different features. This technique permitted DED to be extended to a Zenith (Heathkit) terminal quite easily. (The Zenith does not allow the scrolling region to be changed; in order to minimize accidental scrolling, the scrolling region is cleared as soon as the first character of the next command is typed.)

After DED was finished, a small experiment was performed to test the feasibility of extending it to run on a bitmap display (a Xerox Dolphin). This turned out to be simpler than I had expected, involving essentially a mapping between character positions and bit positions. More interesting was the attempt to use a mouse (rather than arrow keys) to indicate changes in the focus of attention. The basic problem was to invert the mapping of cells in the expression which was prettyprinted to character positions on the screen. A few simple rules seemed sufficient to produce a comfortable location indicator, even if the mouse was not pointing to a character position that was stored in the original table. Although the experiment was not completed, it became clear that a pointing device, especially when combined with a sophisticated menu system, was a significant improvement over the VT100 interface. (An additional major advantage was the larger size of the display, which would permit such features as a split screen for editing two functions simultaneously.) However, the entire process also made me wonder whether a better approach would be to redesign the entire editor and interface from scratch, rather than to continually tack new features onto the initially teletype-oriented INTERLISP editor. [*Editors' note*: This has been done with Interlisp-D.] DED certainly seems to be a valuable step, but is also certainly not the ultimate solution.

4. LESSONS AND SURPRISES

Building programming environments is inherently an experimental process— it is simply impossible to determine beforehand the appropriate way for an environment to appear to the user and to respond to his/her requests. DED is the second display-editor I have built for INTERLISP (but the first that I actually use). What follows are the lessons I learned in the process of building DED and some of the surprises that I encountered.

Perhaps the greatest surprise was the utility of the automatic zoom feature. I had expected that too much zooming in and out would disturb the user's sense of continuity. After all, the user could always zoom in or out, whenever he/she wanted, simply by typing a two-character command. In fact, the "autozoom" feature was added to DED only after experiencing considerable frustration at having to type the zoom commands so frequently. I now consider the autozoom feature to be of great importance, and rarely explicitly command DED to zoom in or out.

Another surprise, although less consequential, was the low utility of the zoom line as a way of determining where I am within the overall expression being edited. I was rather proud of the idea when it occurred to me, but have never actually used it in an editing session. I have left it in DED, since it also serves to separate cleanly the Prettyprint and Interaction Regions.

A third lesson (but no real surprise) was that the current focus of attention could be indicated so well by highlighting only the parentheses around the expression, but not the entire expression. This has turned out to be very comfortable (it is less obtrusive than continually highlighting and unhighlighting large portions of the screen) as well as simple to implement.

The fourth lesson is the importance of the arrow keys for quickly changing the focus of attention within the displayed region. I now use these keys almost to the exclusion of INTERLISP's other attention changing commands. (Except, of course, that I also use the search commands, which are especially useful when combined with automatic zooming.) I had put considerable thought into defining the appropriate action for the keys so that they seemed natural. My initial design was that the right and left arrows would correspond to moving forward and backward within an expression and that the up and down keys would correspond to moving to higher and lower levels within the displayed expression. This seems to be natural to DED's users, even though it does not always correspond to the same physical direction on the display screen. A major improvement in this scheme resulted from having the keys perform some other action if the normal one did not fit the context. For example, if the current focus of attention is on the last element of a list, the right arrow moves up a level before moving to the next element. While one might think that multiple meanings for the keys would be confusing, we have found the opposite to be the case. If the user types a right arrow while at the last element of a list, he/she presumably wants to move somewhere, and the secondary meaning is probably right.

The final lesson (perhaps "observation" is a better term) is that my editing style has changed considerably. I now use a different set of commands (e.g., PCK, PUT and SWAP where I used to use MOVE). But in broader terms, my basic mode of interaction has changed. The prettyprinter with elision provides (for me, at least) a comfortable level at which to view a form—so comfortable that I find myself referring much less frequently to hardcopy listings. Adding display facilities to INTERLISP's structure editor has oriented my editing style much more toward interactivity than it ever was in the past.

REFERENCES

[Greenblatt et al. 1984] R. Greenblatt, T. Knight, J. Holloway, D. Moon, D. Weinreb. The Lisp machine. In *Interactive Programming Environments*.

[Moon 1974] D. Moon. *MACLISP Reference Manual*. Massachusetts Institute of Technology, Project MAC, 1974.

[Sandewall 1978] E. Sandewall. Programming in the interactive environment: the LISP experience. *Communications of the ACM*, 10:1 (March 1978), 35-71; reprinted in *Interactive Programming Environments*.

[Stallman 1981] R.M. Stallman. *EMACS: The Extensible, Customizable Display Editor*. Massachusetts Institute of Technology, Artificial Intelligence Laboratory, Memo 519a, 1981; reprinted in *Interactive Programming Environments*.

[Teitelbaum and Reps 1980] T. Teitelbaum, T. Reps. The Cornell Program Synthesizer: a syntax-directed programming environment. *Communications of the ACM*, 24:9 (September 1981), 563-573; reprinted in *Interactive Programming Environments*.

[Teitelman 1977] W. Teitelman. A display-oriented programmer's assistant. CSL 77-3, XEROX PARC, 1977; reprinted in *Interactive Programming Environments*; see also *Proceedings of the Fifth International Joint Conference on Artificial Intelligence*, Cambridge, Massachusetts, August 1977, 905-915.

[Teitelman 1978] W. Teitelman. *INTERLISP Reference Manual*. Xerox Palo Alto Research Center, Palo Alto, California, December 1978.

15 EMACS: The Extensible, Customizable, Self-Documenting Display Editor

RICHARD M. STALLMAN

Massachusetts Institute of Technology
Cambridge, Massachusetts

EMACS is a display editor which is implemented in an interpreted high level language. This allows users to extend the editor by replacing parts of it, to experiment with alternative command languages, and to share extensions which are generally useful. The ease of extension has contributed to the growth of a large set of useful features. This paper describes the organization of the EMACS system, emphasizing the way in which extensibility is achieved and used.

This is an extended version of a paper which was published in *Proceedings of the ACM SIGPLAN SIGOA Symposium on Text Manipulation,* June 1981, Portland, Oregon, pp. 147-156.

1. INTRODUCTION

EMACS[1] is a real-time display editor which can be extended by the user while it is running.

Extensibility means that the user can add new editing commands or change old ones to fit his editing needs, while he is editing. EMACS is written in a modular fashion, composed of many separate and independent functions. The user extends EMACS by adding or replacing functions, writing their definitions in the same language that was used to write the original EMACS system. We will explain below why this is the only method of extension which is practical to use: others are theoretically equally good but discourage use, or discourage nontrivial use.

Extensibility makes EMACS more flexible than any other editor. Users are not limited by the decisions made by the EMACS implementors. What we decide is not worth while to add, the user can provide for himself. He can just as easily provide his own alternative to a feature if he does not like the way it works in the standard system.

A coherent set of new and redefined functions can be bound into a *library* so that the user can load them together conveniently. Libraries enable users to publish and share their extensions, which then become effectively part of the basic system. By this route, many people can contribute to the development of the system, for the most part without interfering with each other. This has led the EMACS system to become more powerful than any previous editor.

User customization helps in another, subtler way, by making the whole user community into a breeding and testing ground for new ideas. Users think of small changes, try them, and give them to other users. If an idea becomes popular, it can be incorporated into the core system. When we poll users on suggested changes, they can respond on the basis of actual experience rather than thought experiments.

To help the user make effective use of the copious supply of features, EMACS provides powerful and complete interactive self-documentation facilities with which the user can find out what is available.

A sign of the success of the EMACS design is that EMACS has been requested by over a hundred sites and imitated at least ten times.

1.1 Background: Real-Time Display Editors

By a *display editor*, we mean an editor in which the text being edited is normally visible on the screen and is updated automatically as the user types his commands. No explicit commands to "print" text are needed.

As compared with printing terminal editors, display editor users have much less need for paper listings, and can compose code quickly on line without writing it on paper first. Display editors are also easier to learn than printing terminal editors. This is because editing on a printing terminal requires a mental skill like that of blindfold chess; the user must keep a mental image of the text he is editing, which he cannot easily see, and calculate how each of his editing command "moves" changes it. A display editor makes this unnecessary by allowing the user to see the "board".

Among display editors, a *real-time* editor is one which updates the display very frequently, usually after each one or two character command the user

---

[1]EMACS stood for Editing Macros, before we realized that EMACS is composed of functions written in a programming language rather than macros in the editor TECO.

types. This is a matter of the input command language. Most printing terminal editors read a string of commands and process it all at once; a useful feature on a printing terminal. For example, there is usually an "insert" command which inserts a string of characters. When such editors are adapted to display terminals, they often update the display at the end of a command string; thus, the insertion would be shown all at once when it was over. It is more helpful to display each inserted character in its position in the text as soon as it has been typed.

A real-time display editor has (primarily!) short, simple commands which show their effects in the display as soon as they are typed. In EMACS, text (printing characters and formatting characters) is inserted just by typing it; there is no "insert" command. In other words, each printing character is a command to insert that character. The commands for modifying text are non-printing characters, or begin with nonprinting characters. Many-character commands echo if typed slowly; if there is a sufficiently long pause, the command so far is echoed, and then the rest of the command is echoed as it is typed. Aside from this, EMACS acknowledges commands by displaying their effects.

EMACS is not the first real-time display editor, but it derives much appeal from being one. It is not necessary to know how to program, or how to extend EMACS, to use it successfully.

2. APPLICATIONS OF EXTENSIBILITY

To illustrate and demonstrate the flexibility which EMACS derives from extensibility, here is a summary of many of the features, available to EMACS users without the need to program, to which extensibility has contributed. Many of them were written by users; some were written by the author, but could just as well have been written by users.

2.1 Customization

Many minor extensions can be done without any programming. These are called customizations, and are very useful even by themselves. For example, for editing a program in which comments start with <** and end with **>, the user can tell the EMACS comment manipulation commands to recognize and insert those strings. This is done by setting parameters which the comment commands refer to. It is not necessary to redefine the commands themselves. Another sort of customization is rearrangement of the command set. For example, some users prefer the four basic cursor motion commands (up, down, left and right) on keys in a diamond pattern on the keyboard. It is easy to reassign the commands to these positions. It is also possible to rearrange the entire command set according to a different philosophy.

2.2 Operating on Meaningful Units of Text

EMACS can be programmed to understand the syntax of the language being edited and provide operations particular to it. Many *major modes* are defined, one for each language which is understood. Each major mode has the ability to redefine any of the commands, and reset any parameters, so as to customize EMACS for that language. Files can contain special text strings that tell EMACS which major mode to use in editing them. For example, (-*-Lisp-*-)

anywhere in the first nonblank line of a file says that the file should be edited in Lisp mode. The string would normally be enclosed in a comment.

For editing English text, commands have been written to move the cursor by words, sentences and paragraphs, and to delete them; to fill and justify paragraphs; and to move blocks of text to the left or to the right. Other commands convert single words or whole regions to upper or lower case. There are also commands which manipulate the command strings for text justifier programs: some insert or delete underlining commands, and others insert or delete font-change commands.

Many commands are controlled by parameters which can be used to further adapt them to particular styles of formatting. For example, the word moving and deletion commands have a syntax table that says which characters are parts of words. There are two commands to edit this table, one convenient for programs to use and an interactive one for the user. The paragraph commands can be told which strings, appearing at the beginning of a line, constitute the beginning of a paragraph. Such parameters can be set by the user, or by a specification in the file being edited. But normally they are set automatically by the major mode (that is, by telling EMACS what language the file is written in) and do not require attention from the user.

2.3   Redefining Self-Inserting Characters

A very powerful extension facility is the ability to redefine the graphic and formatting characters as commands. These characters, which include letters, digits and punctuation, are normally all defined as commands to insert themselves into the text. Useful alternate definitions for these characters usually insert the character as usual, and then do additional processing which is in some way meaningfully associated with the insertion of that character.

The single most useful command for editing text is the "auto-fill space". It is a program intended to be used as the definition of the space character. In addition to inserting a space, it breaks the line into two lines if it has become too long. With the space character redefined in this way, the user can type endlessly ignoring the right margin, and the text is divided into lines of a reasonable length. Of course, this feature is not always desirable. It is turned on or off by redefining the space command. If the auto-fill space did not exist, any user could write it and also the command to turn it on and off.

A bolder use of redefinition of self-inserting characters is the abbreviation facility, part of the standard EMACS system but still implemented as an extension maintained by the user who wrote it. The abbreviation facility allows the user to define abbreviations for words, and then type the abbreviations in order to insert the words. For example, if "cd" were defined as an abbreviation for "command", typing "i/o-cd" would insert "i/o-command" into the text. Abbreviation expansion preserves case, so "Cd" would expand into "Command". Abbreviation works by redefining all punctuation characters (the list of which can be altered by customization) to run a program which looks at the preceding word and, if it is a defined abbreviation, replaces it with its expansion.

Yet another application of redefining printing characters is automatic parenthesis-matching. When this feature is in use, every time the user inserts a close-parenthesis, the cursor moves briefly to the matching open-parenthesis, then back again. Automatic matching is especially useful in editing Lisp code, but it is helpful with most other programming languages also. It is implemented by redefining the close-parenthesis character.

2.4   Editing Programs

Extensibility is especially useful for editing programs. One might conceivably design in advance all the editing commands needed for editing English text, but each programming language has its own set of useful syntactic operations, which suggest useful editing commands. Because languages differ so much, simple customization is not in general enough to implement familiar operations for a new language. A new extension package is required.

EMACS commands have been written, for many languages, to move over or kill balanced expressions, to move to the beginning or end of a function definition, and to insert or align comments. But the most useful editing operation for programs, and the first one to be implemented for any programming language, is automatic indentation.

The structure of a program can be made clear at a glance by adjusting the indentation of each line according to its level of nesting. Most programming communities attempt to indent code properly but do it manually. Automatic indentation is used mostly by Lisp programmers.

Automatic indentation was traditionally done by a program which would read in an entire source file, rearrange the indentation, and write out a corrected source file. Such a tool has several disadvantages. For one thing, processing the entire file is likely to take a while. For another, the tool insists on imposing its own idea of proper formatting, which the user cannot override. Even after a lot of effort is put into heuristics for good indentation, users are still dissatisfied.

Automatic indentation in EMACS is done incrementally. The Tab character is redefined, as a command, to update the indentation of the current line only, based on the existing indentation of the preceding lines. The Tab command is used on lines whose nesting has changed. With it, the user can indent code properly as it is first typed in. If he does not agree with the Tab command's choice of indentation, he can override it.

Because the indentation function must understand the syntax of the programming language being edited, each language requires a separate indentation function. It is the job of the major mode for each programming language to redefine the Tab character to run an appropriate indenter. Users can always use the same command to indent, no matter what sort of program they are editing. In addition, another editing command can do indentation by calling the current definition of Tab as a subroutine. (One such function is the one which indents several consecutive lines.)

Conventions such as this are vital, in an extensible system, for enabling unrelated extensions to avoid interacting wrong; one user can write an indentation function for a new language, while another user writes new language-independent operations for requesting indentation, and the two automatically work properly together.

Languages which have support for indentation include Lisp, Pascal, PL/I, Bliss, BCPL, Muddle and TECO.

Comprehension of the user's program reaches its greatest heights for Lisp programs, because the simplicity of Lisp syntax makes intelligent editing operations easier to implement, while the complexity of other languages discourages their users from implementing similar operations for them. In fact, EMACS offers most of the same facilities as editors such as the Interlisp editor which operate on list structure, but combined with display editing. The simple syntax of Lisp, together with the powerful editing features made possible by that simple syntax, add up to a more convenient programming system than is practical with other languages. Lisp and extensible editors are made for each other, in this way. We will see below that this is not the only way.

2.5   Editing Large Programs

Large programs are composed of many functions divided among many files. It is often hard to remember which file a given function is in. An EMACS extension called the TAGS package knows how to keep track of this.

The TAGS package makes use of a file called a tag table, which records each function in the program, stating what file it is defined in and at what position in the file. The tag table is made by running a special program named TAGS, which is not part of EMACS. Once the tag table is loaded into EMACS, the command Meta-Period[2] finds the definition of any function, using the information in the tag table to select the proper file and find the function in it.

The positions within the source file, remembered in the tag table, are used to find the function in the file instantly. Changing the file makes the remembered positions inaccurate. If this has happened, Meta-Period searches in both directions away from the remembered position until it finds the definition. So small inaccuracies cause only slight delays.

When many new functions have been added, or moved from one file to another, the TAGS program can reprocess the tag table into an updated one. To make this more automatic, the tag table also remembers which language each source file is written in. This information is needed for recognizing the function definitions in the file.

2.6   Editing Other Things

Interactiveness is useful in many activities aside from editing text. For example, reading and replying to mail from other users ought to be interactive. Many of these activities occasionally involve text editing: for example, editing the text of a reply. If a special editor is implemented for the purpose, it can easily be much more work to write than all the rest of the system. It is easier to write the other interactive system within the framework of an extensible editor.

EMACS has two extensions, RMAIL and BABYL, for reading mail. Commands in RMAIL and BABYL are not like EMACS commands; typical commands include "D" for "delete this message", and "R" for "reply to this message". Editing the text of the reply is done with ordinary EMACS commands.

DIRED is used for editing a file directory. The normal editing commands, as extended, can be used to move the cursor through the directory listing. Other special commands defined only in DIRED delete, move, compare or examine the file whose name is under the cursor.

The INFO extension is designed for reading tree-structured documentation files. These files are divided textually into nodes, which contain text representing pointers to other nodes. INFO displays one node at a time, and INFO commands move from one node to another by following the pointers.

3.   THE ORGANIZATION OF THE EMACS SYSTEM

The primary components of the EMACS system are the text manipulation and I/O primitives, the interpreter, the command dispatcher, the library system, and the display processor.

The text and I/O primitives are used to operate on the text under the com-

---

[2]"Meta" is the name of a shift key on the ideal EMACS terminal. On terminals which do not have this key, the ASCII character Escape is used as a prefix instead.

mand of the program. The interpreter executes programs, using the primitives when called for. The command dispatcher remembers which program corresponds to each possible input character; it reads a character from the terminal and calls the associated function. The library system associates functions with their names and documentation, and allows groups of related functions to be loaded quickly together. The display processor updates the screen to match the text as changed by the text primitives; it is run whenever there is nothing else to do.

3.1   Editing Language vs.
Programming Language

An EMACS system actually implements two different languages, the editing language and the programming language. The editing language contains the commands users use for changing text. These commands are implemented by programs written in the programming language. When we speak of the *interpreter*, we mean the one which implements the programming language. The editing language is implemented by the *command dispatcher*.

Previous attempts at programmable editors have usually attempted to mix programming constructs and editing in one language. TECO is the primary example of this sort of design. It has the advantage that once the user knows how to edit with the system, he need only learn the programming constructs to begin programming as well.

However, there are considerable disadvantages, because what is good in an editor command language is ugly, hard to read, and grossly inefficient as a programming language. A good interactive editing language is composed primarily of single-character commands, with a few commands that introduce longer names for less frequently used operations. As a programming language, it is unreadable. If the editor is to be customizable, the user must be able to redefine each character. This in a programming language would be intolerable!

When the programming language is the editing language, the built-in editing commands and the primitive operations they use have to be written in another language. Then the user cannot change part of the standard system slightly by making a small change to its definition; it has to be reimplemented from scratch as a macro. Since the primitives available are only the commands he uses for editing, this will often be impossible because the necessary primitives will be internal routines that the user cannot call. The primitives that an extension would like to use are not always the same as the editing operations the user wants.

The implementor of a macro processor is encouraged to ignore such deficiencies because he himself does not use the language in implementing the rest of the system. Since it is traditional, in designing a macro language, to ignore the standards of readability, power and robustness typically applied to the design of programming languages, these deficiencies are usually considerable. The original TECO is a good example of this sort of problem.

In EMACS, each language is designed for its purpose. The editing language has single-character redefinable commands. The programming language is TECO, modified and extended to be more suitable for writing well-structured and robust programs, and to provide the primitives needed by editing programs as opposed to editor users. It remains hard to read, so the descendents of EMACS generally use Lisp instead. TECO was used only for reasons of historical convenience.

More information on the requirements extensibility imposes on the system's programming language is in the next chapter.

3.2   The Library System and
the Command Dispatcher

An important part of any practical extensible system is the ability to use more than one extension at one time, and begin using an additional extension at any time. Extensions should be able to override or replace parts of the standard system, or previous extensions. In EMACS the library system is responsible for accomplishing this.

An EMACS library is a collection of function names, definitions and documentation that can be loaded into an EMACS in mid-session. Libraries are read-only and position-independent, so that they can be loaded just by incorporating them into the virtual memory of the EMACS. This allows all EMACS's using a library to share the physical memory. Each library contains its own symbol table which connects function names with definitions, and also with their documentation strings. Libraries are generated from source files in which each function definition is accompanied by its documentation; this encourages all functions to be documented.

When a function name is looked up, all the loaded libraries are searched, most recently loaded first. For the sake of uniformity, the standard EMACS functions also reside in a library, which is always the first one loaded. Therefore, any library can override or replace the definition of a standard EMACS function with a new definition, which will be used everywhere in place of the old. This, together with the fact that EMACS is constructed with explicit function calls to named subroutines at many points, makes it easy for the user to change parts of the system in a modular fashion without replacing it all.

Subroutines are normally called by their full names. The user can also call any command by name, and many commands are primarily intended to be used in that way. However, the most common editing operations need to be more easily accessible. This is the purpose of the command dispatcher, which reads one character and looks it up in the *dispatch table*, a vector of definitions to find the function to be called (the definition-object, not the name).

Functions residing in the dispatch table can be invoked either by the character command or by name. A function which does not appear in the dispatch table can be called only by name. The user calls functions by name by means of a single-character command (Meta-X) whose definition is to read the name of a function and call that function.

Each user has his own patterns of use. Many functions in EMACS are accessible only by name because we expect most users to use them infrequently. If a particular user uses one such command often, he can place the definition in the dispatch table using the function Set Key. The function calling conventions are designed so that almost any function definition will behave reasonably if called by the command dispatcher. If a function tries to read a string argument from its caller, then when called by the command dispatcher it will automatically prompt and read the argument from the terminal instead.[3]

Some libraries contain functions that are intended to be called with single-character commands. The library can arrange to place those functions' definitions in the dispatch table by defining a function called Setup. This will be called automatically when the library is loaded, and it can redefine character commands as needed. However, because EMACS is intended to be customized, no library can reasonably make the assumption that a function belongs on a particular character without allowing the user who loads the library to override

---

[3]The process of reading the argument from the terminal is implemented by a function which the user can replace.

that assumption. For example, a library might wish to redefine Control-S on the assumption that it invokes the search function, but a user might prefer to keep his search on Control-T instead, and he might prefer that same library to alter the definition of Control-T when loaded by him. The author of the library cannot anticipate the details of such idiosyncrasies, but he can provide for them all by following a convention: in the Setup function of the library (TAGS, say), he checks for a variable called TAGS Setup Hook and if it exists, its value is called as a function instead of the usual setting up.

3.3   The Display Processor

The display processor is the part of EMACS which maintains on the display screen an up-to-date image of the text inside the editor. Since the size of the screen is limited, only a portion or "window" can be shown. The display processor prefers to continue to start its display at the same point in the file, so as to minimize the amount of changes necessary to the screen. However, the text where the editor's own cursor is located must appear on the screen so that the terminal's cursor can show where it is. This sometimes forces a new window position to be computed. The user can also command changes in the window position, moving the text up or down on the screen.

The EMACS display processor embodies an unusual principle which makes for much faster responses to the user: display updating has lower priority than cogitation.

Most display editors change the display after each user command. This is the simplest strategy to implement, since each command knows precisely how it has changed the text. But it is very inefficient, not just of the computer's time, but of the user's time, because it makes the user wait for the completion of display updates that have already been made obsolete by further commands waiting to be executed.

Here is an example of the problem. If the user types Carriage Return to create a new line, all the lines below that point need to be redisplayed in their new positions. While this is still going on, if he types an additional Carriage Return to create another new line, the rest of the display update is obsolete; there is no use displaying the rest of the lines in their second positions, only to display them again in their third positions.[4]

The EMACS display processor is best understood as being a separate, lower priority process that runs in parallel with the editing process. The editing process reads keyboard input and makes changes in the text. The display process is always trying to change the screen to match the text; it keeps a record of what is on the screen, and in each cycle of operation finds one discrepancy between the editing buffer and the screen record and corrects it. After each cycle, the display process can be pre-empted by the editing process, which has higher priority. The display process can be thought of as chasing an arbitrarily moving target, the edited text, with a speed limited by the terminal baud rate.

Multiple processes are not actually used in the implementation. Instead, after each line of display output, the display processor updates its data base and polls for input.

An additional benefit of this input-before-output philosophy is that it uses less computer resources when the system is heavily loaded. When not enough

---

[4]This particular sequence of events poses no problem on terminals which can move text up and down on the screen. But the same problem can still result from other events.

computer power is available, EMACS gets behind in processing the user's input. When the first command is completed, more input is available, so no effort is put into display updating yet. By saving computer time this way, EMACS eventually catches up with the user and does its display updating all at once.

Since display updating is not necessarily done at the same time as the editing operation which necessitates it, display updating cannot be the responsibility of the editing command itself. Instead, the display update must be done by somehow comparing the new text with the previous displayed text, or information about it. In EMACS, each editing command returns information on the range of text it has changed, but aside from that the display processor operates independently. This is good for extensibility as well: it is easier to write or change an editing command if it does not have to contain algorithms for updating the screen.

Because the TECO language is not very efficient, the display processor had to be written in assembler language to get adequate performance. This is unfortunate because extensions to the display processor could be very valuable. In later implementations of EMACS, the display processor is written in Lisp along with the editing commands, and can be extended.

4. EXTENSIBILITY AND INTERPRETERS

Despite its syntactic obscurity, TECO is actually one of the best languages to use for implementing an extensible editor. This is because most traditional programming languages simply cannot do the job! Implementing an extensible system of any sort requires features that they intrinsically lack. Specifically, it requires a language with an interpreter and the ability for programs to access the interpreter's data structures (such as function definitions).

Adherents of non-Lisp programming languages often conceive of implementing an EMACS for their own computer system using PASCAL, PL/I, C, etc. In fact, it is simply impossible to implement an extensible system in such languages. This is because their designs and implementations are *batch-oriented*; a program must be compiled and then linked before it can be run. An on-line extensible system must be able to accept and then execute new code while it is running. This eliminates most popular programming languages except Lisp, APL and Snobol. At the same time, Lisp's interpreter and its ability to treat functions as data are exactly what we need.[5]

A system written in PL/I or PASCAL can be modified and recompiled, but such an extension becomes a separate version of the entire program. The user must choose, before invoking the program, which version he wants. Combining two independent extensions requires comparing and merging the source files. These obstacles usually suffice to discourage all extension.

The only way to implement an extensible system using an unsuitable language is to write an interpreter for a suitable language and then use that one. Prime is now implementing an EMACS using a simple Lisp written in PL/I. This technique works because an editor does not require a very efficient interpreter; even the most straightforward Lisp interpreter is more efficient than the TECO interpreter which is empirically observed to be good enough. I would not regard this as implementation "in" the original language, however.

---

[5]It is o.k. to use a Lisp compiler, if there is one. What counts is not using the interpreter all the time, but having it available all the time.

A PASCAL or PL/I implementation which uses an interpreter, and allows the user to access the interpreter data structures sufficiently, could be used just as a Lisp implementation would be used. But such systems are rare, since they are more work to implement than a Lisp system, and inferior in use. They are more work because they must contain all the same basic mechanisms as the Lisp interpreter system, but have more messy details to handle. They are inferior because they merely allow the programmer to write the same program with less effort, whereas the Lisp system in addition allows the program to become simpler. Lisp provides constructs with which the program can take advantage of the interpreter, and of the ability to do run-time type checking (which any system with a garbage collector *must* be able to provide). PASCAL is designed to be compiled, so it gives the program no way to take advantage of these facilities when they are present.

It is also possible to use dynamic linking (the ability to load additional modules of compiled code during execution, and refer to subroutines therein by name) in place of an interpreter. However, dynamic linking operating systems are rarer than good Lisps, harder to implement, and not as convenient for the job. One of the few such operating systems, Multics, has an EMACS written in Lisp. SINE, the EMACS implementation on Interdata computers, uses dynamic linking to load files compiled from a language which resembles Lisp.

5. LANGUAGE FEATURES FOR EXTENSIBILITY

When a language is used for implementing extensible systems, certain control structure and data structure features become vital.

5.1 Global Variables

One difference between Lisp (and TECO) and most other programming languages, which is very important in writing extensible systems, is that variable names are retained at run time; they are not lost in compilation.

In typical compiled languages, variable names are meaningful only at compile time. In the compiled code, uses of one variable name become references to one location in memory, but the name itself has been discarded.

By contrast, Lisp remembers the connection between variable names and their values, so that new programs can be defined.

Global variables are essential for parameters used for customization. EMACS has a variable named Comment Start which controls the string recognized as starting a comment in the text being edited. Its value is supposed to be that string. This variable is used by the comment indenting command to recognize an existing comment. The fact that the variable name is known at run time enables the user to

1. ask to see the value of the string.
2. change the string.
3. define or redefine major modes, for various programming languages, which change the string.
4. define or redefine comment-manipulation commands, which refer to the variable so that they will work on text in various languages.

5.2   Dynamic Binding

Most batch languages use a lexical scope rule for variable names. Each variable can be referred to legally only within the syntactic construct which defines the variable.

Lisp and TECO use a dynamic scope rule, which means that each binding of a variable is visible in all subroutine calls to all levels, unless other bindings override. For example, after

```
(defun fool ( × ) (foo2))
(defun foo2 () (+ × 5))
```

then (fool 2) returns 7, because foo2 when called within fool uses fool's value of x. If foo2 is called directly, however, it refers to the caller's value of x, or the global value. We say that fool *binds* the variable x. All subroutines called by fool see the binding made by fool, instead of the global binding, which we say is *shadowed* temporarily until fool returns.

In PASCAL the analogous program would be erroneous, because foo2 has no lexically visible definition of x.

Dynamic scope is useful. Consider the function Edit Picture, which is used to change certain editing commands slightly, temporarily, so that they are more convenient for editing text which is arranged into two-dimensional pictures. For example, printing characters are changed to replace existing text instead of shoving it over to the right. Edit Picture works by binding the values of parameter variables dynamically, and then calling the editor as a subroutine. The editor "exit" command causes a return to the Edit Picture subroutine, which returns immediately to the outer invocation of the editor. In the process, the dynamic variable bindings are unmade.

Dynamic binding is especially useful for elements of the command dispatch table. For example, the RMAIL command for composing a reply to a message temporarily defines the character Control-Meta-Y to insert the text of the original message into the reply. The function which implements this command is always defined, but Control-Meta-Y does not call that function except while a reply is being edited. The reply command does this by dynamically binding the dispatch table entry for Control-Meta-Y and then calling the editor as a subroutine. When the recursive invocation of the editor returns, the text as edited by the user is sent as a reply.

It is not necessary for dynamic scope to be the *only* scope rule provided, just useful for it to be available.

5.3   Formal Parameters Cannot Replace Dynamic Scope

Some language designers believe that dynamic binding should be avoided, and explicit argument passing should be used instead. Imagine that function A binds the variable FOO, and calls the function B, which calls the function C, and C uses the value of FOO. Supposedly A should pass the value as an argument to B, which should pass it as an argument to C.

This cannot be done in an extensible system, however, because the author of the system cannot know what all the parameters will be. Imagine that the functions A and C are part of a user extension, while B is part of the standard system. The variable FOO does not exist in the standard system; it is part of the extension. To use explicit argument passing would require adding a new argument to B, which means rewriting B and everything that calls B. In the most common case, B is the editor command dispatcher loop, which is called from an awful number of places.

What's worse, C must also be passed an additional argument. B doesn't refer to C by name (C did not exist when B was written). It probably finds a pointer to C in the command dispatch table. This means that the same call which sometimes calls C might equally well call any editor command definition. So *all* the editing commands must be rewritten to accept and ignore the additional argument. By now, none of the original system is left!

5.4   Variables Local to a File

Suppose one file is formatted with comments starting at column 50. Editing this file is easier if the variable Comment Column, which is used (by convention) to decide where to align comments, is always set to 50 whenever this file is being editing. EMACS provides a way to request this; but since it also provides the feature of visiting several files at once, it must take special care to keep each file's variables straight. Suppose one file wants Comment Column to be 50 while another is formatted with 40?

This is solved by allowing each file to have its own local values for any set of variables. Specially formatted text at the end of the file specifies them:

```
Local Modes:
Comment Column:50
End:
```

When a file is brought into EMACS, this local modes list is parsed and the variables and values remembered in a local symbol table. While the file is not selected, its local symbol table contains the local values of the variables. While a file is selected, its local symbol table contains the global values, and the real symbol table contains the file's local values instead.

5.5   Absence of Type Declarations

Most languages require from the user as many declarations as they can get away with; in particular, the data type of every variable or structure field is specified explicitly or implicitly in all programs that use the variable. By contrast, Lisp and TECO allow any variable and any structure slot to have any type, except in unusual circumstances. Many operations are generic; others signal errors if given the wrong type of object. The user can make his functions generic by testing the data types of their arguments with type predicate functions. Some Lisp dialects allow optional data type declarations, which, being optional, can do no harm.

Mandatory compile-time type determination interferes with extensibility in two ways: it makes certain functions hard to write at all (or hard for the user to write), and it makes simple changes to the program require pervasive editing to fix widespread redundant information.

One function which would be impossible, or nearly so, with compile-time type checking, is Edit Options. This fills an editing buffer with the names and values of all defined option-variables, so that the user can edit the values and thereby change his option settings. Even if each variable had a declared type, Edit Options would still have to be prepared to come across variable values of all types. Edit Options is only one of a large class of such functions in EMACS.

Other functions which must be able to pass along values whose types are not known in advance are functionals, which call other, user-supplied functions and save or pass back their results. Normally these must be prepared to accept any type of value from the user-supplied function. Consider the Lisp function MAPCAR: it applies a user-specified function to each element of a list, one at a time, and collects a list of the individual results. So, for example,

```
(MAPCAR '- '(1 2 3))
```

returns the list (-1 -2 -3). If MAPCAR is to be general, it must be able to deal with any type of values, and must be able to put them in a list no matter what types they have.

In Lisp, MAPCAR is a function which could be written by the user. In a strongly typed language, a general MAPCAR facility would have to be built into the compiler, and each use is likely to require specification of a type parameter. The user cannot define new functionals; or at least not generic ones. This means that functionals cannot be part of user extensions.

The other problem with strong typing is that declarations make changes to the program less modular. This is a subtler problem than the other.

Strongly typed languages typically require each module to declare the type of all the data objects that it handles, all the components of any structures, and all the arguments of any functions. This causes declarations for an external variable, or especially a function, to appear in many modules, each of which must be redefined if the data type properties of the external variable or function are changed.

It does no harm if a function whose code assumes that the value of the variable or function FOO is a number also contains a declaration that says so. But another function BAR may merely pass along FOO's value, using code that would be correct no matter what type the value has. Or it may store FOO's value in a list, and it may have to use a different list-structure data type depending on FOO's type. In a typeless language, BAR will require no change if FOO is changed to have values of another type. In a strongly typed language, BAR will have a declaration of FOO. As a result, any extension which changes the type(s) that FOO's value may have, must replace the definition of BAR with a new one differing only in type declarations. Then the extension which changes FOO may conflict with other orthogonal extensions which make real changes in BAR.

The idea that redundant information, such as declarations, makes programming more reliable is based on looking at an individual piece of program source as a timeless object, rather than as something which will certainly be changed even if it is now "correct". This point of view imagines that the development of a program is aimed at a fixed goal, the program that correctly meets the specifications. Redundant descriptions of the specifications provide error checking: an error in one description makes it fail to match the other, which can be detected by the compiler. But this also makes the program rigid. Extensible systems are oriented toward the idea that the specifications *will* change, and that it should be as easy as possible to change the program when that happens.

5.6 Hooks

When an extensible system allows the user to provide a function to be called on certain well-defined occasions, we call it a *hook*. For example, we have already mentioned the hook which is executed whenever a certain library is loaded; for the TAGS library, the hook is named TAGS Setup Hook.

Another important class of hooks is executed when a major mode is entered. Each major mode has its own hook. For example, Text mode's hook is named Text Mode Hook. This hook can be used to request arbitrary actions in advance for each time text mode is entered. Many users always define this hook to turn on Auto Fill mode, so that Auto Fill mode is always on when Text mode is.

Hooks can be associated with variables as well. Then, each time the value of the variable changes, its hook is run. Usually these hooks are used to change other data structures so that they always correspond to the value of the variable. This is often more efficient and more modular than checking the variable itself whenever its value is relevant. For example, changing the value of Auto Fill mode to turn auto-filling on or off calls a function which automatically redefines the Space character's command definition.

Some hooks are attached to specific points within the interpreter or display processor. For example, there is a hook which is called whenever it is time to read a character of input from the terminal. The hook program can supply the character itself. These hooks can be thought of as compensating for the fact that some parts of the system are written in assembler language and cannot simply be redefined by the user.

5.7 Errors and Control Structure

A system for programming editor commands needs more sophisticated facilities for handling errors and other exceptional conditions than most programming systems provide. Let us consider what an error is, and what ought to happen when there is an error.

First of all, what exactly is an error? Sometimes the user asks to do something that cannot be done (a user error). Sometimes a program asks to do something which cannot be done (a program error). Program errors often accompany user errors, but either one can happen without the other.

Program errors can be defined objectively: any event which executes a certain part of the interpreter is a program error. User errors cannot be defined objectively in this way because they are a matter of attitude toward events rather than events themselves. If a command has done nothing, we can regard this either as the response to an error or as normal functioning. And this choice of attitude has no necessary connection with whether the command definition required special code to make it do nothing in the circumstances in question.

When a program error happens, EMACS prints the error message and then gives the user the chance to invoke the error handler to debug it. If he does not do this, control returns to the innermost error return point. Programs can create error return points with a special construct. (We use a Lisp-style syntax in these examples for clarity).

```
(error-return
  (arbitrary-code-here))
```

The end of the error-return construct becomes an error return point which is in effect while the code inside the construct is being executed. Error returns are usually used by loops which read and execute commands of some sort, including the built-in one which reads and displays editing commands.

```
(do-forever
  (error-return
    (read-and-execute-one-command)))
```

Sometimes interpreted functions are called asynchronously or unpredictably. An example is the one which optionally saves the text every so often to reduce the amount lost if the system crashes. If this function gets a program error, it should notify the user, but should not interfere in any way with the user's explicit commands. This requires a construct known in Lisp as *errset*, which prevents *all* normal processing of errors that occur within it. An error occurring within an errset does nothing but return control immediately to the end of the errset.

The programming system does not provide any such uniform handling for user errors because the concept of a user error is not defined at that level. Instead, the designer of each editing command must decide what conditions ought to be considered errors, and what to do in each case. Sometimes the command simply does nothing. Sometimes it rings the terminal's bell and perhaps throws away type ahead. This can be best if we expect that, once the user is told that there is something wrong, it will be obvious what it is. When the cause of the error is less obvious, causing a program error deliberately with a specially chosen error message is a good way of informing him. A special primitive is used to cause a program error with an arbitrary specified error message so that the error-return processing can be invoked.

Sometimes the user error leads naturally to an error in the program, which may be all the handling it needs. This can be so if the program error's error message is an adequate explanation for the user, or if the situation is not deemed likely enough to deserve the effort required to make anything else happen.

The error handler for debugging program errors is an interpreted program itself. This is possible because primitives are provided for examining the function call stack and all other data structures which the programmer would want to examine while debugging. Users have actually written extensions and complete replacements for the standard error handler program.

5.8 Non-local Control Transfers

Returning to the example of the user-written command loop, there has to be a command to exit the loop. How can it be done?

```
(do-forever
  (error-return
    (read-and-execute-one-command)))
```

We do it by means of a non-local control transfer. We create the transfer point by means of a *catch* construct around the loop. The catch creates a named transfer point at the end of the loop, which is accessible only within the loop.

```
(catch
  (do-forever
    (error-return
      (read-and-execute-one-command)))
  exit-my-loop)
```

At any time during the loop, execution of (throw exit-my-loop) transfers control immediately to the end of the catch, thus exiting the loop. The catch and throw constructs were copied from Maclisp.

Like variable names, catch names have dynamic scope: the program can throw to a catch from any of the subroutines called while inside the catch. This is important because ease of extension dictates that each command which the command-reading loop understands be implemented by a separate function, so that the user can redefine one command without replacing the framework of the loop.[6]

6. SELF-DOCUMENTATION AND EXTENSIBILITY

A complex program is much easier to learn if it can answer questions about how to use it. When the program is customizable, it is important for the answers to reflect any customization that has been done. The easiest way to do this is for questions to be answered based on the same tables and data structures that control the functioning of the system. In EMACS, these include the command dispatch table and the loaded libraries.

The most basic kind of question that a user might want to ask is, "What does this command do?" He can inquire about either a function name or a command character. A library contains a documentation string for each function in it, and this is used to answer the question. When the question is about a command character, the dispatch table is used to find the function object which is currently the definition of that character. Then the library system is used to find the name of the function, and then, from that, the documentation string.

The ability to ask what a certain command does only helps users who know what commands to ask about. Other users need to ask, "What commands might help me now?" EMACS attempts to answer this by listing all the functions whose names contain a given substring. Since the function names tend to summarize what the functions do (such as "Forward Word" or "Indent for Comment") and follow systematic conventions, this is usually enough. The list also contains the first line of each function's own documentation, and how to invoke the function with one or two characters, if that is possible.

The documentation for a function is usually just a string of text, but it can also contain programs to be executed to print the documentation, interspersed with text to be printed literally. This comes in handy when the description of one function refers to another function which is usually accessed as a one or two character command. It is better to tell the user the short command, which he would actually use, than the name of the function which defines it. But exactly which command (if any) runs the function in question depends on the user's customization. What we do is to use a program, in the middle of the documentation string, which searches the dispatch table and prints the command which would invoke the desired function. Another application of this facility is for functions which simply load a library and call a function in it. The documentation string for such functions is a program to load the library and print the documentation of the function which would be called.

To help users remember how to ask these questions, we make it simple and standard. A special character, called the Help character, is used. This character is only used for asking for help, and is always available. Help is normally followed by another character which specifies the type of inquiry. If the user does not remember these characters, he can type Help again to see a list of them. To close the remaining loophole of confusion, EMACS prints a message about the Help character each time it starts up.

---

[6]Normally the command reading loop uses the name of the command to compute the name of the function to call. For example, if RMAIL reads the letter N as a command, it calls the function # RMAIL N. This way the user can easily define new commands.

Help is also available in the middle of typing a command. For example, if you start to type the Replace String command and forget what arguments are required, type Help. The documentation of the Replace String function will be printed to tell you what to do next.

Because questions are answered based on the data structures as they are at the moment, many changes in EMACS require no extra effort to update the documentation. It is only necessary to update the documentation of each function whose definition is changed. The format for EMACS library source files encourages this by requiring a documentation string for every function, between the function name and its definition.

7. HISTORY

I began the development of EMACS in 1974 with an improvement to TECO: the implementation of the display processor and a command dispatcher with a small fixed set of commands. These were inspired by the editor E of the Stanford Artificial Intelligence Lab. They were not considered a new editor, but rather one new feature in TECO to join many existing features. The user would give the TECO command Control-R to enter display editing mode, whose commands were suitable only for making local changes to the file. He would exit display editing mode to do anything else.

But once display editing was implemented, it was fairly easy to allow commands to be redefined to call functions written in TECO. TECO already contained considerable facilities for text manipulation, I/O, and programming, so almost immediately many users began to implement large collections of editing commands, powerful enough to do every part of editing. One of the most popular of these systems was TECMAC. Others included MACROS, RMODE, TMACS, Russ-mode and DOC. The need to exit from display editing mode to use TECO directly became less and less frequent until new users no longer learned how.

But TECO was still missing many of the important control and programming constructs which allow programs to be readable and maintainable (for example, named functions and variables!). So the early TECO-based display editors were very hard to maintain. In 1976 the TMACS system experimented with adding named functions and variables, with good results limited by the inefficiency of implementing them with TECO programs. This inspired me to implement EMACS itself.

Writing EMACS involved simultaneously adding to TECO the features which make up the library system and self-documentation, which permitted a new readable programming style, and writing a new set of display editing commands using this style. The design for the commands themselves was based on examining the command sets of the many TECO-based editors for inspiration, and choosing commands so that the most common operations would take few keystrokes. The first operational EMACS system existed in late 1976.

Since then, development has proceeded steadily, most new code being written in TECO. New features are added to TECO itself only to speed up loops such as table searching and s-expression parsing, or to make possible new kinds of I/O or interface operations.

EMACS was developed on the Digital Equipment Corporation PDP-10 computer using MIT's own Incompatible Timesharing System. By 1977, outside interest in EMACS was sufficient to motivate Mike McMahon of SRI International to adapt it to Digital's Twenex ("Tops-20") operating system. EMACS is now in use at about a hundred sites.

7.1   Successors of EMACS

Several post-EMACS editor implementations have copied from EMACS both the specific command set and user interface and the fundamental principle of being based on a programmable interpreter. The motivation for these projects was to transfer the ideas of EMACS to other computer systems. Two of them, now in use, are Multics EMACS, a Honeywell product, and ZWEI, the editor for the MIT Artificial Intelligence Lab Lisp machine.

Because EMACS supplied the implementors with a clear idea of what was to be implemented, their focus was on making the foundations clean. The essential improvement was the substitution of an excellent programming language, Lisp, for the makeshift extended TECO used in EMACS. Lisp provides the necessary language features in a framework much cleaner than TECO. Also, it is more efficient. A Lisp interpreter is intrinsically more efficient than a string-scanning interpreter such as TECO's, and Lisp compilers are also available. This efficiency is important not just for saving a few microseconds, but because it reduces the amount of the system which must be written in assembler language in order to obtain reasonable performance. This opens more of the system to user extensions. Another improvement has been in the data structure used to represent the editing buffer: Multics EMACS developed the technique of using a doubly-linked list of lines, each being a string. This technique is used in ZWEI as well.

Many other editors imitate the EMACS command set and display updating philosophy without providing extensibility. Despite that deficiency, and despite the greatly reduced set of features that results from it, these can be useful editors, though not as useful as an extensible one. For a computer with a small address space or lacking virtual memory, this is probably the best that can be done.[7]

The proliferation of such superficial facsimiles of EMACS has an unfortunate confusing effect: their users, knowing that they are using an imitation of EMACS, and never having seen EMACS itself, are led to believe that they are enjoying all the advantages of EMACS. Since any real-time display editor is a tremendous improvement over what they probably had before, they believe this readily. To prevent such confusion, we urge everyone to refer to a nonextensible imitation of EMACS as an "Ersatz EMACS".

8.   CONCLUSIONS

8.1   Research Through Development of Installed Tools

The conventional wisdom has it that when a program intended for multiple users is to be written, specifications should be designed in advance. If this is not done, the result will be inferior. The place to try anything new is in a research project which users will not see.

Some people know better than this, but they have been silenced.

The development of EMACS followed a path that most authorities would say is a direct route to disaster. It was the continuous deformation of TECO into something which is totally unlike TECO, from the typical user's point of

---

[7]The standard EMACS system is bigger than the entire 64k-byte address space of the PDP-11, despite constant strenuous efforts to reduce its size. And TECO is equally large. The post-EMACS editors are even larger.

view. And during the whole process, TECO and programs containing TECO were the only text editors we had on ITS.[8]

Indeed, there are ways in which EMACS shows the results of not having been completely thought out in advance: such as, in being based on TECO rather than Lisp. But it is still reliable enough to be widely used and imitated. The disaster which would have been forecast has not occurred. Instead, a new and powerful way of constructing editors has been explored and shown to be good.

I believe that this is no accident. EMACS could not have been reached by a process of careful design, because such processes arrive only at goals which are visible at the outset, and whose desirability is established on the bottom line at the outset. Neither I nor anyone else visualized an extensible editor until I had made one, nor appreciated its value until he had experienced it. EMACS exists because I felt free to make individually useful small improvements on a path whose end was not in sight.

While there was no overall goal, each small change had a specific purpose in terms of improving the text editor in general use, and each step had to be individually well designed and reliable. This helped to keep things on the right track. Research projects with no users tend to improve the state of the art of writing research projects, rather than the state of the art of writing usable system tools.

The individual commands of EMACS benefited from a stage of unregulated experimentation also. When the display processor and the capability for extension were created, many users began to write extensions, which developed into the complete editing environments of which EMACS is the most recent. Each command in EMACS benefits from the experimentation by many different users customizing their editors in different ways since that time. This experimentation was possible only because a programmable display editor existed.

New implementations of EMACS can now be carefully designed, because they have the advantage of hindsight based on the original EMACS. However, the implementor must carefully restrict his careful design to the parts of the editor that are already well understood. To go beyond the original EMACS, he must experiment.

But why isn't such a program of exploration doomed to be sidetracked by a blind alley, which will be unrecognized until too late? It is the extensibility, and a flexibility of mind, which solves this problem: many alleys will be tried at once, and blind alleys can be backed out of with minimal real loss.

8.2   Lisp is Loose!

The traditional attitude towards Lisp holds that it is useful only for esoteric amusements and Artificial Intelligence. The appearance of Multics EMACS as a Honeywell product is the death knell of this view. Now, a mainframe manufacturer is offering a system utility program written in Lisp; a program intended for heavy use by the general user community. The special properties of Lisp, which make extensibility possible, are a key feature, even though many of the users will not be programmers. Lisp has escaped from the ivory tower forever, and is a force to be reckoned with as a system programming language.

---

[8]The Incompatible Timesharing System.

8.3 Blue Sky

The programmable editor is an outstanding opportunity to learn to program! A beginner can see the effect of his simple program on the text he is editing; this feedback is fast and in an easily understood form. Educators have found display programming to be very suited for children experimenting with programming, for just this reason (see LOGO).

Programming editor commands has the additional advantage that a program need not be very large to be tangibly useful in editing. A first project can be very simple. One can thus slide very smoothly from using the editor to edit into learning to program with it.

When large numbers of nontechnical workers are using a programmable editor, they will be tempted constantly to begin programming in the course of their day-to-day lives. This should contribute greatly to computer literacy, especially because many of the people thus exposed will be secretaries taught by society that they are incapable of doing mathematics, and unable to imagine for a moment that they can learn to program. But that won't stop them from learning it if they don't know that it is programming that they are learning! According to Bernard Greenberg, this is already happening with Multics EMACS.

9. APPENDICES

9.1 Display Processing

The way EMACS records what remains on the screen, and compares it with what is now in the text being edited, is determined by the representation used for that text. The post-EMACS editors use better text representations that make for easier display updating algorithms.

The representation used in EMACS is a straightforward linear string of characters. A movable gap which can grow and shrink makes it unnecessary for insertion and deletion within a small region of the file to move half of the file up and down. The gap was essential in making it practical to insert characters one at a time, instead of en masse in an "insert" command, but aside from that it is made invisible at all but the lowest levels of software, so essentially the representation is just a linear string. It is the task of the display processor's auxiliary data to make sense out of the amorphous mass of text.

The lowest level of avoiding wasteful output is a checksum of the characters displayed on each line of the screen. If a screen line is about to be rewritten, the new and old checksums are compared. If they match, the rewriting is skipped. Once in every 2^{36} times this will leave old incorrect text on the screen.

Higher levels of display optimization work by preserving information which is a byproduct of writing the display (namely, where in the text string the beginning of each screen line comes) and combining it with information which localizes the regions of the text string in which alteration has taken place. This allows it to restrict display update processing to a horizontal band of screen which contains all the necessary changes (often just one line). While processing the other lines on the screen would do no actual output, because of the checksums, even the time to compute the checksums is noticeable to the user as a delay. The same information can be used to decide when some lines on the screen should be moved up or down. When lines are inserted in the middle of the screen, it is much better to scroll the following lines downward (if the terminal can do this) than to rewrite them all in their new positions.

The record of where in the text string changes have taken place is maintained by requiring every command to return values saying what part of the string it has changed. It can identify a subinterval of the string which contains all the changes made, it can say that no change was made (though the cursor may have been moved), or it can say nothing, which requires the display processor to make no assumptions.

A better way, developed by Bernard Greenberg in Multics EMACS and used in ZWEI, is to represent the buffer as a doubly-linked list containing pointers to strings, one for each line. Newline characters are not actually present, but implicitly appear after each line except the last. This requires the lowest level insert, delete and search subroutines to be more complicated (for example, inserting a string cannot treat Newline characters like other characters), but this is just a finite amount of complexity; and it greatly simplifies efficient display computations. The state of the screen can be remembered in an array of pointers to the string that was displayed on each screen line. When the display is updated, one can compare the strings in the buffer with the strings in the display, both to see whether they are the same objects (the pointers are equal; EQ, in Lisp), and to see whether their contents are the same.

Multics EMACS never changes the contents of a string in the buffer. It creates new strings to replace the old ones when the text changes. Thus, the string pointers in the screen state continue to record the screen as it was.

ZWEI does change the contents of existing strings. To make sure that it does not fail to notice that the text no longer matches the screen, ZWEI maintains a "clock" which increments each time a change is made in the text. Each line records the clock tick of the last modification. Each screen line records the clock tick as of the time it was displayed. If the line in the text matches the line in the screen record, but the tick counts do not match, then the contents of the line have been changed.

Line list representations also eliminate the requirements on commands to say what they have changed. Reducing the need for the programmer to worry about how display will be done is very desirable. Another advantage is that it becomes feasible to have pointers to characters in the text which relocate when insertions or deletions are done, so that they continue to point to the same place in the text.

9.2 Libraries

An EMACS sharable library contains, first of all, a symbol table which can be binary searched for the name of an object to find the object named. The symbol table points at both the names and the definitions using offsets from the beginning of the file, so that the file can be valid at any location in memory. The names and definitions are all examples of the TECO string data type, in the internal TECO format, so that the library does not need to be translated or parsed in any way when it is loaded.

The symbol table points to the documentation of functions in the library as well as their definitions. The documentation for the function Visit File is an object entered in the symbol table with the name ~Doc~Visit File. There is also a string named ~Directory~whose definition contains a list of the names of all the objects in the file which the library wishes to advertise. This is used for documentation purposes, not for looking up names, and it does not contain names of auxiliary objects such as ~Doc~Visit File or ~Directory~.

It is possible to search the symbol table in reverse, to take a definition and find its name. Since one can tell which library an object is in by comparing its address with the range of memory occupied by the library, this makes it possible to find the name of any object which has one. The ability to do this is important, because when the user asks what the character Control-K does, it is desirable to be able to tell him that it runs the function Kill Line. The names themselves are not kept in the dispatch table because looking up a name in the loaded libraries is slow. For other implementations, that is a reasonable strategy.

10. NOTES

10.1 EMACS Distribution

EMACS is available for distribution to sites running the Digital Equipment Corporation Twenex ("Tops-20") operating system. It is distributed on a basis of communal sharing, which means that all improvements must be given back to me to be incorporated and distributed. Those who are interested should contact me. Further information about how EMACS works is available in the same way.

10.2 Further Information

An expanded version of this paper is available as [Stallman 1981]. A complete manual for use (but not extension) of EMACS is [Stallman 1980a] and [Stallman 1980b]. Various lower level implementation strategies for parts of an EMACS-like editor are treated in [Finseth 1980].

10.3 EMACS-Related Editors

These include the true extensible descendents of EMACS, and the editors which preceded EMACS and supplied some of the ideas for it. The many ersatz EMACS editors are not included.

10.3.1 Multics EMACS   Multics EMACS was written in MacLisp by Bernard S. Greenberg of Honeywell's Cambridge Information Systems Lab, starting in 1978. (When first implemented, it could be used only by its author, because he alone had the necessary privileges to patch the Multics operating system so that a program could read one character from the keyboard instead of waiting for a complete line. After seeing the new editor in operation, the other Honeywell people were convinced to make the feature generally available.) Because it is written in Lisp, Multics EMACS is even more extensible than the original EMACS, and as a result it has accumulated even more powerful features. See [Greenberg 1979], [Greenberg 1980b], [Greenberg and Kissel 1979] and [Greenberg 1980a].

10.3.2 SINE   SINE ("SINE Is Not EMACS") is based on compiling Lisp code to run in a non-Lisp editor environment, in which, unfortunately, no interpreter is present. However, the user can load his own compiled files into a running editor. This design was chosen because of the small address space of the machine, an Interdata at the MIT Architecture Machine Group. See [Anderson 1979].

10.3.3 TECMAC   TECMAC was the first editor implemented in TECO to work with the display processor. It developed many of the ideas used in the EMACS user interface. It was retired because, written when TECO was less suited to system programming, it was unable to attain either readability or efficiency. TECMAC was maintained from 1974 to 1976 by John L. Kulp and Richard L. Bryan.

10.3.4   TECO   PDP-10 TECO was originally written by Richard Greenblatt, Stew Nelson and Jack Holloway at the MIT Artificial Intelligence Lab, based on PDP-1 TECO which was written by Murphy in 1962. The TECO in which EMACS is implemented is its direct descendant. The PDP-10 TECO from Digital, a typical example of TECO, is also a descendant of an early version from MIT. It is documented in [TECO].

Ordinary TECO lacks many important programming constructs. In MIT TECO, the constructs may be syntactically ugly, but they exist. So programs can be well organized, and clean except in the lowest level of detail.

10.3.5   TMACS   TMACS was an editor implemented in TECO which began to develop the idea of the sharable library with commands that could be assigned to keys by the user. TMACS was the project of Dave Moon, Charles Frankston, Earl A. Killian, and Eugene C. Ciccarelli. Interestingly, it had no standard command set. The implementors were unable to agree on one, which is what motivated them to work on making customization easier.

10.3.6   ZWEI   ZWEI ("ZWEI Was EINE Initially") is the editor for the Lisp machine. EINE ("EINE Is Not EMACS"), the former editor for the Lisp machine, was also based on EMACS; it was operational for late 1977 and 1978, and was redone to make it cleaner. Both EINE and ZWEI are primarily the work of Daniel Weinreb and Mike McMahon; see [Weinreb 1979].

10.4   Other Interesting Editors

10.4.1   Augment   Augment (formerly known as NLS) is a display editor whose interesting feature is its ability to structure files into trees. Making the tree structure useful required the concept of the viewspec, which specifies that only certain levels in the tree structure will be visible. (This is the sort of feature which cannot be added by a user to EMACS, because it involves modification of the display processor; but it could be added by a user to Multics EMACS or ZWEI. Augment popularized the graphical input device known as the "mouse", which is a small box with wheels or balls on the bottom and buttons on the top, which the user moves on the table with his hand. This device has been copied widely because of its simplicity and low cost.) Augment was designed at SRI International but is now supplied by Tymshare. See [Engelbart and English 1968] and [Seybold 1978].

10.4.2   Bravo   Bravo comes from the Xerox Palo Alto Research Center. Its orientation is toward text formatting, and it can display multiple fonts, underlining, etc. It makes heavy use of a graphical pointing device, the "mouse" (see Augment). It is not programmable and offers no special help for editing programs as opposed to text. For more information, see your local industrial espionage agent.

10.4.3   E   The editor used at the Stanford Artificial Intelligence Lab, E interfaces with a "line editor" (used to edit within a line, on a display terminal) which can also be employed to edit the input to any other program. The line editor does not allow commands to be redefined; since it is part of the time-sharing system, that is not trivial (though possible in principle). (E allows macros to be written using the same language used for editing. These are as powerful as a Turing machine, and as easy to program with.) See the on-line documentation file E.ALS[UP,DOC] of the Stanford Artificial Intelligence Laboratory.

10.4.4   TRIX   TRIX is a language similar to TRAC designed at Lawrence Livermore Lab specifically for writing editors. It has been used to write commands that are specific to particular languages, and to write text formatters. Its fatal flaw is that it was designed for printing terminals. See [Cecil et al. 1977].

10.4.5   TVEDIT   TVEDIT is a distant relative of E (above) which is used at Stanford on the Twenex and Tenex operating systems. These systems do not provide a line editor, so TVEDIT has its own facilities for changes within lines. TVEDIT is a good example of a generally reasonable but nonprogrammable display editor. See [Kanerva 1973].

10.5   Other Related Systems

10.5.1   The Lisp Machine   The MIT Artificial Intelligence Laboratory has built a machine specifically for the purpose of running large Lisp programs more cheaply than ever before. One of its goals is to make the entire software system interactively extensible by writing it in Lisp and allowing the user to redefine the functions composing the innards of the system. Part of the system is an EMACS-like editor (ZWEI; see above) written entirely in Lisp, which shares in this extensibility. See [Weinreb and Moon 1981].

10.5.2   LOGO   LOGO is a language used for teaching children how to think clearly. Unlike conventional computer-aided instruction, which automates a method of teaching which offers little to motivate the student, LOGO invites students to write programs to produce interesting pictures and learn while doing something fun. See [Papert 1971].

10.5.3   MacLisp   The MacLisp language is very suitable for writing extensible interactive programs, and has been used for the implementation of Multics EMACS. See [Moon 1974].

10.5.4   Smalltalk   The Smalltalk language and system is oriented toward writing extensible programs. See [Ingalls 1978].

ACKNOWLEDGMENTS

This report describes work done at the Artificial Intelligence Laboratory of the Massachusetts Institute of Technology. Support for the laboratory's research is provided in part by the Advanced Research Projects Agency of the Department of Defense under Office of Naval Research contract N00014-80-C-0505.

REFERENCES

[Anderson 1979] O.T. Anderson. *The design and implementation of a display-oriented editor writing system.* Undergraduate thesis, Massachusetts Institute of Technology Physics Department, January 1979.

[Cecil et al. 1977] Cecil, Moll, Rinde. *TRIX AC: a set of general purpose text editing commands.* Lawrence Livermore Lab UCID 30040, March 1977.

[Engelbart and English 1968] D.C. Engelbart, W.K. English. A research center for augmenting human intellect. *Proceedings of the Fall Joint Computer Conference*, AFIPS Proceedings Vol. 33, San Francisco, December 1968. 395-410.

[Finseth 1980] C.A. Finseth. *Theory and practice of text editors, or, a cookbook for an EMACS*. Massachusetts Institute of Technology, L.C.S. Technical Memo TM-165, May 1980.

[Greenberg 1979] B.S. Greenberg. Multics Emacs: an experiment in computer interaction. *Proceedings of the Fourth Honeywell International Software Conference*, Bloomington, Minnesota, April 1979.

[Greenberg 1980a] B.S. Greenberg. *Multics Emacs Extension Writers' Guide*, Honeywell Information Systems, Publication #CJ52, Waltham, Massachusetts, 1980.

[Greenberg 1980b] B.S. Greenberg. Prose and CONS (Multics Emacs: a commercial text processing system in Lisp). *Proceedings of the 1980 Lisp Conference*, Stanford, California, August 1980.

[Greenberg and Kissel 1979] B.S. Greenberg, K. Kissel. *Multics Emacs Text Editor User's Guide*. Honeywell Information Systems, Publication #CH27, Waltham, Massachusetts, 1979.

[Ingalls 1978] Dan Ingalls. The Smalltalk-76 programming system, design and implementation. *Conference Record of the Fifth Annual ACM Symposium on Principles of Programming Languages*, January 1978, 9-17.

[Kanerva 1973] P. Kanerva. *TVGUID: A User's Guide to TEC/DATAMEDIA TV-Edit*. Stanford University, Institute for Mathematical Studies in the Social Sciences, 1973 (online document).

[Moon 1974] D. Moon. *MACLISP Reference Manual*. Massachusetts Institute of Technology, Project MAC, 1974.

[Papert 1971] S. Papert. *Teaching children to be mathematicians vs. teaching about mathematics*. Massachusetts Institute of Technology, Artificial Intelligence Laboratory, Memo 249, 1971.

[Seybold 1978] P.B. Seybold. TYMSHARE's AUGMENT: Heralding a New Era. *The Seybold Report on Word Processing*, 1:9 (October 1978), Seybold Publications, Inc., Media, Pennsylvania.

[Stallman 1980a] R.M. Stallman. *EMACS Manual for ITS Users*. Massachusetts Institute of Technology, Artificial Intelligence Laboratory, Memo 554, 1980.

[Stallman 1980b] R.M. Stallman. *EMACS Manual for TWENEX Users*. Massachusetts Institute of Technology, Artificial Intelligence Laboratory, Memo 555, 1980.

[Stallman 1981] R.M. Stallman. *EMACS: The Extensible, Customizable Display Editor*. Massachusetts Institute of Technology, Artificial Intelligence Laboratory, Memo 519a, 1981; reprinted in *Interactive Programming Environments*

[TECO] *TECO Programmer's Reference Manual*. Digital Equipment Corporation, Maynard, Massachusetts, DEC-10-ETEE-D (revised from time to time); see also *PDP-6 Time Sharing TECO*. Stanford University, Stanford Artificial Intelligence Laboratory, Operating Note 34, 1967; see also P.R. Samson. *PDP-6 TECO*. Massachusetts Institute of Technology, Artificial Intelligence Laboratory, AI Memo 81, July 1965.

[Weinreb 1979] D.L. Weinreb. A real-time display-oriented editor for the LISP Machine. Massachusetts Institute of Technology, Department of Electrical Engineering and Computer Science, undergraduate thesis, January 1979.

[Weinreb and Moon 1981] D. Weinreb, D. Moon. *The Lisp Machine Manual*. Massachusetts Institute of Technology, Artificial Intelligence Laboratory, 1981.

16 The LISP Machine

RICHARD D. GREENBLATT, THOMAS F. KNIGHT, JR.,
JOHN HOLLOWAY, DAVID A. MOON, DANIEL L. WEINREB

Massachusetts Institute of Technology
Cambridge, Massachusetts

This report presents an overview of the LISP Machine Project at MIT. The decision to base a sophisticated software system on a personal computer is justified. The principal modules of the specially designed hardware processor are discussed, highlighting its support for the tagged macro-code architecture. Many additions to the LISP language are described. Sections cover system language extensions, input/output improvements, data representation, program representation, new control structures, storage organization, the smart editor, and message passing.

1. INTRODUCTION

LISP is the second oldest computer programming language still in active use, preceded only by FORTRAN. Its origins go back to 1958 [McCarthy 1978], and the landmark *LISP 1.5 Programmers Manual* [McCarthy et al. 1962] was published in 1962. The previous workhorse LISP implementation in use at our laboratory, PDP-10 MACLISP [Moon 1974], directly traces its origins to an earlier PDP-6 implementation started in 1964. Continuous evolution of the system has occurred since then, with the addition of many new facilities, such as fast arithmetic, and array handling. As one would expect, such a process of evolution left behind many historical artifacts and compatibility driven compromises in the final system. In 1973, we felt it was time for a top-to-bottom reconsideration of our existing LISP implementation.

In designing a LISP implementation for a conventional computer, quite frequently fundamental compromises are made necessary by the structure of the machine. Deficiencies are often encountered in procedure calling, handling of run-time typed operands, and management of large virtual memories, for example. In addition, it was evident that large savings in the space occupied by compiled code could be effected by a suitably designed instruction set. We had available experienced hardware designers and a sophisticated hardware design-aid system [Helliwell 1970]. Thus, it was possible for us to design the computer from scratch. Our prototype processor, referred to as CONS, became operational in 1975. The second generation design, called CADR, was completed and usable by mid-1978.

We define a "personal" computer to be one where the processor and main memory are not time-division multiplexed. Instead each person gets his own, at least for the duration of the session. We had experienced personal computation on the PDP-1 and PDP-6 computers before the advent of time-sharing. The move to time-sharing was an economic necessity, and there were many aspects of the personal computing environment we had given up most reluctantly.

By 1973, a number of factors had prompted us to reexamine the situation. Hardware costs had dropped sharply and were forecast to drop more sharply still. Recognition was increasing that personnel costs were becoming a larger and larger share of total costs, and thus personal computers might be justified even if they were somewhat more expensive. In addition, our enthusiasm for the virtues of time-sharing had been tempered by some of our experiences. In particular, every time-sharing system we had ever seen spent the prime-time hours "thrashing"—making poor use of both human and machine resources. In most cases, serious work on large programs could be done only in the middle of the night.

We were impressed by personal computers we saw being developed at Xerox PARC. Work there pointed the way toward combining some of the advantages of time-sharing (notably access to shared file structures) with personal computation.

In addition, we had to contend with the usual demands from our users for "more, bigger, and faster." In this case, the dominant need was for "bigger," i.e., the capability to run larger programs. Our users were severely constrained by the 256K addressing limitation of the PDP-10, and it was clear that the new system must provide a much larger virtual address space. Furthermore, beyond the virtual addressing capability itself, additional features (in garbage collecting and memory management, for example) are necessary to permit efficient execution of multi-million word programs.

While we were improving LISP, we had to be careful to retain the essential strong points of the language. This is harder than it sounds. (See LISP2 [Abrahams et al. 1966], MLISP [Smith 1970], ECL [ECL 1974], MUDDLE [Galley and Pfister 1975], and POP-2 [Burstall et al. 1971] for examples of systems that, in our view, were not successful in this regard). Among such essentials we would list the following:

- Fully parenthesized list-structure notation for program and data,
- Interactive orientation with both a compiler and an interpreter,
- Run-time data typing, requiring a minimum of declarations to obtain runable code if efficiency is not a concern.
- Dynamic linking. That is, the ability to modify, compile and load small sections of a large system without reprocessing the whole thing.
- System-wide symbol identity provided in a uniform fashion. Essentially this means READ (and most particularly, INTERN.)
- Automatic storage allocation and garbage collection.
- No special attributes, characteristics or abilities are reserved to system functions. User written functions are not logically distinguished from system provided ones.
- Well integrated language-extension capability through macros. Highly similar compile-time and run-time environments, allowing the full power of the language to be easily available at macro expand time.

2. WHY A PERSONAL COMPUTER

The personal computer theme was one of two strong influences working to determine the architecture of our LISP Machine (LISP itself being the other). Our decision to make the system a personal computer instead of a multi-user time-sharing system is surprising to many people. One reason is that personal computers provide a higher quality of computation—a steady and predictable resource on which to build a more interactive computing environment.

However, personal computers can be justified on cost-performance grounds alone. In the case of very large programs (in the multi-million-word range for the coming generation of hardware), paging from secondary store is a necessity in any case. There are a number of reasons which make time-sharing an inefficient way to support such large virtual memory requirements.

In today's technology, the secondary memory consists of disk drives whose throughput is limited by mechanical considerations. Thus, the small disks available to the personal computer designer frequently have identical performance, in terms of access time, to the larger disks used in a time-sharing system. The time-sharing system divides among its users a total resource which is not much larger than the resource that the personal computer is able to devote entirely to its single user.

A number of other factors handicap a time-sharing system in its attempt to utilize the limited resources it has available. Consider the sequence of events that occur when a memory reference page faults in a time-sharing system. The running process becomes blocked, and its disk request is put into the disk queue. The main processor goes on to run some other process. Later, the transfer is completed and original process becomes runnable. However, before it can actually resume execution, it must wait for the currently active process to finish its quantum and for any other higher priority processes to run. The result is that a page fault causes a long real-time delay to the process that takes it. This, in turn, limits the ultimate performance available to any one process to a low value. Moreover, as program size goes up, more and more primary memory occupancy time is wasted by such blocked processes.

On the other hand, there are methods for increasing virtual memory efficiency which are available to the personal computer but very difficult to achieve in a time-sharing system. For example, no reasonable way has been found to allow a user process in a time-sharing system to communicate to the system its probable future page requirements. One would have to find a mechanism by which the system could present to the user his current real memory status and some system instantaneous memory demand parameters. Even if one could do this, effectiveness would be very problematical since these data are rapidly changing. In the case of the personal computer, the problem is much more tractable.

The performance of swapping devices is not the only operating system issue which prompted us to favorably consider the personal computer approach. A promising new technique which seems quite difficult to exploit in the context of time-sharing is microcompilation, i.e. translation of user functions directly into microcode. One difficulty with attempting this in a time shared environment is that system security might be compromised. If many users want divergent microcode, the machine state which must be swapped when changing users is also considerably increased. These problems do not arise in the personal computer approach. The speed improvement which can be gained by microcompiling is largely unknown at present; however, from examples which have been hand-coded in microcode, the performance increases have been dramatic in some cases.

The fact the LISP Machine was to be a personal computer meant that absolute costs had to be kept down. The machine would have plenty of performance, but care would be required not to price it out of its intended market. (In fact, for quite a few applications the current machine is too expensive; however, in many of these cases one can project future hardware costs and foresee that within a few years costs will come down to acceptable levels. In such cases one can often justify small numbers of the current machine on the ground that they are needed to develop software for future machines.)

As a result, our machine is almost classically simple; the pdl buffer (which serves as a sort of cache for the pushdown list) is the only major unit whose function could conceivably be taken over by the remaining units in a reasonable fashion. While we wished to minimize hardware costs, we were careful to avoid ugly kludges in the attempt to effect minor hardware savings. In fact, among microcoded machines we have seen, ours has by far the fewest number of weird fields, complex timing restrictions, etc. We feel strongly that increased difficulty in writing and debugging microcode far outweighs any advantages that might be gained by such methods. In addition to being clean, our micromachine is very general: There is no hard-wiring associated with the details of the macrocode instruction set. Instead, all instruction decoding and register-field selection is handled in a general manner by a barrel shifter and masker which is under microprogram control.

3. THE LISP MACHINE
HARDWARE IMPLEMENTATION

Each logged-in user of the LISP Machine system has a processor, a memory, a keyboard, a display, and a means of accessing shared resources. Terminals, of course, are placed in offices and various rooms; ideally there would be one in every office. The processors, however, are kept in a separate machine room. Since they may need special environmental conditions, often make noise, and take up space, they are not welcome office companions. The number of processors is unrelated to the number of terminals, and may be smaller depending on economic circumstance.

The processor is implemented with a microprogrammed architecture. The current processor, called CADR, is a second generation design based on the first generation CONS design. CADR is a very unspecialized machine with 32-bit data paths and 24-bit address paths. It has a large microcode memory (16K of 48-bit words) to accommodate the large amount of specialized microcode to support LISP. It has hardware for extracting and depositing arbitrary fields in arbitrary registers, which substitutes for the specialized data paths found in conventional microprocessors. It does not have a cache, but does have a push-down list buffer, which is described below.

Using an unspecialized processor was found to be a good idea for several reasons. For one thing, it is faster, less expensive, and easier to design and debug. It is also easier to microprogram, which allows us to write and debug the large amounts of microcode required to support a sophisticated LISP system with high efficiency. In addition it makes feasible a compiler which generates microcode, allowing users to microcompile some of their functions to increase performance.

The primary memory is semiconductor RAMs, typically 128k words by 32 bits and expandable to about 1 million words. The full virtual address space is stored on a 16 million word disk secondary memory and paged into primary memory as required. A given virtual address is always located at the same place on the disk. The access time of the primary memory is about 1 microsecond, and of the disk about 25 milliseconds.

In addition, the machine contains an internal 1K word by 32-bit push-down list buffer which holds the top of the LISP stack. This memory forms an integral part of the processor, so an operand can be addressed and used within a single 180-nanosecond processor cycle.

The display is a high-resolution raster-scan TV driven by its own one megabit memory. The standard monitor features a white phosphor, vertical major axis orientation, and a 64-MHz video data rate. Resolution is approximately 800 by 900 points. Characters are drawn entirely by software, and so any type or size of font can be used, including variable-width ones. Several styles can be used at the same time. One of the advantages of having an unspecialized microinstruction such as CADR is that one can implement a flexible terminal in software for less cost than an inflexible, hard-wired conventional terminal. The TV system is easily adapted to support gray scale, standard resolution, and/or color. This system has been shown to be very useful for both character display and graphics.

The keyboard has several levels of control/shifting to facilitate easy single-keystroke commands to programs such as the editor. The keyboard is also equipped with a speaker for beeping, and a pointing device, usually a mouse.

The shared resources are accessed through an 8 million bit/sec peak transfer rate packet-switching network with completely distributed control. This network is similar in many ways to the Ethernet [Metcalfe and Boggs 1976] developed at Xerox PARC. Shared resources available over the network include a highly reliable file system implemented on a dedicated computer equipped with state-of-the-art disks and tapes, specialized I/O devices such as high-quality hardcopy output, special-purpose processors, and connections to the outside world (e.g. other computers in the building, and the ARPANET).

As in a time-sharing system, the file system is shared between users. Time-sharing has pointed up many advantages of a shared file system, such as common access to files, easy inter-user communication, centralized program maintenance, centralized backup, etc. There are no personal disk packs to be lost, dropped by users who are not competent as operators, or filled with copies of old, superseded software.

The complete LISP Machine, including processor, memory, disk, terminal, and connection to the shared file system, is packaged in a single 19″ logic cabinet, except for the disk, which is free-standing. The complete machine would cost about $80,000 if commercially produced. Since this is a complete, fully-capable system (for one user at a time), it can substantially lower the cost of entry by new organizations into serious artificial intelligence work.

4. LISP AS A SYSTEM LANGUAGE

In the software of the LISP Machine system, code is written in only two languages (or "levels"): LISP, and CADR machine microcode. There is never any reason to hand-code macrocode, since it corresponds so closely to LISP; anything one could write in macrocode could be more easily and clearly written as the corresponding LISP code. The READ, EVAL, and PRINT functions are completely written in LISP, including their subfunctions (except that APPLY of compiled functions is in microcode). This illustrates the ability to write "system" functions in LISP.

In order to allow various low-level operations to be performed by LISP code, a set of "sub-primitive" functions exist. Their names by convention begin with a "%", so as to point out that they are capable of performing unLISPy operations which may result in meaningless pointers. These functions provide "machine level" capabilities, such as performing byte-deposits into memory. The compiler converts calls to these sub-primitives into single instructions rather than subroutine calls. Thus LISP-coded, low-level operations are just as efficient as they would be in machine language on a conventional machine.

In addition to sub-primitives, the ability to do system programming in LISP depends on the LISP Machine's augmented array feature. There are several types of arrays, one of which is used to implement character strings. This makes it easy and efficient to manipulate strings either as a whole or character by character. An array can have a "leader", which is a little vector of extra information tacked on. The leader always contains LISP objects while the array often contains characters or small packed numbers. The leader facilitates the use of arrays to represent various kinds of abstract object types. The presence in the language of both arrays and lists gives the programmer more control over data representation.

A traditional weakness of LISP has been that functions have to take a fixed number of arguments. Various implementations have added kludges to allow variable numbers of arguments; these, however, tend either to slow down the function-calling mechanism, even when the feature is not used, or to force peculiar programming styles. LISP-machine LISP allows functions to have optional parameters with automatic user-controlled defaulting to an arbitrary expression in the case where a corresponding argument is not supplied. It is also possible to have a "rest" parameter, which is bound to a list of the arguments not bound to previous parameters. This is frequently important to simplify system programs and their interfaces.

A similar problem with LISP function calling occurs when one wishes to return more than one value. Traditionally one either returns a list or stores some of the values into global variables. In LISP machine LISP, there is a multiple-value-return feature which allows multiple values to be returned without going through either of the above subterfuges.

LISP's functional orientation and encouragement of a programming style of small modules and uniform data structuring is appropriate for good system programming. The LISP Machine's microcoded subroutine-calling mechanism allows it to also be efficient.

Paging is handled entirely by the microcode, and is considered to be at a very low level (lower-level than any kind of scheduling). Making the guts of the virtual memory invisible to all LISP code and most microcode helps keep things simple. It would not be practical in a time-sharing system, but in a one-user machine it is reasonable to put paging at the lowest level and forget about it, accepting the fact that sometimes the machine will be tied up waiting for the disk and unable to run any LISP code.

Microcoded functions can be called by LISP code by the usual LISP calling mechanism, and provision is made for microcoded functions to call macrocoded functions. Thus there is a uniform calling convention throughout the entire system. This has the effect that standard subroutine packages can be written, (for example the TV package, or the EDITOR package) which can be called by any other program. (A similar capability is provided by Multics [Corbato et al. 1965], but not by most other operating systems).

A related feature is dynamic linking. That is, if a function is called which is not currently defined, the system can attempt to find the definition in certain library files. If the definition can be found, it can be loaded and the computation proceeded without interruption visible to the user.

Many of the capabilities which system programmers write over and over again in an ad hoc way are built into the LISP language, and are sufficiently good in their LISP-provided form that it usually is not necessary to waste time worrying about how to implement better ones. These include formatted output, symbol tables, storage management, both fixed and flexible data structures, function-calling, and an interactive user interface.

Our experience has been that we can design, code, and debug new features much faster on and for the LISP Machine than for earlier systems, whether they are written in assembler language or in traditional "high-level" languages.

5. INPUT/OUTPUT

5.1   Low Level

The LISP Machine processor (CADR) has two buses used for accessing external devices: the "XBUS", and the "UNIBUS". The XBUS is 32 bits wide, and is used for the disk and for main memory. The UNIBUS is a standard PDP-11 16-bit bus, used for various I/O devices. It allows commonly available PDP-11 compatible devices to be easily attached to the LISP Machine.

Input/output software is essentially all written in LISP; the only functions provided by the microcode are %UNIBUS-READ and %UNIBUS-WRITE, which know the offset of the UNIBUS in physical address space, and refer to the corresponding location. The only real reason to have these in microcode is to avoid a timing error which can happen with some devices which have side effects when read. Using these primitives even the lowest level I/O routines can be written in LISP. As the system was refined, a few routines have been hand translated to microcode for efficiency, in such areas as the lowest level of character display and the lowest level of the network.

5.2   High Level

Many programs perform simple stream-oriented (sequential characters) I/O. In order that these programs be kept device-independent, there is a standard definition of a "stream": a functional object which takes one required argument and one optional argument. The first argument is a symbol which is a "command" to the stream, such as "TYI", which means "input one character, and return it, or "TYO", which means "output one character". The character argument to the TYO command is passed as the second argument to the stream. There are several other standard stream operations, for several purposes including higher efficiency. If a particular stream does not support some of these, a defaulting mechanism is provided which defines them in terms of other stream operations (thus obtaining correct functionality without, of course, the higher efficiency). Particular device-specific streams can implement additional operations for their own purposes.

Streams can be used for I/O to files in the file system, strings inside the LISP Machine, the terminal, editor buffers, or anything else which is naturally represented as sequential characters.

For I/O which is of necessity device-dependent, such as the sophisticated operations performed on the TV by the editor, which include multiple blinkers and random access to the screen, special packages of LISP functions are provided, and there is no real attempt to be device-independent.

We hold some hope that eventually input-output conventions and network protocols will be developed fully enough to support sophisticated display usage remotely. Currently, however, we do not feel this is practical. Very likely, personal computers will become cheap enough to largely eliminate the need to solve this problem.

6. REPRESENTATION OF DATA

A major reason for designing our own machine instead of using a commercially available one was the opportunity to employ a tagged architecture. That is, instead of fundamentally operating on integers, we consider our machine to operate on objects having both a type code field and a pointer field. This is distinguished from a conventional implementation where a LISP object is represented by just a pointer. In the conventional system, the data type of the object must be determinable from the pointer; usually this means each page of memory can contain only objects of a single type.

Our type field is relatively small (5 bits); it provides for a generous number of system initial data types, but does not allow directly for user defined data types. We feel this was the right decision. The small data-type field conserves storage in the LISP node and is handled efficiently by the microcode. User data types must really be composed out of system generic ones anyway. We have several methods for doing this (see discussion of message passing below). Note this does not bear on the question of whether the user can define a type and have system primitives such as PRINT, EVAL, +, etc. operate on it in a certain fashion. This in fact can be done in the present system but the process of reaching the user-provided primitive performing function has two levels. For example, the system print function first notices it is printing a DTP-ENTITY, and follows certain conventions to determine the user-specified type (CLASS in the parlance of SMALLTALK [Goldberg and Kay 1976]), then proceeds to locate the print function for that type.

The LISP Machine data types are designed according to these criteria: There should be a wide variety of useful and flexible data types. Some effort should be made to increase the bit-efficiency of data representation, in order to improve performance. The programmer should be able to exercise control over the storage and representation of data, if he wishes. It must always be possible to take an anonymous piece of data and discover its type; this facilitates storage management. There should be as much type-checking and error-checking as feasible in the system.

Currently 26 of the possible 32 type codes are in use. We refer to these codes by symbols with the prefix DTP-. Some are classical LISP data types such as DTP-SYMBOL and DTP-LIST, and others represent particular sorts of functional objects like DTP-FEF-POINTER (macrocompiled function) and DTP-U-ENTRY (microcompiled or hand microcoded function). Also discussed below are various data types which function as forwarding pointers (in other words, things which point at the forwarding pointer appear to point directly to what the forwarding pointer points to), and DTP-STACK-GROUP and DTP-CLO-SURE, which are associated with interesting control structure mechanisms.

One side benefit of a tagged machine is its very high degree of inherent error-checking. Every data-memory reference makes a test which can detect an error if data corruption has somehow occurred. We take advantage of this by defining DTP-TRAP, DTP-NULL, and DTP-FREE. All of these cause an immediate trap if referenced by ordinary instructions. (A reference to a DTP-FREE, for example, would indicate that somehow a pointer had been generated to a free storage list. This disaster could be caused by a hardware failure or a bug in the garbage collector.)

Our pointer field is 24 bits wide, allowing a total virtual address space of 16 million 32-bit words. Although this is a factor of 64 larger than the PDP-10, we realize this will be adequate for only a few years. However, in the future we can easily construct a version of the machine with a wider word size and larger address field, and without making current software obsolete. In fact, during the evolution of the present system, we changed the virtual address size from 24 bits to 23 bits and then back to 24, so we are confident we have the virtual address size properly parameterized. We decided to use a 24-bit virtual address (and thus a 32-bit overall word length) for reasons of input-output compatibility and to save hardware and simplify packaging.

Symbols are stored as five consecutive words, each of which contains one object. The words are termed the PRINT NAME cell, the VALUE cell, the FUNCTION cell, the PROPERTY LIST cell, and the PACKAGE cell. The PRINT NAME cell points to a string object which is the printed representation of the symbol. The PROPERTY LIST cell, of course, points to the property list, and the VALUE CELL contains the current value of the symbol (it is a shallow-binding system [Moses 1970]). The FUNCTION cell replaces the task of the EXPR, SUBR, FEXPR, MACRO, etc. properties in MACLISP. When a form such as (FOO ARG1 ARG2) is evaluated, the object in FOO's function cell is applied to the arguments. Thus, in function context, the function cell is treated in an analogous manner to the value cell. The PACKAGE CELL points to the "package" to which the symbol belongs. This is a new feature (a generalization of the OBLIST or OBARRAY [McCarthy et al. 1962] [Moon 1974]) which considerably reduces the chances of encountering naming conflicts when independently written systems are merged. A symbol object has data-type DTP-SYMBOL, and the pointer is the address of the first of these five words.

Storage of list structure is somewhat more complicated. Normally a "list object" has data-type DTP-LIST, and the pointer is the address of a two word block; the first word contains the CAR, and the second the CDR of the node.

However, note that since a LISP object is only 29 bits (24 bits of pointer and 5 bits of data type), there are three remaining bits in each word. Two of these bits are termed the CDR-CODE field, and are used to compress the storage requirement of list structure. The four possible values of the CDR-CODE field are given the symbolic names CDR-NORMAL, CDR-NEXT, CDR-NIL, and CDR-ERROR. CDR-NORMAL indicates the two-word block described above. CDR-NEXT and CDR-NIL are used to represent a list as a vector, taking only half as much storage as usual; only the CARs are stored. The CDR of each location is simply the next location, except for the last, whose CDR is NIL. The primitive functions which create lists (LIST, APPEND, etc.) create these compressed lists. If RPLACD is done on such a list, it is automatically changed back to the conventional two-word representation, in a transparent way, using forwarding pointers.[1]

Thus in the first word of a list node the CAR is represented by 29 bits, and the CDR is represented by 2 bits. CDR is a compressed pointer which can take on only 3 legal values: to the symbol NIL, to the next location after the one in which it appears, or indirect through the next location. CDR-ERROR is used for words whose address should never be in a list object; in a "full node", the first word is CDR-NORMAL, and the second is CDR-ERROR. It is important to note that the cdr-code portion of a word is used in a different way from the data-type and pointer portion; it is a property of the memory cell itself, not of the cell's contents. A "list object" which is represented in compressed form still has data-type DTP-LIST (that is, words which point to such a list have DTP-LIST in their type fields), but the cdr code of the word addressed by its pointer field is CDR-NEXT or CDR-NIL rather than CDR-NORMAL.

In addition to simply saving storage, CDR-coding allows the same identical storage to be referenced simultaneously both as an array and as a list. This can be a convenient feature for the user, and is important to the system in the efficient implementation of "rest" parameters.

Various numeric data types are supported. Most computation is done with FIXNUMs, which are 24-bit signed integers. They are represented by a type code of DTP-FIX, whose "pointer" part is actually the value of the number. Thus a FIXNUM does not require any "CONSed" storage for its representation. However, if the user should generate a result which cannot be contained within 24 bits, the system will automatically switch to the BIGNUM representation, which is a form of DTP-EXTENDED-NUMBER. BIGNUMs can represent integers of arbitrary precision. Ability to deal in a uniform fashion with arbitrarily large integers is a practical necessity for programs such as MACSYMA [Macsyma 1974] which do symbolic algebra.

DTP-SMALL-FLONUMs provide a limited precision floating-point representation, with a 7-bit exponent and 17-bit mantissa. Like FIXNUMs, DTP-SMALL-FLONUMs are "represented in the pointer" and do not require CONSed storage.

DTP-EXTENDED-NUMBER is a catch-all which is used to represent full precision (32-bit mantissa, 11-bit exponent) floating-point numbers as well as BIGNUMS. Provision has been made for a variety of other number types such as complex and big floating (floating point with arbitrary precision mantissa).

One exciting possibility to be developed in the future is true interval arithmetic. That is, a single number would actually contain two numbers bounding the range of the represented value. When two such numbers were multiplied, for example, the lower bound would be computed by multiplying the two lower bounds, with all rounding in the downwards direction.

In all cases, identical macroinstructions are used to operate on any type of number and the microcode automatically converts between the different number representations without the need for explicit declarations by the programmer.

---

[1] The idea of cdr-coding first appeared in print in [Hansen 1969], though this article did not consider the RPLACD problem. However, the idea circulated informally well before this date.

A feature is provided to prevent intermediate numeric results from using up storage and causing increased need for garbage collection. DTP-EX-TENDED-NUMBERs can be initially CONSed in a special area, called EX-TRA-PDL-AREA. This area has the property that pointers to it can exist only in the pdl buffer (a memory internal to the machine which holds the most recent stack frames). Whenever a pointer to EXTRA-PDL-AREA is stored in main memory, its block of storage is copied, and a pointer to the copied object stored instead. When the EXTRA-PDL-AREA area becomes full, all pointers to it can be found quickly by scanning the pdl buffer. Once they have been copied out, EXTRA-PDL-AREA is guaranteed isolated and can be reclaimed, with no need to garbage collect nor to look at other parts of memory. This is an example of the kind of feature that can be implemented with "pointer control" on a tagged machine. Note that these are not at all the same as pdl numbers in MACLISP [Steele 1977], although they both exist for the same reason.

The most important other data type is the array. Some problems are best attacked using data structures organized in the list-processing style of LISP, and some are best attacked using the array-processing style of Fortran. The complete programming system needs both. As mentioned above, LISP Machine arrays are augmented beyond traditional LISP arrays in several ways. First of all, we have the ordinary arrays of LISP objects, with one or more dimensions. Compact storage of positive integers, which may represent characters or other non-numeric entities, is afforded by arrays of 1-bit, 2-bit, 4-bit, 8-bit, or 16-bit elements.

For string processing, there are string arrays, which are usually one-dimensional and have 8-bit characters as elements. At the microcode level, strings are treated the same as 8-bit arrays. Strings are treated differently by READ, PRINT, EVAL, and many other system and user functions: For example, they print out as a sequence of characters enclosed in quotes. The characters in a character string can be accessed and modified with the same array-referencing functions used for any other type of array. Unlike arrays in other LISP systems, LISP Machine arrays usually have only a single word of overhead, so character strings are quite storage-efficient.

There are a number of specialized types of arrays which are used to implement other data types, such as stack groups, internal system tables, and, most importantly, the refresh memory of the TV display as a two-dimensional array of bits.

An important additional feature of LISP Machine arrays is called "array leaders." A leader is a vector of LISP objects, of user-specified size, which may be tacked on to an array. Leaders are a good place to remember miscellaneous extra information associated with an array. Many data structures consist of a combination of an array containing a number of objects all of the same conceptual type and a record containing miscellaneous items of different conceptual types. By storing the record in the leader of the array, the single conceptual data structure is represented by a single actual object. Many data structures in LISP Machine system programs work this way.

Another thing that leaders are used for is remembering the "current length" of a partially-populated array. By convention, array-leader element number 0 is always used.

Many programs use data objects structured as "records;" that is, a compound object consisting of a fixed number of named sub-objects. To facilitate the use of records, the LISP Machine system includes a standard set of macros for defining, creating, and accessing record structures. The user can choose whether the actual representation is to be a LISP list, an array, or an array-leader.

Because this is done with macros, which translate record operations into the lower-level operations of basic LISP, no other part of the system needs to know about records.

Since the reader and printer are written in LISP and user-modifiable, this record-structure feature could be easily expanded into a full-fledged user-defined data-type facility by modifying READ and PRINT to support input and output of record types.

By setting a flag in the array header, one specifies that an array is a NAMED-STRUCTURE. This facility provides an entry to "message-passing," that is, when a system primitive such as PRINT encounters a NAMED-STRUCTURE, it can locate a handler function by following certain conventions and send that function a PRINT message and the original array (SELF pointer). That handler function can then produce a printout more readable than the standard PRINT function ("Picture of House" instead of <DTP-ARRAY-POINTER 234156>, for example). Currently, however, the DTP-ENTITY mechanism provides our preferred entry to message passing, with full CLASS - SUPER-CLASS structure.

Another data type is the "locative pointer." Locatives are used by low-level system programs to point to "cells," memory words which contain pointer quantities but are not part of a list. Examples of such cells are value cells of symbols, array elements, and stack locations. Taking either CAR or CDR of a locative gets the contents of the pointed-to location, and both RPLACA or RPLACD store. It is possible to LAMBDA-bind the location. Because of the tagged architecture and highly-organized storage, it is possible to have a locative pointer into the middle of almost anything without causing trouble with the garbage collector.

7. REPRESENTATION OF PROGRAMS

In the LISP Machine there are three representations for programs. Interpreted LISP code is the slowest, but the easiest for programs to understand and modify. It can be used for functions being debugged, for functions needed to be understood by other functions, and for functions not worth the bother of compiling. A few functions, notably EVAL, will not work when interpreted.

Compiled LISP ("macrocode") is the main representation for programs. This consists of instructions in a conventional machine-language, whose unusual features are described below. Unlike the case in many other LISP systems, macrocode programs still have full checking for unbound variables, data-type errors, wrong number of arguments to a function, and so forth, so it is not necessary to resort to interpreted code just to get extra checking to detect bugs. Often, after typing in a function to the editor, one skips the interpretation step and requests the editor to call the compiler on it, which only takes a few seconds since the compiler is always in the machine and has only to be paged in.

Compiled code on the LISP Machine is stored inside objects called Function Entry Frames (FEFs). For each function compiled, one FEF is created, and a pointer of type DTP-FEF-POINTER is stored in the function cell of the symbol which is the name of the function. An FEF consists of some header information, a description of the arguments accepted by the function, pointers to external LISP objects needed by the function (such as constants and special variables), and the macrocode which implements the function.

The third form of program representation is microcode. The system includes a good deal of hand-coded microcode which executes the macrocode instructions, implements the data types and the function-calling mechanism, maintains the paged virtual memory, does storage allocation and garbage collection, and performs other systemic functions. The primitive operations on the basic data types, that is, CAR and CDR for lists, arithmetic for numbers, reference and store for arrays, etc. are implemented as microcode subroutines. In addition, a number of commonly-used LISP functions, for instance GET and ASSQ, are hand-coded in microcode for speed.

In addition to this system-supplied microcode, there is a feature called microcompilation. Because of the simplicity and generality of the CADR processor, it is feasible to write a compiler to compile user-written LISP functions directly into microcode, eliminating the overhead of fetching and interpreting macroinstructions. This can be used to boost performance by microcompiling the most critical routines of a program. Because it is done by a compiler rather than a system programmer, this performance improvement is available to everyone. The amount of speedup to be expected depends critically on the operations used by the program; simple low-level operations such as data transmission, byte extraction, integer arithmetic, and branching can expect to benefit the most. Function calling, and operations which already spend most of their time in microcode, such as ASSQ, will benefit the least. In the best case one can achieve a factor of about 20; in the worst case, maybe no speedup at all.

Since the amount of microcode-control memory is limited, only a small number of microcompiled functions can be loaded in at one time. This means that programs have to be characterized by spending most of their time in a small inner kernel of functions in order to benefit from microcompilation; this is probably true of most programs. There will be metering facilities for identifying such critical functions.

We do not yet have a microcompiler, but a prototype of one was written and heavily used as part of the LISP Machine simulator. It compiles for the PDP-10 rather than CADR, but uses similar techniques and a similar interface to the built-in microcode.

In all three forms of program, the flexibility of function calling is augmented with generalized LAMBDA-lists. In order to provide a more general and flexible scheme to replace EXPRs vs. FEXPRs vs. LEXPRs, a syntax borrowed from MDL [Galley and Pfister 1975] and CONNIVER [McDermott and Sussman 1972] is used in LAMBDA lists. In the general case, there are an arbitrary number of *required* parameters, followed by an arbitrary number of *optional* parameters, possibly followed by one *rest* parameter. When a function is APPLYed to its arguments, first of all the required formal parameters are paired off with arguments; if there are fewer arguments than required parameters, an error is signalled. Otherwise, any remaining arguments are paired off with the optional parameters; if there are more optional parameters than arguments remaining, then the rest of the optional parameters are initialized in a user-specified manner. The *rest* parameter is bound to a list, possibly NIL, of all arguments remaining after all *optional* parameters are bound. To avoid consing, this list is actually stored on the pdl; this means that the programmer has to be careful how he or she uses it, unfortunately. It is also possible to control which arguments are evaluated and which are quoted.

Normally, such a complicated calling sequence would entail an unacceptable amount of overhead. Because this is all implemented by microcode, and because the simple, common cases are special-cased, we can provide these advanced features and still retain the efficiency needed in a practical system.

In a LISP Machine macrocode function-calling sequence, the CALL instruction precedes the instructions which load the arguments. That is, when compiling (FOO A B), instead of the usual PUSH A; PUSH B; CALL FOO instruction order, we have CALL FOO; MOVE D-NEXT, A; MOVE D-LAST,B. We say that the CALL instruction opens (i.e. allocates, links, and initializes) a pushdown list frame. An instruction with destination D-NEXT stores in the next argument position in the currently open frame. D-LAST not only stores in the next argument position, but activates the frame. Activating the frame means storing the local program counter and transferring control to the indicated function (which was previously stored in the frame when it was initialized by the CALL instruction). Doing things in this manner causes the details of pushdown list allocation to work out much better. It is never necessary to copy the arguments since they are always used in place. Furthermore, when arriving at the called function, the stack is "clean." That is, the arguments are at the most active end of the stack, the return address, etc. having been stored higher up on the stack in the place allocated by the CALL instruction. This way, the called function can easily provide any unsupplied OPTIONAL arguments in such a way that they are contiguous with the remaining arguments. In addition, we have increased structure on the pushdown list because open frames are linked in; in more conventional implementations, they are undifferentiated storage until suddenly made into a frame by a CALL instruction.

We will now discuss some of the issues in the design of the macrocode instruction set. Macroinstructions are 16 bits long and are stored two per word. The instructions work in a stack-oriented machine. The stack is formatted into frames, each one of which contains a bunch of arguments, a bunch of local variable value slots, and a pushdown stack for intermediate results. It also contains a header that points to the function that owns the frame, links this frame to previous frames, remembers the program counter, and flags when this frame is not executing, and may contain "additional information" used for certain esoteric purposes.

Originally we intended to use a frame-allocated stack. That is, each call frame would have been a fixed-length structure. Unfortunately, the overhead of this strategy becomes unacceptably high. We then moved toward a hybrid tree-structured (or spaghetti) stack scheme, but the invention of closures and stack-groups (see the control-structure section), plus the extreme complexity of spaghetti stacks, made us decide to use a simple linear stack. We now believe that the *desiderata* which motivated the introduction of a tree-structured stack are logically unattainable. It would be a nice feature to be able to save efficiently the complete current context, and be able to revert to it later if desired, but attempts to do so (CONNIVER [McDermott and Sussman 1972] and Bobrow-Wegbreit [Bobrow and Wegbreit 1973]) approach only the problem of saving the control state and perhaps the variable state. Without saving also the external state (i.e. the list structure and other data pointed to by the variables), the feature is fatally deficient, and leads to non-modular code. But it is very difficult to see how the external state can be saved in any meaningful way.

The currently active frame is always held in the pdl buffer, so accesses to arguments and local variables require neither memory references nor checks related to the garbage collector, which improves performance. Usually several other frames will also be in the pdl buffer.

The macroinstruction set is bit-compact. The stack organization and LISP's division of programs into small, separate functions mean that address fields can be small. The use of tagged data types, powerful generic operations, and easily-called microcoded functions frequently makes a single 16-bit macro instruction do the work of several instructions on a conventional machine such as a PDP-10.

The primitive operations performed by LISP Machine macroinstructions are higher-level than those of a conventional machine. Since they do data-type checks, there is more run-time error checking than in MACLISP, which increases reliability. Also eliminated is much of the need to make declarations in order to get efficient code. Since a data-type check is being made, the "primitive" operations can decide dynamically which specific routine is to be called. They are all "generic", that is, they work for all data types where they make sense. For example, a single + instruction can add numbers which are fixed, floating, complex, or any other numeric type.

The operations regarded as most important and easiest for macrocode to do are data transmission, function calling, conditional testing, and simple operations on primitive types, such as, CAR, CDR, CADR, CDDR, and the usual arithmetic operations and comparisons. More complex operations are generally done by "miscellaneous" instructions, which call microcoded subroutines, passing arguments on the temporary-results stack.

There are three main kinds of addressing in macrocode: implicit addressing of the top of the stack, macroinstruction operand field, and destination field. Implicit addressing of the top of the stack is the usual way that operands get from one instruction to the next. The macroinstruction operand field is used to reference special variables and to call other functions. It can also address up to 64 arguments to the current function, up to 64 local variables of the current function, the last result popped off the stack, one of several commonly-used constants (e.g. NIL) stored in a system-wide constants area, a constant stored in the FEF of this function, or a value cell or a function cell of a symbol, referenced by means of an invisible pointer in the FEF. The destination field specifies what to do with the result of the instruction. The possibilities are: Ignore it, except set the indicators used by conditional branches; push it on the stack; pass it as an argument; pass it as an argument, then activate the currently open call block; return it as the value of this function; and cons up a list.

When consing-up of lists, one first does a miscellaneous function saying "make a list N long" and then executes N instructions with destination D-NEXT-LIST to supply the elements of the list. After the Nth such instruction, the list-object magically appears on the top of the stack.

Another type of "instruction set" used with macrocode is the Argument Description List (or ADL), which is executed by a different microcoded interpreter at the time a function is entered. The ADL contains one entry for each argument which the function expects to be passed and for each auxiliary variable. It contains all relevant information about the argument: whether it is *required*, *optional*, or *rest*; how to initialize it if it is not provided; whether it is local or special; and data-type checking information. Sometimes the ADL can be dispensed with if the "fast-argument option" is used instead; saving time and memory for small, simple functions. The fast-argument option is used when the optional arguments and local variables are few, are all initialized to NIL, and involve no data-type checking. In addition, the usage of special variables must be uncomplicated. The selection of the fast-argument option, if appropriate, is made automatically by the compiler.

8. CONTROL STRUCTURES

8.1 Function Calling

Function calling is, of course, the basic control structure in LISP. As mentioned above, LISP Machine function calling is made fast through the use of microcode and augmented with optional arguments, rest arguments, multiple return values, and optional type-checking of arguments.

8.2 CATCH and THROW

CATCH and THROW were first used in PDP-10 MACLISP. CATCH is a way of marking a particular point in the stack of recursive function invocations. THROW causes control to be unwound to the matching CATCH, automatically returning through the intervening function calls. They are used mainly for handling errors and unusual conditions. They are also useful for getting out of a complicated piece of code when it has discovered what value it wants to return; this resembles "exit" of BLISS and other ALGOL-like languages except it is dynamic and not lexical.

8.3 Closures

The LISP Machine contains a data type called "closure" which is used to implement "full funarging." By turning a function into a closure, it becomes possible to pass it as an argument with no worry about naming conflicts, and to return it as a value with exactly the minimum necessary amount of binding environment being retained, solving an important case of the classical "funarg problem". Closures are implemented in such a way that when they are not used the high-speed shallow-binding variable scheme operates at full efficiency, and when they are used things are slowed down only slightly. The way one creates a closure is with a form such as:

```
(CLOSURE '(FOO-PARAM FOO-STATE)
         (FUNCTION FOO-BAR))
```

The function could also be written directly in place as a LAMBDA-expression, instead of referring to the externally defined FOO-BAR. The variables FOO-PARAM and FOO-STATE are those variables which are used free by FOO-BAR and are intended to be "closed." That is, these are the variables whose binding environment is to be fixed to that in effect at the time the closure is created. The explicit declaration of which variables are to be closed allows the implementation to be highly efficient, since it does not need to save the whole variable-binding environment. It also allows the programmer to choose explicitly for each variable the option of being dynamically bound (at the point of call) or statically bound (at the point of creation of the closure), a choice not conveniently available in other languages. In addition, the program is clearer because the intended effect of the closure is made manifest by listing the variables to be affected.

The following illustration shows how the closure feature can be used to solve a problem presented in "LAMBDA - The Ultimate Imperative" [Steele 1976a]. The problem is to write a function called GENERATE-SQRT-OF-GIVEN-EXTRA-TOLERANCE, which is to take one argument, which is the factor by which the tolerance is to be increased, and return a function which takes square roots with that much more tolerance than usual, whatever "usual" is later defined to be. The given function SQRT makes a free reference to EPSILON, the tolerance it demands of the trial solution. The reason this example presents difficulties to various languages is that the variable EPSILON must be bound at the point of call (that is, dynamically scoped), while the variable FACTOR must be bound at the point of creation of the function (lexically scoped). Thus the programmer must have explicit control over how the variables are bound.

```
(DEFUN GENERATE-SQRT-OF-GIVEN-EXTRA-TOLERANCE (FACTOR)
(CLOSURE '(FACTOR)
     (FUNCTION
       (LAMBDA (X)
         ((LAMBDA (EPSILON) (SQRT X))
          (* EPSILON FACTOR))))))
```

The function, when called, rebinds EPSILON to FACTOR times its current value, then calls SQRT. The value of FACTOR used is that in effect when the closure was created, i.e. the argument to GENERATE-SQRT-OF-GIVEN-EX-TRA-TOLERANCE.

The way closures are implemented is as follows. For each variable to be closed, an "external value cell" is created, which is a consed-up free-storage cell which contains the variable's value when it is at that level of binding. Because this cell is consed-up, it can be retained as long as necessary, just like any other data, and unlike cells in a stack. Because it is a cell, if the variable is SETQed (assigned to) the new value is seen by all the closures that should see it. The association between the symbol which is the name of the variable and this value cell is of the shallow-binding type, for efficiency; an invisible pointer (see the storage-organization section) in the normal (internal) value cell supplies the connection, eliminating the overhead of searching stack frames or a-lists. If at the time the closure is created an external value cell already exists for a variable, that one is used instead of creating a new one. Thus all closures at the same "level of binding" use the same value cell, which is the desired semantics.

The CLOSURE function returns an object of type DTP-CLOSURE, which contains the function to be called and, for each variable closed over, locative pointers to its internal and external value cells.

When a closure is invoked as a function, the variables mentioned in the closure are bound to invisible pointers to their external value cells; this puts these variables into the proper binding environment. The function contained in the closure is then invoked in the normal way. When the variables happen to be referred to, the invisible pointers are automatically followed to the external value cells. If one of the closed variables is then bound by some other function, the external value cell-pointer is saved away on the binding stack, like any saved variable value, and the variable reverts to normal nonclosed status. When the closed function returns, the bindings of the closed variables are restored just like any other variables bound by the function.

Note the economy of mechanism: Almost all of the system is completely unaffected by and unaware of the existence of closures; the invisible pointer mechanism takes care of things. The retainable binding environments are allocated through the standard CONS operation. The switching of variables between normal and "closed" status is done through the standard binding operation. The operations used by a closed function to access the closed variables are the same as those used to access ordinary variables; closures are called in the same way as ordinary functions. Closures work just as well in the interpreter as in the compiler. An important thing to note is the minimality of consing in closures. When a closure is created, some consing is done; external value cells and the closure-object itself must be created, but there is no extra "overhead." When a closure is called, no consing happens.

Note that, in the compiler, closed variables have to be declared "special." It is a general feature of the MACLISP and LISP Machine compilers, that by default variables are local, meaning that they are lexically bound, available only to the function in which they are bound, and implemented not with atomic symbols, but simply as slots in the stack. Variables that are declared special are implemented with shallow-bound atomic symbols, identical to variables in the interpreter, and have available either dynamic binding or closure binding. They are somewhat less efficient since it takes two memory references to access them and several to bind them.

8.4 Stack-Groups

The stack-group is a type of LISP object useful for implementation of certain advanced control structures such as coroutines, asynchronous processes, and generators. A stack-group is similar to a process (or fork or job or task or control point) in a time-sharing system; it contains such state information as the "regular" and "special" (binding) PDLs and various internal registers. At all times there is one stack-group running on the machine.

Control may be passed between stack-groups in several ways. A stack-group may be called like a function; when it wants to return it can do a STACK-GROUP-RETURN, different from an ordinary function return in that the state of the stack-group remains unchanged; the next time it is called it picks up from where it left off. This is good for generator-like applications which wish to retain control state between invocations; each time STACK-GROUP-RETURN is done, a value is emitted from the generator, and as a side-effect execution is suspended until the next time the generator is called. STACK-GROUP-RETURN is analogous in this way to the AU-REVOIR construct in CONNIVER.

Control can be passed explicitly from one stack-group to another, coroutine-style. Alternatively, there can be a scheduler stack-group which invokes other stack-groups when their requested scheduling conditions are satisfied.

Interrupts cause control of the machine to be transferred to an interrupt-handler stack-group. Essentially this is a forced stack-group call like the calls described above. Similarly, when the microcode detects an error the current stack-group is suspended and control is passed to an error-handling stack-group. The state of the stack-group that got the error is left exactly as it was when the error occurred, undisturbed by any error-handling operations. This facilitates error analysis and recovery.

When the machine is started, an "initial" stack-group becomes the current stack-group, and is forced to call the first function of LISP.

Note that the same scheduler-driven stack-group switching mechanism can be used both for user programs which want to do parallel computations, and for system programming purposes such as network servers and peripheral handlers.

Each stack-group has a call-state and a calling-stack-group variable, which are used in maintaining the relations between stack-groups. A stack-group also has some option flags controlling whether the system tries to keep different stack-groups' binding environments distinct by undoing the special variable bindings of the stack-group being left and redoing the bindings of the stack-group being entered.

Stack-groups are created with the function MAKE-STACK-GROUP, which takes one main argument, the "name" of the stack-group. This is used only for debugging, and can be any mnemonic symbol. It returns the stack-group, i.e., a LISP object with data type DTP-STACK-GROUP. Optionally the sizes of the pdls may be specified.

The function STACK-GROUP-PRESET is used to initialize the state of a stack-group: the first argument is the stack-group, the second is a function to be called when the stack-group is invoked, and the rest are arguments to that function. Both PDLs are made empty. The stack-group is set to the AWAIT-ING-INITIAL-CALL state. Later, when the stack-group is activated (for example by calling it as a function), the specified function will find that it has been called with the specified arguments. If it should return in the normal way (i.e. the stack-group "returns off the top"), the stack-group will enter a "used up" state and control will revert to the calling stack-group (somewhat similar to CONNIVER ADIEU). Normally, the specified function will use STACK-GROUP-RETURN several times; otherwise it might as well have been called directly rather than in a stack-group.

One important difference between stack-groups and other means proposed to implement similar features is that the stack-group scheme involves no loss of efficiency in normal computation. In fact, the compiler, the interpreter, and even the runtime function-calling mechanism are completely unaware of the existence of stack-groups.

Comparing stack-groups and closures, we see that a closure retains its state only in variables while a stack-group can retain both variables and control structure. In other words, with a closure, if the initially called function calls a second function, there is no way for the closure to return before the second function returns. With a stack-group, this is not true: the second function can do a STACK-GROUP-RETURN directly on behalf of the entire stack-group. In this case, the return information to the initially-called function will remain on the stack-group's push-down list, and may be reactivated if the second function returns after the stack-group is resumed.

9. STORAGE ORGANIZATION

9.1 Incremental Garbage Collection

The LISP Machine uses a real-time, incremental, compacting garbage collector. Real-time means that CONS (or related functions) never delay LISP execution for more than a small, bounded amount of time.

This is very important in a machine with a large address space, where a traditional garbage collection could bring everything to a halt for several minutes. The garbage collector is incremental, i.e. garbage collection is interleaved with execution of the user's program; every time you call CONS the garbage collection proceeds for a few steps. Copying can also be triggered by a memory reference which fetches a pointer to data which has not yet been copied. The garbage collector compacts in order to improve the paging characteristics.

The basic algorithm is described in a paper by Henry Baker [Baker 1978]. It is much simpler than previous methods of incremental garbage collection [Dijkstra et al. 1975], [Lamport 1975], [Smith 1970] in that only one process is needed; this avoids interlocking and synchronization problems, which are often very difficult to debug.

9.2 Areas[2]

Storage in the LISP Machine is divided into "areas." Each area contains related objects, of any type. Since unlike conventional LISPs we do not encode the data type in the address, we are free to use the address to encode the area.

---

[2] In [Bishop 1977] Peter Bishop presents a similar feature. However, the development of areas in LISP Machine LISP had been proceeding previously. Bishop, though, considered the problem in the context of a multi-user time-sharing system with protection, which was not done here.

Areas are intended to give the user control over the paging behavior of his program, among other things. By putting related data together, locality can be greatly increased. Whenever a new object is created, for instance with CONS, the area to be used can optionally be specified. There is a default Working Storage area which collects those objects which the user has not chosen to control explicitly.

Areas also give the user a handle to control the garbage collector. Some areas can be declared to be "static," which means that they change slowly and the garbage collector should not attempt to reclaim any space in them. This can eliminate a lot of useless copying. All pointers out of a static area can be collected into an "exit vector," eliminating any need for the garbage collector to look at that area. As an important example, an English-language dictionary can be kept inside the LISP without adversely affecting the speed of garbage collection. A "static" area can be explicitly garbage-collected at infrequent intervals when it is believed that that might be worthwhile.

Each area can potentially have a different storage discipline, a different paging algorithm, and even a different data representation. The microcode will dispatch on an attribute of the area at the appropriate times. The structure of the machine makes the performance cost of these features negligible; information about areas is stored in extra bits in the memory mapping hardware where it can be quickly dispatched on by the microcode. These dispatches usually have to be done anyway to make the garbage collector work, and to implement invisible pointers.

9.3   Invisible Pointers

An invisible pointer is similar to an indirect address word on a conventional computer except the indirection is specified in the data instead of in the instruction. A reference to a memory location containing an invisible pointer is automatically altered to use the location pointed to by the invisible pointer. The term "invisible" refers to the fact that the presence of such pointers is not visible to most of the system, since they are handled by the lowest-level memory-referencing operations. The invisible pointer feature does not slow anything down too much, because it is part of the data-type checking that is done anyway (this is one of the benefits of a tagged architecture). A number of advanced features of the LISP machine depend upon invisible pointers for their efficient implementation.

Closures use invisible pointers to connect internal value cells to external value cells. This allows the variable binding scheme to be altered from normal shallow binding to allocated-value-cell shallow binding when closures are being used, without altering the normal operation of the machine when closures are not being used. At the same time the slow-down when closures are used amounts to only 2 microseconds per closed-variable reference, the time needed to detect and follow the invisible pointer.

Invisible pointers are a necessary part of the operation of the cdr-coded compressed list scheme. If an RPLACD is done to a compressed list, the list can no longer be represented in the compressed form. It is necessary to allocate a full 2-word LISP node and use that in its place. But, it is also necessary to preserve the identity (with respect to EQ) of the list. This is done by storing an invisible pointer in the original location of the compressed list, pointing to the uncompressed copy. Then the list is still represented by its original location, preserving EQ-ness, but the CAR and CDR operations follow the invisible pointer to the new location and find the proper car and cdr.

This is a special case of the more general use of invisible pointers for "forwarding" references from an old representation of an object to a new one. For instance, there is a function to increase the size of an array. If it cannot do it in place, it makes a new copy and leaves behind an invisible pointer.

The exit-vector feature uses invisible pointers. One may set up an area to have the property that all references from inside that area to objects in other areas are collected into a single exit vector. A location which would normally contain such a reference instead contains an invisible pointer to the appropriate slot in the exit vector. Operations on this area all work as before, except for a slight slow-down caused by the invisible pointer following. It is also desirable to have automatic checking to prevent the creation of new outside references; when an attempt is made to store an outside object into this area execution can trap to a routine which creates a new exit-vector entry if necessary and stores an invisible pointer instead. The reason for exit vectors is to speed up garbage collection by eliminating the need to swap in all of the pages of the area in order to find and relocate all its references to outside objects.

The macrocode instruction set relies on invisible pointers in order to access the value cells of "special" (non-local) variables and the function cells of functions to be called.

Certain system variables stored in the microcode scratchpad memory are made available to LISP programs by linking the value cells of appropriately-named LISP symbols to the scratchpad memory locations with invisible pointers. This makes it possible not only to read and write these variables, but also to lambda-bind them. In a similar fashion, invisible pointers could be used to link two symbols' value cells together, in the fashion of MICROPLANNER [Sussman et al. 1970] but with much greater efficiency.

10. THE EDITOR

A very large percentage of the time a user spends working with an interactive system is spent doing some sort of text editing. With extremely few exceptions, users and system designers have failed to appreciate the tremendous effect of a good editor upon programmer productivity. At the MIT Artificial Intelligence Labs, we have used display editors exclusively since 1964 [TECO]. Simply seeing the text to be edited on the display screen is an extraordinarily important thing. Yet, even in 1979, many editors being used every day do not have this feature.

A further large step forward was taken around 1972 with the introduction of "Real Time" editing. This simply means that the editing commands take place immediately as they are typed (in contrast to TECO [TECO] and similar editors, which do not perform commands until an "activate" character is typed). The display is continuously updated so that the user sees the current state of his text at all times.

EMACS [Ciccarelli 1978], our current PDP-10 editor, represents another giant step ahead. EMACS features language specific "major modes," by which the editor command set is automatically specialized to the language in which the file being edited is written. This enables EMACS to do some parsing and "understanding" of the text being edited.

ZWEI [Weinreb 1979] is our editor for the LISP Machine, and we feel it represents an additional major step ahead.

Historically, difficulties in balancing parentheses have been one of the major user objections to LISP. At best, the full parenthesization of LISP was thought to be an evil necessary for the sake of a common representation for program and data. Smart editors such as EMACS and ZWEI have completely changed this picture.

Several editor features combine to achieve this result. To begin with, if the editor cursor is to the right of a close parenthesis, the editor blinks the matching open parentheses. In addition, as the user types in his function, several format effector keys like TAB and LINE-FEED are not simply literally inserted. Instead, they activate an automatic formatting algorithm similar to what has traditionally been called PRETTYPRINT or GRINDEF. The difference here is that the formatting takes place incrementally and instantly, so the user receives immediate confirmation that he is typing arguments to the intended function. Furthermore, should the user decide to alter the system's normal formatting rules, he can do so simply with ordinary editor commands. The complete formatting job is being done simultaneously with typein, so the problem of the system coming along later and undoing the user's formatting (in other words, reapplying the standard formatting rules) does not arise.

A brief on-line demonstration will suffice to convince most observers that it is easier to assure correct operand grouping in LISP than in operator languages like ALGOL if one is using a smart editor.

ZWEI has important features beyond those found in EMACS. For example, as the user is typing in a function call, a single character command retrieves the argument names of the function being called. With the mouse (a graphical input device), the user can point at a function, and be inspecting its source text seconds later. All calls on a function or uses of a global variable can be easily "found." Many of these features are made practically possible by the fact that ZWEI is part of the LISP environment, or by the personal computer nature of the LISP machine, or both.

11. MESSAGE PASSING

The development of message passing within our system is in an early stage. Thus, we will not give here a complete description of our current message passing system(s). Instead, we will confine ourselves largely to descriptions of low level mechanisms which can be employed to implement the mechanics.

"Message passing," as we use the term, refers to a style of program organization. The basic idea is that one has certain kinds of data groupings, called *classes*, which hold state. A particular individual of such a group is called an *instance*. Each *instance* consists of some number of components, called instance variables. (Objects in SIMULA, instances in SMALLTALK, ACTORs in PLASMA, etc. are similar. Our discussion follows most closely the terminology and organization of SMALLTALK.) We will use the term *target* when referring to message receiving groups in general, and the terms NAMED-STRUCTURE, DTP-INSTANCE, and DTP-ENTITY to refer to these *targets* when implemented in particular ways.

Basic operations are performed by sending messages. Sending a message is very similar to calling a function in a traditional organization; however, the function to be called is not named explicitly by the caller. Instead, the caller names an operation (called the message-key), and the system locates the receiving function (or method) by associating the message key with the *target* of the message. Usually, an inheritance mechanism is provided so that the method need not be directly associated with the target, but can instead be associated with the target's *class*, or that *class*'s superclass, etc. In existing systems (to our knowledge) the *classes* must form a strict hierarchy; however, the desire to permit a tangled hierarchy instead (sometimes called the multiple-superclass feature) has been expressed. Each class can specify that its members are to have certain components; an *instance*, then, has as instance variables the union of the components specified by its *class* and all other classes superior to its *class*.

The receiving method must have access to the message (which it does in our system via the normal argument transmission mechanism) and to the target *instance*. The means employed to access the *instance* vary depending on the particular implementation being considered. In our usage, the procedure bodies of the methods are ordinary LISP, indeed the methods themselves are ordinary LISP functions, which are accessed in a somewhat unusual way.

We are of the opinion that true strengths and weaknesses of message passing as a style of program organization are largely unknown. Although message passing systems have been a popular research subject for some time, many of the implementations have had serious practical failings.

The NAMED-STRUCTURE construct, described previously, can serve as a base on which to construct a message passing system. By convention, one of the components of the NAMED-STRUCTURE is a pointer to a handler function. The remaining components of the NAMED-STRUCTURE hold the instance variables. Sending a target a message then consists of calling its handler function with arguments consisting of the message key, a pointer to the target (sometimes referred to as a SELF pointer), followed by additional arguments which are the message itself. The handler function is completely responsible for locating the appropriate method and calling it, or it can simply perform the indicated operation itself. NAMED-STRUCTUREs show how the message passing idea can be implemented within the context of a conventional system, in a reasonably efficient fashion and without the need for special control or data structures. However, we have not chosen to develop this mechanism into a full blown message system, instead we support mainly the PRINT operation. Even so, the improved printout is a welcome aid when debugging programs which deal with plex type data structures.

DTP-INSTANCEs are similar to NAMED-STRUCTUREs, but more optimized for the purpose. Each DTP-INSTANCE contains only a pointer to its *class* in addition to its instance variables. (This pointer can even be implicit as by locating only DTP-INSTANCEs of a single class on a single page, although we have not chosen to do this.) Some storage efficiency is achieved compared to the NAMED-STRUCTURE approach, since formatting information can be stored in the class, rather than being duplicated for each instance (which is necessary with NAMED-STRUCTUREs since each NAMED-STRUCTURE is a free standing array). Since the algorithm for locating methods is built into the system rather than distributed among many handler functions, it is likely to behave in a more uniform fashion. In addition, DTP-INSTANCEs lend themselves to certain optimizations in macrocode structure, which can save both macrocode space and execution time. DTP-INSTANCEs are practically identical to the implementation methods used in SMALLTALK-76 [Ingalls 1978].

The DTP-ENTITY represents a rather different approach. A DTP-ENTITY is a closure over the instance variables. There is no semantic difference between a DTP-ENTITY and an ordinary closure, except that one can assume that a DTP-ENTITY will accept arguments according to certain conventions. The function closed over is a LISP symbol, which represents the *class*. Thus, the access to an instance variable from the point of view of the method is a free variable reference instead of some sort of array reference as it is in the other schemes. In *class* symbol's function cell we store a special data type, DTP-SELECT-METHOD, which implements method selection when seen in function context. The primary advantage of the DTP-ENTITY scheme over the other schemes seems to be that the DTP-ENTITY lends itself to multiple-superclasses.

The problem encountered by the other schemes has to do with ordering the instance variables within the instance. As long as the classes form a strict hierarchy, we can start at the top of the heirarchy and work our way down to the desired class, assigning positions in the instance to components as they are specified by classes. The resulting instance will not only have its components in the correct position for its own class, but they will also be correct for each superclass. However, if we allow the class hierarchy to become tangled, there is no single ordering which will have this property. The DTP-ENTITY scheme avoids this problem because referencing an instance variable is not an array-type reference at all.

The DTP-ENTITY scheme appears to require somewhat greater execution time than the DTP-INSTANCE scheme. The importance of this is not clear, however, since, in our limited experience so far, we tend to use message passing for relatively high level operations. Once it has really been decided "what to do", the work is usually carried out by ordinary LISP functions.

In the future it may prove possible to combine the advantages of the several schemes, or it may be possible to arrange that the choice of scheme can be made dynamically by the system, depending on whether the multiple-superclass feature is in fact in use.

Message passing is an example of a research area to which we feel the LISP Machine is ideally suited. The tagged machine and system flexibility resulting from the entire system being written in a single language (except for microcode) are particularily important here.

12. SOME DESIGN DECISIONS AND LESSONS

In some sense, rather few explicit design decisions were called for in the LISP Machine effort. Many times, what people think of as design decisions are actually attempts to minimize inefficiencies resulting from outside constraints which in turn result from incorrect decisions earlier in the design process (incorrect, at least, when considered from the point of view of the project at hand). Since we were starting from scratch, we had a minimum of this kind of problem to contend with.

Another way to look at it is that there were relatively few "flash of brilliance" type decisions. Instead the decisions resulted from accumulated experience in such a way that it was evident to all concerned what the "right" way to do something was well before we were in a position to actually do it. In many cases, key ideas which were obviously good had been floating around the "hacker" community for many years. The problem was simply that an appropriate system base in which to install them did not exist.

For example, a tagged architecture is a natural for a run-time typed language such as LISP. The tagged machine concept had existed before [Feustal 1972], [Burroughs 1969]; however these machines, while interesting, had never been able to demonstrate convincing practical advantages. We believe this was precisely because they were used to implement compile-time typed languages (usually ALGOL). We also had acquaintance with MDL [Galley and Pfister 1975], which attempted to implement a form of run-time data tagging fairly similar to the LISP Machine, but which had serious efficiency problems. Thus, it was obvious to us that the combination of a tagged machine and a run-time typed language had to win, and there was no need for elaborate studies of the tradeoffs. This commitment was made well before many of our more specific ideas had taken shape, so any detailed study we might have made at the time would have been meaningless anyway. We believe that subsequent events have shown how the LISP system allows the user to take important advantage of the tagged architecture, and we are confident that important new applications of the tagged architecture will be found in the future.

Another question that came up was whether the machine should have 16-bit main data paths or 32-bit ones. It was clear, of course, that 16 bits was not an adequate virtual address space; however, one might conceive of a machine which had 16-bit data paths and processed 32-bit quantities in two sequential whacks. While having less performance than the 32-bit machine, the resulting machine might still be adequate for many purposes and would be cheaper. In the end, we decided against this largely because it would take twice as many microinstructions to get anything done. In addition, there would always be the terrible temptation to try to speed things up by using only a 16-bit quantity in some places; any such decision would very likely be regretted later if not sooner when that quantity bumped into its 65K maximum limit. Going the 32-bit route was probably a wise decision, since that was the "natural" thing to do, so it freed resources to be applied in other areas.

Another similar sort of decision was whether to use 8 bits or 16 as the fundamental unit of macrocode. 8 bits had been used by Deutsch in [Deutsch 1973a]. We decided to use 16 because it allowed for a destination field and a larger number of primitives. We feel this was probably a good choice. 16 bits probably result in less decoding overhead (at least if no special hardware is provided), possibly at the cost of some sacrifice in space occupied by the compiled code. With the adequate virtual memory space and the larger memory sizes of today, this is probably a profitable tradeoff. Code density, while still important, appears to be somewhat less so than it did earlier. We should note too that the exact representation of compiled code is actually quite unimportant from the overall system point of view. It is quite conceivable that one could use several different compiled representations within a single system, some optimized for speed and some for space.

ACKNOWLEDGMENTS

The LISP Machine effort was a group effort, extending over many years, and drew heavily upon the large MACLISP community at MIT. The general experience with MDL had an important bearing, as did a whole range of influences from Xerox PARC. EMACS has its own community of users, and many of these people contributed ideas.

The project was initiated by Richard Greenblatt, who wrote most of the initial operational software. Tom Knight designed the prototype CONS machine. Jack Holloway designed the bus interfaces for both CONS and CADR, designed the CHAOSnet transceiver, and was unofficial chief electrical engineer. Jack also designed the high-resolution TV controller. Dave Moon did much of the work of turning CONS into CADR, designed the disk control, and did yeoman work on software. Virtual memory support, and the real-time garbage collector were mainly his responsibility. He was also mainly responsible for the innovative CHAOSnet protocol. Dan Weinreb wrote the ZWEI editor, and with Dave Moon, wrote the reference manual. Richard Stallman overhauled the compiler, and among other things is the main force behind EMACS. Alan Bawden wrote a finite state machine oriented READ function, and did BIGNUM arithmetic. Bruce Edwards, Howard Cannon, and Mike McMahon made major contributions to LISP machine hardware and software. Tom Callahan was mainly responsible for mechanical construction and parts procurement. Many other people, too numerous to list, made important contributions.

This report describes research done at the Artificial Intelligence Laboratory of the Massachusetts Institute of Technology. Support for the Laboratory's artificial intelligence research is provided in part by the Advanced Research Projects Agency of the Department of Defense under Office of Naval Research contract N00014-75-C-0643.

REFERENCES

[Abrahams et al. 1966] P.W. Abrahams et al. The LISP 2 programming language and system. In *Proceedings of the 1966 Fall Joint Computer Conference*, San Francisco, 661-677.

[Baker 1978] H.G. Baker. List processing in real time on a serial computer. *Communications of the ACM*, 19:4 (April 1978), 280-294.

[Bishop 1977] P.B. Bishop. *Computer systems with a very large address space and garbage collection*. Massachusetts Institute of Technology, Laboratory for Computer Science, TR-178, May 1977.

[Bobrow and Wegbreit 1973] D.G. Bobrow, B. Wegbreit. A model and stack implementation for multiple environments. *Communications of the ACM*, 16:10 (October 1973), 591-603.

[Burroughs 1969] *Burroughs B6500 information processing systems reference manual*. Burroughs Corporation, Detroit, Michigan, 1969.

[Burstall et al. 1971] R.M. Burstall, R.J. Popplestone et al. *Programming in POP-2*. University Press, Edinburgh, Scotland, 1971.

[Ciccarelli 1978] E. Ciccarelli. *An introduction to the EMACS editor*. Massachusetts Institute of Technology, Artificial Intelligence Laboratory, AI Memo 447, January 1978. [*Editors note:* see also [Stallman 1981]]

[Corbato et al. 1965] F.J. Corbato et al. Introduction and overview of the multics system. *Proceedings of the Fall Joint Computer Conference*, Las Vegas, 1965, 185-197.

[Deutsch 1973a] L.P. Deutsch. A LISP machine with very compact programs. *International Joint Conference on Artificial Intelligence*, Stanford, California, August 1973, 697-703.

[Dijkstra et al. 1975] E.W. Dijkstra et al. On the fly garbage collection: An exercise in cooperation. E. W. Dijkstra note EWD496, June 1975.

[ECL 1974] *ECL Programmer's Manual*. Harvard University, Center for Research in Computing Technology, TR-23-74, December 1974.

[Feustal 1972] E.A. Feustel. The Rice Research Computer - a tagged architecture. *Proceedings of the Spring Joint Computer Conference*, 1972, 369-379.

[Galley and Pfister 1975] S.W. Galley, G. Pfister. *The MDL Language*. Massachusetts Institute of Technology, Project MAC Programming Technology Division, Sept 1975.

[Goldberg and Kay 1976] A. Goldberg, A. Kay. *SMALLTALK-72 Instruction Manual*. Learning Research Group, Xerox Palo Alto Research Center, 1976.

[Hansen 1969] W.J. Hansen. Compact list representation: definition, garbage collection and system implementation. *Communications of the Association for Computing Machinery*, September 1969, 499-507.

[Helliwell 1970] R.P. Helliwell. *The Stanford University Drawing System (SUDS)*, developed about 1970. Extensive modifications were later made by J. Holloway.

[Ingalls 1978] Dan Ingalls. The Smalltalk-76 programming system, design and implementation. *Conference Record of the Fifth Annual ACM Symposium on Principles of Programming Languages*, January 1978, 9-17.

[Lamport 1975] L. Lamport. On the fly garbage collection: once more with rigor. Massachusetts Computer Associates CA-7508-1611, Cambridge Massachusetts, August 1975.

[Macsyma 1974] *MACSYMA Reference Manual*. Massachusetts Institute of Technology, Mathlab Group, Project MAC, Cambridge, Massachusetts, September 1974.

[McCarthy 1978] J. McCarthy. The history of LISP. *Sigplan Notices*, 13:8 (August 1978), 217-223.

[McCarthy et al. 1962] J. McCarthy, P. Abrahams, D. Edwards, T. Hart, M. Levin. *LISP 1.5 Programmer's Manual*, MIT Press, Cambridge, Massachusetts, 1962.

[McDermott and Sussman 1972] D.V. McDermott, G.J. Sussman. *The CONNIVER Reference Manual.* Massachusetts Institute of Technology, Artificial Intelligence Laboratory Memo 259, May 1972.

[Metcalfe and Boggs 1976] R.M. Metcalfe, D.R. Boggs. Ethernet: distributed packet switching for local computer networks. *Communications of the Association for Computing Machinery,* 19:7 (July 1976), 395-404.

[Moon 1974] D. Moon. *MACLISP Reference Manual.* Massachusetts Institute of Technology, Project MAC, 1974.

[Moses 1970] J. Moses. The function of FUNCTION in LISP. Massachusetts Institute of Technology, Project MAC, Memo MAC-M-248, June 1970.

[Smith 1970] D.C. Smith. *MLISP.* Stanford Artificial Intelligence Laboratory, Stanford, California, 1970.

[Stallman 1981] R.M. Stallman. *EMACS: The Extensible, Customizable Display Editor.* Massachusetts Institute of Technology, Artificial Intelligence Laboratory, Memo 519a, 1981; reprinted in *Interactive Programming Environments.*

[Steele 1976a] G.L. Steele. *LAMBDA, the ultimate imperative.* Massachusetts Institute of Technology, Artificial Intelligence Laboratory, Memo 353, Feb 1976.

[Steele 1977] G.L. Steele. *Fast arithmetic in MACLISP.* Massachusetts Institute of Technology, Artificial Intelligence Laboratory, Memo 421, September 1977.

[Sussman et al. 1970] G.J. Sussman, T. Winograd, E. Charniak. *Micro-Planner Reference Manual.* Massachusetts Institute of Technology, Artificial Intelligence Laboratory, Memo 203, July 1970.

[TECO] *TECO Programmer's Reference Manual.* Digital Equipment Corporation, Maynard, Massachusetts, DEC-10-ETEE-D (revised from time to time); see also *PDP-6 Time Sharing TECO.* Stanford University, Stanford Artificial Intelligence Laboratory, Operating Note 34, 1967; see also P.R. Samson. *PDP-6 TECO.* Massachusetts Institute of Technology, Artificial Intelligence Laboratory, AI Memo 81, July 1965.

[Weinreb 1979] D.L. Weinreb. A real-time display-oriented editor for the LISP Machine. Massachusetts Institute of Technology, Department of Electrical Engineering and Computer Science, undergraduate thesis, January 1979.

17 UNIX Time-Sharing System: The Programmer's Workbench

T. A. DOLOTTA
Interactive Systems Corporation
Santa Monica, California

R. C. HAIGHT
Bell Laboratories
Murray Hill, New Jersey

J. R. MASHEY
Bell Laboratories
Whippany, New Jersey

Many, if not most, UNIX* systems are dedicated to specific projects and serve small, cohesive groups of (usually technically oriented) users. The Programmer's Workbench UNIX system (PWB/UNIX for short) is a facility based on the UNIX system that serves as a large, general-purpose, "utility" computing service. It provides a convenient working environment and a uniform set of programming tools to a very diverse group of users. The PWB/UNIX system has several interesting characteristics:

• Many of its facilities were built in close cooperation between developers and users.

• It has proven itself to be sufficiently reliable so that its users, who develop production software, have abandoned punched cards, private backup tapes, etc.

• It offers a large number of simple, understandable program-development tools that can be combined in a variety of ways; users "package" these tools to create their own specialized environments.

• Most importantly, the above were achieved without compromising the basic elegance, simplicity, generality, and ease of use of the UNIX system.

The result has been an environment that helps large numbers of users to get their work done, that improves their productivity, that adapts quickly to their individual needs, and that provides reliable service at a relatively low cost. This paper discusses some of the problems we encountered in building the PWB/UNIX system, how we solved them, how our system is used, and some of the lessons we learned in the process.

1. INTRODUCTION

The Programmer's Workbench UNIX system (hereafter called PWB/UNIX for brevity) is a specialized computing facility dedicated to supporting large software-development projects. It is a production system that has been used for several years in the Business Information Systems Programs (BISP) area of Bell Laboratories and that supports there a user community of about 1,100 people. It was developed mainly as an attempt to improve the quality, reliability, flexibility, and consistency of the programming environment. The concepts behind the PWB/UNIX system emphasize several ideas:

• Program development and execution of the resulting programs are two radically different functions. Much can be gained by assigning each function to a computer best suited to it. Thus, as much of the development as possible should be done on a computer dedicated to that task, i.e., one that acts as a "development facility" and provides a superior programming environment. Production running of the developed products very often occurs on another computer, called a "target" system. For some projects, a single system may successfully fill both roles, but this is rare, because most current operating systems were designed primarily for *running* programs, with little thought having been given to the requirements of the program-development process; we did the exact opposite of this in the PWB/UNIX system.

• Although there may be several target systems (possibly supplied by different vendors), the development facility should present a single, uniform interface to its users. Current targets for the PWB/UNIX system include IBM System/370 and UNIVAC 1100-series computers; the PWB/UNIX system, in some sense, is also a target, because it is built and maintained with its own tools.

• A development facility can be implemented on computers of moderate size, even when the target machines consist of very large systems.

Although PWB/UNIX is a special-purpose system (in the same sense that a "front-end" computer is a special-purpose system), it is specialized for use by human beings. As shown in Figure 1, it provides the interface between program developers and their target computer(s). Unlike a typical "front-end," the PWB/UNIX system supplies a separate, visible, uniform environment for program-development work.

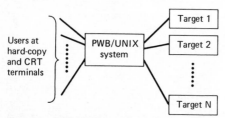

Figure 1. PWB/UNIX interface with its users.

354

Table 1. PWB/UNIX hardware at BISP (10/77)

System name	CPU type	Memory (K-bytes)	Disk (M-bytes)	Dial-up ports	Login names
A	/45	256	160	15	153
B	/70	768	480	48	260
D	/70	512	320	48	361
E	/45	256	160	20	114
F	/70	768	320	48	262
G	/70	512	160	48	133
H	/70	512	320	48	139
Totals	—	3,584	1,920	275	1,422

2. CURRENT STATUS

The PWB/UNIX installation at BISP currently consists of a network of DEC PDP-11/45s and /70s running a modified version of the UNIX system.[1] By most measures, it is the largest known UNIX installation in the world. Table 1 gives a "snapshot" of it as of October 1977.

The systems are connected to each other so that each can be backed up by another, and so that files can be transmitted efficiently among systems. They are also connected by communications lines to the following target systems: two IBM 370/168s, two UNIVAC 1100-series systems, and one XDS Sigma 5. Of the card images processed by these targets, 90 to 95 percent are received from PWB/UNIX systems. Average figures for prime-shift connect time (9 a.m. to 5 p.m., Monday through Friday) and total connect time per day are 1,342 and 1,794 hours, respectively. Because some login names are duplicated across systems, the figure of 1,422 is a bit misleading. The figure of 1,100 *distinct* login names is a better indicator of the size of the user community.

This installation offers fairly inexpensive time-sharing service to large numbers of users. An "average" PWB/UNIX user consumes 25 hours of prime-shift connect time per month, and uses 0.5 megabytes of active disk storage. Heavy use is made of the available resources. Typically, 90 percent of available disk space is in use, and between 75 and 80 percent of possible prime-time connect hours are consumed; during periods of heavy load, CPU usage occasionally exceeds 95 percent.

The PWB/UNIX system has been adopted outside of BISP, primarily for computer-center, program-development, and text-processing services. In addition to the original PWB/UNIX installation, there are currently about ten other installations within Bell Laboratories and six installations in other parts of the Bell System. A number of these installations utilize more than one CPU; thus, within the Bell System, there are over thirty PDP-11s running the PWB/UNIX system and there are plans for several more in the near future.[2] There is also a growing number of PWB/UNIX installations outside of the Bell System.

---

[1] In order to avoid ambiguity, we use in this paper the expression "Research UNIX system" to refer to the UNIX system itself [Ritchie and Thompson 1974] [Ritchie and Thompson 1978].

[2] The number of PDP-11s in the Bell System that operate under the PWB/UNIX system has doubled, on the average, every 11 months during the past 4.5 years.

3. HISTORY

The concept underlying the PWB/UNIX system was suggested in mid-1973 and the first PDP-11/45 was installed late that year. This machine was used at first for our own education and experimentation, while early versions of various facilities were constructed. At first, ours was an experimental project that faced considerable indifference from a user community heavily oriented to large computer systems, working under difficult schedules, and a bit wary of what then seemed like a radical idea. However, as word about the system spread, demand for service grew rapidly, almost always outrunning the supply. Users consistently underestimated their requirements for service, because they kept discovering unexpected applications for PWB/UNIX facilities. In four years, the original PWB/UNIX installation has grown from a single PDP-11 serving 16 users to a network of seven PDP-11s serving 1,100 users. Figure 2 shows two other aspects of the growth of that installation; see [Ivie 1977] [Dolotta and Mashey 1976] for "snapshots" of that installation earlier in its lifetime.

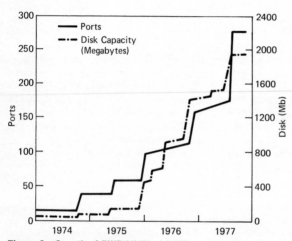

Figure 2. Growth of PWB/UNIX at BISP: number of ports and disk capacity.

4. MOTIVATION FOR THE PWB/UNIX APPROACH

The approach of using small computers to build a development facility for use with much larger targets has both good and bad points. At the outset, the following were thought to be potential problem areas:

- Cost of additional hardware.
- Inconvenience of splitting data and functions among machines.
- Use of incompatible character sets, i.e., ASCII and EBCDIC.
- Limited size and speed of minicomputers, as compared to the speed and size of the target systems.
- Degradation of reliability caused by the increased complexity of the composite system.

Of these, only the last has required any significant, continuing effort; the main problem has been in maintaining reliable communications with the targets in the face of continually changing configurations of the targets, of the PWB/UNIX systems, and of the communications links themselves.

The approach embodied in the PWB/UNIX system offers significant advantages in the presence of certain conditions, all of which existed at the original PWB/UNIX installation, thus giving us a strong motivation for adopting this approach. We discuss these conditions below.

4.1 Gain by Effective Specialization

The computer requirements of software *developers* often diverge quite sharply from those of the *users* of that software. This observation seems especially applicable to software-development organizations such as BISP, i.e., organizations that develop large, data-base-oriented systems. Primary needs of developers include:

• Interactive computing services that are convenient, inexpensive, and continually available during normal working hours (where often the meaning of the expression "normal working hours" is "22 hours per day, 7 days per week").
• A file structure designed for convenient interactive use; in particular, one that never requires the user to explicitly allocate or compact disk storage, or even to be aware of these activities.
• Good, uniform tools for the manipulation of documents, source programs, and other forms of text. In our opinion, all the tasks that make up the program-development process and that are carried out by computers are nothing more than (sometimes very arcane) forms of text processing and text manipulation.
• A command language simple enough for everyone to use, but one that offers enough programming capability to help automate the operational procedures used to track and control project development.
• Adaptability to frequent and unpredictable changes in location, structure, and personnel of user organizations.

On the other hand, users of the end products may have any or all of the following needs:

• Hardware of the appropriate size and speed to run the end products, possibly under stringent real-time or deadline constraints.
• File structures and access methods that can be optimized to handle large amounts of data.
• Transaction-oriented teleprocessing facilities.
• The use of a specific type of computer and operating system, to meet any one of a number of possible (often externally imposed) requirements.

Few systems meet all the requirements of both developers and users. As a result, it is possible to make significant gains by providing two separate kinds of facilities and optimizing each to match one of the two distinct sets of requirements.

4.2 Availability of Better Software

Time-sharing systems that run on large computers often retain significant vestiges of batch processing. Separation of support functions onto an appropriate minicomputer may offer an easy transition to more up-to-date software. Much of the stimulus for PWB/UNIX arose from the desire to make effective use of the UNIX system, whose facilities are extremely well matched to the developers' needs discussed above.

4.3   Installations with Target Systems
from Different Vendors

It is desirable to have a uniform, target-independent set of tools to ease training and to permit the transfer of personnel between projects. File structures, command languages, and communications protocols differ widely among targets. Thus, it is expensive, if not impossible, to build a single set of effective and efficient tools that can be used on all targets. Effort is better expended in building a single good development facility.

4.4   Changing Environments

Changes to hardware and software occur and cause problems even in single-vendor installations. Such changes may be disastrous if they affect both development and production environments at the same time. The problem is at least partially solved by using a separate development system. As an example, in the last few years, every BISP target system has undergone several major reconfigurations in both hardware and software, and the geographic work locations of most users have changed, in some cases more than once. The availability of the PWB/UNIX system often has been able to minimize the impact of these changes on the users.

4.5   Effective Testing of
Terminal-Oriented Systems

It is difficult enough to test small batch programs; effective testing of large, interactive, data-base management applications is far more difficult. It is especially difficult to perform load testing when the same computer is both generating the load and running the program being tested. It is simpler and more realistic to perform such testing with the aid of a separate computer.

5. DESIGN APPROACH

In early 1974, much thought was given to what should be the overall design approach for the PWB/UNIX system. One proposal consisted of first designing it as a completely integrated facility, then implementing it, and finally obtaining users for it. A much different, less traditional approach was actually adopted; its elements were:

• Follow the UNIX system's philosophy of building small, independent tools rather than large, interrelated ones. Follow the UNIX system's approach of minimizing the number of different file formats.
• Get users on the system quickly, work with them closely, and let their needs and problems drive the design.
• Build software quickly, and expect to throw much of it away, or to have to adapt it to the users' real needs, as these needs become clear. In general, emphasize the ability to adapt to change, rather than try to build perfect products that are meant to last forever.
• Make changes to the UNIX system only after much deliberation, and only when major gains can be made. Avoid changing the UNIX system's interfaces, and isolate any such changes as much as possible. Stay close to the Research UNIX system, in order to take advantage of continuing improvements.

This approach may appear chaotic, but, in practice, it has worked better than designing supposedly perfect systems that turn out to be obsolete or unusable by the time they are implemented. Unlike many other systems, the UNIX system both permits and encourages this approach.

6. DIFFERENCES BETWEEN RESEARCH UNIX AND PWB/UNIX

The usage and operation of the PWB/UNIX system differ somewhat from those of most UNIX systems within Bell Laboratories. Many of the changes and additions described below derive from these crucial differences.

A good many UNIX (as opposed to PWB/UNIX) systems are run as "friendly-user" systems, and are each used by a fairly small number of people who often work closely together. A large fraction of these users have read/write permissions for most (or all) of the files on the system, have permission to add commands to the public directories, are capable of "re-booting" the operating system, and even know how to repair damaged file systems.

The PWB/UNIX system, on the other hand, is most often found in a computer-center environment. Larger numbers of users are served, and they often represent different organizations. It is undesirable for everyone to have general read/write permissions. Although groups of users may wish to have sets of commands and files whose use they share, too many people must be served to permit everyone to add commands to public directories. Few users write C programs, and even fewer are interested in file-system internals. Machines are run by operators who are not expert system programmers. Many users have to deal with large quantities of existing source code for target computers. Many must integrate their use of the PWB/UNIX system into existing procedures and working methods.

Notwithstanding all the above problems, we continually made every attempt to retain the "friendly-user" environment wherever possible, while extending service to a large group of users characterized by a very wide spectrum of needs, work habits, and usage patterns. By and large, we succeeded in this endeavor.

7. NEW FACILITIES

A number of major facilities had to be made available in the PWB/UNIX system to make it truly useful in the BISP environment. Initial versions of many of these additional components were written and in use during early 1974. This section describes the current form of these additions (most of which have been heavily revised with the passage of time).

7.1 Remote Job Entry

The PWB/UNIX Remote Job Entry (RJE) subsystem handles the problems of transmitting jobs to target systems and returning output to the appropriate users; RJE per se consists of several components, and its use is supported by various other commands.

The send command is used to generate job streams for target systems; it is a form of macro-processor, providing facilities for file inclusion, keyword substitution, prompting, and character translation (e.g., ASCII to EBCDIC). It also includes a generalized interface to other UNIX commands, so that all or parts of job streams can be generated dynamically by such commands; send offers the users a uniform job-submission mechanism that is almost entirely target-independent.

A transmission subsystem exists to handle communications with each target. "Daemon" programs arrange for queuing jobs, submitting these jobs to the proper target, and routing output back to the user. Device drivers are included in the operating system to control the physical communications links. Some of the code in this subsystem is target-specific, but this subsystem is not visible to end users.

Several commands are used to provide status reporting. Users may inquire about the status of jobs on the target systems, and can elect to be notified in various ways (i.e., on-line or in absentia) of the occurrence of major events during the processing of their jobs.

A user may route the target's output to a remote printer or may elect to have part or all of it returned to the originating PWB/UNIX system. On return, output may be processed automatically by a user-written procedure, or may be placed in a file; it may be examined with the standard UNIX editor, or it can be scanned with a read-only editor (the "big file scanner") that can peruse larger files; RJE hides from the user the distinction between PWB/UNIX files, which are basically character-oriented, and the files of the target system, which are typically record-oriented (e.g., card images and print lines). See [Bianchi and Wood 1976] for examples of the use of RJE.

7.2   Source Code Control System

The PWB/UNIX Source Code Control System (SCCS) consists of a small set of commands that can be used to give unusually powerful control over changes to *modules* of text (i.e., files of source code, documentation, data, or any other text). It records every change made to a module, can recreate a module as it existed at any point in time, controls and manages any number of concurrently existing versions of a module, and offers various audit and administrative features [Rochkind 1975].

7.3   Text Processing and Document Preparation

One of the distinguishing characteristics of the Research UNIX system is that, while it is a general-purpose time-sharing system, it also provides very good text-processing and document-preparation tools [Kernighan et al. 1978]. A major addition in this area provided by the PWB/UNIX system is PWB/MM, a package of formatting "macros" that make the power of the UNIX text formatters available to a wider audience; PWB/MM has, by now, become the de facto Bell Laboratories standard text-processing macro package; it is used by hundreds of clerical and technical employees. It is an easily observable fact that, regardless of the initial reasons that attract users to the PWB/UNIX system, most of them end up using it extensively for text processing. See [Mashey and Smith 1976] for a further discussion of this topic.

7.4   Test Drivers

The PWB/UNIX system is often used as a simulator of interactive terminals to execute various kinds of tests of IBM and UNIVAC data-base management and data communications systems, and of applications implemented on these systems; it contains two test drivers that can generate repeatable tests for very complex systems; these drivers are used both to measure performance under well-controlled load and to help verify the initial and continuing correct operation of this software while it is being built and maintained. One driver simulates a *TELETYPE*® CDT cluster controller of up to four terminals, and is used to test programs running on UNIVAC 1100-series computers. The other (LEAP) simulates one or more IBM 3270 cluster controllers, each controlling up to 32 terminals. During a test, the actions of each simulated terminal are directed by a *scenario,* which is a specification of what *scripts* should be executed by that terminal. A script consists of a set of actions that a human operator might perform to accomplish some specific, functional task (e.g., update of a data-base record). A script can be invoked one or more times by one or more scenarios. High-level programming languages exist for both scripts and scenarios; these languages allow one to specify the actions of the simulated terminal-operator pairs, as well as a large variety of test-data recording, error-detection, and error-correction actions. See [Dolotta et al. 1976] for more details on LEAP.

8. MODIFICATIONS TO THE UNIX SYSTEM

Changes that we made to the UNIX operating system and commands were made very carefully, and only after a great deal of thoughtful deliberation. Interface changes were especially avoided. Some changes were made to allow the effective use of the UNIX system in a computer-center environment. In addition, a number of changes were required to extend the effective use of the UNIX system to larger hardware configurations, to larger numbers of simultaneous users, and to larger organizations sharing the machines.

8.1 Reliability

The UNIX system has generally been very reliable. However, some problems surfaced on PWB/UNIX before showing up on other UNIX systems simply because PWB/UNIX systems supported a larger and heavier time-sharing load than most other installations based on UNIX. The continual need for more service required these systems to be run near the limits of their resources much of the time, causing, in the beginning, problems seldom seen on other UNIX systems. Many such problems arose from the lack of detection of, or reasonable remedial action for, exhaustion of resources. As a result, we made a number of minor changes to various parts of the operating system to assure such detection of resource exhaustion, especially to avoid crashes and to minimize peculiar behavior caused by exceeding the sizes of certain tables.

The first major set of reliability improvements concerned the handling of disk files. It is a fact of life that time-sharing systems are continually short of disk space; PWB/UNIX is especially prone to rapid surges in disk usage, due to the speed at which the RJE subsystem can transfer data and use disk space. Experience showed that reliable operation requires RJE to be able to suspend operations temporarily, rather than throwing away good output. The ustat system call was added to allow programs to discover the amount of free space remaining in a file system. Such programs could issue appropriate warnings or suspend operation, rather than attempt to write a file that would consume all the free disk space and be, itself, truncated in the process, causing loss of precious data; the ustat system call is also used by the PWB/UNIX text editor to offer a warning message instead of silently truncating a file when writing it into a file system that is nearly full. In general, the relative importance of files depends on their cost in terms of human effort needed to (re)generate them. We consider information typed by people to be more valuable than that generated mechanically.

A number of operational procedures were instituted to improve file-system reliability. The main use of the PWB/UNIX system is to store and organize files, rather than to perform computations. Therefore, every weekday morning, each user file is copied to a backup disk, which is saved for a week. A weekly tape backup copy is kept for two months; bimonthly tape copies are kept "forever"—we still have the tapes from January 1974. The disk backup copies permit fast recovery from disk failure or other (rare) disasters, and also offer very fast recovery when individual user files are lost; almost always, such files are lost not because of system malfunctions, but because people inevitably make mistakes and delete files that they really wish to retain. The long-term tape backup copies, on the other hand, offer users the chance to delete files that they might want back at some time in the future, without requiring them to make "personal" copies.

A second area of improvement was motivated by the need for reliable execution of long-running procedures on machines that operate near the limits of their resources. Any UNIX system has some bound on the maximum number of processes permitted at any one time. If all processes are used, it is impossible to successfully issue the fork system call to create a new process. When this happens, it is difficult for useful work to get done, because most commands execute as separate processes. Such transient conditions (often lasting only a few seconds) do cause occasional, random failures that can be extremely irritating to the users (and, potentially, destroy their trust in the system). To remedy this situation, the shell was changed so that it attempts several fork calls, separated from one another by increasing lengths of time. Although this is not a general solution, it did have the practical effect of decreasing the probability of failure to the point that user complaints ceased. A similar remedy was applied to the command-execution failures due to the near-simultaneous attempts by several processes to execute the same pure-text program.

These efforts have yielded production systems that users are willing to trust. Although a file is occasionally lost or scrambled by the system, such an event is rare enough to be a topic for discussion, rather than a typical occurrence. Most users trust their files to the system and have thrown away their decks of cards. This is illustrated by the relative numbers of keypunches (30) and terminals (550) in BISP. Users have also come to trust the fact that their machines stay up and work. On the average, each machine is down once a week during prime shift, averaging 48 minutes of lost time, for total prime-shift availability of about 98 percent. These figures include the occasional loss of a machine for several hours at a time, i.e., for hardware problems. However, the net availability to most users has been closer to 99 percent, because most of the machines are paired and operational procedures exist so that they can be used to back each other up. This eliminates the intolerable loss of time caused by denying to an entire organization access to the PWB/UNIX system for as much as a morning or an afternoon. Such availability of service is especially critical for organizations whose daily working procedures have become intertwined with PWB/UNIX facilities, as well as for clerical users, who may have literally nothing to do if they cannot obtain access to the system.

Thus, users have come to trust the systems to run reliably and to crash very seldom. Prime-shift down-time may occur in several ways. A machine may be taken down voluntarily for a short period of time, typically to fix or rearrange hardware, or for some systems programming function. If the period is short and users are given reasonable notice, this kind of down-time does not bother users very much. Some down-time is caused by hardware problems. Fortunately, these seldom cause outright crashes; rather, they cause noticeable failures in communications activities, or produce masses of console error messages about disk failures. A system can "lock-up" because it runs out of processes, out of disk space, or out of some other resource. An alert operator can fix some problems immediately, but occasionally must take the system down and reinitialize it. The causes and effects of the "resource-exhaustion" problems are fairly well-known and generally thought to offer little reason for consternation. Finally, there is the possibility of an outright system crash caused by software bugs. As of mid-1977, the last such crash on a production machine occurred in November 1975.

8.2 Operations

At most sites, UNIX systems have traditionally been operated and administered by highly trained technical personnel; initially, our site was operated in the same way. Growth in PWB/UNIX service eventually goaded us into getting clerical help. However, the insight that we gained from initially doing the job ourselves was invaluable; it enabled us to perceive the need for, and to provide, operational procedures and software that made it possible to manage a large, production-oriented, computer-center-like service. For instance, a major operational task is "patching up" the file system after a hardware failure. In the worst cases, this work is still done by system programmers, but cases where system recovery is fairly straightforward are now handled by trained clerks. Our first attempt at writing an operator's manual dates from that time.

In the area of system administration, resource allocation and usage accounting have become more formal as the number of systems has grown. Software was developed to move entire sections of a file system (and the corresponding groups of users) from volume to volume, or from one PWB/UNIX system to another without interfering with linked files or access history. A major task in this area has been the formalization and the speeding-up of the file-system backup procedures.

By mid-1975, it was clear that we would soon run out of unique "user-ID" numbers. We resisted user pressure to re-use numbers among PWB/UNIX systems. Our original reason was to preserve our ability to back up each PWB/UNIX system with another one; in other words, the users and files from any system that is down for an extended period should be able to be moved to another, properly configured system. This was difficult enough to do without the complication of duplicated user-IDs. Such backup has indeed been carried out several times. However, the two main advantages of retaining unique user-IDs were:

1. Protecting our ability to move users *permanently* from one system to another for organizational or load-balancing purposes.

2. Allowing us to develop reasonable means for communicating among several systems without compromising file security.

We return to the subject of user-IDs in Section 8.4 below.

8.3 Performance Improvements

A number of changes were made to increase the ability of the PWB/UNIX system to run on larger configurations and support more simultaneous users. Although demand for service almost always outran our ability to supply it, minor tuning was eschewed in favor of finding ways to gain large payoffs with relatively low investment.

For a system such as PWB/UNIX, it is much more important to optimize the use of moving-head disks than to optimize the use of the CPU. We installed a new disk driver[3] that made efficient use of the RP04 (IBM 3330-

---

[3] Written by L. A. Wehr.

style) disk drives in multi-drive configurations. The seek algorithm was re-written to use one (sorted) list of outstanding disk-access requests per disk drive, rather than just one list for the entire system; heuristic analysis was done to determine what I/O request lead-time yields minimal rotational delay and maximal throughput under heavy load. The effect of these changes and of changes in the organization of the disk free-space lists (which are now optimized by hardware type and load expectation) have nearly tripled the effective multi-drive transfer rate. Current PWB/UNIX systems have approached the theoretical maximum disk throughput. On a heavily loaded system, three moving-head drives have the transfer capacity of a single fixed-head disk of equivalent size. The C program listing for the disk driver is only four pages long; this made it possible to experiment with it and to tune it with relative ease.

Minor changes were made in process scheduling to avoid "hot spots" and to keep response time reasonable, even on heavily loaded systems. Similarly, the scheduler and the terminal driver were also modified to help maintain a reasonable rate of output to terminals on heavily loaded systems. We have consciously chosen to give up a small amount of performance under a light load in order to gain performance under a heavy load.

Several performance changes were made in the shell. First, a change of just a few lines of code permitted the shell to use buffered "reads," eliminating about 30 percent of the CPU time used by the shell. Second, a way was found to reduce the average number of processes created in a day, also by approximately 30 percent; this is a significant saving, because the creation of a process and the activation of the corresponding program typically require about 0.1 second of CPU time and also incur overhead for I/O. To accomplish this, shell accounting data were analyzed to investigate the usage of commands. Each PWB/UNIX system typically had about 30,000 command executions per day. Of these, 30 percent resulted from the execution of just a few commands, namely, the commands used to implement flow-of-control constructs in shell procedures. The overhead for invoking them typically outweighed their actual execution time. They were absorbed (without significant changes) into the shell. This reduced somewhat the CPU overhead by eliminating many fork calls. Much more importantly, it reduced disk I/O in several ways: swapping due to forks was reduced, as was searching for commands; it also reduced the response time perceived by users executing shell procedures — the improvement was enough to make the use of these procedures much more practical. These changes allowed us to provide service to many more users without degrading the response time of our systems to an unreasonable degree.

The most important decision that we made in this entire area of reliability and performance was our conscious choice to keep our system in step with the Research UNIX system; its developers have been most helpful: they quickly repaired serious bugs, gave good advice where our needs diverged from theirs, and "bought back" the best of our changes.

8.4   User Environment

During 1975, a few changes that altered the user environment were made to the operating system, the shell, and a few other commands. The main result of these changes was to more than double the size of the user population to which we could provide service without doing major harm to the convenience of the UNIX system. In particular, several problems had to be overcome to maintain the ease of sharing data and commands. This aspect of the UNIX system is popular with its users, is especially crucial for groups of users working on common projects, and distinguishes the UNIX system from many other time-sharing systems, which impose complete user-from-user isolation under the pretense of providing privacy, security, and protection.

Initially, the UNIX system had a limit of 256 distinct user-IDs [Ritchie and Thompson 1974]; this was adequate for most UNIX installations, but totally inadequate for a user population the size of ours. Various solutions were studied, and most were rejected. Duplicating user-IDs across machines was rejected for operational reasons, as noted in Section 8.2 above. A second option considered was that of decreasing the available number of the so-called "group-IDs," or removing them entirely, and using the bits thus freed to increase the number of distinct user-IDs. Although attractive in many ways, this solution required a change in the interpretation of information stored with every single disk file (and every backup copy thereof), changes to large numbers of commands, and a fundamental departure from the Research UNIX system during a time when thought was being given to possible changes to that system's protection mechanisms. For these reasons, this solution was deemed unwise.

Our solution was a modest one that depended heavily on the characteristics of the PWB/UNIX user community, which, as mentioned above, consists mostly of groups of cooperating users, rather than of individual users working in isolation from one another. Typical behavior and opinions in these groups were:

• Users in such a group cared very little about how much protection they had from each other, as long as their files were protected from damage by users outside their group.

• A common password was often used by members of a group, even when they owned distinct user-IDs. This was often done so that a needed file could be accessed without delay when its owner was unavailable.

• Most users were willing to have only one or two *user-IDs* per group, but wanted to retain their own *login names* and *login directories*. We also favored such a distinction, because experience showed that the use of a single login name by more than a few users almost always produced cluttered directory structures containing useless files.

• Users wanted to retain the convenience of inter-user communication through commands (e.g., `write` and `mail`) that automatically identified the sending person.

The Research UNIX `login` command maps a login name into a user-ID, which thereafter identifies that user. Because the mapping from login name to user-ID is many-to-one in PWB/UNIX, a given user-ID may represent many login names. It was observed that the `login` command knew the login name, but did not record it in a way that permitted consistent retrieval. The login name was added to the data recorded for each process and the `udata` system call was added to set or retrieve this value; the `login` command was modified to record the login name and a small number of other commands (such as `write` and `mail`) were changed to obtain the login name via the `udata` system call. Finally, to improve the security of files, a few commands were changed to create files with read/write permission for their owners, but read-only for everyone else. The net effect of these changes was to greatly enlarge the size of the user community that could be served, without destroying the convenience of the UNIX system and without requiring widespread and fundamental changes.

The second problem was that of sharing commands. When a command is invoked, the shell first searches for it in the current directory, then in directory `/bin`, and finally in directory `/usr/bin`. Thus, any user may have private commands in one of his or her private directories, while /bin is a repository for the most frequently used public commands, and /usr/bin usually contains less frequently used public commands. On many systems, almost anyone can install commands in /usr/bin. Although this is practical for a system with twenty or so users, it is unworkable for systems with 200 or more, especially when a number of unrelated organizations share a machine. Our users wanted to create their own commands, invoked in the same way as public commands. Users in large projects often wanted several sets of such commands: project, department, group, and individual.

The solution in this case was to change the shell (and a few other commands, such as nohup and time) to search a *user-specified* list of directories, instead of the existing fixed list. In order to preserve the consistency of command searching across different programs, it was desirable to place a user-specified list where it could be accessed by any program that needed it. This was accomplished through a mechanism similar to that used for solving the previous problem. The login command was changed to record the name of the user's login directory in the per-process data area. Each user could record a list of directories to be searched in a file named .path in his or her login directory, and the shell and other commands were changed to read this file. Although a few users wished to be able to change this list more dynamically than is possible by editing the .path file, most users were satisfied with this facility, and, as a matter of observed fact, altered that file infrequently. In many projects, the project administrator creates an appropriate .path file and then makes links to it for everyone else, thus ensuring consistency of command names within the project.

These changes were implemented in mid-1975. Their effect was an upsurge in the number of project-specific commands, written to improve project communication, to manage project data bases, to automate procedures that would otherwise have to be performed manually, and, generally, to customize the user environment provided by the PWB/UNIX system to the needs of each project. The result was a perceived increase in user productivity, because our users (who are, by and large, designers and builders of software) began spending significantly less time on housekeeping tasks, and correspondingly more time on their end products; see [Bianchi and Wood 1976] for comments on this entire process by some early PWB/UNIX users.

8.5 Extending the Use of the Shell

A number of extensions were made to the shell to improve its ability to support shell programming, while leaving its user interface as unchanged as possible. These changes were made only after a great deal of trepidation, because they clearly violated the UNIX system's principle of minimizing the complexity of "central" programs, and because they represented a departure from the Research (UNIX) shell; these departures consisted of minor changes in syntax, but major changes in intended usage.

During 1974 and early 1975, the PWB/UNIX shell was the same as the Research UNIX shell, and its usage pattern was similar, i.e., it was mainly used to interpret commands typed at a terminal and occasionally used to interpret (fairly simple) files of commands. A good explanation of the original shell philosophy and usage may be found in [Thompson 1975]. At that time, shell programming abilities were limited to simple handling of a sequence of arguments, and flow of control was directed by if, goto, and exit—separate commands whose use gave a Fortran-like appearance to shell procedures. During this period, we started experimenting with the use of the shell. We noted that anything that could be written as a shell procedure could always be written in C, but the reverse was often not true. Although C programs almost always executed faster, users preferred to write shell procedures, if at all possible, for a number of reasons:

- Shell programming has a "shallow" learning curve, because anyone who uses the UNIX system must learn something about the shell and a few other commands; thus little additional effort is needed to write simple shell procedures.
- Shell programming can do the job quickly and at a low cost in terms of human effort.
- Shell programming avoids waste of effort in premature optimization of code. Shell procedures are occasionally recoded as C programs, but only after they are shown to be worth the effort of being so recoded. Many shell procedures are executed no more frequently than a few times a day; it would be very difficult to justify the effort to rewrite them in C.
- Shell procedures are small and easy to maintain, especially because there are no object programs or libraries to manage.

Experience with shell programming led us to believe that some very modest additions would yield large gains in the kinds of procedures that could be written with the shell. Thus, in mid-1975, we made a number of changes to the shell, as well as to other commands that are used primarily in shell procedures. The shell was changed to provide 26 character-string variables and a command that sets the value of such a variable to an already existing string, or to a line read from the standard input. The if command was extended to allow a "nestable" if-then-else-endif form, and the expr command was created to provide evaluation of character-string and arithmetic expressions. These changes, in conjunction with those described in Section 8.4 above, resulted in a dramatic increase in the use of shell programming. For example, procedures that lessened the users' need for detailed knowledge of the target system's job control language were written for submitting RJE jobs,[4] groups of commands were written to manage numerous small data bases, and many manual procedures were automated. A more detailed discussion of shell usage patterns (as of June 1976) may be found in [Mashey 1976].

Further changes have been made since that time, mainly to complete the set of control structures (by adding the switch and while commands), and also to improve performance, as explained in Section 8.3 above.

Although the shell became larger, the resulting extensive use of shell programming made it unnecessary for us to build large amounts of centrally-supported software. Thus, these changes to the shell actually reduced the total amount of software that we had to build and maintain, while allowing each user project to customize its own work environment to best match its needs and terminology. A new version of the shell has been written recently [Bourne 1978a]; it includes most of our additions, in one form or another.

9. WHAT WE HAVE LEARNED

Several UNIX systems have served for many years as development facilities in support of minicomputers and microprocessors. The existence of the PWB/UNIX system shows that the UNIX system can also perform this function

---

[4] Target-system users who interact with these targets via the PWB/UNIX RJE subsystem make about 20 percent fewer errors in their job control statements than those who interact directly with the targets.

quite effectively for target machines that are among the largest of the currently-available computers. The importance of this observation lies in the fact that the PWB/UNIX system can be used to provide a uniform interface and development facility for almost any programming project, regardless of its intended target, or the size of that target.

Our experience also proves that the UNIX system is readily adaptable to the computer-center environment, permitting its benefits to be offered to a very wide user population. Although some changes and additions to the UNIX system were required, they were accomplished without tampering with its basic fabric, and without significantly degrading its convenience and usability.

Finally, why is the PWB/UNIX system so successful? Certainly, most of the credit goes to the UNIX system itself. In addition, success came partly from what we added to the UNIX system, partly because we provided generally good service, and, perhaps most importantly, because, during the entire design and development process, we forcefully nurtured a close, continuing dialogue between ourselves and our users.

Another reason for the success of the PWB/UNIX system is that it adapts very easily to the individual needs of each user group. Without delving into the "Tower of Babel" effect, it appears that each programming group has strong functional (and perhaps social) needs to radically customize its work environment. This urge to specialize has often been carried out at great cost on other systems. On PWB/UNIX systems, users within such a group share files, build specialized send "scripts" for compiling, loading, and testing their programs on target computers, and write commands (shared within the group) that incorporate nomenclature specific to the group's project. Our changes to the shell and to the user environment, along with the basic facilities of the UNIX system, combined to permit the writing of these new commands as shell procedures. The development of such shell procedures requires at least an order of magnitude less effort than the writing of equivalent C programs. The result is that today, on many PWB/UNIX systems, four out of five commands that are executed originate in such user-written shell procedures.

Speaking as developers of the PWB/UNIX system, we believe that our system fosters real improvement in our users' productivity. The contributing factors have all been touched upon above; the most important of these are:

- A single, uniform, consistent programming environment.
- Good, basic tools that can be combined in a variety of ways to serve special needs.
- Protection of data to free the users from time-consuming housekeeping chores.
- Very high system availability and reliability.

Taken together, these characteristics instill confidence in our users and make them want to use our system.

One effect that we did not fully foresee was that our changes to the UNIX system (some made under considerable pressure from our users) would lead to an explosion of project-specific software and an expanded demand for PWB/UNIX service. However, we did keep to our original goals:

- To keep up-to-date with the Research UNIX system.
- To change as little of the Research UNIX system as possible.
- To make certain that our changes did not compromise the inherent simplicity, generality, flexibility, and efficiency of the UNIX system.
- To provide to our users tools, rather than products.

ACKNOWLEDGMENTS

The basic concept of the PWB/UNIX system was first suggested by E. L. Ivie [Ivie 1977]. Many of our colleagues have contributed to the design, implementation, and continuing improvement of that system. Thanks must also go to several members of the Bell Laboratories Computing Science Research Center for creating the UNIX system itself, as well as for their advice and support.

REFERENCES

[Bianchi and Wood 1976] M.H. Bianchi, J.L. Wood. A user's viewpoint on the Programmer's Workbench. *Proceedings of the Second International Conference on Software Engineering*, San Francisco, California, October 1976, 193-199.

[Bourne 1978a] S.R. Bourne. UNIX Time-Sharing System: The UNIX shell. *The Bell System Technical Journal*, 57:6 (July-August 1978), Part 2, 1971-1990.

[Dolotta and Mashey 1976] T.A. Dolotta, J.R. Mashey. An introduction to the Programmer's Workbench. *Proceedings of the Second International Conference on Software Engineering*, San Francisco, California, October 1976, 164-168; [*Editors' note*: see also [Dolotta et al. 1978]]

[Dolotta et al. 1976] T.A. Dolotta, J.S. Licwinko, R.E. Menninger, W.D. Roome. The LEAP load and test driver. *Proceedings of the Second International Conference on Software Engineering*, San Francisco, California, October 1976, 182-86.

[Ivie 1977] E.L. Ivie. Programmers Workbench—a machine for software development. *Communications of the ACM*, 20:10 (October 1977), 746-753. [*Editors' note*: see also [Dolotta et al. 1978].]

[Kernighan et al. 1978] B.W. Kernighan, M.E. Lesk, J.F. Ossanna. UNIX Time-Sharing System: Document Preparation. *The Bell System Technical Journal*, 57:6 (July-August 1978), Part 2, 2115-2135.

[Mashey 1976] J.R. Mashey. Using a command language as a high-level programming language. *Proceedings of the Second International Conference on Software Engineering*, San Francisco, California, October 1976, 169-176.

[Mashey and Smith 1976] J.R. Mashey, D.W. Smith. Documentation tools and techniques. *Proceedings of the Second International Conference on Software Engineering*, San Francisco, California, October 1976, 177-181.

[Ritchie and Thompson 1974] D.M. Ritchie, K. Thompson. The UNIX Time-Sharing System. *Communications of the ACM*, 17:7 (July 1974), 365-375.

[Ritchie and Thompson 1978] D.M. Ritchie, K. Thompson. The UNIX Time-Sharing System. *The Bell System Technical Journal*, 57:6 (July-August 1978), Part 2, 1905-1929.

[Rochkind 1975] M.J. Rochkind. The Source Code Control System. *IEEE Transactions on Software Engineering*, SE-1:4 (December 1975), 364-370.

[Thompson 1975] K. Thompson. The UNIX command language, in *Structured Programming—Infotech State of the Art Report*. Infotech International Ltd., Nicholsen House, Maidenhead, Berkshire, England, March 1975, 375-384.

18 Software Tools in the User Software Engineering Environment

ANTHONY I. WASSERMAN

University of California
San Francisco, California

Software tools are becoming an increasingly important aspect of systematic methods for software development and play a major role in supporting the User Software Engineering methodology. This paper describes the goals of the User Software Engineering methodology, some of the requirements for the methodology, and the characteristics of the tools that have been created to support the methodology. Four major tools are reviewed: the Transition Diagram Interpreter (TDI), Troll, a relational algebra-like interface to a data base management system, the programming language PLAIN, and the Module Control System. The paper concludes with a discussion of the integration of these tools and their use in a Unix-based development environment.

1. INTRODUCTION

But the moment man first picked up a stone or a branch to use as a tool, he altered irrevocably the balance between him and his environment. From this point on, the way in which the world around him changed was different. It was no longer regular or predictable. New objects appeared that were not recognizable as a mutation of something that had existed before, and as each one emerged it altered the environment not for a season, but for ever. While the number of these tools remained small, their effect took a long time to spread and to cause change. But as they increased, so did their effects: the more the tools, the faster the rate of change.

—JAMES BURKE [Burke 1978]

Many computer-based systems may be described as interactive information systems (IIS), providing their users with conversational access to data. Such users are frequently unfamiliar with the technical details of computer hardware and software and view the system only as a tool that may help them (or may possibly be required) in their jobs. Trends toward distributed systems, lower hardware costs, and the criticality of user/program interfaces all indicate the importance of developing tools and techniques specifically for this class of systems.

Accordingly, the User Software Engineering (USE) project was undertaken in 1975 with the objective of creating a methodology to support the specification, design, and implementation of interactive information systems, including the construction of tools that would support the developer of such systems. Attention was specifically focused on the application program developer, who had been traditionally squeezed between the realistic needs of users and the lack of suitable tools for meeting those needs. At that time, virtually all interactive systems were being developed in a haphazard, ad hoc manner, and the emerging techniques for software engineering did not address this very important class of programs.

To improve this development process, the goals of the project combined notions of software engineering and systematic program development with those of user involvement in the software development process.

After considerable study of the state-of-the-art in interactive information systems and tools for their construction, we identified some requirements for the methodology and tools. These requirements included the following key points:

1. *Specification of user interaction.* We needed a tool that could be used to specify the user/program dialogue; furthermore, this tool should produce a representation of the dialogue that was both comprehensible to the user and sufficiently precise for the developer.

2. *Design guidelines for user/program dialogue.* Guidelines were needed to assist the application developer in creating a dialogue between the user and the program; ideally, it should be possible to identify several types of dialogues, where the appropriate dialogue type for a given application can be determined from a study of user, organization, and hardware characteristics.

3. *Experimentation with user/program dialogue.* The user needed the opportunity to work with a "breadboard" of the system to create a hospitable user interface before beginning full-scale development of the production version of the system; it was also felt that availability of such a tool would assist the user in thinking more carefully about how the system would work and how it would be used; this tool could thus also serve as an effective analysis tool, leading to a better specification and eventually to a better system.

4. *Language for implementation of interactive information systems.* We needed a tool that contained the appropriate primitives for creating well-

structured programs; available programming languages either lacked support for the needs of interactive programs or for the objectives of structured programming or both [Wasserman 1974].

5. *Assistance in maintenance of program production library.* We needed to keep track of the documentation associated with the specification, design, implementation, and testing of interactive information systems; in addition, it was necessary to be able to keep track of versions of the system and its individual modules.

6. *Orientation to small and medium-sized machines.* We wanted to take advantage of hardware trends toward distributed systems and mini- and microcomputers; it was assumed that application programs would probably run on such computers and that the development would take place on such computers, regardless of the target machine.

7. *Integration of tools into a suitable development environment.* We decided to build these new tools on top of other tools for common tasks such as program editing, text formatting, language development, and other common software development activities, since it was not reasonable to build these tools from scratch.

These objectives have led to the development of a methodology for the creation of interactive information systems and to the creation of tools that support the methodology. Four principal tools have been developed to date:

1. *TDI (Transition Diagram Interpreter).* A tool for encoding transition diagrams that permits the rapid construction and modification of prototype user/program interfaces, as well as the creation of system prototypes

2. *PLAIN (Programming LAnguage for INteraction).* A procedural programming language derived from Pascal that contains features for building interactive information systems, including strings, patterns and pattern-matching operations, exception-handling, and relations, with a set of operations to support definition and manipulation of relational data bases

3. *Troll.* A tool that provides a relational algebra-like interface to a small relational data base system, used both as the runtime support of PLAIN and as the "backend" of TDI in the construction of system prototypes

4. *Module Control System.* A tool that supports a modular organization of the software system, provides version control, and automatic logging of developer activities

The remainder of this paper provides an overview of the User Software Engineering development methodology, including an historical perspective on the project, with an emphasis on these four tools and their capabilities.

2. SYSTEMATIC SOFTWARE DEVELOPMENT

An important consideration in developing high quality software systems is to follow a systematic approach to software development. The potential benefits of such an approach include:

1. improved reliability;
2. verifiability, at least in an informal sense;
3. improved maintainability, including portability and adaptability;
4. system comprehensibility, as a result of improved structure;
5. more effective management control of the development process;
6. higher user satisfaction.

The unifying notion in this regard is that of software engineering. The term "software engineering" was invented in 1967 to suggest the need to follow an engineering-type of discipline in the creation of computer software. Among the important engineering concepts are those of a "life cycle" and a "methodology" for production, as well as cost and performance prediction.

The life cycle divides the development process into a series of related activities, beginning with analysis and proceeding through specification, design, implementation, and testing, until the product is ready for operational use. This phased approach to development provides milestones and checkpoints where intermediate products, e.g., design documents, are delivered and reviewed. In this way, it is possible to gain greater control over the development process.

Not only should one follow the life cycle in carrying out system development, but one should also have a methodology for this process, using a set of tools for analysis, design, implementation, testing, and project control. The notion of "software engineering" implies that the developer will have a set of tools and procedures that can be applied to different projects. In short, when a development organization is presented with a problem that may require the development of a system, it should be able to follow this methodology from the original concept down through the release of the completed system.

In general, efforts to follow a systematic approach to software development involve putting increased effort into requirements analysis, specification, and design, with the expectation of lower costs for testing and system evolution, since the implemented system will represent a better fit to the user's needs and will operate more reliably than would otherwise be the case.

Clearly, there is much to commend such a systematic approach to software design and development. When developing interactive information systems, though, there is one extremely serious flaw: there may be a long period of time between the early stages of analysis and specification and the actual availability of the system while the systematic procedure is followed. During this time, the user's needs may change significantly, and the user has no system to use in the interim. When the system finally becomes operational, it may do what was originally specified, but user experience with the system may show that what is needed is quite different. As a result, a large part of the systematic development effort may have been wasted as it becomes necessary to redesign and reimplement a system that meets the newly identified needs of the user.

In short, there is some merit to the traditional idea of "let's build one of these and see how it works". If such a system is conceived as a "throwaway" system, intended only to identify user needs or to serve those needs during an interim period while development of a production system is in progress, and it can be built quickly and inexpensively, then there is ample justification for proceeding with this approach. Indeed, integration of this concept of prototyping into a systematic development methodology seems to strike a good balance between the needs of the user and the desire to proceed in a well-disciplined way.

3. TOOL DEVELOPMENT
IN THE USE ENVIRONMENT

In this context, the objectives of the User Software Engineering project become more apparent. USE attempts to span the software development life cycle, giving particular attention to the ideas of prototyping and to the needed features for a programming language directed to the construction of interactive information systems. The USE methodology utilizes tools and techniques developed by others with tools specifically developed for this application area.

An early project decision was to build the USE tools upon the UNIX[1] operating system and its associated tools [Bell 1978] [Kernighan and Mashey 1981]. This decision was made not only because of easy access to Unix-based systems, but also because of its relative simplicity, its orientation toward small computers, and its substantial collection of operational tools. Although some of the Unix tools were less than ideal for our purposes, we felt that no other tool set approached that of Unix, and that it was far more desirable to use a workable set of tools than to go to the effort to create the tools *de novo*.

Tool development in the USE environment focused first on programming languages, since it seemed that there were no programming languages that were well suited for transforming a design into an interactive system of this kind. The observation that "the programming languages designed explicitly for interaction do not [have the structure] for creating modular, well-structured, reliable software" [Wasserman 1974] led to design of the programming language PLAIN (Programming LAnguage for INteraction). The idea behind PLAIN, then, was to provide a tool for the construction of interactive information systems that incorporates concepts of structured programming. PLAIN was also viewed as a possible replacement for MUMPS [O'Neill 1977], used widely in the construction of medical applications programs, despite its poor qualities as a programming language [Wasserman and Sherertz 1976].

The next focus of attention was the specification for interactive information systems. At that time, specifications were largely written in narrative form, showing little or nothing about the system structure or about the way that the user would interact with the system. A specification method for interactive information systems should show both a possible software system structure and the user interaction. In that way, the specification would be user-centered, and would thus encourage increased attention to user needs at an early stage.

The next step was to automate the user/program dialogue that was produced as part of the specification. This led to the development of the Transition Diagram Interpreter (TDI), making it possible for the user to interact with a prototype of the user/program interface.

The development of a relational data base handler and relational algebra-like interface (Troll) was undertaken in parallel with these other efforts. Troll was the interface between the runtime system of PLAIN, which provides relations as a data type, and a relational database management system. More recently, Troll is being integrated with TDI so that prototype systems can be built, not just prototype user interfaces.

Little attention was given to the creation of new design tools, since there appeared to be adequate tools, e.g., Structured Design [Yourdon and Constantine 1978], for architectural design, and program design languages [Caine and Gordon 1975] for detailed design.

Finally, we have built a tool that can assist with management of the development and evolution of system modules. This tool, named the Module Control System, is intended to retain the history of module development, to maintain consistent names for modules throughout their specification, design, and implementation, and to provide version control at the module level.

The USE project has been closely tied to the Unix programming environment, since Unix is aimed at supporting interactive program development, as well as the use of interactive programs (not the same thing!). Furthermore, Unix contained an impressive set of tools for text processing, documentation, language implementation, and file management. One can thus envision the

---

[1] UNIX is a trademark of Bell Laboratories.

USE techniques and tools, combined with Unix tools, as providing a "workbench" [Ivie 1977] for the engineering of interactive information systems.

We now provide a little more detail on each of the USE tools: TDI and the specification method, PLAIN, Troll, and the Module Control System. Description of the integration of Troll and TDI for prototyping purposes appears elsewhere [Wasserman and Shewmake 1981]. Additional detail may be found in the cited references.

4. TDI AND THE USE SPECIFICATION METHOD

Along with recognizing the inadequacy of programming languages for interactive information systems, it was noted that similar weaknesses existed for specification methods. This problem was particularly severe with respect to tying the user input to specific actions. With respect to the User Software Engineering goals, two points were most important:

1. the primitives used in the specification method had to correspond closely to features in PLAIN to simplify implementation of the interactive information system, and subsequent testing and/or verification of the system;

2. the specification method had to support user involvement in the specification process, with the resulting document being comprehensible to computer-naive users and sufficiently precise for developers.

Among the goals that one seeks in a specification method are completeness, consistency, unambiguity, writeability, testability, implementability, modifiability, and, perhaps most important, comprehensibility. Achievement of these diverse goals is difficult, since some of them entail a significant amount of formalism, while others are less suited for the use of formalisms. Accordingly, some blending of formal and informal specification techniques is necessary.

Informally, an interactive information system may be seen as consisting of three major components: the user interface, the operations on the data objects, and the data base (or files). We use an informal narrative notation for our informal specification, but couple it to a more formal transition diagram scheme to provide consistency and to eliminate ambiguity. It is also possible to employ a formal specification language, such as SPECIAL [Roubine and Robinson 1978] or BASIS [Leveson and Wasserman 1981], to describe the system actions.

The user interface of an interactive information system provides the user with a language for communicating with the system, and the normal action of the program is determined by user input. The program may respond in a variety of ways, including the printing of results, requests for additional input, error messages, or assistance in the use of the system.

The critical observation, though, is that the semantics of the system are driven by raw or transformed user input. As with programming languages, the user language in its runtime context determines the semantic actions to be performed; the resemblance between such a user language and an interpreted programming language is quite strong. Accordingly, an effective specification technique for programming languages can be used effectively for specifying user interfaces.

We have chosen to use transition diagrams [Conway 1963] for this purpose. A transition diagram is a network of nodes and directed paths. Each path may contain a token, corresponding to a character string in the primitive alphabet (such as ASCII), or the name of another diagram. If the path is blank, it will be traversed as a default case, i.e., if all other paths leaving a given node fail.

Scanning of the diagram begins at a designated entry point and proceeds until reaching an exit node or a dead end (no successful match on the paths from a given node and no default). A semantic action may be associated with any path; traversal of the path causes the action to occur.

The next aspect of the specification is to define the data base, since the operations in the interactive information system are generally tied to the logical structure of the data base. We follow the ANSI/SPARC framework [Tsichritzis and Klug 1978], focusing primarily on the external model(s) defined in relations. We design a separate external model for each user class, thereby providing a separate view of the data base, typically determined by a different set of operations, thereby producing a user view specification for each user class.

The final step of the specifications is to create a tie between the semantic actions of the transition diagrams and the operations on the data base. Each semantic action must be specified and the method of specification may be chosen from a variety of alternatives. Our preference is to use a narrative form first, and then to use a more formal approach. The specification language can include the semantic actions, including the data base operations.

The specification of the semantic actions in this way is a powerful tool for several reasons:

1. Each of the semantic actions is quite small, since it is associated with the traversal of a single arc of a transition diagram. Thus, an effective decomposition of the system is produced in this way.

2. One may continually rework the individual semantic actions, beginning with a prose description and proceeding through a specification language, a program design language, and finally code. Comparison and tracing from one stage of the software life cycle to another is thereby simplified.

3. The relational data base definition and the syntax of the paths on the transition diagram are extremely well suited to implementation in PLAIN, so that the transformation from the specification of an interactive information system to its realization in a PLAIN program is as straightforward as possible.

Automated support for the specification aid has also been developed. The transition diagram can be specified in a table, showing, for each node, each of the possible exit paths, the target of the path (a node), the token of diagram that must be matched to cause the arc to be traversed, and the name of the semantic action (typically a procedure) to be performed if the arc is traversed.

This information can be encoded in a form similar to that used by the YACC parser generator [Johnson and Lesk 1978], using a text editor. Then a Transition Diagram Interpreter (TDI) can use that table as input and can perform two important tasks:

1. it can check the diagram(s) for consistency, making sure, for example, that there is a path from each node (checking to see that there is a path from entry to exit becomes an exponentially large problem as the number of nodes increases)

2. it can be used to provide a "mockup" of the actual user/system dialogues simply by making the semantic actions into dummy statements.

This latter use is extremely valuable in the specification of interactive information systems. First, it lets the eventual user interact with "the system" at a very early stage in the life cycle and provides a "feel" for the character of the eventual system. If the user has little or no prior experience with information systems, this process helps the user to think about what the system will actually do, and therefore to gain a better idea of the requirements and to see how usable the interface will be.

Without such a tool, the information system remains too abstract for the user, who will not then get to interact with it until it has been built. In such a case, the user will often request changes based on initial usage. As noted above, the cost of evolving the system to accommodate these requests is typically much higher than the cost of meeting the requirements the first time. Hence, the payoff from the TDI is improved user understanding of the interactive information system, giving the user the ability to assist in modification of the requirements and specification at an early stage in the development life cycle.

The subsequent introduction to PLAIN shows that the content and notation of the specification method blends well with the features of PLAIN so that they can work in harmony with one another. Furthermore, the structure of the semantic action specification encourages the use of a program design language at the detailed design stage. In this way, the USE methodology spans the heart of the software development life cycle. An example showing the specification method and a sample implementation is presented in [Wasserman 1979].

5. AN INTRODUCTION TO PLAIN

The design goals of PLAIN fall into two categories: those that support systematic programming practices, and those that support the creation of interactive programs. In practice, these goals mesh in the process of language design, but can be separated when examining the design philosophy.

The design goals for systematic programming were:

1. Support for procedural and data abstraction
2. Support for modularity
3. Control structures to encourage linear flow of control within modules
4. Visibility of data flow and data use
5. Prevention of self-modifying programs
6. Program readability
7. Limited language size

Many of the features of PLAIN with respect to systematic programming are derived from Pascal. However, several other modern languages, including LIS [LIS 1976], CLU [Liskov et al. 1978], Euclid [Lampson et al. 1977], Gypsy [Good 1978], and Ada[2] [Ichbiah et al. 1980], have also influenced the design. These goals, and the way that they are addressed in PLAIN, are explained at greater length in [Wasserman 1980].

The design goals for supporting the construction of interactive programs were:

1. Features for data base management
2. Support for strings and string handling
3. Facilities for exception handling
4. Availability of a rudimentary pattern specification and matching facility
5. Appropriate input/output features
6. Rudimentary timing facilities

With these features, PLAIN programs could be made resilient to user errors, could simplify user interaction with large data bases, and could be made flexible in handling diverse forms of user input. Unlike the case with the system-

---

[2] Ada is a registered trademark of the U.S. Department of Defense.

atic programming goals, there were few, if any, languages that had developed a satisfactory solution for achieving the goals for reliable interactive programs. Accordingly, much of the design effort went into the design of features for string handling, exception handling, pattern-matching, and relational data base management.

We now briefly sketch the features of PLAIN that explicitly support interactive programs. The complete language definition is presented in the Revised Report [Wasserman et al. 1981].

5.1 Data Base Management

A complete set of relational data base management facilities are part of PLAIN. A relation is a built-in data type, and may be seen as a set of records whose storage persistence is separate from the execution time of the programs accessing them. Relations from one or more data bases may be imported into the execution environment of a PLAIN program to perform the desired data base management operations.

One can routinely create and manipulate relations in PLAIN programs. The data base operations in PLAIN are aimed at providing the programmer with some control over the sequence of data base operations, and therefore at incorporating a set of features that permit the programmer to improve the efficiency of the program's data base management. The data base management facilities of PLAIN include:

1. Formation of data base expressions using the following relational algebra-like operations:

• selection of a set of tuples satisfying a certain constraint
• projection on some attributes
• joining two relations on attributes of the same type
• set operations: union, intersection, and difference

2. Assignment of a data base expression to a variable
3. Individual tuple operations: - associative access using key-attribute values - insertion/deletion of tuples - modification of non-key attribute values
4. Iteration through the set of tuples with a for each clause
5. Aggregation operations count, sum, min, max, and avg

These operations, along with some examples, are described further in [Wasserman 1979].

5.2 String Handling in PLAIN

The key decision in the inclusion of string handling facilities was to permit the generalized use of variable length strings as well as the more traditional use of fixed length strings. It is permissible in PLAIN to declare a variable of type string, with no stated maximum length: as in Pascal, it is also permissible to declare arrays of characters for those instances where the variable-length facility is not needed.

Additional operators and functions were provided to support the use of this data type. The binary operations of concatenation, string contains, and string follows (lexical ordering) were introduced, along with functions for string insertion, removal, replacement, and extraction. It is also possible to convert between fixed and variable length strings.

The decision to permit variable length strings, with the necessary implementation overhead associated with heap management, was based on the assumption that string processing would not represent a significant bottleneck in PLAIN programs. Instead, it was felt that most of the execution time would be spent either carrying out data base and input/output operations involving secondary storage devices, or in waiting for user input. This decision also made it possible to generalize the Pascal array declaration facility to allow dynamic array (using the same heap management) declarations, thereby overcoming a common criticism of Pascal.

5.3 Exception Handling in PLAIN

Events that occur during the execution of a program, such as arithmetic overflow, may cause an exception to be raised. Without explicitly handling these exceptions, a program may fail. The interactive user finds such failures to be extremely undesirable, since they may cause the loss of some work. Instead, it is necessary to handle such situations gracefully. PLAIN incorporates built-in exceptions and permits the programmer to define additional exceptions. All exceptions may be raised by using a signal statement, and the built-in exceptions may be raised automatically by the runtime system.

When an exception is raised, an exception handler is invoked. This handler is a PLAIN procedure, to which parameters may be passed. The handler may clear the active exception and provide for continued program execution, may clear the exception and provide for repetition of the statement that caused the exception to be raised, may notify the invoker of the module that received the exception signal, or may cause the program to fail.

The exception-handling mechanism makes it possible to trap exceptional conditions and to take actions that can prevent situations that may be harmful to the user. In short, it is possible to write extremely robust programs, capable of dealing with virtually every type of user or software error situation. This exception-handling scheme is described at greater length in [Dippe 1981].

5.4 Pattern Specification and Matching

The pattern matching facility of PLAIN permits patterns and pattern sets to be declared and used. Pattern matching operators are provided, along with pattern-directed input/output. The pattern declaration facility consists of patterns that are composed of string literals, predefined patterns, user-defined patterns, repetition codes, and pattern sets, each consisting of one or more patterns. The predefined patterns designate commonly used groupings of characters, such as alphabetic characters or digits. Each pattern (or group of patterns) may be preceded by a repetition code, which may be definite or indefinite (0 or more, 1 or more). Pattern specifications are static, similar to those of MUMPS, and unlike the dynamic pattern specifications of SNOBOL4.

The binary pattern matching operators "?=" and "?" test a string to determine if it conforms to a pattern. The keywords **match** and **contains** are available for pattern sets to determine if a string matches any pattern in a pattern set. In each case, the former operation tests for an exact match between the target string and the pattern, while the latter looks for any occurrence of the pattern in the string.

The programmer may specify any context-free grammar using the facility. Thus, in the construction of an interactive information system, all of the valid user inputs, such as command strings, may be specified in patterns, and the user input string may be compared with various patterns, with appropriate action taken depending on the success of the string pattern match. The pattern matching and string handling features of PLAIN are described more completely in [Wasserman and Booster 1981].

5.5   Interactive Systems in PLAIN

It is really the synthesis of these features, rather than any one of them alone, that makes PLAIN a powerful tool for the construction of interactive information systems. For example, relations can be used as the representation mechanism in the declaration of a module (which provides data abstraction facilities) to permit the encapsulation of a set of data base operations that might correspond to a "transaction."

As a more compelling example, consider the following scenario of IIS usage: the user issues commands that are either inquiries on a data base, or modifications to the data base, using a simple language designed specifically for this application, with appropriate diagnostic messages provided in the event of user or system errors.

In general, the main program is a loop that reads user input, branches according to the input, calling the appropriate procedures, and terminates if and when the user issues the command to quit. The legal syntax for the various commands are each specified as patterns, and the patterns are collected into a pattern set. The user input is matched against the pattern set to branch to the appropriate case, including the "illegal command" case. The procedures that are thereby invoked contain data base operations using the data management facilities in PLAIN. Any execution time errors result in the signalling of an exception, so that a handler procedure can handle the exceptional condition without causing the program to crash, instead generating an appropriate message and carrying out any necessary recovery activities.

Unless the programming language has facilities for string handling, pattern matching, exception handling, and data base management, it would be extremely difficult to write programs that conform to this extremely common scenario. This reason is why PLAIN was designed: to provide the application programmer with an appropriate tool for this important class of software systems. This is not to say that PLAIN is not well suited for other kinds of applications, but simply to observe that PLAIN is addressed to a type of application that is not well treated by other programming languages.

6.   TROLL AND THE RELATIONAL DATA BASE HANDLER

Access to a relational data base management system was needed to support the runtime needs of PLAIN. It was also decided to build a relational data base management system explicitly for use with PLAIN. Initial consideration was given to interfacing with an existing data base management system, INGRES [Stonebraker et al. 1976], but INGRES at that time was too large and too inefficient to permit effective experimentation with PLAIN. Furthermore, the needs of PLAIN were less general than those of a general purpose data base management system.

The PLAIN Data Base Handler [Kersten and Wasserman 1981] was designed to be extremely compact and highly modular so that it could serve as a research vehicle in the area of DBMS performance. The interface between the PLAIN translator and the Data Base Handler was defined and the resulting interface language, named Troll [Kersten et al. 1981], is sent by the translator to the Data Base Handler. Troll resembles a low-level query language, and is also suitable as the intermediate language for an alternative data base interface, including programs written in other languages. Before PLAIN was available, for example, Troll has been used with programs written in C and in Pascal, in the former case through the Unix pipe mechanism and in the latter case through a set of procedure and function calls.

The separation of the Data Base Handler from the PLAIN compiler appears to have been a good decision, since the size of the language processor is such that a division was necessary. Furthermore, the separation enhances the overall modularity of the PLAIN implementation, and makes it feasible to use PLAIN in a distributed environment, with the eventual possibility of implementing the Data Base Handler on a "data base machine." It also opened up the possibility of using the Data Base Handler in a variety of different ways within the USE environment, such as for prototype construction and for tool-oriented data bases.

For example, Troll is being used with the TDI to support the creation of system prototypes. Since a semantic action can be associated with any transition, one may, for example, send and/or receive a message from the Data Base Handler via Troll. Thus, one could design a relational data base, load it with sample tuples, and write semantic actions for the TDI that access and/or modify the data base. In that way, one can not only provide a prototype of the user/program interface, but can also provide some of the system function. If one used "real" data, it is conceivable that certain kinds of systems could be implemented with the prototyping tools alone.

It should be noted that there is some disadvantage to the separation of PLAIN and the Data Base Handler, primarily the overhead incurred in interpreting the Troll input within the Data Base Handler. However, we decided that the potential benefits outweighed the risks and that it would be possible to couple the two tools more closely in the future if that proved to be necessary.

7. THE MODULE CONTROL SYSTEM

The design and development of interactive information systems often requires the specification, design, and development of numerous modules, and typically results in the generation of a large amount of documentation. Furthermore, the use of a system over a period of months or years results in changes to the system, resulting in multiple versions or releases of the system. Some machine assistance is essential for managing the different pieces of text and for managing the software development activity that has produced them.

The goal of the Module Control System is to provide a means for handling the required documentation and linking together the documents related at both the system level and the module level. It is intended to be used in both a horizontal (timewise) and vertical manner. Thus, one can examine, for any given module, the specification, design, code, and test data as it existed on any given date. Alternatively, one can link together the object versions of modules as they existed on a given date to produce a linked, executable version of the system.

While PLAIN and the specification tool are intended to support the technical activities associated with the development of interactive information systems, the Module Control System is aimed more directly at the managerial and organizational issues in software creation. Information on the status of every module can be maintained online so that it is possible to monitor project progress and to identify problems. Furthermore, various members of a project team have access to the information, so that some of the traditional communication and interface problems between members of a group can be overcome.

The program developer enters the the Module Control System, and can issue various commands that control different functions, including:

1. definition of a system, to have the system establish a directory to hold information about the various modules that comprise the system, along with other administrative information

2. definition of a module, to have the system create files to store a specification, design, source code, object code, and test data for that module

3. editing of a file to create or modify some aspect of the information stored about a module; the old version will be saved and the new version will be saved as a set of changes to the old version (except for an object module, where the newest is saved and older versions must be specifically recreated). This step is similar to creating a "delta" in the Source Code Control System [Rochkind 1975].

4. definition of a version, consisting of a named set of object modules and associated date

5. linking together of a set of object modules to produce an executable load module for Unix

6. display of statistics about the system and the development effort associated with various phases of the system or with specific modules

The Module Control System may be seen as imposing discipline on the use of the various tools. When one wants to create a new system, one issues either the "build system" or "new system" command, depending on whether or not parts of the system already exist. It is possible to define "policies" that govern the use of tools or the rights of certain developers to modify certain modules. The Module Control System uses many of the Unix tools directly, as well as giving the user direct access to them through a Shell "escape" feature.

8. THE IMPLEMENTATION ENVIRONMENT FOR USE

These four tools (PLAIN, Troll, TDI, and the Module Control System) are the innovative contributions to the USE methodology. As noted earlier, though, these tools have to be integrated into a workbench environment for the application development team, and must therefore be implemented in that environment. We now describe some of the aspects of that implementation.

As noted above, the Unix time-sharing system was selected as the best environment for the developer of interactive information systems, with the idea that PLAIN, Troll, TDI, and the Module Control System would be added to that environment, thereby giving the application programmer the best possible set of tools.

Unix was selected for several reasons, including the following:

1. It was developed to run on small systems, and variants of Unix, Mini-Unix and LSX [Lycklama 1978], had been developed to run on even smaller systems.

2. Unix already possessed a good collection of tools that would assist not only the eventual application developer, but would also assist in the construction of the USE tools. Among the most useful of the Unix tools for our purposes are: a) the text editor (ex), with the vi option to provide full-screen editing; b) the nroff and troff formatting programs, for typewritten and phototypeset output respectively; c) the tbl program for producing tables, and usable with both nroff and troff; d) macro packages (me and ms) to simplify the formatting of text, and to permit the standardized formatting of various documents; e) a fully hierarchical file system, permitting distribution of the various specification, design, and code files into separate directories; f) a systems programming language (C), along with a type checking program (lint) and a source code debugger (sdb); g) a lexical analyzer generator (Lex); h) a parser generator (YACC); i) a standard I/O library that could be used to implement the

I/O operations of PLAIN; j) the "shell" which permits one or more Unix commands to be packaged (in a macro-like way) and executed as if it were a single command; k) a program (make) for combining files and preparing them for execution; l) various programs for checking writing style and spelling (style, diction, spell) in documentation and reports (including this paper); m) an excellent collection of games, including chess, bridge, and adventure, to occupy the developer during less productive interludes

3. The Unix command language (shell commands) are very easy to learn, and the user of the application programs, as well as the application programmer, would not have to learn a complicated operating system command language; indeed, most of the features of Unix could be made completely invisible to the end user.

4. Unix was in widespread use so that the USE tools could be exported to other organizations.

Initial attention was given to the implementation of PLAIN. For reasons described above, it was decided to separate the task into two parts: the translator and the data base handler (DBH). It was next decided to follow an intermediate language approach in the construction of the PLAIN interpreter. The original plan was to generate P-code, the intermediate language of the Pascal compiler, and then use existing P-code software and/or hardware for program execution. After some deliberation, though, it was decided to use EM-1 (Experimental Machine—1) [Tanenbaum 1978] [Tanenbaum et al. 1980], a machine architecture for a hypothetical stack-oriented machine that had been used as the intermediate language in the Pascal compiler developed at the Vrije Universiteit, Amsterdam, for the PDP-11 using the Unix operating system.

The EM-1 architecture assumes a monitor that provides low-level functions that correspond closely to those functions required by the runtime system of a programming language processor. The available EM-1 software included an EM-1 optimizer, an interpreter for EM-1, and an EM-1 to PDP-11 assembler translator, making it possible to either interpret or generate executable PDP-11 object code from EM-1. In short, once a PLAIN-to-EM-1 translator was built, much of the remaining lower-level and runtime procedures were already available, thereby reducing the implementation effort substantially.

The existing Unix tools played a significant role in the implementation of PLAIN. The code and documentation was entered with the text editors. Lex and YACC were used to write the lexical analyzers and parsers for both the PLAIN translator and Troll. The semantic actions of the PLAIN translator and the Data Base Handler were written in C, and the C program checker, Lint, was used to ensure that good programming practices were used in the implementation. Make was used to link together the various object files to produce an executable version of the translator.

The Module Control System has been implemented, in large part, using Unix shell scripts, so that the Module Control System can make use of a wide variety of existing Unix facilities, including the text editor, the loader, file renaming and copying commands, and language compilers. It should be noted that the Module Control System is not in any way restricted to PLAIN programs, but could serve equally well for programs written in C, for example. Indeed, the first version of the Module Control System was oriented to C programs, since C is the implementation language for the USE tools.

In summary, the existing Unix tools greatly aided the development effort. These tools, combined with PLAIN, are the programming environment for the PLAIN application developer. In this way, it can be seen that the Unix tools have been valuable throughout the USE project, and they will be of further use in system development and future tool building.

9. CONCLUSIONS AND FUTURE DIRECTIONS

The four USE tools described here are are intended to have a significant favorable impact on the development of interactive information systems. Development and use of the tools to this point has identified the utility of certain other tools for the development of interactive information systems. We have already undertaken the combination of TDI and Troll to support a sophisticated prototype development facility.

Another important goal is to use graphical tools to assist in the development process, for tasks such as illustrating software structures and transition diagrams. There already exist several powerful graphics packages in the Unix environment, and such a tool could take advantage of those facilities.

The next set of necessary tools are in the data design area. Although the PLAIN Data Base Handler collects some statistics on storage and use of various relations, including the number of disk accesses required for various operations, more sophisticated tools can help to reorganize the data base and to enhance the performance of programs using the data base facilities. Similarly, data base design aids can assist in database creation.

We have been exploring the area of personal development systems to provide proper support for these tools. If the developer can be provided with a personal machine that contains these tools, along with suitable facilities for communication with other users and systems, then it becomes much more practical to support high-bandwidth interfaces such as color graphics and audio input/output [Gutz et al. 1981]. The small size of the USE tools and the availability of Unix on several small machines makes it practical to create a "USE development machine".

In summary, USE is an attempt to build upon a well-understood set of tools by adding some new tools that can aid the developer of interactive information systems. Although we have taken some significant steps toward the creation of a software development methodology for interactive information systems, the present state of USE is only a first step toward the longer term goal of a software development environment combining a methodology with a coherent set of tools whose benefits are real and quantifiable. This longer term goal represents the future direction of the USE project.

ACKNOWLEDGMENTS

This work was supported in part by National Science Foundation grant MCS78-26287. Computing support for text preparation was provided by National Institutes of Health grant RR-1081 to the UCSF Computer Graphics Laboratory, Principal Investigator: Robert Langridge.

REFERENCES

[Bell 1978] *The Bell System Technical Journal*, 57:6 (July-August 1978), Part 2, 1971-1990.

[Burke 1978] J. Burke. *Connections*. Little, Brown, Boston, 1978.

[Caine and Gordon 1975] S.H. Caine, E.K. Gordon. PDL—a tool for software design. *Proceedings of the National Computer Conference*, AFIPS Proceedings Vol. 44 (1975), 271-276.

[Conway 1963] M.E. Conway. Design of a separable transition-diagram compiler. *Communications of the ACM*, 6 (1963), 396-408.

[Dippe 1981] M.D. Dippe. Exception-handling in PLAIN. University of California, Laboratory of Medical Information Science, Technical Report #52, San Francisco, 1981.

[Good 1978] D.I. Good et al. Report on the language Gypsy—Version 2.0 University of Texas at Austin, Certifiable Minicomputer Project, Report ICSCA-CMP-10, 1978.

[Gutz et al. 1981] S. Gutz, A.I. Wasserman, M.J. Spier. Personal development systems for the professional programmer. *Computer*, 14:4 (April 1981), 45-53.

[Ichbiah et al. 1980] J.D. Ichbiah et al. *Reference Manual for the Ada Programming Language*. Advanced Research Projects Agency, U.S. Department of Defense, Arlington, Virginia, 1980.

[Ivie 1977] E.L. Ivie. Programmers Workbench—a machine for software development. *Communications of the ACM*, 20:10 (October 1977), 746-753. *[Editors note: see also* [Dolotta et al. 1978]]·

[Johnson and Lesk 1978] S.C. Johnson, M.E. Lesk. Language development tools. *The Bell System Technical Journal*, 57:6 (July-August 1978), Part 2, 2155-2176.

[Kernighan and Mashey 1981] B.W. Kernighan, J.R. Mashey. The UNIX Programming Environment. *Computer*, 14:4 (April 1981), 12-24; reprinted in *Interactive Programming Environments*.

[Kersten and Wasserman 1981] M.L. Kersten, A.I. Wasserman. The architecture of the PLAIN data base handler. *Software—Practice and Experience*, 11 (1981), 175-186.

[Kersten et al. 1981] M.L. Kersten, A.I. Wasserman, R.P. van de Riet. Troll—a database interface and testing tool. (in preparation) 1981.

[LIS 1976] *The system implementation language LIS*. CII-Honeywell-Bull, Document 4549 EL/EN, Louveciennes, France, 1976.

[Lampson et al. 1977] B.W. Lampson, J.J. Horning, R.L. London, J.G. Mitchell, G.J. Popek. Report on the programming language EUCLID. *SIGPLAN Notices*, 12:2 (February 1977).

[Leveson and Wasserman 1981] N. Leveson, A.I. Wasserman. A methodology for information system design based on formal specifications (submitted for publication) 1981.

[Liskov et al. 1978] B. Liskov et al. *CLU Reference Manual*. Massachusetts Institute of Technology, Laboratory for Computer Science, Computation Structures Group Memo 161, July 1978.

[Lycklama 1978] H. Lycklama. UNIX on a Microprocessor. *The Bell System Technical Journal*, 57:6 (1978), 2087-2101.

[O'Neill 1977] J.T. O'Neill (ed.) *MUMPS language standard*. ANSI Standard X11.1, American National Standards Institute, 1977.

[Rochkind 1975] M.J. Rochkind. The source code control system. *IEEE Transactions on Software Engineering*, SE-1:4 (December 1975), 364-370.

[Roubine and Robinson 1978] O. Roubine, L. Robinson. *SPECIAL Reference Manual*. Technical Report CSG-45, SRI International, Menlo Park, California 1978.

[Stonebraker et al. 1976] M. Stonebraker, E. Wong, P. Kreps, G.D. Held. The design and implementation of INGRES. *ACM Transactions on Database Systems*, 1 (1976), 189-222.

[Tanenbaum 1978] A.S. Tanenbaum. Implications of structured programming for machine architecture. *Communications of the ACM*, 21 (1978), 237-246.

[Tanenbaum et al. 1980] A.S. Tanenbaum, J. W. Stevenson, H. van Staveren. *Description of an experimental machine architecture for use with block-structured languages*. Informatica Rapport IR-54, Wiskundig Seminarium, Vrije Universiteit, Amsterdam, 1980.

[Tsichritzis and Klug 1978] D. Tsichritzis, A. Klug (eds.) The ANSI/X3/SPARC DBMS Framework Report of the Study Group on Database Management Systems. *Information Systems*, 3 (1978), 173-192.

[Wasserman 1974] A.I. Wasserman. Online programming systems and languages: a history and appraisal. Laboratory of Medical Information Science, University of California, San Francisco, Technical Report #6, 1974.

[Wasserman 1979] A.I. Wasserman. The data management facilities of PLAIN. *Proceedings of the ACM SIGMOD Conference*, Boston, Massachusetts, 1979, 60-70.

[Wasserman 1980] A.I. Wasserman. The design of PLAIN—support for systematic programming. *Proceedings of the National Computer Conference*, AFIPS Proceedings Vol 49 (1980), 731-740.

[Wasserman and Booster 1981] A.I. Wasserman, T.W. Booster. *String handling and pattern matching in PLAIN*. Laboratory of Medical Information Science, University of California, San Francisco, Technical Report #50, 1981.

[Wasserman and Sherertz 1976] A.I. Wasserman, D.D. Sherertz. A balanced view of MUMPS. *Proceedings of the ACM SIGPLAN/SIGMINI Symposium on Programming Systems in the Small Processor Environment, ACM SIGPLAN Notices*, 11:4 (April 1976), 16-26.

[Wasserman and Shewmake 1981] A.I. Wasserman, D.T. Shewmake. Automating the development and evolution of user dialogue in an interactive information systems. In L. Methlie (ed.) *Evolutionary Information Systems*. North Holland, 1981.

[Wasserman et al. 1981] A.I. Wasserman et al. Revised report on the programming language PLAIN. *ACM SIGPLAN Notices*, 16:5 (1981).

[Yourdon and Constantine 1978] E. Yourdon, L.L. Constantine. *Structured Design*, Yourdon Press, New York, 1978.

19 A Layered Approach to Software Design

IRA P. GOLDSTEIN

Computer Research Center
Hewlett Packard
Palo Alto, California

DANIEL G. BOBROW

XEROX Palo Alto Research Center
Palo Alto, California

Software engineers create alternative designs for their programs, develop these designs to various degrees, compare their properties, then choose among them. Yet most software environments do not allow alternative definitions of procedures to exist simultaneously. It is our hypothesis that an explicit representation for alternative designs can substantially improve a programmer's ability to develop software. To support this hypothesis, we have implemented an experimental Personal Information Environment (PIE) that has been employed to create alternative software designs, examine their properties, then choose one as the production version. PIE is based on the use of layered networks. Software systems are described in networks; alternatives are separated by being described in different layers. We also demonstrate that this approach has additional benefits as a data structure for supporting cooperative design among team members and as a basis for integrating the development of code with its associated documentation.

Previously published as: CSL-80-5 (December 1980) by Xerox Palo Alto Research Center, 3333 Coyote Hill Road, Palo Alto, California 94304.

1. INTRODUCTION

Most computing environments use files to express alternative designs. Users record significant alternatives in files of different names; the evolution of a given alternative is recorded in files of the same name with different version numbers. In this paper, we argue that this use of files provides an inadequate structure for representing alternatives. We propose a notion of layered networks as a more suitable structure for representing an evolving design (and as an improvement over existing version control systems such as SCCS [Rochkind 1975] that represent software development in terms of changes to lines of source code). Our proposal is based on experience with an experimental system and our analysis of the deficiencies of present source code control systems.

We store software designs in networks whose nodes represent the modules, procedures and other entites of the design, and whose links represent relationships among them. Relationships are asserted relative to a layer. As an example, Figure 1 shows a block diagram of a simple software system and Figure 2 shows its network representation. All of the links in Figure 1 belong to layer A. Figure 3 shows a redesign involving changes to the definitions of procedures P1 and Q1. The new definitions are asserted in layer B whose links are shown dashed. The redesign has altered only the definitions of the procedures and not their comments, declarations or module membership. Hence, layer B contains no links regarding these attributes.

Retrieval is performed with respect to a sequence of layers termed a context: the first value found for each link is returned. The new design is returned with respect to contexts in which layer B dominates layer A. The old design is returned for contexts containing only layer A.

1.1   The Inadequacies of Files

To exemplify the inadequacies of the traditional use of files to represent an evolving software system, consider how the development of the PC system would interact with the storage of its code in a standard file system. Suppose the source code for the two modules of the initial design is stored in files P and C. If a programmer develops an alternative design that requires changes to both modules, how can he store this alternative? Typically, he would create files P' and C' containing the new definitions plus any unaltered code. The result is that shared structure is stored redundantly. If subsequent development leads to modifications to procedures common to both alternatives, then these modifications must be made in both files. The need for redundant editing becomes progressively worse as the number of alternatives grows.

How else might the programmer store his design if he wishes to avoid the need for redundant editing? One option is to place the common code into a separate file. Altering a given procedure common to more than one design would then take place in only one place. The cost of this storage strategy is

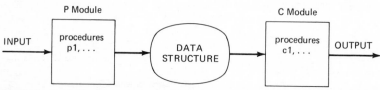

Figure 1. A Block Diagram of the PC System.

388

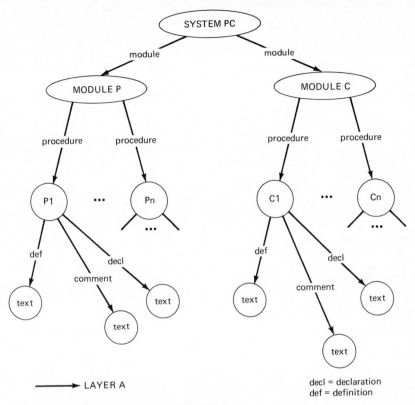

Figure 2. A network representation of the PC system.

that files would no longer serve to group related procedures of a design. Thus, to obtain design flexibility, the programmer would give up an equally important feature—modular representation.

Another option is to use conditional compilation statements in the original source code and avoid the need for multiple files and the associated redundant storage. However, the problem of examining the set of changes common to a redesign is now complicated by the distribution of these changes across many files.

A related problem is coordinating change. The programmer must maintain descriptions of how various alternative designs are distributed among files. Sometimes this is done by adopting conventions in naming files, as we have implicitly done in naming the files for our second design P' and C'. But such conventions are an impoverished means to describe a configuration and fail as the space of alternatives grows in complexity. Explicit descriptions of such configurations that do not depend on naming conventions are preferable.

Finally, there is the problem that designs represented as configurations of files are not reflected in the operational software. The result is that it is cumbersome to examine the structure and performance of a design interactively within the system. Switching from one design to another requires reading and writing the appropriate files.

Thus, the traditional use of files is unsuitable for representing alternative designs for three reasons. (1) Files are inflexible. Their utility to store modular

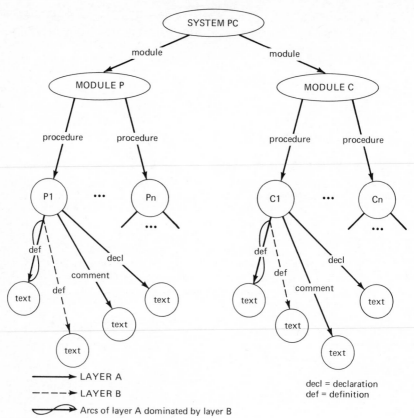

Figure 3. A layered representation of a design change.

parts of a design must be sacrificed to avoid redundant storage of shared structure. (2) File names are impoverished as a vehicle to encode the intended coordination between different files as part of a common design. (3) The representation of alternatives is not integrated into the running software environment.

1.2   Source Code Control Systems

To remedy the first two of these deficiencies, editors have been developed that store changes of source code to a base file. One such system extensively used is the Source Code Control System [Rochkind 1975] [Glasser 1978] developed as part of the Programmer's Workbench for the UNIX system [Ivie 1977]. In SCCS, changes are stored in terms of lines deleted and inserted in a file called a delta. A version of a file is computed from a base with the deltas applied in sequence. Changes do not have to be made in linear sequence; one can have branches in the chain representing alternative developments. A delta can be forced to apply to more than the version it was derived from. A delta also stores the name of the person who made the change, and the reason that it was made. The success of this system in practice—it has been used to control over 3 million lines of code by 500 programmers—makes it clear that having some mechanism for dealing with a finer granularity than files is important.

SCCS has the virtue that shared structured is not stored redundantly. A delta contains only changes. The description of a particular version of a system is specified by a delta sequence. The explanation for the differences between this version and earlier ones is stored in the comments associated with the new delta files.

1.3   Layered Networks

Layers are similar to delta files. Information is not stored redundantly and versions are described by sequences of coordinated changes. However, our approach extends SCCS in several respects:

1. We record changes relative to a network rather than a textual description of source code. The network provides a more structured description of software than text. A change to the first 10 lines in a listing has no intrinsic tie to the objects actually manipulated by the programming environment. Changing a link representing a relationship between two software objects does have such a tie. We have taken advantage of this tie to integrate the layer system into the software environment of the host language. Multiple definitions of a procedure can coexist in the environment and be edited and tested side by side. The capabilities of an experimental programming environment based on layered networks are described in Section 2.

2. We have developed a display interface for supporting a layered design environment. The Programmer's Workbench does not yet have this kind of interface for examining and manipulating code. The user interface is important since a representation for the evolution of designs is of little use if a user cannot manipulate it comfortably. Our primary technique for simplifying the presentation and manipulation of layered networks has been to use the network itself to record knowledge about defaults and constraints, so as to allow the system to assume the initiative in making certain common decisions.

3. We have developed a program librarian described in section 4 that takes advantage of the network machinery to respond to retrieval requests for particular software. Layers and contexts are themselves described in the network, allowing the search requests to include requests for particular designs.

1.4   Previous Research
in Artificial Intelligence

Various kinds of layered databases have been explored in artificial intelligence research as a mechanism for representing alternative world views. (See, for example, [Rulifson et al. 1971]; [Hewitt 1972]; [Sussman and McDermott 1972]; [Hendrix 1975]; [Cohen 1975]). Generally the need to represent alternatives has arisen in planning programs. For example, a robot is analyzing alternative paths to reach some specified location. The terms contexts and layers are drawn directly from CONNIVER [Sussman and McDermott 1972].

Our application of a layered database differs from previous AI research in several respects:

1. Previous applications have focussed on the use of such databases by mechanical problem solvers. We are exploring the use of such databases in a mixed-initiative fashion with the user primarily responsible for their creation and maintenance. This has required that special attention be paid to the user interface.

2. Previous applications have demanded a uniform overhead in space and

time for adopting the context machinery. Using the layered database was an all or nothing proposition in CONNIVER. We are exploring implementations that allow the programmer to trade flexibility for efficiency, decreasing the system's investment in tracking the evolution of particular parts of a design at the price of not being able to represent alternatives simultaneously in primary memory. Thus, employing the design environment is not an all or nothing choice for the user.

3. Previous applications have been to problems from restricted domains and of limited complexity. We have married the layer machinery to the host computing environment in such a fashion that any programming problem can be explored.

2. A DESIGN SCENARIO

PIE is an experimental Personal Information Environment that employs layered networks to manage software development for any project undertaken in its host environment, Smalltalk [Ingalls 1978] [Kay 1974]. Smalltalk is an object-oriented language that extends the notion of class and instance found in Simula [Birtwistle et al. 1973]. This section presents a design scenario that we conducted using PIE to improve Smalltalk's implementation of the abstract datatype for sets.

In choosing a scenario, we faced two difficulties. The first was whether to use an actual Smalltalk example or convert to a hypothetical exercise in a more common programming language. We chose to use Smalltalk to illustrate the actual functionality of the system. However, PIE is largely independent of its host language. It is a system for building descriptions of software and contains few commitments regarding the language's interpreter or other characteristics. Thus, the techniques employed are readily mapped to other programming language environments.

Our second difficulty was choosing how complex a scenario to present. A simple scenario would not illustrate the utility of layers to aid complex design problems, but a complex scenario would be confusing in its own right. To resolve this dilemma, we have chosen a software problem that is simple quantitatively with respect to the number of design changes made, but more complex qualitatively in terms of the different kinds of changes made to the implementation. Our redesign of the implementation for sets will include changes both to the efficiency of the implementation and to its input/output behavior. We consider combining designs, adjudicating differences, describing our design decisions in the network along with the modified software, and coordinating the whole project with associated documentation. A discussion of the application of layers to more complex design problems concludes this section.

2.1   Smalltalk's Implementation of Class Set

Abstract datatypes such as sets are implemented by classes in Smalltalk. A class defines a group of procedures, called methods in Smalltalk, and a set of variables on which they operate. Each method is invoked by a message pattern. Some of these messages are private; others are public messages that the class expects to receive from clients. Particular sets are instances of the class, i.e. each instance has some specified assignments of values to the instance variables of the class. Below is a simplified listing of class Set. Message patterns are shown in boldface and their methods appear below and indented.

The listing is incomplete: for example, the definition of the method for deleting elements from the set is not shown.

Class new title: 'Set' instanceVariables: 'array n'

''Class Set employs an array with a position pointer n to represent sets. The objects of the set are stored in the array from position 1 to n.''

Initialization Protocol

init

''This method is conventionally executed when a new instance of class Set is created. It initializes the instance variables. The array variable is set to an array of size 8 and n is set to 0.''

```
[array ← Array init: 8.
n ← 0.]
```

Public Protocol

has: element

''Testing whether an element belongs to the set is accomplished by iterating through the first n items in the array, checking for equality.''

```
[for: i from: 1 to: n do:
    [if: element = (array lookup: i) then: [return: true]].
return: false]
```

insert: element

''A new element is added to the set if it is not already present.''

```
[if: (self has: element) then: [return: false] else: [self add:
element]]
```

Private Protocol

add: element

''A new element is added by loading it into position n+1 of the array and incrementing the pointer. The array is copied into a larger array if its free position are exhausted.''

```
[if: n=(array length) then: [array ← array growby: 10].
array insert: (n←n+1) with: element.]
```

Printing Protocol

print

''This method prints a set by printing the string 'a set'.''

```
['a set' print.]
```

2.2   A Layered Redesign of Class Set

The first design goal we consider is to improve retrieval time by having the implementation convert from a sequential to a hashtable representation when the cardinality of the set exceeds some bound. The rationale for this redesign is that sequential access is less expensive in storage space and retrieval time when the set is small, but is not economic when the set is large.

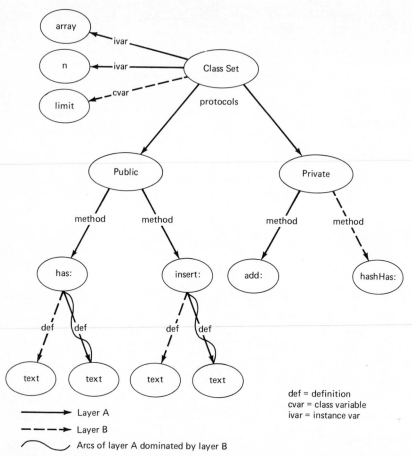

Figure 4. A partial view of a layered network representation for class Set. Layer A describes the original design, Layer B contains modifications. The Hashing Context contains both these layers with layer B dominating layer A.

We begin by generating in PIE a description of the current implementation. PIE is able to generate a network describing any class in Smalltalk from the internal Smalltalk representation for the class. This network is stored as a collection of instances of class Node, a class we created to implement the behavior of a network database. The network generated from the initial implementation is stored in a new layer—say layer A. The layer is placed in a new context which we shall name the hashing context.

The next step in the design process is to define the changes to the present implementation. A layer is created and added to the context to store these changes. This is layer B in Figure 4. Competing assertions in this layer will dominate those in layer A. Competing assertions are shown by links originating from the same point on the circumference of the circle representing the node. Links of layer B that only augment properties asserted in layer A such as the addition of another state variable (e.g. limit) are shown by links with the same label but these links do not originate from a common point on the circumference of the circle representing the node.

Below is part of the PIE-generated listing of the redesigned class with respect to the hashing context. Only parts of the public and private protocols are shown and comments have been removed. PIE has been instructed to highlight new assertions, derived from layer B, by printing them in boldface. The listing shows a new type of variable in the class definition. limit is a class variable. The value of a class variable is available to all instances. limit is used to specify the size at which the internal representation switches from sequential to hashed.

```
Class new title: 'Set' instanceVariables: 'array n' classVariables:
       'limit'
```

Public Protocol

```
     has: element

     [if: n<limit
      then: [for: i from: 1 to: n do:
             [if: element = (array lookup: i) then: [return: true]].
             return: false]
      else: [return: (self hashHas: element)].

     insert: element

     [if: (self has: element) then: [return: false].
      if: n=limit then: [self convertFromSequentialToHash].
      if: n<limit then: [self add: element]
          else: [self hashAdd: element].]
```

Private Protocol

```
     add: element

     [if: n=(array length) then: [array ← array growby: 10].
      array insert: (n ← n+1) with: element.]
```

   hashAdd: element
     . . .
   hashHas: element
     . . .

The user can test his design by installing the hashing context. Installation causes the Smalltalk interpreter to employ the definitions asserted in the specified context. Design changes are not immediately installed. This prevents premature modification of the underpinnings of the system before a design is complete. Hence, PIE maintains a distinction between the description context which is edited, and the execution context.

If further debugging is needed following installation, the programmer can create a new layer to store the changes to his design, then reinstall the context with this layer dominating the old layers. By placing the edits of each debugging session in a separate layer, the programmer can undo a set of changes that have proved unsatisfactory by removing the layer from the context and reinstalling.

Design exercises rarely consist of a single iteration through the design/ debugging loop. In conducting this design exercise, a number of additional layers were added to the hashing context. For example, layer C was added to correct the inconsistent treatment of the limit value. *has: element* treats limit as the lower bound of the hash representation while *insert: element* treats limit as the upper bound of the sequential representation. Layer C debugged the *has: element* procedure to use a < test for comparing the size of the set and the limit value.

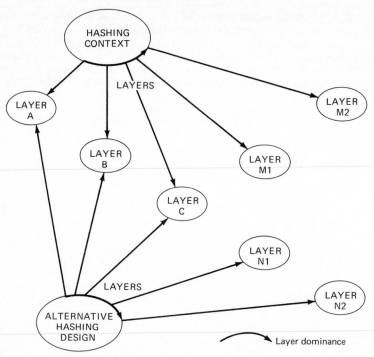

Figure 5. Alternative designs for hashing. The dominance arrow points from least to most dominant layer.

Layers facilitate the comparison of alternatives.[1] For example, we considered different implementations of hashing in the redesign of class Set. Such analyses produced a network of layers as illustrated in Figure 5. The m and n layer sequences represent alternative designs.

2.3   Redesigning The I/O Behavior of Sets

To illustrate the ability of layers to manage interacting designs, we continue our scenario by pursuing a second design goal. This goal is to improve the I/O behavior of sets. Specifically, the goal is for an instance of class Set to print showing its elements enclosed in braces, e.g. as {A,B}, if the size of the set is less than some bound. Presently all instances of class set simply print as 'a set'. This redesign requires that we modify the printing method of class Set.

Before we make this change, we must decide where to store it. Since this is

---

[1] Easy switching facilitated our obtaining comparative performance measures for the original linear design and our mixed linear and hashing design for implementing sets. The parameters which determine performance of a set implementation are: the number of elements in a set; the ratio of membership tests to insertion and deletion; and the proportion of such tests which return false. With two tests for every insertion, and 33% returns of false, the choice of 7 for limit allowed the mixed design to dominate; with five tests for every insertion, limit should be 4 to provide overall better performance for the mixed design.

an independent modification of the code, our philosophy requires that we store these changes in a new layer, D. To make it easier to test and adopt the printing changes independently of the hashing changes, we create a new context, to be called the printing context, for these changes.

This context begins from the initial design of class Set and, therefore, its first layer should be the same as the first layer of the hashing context. If we examine or install this context, we get an implementation of class Set that only has the improved printing behavior. Layer D is added to the printing context to store the changes involved in this redesign. Below is the new method for printing sets stored in layer D.

print

```
[if: (self size)≤4
then: ['{' print.
         for: i from: 1 to: (self size)
             do: [(self element: i) print].
             '}' print.]
else: ['a set' print.] ]
```

This redesign becomes more interesting if we decide to include a modification to the Smalltalk reader that allows the string printed to be reread as a set. To accomplish this, we must modify the reader to recognize braces. We could put the required changes in layer D. Changes recorded in a layer can span module boundaries. But since the reader changes are independent of the altered printing behavior, it is better practice to put this set of modifications in a separate layer, say layer E. We can therefore test the two parts of the design separately, i.e. we can first install layer D to examine the printing behavior, then install layer E to examine the reader.

Layer E could be placed in an entirely separate context, but since we presumably want to adopt both the changes to the reader and to the printing procedure, it makes sense to include this layer in the set printing context. However, since the alterations are modularly stored in a layer, we leave open the option of creating a separate context to store changes to the reader that includes layer E.

The printing context now contains layers that make a coordinated set of changes to more than one module of the system: in this case, both the reader and a particular abstract datatype. This is not an unusual situation—despite a modular design, some modifications inevitably cross module boundaries, since the modularity is based on a particular partitioning of the design space, and such partitionings are not unique.

2.4 Representing Contexts

Layers and contexts are described by PIE in the same network as software is described. Figure 6 shows part of the network representing the hashing and printing contexts. The rationale attribute links a layer or context to a textual description of its purpose and the focus attribute points to the major classes being modified by the design. The layers attribute of a context node points to a sequence of nodes representing the layers.

Describing layers and contexts in the network has two important advantages. First, the user can search for a layer or context using the general network matching machinery provided by PIE. A search is initiated by specifying a description of some node in terms of constraints on the values of its

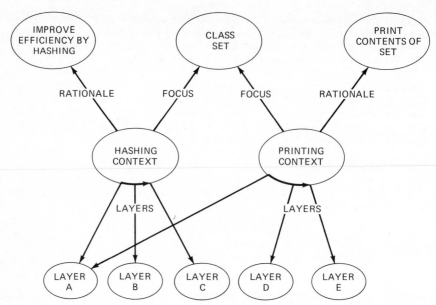

Figure 6. A partial view of the network description of layer and context nodes.

attributes. Thus, a user can search for a node representing a context whose focus is class Set and whose rationale includes the subString *hashing*. The network description escapes the limitation of file systems in which the name of a file is burdened with the description of the file. Second, the user can manipulate layers and contexts using the same network operations used to manipulate code—i.e. the addition, deletion or modification of the attributes of nodes.

2.5   Composite Contexts

After we have debugged our two redesigns of class Set, we will want to combine them. We can do this by creating a composite context built from the layers of the existing contexts. This is the SetRedesign context shown in Figure 7. We have not simply concatenated the layers of the hashing and printing contexts. This would produce the sequence: A, B, C, A, D, E. The second occurrence of layer A would inadvertently dominate the changes in layers B and C.

We may wish to impose the constraint that if new layers are added to the hashing or printing contexts, then they are automatically included in the composite context. This can be accomplished by a capability that PIE provides for defining procedures that are attached to nodes. These procedures are triggered by adding or deleting attributes of the node. By defining such a procedure and attaching it to the layers attribute of the hashing and printing contexts, we can have it synchronize these contexts with the composite context.

Concatenating new layers of the printing context to the hashing context is justified by the independence of the printing and hashing refinements. This is therefore a useful comment to include in the network. Figure 7 illustrates various design comments. Layers B and D are commented as independent refinements, layers D and E as dependent refinements and layer C as a repair for layer B. When layers are combined into new contexts, these comments are checked and the user is alerted to questionable combinations such as adding a layer without its subsequent repairs. This description also allows other programmers to examine the network of contexts and layers and understand their relationships.

Interactions between design decisions can lead to conflicting values in two layers. In SCCS, conflicts are noticed only to the extent that two modifications touch the same line of code. In PIE, the granularity of detected overlap is at the level of the method; if two layers have changed the same method, then there is a potential conflict. In addition, we have in PIE a mechanism for explicitly expressing dependencies among a number of methods. This allows us to find some potential interactions when there is no structural overlap.

To resolve conflicts between layers, a new layer could be added to the composite context that resolved any differences in design decisions. This layer would only apply to the composite design and not to the individual designs since it would not be included in their contexts.

Finally, we could have created a composite context. The concatenated context in Figure 7 is such a context. PIE treats the layer sequence of such a context as the concatenation of the layer sequences of its subcontexts. This

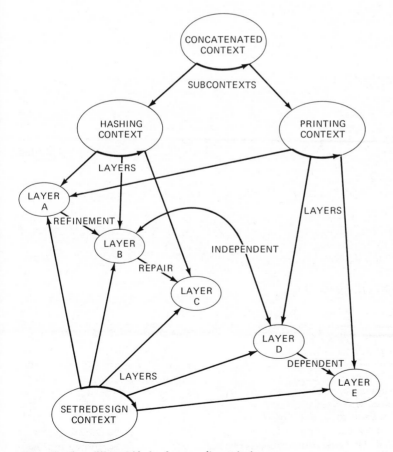

Figure 7. Two different kinds of composite contexts.

combination strategy is appropriate when the constituent contexts are independent. But here, the common use of layer A makes it inappropriate.

2.6 Communicating Contexts

We have discussed this design project so far from the standpoint of an individual programmer. But many projects are collaborative. Layers facilitate cooperative design by supporting on-line interaction that is analogous to two programmers scribbling on a common listing. One programmer can transmit to another programmer a set of changes to the first programmer's design by sending a layer. PIE supplies comparison functions for identifying the changes between layers. Below is a PIE-generated listing of class Set with respect to the redesign context plus a layer transmitted by a collaborator. The collaborator's layer redefines the has: element procedure and includes an annotation stating the rationale for the change.

Class new title: 'Set' instanceVariables: 'array n' classVariables: 'limit'

Public Functions

```
has: element

[if: (self size)<limit
 then: [return: (self seqHas: element)]
 else: [return: (self hashHas: element)].
```

Annotation from Danny received 4/1/80, 3:15pm: I think that a more subroutinized definition will pay off in the long run.

The advantages of this level of intimacy in communication would not ordinarily be sufficient to offset the disadvantages that might arise from an unwanted intrusion by the sender into the recipient's workspace. A programmer might be justifiably reluctant to load a file from a collaborator directly into his workspace. Despite the appeal of being able to examine the new software with design tools in the software environment, the software may contain modifications that overlap and interfere with software developed by the programmer.

Layers avoid this problem. The sender's modifications are contained in a separate layer. Hence, they can be loaded without destroying changes stored in separate layers. The user can install then, examine their performance, then undo them if desired simply by deleting the layer from his context.

2.7 Combining Contexts

Following the receipt of contributions from a collaborator, the need arises to select some of these proposals and combine them with the programmer's existing design. A design environment should make it easy to examine overlapping designs and to select pieces for combination into a joint design. A layered environment facilitates this since coordinated sets of change have been localized into layers. One needs a user interface for comparing layers.

PIE provides several interfaces for comparing layers and contexts. We have already seen the ability of the system to generate listings that highlight contributions from different layers using fonts and faces. A comparison of the differences between the two layers is accomplished using the interface shown in Figure 8. This interface presents the user with a display screen divided into three regions called windows. The upper window shows the (node, attribute)

```
Comparing SetRedesign context with DannysLayer

~Differences~
  Set vars
  has: annotation
  has:  definition
  hashHas: element

~SetRedesignContext~
  has: element
    [If: (self size) < limit
      then: [for: i from: 1 to: n do:
                      [if: (element = array lookup: i) then: [return: true] ]
                return: false]
      else: [return: (self hashHas: element)] ] ]

~DannysLayer~
  has: element
    [if: (self seqMode)
      then: [return (self seqHas: element)]
        else: [return: (self hashHas: element)] ] ]
```

Figure 8.   The Set redesign context is being compared with a collaborator's suggestions. The user has selected the definition attribute of the has: method in the upper pane. The alternative values appear in the lower two panes.

pairs on which two contexts or layers differ. The user can select a pair from this list. The interface then shows the differing values in the two contexts in the middle and lower display windows.

The interface creates a new layer, entitled the merge layer, in which the programmer can selectively copy those (node,attribute,value) triples that he wishes to include in his own context. If the merge layer is then added to his context, it will dominate his old layers and supply the new information.

Figure 8 shows the user comparing his redesign of class Set (stored in the hashing context) with improvements suggested by his collaborator. The user is presently examining the definition of the *has: element* procedure. His collaborator has suggested a more modular definition. The user is about to add this definition to the merge layer, thereby adopting his collaborator's suggestion. A consequence of this is that the user must also assert in the merge layer definitions of the required subroutines: *seqHas: element* and *hashHas: element*.

Understanding such dependencies is facilitated by examining commentary supplied by the designers regarding the rationale of their choices. But this requires that commentary be coordinated with design. Fortunately no additional machinery is required in PIE to address this problem. Commentary such as the rationale of a procedure or its dependencies on other procedures can be stored in the same layer as the one which records the change, thus keeping them coordinated.

For complex designs, the merge process is non-trivial. PIE does not eliminate this complexity. What it does provide is a more finely grained descriptive structure than files in which to manipulate the pieces of the design. It highlights differences explicitly, and provides a place to document dependencies, and the rationale for changes.

2.8   Integrating Software and Documentation

Program comments are ordinarily second class citizens. While the programs may have elaborate structure, the comments are only strings. A uniform net-

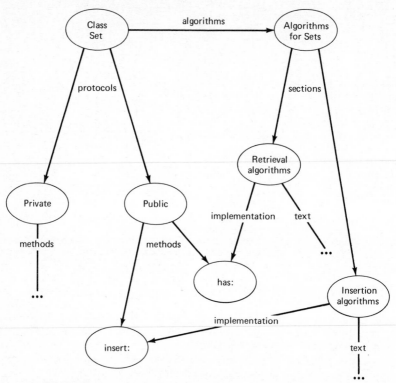

Figure 9. A partial view of a network in which nodes representing code and documentation are interlinked.

work representation facilitates the integration of structured comments with the corresponding software. A node representing a class can point to the node documenting its behavior. Nodes representing procedures of the class can point directly to nodes representing the appropriate parts of the documentation. Comments that apply to more than one part of a software system can point to multiple nodes. The PIE-user interface described in the next section supports the integrated development and perusal of such network structures.

Figure 9 shows a partial view of the network documenting class Set, developed at the same time as the software. The description of the algorithms employed is linked to the procedures implementing these algorithms. A user can enter the network from any node and traverse it as his interests dictate. Hardcopy is generated using user-specified filters on how much of the network to print and on the ordering. Thus, a listing of the source code need not contain the entire discussion of the underlying algorithms—a programmer can choose how much detail to see.

An additional advantage of representing documentation in the network is that layers can be used to represent alternative drafts and coordinate joint authorship. Layers are, after all, a general means to organize an evolving design. An author can explore alternative organizations with layers that modify section links. Revisions of paragraphs can be stored by means of alternate text links. Comments regarding the rationale for a change can be recorded with annotation links and stored in the same layers as the change. Filtered views of the network can highlight or suppress such annotations.

Coauthorship can be facilitated by adopting the convention that a coauthor place his revisions in separate layers. Additional advantages can be obtained if the authors use separate layers for recording different kinds of change: for example, separating spelling corrections or minor style improvements from major revisions or suggestions for altering the content of the document. This separation allows an author to accept without further examination layers from a coauthor containing minor revisions, thereby freeing time to concentrate attention on other layers. The purpose of the layer can, of course, be recorded in the network for examination both by other authors and by various formatting and comparison tools.

Across a period of time, we have built up such conventions regarding the purpose of layers, and have found them crucial for organizing the coauthorship process. We have also found that these conventions apply equally well to software: a layer can be correcting the grammar or style of a module, making minor revisions in its parts, or proposing a major structural change.

2.9   Complex Designs

Massive redesigns can involve changes to hundreds of procedures distributed over dozens of modules. We believe that the machinery described here for layers and contexts provides capabilities that are suitable for such complex real-world software problems based on our analysis of the deficiencies of present source control systems.

As with systems like SCCS and unlike systems that store the entire source code for a package in a single file, we store a set of changes modularly with very little redundant information. This allows forks in designs to be explored and facilitates the creation of specialized configurations from selected subsets of the layers.

Unlike SCCS, we represent software and design configurations in a network that has important structural advantages over textual descriptions. First, the network supports a representation in which there is a natural locus for all of the properties of a given object including both source and compiled code—such properties would typically have to be distributed across a textual listing or even across different files. A designer can readily examine all of the properties of some object by interrogating the network. Second, a network allows us to move two ways across a link. Thus we can move from the nodes describing variables to their classes or vice versa. A designer can therefore traverse the network to explore some the consequences of a redesign. Third, the formalized descriptions of a network support search and matching operations to find desired objects of a design, including layers and contexts themselves. Fourth, the network facilitates the formation of various kinds of composite designs. Hierarchical file directories provide some aid of this kind for file-based source code systems, but are less powerful than the network architecture of PIE. Finally, the network strictly dominates text since a node can have a source code attribute that points at text describing the software.

3.   THE USER INTERFACE

PIE's ability to represent alternative designs comes at the price of a more complex, context-sensitive representation. For this price to be affordable, the user interface must simplify the presentation and manipulation of the database. In this section, we discuss a user interface that has proved successful for expert users, and several alternative interfaces that may be more appropriate for novices. We also discuss the use of additional description provided in the network to specify reasonable default behavior for the interface.

Smalltalk Code Browser			
~CATEGORIES~	~CLASSES~	~PROTOCOLS~	~METHODS~
Kernel Classes	Array	Initialization	delete: element
Data Structures	Dictionary	**Private**	**has: element**
Numbers	**Set**	Public	insert: element
Windows	Vector		
. . .	. . .	~PROTOCOLS~	~METHODS~

has: element
　　　"use sequential access to determine if element is in the set"
　　[for: i from: 1 to: n do:
　　　　[if: (element = (array lookup: i)) then: [return: true]]
　　　return: false]

Figure 10. The Smalltalk Code Browser.

3.1　The Smalltalk Browser

The PIE interface is modelled on the standard Smalltalk interface for examining and altering code. The Smalltalk interface is shown in Figure 10 and is called a browser. It is a display window built from six subwindows called panes. The top pane is the title pane. Below it is a row of four panes that display, from left to right, categories of classes, classes, protocols and methods. The lower pane displays text associated with the most recently selected item. The browser as shown is in a state arrived at by the following process. (1) The user selected the category Data Structures in the upper left pane. (Selected items are shown in boldface.) This selection caused the classes of this category to be displayed in the pane to the right labelled classes. (2) The user then selected the class Set. This caused the protocols of this class to be displayed in the pane labelled protocols. (3) The user then selected the protocol Public, causing the methods of this protocol to be displayed in the pane labelled methods. (4) Finally, the user selected the method has: element causing its definition to appear in the lower pane. The user can now edit this definition using commands associated with the lower pane. Thus the browser allows the user to examine and change any method in the Smalltalk system. It has found wide acceptance in the Smalltalk community.

3.2　The PIE Browser

PIE organizes the representation of Smalltalk code into a network, rather than a hierarchy. The network includes nodes that represent categories, classes, protocols and methods with links describing their hierarchical organization. However, the network includes non-hierarchical relationships. A node representing a method might be linked to more than one protocol in more than one class. Nodes representing code can point to nodes representing documentation and vice versa. Nodes representing methods can point to nodes that describe dependencies between the method definitions.

Figure 11 shows the generalization of the standard Smalltalk browser that we have implemented to examine this network. Moving from one level of structure to the next is a two step process. The first step is to select a node. This causes the names of its attributes to be displayed in the pane immediately below. The lower pane is labelled with the type of the node. The second step is to select an attribute. The value of this attribute is then displayed in the upper pane to the right. The pane in which it is displayed is labelled with the

ORIGIN: Code; Contexts: SetRedesign			
~CATEGORIES~	~CLASSES~	~PROTOCOLS~	~METHODS~
Kernel Classes	Array	Initialization	delete: method
Data Structures	Dictionary	Private	**has: element**
Numbers	**Set**	**Public**	insert: element
. . .	. . .	~PROTOCOLS~	~METHODS~
~ACATEGORY~	~ACLASS~	~APROTOCOL~	~AMETHOD~
classes	**protocols**	**methods**	**definition**
comment	comment	comment	comment
documentation	variables	variables	variables
. . .	. . .	. . .	. . .

~definition of has: node~
has: element
    "Use sequential access   to vector if size < limit,   else use hashing"
[If: (self size) < limit
   then: [for: i from: to to: n do:
               [If: element = (array lookup: i) then: [return: true]]
         return: false]
   else: [return: (self hashHas: element)]]]

Figure 11. The PIE Browser viewing nodes from the SetRedesign context.

attribute name. For example, when the user selects the node representing the Data Structure category, the names of the attributes of this node are shown below in the pane labelled ACategory. These attributes include the category's classes and documentation. The user must then select one of these attributes to see the next level of node structure. In Figure 11, the user selected the classes attribute. This caused the nodes representing the classes of the category to be displayed in the upper pane to the right under the label classes. The user then selected a path through the network that allowed him to reach the *has: element* node.

The definition of the has: element method shown in Figure 11 differs from that shown in Figure 10 since the PIE browser is viewing the network with respect to the SetRedesign context while the Smalltalk Browser was viewing the original Smalltalk specification for class Set. The context being employed for viewing the network is shown at the top of the browse window.

Multiple PIE browsers can be placed on the display screen simultaneously to view designs from different contexts. For example, a second browser could be created and associated with the original SystemCode context. This would allow the user to compare the two designs.

3.3 Alternative Interfaces

We are experimenting with alternative interfaces that display the network in different ways. The goal is to minimize the difficulties new users encounter in mastering the network architecture. We are exploring browsers that display the network as a graph similar to that shown in Figures 3 and 4, as an outline, and as a nested set of boxes. Figure 12 shows these last two views of the new Set design. The outline browser employs a two dimensional layout editor developed by Bob Flegal and Diana Merry of the Xerox PARC Learning Research Group. The box browser is a descendant of a summer project done at Xerox PARC by Bill Finzer of San Francisco State University. We have not yet had sufficient experience with different users to know which interface is the most congenial for unravelling the complexity of context-dependent network de-

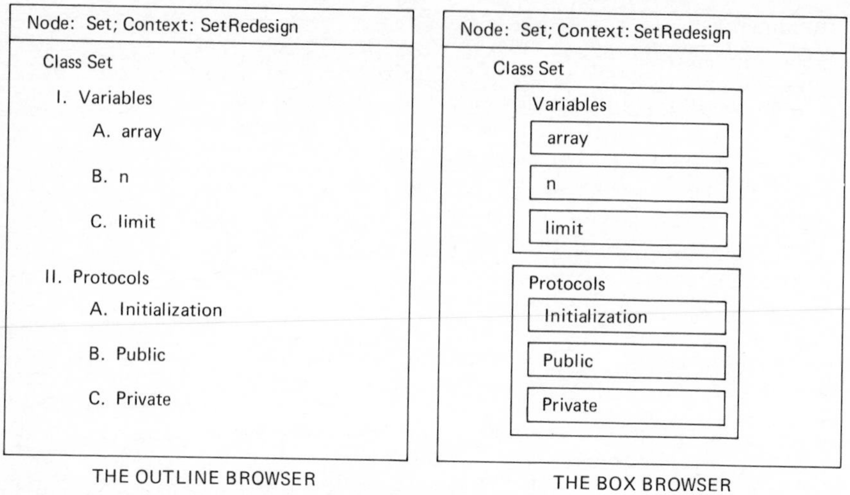

```
┌─────────────────────────────────────┐
│ Node:  Set; Context: SetRedesign    │
│                                      │
│   Class Set                          │
│                                      │
│     I. Variables                     │
│                                      │
│         A. array                     │
│                                      │
│         B. n                         │
│                                      │
│         C. limit                     │
│                                      │
│    II. Protocols                     │
│         A. Initialization            │
│                                      │
│         B. Public                    │
│                                      │
│         C. Private                   │
│                                      │
│                                      │
└─────────────────────────────────────┘
         THE OUTLINE BROWSER
```

```
┌───────────────────────────────────────┐
│ Node:  Set; Context: SetRedesign       │
│                                        │
│   Class Set                            │
│   ┌─────────────────────────────────┐ │
│   │ Variables                       │ │
│   │  ┌──────────────────────────┐   │ │
│   │  │ array                    │   │ │
│   │  └──────────────────────────┘   │ │
│   │  ┌──────────────────────────┐   │ │
│   │  │ n                        │   │ │
│   │  └──────────────────────────┘   │ │
│   │  ┌──────────────────────────┐   │ │
│   │  │ limit                    │   │ │
│   │  └──────────────────────────┘   │ │
│   └─────────────────────────────────┘ │
│   ┌─────────────────────────────────┐ │
│   │ Protocols                       │ │
│   │  ┌──────────────────────────┐   │ │
│   │  │ Initialization           │   │ │
│   │  └──────────────────────────┘   │ │
│   │  ┌──────────────────────────┐   │ │
│   │  │ Public                   │   │ │
│   │  └──────────────────────────┘   │ │
│   │  ┌──────────────────────────┐   │ │
│   │  │ Private                  │   │ │
│   │  └──────────────────────────┘   │ │
│   └─────────────────────────────────┘ │
└───────────────────────────────────────┘
            THE BOX BROWSER
```

Figure 12. Alternative browsers for examining the network. Any item appearing in either browser can be expanded to reveal its substructure.

signs. Perhaps more than one is appropriate, depending on the user's purpose—e.g. obtaining an overview, examining a part of the design in detail, making a coordinated set of changes. Our present plan is to develop a variety of interfaces and analyze their acceptance by various users.

3.4   Self-Description

One problem common to all of these browsers is that the number of choices needed to move from one node to the next is larger than that required by the simpler hierarchy of the original Smalltalk. When a code object is selected in Smalltalk, there is no ambiguity regarding the subordinate objects to be displayed. This is reflected in the fact that the labels of the browser panes are fixed. When a PIE node is selected, however, there is a potential ambiguity regarding which subordinate nodes to be displayed: the selected node may have more than one attribute that points to other nodes. The user must specify the desired attribute. Furthermore, the appropriate context must be chosen for viewing the value of the attribute. Thus, the richer data structure of PIE comes at the price of investing more effort to traverse the information space.

We minimize the effort required by the user by supplying default specifications of expected decisions. These defaults are supplied by means of additional description associated with the node being examined. For example, this description includes a specification of the default attribute and context. As a result, the browser can make an informed guess regarding the desired information to be displayed. By an appropriate choice of defaults, the PIE browser can mimic the behavior of the standard Smalltalk browser. The default attribute of a category is its classes, of a class its protocols, etc. The default context is generally specified in the self-description associated with the class node, since designs generally span entire classes. The user can override defaults by explicit selection. Therefore, the user expends additional effort only when traversing non-standard paths.

We have found that this knowledge-based behavior of the browser is critical to reducing the overhead in employing the system. Selecting the appropriate context and attribute is tedious. Forgetting to select the appropriate context is disastrous. Controlling the interface with meta knowledge stored in the network both improves efficiency and reliability.

4. REMOTE STORAGE

We have not yet discussed how contexts and layers are stored remotely for backup purposes and to provide access by other programmers. In an early implementation, layers and contexts were stored as files in the following way: The layer file contained assertions regarding the contents of the layer, i.e. the (node, attribute, value) triples and was named by a unique identifier associated with the layer. The context file contained the names (identifiers) of layers owned by the context. Thus, loading a design was a multi-step process: the user first examined a file directory for the context with the desired name, retrieved its list of layer identifiers, then loaded these layers from a second file directory.

There are several subtleties and some deficiencies in this scheme. First, how does the loading process identify that an assertion in the filed layer is referring to an existing node? The filed layer does not know the local address of the node and node titles are not unique. Second, how do we deal with changes to layers, since we do not allow multiple versions of a layer? Third, how can we avoid reducing retrieval of filed contexts to examining a list of file names? This seems to return us to the limitations of file names that layers and contexts were intended to eliminate. This section discusses each of these points in turn.

4.1 Identifying Existing Nodes
During The Loading Process

Our method for identifying existing nodes is to assign each node a unique identifier when it is first created. This identifier is unique across all users. It is generated from the time of creation and the serial number of the creating machine, and defines a community wide address space. When a layer is written onto remote storage, relations between nodes are described by the name of the relation and the identifiers of the participating nodes. When the layer is loaded into a new environment, these identifiers are checked against a dictionary of identifiers and existing nodes in the environment. If present, the identifier is replaced by a pointer to the existing node. If not, a new node is created and assigned this identifier. Thus, different PIE systems have their own copies of a node while a particular PIE system has at most only one copy of a node, regardless of the number of layers in which it is referenced.

Unique identifiers are a satisfactory basis for communication when one team member creates a set of nodes, then transmits his layers to another team member for subsequent development. The unique identifiers are included in this transmission. When the second team member returns his contribution, information can be attached to nodes created in the original space.

Unique identifiers provide no help when one team member wishes to attach some information to a node in the workspace of another team member whose unique identifier is not known. He may only know a description of the node, for example, that it represents the "retrieval function for the set module." This problem is treated by allowing the sender to transmit a search request to the recipient. The search request, if successful, returns the identifier of the desired node. Naturally the search will be unsuccessful if the sender formulates his request in terms not understood by the recipient's environment. However, this is generally mitigated by the common vocabularies that team members develop.

Unique identifiers do not deal with the problem of two team members independently creating separate nodes to describe the same object. To cope with this problem, PIE contains functions for comparing the descriptions of nodes. Based on these comparisons, the user must decide if an unintentional coreference has occurred and take appropriate action, such as using one of the nodes as the preferred one and deleting the other.

4.2 Layer Immutability

We avoid multiple versions of a layer by adopting the convention that layers are immutable once they have been stored remotely and made available for public use. Change is limited to adding new layers and updating the context file. Thus, to obtain the latest release, a user reexamines the context file and loads any new layers. To make private modifications to a software design, a new layer is added to the context in which the changes are made, rather than altering the retrieved layers.

There are several advantages to immutability. First, it allows a user to judge if his release is current by comparing the layer identifiers retrieved from the context file with the identifiers of the layers that have been loaded. It is not necessary to load fresh versions of those layers, since they do not change. Second, the immutability convention allows a PIE system to treat local memory as a cache. The local memory stores those layers currently being used. Trying to use a non-local layer causes a fault that initiates a load of that layer from the remote store. If space is unavailable, an existing layer is erased from local memory. The layer need not be rewritten on the remote store if it has been previously filed, since it cannot change.

Immutable layers work well for cooperative design in which updates are not required immediately. They are not appropriate for real time interactions as they do not solve traditional problems of deadlock and resource sharing. Design problems being attacked by a team, however, do not require this level of intimacy. Indeed, designers benefit from being able to examine proposed changes without having them be immediately inserted into their workspace.

4.3 Retrieving Public Contexts

We improved upon our early use of a file directory to store public contexts by providing a PIE system as a public context directory. We have previously discussed how PIE improves upon file directories for a user's local contexts. These contexts are stored in the network and a user can retrieve a context using PIE's search machinery. The network description avoids the limitations of file names. Hence, it was a natural choice to use PIE itself as a public directory.

To store or update a public context, a programmer transmits to the public PIE system a network description of the context. This network fragment contains the name of the context, the identifiers of its layers, and any attribute/value properties such as its rationale and focus that the creator chooses to make public.

The public PIE system can now service requests for a particular software package that range from the name of the context to a network description of its properties. Furthermore, if an ambiguity arises or if the user simply wishes to examine the available software, the public PIE system can support browsing through its network of contexts just as a private PIE system does.

An advantage of a PIE system serving as a public directory is that it can respond differently to different kinds of users. Some users may be designers who want the complete history of a design while other users may only want the completed system. For the former, PIE can deliver the layer identifiers. The programmer can then read these layers into his workspace, and compare their contents with the contents of his own layers. For the latter, PIE can deliver the Smalltalk source code using its standard installation machinery for converting a layered design into running software. In this case, the user need have only a kernel Smalltalk. No PIE machinery is necessary. Thus, the cost of a machine powerful enough to support flexible design need only be borne by those engaged in design. For other members of the environment, a kernel system is sufficient.

The machinery to employ PIE as public context directory is implemented, but we have not tested it on a large user community. We have successfully employed PIE in this way on an experimental basis for collaborative software projects undertaken by the authors.

5.   IMPLEMENTATION

In this section, we discuss the Smalltalk class structure of the PIE system, its performance, and two implementations of layers.

5.1   Class Structure

PIE's classes are grouped into three categories: display, database and semantics. The display category implements the browser shown in Figure 11. In implementing the browser, we took advantage of previously existing Smalltalk classes which provided most of the desired behavior. The PIE browser is built from four classes. The four panes in the top row that display lists of nodes have identical behavior and are instances of one class, the four panes in the middle row that display attributes are instances of a second, and the bottom pane employed for text editing is an instance of a third. A fourth class coordinates the behavior of the individual panes. These four classes are subclasses of existing display classes in Smalltalk and they inherit much of their behavior from their superclasses. Where there are differences, the PIE subclasses have methods that override the behavior of their superclasses. Thus, Smalltalk's hierarchical class structure made it straightforward to define a powerful, individualized display interface.

Multiple browsers can coexist on the screen. Each browser is a different set of instances of the display classes. This allows separate browsers to examine different regions of the network from different contexts. At any time, the user can create a browser whose initial view is centered on the current selection.

The database category contains classes that implement the basic network machinery. Instances of class Node are used for nodes in the network. Each node has a unique identifier, an optional pointer to a meta-node on which default information is stored, and a set of attributes pointing in a context-sensitive fashion to other nodes. Two mechanisms for implementing context-sensitive retrieval are described in Section 5.3.

The semantics category contains classes termed perspectives that are assigned to a node in order to assert that the node represents a particular kind of entity, such as a Smalltalk class or a text document. Perspectives are a type mechanism. Assigning an instance of some perspective class to a node supplies methods that implement the behavior for the type of object that the node represents. For example, perspectives representing Smalltalk code have methods for compiling themselves. The nodes for class Set, its protocols, and its methods all had the appropriate code perspectives assigned. Perspectives representing documents have methods for printing themselves in different formats. The PIE manual has such a perspective, and, hence, can be printed in various filtered formats—with or without footnotes, with or without annotations, with or without paragraph summaries.

It is possible for a node to be assigned more than one perspective when it is sensible to view the entity represented by the node from more than one point of view. One example of this occurs for nodes that represent documents. In addition to the document perspective, they may be assigned a bibliographic perspective. This second perspective supplies the appropriate formatting behavior when the node appears as part of a bibliography.

There is presently a library of 15 perspective classes available for users of PIE including perspectives for describing classes, protocols, methods, documents, user profiles, layers and contexts. However, this category is open-ended and intended to be expanded by the user.

5.2 Performance

PIE runs with excellent response time on a Dorado, a high speed micro-programmable personal computer that runs Smalltalk at approximately one million instructions/second [Lampson and Pier 1980]. The response time is perceived in terms of the time to refresh the browser's panes following a new selection. This response time is satisfactory—a user perceives no delays.

The critical limitation of the present Smalltalk implementation is the size of its virtual memory. Smalltalk-76 [Ingalls 1978] supports an address space of only 32,000 objects. This includes all of the objects defining Smalltalk itself. As a result, there is insufficient space to build large PIE networks. No more than 1,000 nodes can be in the local address space at any one time. Since there are approximately 3,000 methods in Smalltalk, it has not been possible to build a PIE network describing the entire Smalltalk system.

A new Smalltalk implementation soon to be available has a 30-bit virtual memory. Given this capacity, the possibility exists of transforming PIE from its present experimental status to a permanent part of Smalltalk's programming environment.

A PIE/Smalltalk marriage imposes no unavoidable costs on software developed under its auspices. PIE allows a user to trade flexibility for efficiency. Maximal efficiency can be obtained by employing standard Smalltalk mechanisms for defining new code. If this route is chosen, then no evolutionary history is maintained, and no context overhead is paid. However, if the user wishes to maintain a history, then he can convert to a node description of his Smalltalk code and develop his software in a context-sensitive fashion. From this point forward, the evolutionary history is maintained. The price is increased retrieval time and storage space. If these costs become prohibitive, the user can convert back to pure Smalltalk. A solution less extreme than converting to pure Smalltalk is to summarize the dominant assertions of a sequence of old layers into a single new layer, thereby reclaiming some space and speeding retrieval. The user can then continue in a context-sensitive fashion by placing subsequent assertions in a new layer. In either case, the user can store the old layers remotely before deleting them from his local workspace. This allows the user to recreate the history of his design if desired.

The implementation of PIE was a substantial design project in its own right. Hence, once the kernel PIE system reached a sufficient degree of reliability, we applied it to its own development in a number of ways. A major application was to explore the various display interfaces described earlier. Various display projects involved upwards of one hundred changes distributed over more than twenty classes. The layered approach proved particularly useful for exploring closely related designs for the interface since these projects involved a great deal of shared structure. Furthermore, since there was no right design, it was useful to preserve alternatives for a while in order to obtain experience with each of them. Finally, we adopted the convention of asserting changes to program documentation in the same layers as changes to the code. This greatly facilitated keeping the documentation consistent with a rapidly changing prototype.

5.3 Memory Management

We have experimented with two implementations for layered networks. One stores the context-sensitive information in the node, the other in the layer. The node-centered storage is more consistent with the Smalltalk metaphor: each instance of a class knows all of the information regarding its state. The layer-centered design has better memory management behavior.

The node-centered design associates the attribute of a node with a dictionary of layers and values. In this design, retrieval of a value of an attribute a of node n with respect to a context is based on the following algorithm:

1. Retrieve the layer/value dictionary for this attribute stored in the node.
2. Sequentially lookup each layer of the context in this dictionary. If the layer is found in the dictionary, return the associated value. If no layer of the context is found in the dictionary, return "?".

The second design is layer-centered. Layers own a dictionary that associates (node,attribute) pairs with a value. The retrieval algorithm for the value of attribute a of node n with respect to a context is to sequentially lookup (n,a) in the dictionary of each layer in the context. If (n,a) is found, return the associated value. If no layer of the context stores (n,a,) return "?".

To understand the virtues of the layer-centered scheme, we must discuss how the network is stored externally. Layers constitute the unit of secondary storage—i.e., when a user completes a design, he writes the layers defining the design onto secondary store. If the design is subsequently examined, the user must read these layers into his main store. The layer-centered data structure of (node,attribute,value) triples is the format of this external storage.

Given this external format, the layer-centered scheme provides superior performance when the system loads layers from secondary storage into main store. With the layer-centered scheme, the external dictionary can simply be treated as a remote disk page that is mapped into main memory. But if the node-centered scheme is employed, the values in the layer dictionary must be asserted in each node. The result is that loading process must sweep large portions of the virtual memory to access the specified nodes.

Another virtue of the layer-centered scheme relates to the grouping of information. Layers organize coordinated values. Hence, a system designer can specify that attributes from different objects must be swapped into main memory at the same time by placing them in the same layer. This is useful when subsets of the attributes of an object are used for some purposes and not for others. The present implementation of Smalltalk treats an object as an indivisible unit, swapping the entire object at one time. The layer-centered design allows a finer granularity in memory management. The attribute, not the object, is treated as the smallest memory element. The result is that objects are no longer integral blocks of storage. Consequently, the traditional discussion of a Smalltalk system as an interacting collection of integral objects is no longer appropriate. In PIE, a system is an interacting collection of partial descriptions of objects.

6. CONCLUSIONS

The existence of a software problem is widely acknowledged: it is becoming progressively more costly to develop and maintain software systems. Their complexity is growing faster than our ability to manage these systems. We have argued that the use of layered networks to represent design alternatives is one means for managing this complexity for three major reasons: (1) Layered networks are a more flexible tool to represent an evolving design than present file systems. (2) The cognitive complexity for employing these networks can be managed by suitable user interfaces. (3) The computational cost in storage space and retrieval time is reasonable.

Traditionally, structured programming and high level programming languages are offered as means to improve the software development process. Both are based on explicitly representing the structure of a design—structured programming emphasizes modular decomposition while high level programming languages emphasize the description of a module in terms of vocabulary closer to its intent. These techniques are important. However, neither addresses the orthogonal issue of coping with the evolution of a design. Neither is concerned with coordinating change across modules nor do they address the need of a designer to examine alternatives.

Advanced programming environments have tools for describing a system's current state—indexing programs for cross references, file packages for automating the storage and retrieval of a system—but again they are deficient in tools for describing the process of change.

Software evolves. It goes through a life cycle of design, implementation, and redesign. Layered networks are a means to represent an evolving structure and are therefore a useful basis for a software environment. Elements of a software system are represented by nodes in the network: structure by labelled links between these nodes. Modifications to the structure are represented by layers. In particular, refinements are captured by the domination of layers within a context while alternatives are represented by contexts containing different layers. Shared structured is expressed by shared layers.

The techniques described in this paper have been tested in the context of the Smalltalk programming environment. However, they can be applied to any programming system that provides a layered network database and an interactive display interface. We believe that the payoff of such databases for software design and development will more than justify their cost in terms of retrieval time and storage.

REFERENCES

[Birtwistle et al. 1973] G. Birtwistle, O.-J. Dahl, B. Myhrhaug, K. Nygaard. *Simula Begin.* Auerbach, Philadelphia, 1973.

[Cohen 1975] P. Cohen. Semantic networks and the generation of context. *Advance Papers of the Fourth International Joint Conference on Artificial Intelligence*, Tbilisi, U.S.S.R. September 1975, 134-142.

[Glasser 1978] A.L. Glasser. The evolution of a source code control system. In S. Jackson, J. Lockett (eds.). *Proceedings of the Software Quality and Assurance Workshop*, ACM, (1978), 122-125; also in *SICSOFT*, 3:5 (November 1978), 121-125.

[Hendrix 1975] Hendrix, G.G. Expanding the utility of semantic networks through partitioning. *Advance Papers of the Fourth International Joint Conference on Artificial Intelligence*, Tbilisi, U.S.S.R. September 1975, 115-121.

[Hewitt 1972] C. Hewitt. *Description and theoretical analysis (using schemata) of PLAN-NER: a language for proving theorems and manipulating models in a robot.* Massachusetts Institute of Technology, MIT-AI-TR-258, April 1972; see also C. Hewitt. *PLANNER: A language for manipulating models and proving theorems in a robot,* Massachusetts Institute of Technology, memo 168.

[Ingalls 1978] Dan Ingalls. The Smalltalk-76 programming system, design and implementation. *Conference Record of the Fifth Annual ACM Symposium on Principles of Programming Languages,* January 1978, 9-17.

[Ivie 1977] E.L. Ivie. Programmers Workbench—a machine for software development. *Communications of the ACM,* 20:10 (October 1977), 746-753. *[Editors note:* see also [Dolotta et al. 1978]]

[Kay 1974] A. Kay. *SMALLTALK, a communication medium for children of all ages.* Learning Research Group, Xerox Palo Alto Research Center, 1974.

[Lampson and Pier 1980] B.W. Lampson, K.A. Pier. A processor for a high-performance personal computer. *Seventh International Symposium on Computer Architecture,* La Baule, France, May 1980.

[Rochkind 1975] M.J. Rochkind. The source code control system. *IEEE Transactions on Software Engineering,* SE-1:4 (December 1975), 364-370.

[Rulifson et al. 1971] J. Rulifson, R. Waldinger, J. Derksen. A language for writing problem-solving programs. *International Federation of Information Processing,* 1971.

[Sussman and McDermott 1972] G.J. Sussman, D. McDermott. From PLANNER to CONNIVER—a genetic approach. *Proceedings of the Fall Joint Computer Conference,* AFIPS Proceedings (1972).

20 Why Programming Environments Need Dynamic Data Types

JAMES W. GOODWIN

Linköping University
Linköping, Sweden

Data abstraction is a powerful source of program structure and abstraction. There is nothing about it, or the reasons why it works, which restricts it to static applications. Programming environments (PE's) especially need to use data types dynamically, since it is their function to support the programmer in all phases of work with a program. Thus, the PE must proceed smoothly from definition to use to editing of a type.

If the language in which the PE is written permits types to be defined at runtime, then the PE can accurately model the supported program's types in its own. Otherwise, the model will have to be implemented by programming around the language's system of type, simulating the program's types in second order data structures, hiding their nature as types from the language processor's view.

Weakly typed languages provide the desired flexibility, since they impose no strong organization of their own. But there is no reason not to have the advantages of strong typing and good data abstraction within an adequately dynamic framework. The obstacle is not strong typing per se, but the rigid separation of compile and runtime environments. The language EL1 [Wegbreit 1974] shows how to combine strong typing and an emphasis on efficient compilation with the necessary dynamic properties to support good PE's.

©1981 IEEE. Reprinted with permission from *IEEE Transactions on Software Engineering*, SE-7:5 (September 1981), pp. 451-457.

1. DEFINITION OF TERMS

By programming environment (PE), I mean any and all software which the programmer might use in the course of preparing his program, called the supported program. The language processor for the supported language, whether it is an interpreter or a compiler and runtime package, is a only a part of the PE. Debuggers, source code editors, documentation systems, maintenance logs, on-line copies of the specification or requirements, verifiers, program librarians which manage multiple configurations and versions of the supported program, and testbeds are some other parts of the programming environment. The term "supported program" should be taken to include large systems of software, which might exist in multiple releases and configurations, and to include not only code but also manuals, histories, listings, specifications, proofs and so forth.

This definition of "programming environment" is shaped by the belief that the right abstract view of a PE is as a single, integrated, inclusive system. A systematic defense of this belief is beyond the scope of this paper, but I will indicate some of the attitudes motivating it in order to establish context.

Historically, many PE's arose as accumulations of utility programs, conceived and designed completely separately. Some were not conceived as programming aids as such at all (like text editors). Some were conceived as language independent (like DEC loaders and debuggers); this enforced a lowest common denominator approach which prevented language dependent improvements and integration with other tools. Many were unofficial, weekend projects whose usefulness caused them to far outgrow the limits of the original modest design. In reaction to this, I wish to emphasize as much as possible the holistic properties of programming environments. Hence, I resist the characterization of the PE as a tool box. It is much more like one of those huge workshops where a passenger jet is being built. The tools are only a small part of such a shop. More important is the planning, or lack of it, for lighting, noise control, traffic flow, safety, and (not least) for separating the product from the workshop when finished.

As in the aircraft factory, the product under construction is the central object in the PE, and dominates everything else by its presence. Yet there is a great variety of different processes going on at all times around it. There is a great deal of interaction among the various processes, and they call upon one another for information extensively. They are heterarchically, not hierarchically, organized. For example, neither the editor nor the file librarian is properly viewed as controlling the other, but the editor must tell the librarian when sources are changed, and the librarian must tell the editor where to find the sources. The toplevel structure of all these activities is not usefully characterized as an algorithm. It is best viewed as a collection of cooperating processes working in a shared database. The database contains the supported program as well as all the information about it which the various processes must maintain. The unifying principle throughout the various parts of the PE is the focus on the supported program, and on the processes whereby it develops.

1.1 Nominal Type vs. Abstract Type

Suppose a program needs to have a priority sorted queue of tasks. A LISP programmer would say, "I built the queue out of cons cells, numbers and atoms. Those are the types of LISP. The queue is not a type, it's just a data structure." A PASCAL programmer would say, "I defined a new type called **queue**. It's a real type, like any other. I made it up out of primitive types like **integer** and type generators like **array**.

415

In what follows, the term *nominal type* will refer to the notion of type embodied in the language processor. The queue was not a nominal type of LISP because the interpreter does not know anything about queues. LISP has a fixed number of nominal types, and that's it. The queue was a nominal type of PASCAL because the compiler recognizes it, and uses it, for example, when enforcing type correctness.

It is additionally desirable to have a notion of type that is independent of language. Suppose that a programmer, setting aside all thoughts of implementation or the programming language to be used, sat down to analyze his application, and found that a priority sorted task queue would be necessary. Then such a queue is one of the *abstract types* of the analysis. The adjective "abstract" stresses that the type arose in a problem oriented analysis, free of all implementation considerations.

2. COMPARING LANGUAGES

Using the notions of nominal and abstract type, one can compare the different styles in which different languages implement abstract types. At one end of the language spectrum are weakly typed or typeless, late binding, interpreted languages such as LISP, APL and machine language. At the other end are strongly typed, early binding, compiler oriented languages, such as PASCAL [Jensen and Wirth 1977], and SIMULA [Dahl et al. 1972], and more recently the data abstraction languages such as ALPHARD [Shaw et al. 1977], CLU [Liskov et al. 1978][Liskov et al. 1977] and ADA [ADA Reference Manual].

In this paper, LISP and PASCAL are taken as representatives of the two ends of the strong vs. weak typing spectrum. PASCAL was chosen for simplicity's sake. All the points to be made below apply equally to the other strongly typed languages named. Their encapsulation and generic function facilities are much better, and desirable. However, the issue here will be *dynamic* capabilities as against static ones. None of the strongly typed languages named provide any capability to introduce new nominal types at runtime. The only strongly typed language known to me which does provide such capabilities is EL1 [Wegbreit 1974]. The encapsulation and (static) generic capabilities of the data abstraction languages are highly desirable in their own right, but they are not a substitute for dynamic typing, nor do they hinder its implementation. More dynamic typing is an orthogonal dimension along which strong typing mechanisms may be improved. The improvement is that the type abstractions of the language, whatever they are, become applicable in cases where they could not be used before, because the compiler demanded that type information be bound before it became available. As to the choice of LISP (and for simplicity's sake again) an unextended LISP is considered, although major lisp systems today have weakly typed data abstraction facilities like the INTERLISP [Teitelman 1978] record package, and "defstructs" in MACLISP [Moon 1974] and the LISP Machine [Weinreb and Moon 1981].

In LISP, abstract types are realized as data structures, not as nominal types. Nominal types are used as parts of the data structures, but there is no nominal type corresponding to the abstract type desired. PASCAL, on the other hand, promotes the use of user defined nominal types as realizations of abstract types. Ideally, for each abstract type in the analysis of the problem, it will be possible to define a nominal PASCAL type corresponding to and implementing it.

One can say that in LISP, abstract types are realized *outside* the nominal system of type, whereas in PASCAL they are realized *as* nominal types, *within* the system. This means that the LISP language processor cannot distinguish abstract types, and therefore cannot provide support keyed to distinctions between them. For instance, it cannot check (abstract) type correctness, not even at runtime, because it knows nothing of the relation between nominal types, which are accessible to it, and abstract types. In contrast, a PASCAL program models the abstract types in nominal types which the language processor can recognize, permitting it to check type correctness and compile more efficiently.

Although the LISP processor cannot provide support keyed to distinctions between different abstract types, it would be a great mistake to assume that it cannot provide support at all for abstract types. LISP expects that abstract types will be realized outside the nominal system of type, and it provides excellent support for doing so. The support it provides is of a very different nature; it exploits the possibility of writing functions which are defined for all data structures, such as **print, read, copy, subst** and so on. The PE for LISP consists of large programs which are often defined over all data structures: the list editor, the prettyprinter, and so on. In effect, LISP provides a very powerful and expressive generic function capability. In particular, a lisp function like **copy** or the editor will work over abstract types which the author of **copy** or the editor will never see. Nor is it necessary for the programmer who conceives a new abstract type, and chooses a data structure to implement it, to provide code for how to **copy** or edit it. This is elaborated further in section 5 below.

2.1   Can We Have It Both Ways?

The kinds of support which LISP and PASCAL provide for implementing one's abstract datatypes are very different, indeed almost disjoint. It is clear that the strongly typed languages, and especially the data abstraction languages, have an explicit, articulated theory of type, where the weakly typed languages do not. It does not follow, however, that either provides better support for abstract types than the other in any given case; it depends very much on what one happens to need. Ideally, we would like to have it both ways.

It is always possible, in any language, to implement one's abstract types as data structures outside the nominal system of type. FORTRAN does not have linked lists as a nominal type, but much list processing has been done in FORTRAN anyway, implementing lists in arrays. One could do this in PASCAL too, if desired. Presumably it is not a very good idea. PASCAL intends the use of user defined types, it supports that use, and to go outside the nominal system of type in this way sacrifices all the advantages which it is the point of the PASCAL design to provide. PASCAL provides little or no support for working outside its nominal system of type.

But one might be forced to program outside the nominal system of type. Suppose one needed abstract types which must be defined at runtime. In PASCAL, nominal types cannot be defined at runtime, so this need would have to be filled by working outside the nominal system of type. It would probably be done by simulating the desired types using array space, just as in FORTRAN list processing. In such a situation one would be a great deal better off in LISP, because it is supported practice in LISP to write functions which are defined over classes of data structures, including, if desired, data structures (i.e. implementations of abstract types) which arise at runtime.

The next section will show that dealing with dynamically arising types is one of the things the PE designer has to do. Fortunately, it will turn out that the problems are not inherent in the successful parts of the strong typing and data abstraction theories; rather, they are side effects of the conventional way of organizing the PE into wholly separate compile and runtime environments. These problems can be avoided by either doing away with the compiler and interpreting, or, less drastically, by integrating the compiler into the rest of the system in the right way. The language EL1 [Wegbreit 1974] is an existent proof that the dynamic, late binding qualities necessary for a PE can be achieved in a language that also emphasizes strong typing and efficient compilation. This is also discussed more in section 5.

3. ANALOG TYPES AND ANALOG VALUES

What is so special about programming environments, that they should place unusual requirements on the system of type in the language used to implement the PE?

It is the peculiar problem of a programming environment that it has to represent other programs. Many of its most important abstract types are not customers and payrolls and things external to the computer, but entities in the supported program which the PE is helping the programmer to implement: the program's type definitions, runtime values, breakpoints, correctness proofs, specifications, implementations and so on.

The information which the PE may have about entities in the supported program may be conveniently divided into the part used by the language processor, and the rest. The part used by the language processor will be called the *realization* and the rest will be called *further description*.

As an example, if the program entity is a type definition, then the realization of it might be a parse tree in PE language's data, plus perhaps a mapping from operation names defined on that type to their implementations, and whatever else the language processor needs. Further description of it might be maintenance history (date and author of last edit), verification (the last proof or key steps from it), some intermediate results saved by the flow analyzer to expedite reanalysis, and so forth.

The further description of a supported program entity is by definition not used by the actual execution of the program. The realization information, on the other hand, is used not only for execution, but also for many other purposes by various PE subsystems. The flow analyzer and verifier, for example, will often need to examine the definitions of types, procedures and so forth, i.e. their realizations.

In thinking about the design of the PE as a whole, the realization and further description constitute one logical entity, which I call an *analog object*. It is the representation of a supported program entity from the viewpoint of the PE as a whole. From this viewpoint, many operations may be defined on the entity which are not defined from the viewpoint of the supported program. I also use the terms *analog value*, meaning the subset of analog objects which represent values generated in runs of the supported program, and *analog type*, meaning the subset which represent the type definitions in the supported program.

The relation between the PE and the supported program is illustrated in Figure 1. The supported program is drawn containing a type definition called **Customer**, and two values of that type, called **Jones** and **Smith**. The PE is drawn containing analog objects which represent **Customer** and **Jones**, called **Analog Customer** and **Analog Jones**, respectively.

(The reader may wonder what sort of further description the PE could usefully have about ordinary runtime values. The answer is, probably not much, in the case of ordinary values in production program runs. But if one were

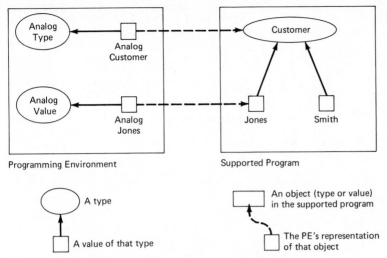

Figure 1. The relation between a PE and the supported program.

testing, for example, then there might be constants intended as inputs to the test, and these would be further described by validity predicates, preconditions for testing, history and comments, filing dates and locations, etc. Or again, in a source level debugging situation, the PE is responsible for presenting run-time values to the user, and it must have a printing capability for these values, even though there might be no such operation defined on them by the supported program.)

It should be noted that the PE must also have many ordinary data structures which are not any kind of analog objects. Calendar dates, source code files, the different programmers on a team, and many other things may be useful for the PE to represent without being part of the supported program.

To summarize, the most important class of abstract types in the design of any PE are the various categories of analog objects. They embody whatever knowledge the PE has about the supported program.

4. WHY DYNAMIC TYPING IS NECESSARY

Both **Analog Customer** and **Analog Jones** are PE values, which must themselves have type. Their abstract types are **Analog Type** and **Analog Value**. These two abstract types are central to the design of the PE, and must be realized by the PE designer in some satisfactory way.

The implementation of the further descriptive information presents no special problems for a static typing scheme. This information will appear in the form of some components like **Date of Last Edit** and **Where to File**. The possible kinds of such information are known, since they depend on the functionality of the PE. If the PE has a subsystem for testing, then operations on analog values to get, set and execute their validity predicates will be needed, otherwise not. This can be determined during PE design.

The realization part of **Analog Type** can also be handled statically. It will consist of a set of component descriptors, where a component descriptor is a substructure specifying the name of the component, the (supported language) type of the component, the dimensions if it is an array component, and so forth. In short, the realization part of **Analog Type** will look very similar to the grammar for type declarations in the supported language.

4.1   New Types Arise at PE Runtime

The limitations which static typing imposes on the PE designer arise in implementing the realization part of analog values. If **Customer** has, say, three components, for name, address and telephone, then **Jones** will have three corresponding values, and **Analog Jones** must represent this at the PE level, in PE data. This data is useful, as noted above, for the whole PE, not just the language processor; the testing tool, for example, will need to look at it to validate Jones after the test. **Analog Jones'** name, address and telephone are perfectly proper parts of him, just as much as the further descriptive parts.

Unfortunately, the realization part of an analog value varies depending on the program type in question—**Customer** in this case. So the PE implementation for Analog Value has to support a certain variability. This variability might be formally expressed in any of the well known or less well known ways: schemata, generators, unions, variants, generics, hierarchies or lattices. But no matter how it is formally expressed, the parameter is the program's definition of **Customer**. And this is not bound until PE runtime, because one of the things the PE is for is to help the programmer define, analyze, and redefine his types.

It must be concluded that it is in the nature of the PE's problem that new variants of one of the PE's most important abstract types arise dynamically, at PE runtime.

4.2   Total Values Are Also Necessary

It is not much use to have total generic functions if one cannot call them and process the results. Total expressions and total variables are also necessary. By "total variable" I mean a variable whose type is reset by each assignment, to agree with the type of the value. Obviously, strong typing requires each use of such a variable to make runtime checks of type correctness (unless the context of use also accepts total values). Analogous remarks apply to total expressions. Untyped or weakly typed languages may be regarded as permitting total variables by simply not maintaining the type information at all. Finally, by "total" I mean *dynamically* total, i.e. the set of types over which the variable ranges cannot be bound at compile time, because new types may be defined at runtime, and the variable must accept assignments of their values too.

In practice, total values require the use of pointers in the language implementation, though not necessarily in its semantics. Union modes as in ALGOL 68 and variant records as in PASCAL are not adequate. First, they require allocating enough space to hold the largest value in the union, which in this case would be the largest value in the system. This is inefficient since most assignments will be of small values or pointer values. Second, it is impossible to anticipate the maximum size of new datatypes which may be defined during the scope of the variable. At some level, the implementation must permit the size of the variable to vary from one assignment to the next, and this will involve using pointers from the stack to some kind of heap. But of course, it is not necessary that this be semantically visible. A strongly typed language, which distinguishes pointer values from immediate ones, could maintain the distinction.

Now, why are total values necessary in PE's? The are necessary because PE's must often deal with values of arbitrary user computations. A typical example arises in the the LISP top loop, which in INTERLISP is augmented by the *history package*. The top loop reads arbitrary expressions from the user, evaluates them, and prints the value. The history package, which is one of the most useful and least widely understood PE tools, keeps a record of recent inputs and their values. This record amounts to a superficial model of the dialog between the programmer and the PE. It supports redisplay of inputs and results; re-execution of inputs with optional modifications; and undoing of selected side effects.

Obviously, the type of the value of an expression cannot be predicted before the input expression is entered. Yet this value must be held on local variables in the top loop, and stored in a data structure called an **event** which is maintained by the history package. These local variables, and the **value** field of an **event**, cannot be declared at the time the PE is compiled more narrowly than "any user computable value".

The need for total values arises not only in the top loop, but anywhere that the PE must deal with analog values *qua* results of arbitrary computations. Tracing, breakpoints, validation and performance monitoring are other important functions of every PE which require dealing with arbitrary fragments of user code, their inputs, and their results.

This section has argued that it is in the nature of the PE's problem that new types arise at runtime and that total values are necessary. This does not imply that one cannot implement a PE in a strictly early binding language, or in a language without total values. It does imply that in this case, some of the most important abstract type information in the system will have to be expressed outside the language's nominal system of type.

5. EXAMPLES OF DYNAMIC DATA TYPING

One might accept the argument that dynamic typing is a necessity at times, while still regarding it as an ugly necessity. Such a point of view conflates efficiency issues with abstraction issues. Static binding of type is primarily an efficiency issue; dynamic types operate to raise the level of abstraction in the program, in exactly the same way that static types do.

Dynamic typing is in fact regularly used by programmers in all sorts of languages; it just is not *nominal* dynamic typing. A look at two of the commoner guises in which it occurs, both of which have independent status as structuring or abstraction mechanisms, will illustrate this.

5.1 Table or Data Driven Programming

One common disguise in which dynamic typing occurs is as table driven or data driven programming. In this style, a procedure is called with an actual parameter whose internal structure (type) is only partly known. The procedure retrieves a tag (type identifier) from the known part. This is then used to index control tables which map desired operations onto their implementations for various values of the tag (variant types of parameter). Tables used in this way are in fact tables of type definitions, and can profitably be integrated into the nominal system of type in the programming language, as a generic function capability.

The method of table driven programming is indifferent to the time when the table entries are stored, so it permits dynamic definition of new types without special mechanisms. In languages which lack even static data abstraction facilities, such as FORTRAN, table driven programming is a well established substitute. It is pervasive in LISP.

One would expect that in a language with good static facilities for defining variant subtypes, there would be less need for this table driven technique. In particular, one would expect that when this kind of table driven technique is used, it should often be the case that the information in the tables can be viewed logically as type information, but cannot be implemented as such, owing to limitations of the implementation of variant types in the language, such as the inability to generate new subtypes dynamically.

An example of the use of generating types dynamically, described by Sandewall [Sandewall 1979b], is a utility program for supporting menu oriented programming. One can view this program as a miniature, specialized PE. It supports both the definition, editing, and maintenance of menus by the menu programmer and their use by an end user, typically in database query applications.

But menu definitions are really type definitions, whose instances are filled-in menus. System routines which prompt for a value for a given blank, or display the current status, are generic functions, where the particular "copy" of the menu being processed is the actual parameter, and the definition of the menu being processed is its type, the type parameter. If the set of menus could be statically fixed, any language with adequate generic functions could be used to express menus elegantly as types within the language. In PASCAL, it would be like having **menu** in addition to **set** and **array**. The missing capabilities are two. First, the type generator **menu** has to be definable within the language, which **set** and **array** are not in PASCAL. This is an ordinary (i.e. static) issue of data abstraction. The need for this capability is becoming more widely recognized, for example in [Shaw and Wulf 1980]. Second, new menus must be definable at runtime. The latter requirement, not mentioned in [Shaw and Wulf 1980], is a dynamic requirement characteristic of PE's and systems similar to them, such as this example.

5.2 Total Functions in LISP

Dynamic definition of data types arises in another guise in LISP. It is possible in LISP to define functions which are *total* in that they are defined over all S-expressions. A few dozen basic functions like **copy, subst, member, append, read, print, assoc, nconc** and the like give the language much of its flavor and economy of expression. In addition to this "subroutine library" of smaller functions, there are some very large functions, "total programs", which are major subsystems of the LISP PE, such as the list editor and the prettyprinter.

Total functions are useful over all abstract types that have ever been defined or ever will be. In effect, they are supergeneric functions, like assignment or equality operators in compiler languages. The abstractive power of such operators is recognized, but as Shaw and Wulf [Shaw and Wulf 1980] point out, this power is usually preempted by the language design and not passed on to the user.

It is especially the dynamic property of being applicable to *future* types which makes total functions significant for PE design. It makes it possible for the PE designer to provide tools to manipulate user defined data structures he will never see. Moreover, he can write it as "user" code in the source language (instead of having to change the compiler). This simplifies maintenance, and makes the same capability available to users, who can then *extend the PE* by defining more such functions, particularly adapted to their problem.

This view of LISP's total functions as supergenerics is very similar to Sandewall's "Superroutines" [Sandewall 1979b].

6. IMPLEMENTING DYNAMIC DATA TYPES

If dynamic definition of new data types could be provided within the nominal type framework of a strongly typed language, then these dynamic techniques could be used with a clear, explicit representation of type, rather than hiding the true types in tables or loose code.

The problem is not a matter of inherent rigidity in strong typing as such, as is sometimes claimed by devotees of LISP and weakly typed languages. After all, strongly typed languages usually have at least some total functions, such as equality operators and I/O procedures, and the control of typing is not lost.

Nor is the problem early binding as such, precisely speaking. The problem is the rigid separation of the whole programming environment into compilation and execution environments. Especially important are the following assumptions:

• First you edit. Then you compile. Then you run. These phases follow one another in strict sequence.
• Information flow backwards in the sequence does not or should not occur.
• Symbolic information from the source code, such as symbolic procedure names and especially type information, should not be necessary in the runtime environment.

The usual interpretation of "early binding" tends to entail these assumptions (especially the last). Therefore it is tempting to summarize by saying, "The problem is not strong typing but early binding." Unfortunately this is not quite accurate. In a system with an incremental compiler, built under the alternative assumptions suggested below, it will still be useful to distinguish between binding type early (in the compiler) and late (in the code produced). It is clearer to attack the above assumptions directly. For the same reason, the term "compiler oriented language" is entirely too broad to identify properly the source of the difficulty. Smalltalk for instance [Goldberg et al. 1982] has an incremental spot compiler instead of an interpreter, and EL1 places heavy emphasis on efficient compilation. Yet they have the flexibility at issue here. The above assumptions might be named the "straight line" model of program development. In contrast, the view motivating this paper has been that program development involves many cooperating processes, with much flow of control and information back and forth among them. Rather than being concerned with squeezing out unnecessary information, this approach is concerned with maintaining maximal information: keeping consistent and up to date descriptions of the supported program from as many different viewpoints as possible. The comparable assumptions behind this view are:

• The operation of the compiler, and the operation of the supported program itself (in whole or in part), are two of many processes going on in the workshop. It is undesirable to freeze in the PE architecture any *a priori* restrictions on their relative timing or the information flow between them.
• Source code, including type definitions, must be represented well in the PE language, as first class datatypes. This more or less requires a SYMBOL datatype, and probably some representation of code at the level of parse trees rather than strings of characters or symbols.
• The programmer is expected to carry out many operations on his program not by hand, but by writing code to manipulate his program: by extending the PE. Scaffolding, testbeds, tailored traces and metering, and small syntactic extensions are some typical examples.

• Type faults occurring during the operation of the supported program must be treated as exception conditions, not as a breakdown in the program logic and an occasion to terminate execution.

(By exception condition is meant that type faults should cause a transfer of control, either to a user provided routine, or to a default routine provided in the PE. When the user provides the routine, he may regard it either as part of the program itself, e.g. automatic type coercions, or as an extension to the PE, as in the data tracing example below).

These assumptions are consistent with strong typing, and with binding as much type information at compile time as the user demands, but they permit dynamic definition of datatypes. For example, here is one way to implement user defined total functions within a strong typing, compiler oriented language. Suppose the user wishes to define **transmit**, a procedure which can send any value over a network connection. (Presumably there is a corresponding **receive** procedure.) Instead of defining it directly, he writes a *function generator* for it. A function generator is a perfectly ordinary function in the language, which takes type definitions into function definitions. When the compiler encounters a call to **transmit** with an argument type **customer**, it applies the function generator to the definition of **customer** and obtains the definition of **transmit** for that type.

The above assumptions are essentially the solution used in EL1 [Wegbreit 1974]. It is no accident that this solution evolved in a language, one of whose primary design goals was to support an ambitious, integrated PE, in a strongly typed, efficiently compilable language. The following example may help to suggest the range of things that PE's could be doing for their users if the boundary between PE and program were not drawn so rigidly.

It is possible in EL1 to write a PE utility to put traces on an arbitrary datum. The datum is made *sensitive*, so that wherever it goes in the system, it causes a type fault on every access. These faults are programmed (automatically, by the utility program which sets the trace in place) to display the trace information or monitor performance or whatever the user specified, and then clear the exception condition by performing the operation originally requested. Such a trace may be installed or removed during execution.

It is quite simple to provide such a utility in the PE, given the context of strong typing with type faults handled as programmable exception conditions. The type of the datum to be traced is copied, creating a new, sensitive type which is identical in every respect but name. Now, either the type mark of the original is altered to address the new type, or a standin for the datum is allocated from the new type, using the same components as the original. The type faults for the sensitive type are now programmed to map operations of the original type onto analogous operations on the sensitive one; the definitions of the new operations are made by copying the definitions of the old ones, changing the type declaration, and adding the trace code at the front. Note that this cannot be directly achieved in either LISP (type control too weak) or the data abstraction languages such as CLU or ADA (type control too static).

7. SUMMARY AND CONCLUSIONS

Dynamic data types do not require that the goals of efficient compilation be abandoned. Rather, they require that the distinction between the compile and runtime environments be removed, and that the explicit use of type information at runtime be recognized as a valid and desirable abstraction technique, not merely a symptom of some deficiency in the type checking.

Dynamic data types are a powerful structuring technique. A function which is written to cover ranges of types yet to be defined is a kind of total function, like built in generics for assignment and equality, but user definable. This raises the level of abstraction at which programs are expressed, for the same reason that static generic facilities do so. Dynamic data types have especially many applications in PE's, where it is necessary to write code to deal with types which will not be defined until runtime. The alternative is to push this type information into tables or other user defined runtime data structures, which means in practice to go back to weak typing for this part of the type information, in order to achieve the necessary late binding.

Similar arguments apply to the need for total variables and values, that is expressions which return and variables which accept values of types which are determinable only at runtime, and may not even have been defined at compile time.

ACKNOWLEDGMENTS

This work was supported by the Swedish Board for Technical Development under Contract Dnr 79-3914.

REFERENCES

[ADA Reference Manual] Department of Defense, *Reference Manual for the Ada Programming Language.* July 1980.

[Dahl et al. 1972] O.-J. Dahl, E.W. Dijkstra, C.A.R. Hoare. *Structured Programming.* Academic Press, 1972.

[Goldberg et al. 1982] A. Goldberg et al. *Smalltalk: Dreams and Schemes* (in preparation).

[Jensen and Wirth 1977] K. Jensen, N. Wirth. Pascal User Manual and report. *Springer Verlag Lecture Notes in Computer Science*, 18, 1977.

[Liskov et al. 1977] B. Liskov et al. Abstraction mechanisms in CLU. *Communications of the ACM*, 20:8 (August 1977), 564-576.

[Liskov et al. 1978] B. Liskov et al. *CLU Reference Manual.* Massachusetts Institute of Technology, Laboratory for Computer Science, Computation Structures Group Memo 161, July 1978.

[Moon 1974] D. Moon. *MACLISP Reference Manual.* Massachusetts Institute of Technology, Project MAC, 1974.

[Sandewall 1979b] E. Sandewall. *Why superroutines are different from subroutines.* Software Systems Research Center, Linköping University, report number LITH-MAT-R-79-28, November 1979.

[Shaw and Wulf 1980] M. Shaw, W.A. Wulf. Toward relaxing assumptions in languages and their implementations. *SIGPLAN Notices*, 15:3 (March 1980).

[Shaw et al. 1977] M. Shaw, W.A. Wulf, R.L. London. Abstraction and verification in Alphard: defining and specifying iteration and generators. *Communications of the ACM*, 20:8 (August 1977), 553-563.

[Teitelman 1978] W. Teitelman. *INTERLISP Reference Manual.* Xerox Palo Alto Research Center, Palo Alto, California, December 1978.

[Wegbreit 1974] B. Wegbreit. The treatment of data types in EL1. *Communications of the ACM,* 17:5 (May 1974), 251-264.

[Weinreb and Moon 1981] D. Weinreb, D. Moon. *The Lisp Machine Manual.* Massachusetts Institute of Technology, Artificial Intelligence Laboratory, 1981.

21 Software Architecture Based on Communicating Residential Environments

ERIK SANDEWALL, CLAES STRÖMBERG,
HENRIK SÖRENSEN
Linköping University
Linköping, Sweden

This paper describes an alternative approach to software architecture, where the classical division of responsibilities between operating systems, programming languages and compilers, and so forth is revised. Our alternative is organized as a set of self-contained environments which are able to communicate pieces of software between them, and whose internal structure is predominantly descriptive and declarative. The base structure within each environment (its diversified shell) is designed so that it can accommodate such arriving software modules.

The presentation of that software architecture is done in the context of an operational implementation, the SCREEN system (System of Communicating REsidential ENvironments).

©1981 IEEE. Reprinted with permission from *Fifth International Conference on Software Engineering*, San Diego, California, March 1981, pp. 144-152.

1. THIS PAPER DESCRIBES ALTERNATIVE PRINCIPLES FOR SOFTWARE ARCHITECTURE

Software design today is based on a number of universally accepted assumptions, particularly about the tasks that ought to be performed by operating systems, compilers, and other software tools, and about what tasks ought to be performed by "application" programs. Each of those tools provides a package of services. For example, the practical operating system provides not only resource management, but also the top-level dialogue which allows the user to switch between various services, and to transfer data between them. The conventional compiler provides a number of services, such as data description (through declarations; also performed by the data base system), consistency checks, and code generation. The "application" program is assumed to be in charge of, e.g., all but the most trivial aspects of the user dialogue for the application.

The purpose of this paper is to question this conventional division of responsibilities between the major parts of software. We describe a different overall architecture of the software which we believe is more appropriate. Our view of software architecture has been implemented as an experimental but fully operational system, called the *SCREEN* ("System of Communicating REsidential ENvironments") system. Although the main results that are reported in this paper are the architectural philosophy and not the piece of university-quality software, we shall make frequent references to *SCREEN*, in order to avoid the possible suspicion that the ideas are mere speculation, and to emphasize that the designs described here are the resuls of practical experimentation over several years.

2. APPLICATION EXAMPLE: AN OFFICE INFORMATION SYSTEM

For concreteness, let us start with one particular class of programs whose treatment relies heavily on the characteristics of *SCREEN*, and use it to explain how the system works and how it is used. In the development of the experimental Linköping Office Information System, LOIS [Sandewall et al. 1979a] [Sandewall et al. 1980a], we wanted to provide support for *information flow* in an office environment, i.e. the scenario where one user is able to instantiate a "transaction" (e.g. a purchase order, or a request to have certain analyses made for a patient), send it to another user who (immediately or later) performs some operation on that "transaction" (e.g. authorizes the purchase order), and passes it on again. (For a survey of some recent work on information flow models, see [Ellis and Nutt 1980]). Within one organization, we will usually have many such information-flow paths, and a many-to-many relationship between flow-paths and users: each path passes by several users, and each user has several paths come by.

In an office environment with personal computers for all employees, we will want each user's personal computer to account for his or her role in each of the information-flow paths that he participates in, and to do so in a well-engineered and coherent dialogue. Thus at run time, the complete system for the organization consists of one sub-system for each user. But at design time, we instead want to design each information-flow application separately, so that the roles performed by different users for this flow are co-ordinated and fit well together.

In our project, we have designed a (primarily graphical) language for describing information flows, and an implementation which supports the design and debugging of an information-flow application, as well as the distribution of the segments of the flow to the separate user stations [Sandewall et al. 1979b] [Sandewall 1979c]. The application calls for an interesting and nontrivial structure in the receiving, "end-user" computing environment.

Let us consider this from the point of view of the end user. We assume that he or she already has an office information system with the standard facilities, such as:

• A computer mail system
• A personal data base system, where he or she may store data, organized according to the user's preferences using simple data definition commands, and where browsing and report generation from the data is also supported
• An agenda facility, which allows the user to maintain notes about pending duties of several types: "make the following phone calls: ...", "talk to the following people around the office...", "meetings: ...", "write the following reports with the following deadlines:...", etc.

Each of these sub-systems uses a repertoire of interactive commands, and some will also use other, orthogonal menus, e.g. the repertoire of agenda classes, or the repertoire of data sets in the personal data base.

When an information flow application has been designed, and broken down into the pieces that are to be sent to the personal sub-systems for each of several users, how is each flow-piece to be *integrated* into its user's personal system? The easiest way is to say that the segment defines one new 'program', parallell to the mail 'program', the agenda 'program', and all the others. For example, the information flow between a ward in a hospital and the chemical laboratory, would generate one program for the head nurse in the ward, which might be called "laboratory data", and which would contain sub-commands such as "order analysis for patient", "look through today's returned analyses", "look at patient's journal" (because returned data for a patient are assumed to be accumulated automatically to the patient's journal), "find out status of pending analysis", etc. (These fragments occur at the beginning and at the end of the flow path for each laboratory request). Some of the other stations for this information flow would contain only one or a few operations, if implemented in the same way.

This straight-forward solution is sometimes also the best one. But very often the system becomes more habitable for the user if the segment of the information flow is incorporated into one of the other services. For example, the administrator who has to look over and authorize purchase orders before they can be processed further, but who also needs to be reminded about this duty in order to do it, would prefer to see her part of the purchase order's path as one further agenda category, where it could rely on the presumed machinery of the agenda facility for reminding the user about deadlines, using appropriate devices such as bells, whistles, or color graphics.

Similarly, the user who is on an information flow because he wants to hoard the information in his personal data base, for later browsing, but who is not interested in seeing it when it arrives, would rather have *his* segment of the information flow connect straight into the personal data base. And finally, the user who files a request for vacation once or twice per year, and gets back a positive or negative answer a few days later, would be best served if the answer comes back as a message in the ordinary computer mail (although the manager who approved the application may have seen it differently).

Programs which effect information flow in an organization are conceptually a limited class of programs, but they are also a class of programs which represent a very large volume of actual data processing. These two circumstances taken together are the rationale for designing a special-purpose language for describing information flows. Other classes of programs which satisfy the same requirements, and for which specialized languages have frequently been designed and implemented, are for programming language processors (see e.g. [Johnson and Lesk 1978]), for report generating programs, for data base queries, and for interactive forms management on a display screen. One of our basic design considerations has been to support such special-purpose languages in general; we shall return to that point.

3. A DIVERSIFIED SHELL PROVIDES POWERFUL SUPPORT FOR APPLICATIONS

Let us now switch from the special case of information-flow programs, to the extrapolation to more general issues. The first point we want to make is that *the computer system's (= the operating system's) top-level dialogue with the user should be considerably more developed than what is customary today* in conventional interactive operating systems. The information-flow application provided an example where the shell should contain basic services such as a mail handler, a personal data base handler, and an agenda facility, and where "application programs" were embedded into the shell at various locations. We shall use the term *diversified shell* for a user dialogue facility with such a repertoire of services, oriented towards certain application situations or computer/user interaction modes.

By employing the term *shell* for the computer's top-level dialogue handler, as previously used in the Multics and Unix [Bourne 1978a] operating systems, we indicate that procedural services and easy coupling of modules are taken for granted in the shell, and that we are adding yet another aspect when going to the diversified shell.

In a conventional operating system, there is only one way of adding more programs, at least from the perspective of the common programmer, and that is by storing the object code for the program as a file, so that it can be invoked by a 'RUN' command. In our concept for an office information system, the mail handler, the agenda handler, and the other parts of the shell define a number of different such points where 'programs' may be added. Each point makes implications about when the program will be invoked, or made available to the user, and what conventions it has to follow in order to operate correctly.

Notice that the increments do not consist *only* of procedures, however. Commands, agenda categories, etc. are data objects which are associated both with procedural information (e.g. the code for executing the command) and descriptive information (e.g. the help text that goes with the command).

Systems programmers who are working with operating systems in practice already use these techniques, for operating systems actually contain additional "dispatch" points where "programs" for specific, system-oriented purposes may be added, e.g. drivers for various types of memory devices or I/O devices. However, these additional dispatch points are not used (and are not supposed to be used) by regular programmers.

The techniques described here are classical in the context of Lisp programming. What we have done is to extend them to classes of applications for which Lisp is not usually being used, and to relate them to issues which are significant for software engineering.

It is interesting to compare also with the CODASYL group proposal for an *end user facility* [Codasyl 1976]. Although that proposal only described an EUF with a fixed set of facilities, it generalizes easily to being a specification for a diversified shell, to which services could be added incrementally.

A corollary of our argument is that *operating systems should serve a very significant role for program structuring.* It is interesting to go back to the classical term "the stored-program computer", where the computer is supposed to contain one single program, and apply it to the personal-computer situation. In this view, **the program** consists of all the various pieces of executable code that are stored in (primary or secondary) memory, for example on files. The top-level structure of that program consists of the operating system, which is able to invoke lower-level parts of **the program** which are stored on files, by doing a RUN operation. In this view, **the program** is also able to amend itself, under user control (usually indirect user control), so that new services are added and old services are sometimes deleted. This is done of course by adding or deleting program files. What we are talking about in this paper is to reform and improve the currently very primitive architecture for **the stored program** of the personal computer, so that its ability to modify itself (i.e. to facilitate its own software maintenance) is recognized as an asset, and supported as much as possible.

From this perspective, it is a pity that the sub-discipline for operating systems thinks of the O.S. as being *essentially* an administrator for shared resources, and nothing else. Brinch-Hansen [Brinch-Hansen 1973] writes:

> An *operating system* is a set of manual and automatic procedures that enable a group of people to share a computer installation efficiently.

The role of the operating system as a skeleton program onto which more specific (sub-) programs are to be attached, is equally important.

A third observation is that *the diversified shell must provide a data repository which can hold those data which are common for the shell and the various programs that are attached to it.* Operating systems in the Multics family (such as Tops-20 and Unix) allow one program to invoke another, i.e. to perform the equivalent of the RUN command. However, if the caller and the callee want to share data, only crude facilities are available. Incremental programming systems such as LISP [Sandewall 1978] [Winston and Horn 1981] [Charniak et al. 1980] and APL provide a model here: they allow one environment to hold a large number of procedures, all of which may be invoked by the user, but which may also invoke each other, and which share the common data space of the LISP "sysout" of the APL "workspace". An operating system might provide that service on a global level and in a less language-dependent way.

One example where such a design would be very useful was provided by Boehm in [Boehm 1980], which describes how a small, interactive application software product was developed in a controlled experiment. One of the hypotheses was that "most of the code in (such a) product is devoted to housekeeping", i.e. error processing, mode management, user amenities, and moving data around. This hypothesis was confirmed by the two independent development teams in the experiment, which used only 2% and 3% of the code for implementing the actual cost model that was the real purpose of the program. The quoted figures seem extreme, but the general observation seems to recur frequently.

In a computing environment where the shell provides a global data repository and an interactive command language, one should be able to implement such applications by writing their core (those 2-3 % of the old code) as programs which operate on data in the global data repository, and rely on services or general-purpose commands that are already in the diversified shell for "moving data around" and other housekeeping chores.

Finally, a *diversified shell is the ideal target structure for special-purpose languages.* In a discussion of the use of program generators, particularly in Unix, Johnson and Lesk [Johnson and Lesk, 1978, p. 2156] write:

Program generators have been used for some time in business data processing, typically to implement sorting and report generation applications. Usually, the specifications used in these applications describe the entire job to be done /.../ In contrast, our program generators might better be termed module generators; the intent is to provide a single module that does an important part of the total job. The host language, augmented perhaps by other generators, can provide the other features needed in the application...

We also use that strategy, but just having module generators leaves open the task of putting together the generated modules into a working system. By contrast, a diversified shell offers to the generators a well-defined framework into which they can insert the generated modules. Also, we prefer using an interpretive technique called superroutines [Sandewall 1979b], rather than the compiler-like technique of a program generator.

4. RESIDENTIAL ENVIRONMENTS SHOULD BE ABLE TO SEND AND RECEIVE PIECES OF SOFTWARE

One of the salient features of our architecture, as implemented in the *SCREEN* system, is that it is organized as a number of *residential environments;* this term was defined in [Sandewall 1978], i.e. almost autonomous systems, each of which has its own diversified shell, and whatever contents have been placed into it. Software updates are often performed by having one environment send a patch of software (programs and/or data) to one or more others. Each environment typically serves one user, and is thought of by that user as one piece of software equipment, or a 'software individual', because it has a unique existence through time, and it changes gradually over time as the result of successive software updates that are sent to it from outside, or made on it by the user.

Environments are similar to ADA *configurations* [Buxton 1980], since they are built up from available modules, but they differ from configurations in being able to receive updates and to modify themselves as well. Implementation-wise, in *SCREEN* they are Interlisp 'sysouts' (analogous to APL 'workspaces') (one environment may be one single 'sysout' or several of them which invoke each other).

This section describes the reasons for, as well as some interesting consequences of, that architecture.

The information-flow scenario above provided one reason why different end users need their private *end-user environments*, i.e. customized systems which have the same shell, but filled with different contents. Other reasons are because each user may need his or her own customized repertoire of data base queries, report specifications, edit macros, etc., and because a user who is able to modify the appearance of his or her system is likely to be more satisfied with it (just like having control of your physical working environment is psychologically valuable).

At the same time, there are strong reasons why the personal systems should not be self-contained, but instead should be able to communicate software between them. Although advanced tools, such as query languages and forms handlers, enable end users to make some software additions by themselves, certainly the end user will need to be helped in some cases by a programmer. The programmer should then be able to implement the new service on *his* personal system, which could contain professional tools for testing and debugging, support for special-purpose languages for professional use, tools for keeping track of what software updates have been sent to which users, and other software development services. Since new services are often implemented using special-purpose tools, rather than a general-purpose programming language, we shall use the term *development environment*, rather than the possibly more narrow term 'programming environment', for the environment used by the 'programmer'.

Although software updates may also be made directly in the end-user environment, the use of separate development environments is advantageous not only because extra tools may be made available, but also because many services may be needed by several users, and because (like in information-flow applications) some services require different but co-ordinated pieces of software to be sent to different end-user environments.

However, if pieces of software are developed in one development environment (DE) and transferred for execution in another environment (EUE), special care must be taken that they are inserted correctly. There are in principle three possible (although non-exclusive) ways of handling that problem:

• DE's contain a lot of "knowledge" about the internal structure of the various EUE's
• There is a central data base which contains descriptions of the structure of the EUE's
• Each EUE contains "knowledge" about its own structure, so that incoming software updates can contain abstract specifications of where they are to be inserted, and the EUE decides actively where the patch should be inserted

We avoid the first approach, because multiple DE's are needed, and *SCREEN* uses a combination of the second and third approaches, with as much use of self-description in the EUE as possible. One touchstone for the design of the self-description has been the following: each environment must be able to re-generate itself, i.e. it must be able to generate a 'program' which, when executed within a blank Lisp system, will load into that system those modules which are necessary in order to re-create a rejuvenated equivalent of the originating environment.

There are potentially other kinds of environments, such as *end-user programming environments*, which enable an end user to specify the system's behavior patterns in application-oriented terms, and *control environments* which autonomously control some aspect of the total system's behavior without user dialogue, e.g. causing certain programs to be run at certain hours (like a batch controller). We have however not yet tried using these openings.

5. STRUCTURES BUILT FROM CONCEPTS (NAMED OBJECTS) PROVIDE AN UPDATABLE STRUCTURE IN EACH ENVIRONMENT

Through the global data base or by other means, the DE's and the EUE's must share some knowledge about the EUE's structure. It is clearly a good idea to express that knowledge in terms of *what* the EUE's do, rather than *how* they do it. For the reasons described above, the mapping from the *what* model to the *how* model is stored in the EUE. It is therefore also natural to store at least parts of the *what* model itself in the EUE.

There is also another good use for that information in the EUE. When the end user has to deal with a continously changing computer system, there must be some characteristics in the system which remain stable, and there should also be a frame of reference which allows the user and the system to communicate about how today's system structure relates to last week's structure.

An analogous problem of finding one's way around in a changing environment occurs in a city where construction often goes on, but only locally. The street map in the city then serves as a framework for the inhabitant, and allows him to accommodate to the changes.

These considerations led to two crucial design decisions: First, *the software structure is organized around concepts, structures, and processes which are seen and used by the end user, or which are useful for describing the application environment.*

In *SCREEN*, e.g. as used for the LOIS office information system, the top-level structure is to give the user a choice between several *contexts* (i.e. subsystems such as mail, agenda, personal data base). Within each context, there are usually additional choices to be made in one or more dimensions, e.g. the choice between commands in most of the contexts, the choice between agenda categories, between data sets in the personal data base, etc.

Secondly, since this basic framework of contexts, commands, categories, etc. is needed for multiple uses when the end-user environment is running, it *is represented explicitly as a data structure*, not only in DE's but also in EUE's. In that data structure, each context name has attached information about what commands are available in it, what local variables are bound in the context, what expressions have to be executed when the context is entered, etc. (We will refer to this structure as a 'data structure', rather than as a 'data base', because it is internal to the environment, rather than globally available data).

The information that is stored in the data structure for each environment, can clearly be viewed as specifications for that environment. In our architecture, these specifications are not a "source" from which the "executable" system is constructed or generated; instead they are *the dominant structure in* the executable system.

The data structure that we use in *SCREEN* is a **frame system** as developed in artificial intelligence research (for an introduction to frames, see e.g. Winston [Winston and Horn 1981, page 291 ff]). It is constructed from named objects (corresponding to what are otherwise often called "concepts") and relationships between them, implemented using "slots". Therefore, the elementary piece of information is the **assignment** of a value to an **object.** (This is an assignment in a static sense - the object has a value - rather than in the dynamic sense of an assignment operation such as the Algol :=). One object may have several **slots,** and an assigned value in each of the slots. The assignment can be given explicitly, inherited, computed when needed, or augmented when needed, all using data-driven procedures (cf. Winston, ibid, page 211 ff).

Concepts are often associated with procedures or other pieces of code. Consider for example the **agenda** (tickler file) facility in the office information system, whose standard version allows the user to ask the EUE to later remind her of phone calls, computer mail that remains to be read, and other duties. An external contributor (e.g. a user, or another environment) may now add more classes of tasks to the agenda, so that an agenda printout may be

```
4 PHONE CALLS TO MAKE OF WHICH 1 ASAP
11 NEW MESSAGES IN COMPUTER MAIL
LISP CONFERENCE PAPERS DUE NEXT WEEK
6 LEAVE OF ABSENCE REQUESTS PENDING
14% OF WORKING TIME THIS WEEK SCHEDULED FOR MEETINGS
```

Here the last three items are the printouts for three additional, and user-specific objects in the type **agenda-tasks.** The agenda facility of course knows how to look up all currently relevant agenda-tasks, and for each of them to look up and invoke the little data-driven procedure which inspects the current data structure to compute the figures, and composes the appropriate printout line. The user can proceed directly from this agenda menu to doing the work it suggests (for example pointing at line 4 will bring her into the routine for looking at and approving leaves of absence), or she may merely find out more about the work (for example look closer at the list of intended phone calls). In all cases, her actions cause the invocation of other programs or data attached to the agenda-task.

In many cases, the user obtains multiple, orthogonal options, again often physically represented by menu choices. For example, the services for handling text files, in the LOIS office information system, work with a number of different object types, including:

• **text files** (the objects of direct interest to the user. Reports from the data base may be implemented by associating some file names with procedures for generating the file automatically when needed)
• **classification categories** of text files: teaching, research, etc.
• **format** of text files: letter, memo, contract, etc. (Each format may be associated with e.g. a procedure which generates the beginning of a file automatically)
• **formatter** used to operate on text files. The formatter object is associated with information both about the pieces of software that make up the formatter, the conventions for calling it, and the command conventions that are used in the text file
• **language** (English, Swedish, etc.) in which the text is written. Has implications, e.g. for the choice of fonts, for the choice of reserved words in the formatter ("page", "chapter", etc.), and for hyphenization rules. Much of this information is best given by procedures associated with the language name.

Classical programming languages such as Simula certainly allow one or more procedures to be associated with identifiers (e.g. Simula class names) in the program. However, the language definition in those cases does not account for treating those same identifiers as known entities at run-time. The examples given above show how many kinds of named objects which are needed at run-time, may also need to be associated with procedures. A **case** statement is in fact a mapping from symbols to pieces of code; our architecture represents that mapping more explicitly by slot assignments.

6. SUPERROUTINES ARE AN IMPROVEMENT OVER PROGRAM GENERATORS

In every applications area, there is a need for special tools. In office automation, tools for data base queries, report generation, and forms handling are commonplace. There are two common strategies for such tools:

• General-purpose programs with parameters, where some aspects of the program's behavior can be controlled by setting the parameters. A description of a form (giving X/Y coordinates for all fields) is an example of a parameter which is a data structure.
• Program generators which translate from a specification language, to a source program in a programming language, which may then be further compiled.

As a rule, program generators may provide greater flexibility. Often they are organized so that there is a fixed top-level structure for the generated program, but some positions in the program called *handles* are variable, and their contents are to be written out in the specification, or are computed from information in the specification.

For example, in the parser generator YACC [Johnson and Lesk 1978], there is one handle where code fragments (written in C) associated with each production in tne syntax, are incorporated into a **case** statement, and one handle called **yylex** where a lexical procedure may be inserted, hand-written or generated using the separate tool Lex.

The procedures or code fragments which are stored as slot values in the data structures of our environments would be contributions to program generators that we might have in our system. However, since the procedures are already in the environment used at execution time, no program generation is in fact necessary - these code fragments can be called directly.

The technique that we are using then has been called *superroutines* [Sandewall 1979b]. It is the interpretive equivalent of program generators. The superroutine is identical to the 'fixed, top-level structure' for the generated program, but it is available at run-time, and the variable parts of the program are either computed when needed and executed immediately, or stored in the data structure, and retrieved and executed when needed.

In another view, the superroutine is a generalization of the parameterized program, where the parameters are not restricted to flags or codes, but they may also be procedures or pieces of programs, which are stored in the data structure, and invoked indirectly through data access chains.

For example, *SCREEN* contains a superroutine for forms handling called IFORM, which accepts a form layout description as a parameter, and where each field in the form may be associated with a number of procedures, as:

- A procedure for checking the correctness of values entered by the user
- A procedure for transforming values entered by the user, to their appropriate, internal form, and for performing any forward side effects of the entry of these data
- An inverse procedure for printing out values in the data base in appropriate format on the screen

as well as a number of others. The major advantages of the interpretive character of the superroutine are that errors are more easily controlled, updates are performed more easily, and it is easier to make multiple use of the same information (i.e. information is more "declarative" rather than "procedural").

Superroutines may be said to be interpreters for special-purpose languages, e.g. the forms description language. However, one must realize that the forms description (as well as several other of the special-purpose languages) is only used internally in the data structure of the environment. For the user, the forms description is entered by "drawing" the form on the screen, and is edited in the same fashion. It would in fact be better to reserve the term 'language' for the expressions typed by the user *and* by the computer during that dialogue, and to use the term 'knowledge representation' for the large expression in a formal language that describes the whole form. Thus superroutines are more precisely used as *interpreters for special-purpose knowledge representations* (which have often been communicated using special-purpose dialogue languages).

SCREEN environments contain a limited and fairly fixed repertoire of superroutines (for command dialogue, form-oriented dialogue on the screen, report generation, search in the data base, etc., as well as for a number of system-oriented purposes), together with a large structure of conceptual entities which store information ranging from specifications and documentation, to information which directs the superroutines. Also, it should be clear at this point that *the diversified shell is just one of those superroutines* - it is a fixed procedure with a lot of handles, where the contributions from various applications are attached.

With some simplification, we may then distinguish two kinds of contents in environments: fixed, procedural parts, namely the diversified shell and the library of superroutines, and a data structure part which is variable in the sense that it is tailored to each user, and that it changes over time, more fluently than the procedural parts. These two parts interrelate because the procedural parts often access the data structure to retrieve procedures which are immediately invoked, and which in their turn may often call one of the standard superroutine tools.

7. ON PROGRAMMING TECHNIQUES AND PROGRAMMING STYLE

Environments organized with those two kinds of contents encourage the programmer to make software updates by extending the data-structure part of an environment. Some heuristics for the programmer (or more generally, the person that develops or extends the software) are:

• When a system is extended with new features which are analogous to existing ones, for example support for additional output devices, or introduction of a new kind of structured inter-user messages, try making the extension by introducing additonal named objects into the environment, and providing it with the descriptive information that is needed for execution, documentation, and maintenance;

• For all kinds of system extensions, always look out for concepts which are defined in the application, and try to organize the software around it. This technique is useful both because it suggests a structure for the software, and because it prepares the ground for future addition of analoguous features.

For the end user, this software structure hopefully means that he or she can often form a reasonable model of how the software works and how it changes. Users can frequently communicate in terms of embedded languages, at least with a programmer and sometimes (given enough support software) even with the computer system.

The use of application-oriented concepts as a software framework also makes it easier to arrange that the system's behavior, and the changes in its behavior, is comprehensible for the end user. When operating the system, the end user regularly encounters situations where he has a choice of options, be they commands, formats, data set, language, or whatever, and where changes during the evolution of the software are often merely reflected by additions to a menu, or warning texts that a certain, previously existing item has been changed. Requests for software changes that are sent from the user to a software developer are of course organized in the same ways.

Not surprisingly, updates that are sent from one environment to another often have the same structure, i.e. they consist of definitions for a small number of new objects, assignments to slots for these objects, and assignments to new slots for old objects which already exist in the receiving environment.

This style of working with software marks another departure from old habits. When working with traditional programming languages, we become used to thinking of data as an appendix to the program: the program *is essentially* an algorithm, and it *contains* declarations, and data structures are *created* dynamically as the program is executed. Using *SCREEN*, we think instead of the update as being essentially *a collection of data*, built from objects and relationships, although some attributes of some of those objects may be interpretable as procedures.

8. INCREMENTAL ADVISING IS USEFUL WHEN THE APPLICATION DOES NOT NATURALLY OFFER NAMED OBJECTS (CONCEPTS)

The technique of making software updates by introducing new, named objects, or adding slot assignments to existing objects, is not always sufficient. Although we can always resort to conventional code updates or classical Interlisp-style advising [Teitelman 1978], other and more precise techniques are desirable.

Incremental advising is such a technique. When it is used, a procedure may contain a named *advice point*, i.e. a point to which incremental code ("advice") may be added, and other modules may contain advice to the advice point. (An update message that is sent from one environment to another may constitute such a module). Each piece of advice therefore has the form 'module M gives advice to advice point P that <code>'. Several pieces of advice may be given from different modules to the same advice point, and the origins of these pieces of advice are maintained separately, so that individual pieces of advice may be deleted, or passed on to other environments.

Advice points may be either named objects (like ordinary procedures) or slots of arbitrary objects (i.e. the advice point is a data driven procedure).

Incremental advising is used for many purposes in the software for the *SCREEN* system itself, and in the superimposed LOIS office information system. For example, there are advice points for the entry and exit of a context, for temporary detachment from an environment (Interlisp 'sysout' function) and for the corresponding resumption; for the regeneration of an environment, and so forth. Various services give incremental advice to these advice points; for example, the resumption of an environment has incremental advice for bringing it up to date with what may have happened while it was asleep, e.g. picking up various kinds of messages, as contributed by modules that make use of the respective kinds of messages.

9. TOOLS FOR ADMINISTRATING LARGE NUMBERS OF NAMED OBJECTS SHOULD BUILD 'UPWARDS' FROM THE ELEMENTS OF THE DATA STRUCTURE

The number of objects and slot assignments grows quite rapidly. The present LOIS system already contains many hundreds of them. Conceptual tools and software tools for administrating them are therefore necessary. *SCREEN* suggests and supports a certain uniform structure on the data. This structure is useful both inside environments, and for defining the extraction of modules from environments and the incorporation of modules into environments. The structure is based on two orthogonal concepts, the *block* concept and a fairly conventional *type* concept. They can be characterized as pragmatic and semantic, respectively: types characterize what data have the same structure; blocks describe what data are to be processed or used together.

The type concept is the familiar one: each object has a type, which implies the existence of certain slots in the object, and sometimes also restrictions on the possible value in the slot. We allow for both the conventional type mechanism, where the type name is a new object whose type is **types**, and for A.I.-style **IS-A** hierarchies where slots and slot values may be inherited from superior objects in the hierarchy.

While the data structure is resident in an environment, it is viewed as merely a large collection of slot-value assignments. When information is to be transferred from one environment to another, one usually has to transfer a number of slot assignments. Some possible strategies are to let the sending environment compute by a dependency analysis which slot assignments will be needed by the receiver for a given purpose, or to let the receiving environment ask for assignments when they are needed. Both of these strategies are likely to be time-consuming. We have therefore chosen instead to use a *block* concept for meeting the same objective.

In principle, a block is simply a set of object/slot pairs. Relative to the current contents of an environment at one point in time, it defines a set of object/slot/value triples. Some operations on blocks that may be performed within environments are:

• *Dumping* the block, i.e. putting its set of object/slot/value triples in textual form on a file (sequential file or direct-access file)

• *Loading* the block, i.e. an environment may incorporate the contents of a block as dumped by another environment

• *Checking* well-formedness of the contents of a block within an environment

• *Presentation* of a block (or the union of several blocks) to the user in a well readable format

The block concept originates from the Interlisp *makefile* technique [Teitelman 1978], where blocks are dumped to and loaded from sequential text files. We have used that facility in *SCREEN*, but the sequential-file technique has many draw-backs, and we are gradually shifting to a direct-access technique. The use of blocks for other purposes besides dumping and loading has also turned out to be very convenient. In particular, blocks are the donors of incremental advice as described in the previous section.

The important lesson to be learned from that experience is: in designing tools for controlling masses of software, do not start by assuming the currently available storage devices (e.g. text files), and then think of ways of filling them with contents. Instead, *first make clear what are your elements of information, then how you want to group it, then what operations you have on those aggregates of information, and finally, how you want to store them.* If you still think you can use ordinary text files, you have probably done something wrong.

10. THE META LEVEL SHOULD BE HANDLED IN THE SAME WAY AS THE OBJECT LEVEL

The currently running, *SCREEN*-based software consists of about ten environments, containing software that is organized as several hundred blocks, and using named objects in about one hundred different types, each with potentially a considerable number of slots. The whole system is required to change dynamically, not only because of evolving research ideas, but also because of new application requirements.

It goes without saying that maintenance tools are needed for such a structure. In fact, one additional reason for organizing software using the frame-oriented data structure was the idea that documentation could be integrated into the same data structure in a simple, convenient, and natural fashion.

That hypothesis has in fact been confirmed when working with the system. It has been natural to store various kinds of documentary information in the *SCREEN* environments. Also, just as named objects and object types are introduced for various applications, the task of software maintenance gives rise to a number of object types: *environments* (each of which has a name), modules or what we call *blocks* (each of which of course has a name also), *facilities,* i.e. software development undertakings (the handling of fonts could, e.g. be one facility, containing a font generator, a font editor, an addition to the formatter for accounting for fonts, etc. Thus a facility contains a number of blocks, subsets of which are given to different environments, and it is also associated with a set of programmers, a set of documents, etc.)

An extensive description of the documentation structure that is built within the *SCREEN* system has been published elsewhere [Sandewall et al. 1980b]. Let us just emphasize again one crucial characteristic, namely that the meta level task of describing the system is handled in the same way as object level tasks, and using the same techniques and the same software tools.

11. CONCLUSION

Software design has been sub-divided into the tasks of designing operating systems, programming languages, program generators, data base systems, and so forth. Sub-disciplines of computer science and software engineering have dedicated themselves to studying each of these kinds of software. Unfortunately, the top-level design is obsolete. It does not change easily, partly because of old habits, and perhaps also because each sub-discipline focuses on its own task, and takes the rest of the world more or less for granted. The purpose of this paper has been to suggest that we should take a fresh look at those basic design assumptions.

ACKNOWLEDGMENTS

The philosophy of software architecture that has been described here is based on the philosophy that is prevalent in the A.I. community of Lisp users. In particular, we owe a lot to discussions with David Barstow, Cordell Green, Howard Shrobe, Gerry Sussman, and Terry Winograd.

The authors of this paper have worked jointly on the *SCREEN* software. The paper was written by Erik Sandewall.

This research was supported by the Swedish Board of Technical Development under contract Dnr 79-3919 and 79-3921.

REFERENCES

[Boehm 1980] B.W. Boehm. Developing small-scale application software products: Some experimental results. In S.H. Lavington (ed). *Information Processing 80*, North-Holland, 1980, 321-326.

[Bourne 1978a] S.R. Bourne. The UNIX shell. *The Bell System Technical Journal*, 57:6 (July-August 1978), Part 2, 1971-1990.

[Brinch-Hansen 1973] P. Brinch-Hansen. *Operating System Principles*. Prentice-Hall, 1973.

[Buxton 1980] *DoD Requirements for Ada Programming Support Environments, STONEMAN*. DoD High Order Language Working Group, February 1980.

[Charniak et al. 1980] E. Charniak, C. Riesbeck, D. McDermott. *Artificial Intelligence Programming*. Lawrence Erlbaum Associates, Hillsdale, N.J., 1980.

[Ellis and Nutt 1980] C.A. Ellis, G.J. Nutt. Computer science and office information systems. *ACM Computing Surveys*, 12:1 (March 1980), 27-60.

[Johnson and Lesk 1978] S.C. Johnson, M.E. Lesk. Language development tools. *The Bell System Technical Journal*, 57:6 (July-August 1978), Part 2, 2155-2176.

[Sandewall 1978] E. Sandewall. Programming in the interactive environment: the LISP experience. *Communications of the ACM*, 10:1 (March 1978), 35-71; reprinted in *Interactive Programming Environments*.

[Sandewall 1979b] E. Sandewall. *Why superroutines are different from subroutines.* Software Systems Research Center, Linköping University, report number LITH-MAT-R-79-28, November 1979.

[Sandewall 1979c] E. Sandewall. A description language and pilot-system executive for information-transport systems. *Proceedings of the Conference on Very Large Data Bases,* Rio de Janeiro, 1979.

[Sandewall et al. 1979a] E. Sandewall et al. Linköping Office Information System - an overview of facilities and design. *Data,* Copenhagen, January-February 1979.

[Sandewall et al. 1979b] E. Sandewall, E. Jungert, G. Lönnemark, K. Sunnerud, O. Wigertz. A tool for design and development of medical data processing systems. *Proceedings of Medical Informatics,* Berlin, September 1979.

[Sandewall et al. 1980a] E. Sandewall et al. Provisions for flexibility in the Linköping Office Information System. *Proceedings of the National Computer Conference,* AFIPS Proceedings (1980).

[Sandewall et al. 1980b] E. Sandewall, H. Sörenson, C. Strömberg. A system of communicating residential environments. *Proceedings of the LISP Conference,* Stanford, California, 1980.

[Teitelman 1978] W. Teitelman. *INTERLISP Reference Manual.* Xerox Palo Alto Research Center, Palo Alto, California, December 1978.

[Winston and Horn 1981] P.H. Winston, B.K. Horn. *LISP.* Addison-Wesley, 1981.

Artificial Intelligence in Interactive Programming Environments

Artificial intelligence offers the potential for significantly enhanced support for the programmer. This potential was recognized long ago, both with the goal of fully automatic programming and with the more limited goal of supporting human programmers. (Winograd, in the first paper of this book, mentioned these goals.) Unfortunately, these goals are far from realized. The papers in this section address these issues, but no current programming environments incorporate any of the techniques discussed.

Rich and Shrobe discuss the Programmer's Apprentice, a project largely motivated by Winograd's earlier paper. Their goal is to develop a system with sufficient understanding of programming techniques to enable the maintainence of a high-level description of the code being developed by a human user. Waters describes one of the later developments of this project: an editor for LISP programs which can relate certain high-level descriptions to the code displayed on the screen.

Kant and Barstow discuss an automatic programming project which incorporated knowledge both about certain programming techniques and about efficiency trade-offs. The refinement paradigm which they employed represents a kind of design history of the program, similar in many ways to the structure used by the PDS, as described by Cheatham et al. in an earlier paper.

The common theme of all of these projects is the need to codify large amounts of knowledge about programming in a form that computers can use effectively.

22 Initial Report on a LISP Programmer's Apprentice

CHARLES RICH, HOWARD E. SHROBE

Artificial Intelligence Laboratory
Massachusetts Institute of Technology
Cambridge, Massachusetts

This paper reports on the initial design and partial implementation of an interactive programming environment to be used by expert programmers. The system is based on three forms of program description: (i) definition of structured data objects, their parts, properties, and relations between them, (ii) input-output specification of the behavior of program segments, and (iii) a hierachical representation of the internal structure of programs (plans). The plan representation is of major theoretical interest because it includes not only data flow and control flow relationships between sub-segments of a program, but also goal-subgoal, prerequisite, and other logical dependencies between the specifications of the sub-segments. Plans are utilized both for describing particular programs and in the compilation of a knowledge base of more abstract knowledge about programming, such as the concept of a loop and various specializations, such as enumeration loops and search loops. We also describe a deductive system which can verify the correctness of plans involving side-effects on complex data with structure sharing.

1. INTRODUCTION

The first computers had limited computing ability and were very difficult to program. Since that time, hardware improvements have increased the computational power of the typical computer by several orders of magnitude. Some of this additional computing power has been used to make computers easier to program by developing assemblers, compilers, operating systems, and so on. Despite these tools, modern day computer programming seems to have encountered a complexity barrier. This complexity is not due simply to the size of programs, but also to the fact that as size increases, the number of interactions between modules grows much more quickly. This difficulty is felt particularly strongly in artificial intelligence research, where present day programs are already too large to be improved upon in their present form, and yet fall far short of the levels of performance to which the field aspires.

Many avenues are currently being investigated in the search for ways to overcome the current crisis in software engineering. Some seek to bring the experience and techniques of formal mathematics to bear on the problem. For example, Floyd [Floyd 1967] and Hoare [Hoare 1969] [Hoare 1971] [Hoare 1972] started a major branch of program verification research whose goal is to develop formal logical systems in which desired properties of a program can be proven as theorems. Others have followed past example by seeking to use the computer itself to help reduce the difficulty of programming. The design of new programming languages and language processors is currently a very active field, including Hewitt et al. [Hewitt et al. 1973], Liskov et al. [Liskov et al. 1977], and Wulf et al. [Wulf et al. 1976b], to name a few. Useful code manipulation and bookkeeping tools, such as editors, indexers, and spelling correctors have also been implemented for existing languages. In the best cases, these tools have been integrated into coherent programming environments, as for example Interlisp [Teitelman 1978] or the Programmer's Workbench [Dolotta and Mashey 1976]. The ultimate form of using the computer itself to solve the software problem is automatic programming. The goal of this research is to create a system which will automatically generate correct and reasonably efficient code which satisfies given high-level, application-oriented specifications. Unfortunately it does not appear that this goal will be attainable in the near future [Balzer 1973].

Our approach to the software problem lies between language-oriented programming tools on the one hand, and automatic programming on the other. Language-oriented tools have essentially reached the limit of their potential without the addition of a major new kind of knowledge about the subject programs. Part of this knowledge is the same as required for automatic programming, i.e. an understanding of the application domain and the way that parts of a program, which exist in the abstract world of the computer memory, relate to concrete objects and operations in the real world. Another part of this knowledge is to a great extent independent of the application domain. This consists of the basic algorithms and data structuring techniques of programming such as those compiled by Knuth [Knuth 1968a].

Given knowledge of basic programming technique and the ability to assimilate application domain concepts, it becomes possible for a computer system to understand a user's program in a much deeper sense and therefore to cooperate with him more effectively in the design, implementation, and maintenance of the program. We call such a system a *programmer's apprentice*. An apprentice need not be capable of programming by itself, but can aid the expert programmer by checking his work in various ways. We see this as a realistic interim solution to current software problems and as an evolutionary path towards the more ambitious goals of automatic programming. Similar solutions have been suggested by Floyd [Floyd 1971] and Winograd [Winograd 1973] although there are methodological distinctions between their proposals and our work.

Work is in progress on this project in the form of three Ph.D. dissertations [Rich 1977] [Shrobe 1978] [Waters 1976]. This paper reports on the theoretical framework we have worked out to support the construction of a programmer's apprentice. A longer and more detailed progress report is available in [Rich and Shrobe 1976]. The primary value of this framework thus far has been to identify the sub-problems which are being pursued in the three dissertations. Each dissertation also includes an experimental implementation of one important component of the programmer's apprentice. This phase of research will soon be followed by a unified implementation to demonstrate the feasibility of the kind of integrated system we describe here.

2. A SCENARIO

To explain our concept of a programmer's apprentice in more detail, we first present an imagined scenario which traces the design, coding, and later modification of a hash table deletion program. The only major feature of the following scenario which is not currently part of our research goals is the use of free English dialogue. Although we feel certain that the system we are designing will be able to support a sophisticated natural language "front-end", we have made no efforts in this direction.

[The scenario starts at a point when many design choices have already been documented with the apprentice. In particular, the input-output specifications of the lookup, insert, and delete routines have been given and the basic data structures have been chosen. The hash table has been implemented as an array of linked lists. Each list is called a "bucket". Each entry in the table is a dotted-pair whose CAR is the key part.]

PRGMR: The plan for the delete routine has three main steps: first hash the input key to get an index; then fetch the bucket corresponding to that index from the table; and finally splice out all entries in the bucket whose key part is equal to the input key.

[The apprentice uses the programmer's outline of the design to build an abstract representation of the program's intended structure, called a "plan". Notice the programmer assumes that the apprentice knows many basic programming techniques such as "splicing out" (deleting elements from a linked list.)]

APPRENTICE: I'm sorry, but I can't verify that this plan satisfies the specifications for delete. In particular, when the key of the first entry in a bucket is equal to the input key, I can't prove that all entries with keys equal to the input key are not members of the table after the delete. In such cases, the bucket after splicing out entries is not identical to the bucket before splicing out entries.

[The apprentice has symbolically evaluated the plan and discovered an error. In general, it is the responsibility of the programmer to supply corrections.]

PRGMR: OK, then modify the plan as follows. Compare the bucket after splicing with the bucket before splicing. If they are not identical, store the new bucket in the table under the index.

APPRENTICE: That seems to fix the bug.

PRGMR: Here's the code.

```
(DEFINE DELETE (KEY)
  ;; hash table delete routine.
  (PROG (BKT1 BKT2)
        (SETQ BKT1 (TBL (HASH KEY)))
        (SETQ BKT2 (BKT-DELETE KEY BKT1))
        (COND ((NOT (EQ BKT1 BKT2))
                ;; special case when first entry in bucket deleted.
                (STORE (TBL (HASH KEY)) BKT1)))))
```

APPRENTICE: I'm sorry but this code is not consistent with your plan. In the special case you are storing the bucket before splicing, rather than the bucket after splicing. Did you mean (STORE (TBL (HASH KEY)) BKT2)?

PRGMR: Yes, fix the code. Also, you can code BKT-DELETE as the standard list deletion algorithm.

APPRENTICE: Here it is.

```
(DEFINE BKT-DELETE (KEY BUCKET)
  ;; list deletion routine coded by apprentice.
  (PROG (CURRENT PREVIOUS)
        (SETQ PREVIOUS NIL)      ;initialize trailing ptr.
        (SETQ CURRENT BUCKET)    ;initialize ptr to current entry.
    LP  (COND ((NULL CURRENT)
                (RETURN BUCKET))
              ((EQUAL (CAAR CURRENT) KEY)
                ;; splice out entry.
                (COND (PREVIOUS (RPLACD PREVIOUS (CDR CURRENT)))
                      ;; special case when first element in list deleted.
                      (T (SETQ BUCKET (CDR BUCKET))))
                (SETQ CURRENT (CDR CURRENT))
                (GO LP))
              (T (SETQ PREVIOUS CURRENT)
                 (SETQ CURRENT (CDR CURRENT))
                 (GO LP)))))
```

[This is the implementation of a standard algorithm. Notice that the apprentice provides comments on generated code and attempts to use mnemonic variable names from the programmer's design. In a cooperative programming environment, code written by the programmer and by the apprentice may be freely mixed; in fact each may edit the other's work.]

[... Some time later it is necesary to make a modification of the original design. The apprentice helps the (perhaps new) programmer maintain consistency.]

PRGMR: I want to make a change in the representation of buckets in the hashing programs. A bucket now has two parts: a count field and a list of entries as before. The count field will contain an integer equal to the length of the list of entries. Let a bucket be a dotted-pair whose CAR is the count and whose CDR is the list of entries.

APPRENTICE: The proposed change will affect LOOKUP, INSERT, and DELETE.

PRGMR: What are the problems in DELETE?

APPRENTICE: After fetching the bucket you test the key of its first element. But in this new implementation, the CAR of a bucket is a number not an entry. Secondly, the input to BKT-DELETE is a bucket, but it requires a list of entries.

PRGMR: Explain the plan for BKT-DELETE please.

APPRENTICE: BKT-DELETE is implemented as the standard list deletion plan. Inputs are a key and a list of entries. The plan is a search loop using two pointers: a pointer to the current entry which is initialized to the input list, and a trailing pointer which is initialized to NIL. On each iteration it tests the key of the first element of the current list. If it is equal to the input key, it splices the current element out of the list by RPLACD'ing the trailing pointer.

PRGMR: Change the specifications of this BKT-DELETE to expect as input a bucket of the new type, rather than a list of entries. Also change the initialization of the pointers to read:

```
(SETQ PREVIOUS BUCKET)
(SETQ CURRENT (CDR BUCKET))
```

APPRENTICE: OK. Now the special case tests in BKT-DELETE and DELETE are not necessary since PREVIOUS is never NIL and therefore elements are always deleted by side-effect.

PRGMR: Remove the unnecessary tests.

APPRENTICE: OK. By the way, there is currently no code to maintain the count field.

[... and so the session continues with the apprentice looking over the programmer's shoulder.]

3. OVERVIEW OF THE THEORY

The major theoretical problem in building a programmer's apprentice is to develop a computer representation of programs and knowledge about programs which can facilitate smooth and natural interaction between the programmer and the apprentice. This kind of problem falls within the paradigm of artificial intelligence research.

Our system is based on three forms of program description: (i) definition of structured data objects, their parts, properties, and the relations between them, (ii) input-output specifications of program behavior, and (iii) a hierarchical representation of the internal structure of programs, called *plans*. The major new part of this work is the plan representation, which includes not only the data flow and control flow relationships between parts of a program, but also goal-subgoal, prerequisite, and other logical dependencies. Plans are utilized in the apprentice both for describing particular programs, and for the compilation of a knowledge base (*plan library*) of general knowledge about programming, such as the concept of a loop and its various specializations such as enumeration loops and search loops.

An important observation to be made from the scenario is that there are two different levels at which the apprentice needs to understand and describe the structure of a program. First there is what we call the *surface plan*, a description of the control flow and data flow between the parts of the program. This information is explicitly stated in the program code. However, the apprentice also needs an understanding of the logical structure of the program, called the *deep plan*, which explains how and why the program works. The deep plan is not explicit in the code, but sometimes shows up in comments such as "special case for deleting first entry of bucket".

In the surface plan for a program, each operation or data structure is described by its universally true (or *intrinsic*) specifications. For example, the LISP function CAR always returns the left half of the dotted-pair which is its argument. However, different instances of the CAR function may be used for different purposes. Deep plans assign a purpose (or *extrinsic*) description to each part of a program. For example, one instance of CAR in the scenario is used to extract the count field from a bucket, another is used to extract the key part of an entry. A major deficiency of current approaches to program description, such as the Floyd-Hoare method [Floyd 1967] [Hoare 1969] [Hoare 1971] [Hoare 1972], has been to concentrate on surface plans and intrinsic specifications because these are easily accessible from the code. Languages such as CLU [Liskov et al. 1977] and Alphard [Wulf et al. 1976b] can make up for this deficiency to some extent by raising the abstraction level of the programming language so that purposes are more obvious in the source code.

Hierarchy is another major tool employed by programmers to help understand programs. Depending on the task at hand, the units of description (*segments*) can be very large or small. The plan for a program is hierarchical, so that a large segment can be described in more detail if necessary by expanding its internal plan. For example, at a high level of description the entire DELETE function is a single segment. Its internal plan has three sub-segments: hashing, fetching the bucket, and list deletion. List deletion as a segment also has an internal plan, and so on. Our use of hierarchy, however, is much less rigid than what is advocated by proponents of top-down programming or the virtual-machine method [Dahl et al. 1972]. In the engineering of real-world programs, it is common for strict hierarchy to be violated, usually for the sake of efficiency. For example, the internal plans for two segments may overlap so that a single sub-segment has two different purposes, one in each plan.

Closely related to hierarchy is the notion of abstraction. The apprentice's knowledge base of programming expertise must be expressed at a sufficient level of generality to be applicable to many different programs. Our representation system employs data abstractions of a type similar to CLU or SIMULA in which a data type is defined by its operations and properties. In the apprentice, however, we have combined this data abstraction technique with our plan representation, which abstracts the logical structure of procedures.

4. OVERVIEW OF THE SYSTEM

Figure 1 shows and names the main knowledge structures (denoted by rectangles) and processes (denoted by ovals) in our system. The left side of the figure shows the kinds of program description that are most directly involved in coding activity. The right side shows the deeper knowledge used in program design.

At the leftmost of the figure is a box labelled to indicate that LISP code (with comments) is a main user input to the system. We feel it is important to have at the ground level actual code that can be run by a standard LISP interpreter. The first level of abstraction above raw LISP code is the surface

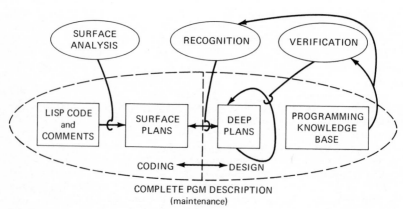

Figure 1. Overview of the System.

plan, which is obtained from LISP code by *surface flow analysis*. The surface flow analyzer is the only programming language dependent component in the system. Given LISP code for a program, it generates a surface plan which represents the program's control flow and data flow in a more convenient and abstract form.

On the design side of the diagram are the deep plans for particular programs under construction and the programming knowledge base, which contains very general deep plans and knowledge about how to verify them. More is said about these later and in [Rich and Shrobe 1976].

For the apprentice to understand a particular program means that it has connected three levels of description of the program: code, surface plan and deep plan. One way this can happen is for the programmer, as in the scenario, to initially specify and have the apprentice verify a deep plan. An important and novel feature of this approach is that the deductive system operates on plans rather than directly on LISP code. This achieves a useful factorization of the verification problem. When the programmer then writes the actual code, the apprentice checks to see that it is compatible with the programmer's intentions by first generating the surface plan and then *recognizing* the correspondence between segments in the surface plan and segments in the deep plan. The recognition component must be able to use general programming knowledge and specific programmer-supplied commentary to aid in establishing a plausible correspondence. The net result of this interaction with the apprentice is a complete description of the program at both the surface and deep levels, which will support explanation and aid in program maintenance.

Initial implementations of the deductive system and of the LISP flow analysis component have been completed; the recognition component is under development. Our current implementation defines and operates on most of the important knowledge representations required to support the introductory scenario. However it is fragmentary and has none of the interactive facilities which would make it usable by a real programmer.

5. THE SCENARIO REVISITED

We return now to the introductory scenario to describe the operation of our system in more detail. We will introduce the various representations and forms of processing we have developed as they would be invoked in the hash table example. The reader is referred to [Rich and Shrobe 1976] for more details than given here.

> [The scenario starts at a point when many design choices have already been documented with the apprentice. In particular, the input-output specifications of the lookup, insert, and delete routines have been given ...]

The apprentice's basic unit of behavioral description is a *segment*. Data objects flow into a segment and new or side-effected data objects flow out. The point of time just before the segment executes is called its *input situation*; the point of time just after is called its *output situation*. A segment is defined by its *specs*, which are a formal statement of input expectations (conditions on or relationships between input objects that are expected to hold in the input situation) and output assertions (conditions that will hold on the input and output objects in the output situation). In terms of code, a segment may correspond to a function definition, the body of a conditional, or several lines of open code. The degree of aggregation is flexible, allowing the programmer and the apprentice to work at the level of detail which is most convenient at the time. The specifications of the hash table deletion segment are as follows.

```
(DEFSPECS delete-segment
   (INPUTS: key1 table1)
   (OUTPUTS: table2)
   (EXPECT: (hashtable table1)
            (hashkey key1))
   (ASSERT: (hashtable table2)
            (side-effected table1)
            (id table1 table2)
            (forall (member table1 =entry)
                if  (keypart =entry key1)
                then (not (member table2 =entry))
                else (member table2 =entry))
            (forall (member table2 =entry)
                    (member table1 =entry)))))
```

These specifications state that DELETE-SEGMENT takes as inputs a hash key and a hash table. The net result of this segment (its output) is an updated hash table containing all the same entries as the input table except for those which have the input key. The SIDE-EFFECTED clause above signals that TABLE1 has been modified to produce the desired results, while the ID clause states that TABLE1 and TABLE2 are two names which refer to the same object, the hash table, in different situations.

We make the convention that clauses which mention an output object refer to the output situation of the segment, while clauses which mention only input objects refer to the input situation. Since TABLE1 is an input name while TABLE2 is an output name, we can conveniently talk about the state of the table before deletion by using the name TABLE1 and to the state of the table after deletion by using the name TABLE2. We may also state relationships between these two states of the table by using quantified statements in which certain of the clauses mention only input objects and certain mention output objects. Thus the first quantified statement in the above specs is equivalent to the following statement in which the situations have been made explicit.

```
(FORALL (member table1 =entry)        IN *input-situation*
    IF  (keypart =entry key1)         IN *input-situation*
    THEN (not (member table1 =entry)) IN *output-situation*
    ELSE (member table1 =entry)       IN *output-situation*)
```

INPUT-SITUATION and *OUTPUT-SITUATION* are special variables which, when reasoning about this segment, are bound to the appropriate input and output situations. Our system will accept specs written in this more explicit manner, although we have found the earlier abbreviated form more convenient. Notice that this quantified statement represents a side-effect to the hash table by specifying which facts of the input situation remain true in the output situation and which are to be updated.

> [...the basic data structures have been chosen. The hash table has been implemented as an array of linked lists. Each list is called a "bucket". Each entry in the table is a dotted-pair whose CAR is the key part.]

We want the apprentice to use a description of data structures which is close to the kind of explanations commonly given by programmers as above. One of the most common data structure notions is that there are object types which are characterized by their decomposition into parts and the relations that hold between these parts. Table 1 shows how we have taken this approach to describing the structure that is common to all hash tables.

Table 1. Abstract Description of Hash Tables

```
(OBJECT-TYPE hashtable)
(OBJECT-TYPE hashbucket)
(OBJECT-TYPE entry)
(OBJECT-TYPE hashkey)

(PART (keypart entry hashkey))

(INDEXED-PART (bucketpart hashtable index hashbucket))

(PROPERTY (size hashtable natural-number))

(RELATION (member hashtable entry))
(RELATION (member hashbucket entry))

(FUNCTION (hash hashkey hashtable index))

(RELATION-DEFINITION
    (member hashtable entry) <=>
    (member [bucketpart hashtable
                        [hash [keypart entry] hashtable]]
            entry))
```

The first four statements in Table 1 define four object types: HASHTABLE, HASHBUCKET, ENTRY and HASHKEY. The next statement defines a part relationship and a type restriction on that part: ENTRY's have a part called the KEYPART which is of type HASHKEY.

Some objects, for example arrays, have many parts which are indentified by a numerical index rather than distinctive names such as KEYPART. This is represented by an INDEXED-PART statement. Table 1 defines hash tables to have an indexed part called BUCKETPART which is restricted to be of type HASHBUCKET.

Table 1 also defines certain properties, relations and functions which are relevant to hash tables. A hash table has a SIZE, which is a natural number. There is a MEMBER relation between entries and the hash table, and between entries and hash buckets. Finally there is a HASH function which, given a hash key and a hash table, computes an index.

Notice that PROPERTY, RELATION and FUNCTION statements specify only the name of a particular relationship and restrictions on the types of the arguments. Many properties and relations between objects can be further defined in terms of the objects' internal part structure, and are thus subject to change if a part is changed. For example, changes to the buckets of a table affect what is a member of the table. Our current system can reason about such side-effects, as will be seen later in the paper. The information required to do this kind of reasoning is expressed in RELATION-DEFINITION's and PROPERTY-DEFINITION's.

The RELATION-DEFINITION in Table 1 states that an entry is a member of the hash table if and only if it is a member of the bucket indexed by hashing the key part of the entry. The square brackets in the definition denote functional terms. Thus if (KEYPART ENTRY1 KEY1) is a predicate which means it is true that KEY1 is the key part of ENTRY1, then [KEYPART ENTRY1] is read *the object which is* the key part of ENTRY1.

The way the programmer has chosen to implement the abstract structure of a hash table using an array, lists, and dotted pairs is represented by the

Table 2. Description of Hash Table Implementation

```
(IMPLEMENTATION-PART (implementing-array hashtable array))

(IMPLEMENTATION-DEFINITION
    (bucketpart hashtable index hashbucket) <=>
    (item [implementing-array hashtable] index hashbucket))

(IMPLEMENTATION-DEFINITION
    (size hashtable natural-number) <=>
    (upperbound [implementing-array hashtable] natural-number)


(IMPLEMENTATION-PART (implementing-list hashbucket list))

(IMPLEMENTATION-DEFINITION
    (member hashbucket entry) <=>
    (member [implementing-list hashbucket] entry))


(IMPLEMENTATION-PART (implementing-pair entry dotted-pair))

(IMPLEMENTATION-DEFINITION
    (keypart entry key) <=>
    (car [implementing-pair entry] key))
```

apprentice as shown in Table 2. Each abstract object type is implemented by one or more concrete objects, called its *implementation parts*. Implementation parts are defined using a syntax similar to PART statements. This scenario shows a comparatively simple example of data structure implementation, since in each case a single abstract object is implemented using a single implementation part. Many implementation strategies combine two or more data objects to achieve the desired abstract behavior, as for example using an array and two pointers to implement an input-output queue.

In addition to naming the parts of a data implementation, the parts and properties of the implemented object are mapped down via IMPLEMENTATION-DEFINITION's onto parts and properties of the implementing objects. Thus Table 2 states that for this example the buckets of the hash table correspond to the items of the implementing array, and the size of the hash table corresponds to the upper bound on the index of the array (assuming here that the object type ARRAY and its parts and properties are pre-defined). Table 2 describes the implementation of the buckets as lists and entries as dotted pairs similarly.

> PRGMR: The plan for the delete routine has three main steps: first hash the input key to get an index; then fetch the bucket corresponding to that index from the table; and finally splice out all entries in the bucket whose key part is equal to the input key.

We view programs as being constructed of input-output segments connected by control and data flow. This is not the only possible way to think about programs, but it is one which many practicing programmers find intuitive. Because the apprentice is intended to be an interactive system, this naturalness of representation has been an important design criterion throughout. We represent the control and data flow between segments in a plan graphically

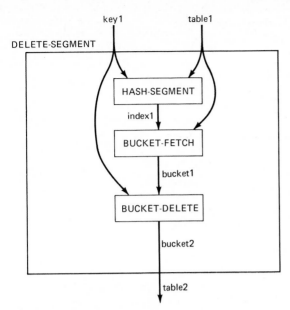

Figure 2. Plan for Delete Routine.

as shown in Figure 2 (the graphical representation is then straightforwardly encoded in an associative data base).

Sub-segments in a plan have specifications which come from two sources. The programming knowledge base contains specifications and plans for many standard programming building blocks, such as splicing elements out of a linked list. A programmer can simply make use of these to build up a more complex plan for his particular application. He may also find it convenient to define new types of segments which help him organize his plan. These new specifications can then, if desired, be assimilated into the programming knowledge base so that they are available for use in designing other similar programs. In this scenario we assume that HASH-SEGMENT, BUCKET-FETCH and BUCKET-DELETE are common building blocks for hashing programs whose specifications, shown in Table 3, have been entered before the scenario begins.

The specifications for BUCKET-DELETE make use of *cases* to express conditional behavior. EXPECT and ASSERT clauses which are not nested within any case apply in all situations. Thus in any execution of BUCKET-DELETE a bucket will be returned which contains exactly those entries of the input bucket whose key part is not equal to the input key. Furthermore, this effect is achieved by side-effecting the input bucket. This part of the specs is followed by a case structure with a WHEN clause to specify the conditions of applicability of the particular case, which are checked to make sure they are mutually exclusive. CASE1 says that when the first entry in the bucket has a different key than the input key, the output bucket will be identical to the input bucket. CASE2 states that this will not be true when the first entry has the same key as the input key. These specifications reflect the behavior of the standard list deletion plan which deletes internal elements by re-routing the pointer from the previous element, and deletes leading elements by returning a pointer to a place in the list which is immediately behind all such deleted elements.

Table 3. Specifications for Sub-segments in Plan

```
(DEFSPECS hash-segment
   (INPUTS: key1 table1)
   (OUTPUTS: index1)
   (EXPECT: (hashkey key1)
            (hashtable table1))
   (ASSERT: (hash key1 table1 index1)
            (integer index1)
            (> index1 0)
            (not (> index1 [size table1])))))

(DEFSPECS bucket-fetch
   (INPUTS: index1 table1)
   (OUTPUTS: bucket1)
   (EXPECT: (hashtable table1)
            (integer index1)
            (> index1 0)
            (not (> index1 [size table1])))
   (ASSERT: (bucketpart table1 index1 bucket1)))

(DEFSPECS bucket-delete
   (INPUTS: key1 bucket1)
   (OUTPUTS: bucket2)
   (EXPECT: (hashbucket bucket1)
            (hashkey key1))
   (ASSERT: (hashbucket bucket2)
            (side-effected bucket1)
            (forall (member bucket1 =entry)
                if   (keypart =entry key1)
                then (not (member bucket2 =entry))
                else (member bucket2 =entry))
            (forall (member bucket2 =entry)
                    (member bucket1 =entry)))
   (CASE1 (WHEN:   (not (keypart [first bucket1] key1)))
          (ASSERT: (id bucket1 bucket2)))
   (CASE2 (WHEN:   (keypart [first bucket1] key1))
          (ASSERT: (not (id bucket1 bucket2))))))
```

6. THE DEDUCTIVE SYSTEM

[The apprentice symbolically evaluates the plan and discovers an error. ...]

The apprentice discovers errors using an innovative system for deductive reasoning about program behavior. In contrast to most other such systems [Deutsch 1973b] [Igarashi et al. 1973] [King 1969] [King 1971] [King 1976] it is capable of reasoning about the behavior of programs involving side-effects on complex data with structure sharing. (A more recent system by Suzuki [Suzuki 1976] also is capable of dealing with such side-effects in PASCAL programs). Other innovative features include the use of a situational data base to maintain a representation of intermediate states in a program's execution and the use of anonymous objects to represent partial knowledge.

The basic action of the deductive system is a form of symbolic evaluation called *specs application*. The specs of a segment are applied to a set of input objects in a particular input situation resulting in a set of output objects (some of which may be input objects which have been subjected to a side-effect), and a new output situation. The process consists of the following three steps:

• Variables in the INPUTS clause are bound to objects in the input situation according to the data flow specified in the plan.

• The EXPECT clauses are verified in the input situation. If the EXPECT's cannot be satisfied, there is a bug in the plan.

• A new output situation is created in which the ASSERT clauses are asserted, substituting the appropriate input object names and creating new object names for newly referenced OUTPUT objects. (Objects which are outputs by virtue of the fact that they have been subjected to a side-effect continue to use their original names.)

This is similar to the way subroutines are handled by Hantler and King [Hantler and King 1976].

To verify an entire plan, an initial situation is created in which the EXPECT clauses of the main segment are asserted. The sub-segments of the plan are then symbolically evaluated, creating a tree of situations which follow from this initial situation. A tree rather than a simple sequence of situations arises when the specifications of some of the sub-segments have cases. After all sub-segments have been evaluated, an attempt is made to show that the ASSERT clauses of the main segment hold in the final situation(s). If this final proof is successful then the plan is correct; if there is a bug in the plan then part of the proof will fail. The deductive machinery is structured in such a way that diagnostic messages can be constructed to describe the logical error in terms of the programmer's plan.

Any segment for which specs are available can be used as a sub-segment in a plan. In particular, a segment may be used as one of its own sub-segments, forming a recursive program. Since loops may be represented as recursions with a single recursive call, we have no special mechanism for handling loops other than those used for recursive plans. The specification of the recursive segment serves both as a set of overall goals to be achieved and as the "loop invariant" as in the method of subgoal induction [Morris and Wegbreit 1976].

We will now see how these techniques enable the apprentice to detect the bug in the programmer's initial plan for DELETE-SEGMENT.

First an initial situation is created in which the EXPECT's of DELETE-SEGMENT are asserted. Anonymous objects A-KEY and A-TABLE are created to represent its inputs. Anonymous objects are objects whose identity is uncertain. Given two objects at least one of which is anonymous, it is impossible to know *a priori* whether or not they are identical. The situational data base starts out as follows:

```
(hashkey a-key)              SITUATION-0
(hashtable a-table)
```

Following the programmer's outline of the plan, HASH-SEGMENT is now applied to A-KEY and A-TABLE. This segment is *applicable* in this situation since its EXPECT's are satisfied. A new situation is created to represent the state of knowledge about the data objects after HASH-SEGMENT has executed. The ASSERT clauses are asserted in this situation, including the creation of another anonymous object, AN-INDEX, to represent the output of HASH-SEGMENT.

```
(hash a-key a-table an-index)    SITUATION-1
(integer an-index)
(> an-index 0)
(not (> an-index a-size))
(size a-table a-size)
```

Notice that the apprentice has created another anonymous object A-SIZE to represent the referent of [SIZE TABLE1] in the specifications of HASH-

SEGMENT. Had the size of A-TABLE been known in the current (or any previous) situation, the bracketed expression would have been replaced by that object and no new object would have been created.

The apprentice now goes on to apply the specs of BUCKET-FETCH and BUCKET-DELETE. The EXPECT clauses of BUCKET-FETCH are easily shown to be satisfied. However, BUCKET-DELETE has a case structure which requires special handling. In symbolically evaluating such segments, the apprentice first attempts to prove all EXPECT clauses which are not in any case. If this is successful, it then considers each case in turn.

If all the EXPECT's of a case can be proved, then the case is applicable and no further cases need be considered; the ASSERT clauses of this case are asserted in the output situation. If any EXPECT of the current case can be shown to be false, then the case is *inapplicable*, and no assertions are added. Finally, if there is a clause which can neither be proved nor disproved then the case has *unknown applicability*. Two output situations are created, one representing the possibility that the clause is applicable, the other representing the possibility that it is not. CASE1 and CASE2 of BUCKET-DELETE in this plan are of unknown applicability, and so two output situations, 3A and 3B, are created. Notice that in the snapshot of the situational data base below, we are not showing all assertions present in each situation, but only those we will need to talk about in the following discussion.

```
(hashtable a-table)                                      SITUATION-0
(hashkey a-key)

(hash a-key a-table an-index)                            SITUATION-1

(bucketpart a-table an-index a-bucket)                   SITUATION-2

(forall (member a-bucket =entry)                         SITUATION-3
   if   (keypart =entry a-key)
   then (not (member a-new-bucket =entry))
   else (member a-new-bucket =entry))

(id a-new-bucket a-bucket)                               SITUATION-3A

(not (id a-new-bucket a-bucket))                         SITUATION-3B
```

Symbolic execution of the programmer's plan is now complete. This means that the apprentice should be able to prove the ASSERT clauses of DELETE-SEGMENT in each of the final situations 3A and 3B. DELETE-SEGMENT has two quantified statements as output assertions: the first one states that all members of the input table will be members of the output table, except for those with the input key; the second one states that all members of the output table are also members of the input table. We will only demonstrate the proof of the first quantified statement here, starting with SITUATION-3A. The specific assertion to be proved is obtained from the specs by substituting the appropriate object names and situations. Notice that in specs the identical table in the input and output situations is distinguished by the use of different names (TABLE1 and TABLE2), whereas in the proof we have to be explicit about the situation in which we are describing the object A-TABLE.

```
(FORALL (member a-table =entry)                   IN situation-0
    IF   (keypart =entry a-key)                   IN situation-0
    THEN (not (member a-table =entry))            IN situation-3a
    ELSE (member a-table =entry)                  IN situation-3a )
```

The deductive system uses only restricted universal quantification. Quantified statements are proved by creating an anonymous object about which nothing is known except that it satisfies the class restriction. Anything that can be shown to be true of this anonymous object must be true of all objects of the class. Thus to start the proof of the above quantified statement an anonymous object AN-ENTRY is created and (MEMBER A-TABLE AN-ENTRY) is asserted in SITUATION-0. The IF-THEN-ELSE part of the quantified statement causes two alternative assumptions to be made about AN-ENTRY. First it is assumed (KEYPART AN-ENTRY A-KEY). From these assumptions, together with facts already in the data base and the definition of membership in a table given earlier, it follows that (MEMBER AN-ENTRY A-BUCKET) in SITU-ATION-2.

The quantified statement in SITUATION-3, which represents one of the effects of BUCKET-DELETE, states that every member of A-BUCKET whose key is A-KEY in SITUATION-2 will not be a member of A-NEW-BUCKET in SITUATION-3. Thus AN-ENTRY is not a member of A-NEW-BUCKET in SITUATION-3.

Furthermore in SITUATION-3A, A-NEW-BUCKET is assumed identical to A-BUCKET. It then follows that AN-ENTRY is not a member of A-TABLE since it is not a member of the bucket hashed to by its key. Thus the THEN part of the quantified statement is proved.

The ELSE part of the quantified statement says that an entry whose key is not A-KEY should remain a member of A-TABLE. This is proved by creating a new situation for hypothetical reasoning in which it is assumed (NOT (KEY-PART AN-ENTRY A-KEY)). Since the key part of AN-ENTRY is now unknown there are two sub-cases: AN-ENTRY may still happen to hash into the same bucket, A-BUCKET, as entries with A-KEY; or AN-ENTRY may be a member of some other bucket. If AN-ENTRY is a member of A-BUCKET, it follows from the specs of BUCKET-DELETE in SITUATION-3 that AN-EN-TRY is a member of A-NEW-BUCKET, and thus is still in the table. On the other hand, if AN-ENTRY is not a member of A-BUCKET then it is a member of some other bucket which was not side-effected, so AN-ENTRY continues to be a member of that bucket and therefore of A-TABLE.

The apprentice is now satisfied that the plan works correctly if CASE1 of BUCKET-DELETE is the applicable case. It must now consider how the plan would operate if CASE2 were applicable. The quantified statement to be verified in this case is the same as above except that now the terminal situation is SITUATION-3B.

```
(FORALL (member a-table =entry)          IN   situation-0
   IF   (keypart =entry a-key)           IN   situation-0
   THEN (not (member a-table =entry))    IN   situation-3b
   ELSE (member a-table =entry)          IN   situation-3b)
```

SITUATION-3B represents the situation produced by BUCKET-DELETE when the key of the first element of A-BUCKET is A-KEY. In this case the output A-NEW-BUCKET is not identical to the input bucket (typically it will be some sub-list of the input bucket). These changed assumptions produce only minor changes in the proof outlined above.

As above the apprentice assumes an anonymous member of the table, AN-ENTRY, with anonymous key, A-KEY, which hashes into A-BUCKET. The quantified statement in SITUATION-3 then asserts that AN-ENTRY is not a member of A-NEW-BUCKET in SITUATION-3. However, in SITUATION-3B A-NEW-BUCKET is not identical to A-BUCKET, so that the apprentice cannot tell whether AN-ENTRY has been deleted or not. This is the reasoning which underlies the error message in the scenario:

> APPRENTICE: I'm sorry, but I can't verify that this plan satisfies the specifications for delete. In particular, when the key of the first entry in a bucket is equal to the input key, I can't prove that all entries with keys equal to the input key are not members of the table after the delete. In such cases the bucket after splicing out entries is not identical to the bucket before splicing out entries.

7. BUILDING PURPOSE LINKS

The apprentice performs deductions by invoking rules from the programming knowledge base triggered by the facts in the situational data base. As each deduction is made, a note is entered into a special plan data base recording the dependency between the newly deduced fact, the triggering facts, and the rule invoked. For example, when the apprentice deduces that AN-ENTRY is not a member of A-TABLE it records the dependence of this fact on the rule for membership in the table and the facts that triggered the rule:

```
((not (member a-table an-entry)) IN situation-3a

    DEPENDS-ON

(RELATION-DEFINITION
  (member hashtable entry) <=>
  (member [bucketpart hashtable
                      [hash [keypart entry] hashtable]]
          entry))
(keypart an-entry a-key) IN situation-0
(hash a-key a-table an-index) IN situation-1
(bucketpart a-table an-index a-bucket) IN situation-2
(not (member a-bucket an-entry)) IN situation-3)
```

Similarly whenever a fact is entered into the situational data base through specs application an entry is made in the plan data base showing the dependence of this fact on the appropriate clause of the responsible segment's specs. Finally, whenever the apprentice proves that a spec clause is satisfied, it makes a record of which clause initiated the proof.

The entries in the plan data base provide a logical chain of dependencies between specs clauses, showing how the ASSERT's of one group of sub-segments interact to satisfy the EXPECT's of other sub-segments or the ASSERT of the enclosing segment. Such logical dependencies are called *purpose links*: if they justify a sub-segment's EXPECT clause they are called *prerequisite links*; if they justify the ASSERT of the enclosing segment they are called *achieve links*. A deep plan is a pattern of purpose links explaining the logical structure of the program. The deep plan is a crucial representation in the apprentice because it allows the programmer and the apprentice to share an understanding of the purpose of every part of the program.

When the programmer attempts to modify a section of the code, it is the purpose links which explain what other segments will be affected and in what ways. ASSERT clauses which are not connected to any purpose link, for example, reflect aspects of a sub-segment's behavior which are irrelevent to the task at hand, and which may be changed easily. In other cases, the purpose links will show what behaviors may be added without affecting the program's behavior.

8. CODING AND PLAN RECOGNITION

PRGMR: Here's the code...

APPRENTICE: I'm sorry, but this code is not consistent with your plan...

Eventually a programmer will refine his plan to the point where coding may begin. In order to assist the programmer further, the apprentice must recognize the correspondence between parts of the code and segments in some deep plan. Although the general problem of recognizing the plan of arbitrary code with no prior expectations is extremely difficult, we expect recognition to be quite practical given an interactive environment with strong expectations provided by the design phase and the programmer's comments. Thus discrepancies between the plan and the actual code discovered during recognition may be brought to the programmer's attention as potential bugs.

This raises the question of why have LISP code at all, given deep plans which describe the programmer's intentions in a much more perspicuous form? There are two reasons for keeping code around. The first reason is the serious shortcoming of current specification languages which might be used to describe segments in the deep plan. Specification techniques have not yet been developed which capture all the important design criteria used by practicing programmers. Furthermore, our deep plan representation is *intended* to be a level of abstraction which ignores many efficiency issues. Until we have a theoretical basis for dealing with space-time trade-offs and the like, we cannot give the programmer any better way of expressing his efficiency-determined design choices than letting him actually write the crucial code, as long as it is compatible with the deep plan. We feel this is a realistic approach to building a usable programmer's apprentice system in the near future.

The first step in plan recognition is the construction of the surface plan using a symbolic interpreter which mimics the operation of the standard LISP interpreter. The major difference between symbolic interpretation and real interpretation is that it is not possible in general to decide which branch of a conditional to take on the basis of a symbolic value. A symbolic interpreter must split control flow and follow both paths, leading to an eventual join.

Program loops are handled in our symbolic interpreter by proceeding forward normally until a jump is made to a point in the code that has already been evaluated. When this occurs, a join in control flow is constructed and a special analysis of the data flow is performed based on the following observation: the only thing wrong with the way the loop body has been already evaluated is that potential data flow between the outputs of the loop body and inputs of the loop body have been missed. This is remedied by first *grouping* the segments in the loop body, which has the effect of calculating the net inputs and outputs of the group of segments, and then adding extra data flow links for any free variable outputs that are also inputs. Notice that this approach to analyzing loops results in a plan that is essentially a recursion, i.e. the outputs of the segment feed back into the inputs.

In the uniform syntax of LISP, control flow and data flow primitives such as PROG, COND, SETQ and RETURN appear as function calls. However these special forms do not give rise to segments in the surface plan. These forms are viewed as *connective tissue* between the segments of code in the program that actually do something (i.e. have i/o specifications). This leads to a surface plan which has almost no hierarchy. There are only two kinds of aggregation that are assumed at this level of analysis: the segments in a LAMBDA body are grouped, and the body of each loop is grouped into a single segment. However, the symbolic interpretation of certain special forms such as COND does leave behind suggestions for likely groupings. Later in the recognition process these suggestions, together with deeper knowledge of programming and plans, are used to impose further structure on the initial flat plan, producing greater correspondence with the more hierarchical deep plan.

The second phase of plan recognition consists mostly of grouping the surface plan and assigning more extrinsic specifications. Grouping is simply the operation of drawing a segment boundary around a number of segments at the same level in the surface plan, thereby creating a new segment, and calculating the net data flow and control flow between the new segment, its subsegments, and other segments now at the same level.

As grouping proceeds, an attempt is made to identify each group with a segment of the deep plan. Identification of a surface plan segment with a deep plan segment is possible only if the data and control flow links surrounding the surface plan segment are consistent with the data flow and purpose links surrounding the deep plan segment. If so, the identification suggests a more extrinsic description of the segment than is apparent from the code alone. If the proposed identification is valid, then this extrinsic specification must be deducible from the intrinsic specifications of the grouped sub-segments. If all the segments in the surface plan can be grouped and identified with segments in some deep plan, then the program has been recognized.

Failure to recognize a plan leads to either of two courses of action. Possibly the surface plan can be regrouped to identify in a different way with segments of a deep plan. However, if the program is sufficiently constrained so that no such regrouping is possible, the failure is reported to the programmer as a coding bug, as in the scenario:

> APPRENTICE: I'm sorry but this code is not consistent with your plan. In the special case you are storing the bucket before splicing, rather than the bucket after splicing. Did you mean (STORE (TBL (HASH KEY)) BKT2)?

The apprentice has determined that the STORE instruction in the code corresponds to the deep plan segment which inserts the updated bucket into the table. However the data flow link in the surface plan fails to correspond to that of the deep plan; the input to STORE should be the output of BUCKET-DELETE (i.e. the updated bucket), instead it is BUCKET-FETCH's output. The apprentice therefore reports this as a coding bug, using deep plan concepts to frame the explanation.

9. A LIBRARY OF PLANS

In order to be useful, the apprentice must have inherent knowledge of many common programming techniques. Plans are a way of representing not only the structure of particular programs, but also of capturing the structure common to many programs. For example, the *search loop* plan captures the essential similarity between programs which search arrays, lists, and any other data structures which can be linearly enumerated. This deep plan represents not only what is common between these data structures, but also the typical procedural steps that are used to search them: an initialization, a test for exhaustion of the enumeration, a test on the current element to see if it is the one being searched for, and a bump step to the next element in the enumeration.

The structure of the plan library is a major area of research which we have only begun to attack. However, several important criteria have been established. The library should be structured to capture the significant generalizations among plans. For example, search loops with early exits should be representable as incremental specializations of the general search loop. It is also crucial that the structure of the plan library allow a smooth interaction between plan specialization and the selection of data structures. Thus once it is decided that the linear structure to be searched is an array, it should be easy to transform the general search loop plan into an array searching plan while maintaining a representation of those parts of the logical structure which still apply.

These features suggest a plan library organized around a hierarchy with the topmost distinctions made on the basis of the loop and recursion structure of the plans, e.g. iterative loops, single recursions, double recursions, and so on. Loops, for example, can then be sub-categorized into search loops, counting loops, approximation loops, and so on. We are currently investigating how to make these ideas more precise. A similar library of programming knowledge has been constructed by Barstow [Barstow 1977]. However, his library is implemented as a rule-based system oriented towards program synthesis and is weak in its representation of the logical structure of programs.

10. PROGRAM MAINTENANCE

What has been achieved in the apprentice environment is an important factorization of the software design problem. The programmer and the apprentice first work at the plan level developing a consistent structure of interdependent segment specifications. Only then does coding begin, with the apprentice looking over the shoulder of the programmer to make sure the code correctly implements the plan. Finally, once a program has been completely designed and coded in this manner, the apprentice will have built up a very rich description which forms the basis for an interactive documentation facility. Furthermore, the descriptions built up by the apprentice can help the programmer to maintain a consistent design as new requirements force evolutionary changes to be made.

> PRGMR: I want to make a change in the representation of buckets in the hashing programs. A bucket now has two parts: a count field and a list of entries as before. The count field will contain an integer equal to the length of the list of entries. Let a bucket be a dotted-pair whose CAR is the count and whose CDR is the list of entries.

> APPRENTICE: The proposed change will affect LOOKUP, INSERT, and DELETE.

> PRGMR: What are the problems in DELETE ?

> APPRENTICE: After fetching the bucket you test the key of its first element. But in this new implementation, the CAR of a bucket is a number not an entry. Secondly, the input to BKT-DELETE is a bucket but it requires a list of entries.

In verifying the plans for LOOKUP, INSERT, and DELETE the apprentice recorded the dependence of parts of the proofs on design decisions such as the implementation of buckets as lists of entries. The programmer here is proposing to change this IMPLEMENTATION-DEFINITION. The apprentice therefore checks to see what segments in the plans depend on this definition for their correct operation. It finds, for example, that in the plan for BUCKET-DELETE the key extracting segment has an EXPECT clause requiring that its input be an entry. In the verification this EXPECT depended on the data flow in the plan, the implementation of buckets as lists, and a type restriction requiring every member of a bucket to be an entry. The fact that this purpose link will no longer hold if the IMPLEMENTATION-DEFINITION is changed is reported to the programmer as above.

PRGMR: Explain the plan for BKT-DELETE please.

APPRENTICE: BKT-DELETE is implemented as the standard list deletion plan. Inputs are a key and a list of entries. The plan is a search loop using two pointers: a pointer to the current entry which is initialized to the input list, and a trailing pointer which is initialized to NIL. On each iteration it tests the key of the first element of the current list. If it is equal to the input key, it splices the current element out of the list by RPLACD'ing the previous pointer.

PRGMR: Change the specifications of this BKT-DELETE to expect as input a bucket of the new type, rather than a list of entries. Also change the initialization of the pointers to read...

The apprentice has recognized the plan for the BKT-DELETE program as a specialization of the general search loop plan in the plan library. This particular search loop uses two pointers and operates by splicing out the appropriate entries. Thus the plan library provides standard programming concepts which the apprentice uses to give explanations which are easily understood by the programmer, and which the programmer can use to instruct the apprentice. This also demonstrates how the apprentice can help maintain not only the program but its documentation as well.

11. FURTHER WORK

Work is continuing on this project in the form of three Ph.D. theses currently in progress. Shrobe [Shrobe 1978] is continuing to develop the theory and implementation of the deductive system. Rich [Rich 1977] is implementing the plan recognition component together with a plan library which will codify many of the basic techniques of non-numerical programming in LISP. Finally, Waters [Waters 1976] is taking a plan-based approach to the task of building a system to understand FORTRAN programs in the IBM Scientific Subroutine Package.

ACKNOWLEDGMENTS

This paper describes research done at the Artificial Intelligence Laboratory of the Massachusetts Institute of Technology. Support for the Laboratory's artificial intelligence research is provided in part by the Advanced Research Projects Agency of the Department of Defense under Office of Naval Research Contract N00014-75-C00643.

REFERENCES

[Balzer 1973] R.M. Balzer. *Automatic programming.* University of Southern California, Information Sciences Institute, 1973.

[Barstow 1977] D.R. Barstow. *Automatic construction of algorithms and data structures using a knowledge base of programming rules.* Stanford University, Stanford Artificial Intelligence Laboratory, Memo AIM-308, November 1977.

[Dahl et al. 1972] O.-J. Dahl, E.W. Dijkstra, C.A.R. Hoare. *Structured Programming.* Academic Press, 1972.

[Deutsch 1973b] L.P. Deutsch. *An interactive program verifier.* University of California, doctoral dissertaion, Berkeley, California, June 1973.

[Dolotta and Mashey 1976] T.A. Dolotta, J.R. Mashey. An Introduction to the Programmer's Workbench. *Proceedings of the Second International Conference on Software Engineering*, San Francisco, California, October 1976, 164-168; [*Editors' note*: see also [Dolotta et al. 1978]]

[Floyd 1967] R.W. Floyd. Assigning meaning to programs. In J.T. Schwartz (ed.) *Mathematical Aspects of Computer Science*, American Mathematical Society, Providence Rhode Island, 19 (1967), 19-32.

[Floyd 1971] R.W. Floyd. Toward interactive design of correct programs. *International Federation of Information Processing*, 1971.

[Hantler and King 1976] S.L. Hantler, J.C. King. An introduction to proving the correctness of programs. *ACM Computing Surveys*, 8:3 (September 1976).

[Hewitt et al. 1973] C. Hewitt, P. Bishop, R. Steiger. A universal modular actor formalism for artificial intelligence. *Proceedings of the Third International Joint Conference on Artificial Intelligence*, Stanford, California, August 1973, 235-245.

[Hoare 1969] C.A.R. Hoare. An axiomatic basis for computer programming. *Communications of the ACM*, 12:10 (October 1969), 576-580,583.

[Hoare 1971] C.A.R. Hoare. Proof of a program: Find. *Communications of the ACM*, 14:1 (January 1971), 39-45.

[Hoare 1972] C.A.R. Hoare. Proof of correctness of data representations. *Acta Informatica* 1:4 (1972), 271-281.

[Igarashi et al. 1973] S. Igarashi, R. London, D. Luckham. *Automatic program verification I: a logical basis and its implementation*. Stanford Artificial Intelligence Memo 200, May 1973.

[King 1969] J.C. King. *A program verifier*. Carnegie-Mellon University, Computer Science Department, doctoral dissertation, 1969.

[King 1971] J.C. King. Proving programs to be correct. *IEEE Transactions on Computers*, 20:11 (November 1971).

[King 1976] J.C. King. Symbolic execution and program testing. *Communications of the ACM*, 19:7 (July 1976).

[Knuth 1968a] D.E. Knuth. *The Art of Computer Programming, Vols. 1-3*. Addison-Wesley, Reading, Massachusetts, 1968,1969,1973.

[Liskov et al. 1977] B. Liskov et al. Abstraction mechanisms in CLU. *Communications of the ACM*, 20:8 (August 1977), 564-576.

[Morris and Wegbreit 1976] J.H. Morris, B. Wegbreit. *Subgoal induction*. Xerox Palo Alto Research Center, CSL-75-6, July 1976.

[Rich 1977] C. Rich. *Plan recognition in a programmer's apprentice*. Massachusetts Institute of Technology, Artificial Intelligence Laboratory, Working Paper 147, May 1977.

[Rich and Shrobe 1976] C. Rich, H.E. Shrobe. *Initial report on a LISP programmer's apprentice*. Massachusetts Institute of Technology, Artificial Intelligence Laboratory, Technical Report 354, December 1976.

[Shrobe 1978] H.E. Shrobe. *Plan verification in a programmer's apprentice*. Massachusetts Institute of Technology, Artificial Intelligence Laboratory, Working Paper 158, January 1978.

[Suzuki 1976] N. Suzuki. *Automatic verification of programs with complex data structures*. Stanford Artificial Intelligence Laboratory Memo AIM-279, Stanford, California, February 1976.

[Teitelman 1978] W. Teitelman. *INTERLISP Reference Manual*. Xerox Palo Alto Research Center, Palo Alto, California, December 1978.

[Waters 1976] R.C. Waters. *A system for understanding mathematical Fortran programs*. Massachusetts Institute of Technology, MIT/AIM-368, August 1976.

[Winograd 1973] T. Winograd. Breaking the complexity barrier (again). *Proceedings of the ACM SIGIR-SIGPLAN Interface Meeting*, November 1973; reprinted in *Interactive Programming Environments*.

[Wulf et al. 1976b] W.A. Wulf, R.L. London, M. Shaw. An introduction to the construction and verification of Alphard programs. *IEEE Transactions on Software Engineering*, SE-2:4 (December 1976).

23 The Programmer's Apprentice: Knowledge Based Program Editing

RICHARD C. WATERS

Artificial Intelligence Laboratory
Massachusetts Institute of Technology
Cambridge, Massachusetts

An initial implementation of an interactive programming assistant system called the programmer's apprentice (PA) is described. The PA is designed to be midway between an improved programming methodology and an automatic programming system. The intention is that the programmer will do the hard parts of design and implementation while the PA will assist him wherever possible. One of the major underpinnings of the PA is a representation (called a plan) for programs which abstracts away from the inessential features of a program and represents the basic logical properties of the algorithm explicitly.

The current system is composed of five parts: an analyzer that can construct the plan for a program; a coder that can create program text corresponding to a plan; a drawer that can draw a graphical representation of a plan; a library of plans for common algorithmic fragments; and a plan editor which makes it possible for a programmer to modify a program by modifying its plan. The greatest leverage provided by the system comes from the fact that a programmer can rapidly and accurately build up a program by referring to the fragments in the library and from the fact that the editor provides commands specifically designed to facilitate program modification.

© 1982 IEEE. Reprinted with permission from *IEEE Transactions on Software Engineering*, SE-8:1 (January 1982).

1. INTRODUCTION

The upper part of the diagram in Figure 1 represents a typical programming environment. The environment is built up out of a number of components (such as a text editor, an interpreter, and a compiler). These components communicate with each other in terms of program code. The components may be highly integrated into a unified environment or, more typically, they may be connected only in that they all operate on the same programming language.

The programmer is the active agent in the picture. He issues commands directing the components in the environment in order to create and modify programs. The programmer's apprentice system (PA) is an additional active agent which assists the programmer with the task of programming. There are three important points about the way the PA fits into this picture. First, it is not intended to replace the programming environment, but rather to augment it. It will communicate with the rest of the environment in terms of code, and commands. Second, the programmer can still communicate directly with the rest of the environment. This gives him a trap door so that he is not always required to work through the PA.

Third, there is an underlying philosophy that there is a fundamental division of labor between the programmer and the PA. The PA will act as a junior partner and critic, keeping track of details and assisting in the documentation, verification, debugging, and modification of a program while the programmer does the really *hard* parts of design and implementation. In order to cooperate with a programmer, the PA must be able to *understand* what is going on. From the point of view of artificial intelligence, one of the central developments of the programmer's apprentice project has been the design of a representation (called a *plan*) for programs and for knowledge about programming which serves as the basis for this understanding. An important component of the PA is a library of plan fragments describing standard algorithms and data structures.

Rich and Shrobe [Rich and Shrobe 1976] [Rich and Shrobe 1978] laid out the initial design for the PA and for plans (see Section 4). The author [Waters 1976] designed a limited system intended to operate in the domain of mathematical Fortran programs and extended the idea of a plan by developing a theory of how plans could be segmented [Waters 1978] [Waters 1979] (see Section 5). More recently, Rich [Rich 1980] [Rich 1981] has further developed the plan formalism (see Section 11) and designed a much more comprehensive library of plans representing many of the standard cliches in non-numerical programming.

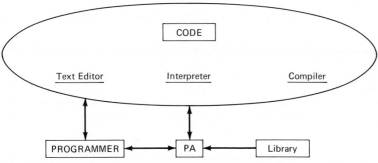

Figure 1. Adding a new agent into the programming environment.

This paper describes an initial implementation of the PA recently completed by the author. This system is an editor which allows a programmer to build up a program from prototypical fragments, and to modify a program in terms of its logical structure. In both cases the system gains most of its power from the fact that all of these actions are performed on the plan for the program rather than on the program text. It should be noted that the current system is intended as a pre-prototype proof of principle. It is neither efficient nor robust. However, it demonstrates the feasibility of some of the basic ideas behind the PA.

Section 2 gives a scenario of the use of the current system pointing out some of the key features of the interaction. Section 3 outlines the architecture of the system. The plan formalism which underlies the system is briefly discussed in Section 4. Sections 5-9 describe the five components of the system and how they are implemented. Section 10 presents another scenario and examines several issues in more depth. Section 11 discusses the weaknesses of the current system, and how these problems will be addressed in the second implementation of the PA which is now under way.

2. A SCENARIO

This section presents a brief scenario showing an actual interaction with the current system. The programmer communicates with the system by typing pseudo English commands on a video terminal. The screen of the terminal is divided into two regions (see Frame 1). The top region shows what the programmer types. The lower region is used by the system to display code for the program being worked on. The part of the program that the system's attention is focused on is highlighted on the display (this is indicated by underlining in the figures below). The last line of the lower region is a description identifying the highlighted section.

In the first frame, the programmer begins the definition of a square root program, specifying its parameter. The code produced by this step is very fragmentary because the description of the program is very fragmentary.

```
>Define a program SQRT with a parameter NUM.


(DEFINE SQRT (NUM) ...)




The program SQRT.
```

Frame 1

The programmer then starts to build up his program. He fills in the top level structure of the program by referring to the algorithmic fragment "successive approximation" (see Frame 2). References like this one have meaning to the system because it has a library of algorithmic fragments represented as plans. The code produced at this step indicates what the system understands a successive approximation to be. The process starts at some (unspecified) initial value. On each cycle, the current value (in the variable RESULT) is tested by some (unspecified) predicate. If the test succeeds the value is returned. If it fails, then some (unspecified) approximation step is used to improve the result.

```
>Implement SQRT as a successive approximation.


(DEFINE SQRT (NUM)
   (PROG (RESULT)
         (SETQ RESULT ..initialization..)
      LP (COND (..test.. (RETURN RESULT)))
         (SETQ RESULT ..approximation..)
         (GO LP)))

The successive approximation program SQRT.
```
Frame 2

The symbols "..initialization..", "..test..", and "..approximation.." represent those parts of the algorithm which are not yet implemented. The programmer can use these names when referring to these parts.

In Frame 3, the programmer continues to build his program by filling in the initialization and approximation slots in the program. The initialization is implemented as a constant. The approximation is implemented using a simple library cliche "average". Note that references to library fragments and simple program text literals can be freely intermixed. The programmer used the literal "(/ NUM RESULT)" because that was easier than specifying what he wanted any other way.

```
>Implement the initialization as '1.
>Implement the approximation as an average of 'RESULT
and '(/ NUM RESULT).

(DEFINE SQRT (NUM)
   (PROG (RESULT)
         (SETQ RESULT 1)
      LP (COND (..test.. (RETURN RESULT)))
         (SETQ RESULT (/ (+ RESULT (/ NUM RESULT)) 2)
         (GO LP)))

The average approximation of the program SQRT.
```
Frame 3

The programmer then implements the "test" of the program as an "equality within epsilon" (see Frame 4). This library cliche embodies the concept of comparing two things to see if they are sufficiently close together. This cliche in turn has three parts (the two items to compare and the comparison criterion) which need to be specified.

```
>Implement the test as an equality within epsilon.


(DEFINE SQRT (NUM)
   (PROG (RESULT)
         (SETQ RESULT 1.0)
      LP (COND ((< (ABS (- ..arg.. ..arg..)) ..epsilon..)
                (RETURN RESULT)))
         (SETQ RESULT (/ (+ RESULT (/ NUM RESULT)) 2))
         (GO LP)))
The equality within epsilon test of the program SQRT.
```
Frame 4

The programmer completes the program by filling in the slots in the equality within epsilon test. The first five frames show one of the dominant modes of interaction with the current system. This mode supports the top down construction of a program. The programmer builds up the program by pulling in fragments from the library, and then filling in their unspecified parts with literal pieces of code, or with other fragments from the library.

```
>Implement the first arg as '(* RESULT RESULT); the second
 arg as 'NUM; and the epsilon as '.0001.



(DEFINE SQRT (NUM)
  (PROG (RESULT)
        (SETQ RESULT 1.0)
    LP (COND ((< (ABS (- (* RESULT RESULT) NUM)) .0001)
             (RETURN RESULT)))
        (SETQ RESULT (/ (+ RESULT (/ NUM RESULT)) 2))
        (GO LP)))

The epsilon of the test of the program SQRT.
```

Frame 5

The next three frames illustrate a completely different mode of interaction with the system: modification. Typically, program construction (and certainly debugging) involves a lot of modification as the program evolves into an acceptable implementation. In Frame 6, a programmer recalls the program SQRT so that he can modify it. (This could be done six months later by a different programmer than the one that initially constructed the program; and it could be done even if the program had not originally been constructed using the system.)

```
>Recall the program SQRT.



(DEFINE SQRT (NUM)
  (PROG (RESULT)
        (SETQ RESULT 1.0)
    LP (COND ((< (ABS (- (* RESULT RESULT) NUM)) .0001)
             (RETURN RESULT)))
        (SETQ RESULT (/ (+ RESULT (/ NUM RESULT)) 2))
        (GO LP)))
The program SQRT.
```

Frame 6

The programmer has decided that he doesn't like the algorithm in the SQRT program because it does an unnecessary multiplication in the equality within epsilon test. He decides that it would be just as good to compare "RESULT" and "(/ NUM RESULT)" as to compare "(* RESULT RESULT)" and "NUM". Note that this is a good example of the division of labor between the PA and the programmer. Deciding that this is a change which should be made is a hard decision which the programmer must make. This is particularly true since this is not a correctness preserving change. The programmer has just decided that the differences are not relevant to his needs. Once the programmer has decided what he wants to do, the system provides facilities to help him make the modification.

```
>Replace the - in the test with '(- RESULT (/ NUM RESULT)).


(DEFINE SQRT (NUM)
  (PROG (RESULT)
        (SETQ RESULT 1.0)
    LP  (COND ((< (ABS (- RESULT (/ NUM RESULT))) .0001)
               (RETURN RESULT)))
        (SETQ RESULT (/ (+ RESULT (/ NUM RESULT)) 2))
        (GO LP)))

The - action of the initialization of the test of ...
```

Frame 7

First, (see Frame 7) the programmer changes the test so that it compares the appropriate quantities. In Frame 8, the programmer then instructs the system to share the division just added to the test with the second division in the approximation step.

```
>Share the / in the test and the second / in the approximation.


(DEFINE SQRT (NUM)
  (PROG (RESULT X)
        (SETQ RESULT 1.0)
    LP  (SETQ X (/ NUM RESULT))
        (COND ((< (ABS (- RESULT X)) .0001)
               (RETURN RESULT)))
        (SETQ RESULT (/ (+ RESULT X) 2))
        (GO LP)))
The transducer of the program SQRT.
```

Frame 8

This is a good example of a command which is easy to understand, and easy to state, but which is not so easy to do. There are two primary difficulties. First, looking at the program text, it is not easy to tell whether or not the sharing is possible. The fact that the two divisions are expressed using the same text string does not imply that they correspond to divisions of the same quantities. Potentially, the whole program must be checked to see that there are no side-effects or other modifications to the variables involved. Second, once it has been determined that the sharing is permissible, relatively global changes may have to be made in the code. Here a temporary variable must be introduced. As will be discussed below, the system gets considerable leverage on both of these problems because it is not operating on program text, but rather on the plan for the program.

Once an orthogonal change like sharing is made in a program, the program must be reanalyzed in order for editing to continue. Here the program is no longer a simple successive approximation. It has an additional component (highlighted in Frame 8) that precomputes "(/ NUM RESULT)" on each cycle of the loop. The descriptive line at the bottom of Frame 8 identifies this component as a "transducer". The name "transducer" is used by the system to identify a part of a loop which simply computes a value used by other parts of the loop on the same cycle of the loop.

The purpose of the current system is to make it possible for a programmer to edit a program as an algorithmic structure rather than a syntactic one. To this end, the system provides a vocabulary for referring to algorithms and their parts. The library makes it possible for the programmer to refer to common algorithms by name. These algorithms have named parts which he can use when manipulating the program. The *verbs* provided by the system (such as "implement", "replace", and "share") make it possible for the programmer to specify actions directly in terms of the algorithm. Except inside literals, there are no references to programming language constructs.

3. ARCHITECTURE OF THE CURRENT SYSTEM

The current system is composed of five modules as shown in Figure 2. Given the text for a piece of a program, the analyzer module can construct a plan corresponding to it. The coder module performs the reverse transformation, creating program text corresponding to a plan. The drawer module can draw a graphical representation of a plan. The library contains common program fragments represented as plans. The plan editor makes it possible for the programmer to modify a program by modifying its plan.

The system maintains two representations (program text and a plan) for the program being worked on. If the programmer uses the plan editor to change the plan, then the system uses the coder to determine what the new program text should be. If the programmer uses an ordinary text editor to change the program text, then the analyzer is used to determine what the resulting plan should be. It should be noted that the existence of the analyzer means that the system can be used to modify programs that were not originally constructed using the system. For example, it would have been possible to modify SQRT beginning with Frame 6 even if the program had not originally been constructed using the system.

As shown in the scenario in the last section, the leverage provided by the system comes primarily from two things. First, the programmer can rapidly and accurately build up a program by referring to the fragments in the plan library. Second, the editor provides a variety of commands specifically designed to facilitate program modification.

There is a similarity between this system and a programming language syntax editor (such as Mentor [Donzeau-Gouge et al. 1975], the Cornell Program Synthesizer [Teitelbaum 1979], or Gandalf [Feiler and Medina-Mora 1981]) in that the system operates on an underlying representation for the program rather than on its textual representation. In both cases many simple errors are prevented because it is no longer possible to even state them.

There are, however, three key differences between this system and a programming language syntax editor. First, this system does not depend on the syntax of any particular programming language. All of the operations of the system are performed on plans. Except for parts of the coder and analyzer modules, the whole system is essentially programming language independent.

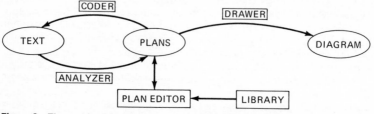

Figure 2. The architecture of the current implementation of the PA.

For example, if the coder was changed so that it produced Fortran instead of Lisp, then the scenario in the last section would create a Fortran program instead of a Lisp program. It would not be necessary to change any other component of the system, or any of the programmer's commands. If the analyzer was modified, the programmer could use Fortran literals instead of Lisp literals.

Second, the existence of the plan library changes the character of the interaction. The only prototypes known to the typical syntax editor are ones related to the basic syntactic constructs of the language. Third, this system specifically supports non-local modifications such as sharing. The typical syntax editor only supports the addition and deletion of individual syntactic units.

There is also a similarity between the current system and a transformational program development system such as TI [Balzer 1981], PSI [Barstow 1977] or PDS [Cheatham 1981]. The key similarity is that both approaches rely heavily on libraries of standard programming cliches (represented as transformations in a transformational system and as plans in the PA). However, there is a considerable difference in their approaches to the way this knowledge is used.

In the transformational approach a program is first completely specified at an abstract level and then a transformational component selects (more or less automatically) transformations (which are intended to be correctness preserving) in order to implement the program in an efficient way. There is, however, no support for creating or modifying the abstract specification itself. The current implementation of the PA is both more modest in its goals, and more flexible. A program does not have to be specified at an abstract level; there is no automatic selection of cliches to use; the addition of a library cliche into a program is not expected to be a correctness preserving process; and the system supports program creation and modification at all levels. Future implementations of the PA will include some automatic cliche selection and are intended to support the kind of programming style pioneered by research on transformational systems, in addition to the interactive programming style presented here.

4. PLANS

The importance of plans as the underlying representation used by the system cannot be overemphasized. The utility of the plan representation stems from the fact that it is specifically designed to make the kind of tasks performed by the system easy. In order to do this, the plan representation is designed to make all of the information the system needs to know explicit and local in a plan.

A plan is like a flow chart except that the data flow as well as the control flow is represented by explicit arcs. (As an example, Figure 3 shows a diagram for a simple plan.) The basic unit of a plan is a *segment* (drawn as a box in a plan diagram). A segment corresponds to a unit of computation. It has a number of *input ports* and *output ports* which specify the input values it receives and the output values it produces. It has a set of specifications (not shown in the figure) which give preconditions which must be true of the inputs in order for the segment to execute properly, and postconditions which describe what will be true after the segment is executed.

Control flow from one segment to another is represented by an explicit arc (drawn as a dashed arrow) from the first segment to the second segment. Similarly, data flow from the output of one segment to the input of another is represented by an explicit arc (drawn as a solid arrow) from the appropriate port of the first segment to the appropriate port of the second segment.

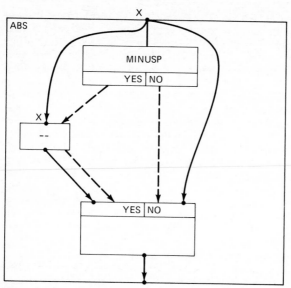

Figure 3. An example plan for (COND ((MINUSP X) (- X)) (T X)).

In addition to segments corresponding to primitive computations there can be intermediate segments containing groups of inner segments. All of the data flow between segments outside of an intermediate segment and segments inside an intermediate segment is channeled through input and output ports attached to the intermediate segment. All of the computation corresponding to a single subroutine is grouped together into one outermost segment.

An important feature of the plan representation is that it abstracts away from inessential features of a program. Whenever possible it tries to eliminate features which stem from the way things must be expressed in a particular programming language, and keep only those features which are essential to the actual algorithm. For example, a plan does not represent a data flow in terms of the way it could be implemented in any particular programming language (e.g. with variables, or nesting of expressions, or parameter passing). Rather, it just records what the net data flow is. (For the convenience of the coder, a plan can have annotations which suggest what variable names are appropriate for a particular data flow.) Similarly, no information is represented about how control flow is implemented. One result of this abstraction is that plans are much more canonical than program text. Programs which vary only in the way their control flow and data flow is implemented all correspond to the same plan.

Another important feature of the plan representation is that it tries to make things as local as possible. For example, each data flow arc represents a specific communication of data from one place to another and, by the definition of what a data flow arc is, the other data flow arcs in the plan cannot have any effect on this. The same is true for control flow arcs. As a result, if there is no data flow or control flow between two segments, then they can have no effect upon each other.

It is the locality of the data flow which makes it easy for the system to determine that sharing is possible in Frame 8 above. In the plan, the two divisions obviously compute the same value because they receive their inputs by data flow from the same places.

Due to the locality of data flow and control flow, plans have the property of *additivity*. It is always permissible to put two sections of plan side by side without their disturbing each other. This is why it is easy for the system to build up a program from fragments as shown in the scenario above. All it has to do is just paste the pieces together. It does not have to worry about issues like variable name conflicts, because there are no variables.

A third important feature of plans is that the intermediate segmentation breaks a plan up into regions which can be manipulated separately due to the property of *substitutability*. It is always permissible to replace any segment with another segment as long as the two are *externally* indistinguishable in that they have the same ports and the same specifications. This is possible because the plan representation is designed so that nothing outside of a segment can depend on anything inside that segment.

5. THE ANALYZER

The analyzer (described in [Waters 1979] and more fully in [Waters 1978]) automatically produces a plan corresponding to a program. This is done in three steps: source translation, surface analysis, and segmentation. In the source translation step, a language specific module parses the program text and converts it into a Lisp-like intermediate form. Source translators currently exist for Fortran and for Cobol. None is needed for Lisp.

The surface analyzer runs over the intermediate form like an evaluator creating a *surface* plan as it goes. A *surface* plan is composed solely of a large number of terminal segments corresponding to primitive operations (such as " + " and "*") grouped into one large segment and connected by data flow and control flow. The surface analyzer has detailed knowledge of the constructs which implement data flow and control flow. However, it does not have any knowledge of what the primitive functions do.

A surface plan is *flat* in that it has no hierarchical structure. The segmentation step introduces intermediate segmentation reflecting the logical structure of the plan. The primary goal of this process is to group segments which interact heavily close together, and keep segments which interact little, if at all, far apart. The segmentation is done in terms of six basic configurations called plan building methods (PBMs). It proceeds bottom up based on the topology of the control flow and data flow by locating minimal configurations which can be grouped together inside intermediate segments in accordance with the PBMs.

In general, the PBMs correspond to basic structured programming constructs: expressions, complex predicates, conditional expressions, and loops. The primary innovative feature is that loops are analyzed as compositions of fragments of looping behavior communicating by means of temporal sequences (streams) of values, rather than as repetitively executed pieces of straight-line code (see [Waters 1979]). For example, the loop in Figure 4 would be analyzed as a composition of four loop fragments as shown in Figure 5.

The first fragment (a generator) counts up by 1 from 1 creating an unbounded temporal sequence of values {1,2,...}. The second fragment (a terminator) tests the sequence of integers produced by the generator and stops the loop when an integer greater than N is found. This has the effect of truncating the sequence of integers to the sequence {1,2,...N}. (Both of these fragments are part of the DO construct.) The third fragment (a filter) restricts the truncated sequence of integers by selecting only those integers which correspond to positive elements of the vector A. The last fragment (an accumulator) computes the sum of the elements of A corresponding to the integers in the re-

```
Z = 0;
DO I=1 TO N;
   IF A(I)>0
      THEN Z = Z+A(I);
END;
```

Figure 4. An example loop.

```
generator            terminator              filter         accumulator
I=1;                 IF I>N THEN             IF A(I)>0 THEN  Z = 0;
                       GOTO EXIT;                            Z = Z+A(I);
I= +1;
```

Figure 5. The example in Figure 4 analyzed by PBMs.

stricted sequence produced by the filter. In the loop as a whole, the four fragments are cascaded together so that the loop computes the sum of the positive members of the first N elements of A.

From the point of view of the system being described here, this analysis is important because it provides very convenient intermediate segmentation. For example, if the programmer wanted to change the loop above into one which computed the product of all of the elements in the vector, he would only have to remove the filter, and replace the summation accumulator with a product accumulator.

The current analysis system is incomplete in that it stops after segmenting a program in terms of PBMs. At the current time, if a program is constructed using a text editor rather than using the plan editor or if it is modified (as in Frame 8 above) then the ensuing analysis is not able to determine the relationship between the program and the library cliches. As a result, further references to parts of the program cannot make use of the names of cliches and their parts but rather only to the PBMs and their parts.

Brotsky [Brotsky 1981] is working on adding a fourth stage to the analysis component of the system so that it can analyze a program in terms of all of the fragments in the library, not just in terms of the six PBMs. The fact that analysis in terms of PBMs is done first should simplify this task because it breaks the program up into a number of small pieces. The recognition process should be able to avoid combinatorial explosion by looking at each piece separately, rather than searching through the entire program at once. Once complete analysis is possible, the system will be able to apply the full force of the knowledge in the plan library to bear on a program whether or not the program was originally built up using the system, and whether or not it has been modified.

6. THE CODER

The coder takes in a segmented plan and creates the code for a Lisp program corresponding to it. This process is relatively straightforward. The structure of the program produced closely follows the structure of the segmented plan. In general, each terminal segment in the plan is implemented as a function call, and each non-terminal segment in the plan is implemented using a syntactic construct corresponding to its PBM. For example, a segment whose PBM is conditional will usually be coded using a COND. There are only three areas of real difficulty: determining how to implement the data flow in the plan, dealing with loops, and dealing with the fact that a plan may be fragmentary.

The data flow is a problem because the plan formalism deliberately does not represent much information about how data flow should be implemented. The coder is forced to discover how to use variables and nesting of function calls in order to implement the required data flow. When deciding how to implement the data flow in a plan, the coder first identifies every place where the nesting of function calls can be used. It then identifies related groups of data flow arcs that can be implemented using the same variable. Its basic goal is to use the smallest number of variables possible. In order to get mnemonic names for these variables, it uses any suggestions recorded in the plan. It has to be particularly careful to make sure that there is no conflict when the same name is suggested for two different groups of data flow arcs.

In order to produce Lisp code for a loop analyzed as a composition of loop fragments, the fragments must first be combined together into a single loop. This process (see [Waters 1978]) is designed so that the validity of the simple logical analysis in terms of composition will be preserved. The fragments are taken apart, and their pieces are reassembled into the resulting loop. The arrangement of the pieces in the loop is dictated by the data flow communicating temporal sequences of values between the fragments. The key idea is that if a piece of one fragment uses a temporal sequence created by a piece of another fragment, then the consuming piece should be placed after the producing piece in the resulting loop. The action of a filter is produced by placing the pieces which receive its outputs within the scope of a conditional predicated on the filter's test. Similar problems have been attacked by the people working on compilers for APL (see for example, [Guibas and Wyatt 1978]).

The coder is used for two purposes. It is used to create code corresponding to a plan so that this code can be used by the system to communicate with other parts of the programming environment such as compilers and interpreters. More importantly, it is used to create code which is used as a display to show the programmer a summary of the current state of the program he is working on. In this role it is important to be able to produce code while the plan is still fragmentary. There are two basic ways in which a plan can be incomplete. First, a data flow arc can be missing causing the input value to a segment to be undefined. Second, a segment can be empty in that its internal computation is unimplemented. In either case the coder uses "..*name*.." where *name* is the logical name for the input or segment (for example "..test.." or "..approximation.." see Frame 2 above) in lieu of code for the data flow or segment in question.

7. THE DRAWER

The drawing module (implemented by D. Chapman) can produce a plan diagram corresponding to a plan. The plan diagram in Figure 3 was produced by the drawer as were the diagrams in Figures 9, 10, & 11 below. [*Editor's note:* The drawings in this book are artist renderings based on diagrams produced by the drawer.] Creating an aesthetic two dimensional depiction of an arbitrary graph is a known hard problem. The drawer is able to produce reasonable results for simple plans by taking advantage of a number of constraints. First of all, it is oriented toward drawing segmented plans. It takes heavy advantage of the fact that a segmented plan is a hierarchy of segments within segments where each segment has only a few subsegments. It determines the arrangement of the diagram top down one segment at a time so that it only has to deal with a small graph at any one time. In order to make the diagram legible, the drawer omits the plan inside an intermediate segment unless there is sufficient space to draw it clearly. In general, it is only able to draw the top two or three levels of a plan.

In order to arrange a set of subsegments aesthetically, it uses a number of templates. The class of templates to use for a particular set of subsegments is chosen based on the PBM of the segment containing the subsegments. A specific template to use is then chosen from this class based on features of the way the subsegments are interconnected. The template specifies where the segments and the control flow between them should be placed. The drawer then adds in inputs, outputs, and data flow attempting to minimize line crossings.

8. THE PLAN LIBRARY

The plan library is a collection of plans for common algorithmic fragments. There are fragments corresponding to the six PBMs (e.g. conditional, predicate, loop, etc.). In addition, there are a variety of more specific programming cliches such as those referred to in Section 2 (e.g. successive approximation, equality within epsilon, and average) and those in Figure 5 (e.g. counting up, stopping at a given number, selecting out the positive elements, and summing up).

The library makes two basic things available to the programmer. First, he can include a fragment in the program he is constructing by referring to it by *name* (e.g. "conditional", "successive approximation", "summation", etc.). Second, each fragment has named *roles* some of which may be unfilled. For example, a successive approximation has some unfilled "test", a summation has an "accumulation" role which is specified to be +, and it has a "sequence" role (the temporal sequence to be summed) which is unfilled. When a fragment is instantiated its role names are carried over as well. The programmer can then use them when referring to the program he is constructing (e.g. "test of *successive approximation*", "accumulation of *summation*", "sequence of *summation*").

The idea of having a library of program fragments is not a new one. It has been argued for a long time that programmers should not have to reinvent the wheel every time they write a program. There have been libraries of subroutines, macros, and transformations. However, none of these things seems to have really solved the problem.

This library is different in approach (even though it is trying to represent the same information) because the fragments are represented as plans. This is more useful than any collection of fragments expressed in a way which depends on a programming language for four reasons. First, it is programming language independent. Second, the plan fragments are more canonical. A given plan can be realized as code in many different ways. Third, many fragments are so fragmentary that they do not correspond to any syntactically reasonable section of code. Fourth, due to the additivity property of plans, having the fragments represented as plans makes it easier to combine them.

An important feature of a library is its size. The current library is just a small prototype. It contains only the fragments needed by the examples in this paper. In order to extend it so that it had reasonable coverage it would have to become much larger. Both in [Barstow 1977] and in [Rich 1980] it is argued that it is possible to get reasonably good coverage of a small but significant part of programming knowledge by using a few hundred carefully chosen fragments. Based on this, in order to get good coverage of programming in general the library will certainly have to have several thousand fragments. Hopefully, it will not need more that ten thousand. The improved library designed by Rich [Rich 1980] should make it possible to effectively access that many fragments.

9. THE PLAN EDITOR

The plan editor provides a set of commands which a programmer can use to modify the program he is working on, by modifying its plan. The central feature of this interaction is the vocabulary that the programmer uses. The semantics of this vocabulary are based on the plan notation and the plan fragments in the library.

The basic objects known to the system are the objects in a plan: segments, input and output ports of segments, data flow, and control flow. Various adjectives are available for referring to particular kinds of objects. For example, "constant *segment*", "function call *segment*", "first *segment*", "free variable *input*", or "side-effect *output*". Part name expressions refer to the relationships between objects. For example, "subsegment of *segment*", "input of *segment*", "use of *output*", or "source of *data flow*". As discussed above, the fragments in the plan library and their roles can be referred to by name.

A programmer can refer to a specific part of the plan for the program he is working on by using the word "the" (e.g. "the test of the program SQRT"). Complex references can be built up by nesting simple ones (e.g. "the use of the output of the approximation of the program SQRT"). These phrases make it possible for the programmer to identify parts of the program based on their role in the algorithm, rather than based on their location in the text, or by their relationship to the parse tree for the program (as in a programming language structure editor). As a convenient method of reference, the pronoun "it" can be used to refer to the object which is the current focus of the system's attention (the area of the display which is highlighted). In addition, program names and variable names can be used to refer to the associated objects.

The word "a" is used to create an instance of something. For example, "a successive approximation", or "a side-effected free variable output TBL". The programmer can also use literal pieces of program text (such as "'(/ NUM RESULT)") in order to create a new fragment of plan. (The analyzer is used to convert the text into a plan.)

The editor provides a variety of verbs which specify actions to be performed. Two of these: "define" (a new program) and "implement" (an unfilled role of a plan fragment), are used to build up a program by combining prototypes from the library. As this is being done, the system annotates the resulting plan so that it embodies an analysis of the program in terms of the fragments used to create it.

Another group of commands (such as "add" (some object to the plan), "remove" (some object from the plan), "replace" (some object with another), "share" (two segments together as a single instance), etc.) are used to modify a plan. The primary leverage here is that it is much easier to make changes to a plan without causing unwanted side-effects, than it is to make changes to program text without causing unwanted side-effects. This is due to the fact that in a plan things are represented explicitly, locally, and irredundantly so that in general if some feature of the plan is changed, it doesn't affect any other feature of the plan. In contrast, consider the use of variables in a programming language. Using a variable to implement a data flow in one place can have arbitrary effects on other data flows that happen to be implemented using the same variable.

Note that the process of modification interacts strongly with the process of constructing a plan from prototypical fragments. As mentioned above, the plan embodies an analysis of the program in terms of the fragments used to create it. Once an orthogonal modification is made to the program, it must be reanalyzed in order to determine what fragments correspond to its new structure.

Whenever possible this reanalysis is done incrementally so that only the immediate neighborhood of the change is affected. If complete reanalysis is required, then information about the specific library cliches used to build up the plan is lost due to the fact that the current analyzer can only analyze a program in terms of the PBMs.

The plan editor also makes available several commands for displaying information to the programmer. For example, he can ask what parts of the plan are still incomplete, he can ask the system to describe parts of the plan, or he can ask the system to display the parts of the program which correspond to a part of the plan.

The verbs and referring phrases described above are combined into a very simple pseudo English (see the frames in Section 2). It should be noted that no attempt is being made to argue that this pseudo English is the best form of input to the system. As it stands it is probably too verbose. Further, if natural language input is going to be used, then a better parser must be used, because the pseudo English is too simple to be very natural. What is being argued is that the basic concepts which the vocabulary expresses are important.

10. A NON-NUMERIC EXAMPLE

In this scenario, the programmer is constructing a function DELETE which will delete (by side-effect) an occurrence of a symbol from a set implemented as a hash table. As shown in Figure 6, the hash table is a vector of lists (called buckets). Each symbol in the set is placed in one of the buckets. To simplify the deletion process, the hash table is implemented using buckets which have header cells of NIL.

```
The set {A B C D E F G I} is stored as:
          [(NIL A D G)
           (NIL B E)
           (NIL C F I)]
```

Figure 6. An example of the hash table implementation.

The programmer has already coded the function in Figure 7 which takes in a symbol, and returns the appropriate bucket of the hash table. The function works by generating a unique number corresponding to the symbol, taking the remainder of this number after dividing by the size of the table, and then using this remainder to index into the table. Note that the hash table itself (TBL) as well as its size (TBLSIZE) are free variable inputs to this function.

```
(DEFINE HASH (SYMBOL)
  (ARRAYFETCH TBL (REMAINDER (MAKNUM SYMBOL) TBLSIZE)))
```

Figure 7. The hashing program.

Frame 9 shows the programmer starting to build up his program. First, he defines a skeletal function specifying only its name and its argument. He then implements the program as a "trailing pointer list enumeration loop". (The coder uses a PSETQ (parallel assignment) in the code it produces because that is easier than trying to determine what order the assignments should be done in.)

The reader might well complain at this point that "trailing pointer list enumeration loop" is a very cumbersome name and that no one would want to have to remember it or use it. There are several points to be made. The actual name itself is not important. What is important is that the process of moving a pointer (here CURRENT) down a list starting at the second element while maintaining a second (trailing) pointer (here PREV) pointing to the

```
>Define a program DELETE with a parameter SYMBOL.
>Implement it as a trailing pointer list enumeration loop with an
  initialization '(HASH SYMBOL).


(DEFINE DELETE (SYMBOL)
   (PROG (CURRENT PREV)
         (SETQ PREV (HASH SYMBOL))
         (SETQ CURRENT (CDR PREV))
     LP (COND ((NULL CURRENT) (RETURN NIL)))
        (PSETQ PREV CURRENT
               CURRENT (CDR CURRENT))
        (GO LP)))


The trailing pointer list enumeration loop program DELETE.
```

Frame 9

preceding list element (see Figure 8) is a common algorithm that is known both to programmers and to the system. The name is used because there has to be some way to refer to the fragment so that the programmer can pull it into his program when he wants it. Just as in Interlisp a programmer has to know the names of the functions in the manual in order to use them, the user of this system has to know the names of the prototypes in the library. Section 11 shows how the next implementation of the PA will reduce the need for the programmer to know idiosyncratic names like this.

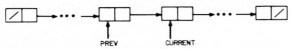

PREV   CURRENT

Figure 8. Trailing pointer list enumeration.

In Frame 10 the programmer adds a second terminator into the loop. The test of this terminator stops the loop if an element identical to the input symbol is found. The second terminator causes the loop to have two exits. The system responds to this by embedding the loop as the test of a conditional. The system notifies the programmer of this change because it is a somewhat non-obvious one, and because it changes the way things can be referred to by adding an additional level of nesting into the plan.

```
>Add a terminator with a test '(EQ (CAR CURRENT) SYMBOL) into the
loop after the first terminator of the loop.
Since the loop now has two exits, I assume that you intend DELETE
to be a conditional with the loop as its test.


(DEFINE DELETE (SYMBOL)
   (PROG (CURRENT PREV)
         (SETQ PREV (HASH SYMBOL))
         (SETQ CURRENT (CDR PREV))
     LP (COND ((NULL CURRENT) (RETURN ..action..)))
        (COND ((EQ (CAR CURRENT) SYMBOL)
               (RETURN ..action..)))
        (PSETQ PREV CURRENT
               CURRENT (CDR CURRENT))
        (GO LP)))

The second terminator of the test of ...
```

Frame 10

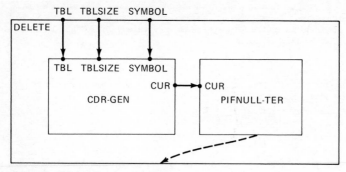

Figure 9. The plan before Frame10.

In order to see what is going on here more clearly, look at the plan diagrams in Figures 9 & 10. The first diagram shows the plan before the second terminator is added. In this plan DELETE is a loop with two parts: a generator that enumerates successive CDRs of the appropriate bucket in the hash table, and a terminator which terminates the loop when the end of this list is reached.

When the second terminator is added (see the upper box inside Figure 10) the loop becomes a two exit loop. (If the programmer had wanted the loop to have only one exit, but with a compound exit test, then he would have asked to add something to the test of the first terminator rather than adding a new terminator.) The system reasons that if the programmer wants two exits then

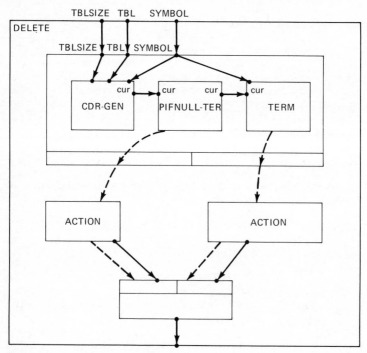

Figure 10. The plan after Frame 10.

it must be that he intends to do different things after the two exits. However, it assumes that after these actions he wants to rejoin the control flow and exit the program as a whole at a single point. To achieve these two things the system embeds the loop in a conditional as shown in Figure 10.

Note that the plan in Figure 10 has exactly the same top level form as the plan in Figure 3. They are both conditionals. However, the code corresponding to these two programs looks very different. In Figure 3 a COND is used while in Frame 10 the two actions of the conditional are embedded in the two exit paths from the loop. This difference is an artifact of the particular control constructs available in Lisp, and of the desire for compactness of the code. The plan representation transcends these stylistic issues and shows that the two programs have an essential similarity. Each one performs a test and then selects an action based on the outcome of that test.

One might well ask: since the system is actually working on a plan, and the programmer's requests refer to that plan and not to the code, why does the system show the programmer code, instead of the plan? The answer is that though it is clearly not optimal, code is better than anything else the current system is able to show the programmer. The purpose of the lower section of the screen is to display a summary of what has happened in the editing session. This summary should be as concise, complete, and unambiguous as possible. The problem with displaying plans is that so far, no concise representation has been developed for them. Plan diagrams are not concise enough. This can be seen from the fact that the plan diagram in Figure 10 only shows about half of the plan for DELETE (the internal plans for the subsegments of the loop have been elided).

Code is concise, unambiguous, and familiar. It has the additional advantage that using it in the display makes the interface between the system and the rest of the programming environment obvious, and highlights the nature of the basic user escape which is built into the system. At any time, the programmer can use an ordinary text editor to make an arbitrary change to the program he is working on.

The only problem with code is that it doesn't reflect the hierarchical structure of the plan accurately enough. One way to solve this problem would be to extend the programming language so that it resembled the plans more closely. Note that this has been done to a certain extent in order to be able to produce code corresponding to an incomplete plan. Additional extensions may eventually be made. However, for the time being, designing a more appropriate language has been postponed, so that the research effort can be focused on the central issues underlying the PA.

Returning to the scenario, in order to demonstrate another capability of the current system, the programmer asks what needs to be done (see Frame 11). The system keeps track of all of the aspects of the plan which are incomplete. It replies that the two actions still need to be implemented. The programmer then finishes the program by specifying these actions. Note that he refers to the simple programming cliche "splice out".

The last frame demonstrates some other capabilities of the current system. In response to the request "describe", the system can report out simple features of the plan. Here, the programmer asks for a description of the inputs and outputs of the program. Note that the system has figured out that TBL and TBLSIZE are free variable inputs to DELETE since they are free variable inputs to HASH.

More interestingly, the system realizes that TBL is also an output of DELETE. The system deduces this, even though it is not at all obvious from the way the programmer built the program up, because it has a simple model of

```
>What needs to be done?
Implement the first action of the program DELETE.
Implement the second action of the program DELETE.

>Implement the second action of the program as a splice out
of 'PREV.

>Implement the first action of the program as 'NIL.
```

```
(DEFINE DELETE (SYMBOL)
  (PROG (CURRENT PREV)
        (SETQ PREV (HASH SYMBOL))
        (SETQ CURRENT (CDR PREV))
     LP (COND ((NULL CURRENT) (RETURN NIL)))
        (COND ((EQ (CAR CURRENT) SYMBOL)
               (RPLACD PREV (CDDR PREV))
               (RETURN NIL)))
        (PSETQ PREV CURRENT
               CURRENT (CDR CURRENT))
        (GO LP)))
The NIL action of the program DELETE.
```

Frame 11

side-effects which allows it to understand many common situations where side-effects are used. It knows that if a program side-effects some part of a structure, then the structure as a whole is also side-effected. Here, the RPLACD potentially changes PREV which through a chain of CDRs is part of the list returned by (HASH SYMBOL). Because HASH has already been defined the system knows that the list it returns is part of the vector TBL and that therefore TBL is potentially modified by DELETE and should therefore be an output. It is very important that the system be able to make this kind of deduction, because much of what goes on in the system depends on the fact that the data flow is correct. If some more complex side-effect were going on the programmer would have to tell the system about it so that the effect would not be overlooked.

```
>Describe the ports of DELETE.
The SYMBOL parameter
The TBL free variable input
The TBLSIZE free variable input
The return value
The TBL side—effect output
>Display the source of the TBL output.
>Draw the program.
```

```
(DEFINE DELETE (SYMBOL)
  (PROG (CURRENT PREV)
        (SETQ PREV (HASH SYMBOL))
        (SETQ CURRENT (CDR PREV))
     LP (COND ((NULL CURRENT) (RETURN NIL)))
        (COND ((EQ (CAR CURRENT) SYMBOL)
               (RPLACD PREV (CDDR PREV))
               (RETURN NIL)))
        (PSETQ PREV CURRENT
               CURRENT (CDR CURRENT))
        (GO LP)))
The TBL side—effect output of the RPLACD action of ...
```

Frame 12

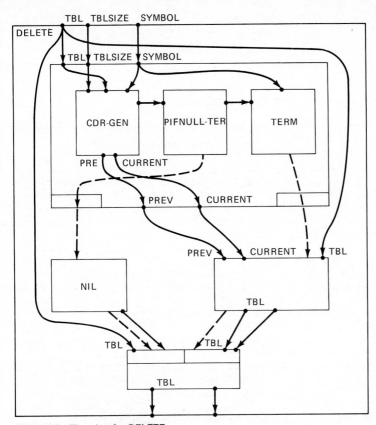

Figure 11. The plan for DELETE.

With the second request in Frame 12 the programmer asks the system to show him where the side-effect output comes from. The system highlights the call on RPLACD indicating the source. Finally, the programmer asks the system to draw a plan diagram corresponding to the program. The diagram produced by the drawing module is shown in Figure 11.

11. THE NEXT IMPLEMENTATION OF THE PROGRAMMER'S APPRENTICE

Figure 12 shows the commands from the scenario above which were necessary in order to construct the program DELETE. One important way to evaluate these commands is to consider the level of understanding exhibited by the current system. There are four classes of things that it understands. It understands the basic plan notions (segments, inputs, outputs, data flows etc.) and how they can be referred to. It understands the PBMs (expression, conditional, loop, etc.). It understands the verbs in the commands (define, implement, add, etc.). Finally, it understands the fragments in the plan library (trailing pointer list enumeration loop, splice out, etc.), but only in that it can retrieve them by name, and interpret references to their roles.

>Define a program DELETE with a parameter SYMBOL.
>Implement it as a trailing pointer list enumeration loop with an initialization '(HASH SYMBOL).
>Add a terminator with a test '(EQ (CAR CURRENT) SYMBOL) into the loop after the first terminator of the loop.
>Implement the second action of the program as a splice out of 'PREV.
>Implement the first action of the program as 'NIL.

Figure 12. The commands used to construct DELETE.

However, there are three very important things that the current system does not understand. First, it does not understand anything about data structures. Prior to the scenario, the hash table was described for the benefit of the reader, but the programmer said nothing about it to the system. He just chose the correct algorithmic fragments for working on the data structure he had in mind. Second, the current system understands nothing about specifications. Again, the programmer just chose the correct fragments to implement the specifications he had in mind. Third, the current system understands nothing about interrelationships between the fragments in the library.

The original design of plans included the notion of specifications. However, this feature was not used in the current system. Rich [Rich 1980] [Rich 1981] has extended the plan formalism so that it can be used to represent knowledge about data structures and about interrelations between plans for data structures, plans for algorithmic structures, and specifications. He has also designed and is implementing a much more comprehensive plan library of common programming cliches in the domain of non-numerical programming using the improved plan formalism. Together with the components described here, this new library will serve as the basis for the next implementation of the PA.

Using the next implementation of the PA, the programmer will be able to create the program DELETE using a sequence of commands like the ones shown in Figure 13. In the figure it is assumed that the library contains plans representing knowledge about hashing in general, but that it does not contain plans corresponding to either the exact hash table implementation the programmer has in mind, or to the exact deletion algorithm to be used.

First, before constructing the program HASH the programmer tells the PA about the data structure being used by saying "TBL is a global vector of size TBLSIZE implementing a set as a hash table whose buckets are lists with header cells of NIL". This command refers to several data structure terms (i.e. set, hash table vector, bucket (part of a hash table), list, header cell (part of a list), NIL). The system understands these terms due to the presence of plans for common data structures in the new plan library. Based on this description the system builds up a plan for the data structure.

The programmer then gives a specification for the program HASH "Define a program HASH which maps a given SYMBOL into the corresponding bucket in TBL". This refers to a number of specification terms understood by the system (i.e. map, corresponding). Based on this, the system constructs specifications and an outer segment for the function HASH.

If the library contained a plan for the exact mapping function the programmer wanted to use in HASH, he could refer to it by name. Alternately, he could implement hash by building it up from simple library cliches. However, he might well feel that it was easier to just type in the body of HASH using literal program text as in the figure. In this case the extended analysis component being implemented by Brotsky would be used to analyze the code in order to recognize what the mapping function is, and in order to verify that the code does not obviously contradict the specifications for HASH.

Once HASH is constructed, the programmer starts to construct DELETE by

In order to create HASH:
```
>TBL is a global vector of size TBLSIZE implementing a set as a hash
 table whose buckets are lists with header cells of NIL.
>Define a program HASH which maps a given SYMBOL into the corresponding
 bucket in TBL.
>Implement it as '(ARRAYFETCH TBL (REMAINDER (MAKNUM SYMBOL) TBLSIZE)).
```
In order to create DELETE:
```
>Define a program DELETE which removes a given SYMBOL from TBL.
>Implement DELETE so that it searches the bucket in TBL corresponding
 to SYMBOL and splices out the occurrence of SYMBOL, if there is one.
```

Figure 13. Commands needed in the next implementation of the PA.

setting up the outer segment and giving its specifications "Define a program DELETE which removes a given SYMBOL from TBL".

He then describes the algorithm to be used by using the command "Implement DELETE so that it searches the bucket in TBL corresponding to SYMBOL and splices out the occurrence of SYMBOL, if there is one". This final command corresponds to the last four commands in Figure 12. He is able to be more concise here because, due to the interrelationships in the new library, the system will be able to reason about how the choice of one fragment determines the choice of other fragments.

The programmer specifies that he wants to search "the bucket in TBL corresponding to SYMBOL". Because of the specifications the programmer gave for HASH, the system knows that this bucket can be calculated by calling "(HASH SYMBOL)".

"Search" is an abstract fragment that specifies that in order to search something a program must enumerate the things in the structure and check each item to see if it is the one desired. There are two exits from the search depending on whether the desired item is found or not. Due to the fact that the programmer said that the buckets in the hash table were lists, the system knows that it must do a list enumeration in order to search it. The programmer specifies that the predicate he wants to use in the search is one which tests for an "occurrence of SYMBOL".

Finally, the programmer specifies that what he wants to do when he finds the occurrence of SYMBOL is "splice (it) out". The system has the same fragment for splice out that is used in Figure 12, but additionally it knows that in order for a splice out to work, there has to be a trailing pointer. As a result, it reasons that it needs to do a trailing pointer list enumeration (a special kind of list enumeration) in the search.

Note that because the new system will be able to do the above kind of simple reasoning, the programmer will not have to use specific fragment names such as "trailing pointer list enumeration loop", but rather can, in general, rely on more abstract terms such as "search". Another important benefit to be gained from this kind of reasoning is that the system can do simple consistency checking, and complain whenever the programmer tries to combine incompatible fragments. The current system only complains when the programmer violates the basic semantics of the plan representation.

Looking further in the future there are several other kinds of knowledge which should be added to the PA. For example, both the current system and the next one are oriented toward understanding how a program does what it does. There is little or no representation of why it does it the way it does as opposed to some other way. This problem can be addressed by adding knowledge of efficiency issues into the system. In addition, the current plan representation is oriented toward representing single programs and small clusters of programs. It needs to be extended so that it can represent large scale system organizations. Finally, the knowledge now being represented is limited to general knowledge about programming. In order to be more useful to a programmer in a particular domain, the library will have to be extended so that it contains a variety of fragments pertaining to the particular domain of use. In the long run, as the PA gains more and more knowledge in more and more areas, it will be able to take on increasingly large portions of the programming task.

ACKNOWLEDGMENTS

This report describes research done at the Artificial Intelligence Laboratory of the Massachusetts Institute of Technology. Support for the laboratory's artificial intelligence research has been provided in part by the Advanced Research Projects Agency of the Department of Defense under Office of Naval Research contracts N00014-75-C-0643 and N00014-80-C-0505, and in part by National Science Foundation grant MCS-7912179.

REFERENCES

[Balzer 1981] R.M. Balzer. Transformational implementation: an example. *IEEE Transactions on Software Engineering*, SE-7:1 (January 1981).

[Barstow 1977] D.R. Barstow. *Automatic construction of algorithms and data structures using a knowledge base of programming rules.* Stanford University, Stanford Artificial Intelligence Laboratory, Memo AIM-308, November 1977.

[Brotsky 1981] D.C. Brotsky. *Program understanding through cliche recognition.* Massachusetts Institute of Technology, Masters thesis proposal, August 1981.

[Cheatham 1981] T.E. Cheatham, Jr. An overview of the Harvard Program Development system. In H.Hunke (ed.) *Software Engineering Environments*, North-Holland, 1981, 253-266.

[Donzeau-Gouge et al. 1975] V. Donzeau-Gouge, G. Huet, G. Kahn, B. Lang, J.J. Levy. A structure oriented program editor: a first step towards computer assisted programming. *International Computing Symposium*, Antibes, France, 1975; also IRIA, Rapport Laboria 114, Avril 1975.

[Feiler and Medina-Mora 1981] P. Feiler, R. Medina-Mora. An incremental programming environment. *Proceedings of the Fifth International Conference on Software Engineering.* San Diego, California, March 1981. [*Editors' note:* see also [Medina-Mora and Feiler 1981]]

[Guibas and Wyatt 1978] L.J. Guibas, D.K. Wyatt. Compilation and delayed evaluation in APL. *Proceedings of Fifth ACM Conference on the Principles of Programming Languages*, 1978.

[Rich 1980] C. Rich. *Inspection methods in programming.* Massachusetts Institute of Technology, Artificial Intelligence Laboratory, MIT/AI/TR-604, August 1981.

[Rich 1981] C. Rich. A formal representation for plans in the Programmer's Apprentice. *Proceedings of the Seventh Internation Joint Conference on Artificial Intelligence*, Vancouver, August 1981.

[Rich and Shrobe 1976] C. Rich, H.E. Shrobe. *Initial report on a LISP programmer's apprentice.* Massachusetts Institute of Technology, Artificial Intelligence Laboratory, Technical Report 354, December 1976.

[Rich and Shrobe 1978] C. Rich, H. Shrobe. Initial report on a LISP programmer's apprentice. *IEEE Transactions on Software Engineering*, 4:6, November 1978, 456-467; reprinted in *Interactive Programming Environments*.

[Teitelbaum 1979] T. Teitelbaum. *The Cornell Program Synthesizer: a microcomputer implementation of PL/CS.* Cornell University, Department of Computer Science, Tech. Report No. TR79-370, June 1979.

[Waters 1976] R.C. Waters. A system for understanding mathematical Fortran programs. Massachusetts Institute of Technology, MIT/AIM-368, August 1976.

[Waters 1978] R.C. Waters. *Automatic analysis of the logical structure of programs.* Massachusetts Institute of Technology, MIT/AI/TR-492, December 1978.

[Waters 1979] R.C. Waters. A method for analyzing loop programs. *IEEE Transactions on Software Engineering*, SE-5:3 (September 1979).

24 The Refinement Paradigm: The Interaction of Coding and Efficiency Knowledge in Program Synthesis

ELAINE KANT

Carnegie-Mellon University
Pittsburgh, Pennsylvania

DAVID R. BARSTOW

Schlumberger-Doll Research
Ridgefield, Connecticut

A refinement paradigm for implementing a high-level specification in a low-level target language is discussed. In this paradigm, coding and analysis knowledge work together to produce an efficient program in the target language. Since there are many possible implementations for a given specification of a program, searching knowledge is applied to increase the efficiency of the process of finding a good implementation. For example, analysis knowledge is applied to determine upper and lower cost bounds on alternate implementations, and these bounds are used to measure the potential impact of different design decisions and to decide which alternatives should be pursued. In this paper we also describe a particular implementation of this program synthesis paradigm, called PSI/SYN, that has automatically implemented a number of programs in the domain of symbolic processing.

© 1981 IEEE. Reprinted with permission from *IEEE Transactions on Software Engineering*, SE-7:5 (September 1981), pp. 458-471.

1. INTRODUCTION

One approach to reducing software costs is to specify systems in a very high-level language and use an automatic system to produce efficient code in a lower level language. We assume that it is possible to develop specification languages that are easy for people to understand and make changes in. The problem is then to develop a translation system. This problem differs from that of traditional compiler optimization in several ways. Since the source language is more abstract, many more combinations of implementations are possible, and the best should be chosen. For the sake of target program efficiency, we would like to allow different instances of the same high-level constructs to be implemented differently within the same program. For the sake of efficiency in the translation process, we would like to reimplement selective parts of the system when changes are made to the specification—only those parts of the program affected by the change (including parts whose efficiency is affected) should have to be reimplemented. For this and other reasons, we will save a history of how the implementation is related to the specification and of what implementation decisions were made and why.

This paper describes a general refinement paradigm for implementing high-level specifications in a low-level target language. Coding and analysis knowledge work together to produce an efficient program in the target language. Since there are many possible implementations, searching knowledge is applied to make the program synthesis process (the "compilation") itself efficient. We believe that the paradigm is similar to those used by good programmers.

We also describe a particular implementation of the paradigm, PSI/SYN. This system was developed as part of a larger program synthesis system, called PSI [Green et al. 1979], in which programs are specified by a dialogue with PSI's acquisition phase using a subset of English and example input/output pairs. PSI/SYN functions both as the synthesis phase of PSI and as an independent system whose specifications are in a formal high-level language. Within PSI/SYN, coding knowledge is represented as coding rules in a subsystem called PECOS ([Barstow 1979a], [Barstow 1979b]) and the efficiency knowledge (analysis and searching rules) is in a subsystem called LIBRA ([Kant 1979a], [Kant 1979b]).

2. THE REFINEMENT PARADIGM

2.1 Refinement Trees

PSI/SYN is based on a refinement paradigm similar to paradigms discussed with respect to programming methodology (for example, see [Wirth 1971a] or [Dahl et al. 1972]). The original specification, described in terms of abstract concepts, is transformed through a sequence of descriptions using successively more refined constructs. The end result is the fully implemented program using the constructs of the target language. The process may be diagrammed as shown below in Figure 1. The first description is the abstract specification, and the last is the fully implemented program; each intermediate description is slightly more concrete than the previous one. Each step in such a *refinement*

Figure 1. A refinement sequence.

488

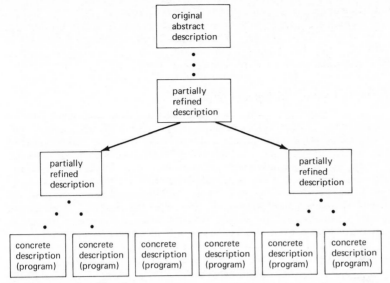

Figure 2. A refinement tree.

sequence is produced by applying a single *coding rule*. Note that the constructs used within any particular description need not all be at the same level of abstraction.

Since more than one rule may be applicable at some step in a refinement sequence, the concept may be generalized to a *refinement tree*, as shown in Figure 2. The root of the tree is the original specification, the leaves (terminal nodes) are alternative implementations, and each path is a refinement sequence. Intermediate nodes are partially implemented program descriptions.

Although the paradigm does not require it, we believe that the steps in the refinement sequences should be relatively small. Most steps involve the application of a single refinement rule to a single instance of an abstract construct. The effect is essentially a replacement of the instance by a description in terms of slightly more refined constructs. For example, in PSI/SYN the process of refining a collection[1] into a linked-list representation actually involves four different rules, tracing through the intermediate constructs of "explicit collection," "stored collection," and "sequence." Our preference for the smaller rules and changes is motivated largely by a concern for modularity in the programming knowledge and a desire to have every design decision reflected explicitly in the tree. The price paid, of course, is that our refinement trees can be quite large. It may take five or so steps to completely refine one abstract concept, and for an entire program of about twenty lines of specification, some refinement sequences may be as long as a thousand steps.

An important feature of such trees is that the nodes (program descriptions) all represent "correct" programs (assuming correctness of the coding rules). Each node represents a step in a path from the abstract specification to some concrete implementation of it. When paths cannot be completed (as happens

---

[1] The term "collection" is used since the rules do not distinguish between multisets, which may have repeated elements, and sets, which may not.

occasionally), the cause is generally the absence of rules for refining a particular construct within a program description, rather than any inherent problem of the description itself. The use of refinement rules enables the system to proceed directly toward correct implementations, without any need for testing different combinations of primitive constructs to see if they are correct.

2.2   A Search Space of Correct Programs

Different implementations of abstract concepts are often appropriate under different situations. Given some measure of "appropriateness" (for example, an efficiency measure), the refinement tree provides a space that can be searched for the most appropriate implementation. Our experience with such trees suggests that they provide a relatively convenient way to deal with the variability and complexity that seem a necessary part of real-world programming.

Theoretically, the system could build the entire search tree, compute the efficiency measure of each terminal node, and select the best. Since the number of reasonable implementations of a given abstract algorithm can be combinatorially high (tens or even hundreds for small specifications), techniques for pruning the tree and limiting the search are clearly needed. Our approach combines many variants of the standard techniques; for example, it employs heuristic rules to prune the coding rules and estimates program costs to prune the tree (with branch and bound) and to guide its construction according to a mixture of best-first search with look-ahead and dynamic programming.

Within the framework of this search space, the roles of coding and efficiency knowledge can be simply stated. Coding knowledge plays the role of a "legal move generator" for a space of correct programs. Efficiency knowledge plays two separate roles. First, analysis knowledge is used to determine the cost of executing the programs represented by nodes in the space; that is, analysis knowledge plays the role of an "evaluation function." Second, searching knowledge is used to reduce the cost of finding the desired (or at least, an adequate) terminal node in the tree.

2.3   The Role of the Target Language

While any implementation of the refinement paradigm must necessarily involve some target language, the paradigm itself seems to be independent of any particular programming language. At some point in the refinement process, the descriptions begin to be expressed in terms of the target language. As refinement progresses, target-specific constructs play an increasingly dominant role in the descriptions. In fact, a terminal node in the tree is characterized by the fact that the description is expressed solely in target-specific terms: it is a program in the target language.

Since different target languages have constructs corresponding to different levels of abstraction, the languages can take over at varying points in the refinement process. For example, a language in which sets were implemented directly could take over much earlier than a language like LISP. The same language may even support different levels of abstractions. For example, PASCAL has a set data type but not a linked-list data type; LISP has linked-lists but not sets.

2.4   Implementation

We have implemented this refinement paradigm twice. In the first implementation, we viewed the coding knowledge as being "in charge" of the process. When choice points were encountered (that is, when more than one coding rule was applicable), efficiency knowledge was used to select the best alternative. The details of the first implementation are available elsewhere [Barstow and Kant 1976]. Our principal conclusion was that the bandwidth for communication between coding and efficiency knowledge was too low.

In the second implementation, PSI/SYN, we reversed our model of who was in charge. The part of efficiency knowledge referred to earlier as "searching knowledge" controls the application of coding and analysis knowledge to build the part of the space that is actually explored in the process of finding the desired program. In this implementation, processing goes through a series of cycles, each consisting of the following steps:

1. Pick some node of the refinement tree to expand, based on cost estimates for the active nodes (which are non-terminal leaves).

2. Pick some part of the program described by that node to refine, based on the relative importance of different parts.

3. Find the coding rules that can be used to refine that part.

4. Prune those rules that fail to satisfy plausibility requirements.

5. Expand the tree by applying each of the remaining coding rules to create new program description nodes.

6. Compute cost estimates for the new nodes by applying the analysis rules.

In this process, branch-and-bound techniques are used to limit the search based on the cost estimates for the nodes in the refinement tree. Two cost estimates are associated with each node: "optimistic" (lower bound) estimates are computed assuming that each abstract construct can be implemented in the most efficient way without regard to possible interactions among the decisions; "achievable" (upper bound) estimates are computed assuming that each abstract construct will be implemented with a default technique that is known *a priori* to be feasible and free from interactions. It is not necessary to expand any node whose optimistic cost estimate is greater than the achievable cost estimate for some other node. These techniques are used primarily in step 1.

In addition, resource-management techniques are used to ensure that limited resources will be spent on the decisions that are most critical. Analysis techniques are used to determine the relative importance of different decisions (reflected in step 2), and, for the less important decisions, more weight is attached to plausibility criteria (reflected in step 4).

In a sense, PSI/SYN's coding rules define programming constructs implicitly in terms of more and less abstract constructs. In implementing the refinement paradigm, we have found it helpful to include more explicit characterizations of the constructs. We call these characterizations *prototypes*. For example, the analysis knowledge makes use of default implementation costs that are associated with individual constructs. The intermediate constructs also provide convenient "hooks" for incorporating PSI/SYN's knowledge about its own behavior. For example, the plausibility criteria are associated with individual constructs. Also, the analysis rules need to know the structure of each construct to compute its time and space costs. In general, we have found it important to include in PSI/SYN's knowledge base descriptions of a variety of different kinds of relationships among the programming constructs that PSI/SYN employs.

3. AN EXAMPLE

To illustrate the refinement paradigm, we will show how PSI/SYN constructs a simple retrieval program. The problem is to write a program, called NEWS, whose behavior is described by the following abstract algorithm:

Read in a database of news stories. Each story has an associated collection of key-words. Repeatedly accept a keyword and print out a list of the names of the stories in the database that contain that keyword. If the keyword "quit" is entered, stop the process.

A human-readable form of PSI/SYN's specification-language version of NEWS is given in Figure 3. (This version is a translation of the internal specification given to PSI/SYN. The internal representation is a kind of semantic net; its exact description is not relevant to this discussion.) As part of the specification, the user can provide information about data structure sizes and about the probabilities of taking different branches of a conditional. If the relevant information is not provided in the specification, PSI/SYN will ask the user for it at the beginning of the synthesis session.

3.1 Alternate Implementation Paths for NEWS

PSI/SYN can generate several versions of NEWS. Under different assumptions about the size of the database or the cost function to be used, different implementations are selected. A refinement tree showing several implementations and the critical decision points is presented in Figure 4. Only nodes involving a choice of coding rules are shown. Achievable and optimistic cost estimates for each node are given in parentheses. (Cost estimates are in millisecond-pages, a result of a cost function that contains a product of running time measured in milliseconds and space measured in pages, and have been rounded for convenience of explanation.) The major choices to be made are the representation for the *database* mapping from stories to keywords and the representation for the *keywords* collection. One refinement sequence, leading to node G in the search tree of Figure 4, is explained in more detail in the following sections. It involves representing *database* internally as a hash table of stories, with each story in turn having a hash table to represent *keywords*. The cost function used in this case is the product of running time and number of pages in use. In this run, PSI/SYN questions the user to determine critical parameters. It finds that the expected number of stories in the database is 80, the average number of keywords per story is 100, the expected number of

NEWS

DATA STRUCTURES
```
database: mapping from story to keywords;
story: string;
keywords: collection of key;
key: string;
command: alternative "quit" or key;
```

ALGORITHM
```
database ← input();
loop:
     command ← input();
     if command = "quit" then exit;
     forall S in domain-of(database) when command
          in database[S] do output(S);
     repeat;
```
Figure 3. Initial program description for NEWS.

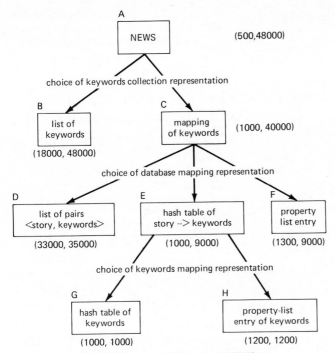

Figure 4. Overview of alternate refinements of NEWS.

iterations of the loop is 300, and the probability that the command is a keyword of the average story is .01. PSI/SYN eventually chooses a hash-table representation for *keywords* because there are many keywords for each story. The time to convert the collection of keywords into a hash table (from the linked-list representation used for input) is balanced by the time savings from the membership test, which is faster as a hash-table lookup than as a search through a list of keywords (for large keyword collections). The *database* representation decision is similar. Both choices are reinforced by the fact that the main loop is executed many times before exiting with "quit." (This is about the best possible implementation given PSI/SYN's current set of coding rules.)

Under other assumptions, a path through node B would be taken and a linked-list representation would be selected for *database*. For example, if the loop is executed only a few times or if the number of keywords associated with a story is small, then the time required to convert the database from the list of pairs (*<story, keywords>*) representation to a hash-table representation is not outweighed by the fast hash-table lookup operations. If space is a critical factor in the cost function, another path through B might be taken in which the original representation of a list of pairs is preserved. This avoids using any more space than absolutely necessary, but at a cost in time.

A different tree than the one pictured in Figure 4 may also be searched under different assumptions. Suppose there are only a few keywords per story, many stories, and a cost function dominated by running time. Then the representation of the *database* mapping would be a more critical decision than the representation of the *keywords* collection because the time for the membership test would not differ greatly for the different representations. Section 5 describes how critical decisions are identified by the potential impact method.

If fewer resources are available for synthesis than in the examples described above, then some of the choices may be made by heuristic rules rather than by efficiency computations. For example, nodes F and H will not be considered if a plausibility rule that prefers hash-table representations to property-list entries is applied.

3.2   Initial Refinements in NEWS

The following sections show more details of the refinement sequence leading to node G. Recall that a dialog with the user revealed that about 80 stories, 100 keywords per story, and 300 loop iterations are expected and that the probability that the command is a keyword is .01.

PSI/SYN first calls on the coding rules to make refinements that do not involve any decisions. For example, the format of the *database* on input is refined to a LISP list of pairs (*<story>*, *<keywords>*), where *keywords* is a LISP list of *keys*. These are the default input formats.

Also, the "forall" statement enumerating the domain of *database* is refined into an explicit enumeration of the items of the domain by the following coding rule (which is the only one applicable):

• The process of performing an action A for all elements of a collection may be implemented as a total enumeration of the elements; if a predicate is specified, the action for each element consists of testing the predicate and performing A if the test succeeds; if no predicate is specified, the action for each element is A.

To decide how to refine the enumeration, more information about the representation of the domain is needed. In this case, the following rules about plausible implementations are sufficient to constrain the choice to a single possibility:

• If the only uses of a collection A are for enumerations over A, and if B is another representation for A that is easily enumerable, then use the same representation for A and B.

• If all the uses of a collection are for enumerations, or as pointers to positions in it, or as tests of the state of the enumerations, and if the target language is LISP, then refine the collection into a linked-list.

These rules determine that the domain collection, which is used only for enumeration and is not an alternate representation of some other collection, should be refined into a linked-list. Therefore, the following sequence of coding rules is applied:

• A collection may be represented explicitly.
• An explicit collection may be stored in a single structure.
• A stored collection may be represented using a sequence.
• A sequence may be represented as a linked-list.

Some of the details of constructing the domain list and the enumeration of the domain are postponed by resource management rules because it is predicted that no decisions will be involved and the cost estimate for that part of the program will not change significantly. Other choices that arise and cannot be resolved by rules about plausible implementations are also postponed until other useful refinements or design choices are made.

3.3   Identifying the Most Important Decision

All of the changes above take place before node A of Figure 4 is reached. The partial program description at this stage of the refinement is shown in Figure 5.

NEWS

DATA STRUCTURES
```
database: LISP list of pairs (story,keywords);
dbl: mapping from story to keywords1;
story: string;
keywords: LISP list of key;
keywords1: collection of key;
key: string;
command: alternative "quit" or key;
```
ALGORITHM
```
database ← input();
ddb ← domain-of(database);
loop:
     command ← input();
     if command = "quit" then exit;
          enumerate-items S in ddb
               if member(command,database[S])
               then output(S);
          repeat;
```
Figure 5. Intermediate program description for NEWS.

During this refinement, several choices were postponed. These choices are 1) how to refine the *database* mapping used inside the "forall" (which is now an "enumerate-items"), and 2) how to refine the *keywords* collection within that mapping. What are the effects of the two choices to be made in this example?

The internal representation of *database*, called *dbl*, is used to retrieve the map value *keywords* of stories once per story per command. Possible implementations for mappings range from a linked-list format that makes retrieval linear in the number of stories to associative structures that have constant expected retrieval time. The keyword collections in *dbl* (called *keywords1*) are used in the "member(*command,database[S]*)" test. This test is executed once per story for each iteration of the loop. Possible implementations give membership tests with times ranging from linear in the number of keywords to constant.

Since the user said that the number of keywords is greater than the number of stories, the keyword representation choice has the largest difference in cost between the default implementation and the optimistic estimate of the cost when the right decision is made. Thus, this part of the code is more likely to be a bottleneck in the final program if care is not taken in the representation choice. According to a resource management rule about making important decisions first, the next step is to look at the possible refinements of *keywords1*.

To make this decision, search resources must be assigned. Currently the resources measured are the CPU time used in carrying out the refinements and the number of construct instances in the program descriptions. The resources needed to complete a program implementation without making choices are estimated and subtracted from the total available resources. Decision-making resources from the remainder are assigned in proportion to the estimated importance of the decision. Then, separate program descriptions are set up in which each of the alternate coding rules are applied. In this decision, the applicable rules allow either refining *keywords1* into an explicit collection, leading to node B, or into an explicit mapping, leading to node C.

3.4 Exploring Two Implementations for *KEYWORDS1*

PSI/SYN's goal is to refine the alternatives (B and C) enough that the comparison among implementations will be informative. The resources previously divided among the alternatives give upper limits on the time and space to be spent on getting more accurate estimates of the program costs of the implementations being explored. As part of the resource-management strategies, each program description has a "purpose" to be fulfilled and a set of program parts that is to be the focus of attention of processing. In this case, the *keywords1* data structure, the representation conversion from the input representation, and the membership test are included in the focus set. Processing of the program description continues until the resources run out or until there are no more tasks relevant to refining the parts of the program under focus.

In the first program description, node B, the explicit-collection rule is applied and refinement proceeds until all relevant tasks are satisfied (resources are sufficient). At the conclusion, the keyword collection for each story has been refined, after the application of several coding rules, into a LISP list, and the membership operation has been refined into a list search.

Refinement of node C, the program description in which the explicit-mapping rule was applied, also halts because all relevant tasks have been accomplished. Here the keyword collection is refined to a mapping and membership is tested by seeing if there is a mapping for the given key. There is also a representation conversion since the keyword collection is represented as a list in the input.

The efficiency rules then compute optimistic and achievable bounds on the cost of the whole program for each program description. In the linked-list implementation, node B, the optimistic estimate is 18000 millisecond-pages, and the achievable bound is 48000 (Section 5 gives more details about how these bounds are computed). The optimistic and achievable cost estimates for the mapping representation, node C, are 1000 and 40000 respectively. Branch and bound is applied to eliminate any implementations with optimistic estimates worse than the achievable estimate of some other implementation. Neither implementation is eliminated in this case, though later in the refinement of NEWS this technique will be fruitful. In general, the comparison of alternatives includes all active program descriptions, not just those involved in the most recent decision. In this case, node C has the best optimistic estimate and is chosen for further refinement.

3.5 Refining the Rest of NEWS

The remaining decisions include choosing a refinement for the explicit-mapping of *keywords1* and choosing a refinement for *db1*. The database decision *(db1)* is chosen by resource management rules as the most important decision to be made. (If resources were running out at this stage, the rules about plausible implementations would make standard refinement choices to avoid the expense of comparing alternate implementations.)

Three program descriptions are set up to consider the three applicable refinement rules—one to consider refining the *db1* mapping to a list of pairs (node D), one to consider a stored mapping (node E), and one to consider a distributed mapping (node F). The relevant parts of the program, those related to the *db1* decision, are then refined in each program description. For example, the stored mapping is refined to a hash table. Next, the resulting program descriptions are compared with each other and with other program descriptions that have been temporarily abandoned, such as node B. As Figure 4 shows, nodes B and D can be eliminated from further consideration because even their optimistic bounds are worse than the achievable bound on node E. The most promising implementation, node E, is then chosen and refinement continues.

The final decision to be made is how to represent the *keywords1* collection, which has been refined into a mapping. As in the refinement of node C, there are three applicable coding rules, but in this case the "collection of pairs" rule is eliminated by a rule about plausible implementations. This plausible-implementation rule (which was not applicable in the developments at node C) states that when refining a mapping that is itself a refinement of a collection, it is not worth pursuing the collection-of-pairs implementation. Thus, only two coding rules are considered. These rules are both tested, in nodes G and H. The stored mapping, leading to the hash table representation in node G, proves to be the best choice. At this point, the cost estimate is precise enough to eliminate all the other possibilities.

Thus, the best possibility is the implementation of both the keyword collection and the mapping *db1* as hash tables. As refinement continues, several other choices of coding rules are resolved by rules about plausible implementations. These decisions include the choice to recompute rather than store values that are easy to compute. The program description is finally refined into the one page LISP program given in Figure 6.

4. CODING KNOWLEDGE

PSI/SYN's coding knowledge is represented in the form of refinement rules, each of which describes a technique for implementing an abstract construct in terms of (slightly) more concrete constructs. Several of PSI/SYN's coding rules are given below as English paraphrases of the internal representation; the details of the representation language are available elsewhere ([Barstow 1979a], [Barstow 1979b]):

• A collection may be represented as a mapping of objects to Boolean values; the default range object is FALSE.

• If the enumeration order is linear with respect to the stored order, the state of an enumeration may be represented as a location in the sequential collection.

• If a collection (or mapping) is input, its representation may be converted into any other representation before further processing. If it is used inside an enumeration construct, its representation may be converted into any other representation during the loop's initialization.

• If a linked-list is represented as a LISP list without a special header cell, then a retrieval of the first element in the list may be implemented as a call to the function CAR.

• An association table whose keys are integers from a fixed range may be represented as an array subregion.

The concepts covered by PSI/SYN's coding rules are all taken from the domain of symbolic programming. They deal generally with three categories of implementation techniques: representation techniques for collections, enumeration techniques for collections, and representation techniques for mappings. Overviews of these three categories of rules are given below. (In addition, PSI/SYN includes rules about low-level aspects of symbolic programming and about programming in LISP, but these will be omitted from this discussion.)

4.1   Representation of Collections

Conceptually, a collection is a structure consisting of any number of substructures, each an instance of the same generic description. (As noted earlier,

```
(NEWS [LAMBDA NIL
      (PROG (DDB DATABASE)
            [SETQ DATABASE (CONS (QUOTE "HEAD")
                                 (PROGN (PRIN1 "DATABASE?") (TERPRI) (READ]
            (SETQ DDB (PROG (G1 C1)
                            (SETQ C1 (CONS (QUOTE "HEAD") (QUOTE NIL)))
                            (SETQ G1 DATABASE)
                       RPT1 (COND ((NULL (CDR G1)) (GO L1)))
                            (RPLACD C1 (CONS (CAR (CAR (CDR G1))) (CDR C1)))
                            (SETQ G1 (CDR G1))
                            (GO RPT1)
                       L1    (RETURN C1)))
            (PROG (DB1)
            (SETQ DB1 (PROG (G2 C2)
                            (SETQ C2 (HARRAY 100))
                            (SETQ G2 DATABASE)
                       RPT3 (COND ((NULL (CDR G2)) (GO L2)))
                            (PUTHASH (CAR (CAR (CDR G2)))
                                     (PROG (G3 X C3)
                                           (SETQ C3 (HARRAY 100))
                                           [SETQ G3 (CDR (CAR (CDR G2]
                                      RPT4 (COND ((NULL G3) (GO L3)))
                                           (SETQ X (CAR G3))
                                           (PUTHASH X T C3)
                                           (SETQ G3 (CDR G3))
                                           (GO RPT4)
                                      L3   (RETURN C3))
                                     C2)
                            (SETQ G2 (CDR G2))
                            (GO RPT3)
                       L2   (RETURN C2)))
            RPT2 (PROG (KEY COMMAND)
                       (SETQ COMMAND (PROGN (PRIN1 "COMMAND?")
                                            (TERPRI) (READ)))
                       (COND ((EQ COMMAND (QUOTE XYZZY)) (GO L4)))
                       (SETQ KEY COMMAND)
                       (PROG (G4 Y)
                             (SETQ G4 DDB)
                        RPT4 (COND ((NULL (CDR G4)) (GO L5)))
                             (SETQ Y (CAR (CDR G4)))
                             (COND ((GETHASH KEY (GETHASH Y DB1))
                                    (PRINT Y)))
                             (SETQ G4 (CDR G4))
                             (GO RPT4)
                        L5   (RETURN)))
            (GO RPT2)
      L4    (RETURN]))
```

Figure 6. The final LISP program for NEWS.

PSI/SYN's rules do not distinguish between sets and multisets.) The diagram in Figure 7 summarizes the representation techniques that PSI/SYN currently employs for collections, as well as several (indicated by dashed lines) that it does not. Each branch in the diagram represents a refinement relationship. For example, a sequence may be refined into either a linked-list or an array subregion. These refinement relationships are stored in the knowledge base as refinement rules. Of course, the diagram doesn't indicate all of the details that are included in the rules (for example, that an array subregion includes lower and upper bounds as well as allocated space). As can be seen in the diagram of Figure 7, PSI/SYN knows primarily about the use of Boolean mappings and sequences. Although "distributed-collection" occurs in a dashed box, PSI/SYN can implement a collection using property list markings by following

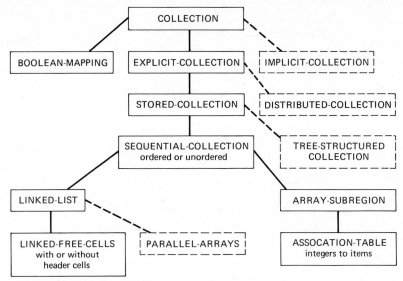

Figure 7. Overview of collection representations.

a path through a Boolean mapping to a distributed mapping. The most significant missing representations are the use of trees (such as AVL trees or 2-3 trees) and implicit collections (such as lower and upper bounds to represent a collection of integers).

Note the extensive use of intermediate-level abstractions. For example, there are four constructs between "collection" and "linked free cells". As noted earlier, such intermediate levels help to economize on the amount of knowledge that must be represented and also facilitate making choices.

4.2   Enumerations over Stored Collections

In its most general form, enumerating the elements of a collection may be viewed as an independent process or coroutine. The elements are produced one after another, one element per call. The process must guarantee that every element will be produced on some call and that each will be produced only once. In addition, there must be some way to indicate that all of the elements have been produced, as well as some way to start up the process initially. The process of constructing an enumerator for a stored collection involves two principal decisions: selecting an appropriate order for enumerating the elements, and selecting a way to save the state of the enumeration.

There are several possible orders in which the elements can be produced. If the enumeration order is constrained to be according to some ordering relation, then clearly that order should be selected. If it is unconstrained, a reasonable choice is to use the stored (first-to-last) order, either from the first cell to the last (for linked-lists) or in order of increasing index (for arrays). In some cases, it may be useful to use the opposite (last-to-first) order.

The enumeration state provides a way for the enumerator to remember which elements have been produced and which have not. There are many ways to save such a state. Whenever the enumeration order is first-to-last (or last-to-first), an indicator of the current position is adequate: all elements before (or after, for last-to-first) the current position have been produced and all

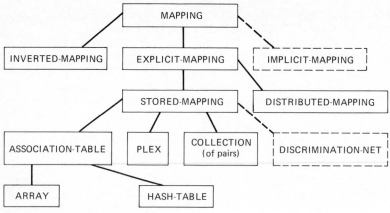

Figure 8. Overview of mapping representations.

elements after (before) the position have not. PSI/SYN's rules handle these cases, as well as the case in which the enumeration order is constrained and the collection is kept ordered according to the same constraint, in which case a position indicator is also adequate for saving the state.

The situation is somewhat more complex for nonlinear enumerations (in which the enumeration order is not the same as the stored order or its opposite); finding the next element typically involves some kind of search or scan of the entire collection. During such a search, the state must be interrogated somehow to determine whether the element under consideration has already been produced. There are basically two kinds of nonlinear enumeration states, destructive and nondestructive. PSI/SYN's rules deal with one destructive technique, the removal of the element from the collection. A technique not covered by the rules is to overwrite the element. The rules also do not cover any nondestructive techniques.

4.3   Representation of Mappings

A mapping is a way of associating objects in one set (range elements) with objects in another set (domain elements).[2] A mapping may (optionally) have a default image: if there is no stored image for a particular domain element, a request to determine its image can return the default image. For example, when a Boolean mapping is used to represent a collection, the default image is FALSE. The diagram of Figure 8 summarizes representation techniques for mappings. As with collection representations, there are several intermediate levels of abstraction for mappings. Note that an association list representation is determined by following the path from a "mapping" to a "collection" whose elements are domain/range pairs; the refinement path in the collection diagram given earlier then leads to a linked-list of pairs. Property lists give a distributed mapping whose domain is the set of atoms. A plex (or record structure) with several fields would constitute a mapping whose domain is the set of field names. The most significant mapping representations missing from PSI/SYN's rules are implicit mappings (such as function definitions) and dis-

---

[2] PSI/SYN's rules only deal with many-to-one mappings and not with more general correspondences or relations.

crimination nets. The rules currently deal with only one small aspect of hash tables: the use of INTERLISP's hash arrays.

5. ANALYSIS KNOWLEDGE

PSI/SYN uses analysis knowledge to make cost estimates for a program description (or any part of one) at any stage of the refinement process and uses the resulting efficiency information for branch-and-bound comparisons, to identify potential bottlenecks in the target program, and for quantitative descriptions in the plausible-implementation rules. Given a program description and a cost function, PSI/SYN's *analysis-maintenance rules* incrementally update the analysis information associated with the developing program; the *cost-estimation rules* compute summary cost information as needed. The lowest-cost implementation may vary under different assumptions about the input data characteristics and the cost function. The execution cost function can be any (user-supplied) polynomial in run time and storage use that reflects the performance measure desired by the user (for example, the product of space and the square of time).

The top-down, incremental analysis process allows cost estimation for programs that would be difficult to analyze if only the target program were given. Another advantage of combining the stepwise refinement with this sort of analysis is that classes of implementations can be compared by considering the cost estimates for intermediate program descriptions rather than by explicitly expanding the refinement tree to compare many target-language programs. For example, in NEWS, the collection of keywords corresponding to a news story can be refined into a mapping (leading to a hash table, bit mapping, or property list) or to a sequence (leading to a linked-list or array, ordered or unordered). Since the collection is used primarily for membership tests, PSI/SYN estimates that the mapping representation will give a faster execution time (a small constant) than the sequence (time is linear in the number of keywords) and therefore decides that the mapping refinement can be made without explicitly considering the list and array representations.

5.1   Updating Analysis Information

Information about the run-time characteristics of a program is needed to analyze efficiency; this includes statement running times and execution frequencies, data structure sizes, and data structure usage (where created, referenced, and modified). The user provides the needed information for the abstract specification, and then PSI/SYN updates the analysis information during refinement and keeps it associated with the relevant construct instances in the program descriptions of the refinement tree. In the NEWS program, the information provided with the specification is the expected number of stories (80), the average number of keywords per story (100), the probability that the command item is in a story (.01) and the number of times the main loop in the program will be executed for a given database (300). In later stages, information such as the size of the hash table is added.

PSI/SYN makes analysis transformations in parallel with refinements so that more accurate cost estimates can be associated with succeeding nodes in the search tree. Some of the analysis-maintenance rules are associated with particular coding rules. For example, when a "subset(A, B)" test is refined to "true-for-all x in A, member(x, B)," the probability that x is a member of B is computed automatically (as a function of the probability p that the subset test is true) by an analysis-maintenance rule associated with that coding rule. Many rules, such as those for analyzing Boolean combinations, are associated with coding constructs rather than with specific coding rules. For example, the probability of an "and" statement being executed is the product of the probabilities of all its arguments (assuming independence). Similarly, when new operation instances are added to a program description, the prototype for the operation is checked to see whether the arguments to the operation are modified or merely inspected so that the reference information for the data structure instances in the program can be updated.

5.2 Estimating Execution Costs

Cost-estimation rules use analysis information to estimate program execution costs. Rules for finding the space for data structures and the running time for operations are attached to the prototypes for the corresponding constructs. For example, a rule attached to the hash-table prototype says to estimate storage as 1.5 words times the size of the set being stored. Two rules are stored for run times of operations to give upper and lower bound estimates. The upper bound is an achievable estimate that is calculated by introducing standard (or default) implementation choices for each programming construct and by assuming that the standard implementation choices are made for the rest of the refinement process. For example, the achievable estimate for a membership test assumes that the default implementation of a collection is a list (when LISP is the target language) and that the average running time is therefore a constant times $n(1 - .5p)$, where p is the probability that the test succeeds and n is the size of the set. For the membership test in NEWS (with a constant of .015), this is $.015(100(1 - .005))$, which is approximately 1.5 milliseconds. The lower bound is an optimistic cost estimate that is based on lower bounds for implementations known to the program, not a theoretical lower bound or a best-case value. For the membership test, for example, the optimistic bound is a small constant (.01) because representing the set with a mapping such as a hash table is a possibility.

The cost estimate functions for the target-language constructs obviously have to be hand-coded. However, the cost-estimation rules for constructs that can be constructed from lower-level constructs (typically in more than one way) should *not* be arbitrary functions since consistency must be maintained. PSI/SYN uses a bottom-up process for constructing the time-estimation rules from time-estimation rules for other constructs. This process is described in more detail in [Kant 1979b].

In addition to the rules about the time and storage for the individual programming constructs, there are a small number of rules about how to combine the cost estimates for individual constructs into cost estimates for a control structure, including for the entire program. Cost estimates are generally prepared only when requested by other components, such as resource management rules, and can be made at varying levels of detail and precision, depending on the resources available for the computation. For example, the space in use for the program can be re-estimated for each statement, for each control block, or just taken as the maximum over the whole program; similarly, the number of executions of a loop can be calculated exactly or estimated. A standard cost-computation process uses different cost-prototypes to make either optimistic or achievable cost estimates and to perform either a quick estimate or a more detailed (and usually more expensive) analysis. To calculate a global achievable cost for a partial program description, the cost-estimation rules simply combine the achievable costs estimates (of the desired level of precision) for the individual constructs. Global optimistic costs are estimated by assuming optimistic costs for each of the constructs in the program and by assuming that no representation conflicts occur.

Rather than having many specific rules for each construct, PSI/SYN uses only a few general cost-estimation rules that inspect the information in the prototypes. General prototypes of construct classes (such as enumerations) and specific prototypes for each construct (such as the "forall" statement) make the structure of the constructs explicit. For example, the prototypes tell how to find the substructures of a data structure, how to find the arguments to an operation, and how to tell which parts of a control construct are local memory, loop initialization, loop exits, and loop body. Cost-estimation rules can then use this information. For example, one rule computes the time used by a control-structure construct and its subparts by summing the time for loop initialization steps, the product of loop-exit probabilities and the time for the corresponding exit actions, and the product of the number of loop executions and the time for one iteration.

Using these cost-computation rules, PSI/SYN estimates that the achievable cost of the program of Figure 5 is $(a + 300(b + 80(c + d)))$, where a is the achievable cost to input the database and find its domain, b is the cost to input and test the command, c is the cost for the membership test inside the enumerate-items, and d is the cost to find the keywords corresponding to the command. (The cost function in NEWS is a space-time product, but since space is measured in pages and in this example everything fits on one page, cost is the same as time.) Since other rules estimate that a is approximately 10 and b, .05, and since c is approximately 1.5 (the achievable time for a membership test as described above) and d is approximately .5 (for reasons similar to the membership test analysis), then the global time (and cost) is therefore $10 + 300(.05 + 80(2))$, or about 48000, as noted in Section 3. Similarly, substituting $(.01 + .01)$ for $(c + d)$ gives an optimistic time (cost) of about 500.

5.3 Computing Potential Impacts

Maintaining both optimistic and achievable estimates permits the assessment of a decision's *potential impact*. This is the difference between the achievable cost estimate and the execution cost estimate when optimistic costs are used for all parts of the program involved in the decision (and achievable estimates are used for parts not involved in the decision). This measure of potential impact is used to identify critical choices and to assign resources. For example, consider the potential impact of the decision about the *keywords* representation in the NEWS. The set of *keywords* (computed by database[S]) are referenced in the "member(command, database[S])" operation. From the cost expression given above, the potential impact is about $24000(2-.51)$, or 35760 millisecond-pages (ignoring differences in the optimistic and achievable estimates of a and b, which are small; PSI/SYN does compute the exact value). A similar calculation for the effect of how *database* is represented yields $24000(2-1.51)$ or 11760, so the *keywords* decision is more important.

6. SEARCHING KNOWLEDGE

PSI/SYN controls the search for an efficient implementation with two types of searching rules that sometimes call on the coding rules to generate legal implementations and sometimes on the cost-estimation rules to provide an evaluation function for the alternate implementations. Agendas of synthesis tasks, one associated with each node in the refinement tree, serve as the workspace for recording the state of the search.

Resource-management rules choose a node (program description) in the refinement tree, and then a part of that program, to work on. These rules assign priorities to tasks to ensure that the tasks are carried out within the limits of the resources. When refining a part of a program, all relevant coding rules are retrieved and tested for applicability. If more than one rule is applicable, *plausible-implementation rules* help decide which coding rule to apply. These rules contain precomputed analyses that may restrict the possible coding rules to those that seem reasonable in the given program situation, thus pruning the search tree. If several coding rules are judged to be plausible, separate children of the current node are produced by each of the rules. The alternatives are refined and compared under the control of resource-management rules.

PSI/SYN's search space has several interesting regularities that influence the search strategies used. First of all, most of the implementations in terms of known coding constructs are reachable, so refinement failure only occurs when no coding rules are applicable, which happens only rarely. Secondly, the current set of coding rules generates a fixed set of programming constructs, which can be partially ordered by level of abstraction. The ordering on the constructs allows the plausible-implementation rules to predict good paths. Because most implementations are reachable and because the potential refinements of abstract constructs can be found from the partial ordering, the analysis rules can compute reasonably tight bounds on the costs of implementations even when the programs are specified in terms of abstract constructs. Of course, the rules may fail to predict the costs correctly if all lower bounds are not simultaneously achievable. In such cases, an implementation can often be constructed by using representation changes, but at a higher cost than originally expected.

The size of the search space is rather large because more than one representation of the same type of data structure (or operation) is allowed. PSI/SYN allows different representations of the same data type, and even different representations of one instance of a data structure at different points in the program. If several representations of the same data were maintained at the same time, which is a reasonable implementation technique, the search space would be even larger. Thus, it is important for the searching knowledge to limit the possibilities considered. The plausible-implementation rules are one technique by which PSI/SYN ensures that multiple representations are only considered when there is a chance that they improve efficiency.

6.1 Assigning Priorities to Decisions

Unfortunately, coding decisions cannot always be made independently. For example, if the cost function involves a product of space and time, then the terms of the cost expression representing the product of the space occupied by one data structure and the time for operations not involving that data can be significant. Since all combinations of implementations cannot be considered in equal detail, the quality of the decisions depends on the order in which they are considered and on the depth to which the consequences of alternatives are explored before making a commitment. PSI/SYN's resource-management rules schedule tasks and allocate synthesis resources to balance the final program performance with the cost of choosing and constructing the implementations. These rules seem largely domain-independent. They make sense only in the context of a search space with properties similar to those described above, but do not depend on the domain being program synthesis.

PSI/SYN has three types of resource-management rules:

- *Priority-setting rules* limit the resources available to explore a particular branch in the refinement tree and decide which branches should be pursued in which order. These rules enforce global strategies such as branch and bound and best-first search with look-ahead. These rules, combined with a plausible-implementation rule that eliminates implementations that are worse in space and time than their alternatives, produce behavior similar to a dynamic programming algorithm. (See [Tompa and Ramirez 1980] for a good discussion of dynamic programming in implementation selection.)

- *Task-ordering rules* determine the order for attempting different refinement tasks within a particular branch of the refinement tree. Ordering principles include postponing choices of coding rules while working on more clearcut refinements to gather additional information, exposing choices by early expansion of complex programming constructs such as "subset," and postponing low-level coding details until the major decisions have been made.

- *Choice-ordering rules* find an order for considering the decisions that must be made if several have been postponed along a particular branch of the refinement tree. One of these rules suggests allocating the most resources to the decisions that are likely to lead to bottlenecks and making those decisions first. The decisions with the highest potential impact (as defined in the section on analysis) are assumed to be those most likely to lead to bottlenecks. However, these values are adjusted to reflect the accuracy of the cost estimates for the current level of program development and the expected cost of completing the refinement process (based on the minimum number of refinements needed to complete the program). Without this, a highly refined implementation might be abandoned in favor of a very abstract description with a slightly better optimistic estimate that is probably not achievable.

6.2   Grouping Related Implementation Decisions

The number of implementations constructed for comparison can be reduced by grouping related refinement decisions. This reduces both the number of decisions and number of interactions between decisions. Better decisions can be made at a lower cost since, for example, all uses of a data structure will be considered at once.

Whenever possible, a program is factored into "cost-wise independent" groups—program parts that are independent (or nearly so) in terms of the global cost function. These parts are then refined separately without considering interactions with other program parts. A more frequently realizable technique is for the resource-management rules to apply the "information-structure" grouping. In this method, related decisions such as the representation of a data structure and the implementation of all operations that reference it are considered as a group, which makes cost tradeoffs more explicit. Before choosing an implementation of one program part, the efficiency rules identify the related program parts and base the decision on the group's global cost impact. Also, when alternate choices of implementations are compared along different branches of the refinement tree, refinements are initially limited to those parts of the program related to the decision group.

6.3   Suggesting Plausible Implementations with Stored Analyses

The plausible-implementation rules are used to filter the coding rules. They help compare implementations without the expense of explicit construction and evaluation of the global execution costs of all alternatives. For example, if implementation X is better than implementation Y in both space and time, then Y can be eliminated without comparing the global costs of the programs that would result. The plausible-implementation rules typically describe the situations under which data structure representations are or are not appropriate, under which different sorting operations are plausible, or under which more than one representation for a data structure should be considered. For example, these rules determine that it is worth considering an additional representation for the database inside the loop of the NEWS program to facilitate faster access and membership testing. When the domain of the database is extracted and used only for enumeration, the plausible-implementation rules suggest a sequential representation. When the keyword collection decision is considered, the plausible-implementation rules for refining collections are checked. One of them says that for collections used only for membership tests and for inserting and deleting elements, some reasonable implementations are a linked-list and a mapping function such as a hash table.

The plausible-implementation rules are structured condition-action rules. The condition of a rule about data structures, for example, states the critical uses of a data structure that make the rule relevant. Analysis information such as the size of a data structure and the number of executions of a statement may be used in the rule condition. The rule action can set a Boolean combination of constraints for a set of program parts requiring that they be refined, or not refined, to a particular programming construct. A three-valued propositional logic (satisfied, possible, impossible) is used to check constraints.

The reliability of plausible-implementation rules may vary. In theory, a "reliability index" could be associated with each rule; in practice, two classifications are defined. A more reliable set of decision rules is always applied. They are assumed to be correct, and must explicitly set backup points if failure is anticipated. The less reliable rules are used only when a quick decision is needed and more accurate comparisons are not affordable or not potentially profitable. These rules contain the standard implementation choices. For example, one rule says to use lists rather than arrays to represent sequences in LISP.

7. ANOTHER EXAMPLE

The following problem is taken from Knuth's textbook series [Knuth]:

7.1-32. [22] (R. Gale and V. R. Pratt.) The following algorithm can be used to determine all odd prime numbers less than N, making use of sets S and C.

P1. [Initialize] Set $j \leftarrow 3$, $C \leftarrow S \leftarrow \{1\}$. (Variable j will run through the odd numbers 3, 5, 7, ... At step P2 we will have

$$C = \{n|n \text{ odd}, 1 \le n < N, n \text{ not prime, and } \mathrm{gpf}(n) \le p)(j)\},$$
$$S = \{n|n \text{ odd}, 1 \le n < N/p(j), \text{ and } \mathrm{gpf}(n) \le p(j)\},$$

where $p(j)$ is the largest prime less than j and $\mathrm{gpf}(n)$ is the greatest prime factor of n; $\mathrm{gpf}(1) = 1$.)

P2. [Done?] If $j \ge N/3$, the algorithm terminates (and C contains all the nonprime odd numbers less than N).

P3. [Nonprime?] If $j \epsilon C$ then go to step P5.

P4. [Update the sets.] For all elements n in S do the following: If $nj < N$ then insert nj into S and into C, otherwise delete n from S. (Repeat this process until all elements n of S have been handled, including those which were just newly inserted.) Then delete j from C.

P5. [Advance j.] Increase j by 2 and return to P2.

Show how to represent the sets in this algorithm so that the total running time to determine all primes $< N$ is $O(N)$. Rewrite the above algorithm at a lower level (i.e., not referring to sets) using your representation.

[Notes: The number of set operations performed in the algorithm is easily seen to be $O(N)$, since each odd number $n < N$ is inserted into S at most once, namely when $j = $ gpf(n), and deleted from S at most once. Furthermore we are implicitly assuming that the multiplication of n times j in step P4 takes $O(1)$ units of time. Therefore you must simply show how to represent the sets so that each operation needed by the algorithm takes $O(1)$ steps on a random-access computer.]

Since PSI/SYN's rules do not cover enumeration over collections that are being modified during the enumeration, a slightly modified version of the original algorithm was given to PSI/SYN. In this version, the set S has been replaced by two collections $S1$ and $S2$, and the collection P is created to output the set of primes (the complement of C).

The key here is to implement the collections $S1$, $S2$, and C differently. The only operations being performed on $S2$ are addition, removal, and taking "any" element. The "any" operation suggests that a Boolean mapping may be inappropriate and the frequent destructive operations suggest that an array may be relatively expensive. Thus, an unordered linked-list is a reasonable selec-

DATA STRUCTURES
```
N, J, K, X: integer
C, S1, S2, P: set of integer
```

ALGORITHM
```
N ← input();
J ← 3;
C ← {1};
S1 ← {1};
loop:
    if 3*J ≥ N then exit;
    if J is not a member of C then
        S2 ← S;
        S ← { };
        loop until S2 is empty:
            for any X in S2:
                remove X from S2;
                if J*X < N then
                    add X to S1;
                    add J*X to S2;
                    add J*X to C;
        remove J from C;
    J ← J + 2;
    repeat;
K ← 3;
P ← { };
loop:
    if N < K then exit;
    if K is not a member of C
        then add K to P;
    K ← K + 2;
    repeat;
output P as a linked-list.
```

tion. Since the value of $S1$ is assigned to $S2$, a representation conversion can be avoided by using the same representation for both collections. This is especially useful here, since the only operation applied to $S1$, the addition of elements, is relatively simple with unordered linked-lists. The only operations applied to C are addition, removal, and two membership tests. Such operations are fairly fast with Boolean mappings. Since the domain elements of the mapping are integers with a relatively high density in their range of possible values, an array of Boolean values is a reasonable representation of C. PSI/SYN derived this implementation, and the resulting program exhibited linear behavior when it was tested.

8. RELATED RESEARCH

A logical extension of historical attempts to automate programming is to "compile" a very high level language. This is perhaps best exemplified by work on SETL [Schwartz 1975]. SETL's specification language contains primarily mathematical concepts similar to PSI/SYN's sets and mappings. The implementation involves choosing from a small number of parameterized implementations by an algorithmic procedure based on sophisticated analysis of data flow and subset relations between sets. A wider variety of implementations is allowed in systems designed by Low and Rovner ([Low 1978], [Rovner 1976]), with choices based on partitioning data structures into equivalence classes and using hill-climbing to select combinations of implementations. Programs are analyzed by monitoring default implementations. These approaches use only one level of refinement—they go from the high-level construct to the alternatives represented in the target language. Rovner's system can be noted for allowing multiple representations and for using heuristics for decision making that are built in but clearly identified. Other approaches to implementation selection use dynamic programming algorithms ([Morgenstern 1976], [Tompa and Ramirez 1980]).

Support for more gradual implementation (as well as for verification) is provided by languages such as CLU and Alphard ([Liskov et al. 1977], [Wulf et al. 1976a]), in which a human user is allowed to define intermediate types or encapsulations. Automatic choice among alternatives is not available. Recently, work on specifying and verifying performance properties of programs has begun [Shaw 1979]. There has also been some work on automatic implementation selection systems with a few intermediate levels of refinement ([Morgenstern 1976], [Rosenschein and Katz 1977], [Rowe 1976]). In addition, knowledge-based approaches similar to PSI/SYN have been successful in implementing lower-level language compilers ([Cattell 1978], [Fraser 1977]).

There has been much recent work on transformations as a method for developing programs ([Balzer 1981], [Burstall and Darlington 1977], [Cheatham et al. 1979b]). The last of these systems, PDS, with its explicit maintenance of a "family tree" of programs, is most clearly related to PSI/SYN's refinement paradigm. PDS allows a user to apply transformations that can refine abstract concepts or extend existing constructs and also provides some analysis tools. Work by Wegbreit ([Wegbreit 1976]) includes goal-directed transformations that explicitly use efficiency information based on theoretical lower bounds to drive search.

Another approach to automatic programming involves the use of theorem proving (for example, by Manna and Waldinger in [Manna and Waldinger 1979]). Axiomatic definitions of program properties, rather than rules, are used to describe implementation techniques. This approach has been reasonably successful with the addition of some programming and domain-specific knowledge to the mathematical axioms.

Green and Barstow's sorting work [Green and Barstow 1978] is another example of an application of the refinement paradigm. Also closely related in some ways is the plan-analysis approach in the Programmer's Apprentice project ([Rich 1980], [Shrobe 1979]).

9. OBSERVATIONS

9.1 The Knowledge-Based Approach

The knowledge-based approach (the use of rules and prototypes) of our implementation of the refinement paradigm has proved to be quite successful. It provides a framework that facilitates the codification of programming knowledge, which is an experimental development process. New implementation techniques can be added simply by adding new coding rules. As new coding knowledge is added, the corresponding analysis knowledge is also added so that the system can always analyze what it can create. The knowledge-based approach also allows the system to include knowledge about its own capabilities, such as searching rules that know about the current deadends in the coding rules. Once a reasonably stable system is developed, it might be possible to "compile" a more efficient implementation, but during development, the knowledge-based approach seems most appropriate.

We have also found that relatively small steps in the refinement sequences make the coding rules more modular and make it easier to reflect the design decisions explicitly in the search tree. The small or medium sized steps correspond roughly to human-sized steps of decision making, which makes it easier for people to build and understand the system. For example, new target languages can be produced by adding new low-level coding rules. Also, the operation of the system is more efficient because the intermediate level abstractions provide islands in the search space from which classes of implementations can be considered as a group. The job of analysis is also easier if the step size is small and the analysis can go hand in hand with refinement.

9.2 The Interaction of Coding and Efficiency Knowledge

Our first experience with writing a program synthesis system convinced us that the interaction between coding, analysis, and search knowledge is inherently complex and that a high bandwidth for communication between the different types of knowledge is a necessity. The refinement paradigm provides an organization in which that kind of communication can be achieved. The search tree serves as a workspace in which the coding decisions or analysis conclusions can be recorded for use by any type of rule. The prototypes provide a static representation of programming constructs that can be used, for example, to allow analysis rules to interpret coding knowledge and to attach analysis processes to either general coding constructs or particular coding rules. Searching knowledge can include domain-independent concepts such as tree search or branch and bound, and can make use of domain-specific information about coding rules in something like the plausible-implementation rules. The refinement paradigm also allows resource-limited searching to focus effort on the parts of a program that the analysis knowledge identifies as important.

Optimizing compilers also include both coding and efficiency knowledge, but the communication between the different types of knowledge is usually less explicit. Most optimizing compilers make relatively local, syntactic transformations to increase efficiency. The transformations are always applied, without checking whether they improve performance for a particular program or for specific input data characteristics (such as list length). This prohibits the use of transformations that may optimize significantly in some situations but produce less efficient code in others. Traditional optimizing compilers cannot make major global improvements such as changing an algorithm. They tend to optimize by redistributing existing code, spreading around the coding decisions without leaving a record or what they have done, or why.

9.3   Limitations

The refinement paradigm seems general enough to be extended along several dimensions, but we have not tested this hypothesis in the PSI/SYN system. For example, what would happen if we attempted to write larger programs or systems of programs is an open question. We believe that the current search techniques would be sufficient to combat combinatorial explosion, but we did not test this hypothesis because the current implementation would not be able to hold all the intermediate representations of large programs in core. And although the coding rules cover the most common implementation techniques, many other coding rules could be added. Also to be determined is the feasibility of the analysis of more complex programs resulting from the addition of new coding rules.

Considering the refinement paradigm as a software design technique raises some other interesting issues. We have considered design decisions related to implementation, but what about design considerations for program specification and maintenance? We have not addressed the issues of specifying program decompositions or explaining implementation decisions to the user. The paradigm does not seem inconsistent with these activities, but again, we have not rigorously tested these hypotheses. Also, the current approach assumes that when modifications are to be made, the original specification is changed and the whole program is re-implemented; there is no obvious way to move back into the middle or compute which of the design decisions are affected by the change(s).

There are several dimensions along which it does seem fruitful to extend the paradigm. For example, it could be of value in the algorithm design process and as part of a system development repository (see the following sections).

9.4   Algorithm Design

In our use of the refinement paradigm, we have focused on the process of algorithm implementation as opposed to algorithm design. (Of course, it is difficult to draw a clear boundary between the two activities: is it "design" or "implementation" to refine an enumeration by deciding to enumerate the items of a set in increasing order and to save the state by deleting enumerated items?) Nonetheless, we believe that the paradigm will also be of value in the algorithm design process. We expect that algorithm design through refinement will be characterized by the following features:

1. The refinement rules will often be of the form: "If the problem is of type X, then try using strategy Y."

2. As a consequence, the initial period of refinement will be subject to many more deadend paths than later periods of the implementation process.

3. In testing the applicability conditions of the rules, there will be a need for a much stronger deductive component.

4. The analysis will be more difficult for design than for implementation.

In fact, we believe that there will be a gradual transition from the design to the implementation phases, and that the refinement process will change gradually from one to the other. An extended discussion of the roles of knowledge and deduction in the algorithm design process is available elsewhere [Barstow 1981].

9.5 A System Development Repository

One of the important directions for future development in automatic programming systems will be the development of models of the design process, including ways to encode the decisions that were made in the development process and the relationships between specifications and low level implementations. As such models are developed, the result of programming will no longer simply be a program in some target language, but rather a detailed description of the entire design and development process, what we may call a "system development repository" (SDR). Such an SDR should be of great assistance in maintaining and enhancing a program, since it would allow the maintainer to "understand" the program more easily by providing direct access to every decision and the reasons for making it.

An SDR will be much more than simply a textual database; it will contain a highly structured and interrelated body of knowledge about a particular program and its design. In building such an SDR, it will be important to exploit whatever structures are naturally available as part of the programming process. We feel that the refinement paradigm provides such a structure—the refinement tree for a program constitutes an elementary form for an SDR, since all of the design and development decisions are encoded explicitly. Since the coding and analysis rules are understandable by a person as well as by a machine, pointers from the tree into the base of programming knowledge should be of great value in understanding the resulting program.

ACKNOWLEDGMENTS

The authors would like to thank C. Green for providing a supportive environment and technical suggestions for the development of the PSI system. The research has also benefited from interaction with other members of the PSI group. B. McCune helped develop the specification language; J. Ludlow helped clarify the coding rules; they and R. Gabriel, J. Phillips, T. Pressburger, L. Steinberg, and S. Tappel provided much help and encouragement. They would also like to thank J. Bentley, and the referees, for their helpful comments on previous versions of the paper.

The research reported herein was conducted while the authors were at Stanford University.

The work was supported by a National Science Foundation Fellowship, by a Fannie and John Hertz Foundation Fellowship, by the Stanford Artificial Intelligence Laboratory under ARPA Order 2494, Contract MDA903-76-C-0206, and by Systems Control, Inc. under ARPA Order 3687, Contract N00014-79-C-0127.

The views and conclusions contained in this paper are those of the authors and should not be interpreted as necessarily representing the official policies, either expressed or implied, of any funding agency.

REFERENCES

[Balzer 1981] R.M. Balzer. Transformational implementation: an example. *IEEE Transactions on Software Engineering*, SE-7:1 (January 1981).

[Barstow 1979a] D.R. Barstow. *Knowledge-based Program Construction.*New York: Elsevier North-Holland, 1979.

[Barstow 1979b] D.R. Barstow. An experiment in knowledge-based automatic programming. *Artificial Intelligence* 12:2 (August 1979), 73-119.

[Barstow 1981] D.R. Barstow. The roles of knowledge and deduction in algorithm design. In D. Michie and Y'H. Pao (eds.), *Machine Intelligence 10.* J. Wiley (Halsted Press), 1982.

[Barstow and Kant 1976] D.R. Barstow, E. Kant. Observations on the interaction between coding and efficiency knowledge in the PSI program synthesis system. *Proceedings of the Second International Conference on Software Engineering*, San Francisco, California, October 1976, 19-31.

[Burstall and Darlington 1977] R.M. Burstall, J. Darlington. A transformation system for developing recursive programs. *Journal of the ACM* 24:1 (January 1977).

[Cattell 1978] R.G.G. Cattell. *Formalization and automatic derivation of code generators.* Carnegie-Mellon University, Department of Computer Science, Tech. Rept. CMU-CS-78-115, April 1978.

[Cheatham et al. 1979b] T.E. Cheatham, Jr., J.A. Townley, G.H. Holloway. A system for program refinement. *Proceedings of the Fourth International Conference on Software Engineering*, Munich, Germany, September 1979, 53-63; reprinted in *Interactive Programming Environments.*

[Dahl et al. 1972] O.-J. Dahl, E.W. Dijkstra, C.A.R. Hoare. *Structured programming.* Academic Press, 1972.

[Fraser 1977] C.W. Fraser. *Automatic generation of code generators.* Yale University, Department of Computer Science, doctoral dissertaion, 1977.

[Green and Barstow 1978] C.C. Green, D.R. Barstow. On program synthesis knowledge. *Artificial Intelligence*, 10:3 (November 1978), 241-279.

[Green et al. 1979] C.C. Green, R.P. Gabriel, E. Kant, B. Kedzierski, B. McCune, J. Phillips, S. Tappel, S. Westford. Results in knowledge-based program synthesis. *Proceedings of the Sixth Internation Joint Conference on Artificial Intelligence*, Tokyo, Japan, August 1979, 342-344.

[Kant 1979a] E. Kant. A knowledge-based approach to using efficiency estimation in program synthesis. *Proceedings of the Sixth Internation Joint Conference on Artificial Intelligence*, Tokyo, Japan, August 1979, 457-462.

[Kant 1979b] E. Kant. *Efficiency considerations in program synthesis: a knowledge-based approach.* Stanford University, Computer Science Department, Tech. Rept. STAN-CS-79-755, September 1979.

[Knuth] D.E. Knuth. Bit manipulation (draft of section 7.1 of *The Art of Computer Programming*).

[Liskov et al. 1977] B. Liskov et al. Abstraction mechanisms in CLU. *Communications of the ACM*, 20:8 (August 1977), 564-576.

[Low 1978] J.R. Low. Automatic data structure selection: an example and overview. *Communications of the ACM*, 21:5 (May 1978).

[Manna and Waldinger 1979] Z. Manna, R. Waldinger. Synthesis: dreams = > programs. *IEEE Transactions on Software Engineering*, SE-5:4 (July 1979).

[Morgenstern 1976] M. Morgenstern. *Automated design and optimization of management information system software.* Massachusetts Institute of Technology, Laboratory for Computer Science, doctoral dissertation, September 1976.

[Rich 1980] C. Rich. *Inspection methods in programming.* Massachusetts Institute of Technology, Artificial Intelligence Laboratory, MIT/AI/TR-604, August 1981.

[Rosenschein and Katz 1977] S.J. Rosenschein, S.M. Katz. Selection of representations for data structures. *Proceedings of the Symposium on Artificial Intelligence and Programming Languages*, Rochester, New York, August 1977, 147-154 (published as *SIGPLAN Notices*, 12:8 and *SIGART Newsletter*, 64).

[Rovner 1976] P.D. Rovner. *Automatic representation selection for associative data structures.* Tech. Rept. TR10, The Unviersity of Rochester, Computer Science Department, September, 1976.

[Rowe 1976] L.A. Rowe. *A formalization of modelling structures and the generation of efficient implementation structures.* University of California at Irvine, Computer Science Department, doctoral dissertation, June 1976.

[Schwartz 1975] J.T. Schwartz. *On programming: an interim report on the SETL project, revised.* New York University, Computer Science Department, Courant Institute of Mathematical Sciences, June 1975.

[Shaw 1979] M. Shaw. *A formal system for specifying and verifying program performance.* Carnegie-Mellon University, Department of Computer Science, Tech. Rept. CMU-CS-79-129, June 1979.

[Shrobe 1979] H.E. Shrobe. *Dependency directed reasoning for complex program understanding.* Massachusetts Institute of Technology, Artificial Intelligence Laboratory, Tech. Rept. 503, April 1979.

[Tompa and Ramirez 1980] F. Tompa, R. Ramirez. *An aid for the selection of efficient storage structures.* University of Waterloo, Department of Computer Science, Tech. Rept. CS-80-46, October, 1980.

[Wegbreit 1976] B. Wegbreit. Goal-directed program transformation. *IEEE Transactions on Software Engineering*, SE-2:2 (March 1976); also in *Third Annual Symposium on Principles of Programming Languages, ACM SIGPLAN/SIGACT*, January 1976.

[Wirth 1971a] N. Wirth. Program development by stepwise refinement. *Communications of the ACM*, 14:4 (April 1971).

[Wulf et al. 1976a] W.A. Wulf, R.L. London, M. Shaw. *Abstraction and verification in Alphard: an introduction to language and methodology.* Carnegie-Mellon University, Department of Computer Science, 1976.

The Future
of Interactive
Programming
Environments

The papers in this final section each reflect different aspects of what we may expect to find in future interactive programming environments. Winograd, in another prophetic paper, stresses the view that programming will become a process not of writing new programs but rather of modifying old ones. (Sandewall et al. discussed this view in their earlier paper.) Winograd's perspective is many years in the future. The next two papers describe views of what we may expect in the shorter term. Buxton and Druffel describe the motivation for the STONEMAN requirements for Ada environments. Fahlman and Harbison describe the Spice project, an attempt to build an environment specifically tailored to personal computer workstations, of which machines such as the Lisp Machine were early examples.

Building interactive programming environments is still largely an experimental process. In the final paper, we have tried to summarize some of the lessons that have been learned from earlier experiments, as well as some of the implications for the practice of software engineering.

25 Beyond Programming Languages

TERRY WINOGRAD
Stanford University
Stanford, California

As computer technology matures, our growing ability to create large systems is leading to basic changes in the nature of programming. Current programming language concepts will not be adequate for building and maintaining systems of the complexity called for by the tasks we attempt. Just as high-level languages enabled the programmer to escape from the intricacies of a machine's order code, higher-level programming systems can provide the means to understand and manipulate complex systems and components. In order to develop such systems, we need to shift our attention away from the detailed specification of algorithms, towards the description of the properties of the packages and objects with which we build. This paper analyzes some of the shortcomings of programming languages as they now exist, and lays out some possible directions for future research.

© 1979, Association for Computing Machinery, Inc. Reprinted from *Communications of the ACM*, 22:7 (July 1979), pp. 391-401.

1. INTRODUCTION

Computer programming today is in a state of crisis (or, more optimistically, a state of creative ferment). There is a growing recognition that the available programming languages are not adequate for building computer systems. Of course, as any first year student of computation theory knows, they are logically sufficient. But they do not deal adequately with the problems we face in our day-to-day work of programming. We get swamped by the complexity of large systems, lost in code written by others, and mystified by the behavior of our almost debugged systems. When we look to the integrated multiprocessor systems that will soon dominate computing, the situation is even worse.

This crisis in software production is far greater (in overall magnitude at least) than the situation of the early 50's that led to the development of high-level languages to relieve the burden of coding. The problems are harder to solve, and the costs of not solving them are in the hundreds of millions. "The symptoms appear in the form of software that is nonresponsive to user needs, unreliable, excessively expensive, untimely, inflexible, difficult to maintain, and not reusable" [Fisher 1978, p. 26]. There are many ways to improve things a little, and they are being tried. But to achieve a fundamental jump in our programming capacity, we need to rethink what we are doing from the beginning.

2. THE PROBLEM

I believe that the problem lies in an obsolete view of programming and programming languages. A widely accepted view can be paraphrased:

> The programmer's job is to design an algorithm (or a class of computations) for carrying out a task, and to write it down as a complete and precise set of instructions for a computer to follow. High level programming languages simplify the writing of these instructions by providing basic building blocks for stating instructions (both control and data structures) that are at a higher level of the logical structure of the algorithm than those of the basic machine.

This view has guided the development of many programming languages and systems. It served well in the early days of computing, but in today's computational environment, it is misleading and stultifying. It focuses attention on the wrong issues, and gives the most important aspects of programming a second-class status. It is irrelevant in the same sense that binary arithmetic is irrelevant—the things it deals with are a necessary part of computing, but should play a subsidiary rather than central role in our understanding.

As computer technology (for both software and hardware) matures, our growing ability to create complex systems has led to three basic changes in the nature of programming.

1. *Computers are not primarily used for solving well-structured mathematical problems or data processing, but instead are components in complex systems.*

According to Department of Defense studies [Fisher 1978], more than half of DoD software costs are associated with "embedded computer systems". An embedded computer system is "one that is logically incorporated in a larger system—e.g. an electromechanical device, a tactical system, a ship, an aircraft, or a communications system—whose primary function is not computation". Of course, embedded computer systems are not unique to the DoD. Many computer scientists spend the majority of their time dealing with embedded computer systems such as message systems and text editing and formatting sys-

518

tems. The example discussed below is a large embedded system in a university context. As the micro-computer revolution continues, this change will become even more extreme. There will be computers embedded in every conceivable kind of electrical and mechanical system, and applications like text editing and message processing will become widespread on the scale of today's telephone network.

As Fisher [Fisher 1978] notes, "embedded computer software often exhibits characteristics that are strikingly different from those of other computer applications. Many embedded computer applications require software that will continue to operate in the presence of faults ... the applications may require the monitoring of sensors, control of equipment display, or operator input processing. They must interface special peripheral equipment... Software must sometimes be able to respond at periodic (real time) intervals, to service interrupts within limited times, and to predict computation times... In many applications ... it is necessary to access, manipulate and display large quantities of data. Much of this data is symbolic or textual rather than numeric, and must be organized in an orderly and accessible fashion."

2. *The building blocks out of which systems are built are not at the level of programming language constructs. They are "subsystems" or "packages," each of which is an integrated collection of data structures, programs, and protocols.*

By making use of existing modules, a programmer can deal with design at a higher level, creating an integrated system with capacities far greater than a program that could be built with the same effort "from scratch." Components for general tasks (such as memory management, user interface, file management and network communication) can be designed once, rather than reconstructed for each system that needs the capability. Unfortunately, in current programming practice this is more of an ideal than a reality. The difficulties of using existing packages often make it easier to replicate their function than to integrate them into a system. The only way such packages are generally used is by building programs within an "operating system" that provides facilities within a uniform environment. Only those packages that are needed by the majority of users find their way into operating systems, and the facilities for using them are complex and ad hoc relative to modern programming languages. We need better ways to deal with the problems of "programming in the large."

As noted in an IBM report on large software systems [Belady 1978, p. 6], "...the understanding of how programs work individually and in cooperation with each other... remains very difficult to generalize, teach, communicate, or even preserve, due to lack of easy 'externalization' i.e. representation, of ideas." Once we begin to deal with networks of processors, it will become even more important to deal explicitly with properties of systems which integrate many independent components.

3. *The main activity of programming is not the origination of new independent programs, but in the integration, modification, and explanation of existing ones.*

This third change grows from the first two. As we are able to build more complex programs, we develop systems that grow to fit an environment of needs, rather than carrying out a single well-specified task. An embedded system (such as one for airline reservations or text preparation and formatting) evolves over many years, increasingly coming to fit the needs of those who use it, and incorporating new capacities as hardware advances make them practical. The DoD study [Fisher 1978, pp. 24-25] noted that "The programs are frequently large (50,000 to 100,000 lines of code) and long-lived (10 to 15 years)... Change is continuous because of evolving system requirements—annual revisions are often of the same magnitude as the original development.... the majority of costs are incurred in software maintenance rather than development."

As additional needs and possibilities arise, it should be possible to modify and combine existing well-tested systems rather than build new ones. In most cases, the needs for continuity in the use of the system (including "upward compatibility" for existing data and user programs) make it impractical to start from scratch. Using current programming techniques, systems often reach a point where the accretion of changes makes their structure so baroque and opaque that further changes are impossible, and the performance of the system is irreversibly degraded. The situation is further complicated by the fact that modifications are often done not by the original builders, but by new programmers with an incomplete or inaccurate understanding of the system. Wulf [Wulf 1977] points out "Another component of the software crisis is less commonly recognized, but, in fact, is often more costly...namely, the extreme difficulty encountered in attempting to modify an existing program....The cost of such evolution is almost never measured, but, in at least one case, it exceeded the original development cost by a factor of 100."

The difficulties in building and modifying large systems have long been recognized and lamented. They have led to various schools of "structured programming," and to the emphasis on restriction and discipline in the design and use of programming languages. There is a large body of lore shared by practicing programmers, providing ways to recognize the problems and guidelines for avoiding the most obvious of them. These include bodies of standards and conventions designed to avoid misunderstanding and miscommunication. But ultimately the solution lies not in greater discipline but in more adequate tools.

3. TOWARDS A SOLUTION

Just as high-level languages enabled the programmer to escape from the intricacies of a machine's order code, higher-level programming systems can provide help in understanding and manipulating complex systems and components. We need to shift our attention away from the detailed specification of algorithms, towards the description of the properties of the packages and objects with which we build. A new generation of programming tools will be based on the attitude that what we say in a programming system should be primarily declarative, not imperative:

The fundamental use of a programming system is not in creating sequences of instructions for accomplishing tasks (or carrying out algorithms), but in expressing and manipulating descriptions of computational processes and the objects on which they are carried out.

> To some extent, this attitude coincides with current work on specification languages, structured programming formalisms, and denotational theories of programming semantics. All of these emphasize the description of the results of computations, rather than instructions for carrying them out. Dijkstra [Dijkstra 1976] for example, describes a methodology for understanding programs in terms of predicate transformers from an initial state to a final state.

A predicate transformer is "a rule telling us how to derive for any post-condition R the corresponding weakest pre-condition...for the initial state such that the attempted activation will lead to a properly terminating activity that leaves the system in a final state satisfying R." He argues that "a program written in a well-defined programming language can be regarded as a mechanism, a mechanism that we know sufficiently well provided we know the corresponding predicate transformer". Languages such as Lucid [Ashcroft and Wadge 1977] carry this philosophy directly into the programming formalism. Lucid is a strictly denotational language, and the statements of a Lucid program can be interpreted as true mathematical assertions about the results and effects of the program.

There is a critical difference, though, which is lost if we look only at the distinction between imperative and declarative. In stating that a programming system helps us to manipulate "descriptions of computational processes," we are saying something quite different from "assertions about the results and effects." In order to clarify this, it is useful to distinguish three types of specification:

1. Program specification: a formal structure which can be interpreted as a set of instructions for a given machine. This is the imperative style of traditional programming languages.

2. Result specification: a process-independent specification of the relationships between the inputs (or initial state), internal variables, and outputs (or resulting state) of the program. This is the specification style advocated by Dijkstra and in work on program verification and program transformation.

3. Behavior specification: a formal description of the time-course of activity of a machine. Any such description selects certain features of the machine state and action (e.g. input and ouput activities, use of memory resources, communication events among processes), without specifying in full detail the mechanisms which generate these.

A behavior specification is like a result specification in that it characterizes what will be done, rather than giving commands for how to do it. It is different in that it is explicitly concerned with issues of sequence, and potentially with real-time measures as well. In practice, result specifications for systems of significant size factor the specification, often using sequence as a dimension of factorization. In a behavior specification, the time-course description is an essential part of the description of what the system as a whole does, not a convenience for factoring it into result-producing modules.

Programming in the future will depend more and more on specifying behavior. The systems we build will carry out real-time interactions with users, other computers, and physical systems (e.g. for process control). In understanding the interaction among independent components, we will be concerned with detailed aspects of their temporal behavior. The machine must be thought of as a mechanism with which we interact, not a mathematical abstraction which can be fully characterized in terms of its results.

Current languages provide only scattered specialized mechanisms for description of either results or process. Declarations are a ubiquitous form of low-level description, and assertions about the state of a computation are occasionally included. But if we look at what a programmer would say about a program to a colleague who wanted to work on it or use it, very little of the description appears anywhere in the "code." If (either because of idealism or coercion) the programmer has included comments, they can provide useful, but local, description. If further (almost always through coercion) the program has been documented, there may be more global descriptions. In large systems, documentation will include a careful specification of protocols and conventions not belonging to any one program, but vital to the system as a whole. It may also include process descriptions along with the result descriptions. But these various pieces of description are scattered, and for the most part not accessible in any systematic fashion.

I want to turn the situation on its head. The main goal of a programming system should be to provide a uniform framework for the information that now appears (if at all) in the declarations, assertions, and documentation. The detailed specification of executable instructions is a secondary activity, and the language should not be distorted to emphasize it. The system should provide a set of tools for generating, manipulating, and integrating descriptions both of results and processes. The activity that we think of as "writing a program" is only one part of the overall activity that the system must support, and emphasis should be given to understanding, rather than creating programs.

The rest of this paper explores some of the consequences of this view, and makes some suggestions as to what a higher-level programming system might look like. It is an attempt to lay out the problems, not to solve them. It will take many years of research before these speculations can be backed up with concrete evidence.

4. A MOTIVATING EXAMPLE

One of the best ways to understand a general view of computing is to look at the examples used by those who hold it. Both Knuth's opus, *The Art of Computer Programming* [Knuth 1968a], and Dijkstra's *A Discipline of Programming* [Dijkstra 1976] begin by discussing the Euclidean algorithm. In a clear and simple way it exemplifies the basic notions of algorithm and program as a mathematical abstraction. The LISP 1.5 Manual [McCarthy et al. 1962] includes the LISP interpreter written in LISP, illustrating the manipulation of symbolic structures, and the ability to treat the programs themselves as symbolic data. The view proposed in this paper is best illustrated by an example at a very different level.

Imagine that you have come to work as a system designer and programmer for a large university. You are given the following system development task:

The current situation: The university administration has a computer system for scheduling and planning room usage. Users at several sites on campus access the system through interactive graphics terminals that display building floorplans as well as text and other graphic data. There is a minicomputer running each cluster of terminals, connected to the central campus facility by a communication network. Each cluster has a device capable of printing out floorplans and graphic data like that displayed on the terminals. Large-scale data storage is at the central campus computer facility.

The system keeps track of the scheduled usage of all rooms, such as long-term lab and office assignments, regular class schedules, and special events. It is able to answer questions about current scheduled usage and availability. Querying is done from the terminals, through structured graphic interaction (menus, standardized forms, pointing, etc.) and a limited natural language interface. The system does not make complex abstract deductions, but can combine information in the data base to answer questions like "Is there a conference room for 40 people with a projection screen available near the education building from 3 to 5 on the 27th?" Users with appropriate authorization enter new information, including the scheduling of room use and changes to the facilities (including the interactive drawing of new or modified floorplans). In addition to the current assignments, the system keeps a history of usage for analysis. Standard statistical information and data representations (such as tables, bar charts, graphs, etc.) are produced on demand for use in long-range planning.

Your assignment: The dean wants the system to provide more help in making up the quarterly classroom assignments. It should be possible to give it a description of the courses scheduled for a future quarter and have it generate a proposed room assignment for all courses. In deciding on assignments, the system should consider factors such as expected enrollment (using past data and whatever new information is available on estimated enrollments), the proximity of rooms to the departments and teachers involved, the preference for keeping the same location over time, and the nature of any special equipment needed. It should print out notices for each teacher, department, dean, and building supervisor, summarizing the relevant parts of the plan. Any of these people should be able to use the normal querying system to find out more about the plan, including the motivations for specific decisions. Properly authorized representatives of the dean's office should be able to request changes in the plan through an interactive dialog with the system, in which alternatives can be proposed and compared. When a change is made, the system should readjust whatever is necessary and produce new notifications for the people affected.

A system like this is just at the edge of our programming powers today. It would take many programmer-years of effort to build, and would be successful only if the project were managed extraordinarily well, even by the standards of the most advanced programming laboratories. But it is not hard because of the intrinsic difficulty of the tasks the system must carry out. It combines hardware and software facilities that have been demonstrated in various combinations a number of times. Even the question-answering and assignment-proposing components are within the bounds of techniques now considered standard in artificial intelligence.

The problem lies in the difficulties of organizing complex systems. The integration of all of the components of the "initial system" would be a major achievement, calling on our best design tools and methodologies. The idea that a new programmer could come in to such a system and make changes widespread enough to handle the "assignment" is enough to make an experienced programmer shudder. It would be hard enough to add new types of questions (such as explanations for decisions), new information (such as distances and estimated enrollments), and new output forms (such as schedule summaries for departments). But even more, we are trying to integrate a new kind of data (projected plans) into a system that was originally built to handle only a single current set of room assignments and a record of their history. These projected plans must be integrated well enough for all of the existing facilities (including floorplan drawing, question answering, statistics gathering, etc.) to operate on them just as they do with the initial data base.

5. THREE DOMAINS OF DESCRIPTION

A system of this complexity can be viewed in each of three different "domains," subject, interaction, and implementation. Each viewpoint is appropriate (and necessary) for understanding some aspects of the system and inappropriate for others. We will look at the example from each of these viewpoints in turn, then discuss how they might be embodied in a programming system.

5.1 The Subject Domain

This system, like every practical system, is about some subject. There is a world of rooms and classes, times and schedules, that exists completely apart from the computer system that is understood as referring to them. The room or the course can't be in the computer—only a pattern of bits which we interpret as a description of it. One of the primary tasks in programming is to develop a set of descriptions that are adequate for talking about the objects being represented. There are descriptions for things we think of as objects (e.g., buildings, rooms, courses, departments) and also for processes (e.g., the scheduling of events). These descriptions are relative to the goals of the system as a whole, and embody a basic view of the problem. For example, what it takes to represent a room would be different for this system and for a system used by contractors in building construction.

All too often, the development of descriptions in this domain is confused with the specification of data structures (which are in the domain of implementation). In deciding whether we want a course to be associated with a single teacher, or to leave open the potential representation of team-teaching, we are not making a data structure decision. The association of a teacher (or teachers) with a course may be represented in many different data structures in many different components of the system. One of the most common problems in integrating systems is that the components are based on different decisions in the subject domain, and therefore there is no effective way to translate the data structures.

Current work on data structure abstraction [Geschke et al. 1977] [Geschke and Mitchell 1975] [Liskov et al. 1977] [Shaw et al. 1977] is a step towards the systematic separation of subject domain decisions from their implementation. Representation languages in artificial intelligence provide additional structure for stating the relationships among abstractions [Bobrow and Raphael 1974] [Bobrow and Winograd 1977a] [Bobrow and Winograd 1977b] [Davis 1978] [Fikes and Hendrix 1977]. A programming system needs to provide a powerful set of mechanisms for building up and maintaining "world views"—coherent sets of description structures in the subject domain that are independent of any implementation. Each component can then implement part or all of this in a way that will be consistent with both the structure of that component and the assumptions made in other components.

A complex system like the one described above will need hundreds of different categories of objects. Some of these (such as classrooms and courses) will be unique to the system. Others (such as times and dates, schedules, physical layouts) will be shared across a wide range of systems. They will be related into hierarchies of abstraction. We can think of a seminar, a course, and a special lecture as examples of a more general class of event, all having a time, a place, etc. For some purposes, this is the right level of generality. For other purposes, we need to distinguish carefully and use special information associated with each. A major part of building up systems will be the systematic development of descriptions that provide a uniform medium for describing objects and their interactions.

5.2   The Domain of Interaction

Every functioning system can be viewed as carrying on an interaction with its environment. As we will discuss in a moment, the choice of "system" and "environment" is relative to a specific viewpoint, but for the moment let us consider the system as viewed by the users. In this domain, the relevant objects are those that take part in the system's interactions: users, files, questions and answers, forms, maps, statistical summaries and notifications to departments. The processes to be described are those like querying the system, describing a new event to be scheduled, and proposing a schedule for a new quarter.

The domain of interaction is concerned with descriptions that are largely orthogonal to those in the subject domain. We can talk about a question as having certain characteristics (e.g., looking for a yes-no answer) independently of whether it is about a room or a lecture. We can talk about the filling out of a form without reference to its specific contents. It is also (and more importantly) independent of the domain of implementation. From the traditional viewpoint, this independence is a bit more difficult to see than the independence of interaction and subject matter. Whereas a subject domain object (like classroom) clearly cuts across large parts of the system, an interaction object (like a question or the process of filling out a form) is typically handled by a single component and described in terms of its implementation. But for the same reasons we want to keep subject domain descriptions independent of their implementations, we must do the same with interaction descriptions.

This view can be applied recursively to sub-parts and components of the system. In looking at one part (such as the on-site processor and its cluster of terminals) we can view it as an independent system interacting with an environment including both the users and the other parts of the overall system, such as the centralized data store. Even within a single implementation module (e.g., the question-answerer), we often want to describe what is happening as an interaction between several conceptual subsystems (the parser, the semantic analyzer, etc.). As with the larger system, it is vital to keep in mind the distinction between the interaction domain and the implementation domain. In order to usefully view a system as made up of two distinct subsystems, they need not be implemented on physically different machines, or even in different pieces of the code. In general, any one viewpoint of a component includes a specification of a boundary. Behavior across the boundary is seen in the domain of interactions, and behavior within the boundary is in the domain of implementation. That implementation can in turn be viewed as interaction between sub-components.

It is in the domain of interaction where there is currently the most to be gained from developing bodies of descriptive structures to be shared by system builders. There are already many pieces that can be incorporated, including protocols (e.g., network communication protocols, graphics representation conventions), standardized interaction facilities (e.g., ASKUSER and DLISP (Display LISP) in Interlisp [Teitelman 1977] [Teitelman 1978], the Smalltalk display programs [Ingalls 1978]), front-end query packages (in various artificial intelligence programs), database standards, and so forth. Currently each of these is in a world and formalism of its own. Given a sufficiently flexible tool for describing and integrating interaction packages, this level of description will be one of the basic building blocks for all systems.

5.3 The Domain of Implementation

Every computer system operates on a set of physical devices with hardwired mechanisms for storing and manipulating data. It is in this domain that we normally think of programming. The detailed choice of algorithms, data structures, and configuration is determined by properties of the hardware and of the descriptive languages we have available for specifying its behavior. However, it would be a mistake to equate this domain with our current notions of programming. The objects in this domain include everything from individual memory bits and subroutines to subsystems (e.g., the file system, the memory management system, the operating system), running processes, hardware devices, and code segments. They include those things we talk about in programs, those we talk about in the debugger, and those found in the machine and hardware manuals. In this domain, as in the others, a uniform system for description is needed, which is not primarily a language for specifying a set of instructions.

In addition to all those things that are directly derivable from the code, the manuals, and the state of the machine, there is also a body of process description. For example, it may be a property of a specific memory-management package that it periodically undergoes a garbage collection period of up to 5 seconds during which no new memory allocations can be made. Such "performance" characteristics may be vital for understanding the interactions of a component with the rest of the system, but are not explicit in its code. Other descriptions bring into focus things that may be implicit in the code. A file system may delete a file if its creation process is interrupted in certain ways that would leave it in danger of being inconsistent. The code that does this may be distributed through various checks and actions, but for the programmer attempting to understand the program it is necessary to have a coherent overview of what is happening.

Similarly, many of the things we think of as properties of data structures are actually conventions spread through the code that manipulates them. Much of the work in structured programming has been to isolate these conventions into access functions that go into a "module" with the data structures [Geschke et al. 1977] [Liskov et al. 1977] [Shaw et al. 1977]. The object-oriented style of programming encouraged by Smalltalk [Ingalls 1978] is another attempt to provide this kind of modularity. A system for implementation description would provide for stating these in a more general way along with those things that now appear only in the comments. As with procedures, data structures can also have implicit properties (e.g. the expected maximal size of variable length fields) that need to be stated explicitly in order for a person to understand how they will interact with other components.

The boundary between hardware and software has become increasingly blurred in the past few years through developments such as micro-code, uniform logic arrays, and the extensive use of virtual machine architecture. A programming system based on description would go further in unifying our approach to different levels of architecture. The emphasis is on an overall description of a component rather than the instructions needed to cause some piece of hardware to run it. A piece of software and a piece of hardware designed to achieve the same purpose would have descriptions that differed in details (e.g. timing), and in the specific aspect that described the code (or logic circuits) used to carry out the steps. They might be identical in the domain of interaction, and even to a large degree in the domain of implementation (for example in the logical description of their data structures).

6. A SKETCH OF A HIGHER LEVEL PROGRAMMING SYSTEM

So far, we have been talking in a general way about the different domains of description and the kinds of things that might be said about a component or system from each of their viewpoints. This does not yet provide a coherent picture of what a program will be. What do we see on the printed page or on the screen? How is it organized? How do we do anything with it?

Once again, it is important not to let our preconceptions get in the way. Notions such as code, listing, file, and compilation are based on the idea of a program as a set of instructions. There need not be any directly corresponding objects in a higher-level system. Instead, it should be based on something much more like what we now think of as an artificial intelligence system, with its "knowledge base" of assertions and procedures. There will be a set of interrelated descriptions, stored in a form that makes it possible to retrieve, manipulate and display them. These will include prototypes for categories of objects and processes (like classroom, and filling out a form), and instances, which correspond to individual objects and processes in one of the domains (such as the course CS 365 in Winter 1978, the contents of the third page of next quarter's schedule, and the process currently running in the data-base server). Instances can be described by more than one prototype, and prototypes are related into hierarchies with different degrees of abstraction. The details of all this are still a matter for extensive research. One set of possibilities is being explored in KRL [Bobrow and Winograd 1977a] [Bobrow and Winograd 1977b], but the basic idea of higher level systems could be implemented using other descriptive representations, such as semantic networks [Brachman 1977] [Fikes and Hendrix 1977] [Levesque 1977] [Woods 1975] and other frame based systems [Davis 1978] [Goldstein and Roberts 1977].

In addition to the basic description system, there will be a wide range of commonly useful prototypes and instances. Some of them (e.g., graphics formats, dates and times, communication protocols) will be in the subject and interaction domains. Others (such as the data structures used in a particular data base) will be in the implementation domain. Some (such as descriptions of specific pieces of hardware and software that are being used) will be specific to the programming system. Others (such as those for abstract objects like sets and sequences, and for process structures) will be very general. In approaching a problem, a programmer will make use of this vocabulary of concepts and descriptive categories, both for interfacing with existing components and organizing new ones.

Earlier in the paper, we discussed the need for programming systems based on the description of both results and processes. In the light of the above discussion, we can see that this applies not only to the implementation domain, but to the others as well. By shifting emphasis away from programs made up of instructions (which are necessarily in the implementation domain) to description of processes and results, it becomes possible to integrate descriptions in all three domains within a single formalism.

A programmer's use of a higher level system will be highly interactive. Since the understanding of a component comes from having multiple viewpoints, no single organization of the information on a printed page will be adequate. The programmer needs to be able to dynamically reorganize the information, looking from one view and then another, going from great generality down to specific detail, and maneuvering around in the space of descriptions to view the interconnections. This will require an interface that is more sophisticated than the question-answering interfaces now used on artificial intelligence knowledge bases. It seems likely that pictorial representations, interactive graphics, and "intelligent summarizing" will play a large role. Some current software development techniques (such as the Structured Analysis Design Technique [Dickover et al. 1977]) emphasize the importance of multiple viewpoints of analysis in documentation and design.

Of course, there always remains the task of providing a description of each component that is detailed enough to allow the system to run it. This will be part of providing a broader description, and may be done in stages. A very abstract specification of what a component does will be sufficient for a kind of "high-level debugging" in which its interactions with other components can be analyzed and described without carrying out the steps at the the lowest level. There is a whole range of operations that are now thought of as "automatic programming", which will enable the programmer to let the system fill in details once the overall behavior of the component has been specified. Some of this will be based on standardized defaults, others on automated analysis of performance characteristics. It will all be based on the availability of descriptions in the implementation domain of the various machines and subsystems being used.

As systems become more complex, the level of desirable invisibility will rise. Current high-level programming languages do not give the user the opportunity to decide just how the hardware registers of the machine will be used to store variables, since there is much more to be gained by a uniform integrated approach to their use by the compiler. Similarly, much of what we now think of as data structure and algorithm specification will be handled by programs that can take into account much more complex efficiency considerations than are practical for a human programmer.

In summary, a programmer will use a programming system that contains a base of knowledge about the system he or she is working on, and of other potential components and concepts of programming that might be of use. The programmer will modify the descriptions of previously described components, and create high-level descriptions of new ones to be added. These modifications and additions may be from the viewpoints of all of the different domains, and will be done in cooperation with the system, which checks for consistency, looks for consequences of new information, etc. Checking and debugging will be done at a variety of levels as the description becomes more detailed. The system will attempt to fill in details that are needed to completely specify the implementation, so the system as a whole can be run. The debugging process will make use of sophisticated reasoning processes that can use all of the different domains of description in analyzing and reporting what is happening.

7.   WHAT NEEDS TO BE DONE

The notion of higher-level programming systems is not new. Integrated programming environments have been one of the major areas of development in LISP systems [Sandewall 1978], and one of the major reasons for the DoD common language effort [Fisher 1978] is to encourage the development of programming tools which are too complex and costly to be justified in a single project, or even a single specialized language. These systems, however, have evolved within the standard view of programming, and although they contain many useful ideas, they are far from achieving the goals discussed above. We need further research in three distinct but interrelated areas: the development of an effective descriptive calculus; the creation of a body of descriptive concepts for computational processes; and the building of a complex integrated system which uses them.

7.1   A Descriptive Calculus

The main thrust of these ideas depends on the ability to create and manipulate descriptions in an effective, understandable way. There are existing formalisms for description (for example, the predicate calculus) which are clear and well-understood, but lack the richness typical in descriptions which people find useful. They can serve as a universal basis for description but only in the same sense that a Turing machine can express any computation. They lack the higher-level structuring which makes it possible to manipulate descriptions at an appropriate level of detail. As Dijkstra [Dijkstra 1977, p. 5] observes:

> That the first-order predicate calculus was the most suitable candidate for the characterization of machine states was assumed right at the start; early experiences,

however, were not too encouraging, because it only seemed practicable in the simplest cases, and we discovered the second consequence: the large number of variables combined with the likely irregularity of the subsets to be characterized very quickly made most of the formal expressions to be manipulated unmanageably long.

The requirements for a descriptive language of the kind I propose are quite different from those used in the mathematical foundations of computation, or for program verification. Work in these areas (see, for example the collection of papers in [Neuhold 1978]) emphasizes the use of descriptive languages in rigorous proofs of the properties of programs. A higher-level programming system must instead emphasize the use of descriptive languages for communication. The concentration must be on those aspects which aid in giving a person a clear overall understanding (at variable levels of detail and from multiple points of view), rather than on those aspects which increase the mathematical tractability of the descriptions.

Wulf [Wulf 1977] describes the motivations for the programming language Alphard in similar terms:

> The 'software crisis' is the result of our human limitations in dealing with complexity. To 'solve' the problem we must reduce the 'apparent complexity' of programs, and this reduction must occur in the program text.... we know something about the way humans have traditionally dealt with understanding complex problems...and we can try to mold the expression of a program so that it facilitates these techniques.

If we look at the ways in which people have "traditionally dealt with understanding complex problems", we find many features of natural language which serve to reduce complexity by allowing imprecision when precision is not required. This is not an excuse for avoiding all precision, or a justification for "natural language programming." We need to understand the deep psychological properties of how people understand language, not mimic its superficial forms. The justification is not that natural language is "better" in some abstract sense, but that it is what we as people know how to use. As discussed above, the most essential feature of a programming formalism is its understandability by programmers. We cannot turn programmers into native speakers of abstract mathematics, but we can turn our programming formalisms in the direction of natural descriptive forms.

There are artificial intelligence formalisms (such as semantic networks [Brachman 1977] [Fikes and Hendrix 1977] [Levesque 1977] [Woods 1975] and KRL [Bobrow and Winograd 1977a] [Bobrow and Winograd 1977b]) with increased dimensions of expressiveness, but these are not yet at a level of precision which would make them sufficiently understandable to be used in a system of the required complexity. The characteristics which they explore (and which will need to be part of a formalism to be used in a higher-level programming system) include:

1. *Prototype hierarchies.* The nouns and verbs of a natural language can be organized into hierarchies (or taxonomies) which capture much of the logical structure of what they describe. We know that a dog is an animal, and the answers to questions about dogs will often be derived through general properties of animals. Systems such as semantic networks treat these deductions specially, rather than dealing with them uniformly as a set of universally quantified implications. This leads to greater efficiency for the common calculations, and provides a structure which makes it much easier for a programmer to organize a knowledge base. These hierarchies contain information which could be thought of as a set of independent facts, but has additional structure in the same sense that a structured program structures a set of steps and jumps.

2. *The centrality of defaults.* Most logical calculi are optimized for handling generalizations which are either true or false. They do not provide means for stating generalizations that are not completely universal, but are "usual" or "normal" or "expected". In natural descriptions of any kind, people draw heavily on the ability to use information of a less formal sort, and to use a kind of ceteris paribus reasoning in which a standard fact is assumed true unless there is an explicit reason to believe the contrary. One of the major directions in artificial intelligence representation research is the attempt to provide this capability in a formally clear system. The notion of a default value is familiar to every programmer, but its place in a formal calculus needs to be carefully worked out.

3. *The suppression of exceptional details.* One of the major reasons for using precise formalizations is that they make everything explicit. For some purposes this is good, but there are times when understanding can come only through the suppression of detail. If we are trying to formally describe a program which normally has simple input-output behavior (e.g. one that copies data from one place to another) we want to describe that behavior in a way which highlights that simplicity. If there are exceptional cases (e.g. when the storage allocator fails to find a sufficient block), these need to be described, but in a secondary place. The basic description of an object cannot be cluttered up with all of the details needed for handling the contingencies. Formalisms used in denotational semantics for programs demonstrate this problem well. In order to deal with a special escape at all, they demand that even the simplest programs be described as operating on continuations, environments, etc. and this description permeates every level of what is said.

4. *Multiple levels of abstractions and instances.* In dealing with programs and processes, we run into complexities involving the instantiation of general classes. For example, a specific algorithm (such as Euclid's algorithm) can be thought of as an instance of a general class (numerical algorithms), or as a class whose instances are programs implementing the algorithm. Each of those programs is in turn both an instance (of the class of formal objects known as programs) and a description of a class of process instances, each of which is carrying it out. If we look at the finer structure of programs, such as the instantiation of variables or pieces of code within loops, similar phenomena arise. Higher-order and typed logics deal in certain ways with the notion of a class (predicate) which is also an instance, but their austerity makes them inadequate for capturing the rich set of ways in which people interleave levels of abstraction. Artificial intelligence formalisms have not yet dealt adequately with these issues, which are currently a topic of active investigation.

7.2 A Basis for Describing Processes

Given a formalism for descriptions in general, we need prototypes for describing those things which are common to all of our programs (e.g., processes, programs, data structures, communication acts). This is a necessary kind of library, just as a library of standard data structures and statistical routines is a necessary part of a system for statistical manipulations. It need not be fixed once and for all, but a good deal of it must be in place before the system is usable, and it must be held relatively uniform if the system is to be extendable.

The domain I believe is currently ripest for exploration is the description of processes. Traditional mathematics provides us with a broad variety of concepts for what I have called "result specifications", and they are being applied to programming (for example [Dijkstra 1976]). In describing processes, we are on shakier ground. There are many promising ideas floating around that need to be captured in a more precise form. The success of higher-level programming systems will depend on having a coherent body of descriptive categories which can capture a variety of modes for process description. There is a beginning of comprehensive work in this area, such as the development of the Delta language for system description [Holbaek-Hanssen et al. 1975], but most of the work so far has dealt with one or another aspect in isolation.

7.2.1 Modularity and structured procedures   There has been a good deal of attention in recent years to the higher-level structure of control constructs. In addition, languages based on data abstractions (such as CLU [Liskov et al. 1977], Alphard [Shaw et al. 1977] and Mesa [Geschke et al. 1977] [Geschke and Mitchell 1975]) provide for larger modules which encapsulate collections of data structures and procedures. Beginning from a different point of view, structured system description languages [Dickover et al. 1977] [Holbaek-Hanssen et al. 1975] provide conceptual tools for describing the overall structure of large systems. We need a consistent way of talking about modularization and interaction between semi-independent modules which can be applied to system structure at all different levels of detail.

7.2.2 Structured data objects   Work on programming language constructs often emphasizes the structure of the sequence of operations, in terms of loops, recursive calls, etc. [Dijkstra 1976]. A related notion in describing processes is the ability to hide detail by allowing the combination of objects into a larger "structured object", and to define unitary operations on this higher level object which invoke collections of operations on the components. This has been explored for simple mathematical objects (e.g. lists in LISP's MAP functions [McCarthy et al. 1962], vectors and arrays in APL [Falkoff and Iverson 1973], sets in SETL [Schwartz 1975] and VERS [Earley 1974]), and seems applicable to more specialized semantic objects (in all of the three domains) as well. In many cases, much of what is now thought of as control structure can be implicit in the data structure, leading to notions of "nonprocedural" or "procedureless" languages [Goldsmith 1974] [Leavenworth and Sammet 1974]. The interaction between control and data structure needs to be put into a theoretical framework.

7.2.3 Program factoring—objects and procedures   In viewing a process as a structured sequence of individual steps, there are different ways to think about what each of those steps is. Most programming languages lead the programmer to think in terms of operations (either primitive or programmer-defined) to be carried out on arguments. Some (such as Simula [Birtwistle et al. 1973], Smalltalk [Ingalls 1978] and Plasma [Hewitt and Smith 1975]) think of typed objects which receive and interpret messages. Instead of organizing code around a single procedure (e.g. print or plus) which selects its action according to data type, they define classes (such as integer, list, etc.) which select what to do on the basis of the message. Artificial intelligence languages take a more general approach in using pattern directed invocation [Bobrow and Raphael 1974] [Davis 1977]. Each step specifies a pattern (or goal) to be achieved. A data base of pattern-action pairs is accessed to decide what steps to carry out. Each of these viewpoints is best for some aspects of programming, and we need to understand how to integrate them into a larger framework.

7.2.4 States and transitions   There are two complementary ways of looking at a computational process—as a sequence of operations, or as a sequence of states. This duality has been exploited in the mathematical theory of computation, but has not really been integrated into programming languages. Transition nets and Petri nets [Holt 1971] [Lauer and Campbell 1975] are state-oriented, rather than operation-oriented. Production systems [Rychener 1977] are state-oriented, with each production specifying a partial state description, and an appropriate transition function (not the name of the new state, but a set of operations which produce the new state). Languages which provide ways of specifying actions to be taken on special conditions [Goodenough 1975] are really mixing state-transition description with the normal operation sequence. As with the operation/object distinction above, the goal is to find a synthesis which allows a process to be described using a mixture of the conceptual viewpoints, and to be run on the basis of that description.

7.2.5 Interacting processes and communication The notions above deal primarily with a single process. The most significant direction in computing over the coming years will be towards multiple processes, both virtual (e.g. organizing a speech system as a series of separate processes, even if it runs on a single PDP-10 [Barnett 1975] [Lesser 1975]) and actual (e.g. networks of computers cooperating on a single task). There are a number of issues which have been dealt with by system designers at lower levels (like operating systems) which have not found their way into higher level languages. There is also a wealth of metaphors provided by thinking of a computation as being carried on by a collection of independent individuals which must communicate by exchanging messages in a common language. We can draw many analogies from human communication—What language do they talk? Which subsystems need to be multi-lingual? What are the discourse rules for establishing and controlling message flow? Is it possible to learn a second language? How can two processes make use of shared knowledge to increase the efficiency of communication? How can one process make use of an internal model of another process, in order to facilitate communication and cooperation?

7.3 A Complex System

The kind of higher level programming system discussed in this paper is itself a massive and complex system. Its subject matter is not an external one, like room-scheduling, but the reflective one—the subject of programming. Much of the other work mentioned in this paper provides a starting point. Integrated programming systems, languages based on data abstraction, and representation languages are examples of work which can be incorporated. It is unlikely that a "crash program" to produce a unified higher level programming system would succeed today. There will have to be a careful program of bootstrapping to get from today's languages and systems to one like I have described. The reason for writing a paper of this sort (rather than setting out to build a system) is the recognition that the relevant ideas need more development, and the hope that people will turn their attention to them.

ACKNOWLEDGMENTS

In a paper of this kind, it is impossible to properly credit the sources of the ideas. It grew out of ongoing interactions with people who hold similar ideas in different forms, and it is really just an expression of the current state of my intellectual environment. My joint work with Danny Bobrow and Brian Smith on the theoretical foundations of KRL has been a primary source of ideas, and the rest of the Stanford/Xerox KRL research group (David Levy, Mitch Model, Richard Fikes, Don Norman and Henry Thompson) have been involved in all stages of our thinking. Stanford computer science students in the CS365 seminar in 1977 pushed and probed on many of the ideas about procedures, which in turn came from the authors of the papers we read there (included in the list of references). The Xerox PARC environment has been a context in which the problems of "programming in the large" are well understood, and has provided a wealth of ideas and examples, including the work of Alan Kay and his group on Smalltalk, the implementation of the Mesa programming language, the development of programming environments by Warren Teitelman and Larry Masinter, Bob Sproull's understanding of graphics systems and protocols, and Peter Deutsch's views on system organization and programming environments. In addition, the cybernetic notions of Humberto Maturana as introduced to me by Fernando Flores have led to subtle but very important shifts of perspective in the way I look at systems of all kinds. I am also grateful to Alan Perlis, Peter Deutsch, Jim Horning and the referees for extensive and insightful comments on earlier drafts of this paper.

REFERENCES

[Ashcroft and Wadge 1977] E.A. Ashcroft, W.W. Wadge. Lucid, a non-procedural language with iteration. *Communications of the ACM* 20:7 (July 1977), 519-526.

[Barnett 1975] J. Barnett. Module linkage and communication in large systems. In D.R. Reddy (ed.), *Speech Recognition*, 1975, 500-520.

[Belady 1978] L.A. Belady. *Large software systems*. IBM Watson Research Center, Research Report RC6966, Yorktown Heights, January 1978.

[Birtwistle et al. 1973] G. Birtwistle, O.-J. Dahl, B. Myhrhaug, K. Nygaard. *Simula Begin*. Auerbach, Philadelphia, 1973.

[Bobrow and Raphael 1974] D.G. Bobrow, R. Bertram. New programming languages for AI research. *ACM Computing Surveys* 6:3 (September 1974).

[Bobrow and Winograd 1977a] D.G. Bobrow, T. Winograd and the KRL Research Group. Experience with KRL-0: One cycle of a knowledge representation language. *Proceedings of the Fifth International Joint Conference on Artificial Intelligence*, Cambridge, Massachusetts, August 1977, 213-222.

[Bobrow and Winograd 1977b] D.G. Bobrow, T. Winograd. An overview of KRL, a knowledge representation language. *Cognitive Science* 1:1 (January 1977), 3-46.

[Brachman 1977] R. Brachman. What's in a concept: Structural foundations for semantic networks. *International Journal of Man-Machine Studies*, 9 (1977), 127-152.

[Davis 1977] R. Davis. Generalized procedure calling and content directed invocation. *Proceedings of the Symposium on Artificial Intelligence and Programming Languages*, Rochester, New York, August 1977 (published as *SIGPLAN Notices*, 12:8 and *SIGART Newsletter*, 64).

[Davis 1978] R. Davis. Knowledge about representations as a basis for system construction and maintenance. In F. Hayes-Roth, D.A. Waterman (eds.), *Pattern Directed Inference Systems*, Academic Press, 1978.

[Dickover et al. 1977] M.E. Dickover, C.L. McGowan, D.T. Ross. Software design using SADT. *Proceedings of the ACM National Conference*, 1977.

[Dijkstra 1976] E.W. Dijkstra. *A Discipline of Programming*. Prentice-Hall, 1976.

[Dijkstra 1977] E.W. Dijkstra. On the interplay between mathematics and programming. E. W. Dijkstra note EWD641, 1977.

[Earley 1974] J. Earley. High level operations in automatic programming. *SIGPLAN notices* 9:4 (1974), 34-42.

[Falkoff and Iverson 1973] A.D. Falkoff, K.E. Iverson. The design of APL. *IBM Journal of Research and Development*, 1973, 324-334.

[Fikes and Hendrix 1977] R. Fikes, G. Hendrix. A network-based knowledge representation and its natural deduction system. *Proceedings of the Fifth International Joint Conference on Artificial Intelligence*, Cambridge, Massachusetts, August 1977, 235-246.

[Fisher 1978] D.A. Fisher. Dod's Common Programming Language Effort. *Computer*, March 1978, 25-33.

[Geschke and Mitchell 1975] C.M. Geschke, J.G. Mitchell. On the problem of uniform references to data structures. *IEEE Transactions on Software Engineering*, June 1975, 207-219.

[Geschke et al. 1977] C.M. Geschke, J.H. Morris, Jr., E.H. Satterthwaite. Early experience with Mesa. *Communications of the ACM*, 20:8 (August 1977), 540-552.

[Goldsmith 1974] C. Goldsmith. The design of a procedureless programming language. *SIGPLAN Notices* 9:4 (1974), 13-24.

[Goldstein and Roberts 1977] I.P. Goldstein, R.B. Roberts. A knowledge-based scheduling program. *Proceedings of the Fifth International Joint Conference on Artificial Intelligence*, Cambridge, Massachusetts, August 1977, 257-263; also MIT AI-MEMO 405 (February 1977).

[Goodenough 1975] J. Goodenough. Exception handling: issues and a proposed notation. *Communications of the ACM* 18:12 (December 1975), 683-696.

[Hewitt and Smith 1975] C. Hewitt, B. Smith. Towards a programming apprentice. *IEEE Transactions on Software Engineering*, SE-1:2 (March 1975), 26-45.

[Holbaek-Hanssen et al. 1975] E. Holbaek-Hanssen, P. Handlykken, K. Nygaard. *System description and the Delta language*. Delta project report #4, Norwegian Computing Center Publication #523, September 1975.

[Holt 1971] A. Holt. Introduction to occurrence systems. In Jacks (ed.), *Associative Information Techniques*. Elsevier, 1971, 175-203.

[Ingalls 1978] Dan Ingalls. The Smalltalk-76 programming system, design and implementation. *Conference Record of the Fifth Annual ACM Symposium on Principles of Programming Languages*, January 1978, 9-17.

[Knuth 1968a] D.E. Knuth. *The Art of Computer Programming, Vols. 1-3*. Addison-Wesley, Reading, Massachusetts, 1968,1969,1973.

[Lauer and Campbell 1975] P.E. Lauer, R.H. Campbell. A description of path expressions by Petri nets. *Second ACM Symposium on Principles of Programming Languages*, 1975, 95-105.

[Leavenworth and Samet 1974] B. Leavenworth, J. Sammet. An overview of nonprocedural languages. *SIGPLAN Notices* 9:4 (1974), 1-12.

[Lesser 1975] V. Lesser. Parallel processing in speech understanding systems: a Survey of design problems. In D.R. Reddy (ed.), *Speech Recognition*, 1975, 481-499.

[Levesque 1977] H. Levesque. *A procedural approach to semantic networks*. University of Toronto, Department of Computer Science, TR-105, 1977.

[Liskov et al. 1977] B. Liskov et al. Abstraction mechanisms in CLU. *Communications of the ACM*, 20:8 (August 1977), 564-576.

[McCarthy et al. 1962] J. McCarthy, P. Abrahams, D. Edwards, T. Hart, M. Levin. *LISP 1.5 Programmer's Manual*, MIT Press, Cambridge, Massachusetts, 1962.

[Neuhold 1978] E.J. Neuhold (ed.) *Formal Description of Programming Languages*. North-Holland, 1978.

[Rychener 1977] M. Rychener. Production systems: a case for simplicity in AI control structures. Draft of paper submitted to ACM National Conference, 1977.

[Sandewall 1978] E. Sandewall. Programming in the interactive environment: the LISP experience. *Communications of the ACM*, 10:1 (March 1978), 35-71; reprinted in *Interactive Programming Environments*.

[Schwartz 1975] J.T. Schwartz. *On programming: an interim report on the SETL project, revised*. New York University, Computer Science Department, Courant Institute of Mathematical Sciences, June 1975.

[Shaw et al. 1977] M. Shaw, W.A. Wulf, R.L. London. Abstraction and verification in Alphard: defining and specifying iteration and generators. *Communications of the ACM*, 20:8 (August 1977), 553-563.

[Teitelman 1977] W. Teitelman. A display-oriented programmer's assistant. CSL 77-3, XEROX PARC, 1977; reprinted in *Interactive Programming Environments*; see also *Proceedings of the Fifth International Joint Conference on Artificial Intelligence*, Cambridge, Massachusetts, August 1977, 905-915.

[Teitelman 1978] W. Teitelman. *INTERLISP Reference Manual*. Xerox Palo Alto Research Center, Palo Alto, California, December 1978.

[Woods 1975] W. Woods, What's in a link? In D. Bobrow, A. Collins (eds.), *Representation and Understanding*, Academic Press, 1975.

[Wulf 1977] W.A. Wulf. Some thoughts on the next generation of programming languages. In A.K. Jones (ed.), *Perspectives on Computer Science*, Academic Press, 1977.

26 Rationale for STONEMAN

JOHN N. BUXTON

University of Warwick
Coventry, England

LARRY E. DRUFFEL

Defense Advanced Research Projects Agency
Arlington, Virginia

Full advantage of the new DoD programming language, ADA, will be realized only when a complete and sophisticated programming support environment is provided. A detailed requirements definition (STONEMAN) for such a support environment has been evolved through extensive cooperation with the DoD, software contracting and computer science communities. This paper summarises the STONEMAN, provides motivation for the requirements and clarifies some underlying concepts.

© 1980 IEEE. Reprinted with permission from *Fourth International Computer Software and Applications Conference, October 1980, Chicago, Illinois, pp. 66-72.*

1. INTRODUCTION

As part of its overall strategy for managing computer resources embedded in major weapon systems, the Department of Defense has undertaken the introduction of a new language, ADA, for the development of application software. This widely advertized project began in 1975 with the first definition of requirements [Tinman 1976] which evolved into a firm specification [Fisher and Wetherall 1977] [Steelman 1978]. Competitive design of the language was narrowed from four contractors to two in 1977 and finally to one in the spring of 1978. The initial ADA design was made available to the public when the language manual [ADA Preliminary Manual 1979] and rationale [Ichbiah et al. 1979] were published in April 1979. For the ensuing nine months, concentrated test and evaluation of the language was carried out by volunteer teams from DoD, industry and academia. Following the test and evaluation phase, [ADA Phase II Reports 1980] a final design revision phase produced the language which is now publicly available for use [Ichbiah et al. 1979].This process has been well documented [Whitaker 1977] [Fisher 1978] [Carlson 1980] [Druffel 1979].

Early in the language design process, DoD realized the need for a complete programming support environment for the new language. A workshop was held to initiate discussion in this area in 1978 [Standish 1978]. An early specification which described both policy and technical issues associated with the language environment was widely circulated in July 1978. [Pebbleman 1978] Based on comments received, the document was revised and recirculated. [Pebbleman 1979]

As the DoD began to address the specific policy issues, it became apparent that a separate document was needed to address the technical issues. The first step in its preparation was to assess the current support systems for DoD projects. After consideration of other relevant work [UK MoD ADA Study 1979] [Fisher and Standish 1979] [Elzer 1979] and extensive circulation of drafts for discussion, [Buxton and Stenning 1979a] [Buxton 1979] the Preliminary STONEMAN [Buxton 1980] was published to describe initial thoughts on the technical requirements for an ADA program support environment.

Preliminary STONEMAN served as a focus for a conference in San Diego in October 1979 [ADA Environment Workshop 1979] to discuss the specific issues associated with programming environments as applied to ADA. The three day conference, attended by over 200 participants from academia, industry and government, served to refine the requirements definition. From this conference and through private coordination, a STONEMAN Draft [Buxton and Stenning 1979b] document was evolved and circulated for final review. Again, extensive comment influenced the final STONEMAN document published in February 1980. [Buxton 1980].

In January 1980, Air Force Systems Command's Rome Air Development Center (RADC) issued a draft request for proposal based on the Draft STONEMAN. Influenced by STONEMAN and by industry comments to the Draft RFP, RADC produced an RFP in May 1980 for a competitive design of an ADA Program Support Environment (APSE). Multiple contractors were chosen in September 1980 to proceed with initial phases of an APSE design.

2. THE EMBEDDED COMPUTER

To fully appreciate the motivation for many of the requirements, it is useful to understand the characteristics of embedded computer environments. Although there are certainly similarities between the software development process for automatic data processing (ADP) and that for computers embedded in major weapon systems, the latter have some rather stringent characteristics not generally found in ADP. The requirment for real-time interactions such as the monitoring and control of unique system components introduce timing dependencies. These functions often require handling of interrupts within specified times and introduce special interface considerations.

Because the computer is embedded in a larger weapon system which is also under development, the specification must be flexible. They are often based on prototype equipment or simulations and are sometimes imprecise or generalized. As a result, the designer must interact with the user, often developing experimental software design through an evolutionary sequence of prototype stages.

Many of the computers embedded in weapon systems are designed for the operational environment and not well suited for software development. Consequently only minimal support systems are available. In some cases, the development is done entirely in assembly language with only an essential set of tools. However, the trend is to develop the software on a host machine in a high order language and to perform the testing primarily on the target machine. With this host/target arrangment, the compiler is viewed primarily as a means of generating and documenting assembly code.

Testing is necessarily carried out in a variety of ways. Syntactic and static semantic errors can be resolved simply at the source code level. Further testing on the host is difficult unless an instruction level simulator for the target exists. Most testing takes place in the software test lab using some sort of target configuration, which may be free standing, connected to a simulator which provides simulated real time inputs, or connected to a hardware operations console often equipped with a monitor computer to trace data bus traffic and execution of test runs. Program size and timing problems are resolved at this level with extensive patching and retesting. A full recompile cycle with optimizing and reconfiguration can vary in length from days to weeks depending on the size of the project, extent of software tools, etc. It is not uncommon for the cost of the testing phase to exceed the cost of the development phase.

Much of the embedded computer memory may contain data: fixed data such as flight performance details and mission dependent data such as the maps for the area to be covered by a specific mission. Although code is rarely classified, data is often classified and can only be handled in a secure environment. Once the system is operational, the software is considered part of the product and is either maintained by the customer or through separate contracts, often by an organization not associated with the original development. Since the computer is by definition embedded in some larger system, it must change in response to the larger system design perturbations. For a computer in a major weapons system such as an aircraft, the annual extent of those changes may equal the magnitude of the original software package.

In general, the tools used to support a project are minimal, often limited to vendor supplied compiler, linker, and perhaps an editor. Special purpose tools are built to support a specific project, either by building from scratch or by modifying other tools. Such tools may include overlay optimizers for disk or drums, load tape builders, patch override consolidators and the like. An environment simulator is particularly important as a project specific tool. The tools available are not well integrated nor do they form a complete set. Error reporting and configuration control schemes are generally separate items which may be handled as data processing tasks or controlled manually.

3. GENERAL REQUIREMENTS

The requirements for an ADA program support environment (APSE) must be developed in the context of those characteristics described for embedded computers. Clearly, tools must be developed to support the developer and the maintainer as well as the manager. The ADA language is aimed at portability of programs and of programmers. The DoD embedded computer world is dynamic in terms of programmer ability. Consequently, it is important that programmers find a consistent environment as they move from one project to another. The tools must not only be portable from one machine to another, but must provide the programmer a consistent interface.

The environment must support the entire software life cycle. It must provide a coordinated and complete set of tools which are applicable to all stages of program development and which provide consistent support, not only for development but for continued change and update in the later stages of the life cycle.

The tool set must not only support the appropriate functions, but must be integrated into a consistent environment. Individual tools must be able not only to access the applications program but also to communicate with one another. This interface between tools must be independent of the host machine.

In more detail, an APSE must facilitate program development and maintenance for embedded computer system projects involving ADA programs, with the intent of improving long-term cost effective software reliability. It must support all functions required by a project team. These functions include project management control, documentation and recording, and long-term configuration and version control. Support must be provided to projects throughout the software life cycle from requirements and design through implementation to long term maintenance and modification. It must reflect the priorities for software quality in military embedded computer applications; that is, reliability, performance, evolution, maintenance and responsiveness to changing requirements.

An APSE must be designed to exploit, but not demand, modern high capacity and high performance host system hardware. It must be a highly robust system that can protect itself from user and system errors, that can recover from unforeseen situations, and that can provide meaningful diagnostic information to its users. It must facilitate the easy movement of project support from one host machine to another.

An APSE must provide a well-coordinated set of useful tools, with uniform inter-tool interfaces and with communication through a common database which acts as the information source and product repository for all tools. Tools will be designed where appropriate to have separable limited function components that are composable, user selectable and communicate through the common database. It must facilitate the development and integration of new tools and the improvement, updating and replacement of tools.

The structure of an APSE should be based on simple overall concepts which are straightforward to understand, easy to use and few in number. Wherever possible, the concepts of the ADA language will be used in the APSE. High priority will be given to human engineering requirements in the design. The system shall provide a helpful user interface with adequate response times for interactive users and turn-around time for batch users. Communications between users and tools shall be according to uniform protocol conventions.

4. THE APSE/MAPSE/KAPSE MODEL

There are three principal features of an APSE: the database, the (user and system) interface and the toolset. The database acts as the central repository for information associated with each project throughout the project life cycle. The interface includes the control language which presents an interface to the user as well as system interfaces to the database and toolset. The toolset includes tools for program development, maintenance and configuration control supported by an APSE.

The STONEMAN develops an approach to portability by giving requirements for two lower levels within the APSE; the Kernel (KAPSE) and the Minimal toolset (MAPSE). This approach is illustrated by Figure 1. The levels in Figure 1 are defined below:

1. *Level 0*.   Hardware and host software as appropriate.
2. *Level 1*.   Kernel ADA Program Support Environment (KAPSE), which provides database, communication and run-time support functions to enable the execution of an ADA program (including a MAPSE tool) and which represents a machine-independent portability interface.
3. *Level 2*.   Minimal ADA Program Support Environment (MAPSE) which provides a minimal set of tools, which are both necessary and sufficient for the development and continuing support of ADA programs. These tools will be written in ADA and supported by the KAPSE.
4. *Level 3*.   ADA Program Support Environments (APSEs) which are constructed by extensions of the MAPSE to provide fuller support of particular applications or methodologies.

The model provides a consistent user interface through the KAPSE, which defines the host system interface. Additional tools, written in ADA, can easily be added and subsequently transported to another APSE. Thus the KAPSE may be viewed as a virtual machine for ADA programs, including tools written in ADA.

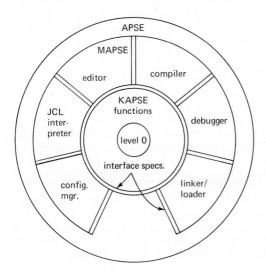

Figure 1. The Level Structure of an ADA Program Support Environment.

It may be anticipated that many systems which offer the use of ADA as a programming language will come into existence without full, or indeed any, regard to the requirements of STONEMAN. For example, translators will be implemented within existing support environments hosted on existing operating systems, together with existing software tools and techniques and possibly with the implementation of some further ADA-related tools. In cases where there is a large current investment in software projects, written originally in other languages and for which long term maintenance must be continued and improved, a viable policy may be to implant APSE-built tools into the existing environment for maintenance. This could provide valuable technology transfer at the environment level rather than the language level.

In other cases, ADA support environments will be constructed offering the use of the language together with a range of facilities which differ markedly in content and/or structure from those proposed by STONEMAN. For example, highly-integrated top-down development systems may be produced in some programming research establishments, meeting the APSE requirments but not reflecting the KAPSE/MAPSE structure.

Such systems represent entirely valid approaches to use of the ADA language. However, the long-term goal of the STONEMAN is to evolve an integrated system with a maximum level of portability. In order to achieve this long-term goal of portability of software tools and application systems dependent on them, it is intended that conventions and, eventually, standards be developed at the KAPSE interface level.

5. THE DATABASE

The database is the central feature of the support system. For each project supported by the APSE, all relevant information is stored within the database throughout the lifetime of the project. Furthermore, the system and all its software tools are stored within the database. Communication between tools takes place primarily via the database and information such as intermediate results is stored within the database for future use by other tools. Communication within the database is therefore widespread and far-reaching, in that all tools exchange information via objects in the database. The STONEMAN proposes that communications throughout the system take place in unified and consistent protocols via a universally accessible "virtual interface." This is further discussed below in the section entitled "Interfaces and User Communication."

The database preserves information relevant to a project throughout its lifetime in order that at any stage in its development it is possible to reconstruct any earlier stage in the project. This is necessary so that earlier design decisions can be reconsidered in the light of current changes in requirements.

At the present state of development of software engineering, information such as requirements or design documentation which arises early in the life cycle will normally be mainly textual in nature rather than rigorously expressed in formal languages and so the database is required to permit the storage of relatively informal relationships between such objects. At later stages, for example during implementation and testing through prototype stages to eventual production releases of the project, a rigorous mechanism is required to provide full control over the consistency and correctness of the different versions and configurations of the system.

6. DATABASE STRUCTURE

A separately identifiable collection of information in the database is known as an object in the STONEMAN. An object has a name by which it may be uniquely identified in the database, it has attributes and it contains information. Typically, an object may contain a separately compilable ADA program unit, a fragment of ADA text, a separable definition, a file of test data, a project requirements specification, an aggregation of other object-names (i.e., a configuration as described below), a documentation file, etc. The attribute list is open-ended but each object will have mandatory categorization or type information, history recording and access control attributes.

All objects in the database are uniquely identifiable; however, a group of objects may exist as related versions which may meet the same or closely related external specifications and may therefore by regarded as different versions of the same "abstract object." Within such a group, the user may specify that one object is the "preferred version" which is to be used whenever the user does not indicate a specific one.

Different collections of objects in a project may be brought together to form different groupings or "software configurations." The different configurations are needed in response to, for example, differing categories of user requirement or differences between peripheral devices on various target systems. Some configurations are long-lived, such as major system releases, and others may be temporary test-beds for development purposes. The relationships between objects in different configurations are in general complex, partially overlapping and not well-structured. Some configurations are related in time, such as consecutive "releases;" others co-exist in time as separate "models." Note that configurations are themselves objects and may therefore exist in version groups.

The system must contain tools to enable the generation, release and subsequent control of a project which exists in multiple configurations. In order to achieve this, it is generally necessary to be able to determine for any configuration the precise history of the construction of each of its components and therefore one of the mandatory attributes for each object in the database will be the history record.

The need to reconstruct, during the maintenance and continuing evolution of a project, the detailed history of its earlier stages raises interesting questions as to the amount of material that can realistically be recorded and accessed in a practical database. The STONEMAN takes a rather strong position by proposing that all relevant material be recorded on the grounds that it is not possible in principle to determine what can safely be thrown away. Large projects would clearly require an archiving system and may use sophisticated implementation techniques such as coalescing closely related versions.

In addition to the strong relationships in the database between versions and configurations, there is a need for the recording of weaker links between objects. In this area the STONEMAN introduces the concept of a "partition;" essentially a loosely structured grouping of objects intended to implement a system of managerial or access control. For example, teams of programmers on a project may share a partition which gives them collective access to shared information. Clearly, such groupings may well cut across configuration and version boundaries and may include other categories of information such as specifications and documentation files.

Because of its central importance to the system, the database and all its access functions are regarded as part of the KAPSE, in the same way as the local host operating system is subsumed within the KAPSE. By this means, portability of projects from APSE to APSE becomes a realizable goal.

7. INTERFACES AND USER COMMUNICATION

The STONEMAN develops the concept of a single unified interface mechanism which handles all communication within the APSE. The behavior of the interface can be illustrated by considering a typical user connection to the system, which takes place via a terminal device and supporting device driver routines. The first requirement is that of establishing user identification and the interface provides the necessary LOGON and LOGOFF services. These are implemented by the KAPSE and in many cases the KAPSE facilities may be little more than those offered by the underlying host operating system.

The user next requires the ability to run a program; possibly from his own files or more often a system-provided software tool, which is also in principle an ADA program. This program initiation facility is also provided by the KAPSE. Inherently, this is not representable in ADA language terms as essentially it enables a data structure produced by an ADA program (e.g., the compiler or linker) to be itself executed as a program. The facilities LOGON, LOGOFF and INITIATE constitute a minimal command language or job control language using the basic KAPSE facilities.

While the program is running, asynchronous communication with the job may be required if the user is working in an interactive mode. An APSE should provide a set of standard functions to implement various levels of communication with an executing program via a parameterized list of standard control keys. Asynchronous communication is normally concerned with the interaction, suspension or termination of executing programs; initiation is inherently a more orderly process and so is normally carried out by command rather than by control key operations.

During a session, the user may well communicate with various tools. In so far as possible, the interface should be consistent and similar functions should be expressed in similar terminology. Furthermore, tools themselves will initiate other tools and this will be done via the unified interface, using the same invocation mechanism as that accessed directly by the user. Such a facility should be provided as a library procedure and hence callable from programs.

Finally, in more complex situations, there is a need to store sequences of commands; for example, to run frequently repeated job sequences. This can be performed by writing ADA programs consisting primarily of calls on the program initiation library procedure. This approach, which was suggested by Stenning et al, [UK MoD ADA Study 1979] is one way to provide the full power of ADA as a command language.

Alternatively a more fully interpretive approach could be taken whereby the "model of program execution" incorporates the user at a control point somewhere in a nested hierarchy of executing ADA programs within the APSE. In this case, which is analogous to systems such as Interlisp, there is little meaningful distinction between ADA as a programming language and as a command language. In this model, the asynchronous functions provided by the control keys are primarily concerned with changing the user control point. This approach has been described by Fisher [Fisher 1979].

A third line is to consider the features needed in a command language to be more than the minimal MAPSE facilities outlined above and to be in some respects orthogonal to concepts in ADA. The objects of discourse in a command language are constants, literals and database objects rather than variable data structures. Furthermore, it may well be that a command language is inherently declarative, not procedural. This approach could lead to provision of a Command Language Interpreter as a separate tool, available to the user via the LOGON function, on the grounds that the benefits of a fully suitable command language outweigh the addition of a further language to the system.

At the present stage of development and study of environments for ADA, the approach in the STONEMAN is to indicate these possibilities while refraining from specifying a choice, on the grounds that a premature choice would hinder rather than help the development of effective APSEs.

8. THE TOOLS

The STONEMAN is a generic document and does not address the question of tools in much detail beyond defining general functions. To some extent this is justified on the grounds that specific APSEs may be addressed to the support of rather different environments, which require different methodologies and correspondingly different tools.

In general, two alternative approaches have been considered. The first is "traditional" in that separate tools such as compiler, editor, debugger, link-loader and configuration controller can be distinguished. Such systems tend to emphasize the support of the implementation phase of a project and support to the earlier phases may well be mainly textual. In the second approach, the paradigm of the construction of a system is more integrated and may proceed in top-down fashion from very high level statements of overall requirements and design, by processes of successive refinement and transformation, to the eventual implementation. The intention of the STONEMAN is to recognize both approaches. In particular, these differing approaches and particularly the requirements at the APSE level are non-specific between them. At the present time, the former approach is preferable within the DoD and more readily leads to the important goal of portability. The further requirements for MAPSEs and the KAPSE therefore emphasize the former approach.

9. THE MAPSE TOOLSET

The STONEMAN proposes a minimal set of software tools which are both necessary and sufficient for the support of ADA programming, including the preparation of further tools. These are all themselves regarded as written in ADA and using the basic facilities of the KAPSE.

The choice of specific tools and the divisions of functionality between tools is to some extent arbitrary and the set proposed represents a rather traditional and limited point of view. It is clear that the set must contain an editor for source program and documentation preparation, a translator and linkers and loaders for object code machines. It is equally clear that some static and dynamic analysis and debugging tools must be provided, though in some existing environments little is available in these areas.

A tool of particular interest called for in the MAPSE is the configuration manager. Even at the MAPSE level it is proposed that this tool address the central issue of version and configuration control. Systems exist concurrently in different versions or releases, operating in different configuration both of hardware and software and embodying complex sub-systems and components which also may exist in different configuration and versions. This area is essentially that of "programming-in-the-large" [DeRemer and Kron 1976] and is the subject of much current research by several workers in the field [Cooprider 1979] [Tichy 1979] [Buxton].

10. CONCLUSION

The requirements set forth in the STONEMAN outline a coordinated and integrated plan for the support of software projects in the ADA language. The individual requirements are all regarded as being within the state of the art at the present time and hence contain no specific high-risk features. Nevertheless, we realize that the set of requirements taken as a whole presents a substantial technical challenge to system designers and implementers. We are confident that the challenge can be met and we expect that the way ahead will be by an evolutionary development of APSE prototypes in response to initiatives taken by the DoD and others.

ACKNOWLEDGMENTS

It is with great pleasure that the authors acknowledge the contributions of many friends and colleagues to the effort on which this paper is based and without whom the work could not have been successfully completed. Although the number of contributors is too great for complete enumeration, the following major contributors are most gratefully acknowledged.

The early documents comprising the Pebbleman series were authored by W.E. Carlson, P.F. Elzer, D.A. Fisher and W.A. Whitaker and revised with substantial input from T.E. Cheatham, P. Cohen, and T.A. Standish.

The STONEMAN benefitted from major contributions by Vic Stenning and its evolution resulted from helpful criticisms from a large number of people at various stages of the project. These include, in addition to these listed above: R.M. Balzer, R.F. Brender, P. Cohen, S. Crocker, R.A. Converse, M.E. Devlin, R. Firth, M.F. Fischer, R.L. Glass, N. Habermann, H. Hart, G. Hayes, L. Klos, D.S. Johnson, M.M. Lehman, H.F. Ledgard, L. Maclaren, U. Merz, D. Notkin, I.D. Pyle, W.E. Riddle, D.F. Roberts, P. Santoni, E. Satterthwaite, R.S. Snowden, S.L. Squires, T.A. Straeter, J.A. Townley, P. Wegner, V.L. Voydock, and S. Zeldin.

REFERENCES

[ADA Environment Workshop 1979] *Proceedings of the ADA Environment Workshop*, DoD High Order Language Working Group, San Diego, November 1979.

[ADA Phase II Reports 1980] *DoD Common High Order Language ADA Design—Phase II Reports and Analyses*, microfiche ref. ADA-88-1-M, January 1980.

[ADA Preliminary Manual 1979] Preliminary ADA Reference Manual, *ACM SIGPLAN Notices, Part A*, June 1979.

[Buxton] J.N. Buxton. A note on system construction systems (to be published).

[Buxton 1979] J.N. Buxton. *STONEMAN Material*. September 1979.

[Buxton 1980] *DoD Requirements for ADA Programming Support Environments, STONEMAN*. DoD High Order Language Working Group, February 1980.

[Buxton and Stenning 1979a] J.N. Buxton, V. Stenning. *STONEMAN Informal Draft*. August 1979.

[Buxton and Stenning 1979b] J.N. Buxton, V. Stenning. *STONEMAN Draft*. December 1979.

[Carlson 1980] W.E. Carlson. ADA: a standard programming language for defense systems. *SIGNAL*, March 1980.

[Cooprider 1979] L.W. Cooprider. *The representation of families of software systems*. Carnegie-Mellon University, Computer Science Department, doctoral dissertation, April 1979.

[DeRemer and Kron 1976] F. DeRemer, H. Kron. Programming-in-the-large versus programming-in-the-small. *IEEE Transactions on Software Engineering*, June 1976.

[Druffel 1979] L.E. Druffel. ADA: How will it affect course offerings? *Interface*, I(1979).

[Elzer 1979] P.F. Elzer. *Some observations concerning existing software environments.* Donier Systems GMBH Report, May 1979.

[Fisher 1978] D.A. Fisher. DoD's Common Programming Language Effort. *Computer,* March 1978, 25-33.

[Fisher 1979] D.A. Fisher, Private communication. 1979.

[Fisher and Standish 1979] D.A. Fisher, T.A. Standish. *Initial thoughts on the pebbleman process.* IDA Paper P-1392, June 1979.

[Fisher and Wetherall 1977] D.A. Fisher, P. Wetherall. *DoD Requirements for High Order Computer Programming Languages, Revised IRONMAN.* DoD High Order Language Working Group, July 1977.

[Ichbiah et al. 1979] J.D. Ichbiah et al. Rationale for the Design of the ADA Programming Language. *ACM SIGPLAN Notices, Part B,* June 1979.

[Pebbleman 1978] *DoD requirements for the programming environment for the common high order language, PEBBLEMAN.* July 1978.

[Pebbleman 1979] *DoD requirements for the programming environment for the common high order language, PEBBLEMAN revised.* January 1979.

[Standish 1978] T.A. Standish (ed.) *Proceedings Irvine Workshop on Alternatives for the Environment, Certification and Control of the DoD Common High Order Language,* June 1978.

[Steelman 1978] *DoD Requirements for High Order Computer Programming Languages, STEELMAN.* DoD High Order Language Working Group, June 1978.

[Tichy 1979] W.F. Tichy. Software development based on module interconnection. *Proceedings of the Fourth International Conference on Software Engineering,* Munich, Germany, September 1979.

[Tinman 1976] *DoD Requirements for High Order Computer Programming Languages, TINMAN.* DoD High Order Language Working Group, June 1976.

[UK MoD ADA Study 1979] *United Kingdom MoD ADA Support System Study.* System Designers Ltd.,/Software Sciences Ltd., 1979.

[Whitaker 1977] W.A. Whitaker, The U.S. Department of Defense common high order language effort. *SIGPLAN Notices,* February 1977.

27 The Spice Project

SCOTT E. FAHLMAN, SAMUEL P. HARBISON

Carnegie-Mellon University
Pittsburgh, Pennsylvania

Many computer science researchers believe that networks of powerful personal computers will soon replace timesharing systems as the predominant computing environment for research and computer-aided design. The Spice project is a long-term research project whose goal is to develop an advanced, integrated, portable computing environment for these personal machines. In this paper we describe some of the advantages of personal machines over timesharing, what an advanced personal computing environment might look like to the user, and the features of Spice that we believe will be important in achieving these goals.

1. THE ADVENT OF PERSONAL COMPUTING

Timesharing evolved as a way to provide users with the power of a large interactive computer system at a time when such systems were much too expensive to dedicate to a single individual. The size of these systems made a qualitative difference in the kinds of service they provided, and the fact that many users ran on the same machine made possible a level of user cooperation and communication that could not have been achieved otherwise. This in turn opened up a range of new applications in man/machine communication: computer-aided design, computer-aided instruction, on-line libraries, electronic mail, etc.

Recent advances in hardware technology are opening up new possibilities. The level of capital investment which today provides each user with a small slice of a timeshared machine and a crude CRT terminal will, by the mid-1980's, provide the same user with his own powerful machine, far more powerful than today's microprocessors and equipped with such features as high-resolution color graphics and audio I/O devices. This development will enable the user to avoid many of the compromises and limitations inherent in timesharing. New high-speed network technologies make it possible to move to this personal computing environment without foregoing the attractive features of timesharing: shared information, good inter-user communication, and the sharing of expensive peripherals. We are entering a new world of versatile personal computers, as different from the world of timesharing as that world was from batch processing. It will take years of work at many different installations to learn how best to exploit these new opportunities.

The Spice project at Carnegie-Mellon University is one attempt to explore the possibilities of this new world. The goal of Spice is to develop an integrated research computing environment based on a network of very powerful personal computers. Machines of this power may be too expensive for widespread individual use today, but we believe that by the mid-1980's they will be easily affordable by most researchers.

The personal computing environment will consist of a set of powerful personal computers and peripheral devices linked together by a high-speed network. Each of the personal computers will be powerful enough to satisfy all of the computing needs of an individual user most of the time, but they will be inexpensive—something like $20,000 each. The network will allow the personal computers to communicate with one another and with shared resources such as printers and the central file system.

An environment such as this can have all the benefits of timesharing systems: the capital allocated to an individual user is acceptably small, and inter-user communication and cooperation is still easy, given the right software environment. Furthermore, the personal computing network offers a number of important advantages over conventional timesharing systems:

• *Response time.* By response time we mean the time the system takes to respond to a user request, whether it be a simple text editing command or the compilation of a large program. A user generally has some notion of an "acceptable" response time for various activities. He may be willing to wait two minutes for a compilation, for instance, but no more than a fraction of a second for a simple text editing operation. If the response is too slow, his tendency will be to move to a faster program, even if it offers less functionality.

In a timesharing system the response fluctuates unpredictably, depending on what the other users are doing. Programs that require fast response must be kept fairly simple if they are to be usable during "peak load" periods. In a personal computing environment the response is constant and predictable.

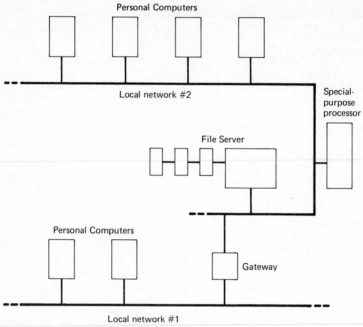

Figure 1. A personal computing environment.

Furthermore, it is likely to be better than the average response from the timesharing computer for two reasons:

1. A personal computer will often have a better cost/performance ratio. Large timesharing systems push the leading edge of computer technology, where increases in performance come at a high incremental cost. Personal computers are able to use more conventional technology and, since more identical units are built, can be mass-produced for added savings.
2. A personal computer can provide a much higher bandwidth between the display screen and the processor than is common on timesharing systems. The personal machine's processor can provide the intensive bursts of computing that are necessary if complex graphics are to be displayed in real time. This kind of service is very hard to provide on a timeshared machine.

With better response, especially at the user interface, the personal computer will support applications that know more about the user and can do more for him.

• *Total computing power.*   Given the right software environment, the network of personal computers can be viewed as a large multicomputer with a total processing power far in excess of that obtainable from a single computer at a comparable cost. Carefully designed system software can make it easy for large applications to harness this power by distributing pieces of their work to idle personal computers on the network or to specialized processors that can concentrate on particular computational tasks without any concern for providing a friendly environment to general users.

• *Incremental expandability.*   When a timesharing system becomes overloaded, the usual solution is to suffer as long as possible and then obtain a second large computer. The subsequent problems of load balancing and communication between the two machines—especially if the hardware *and* software are not identical—can result in a major upheaval in the user community. Personal computing offers a great advantage in this area because the system can be expanded by small increments whenever the need arises. Furthermore, the network protocols conveniently isolate communication, making it easier to accommodate a variety of machines and operating systems on the local network.

• *Reliability*.   There is no reason to suspect that a single personal computer will be any more reliable than a large timesharing computer. However, when reliability is measured as the *availability* of resources to the user community, personal computers have a distinct advantage: failures in a personal computer affect only one user, and he can often simply move to another computer. Furthermore, hardware and software can be tested in actual use on a few machines with minimal danger to the user community as a whole. Shared resources are still critical, but they can be made reliable by distributing them (as in the case of file systems and printers, for instance) or by making them ultra-reliable (as in the case of the network itself).

• *Mutability*.   A timesharing system is much like commercial television in the United States: it must meet the needs of the large "average" audience at the expense of individuals with extraordinary tastes or needs. A personal computing network is relieved of this burden because individual computers can differ in cost and power and can use different system software to meet each individual's needs. This mutability is especially important in universities and other research communities where the computer will be a general "workbench" for many specialized tasks.

• *Security*.   The protection of information is a complex problem that is not magically solved by this new environment. However, the network does give an installation the flexibility to isolate individual computers and the information they contain. If a few people need to work with particularly sensitive information, for instance, their computers can be detached from the main network and located on a second, smaller network. The second network can be physically isolated from the rest of the environment or it can be connected through a secure gateway processor.

2. SOME PERSONAL COMPUTING SCENARIOS

Beyond these advantages, we believe the new capabilities offered by personal computers will give rise to an environment that is qualitatively different from current ones. It is hard to describe in abstract terms how one computing environment differs from another; many subtle differences can be appreciated only when they have been experienced first-hand. Since we are unable to convey such experience on paper, we will have to describe the feel of this kind of computing by way of some imaginary scenarios. Most of the individual elements in these scenarios have already been achieved in one system or another; the challenge for the future is to put all of these elements together in a single system and to provide a fertile environment for further development.[1]

---

[1] Some illustrative efforts include: The Programmer's Workbench from Bell Labs [Dolotta et al. 1978] and the Programmer's Assistant from Xerox [Teitelman 1977]; text systems such as [Knuth 1979] [Kernighan et al. 1978] [Macdonald et al. 1980] [Reid and Walker 1980]; and circuit design systems such as SCALD [McWilliams and Widdoes 1978] and others from Bell Labs [Fraser 1978].

2.1 The Programmer's Workbench

A programmer is installing a new feature in a large, complex system. He "opens" the system for modification, examining the module structure to locate the pieces that must be changed. These pieces the programmer "checks out," so that other programmers will be warned that the modules are being modified. As he makes modifications, the programmer uses a "top-down" programming style, leaving program fragments unspecified or inventing variables and constants to be defined later. The editor, actually a part of an integrated program development system, quietly keeps track of incomplete procedures, undeclared variables, and needed documentation, providing this information when requested. The editor can also detect syntax errors, keep the text in a standard format, and call up documentation on procedures, modules, and entire systems.

When he finishes his modifications, the programmer constructs an experimental system "configuration," merging his changes with the rest of the system for a test—without affecting users of the standard system. The programmer tests and debugs the system using only source-level concepts and interactions, using a variety of software probes to monitor the program's progress. The programmer can make changes interactively—changes that are either temporary to the debugging session or permanent. As he becomes more confident, the programmer applies his system to an "acceptance trial" of standard test cases, altering and augmenting those cases with specific tests relevant to his new features.

With testing finished, the programmer installs the new system, his changes becoming visible to users and other programmers for the first time. If problems with the new system develop, the previous module versions—or the entire previous system —can be "rolled back."

2.2 The Writer's Workbench

An author working on his manuscript uses tools that resemble those used by the programmer. The author makes revisions in chapters and rearranges text; he becomes dissatisfied with a revision and recalls the original copy, only to decide a few weeks later to go back to the revision. He notes prose that seems awkward and needs further work; his computer keeps a list of these notes so that he can return to them tomorrow—or next month. An author of fiction might suddenly decide that a character in his novel must be rewritten; the computer locates every reference to the character so that a consistent and progressive development can be made. An author of technical manuals might wish to include figures or tables from a standard library or generate them on the spot from a data base.

The numbering of chapters, figures, and tables is handled automatically, as are cross references to pages or figures, the table of contents, and the index. When the author finds himself searching for a particular word, he can invoke a thesaurus, a dictionary or an encyclopedia at the touch of a key. He can go back to his earlier books to locate an inspired phrase. And, of course, the computer watches for spelling and simple grammatical errors. At all times, the author sees neat and properly formatted text on his display. If he wants printed copy, he can have it in minutes from a page-per-second laser printer.

When he finishes his revisions, the author sends the final draft to his editor over a telephone or satellite link. The editor checks the manuscript, adds illustrations and cover art (created on the Illustrators' Workbenches in the publisher's art department) and forwards the whole thing to a phototypesetter and engraver. The printer will have camera-ready copy—and color plates for the cover art—in less than a day.

2.3 The Engineer's Workbench

A logic designer is working on a new VLSI chip. As he draws the layout on his color screen, using a mouse and menu system, a constraint-checking program is monitoring his work, adjusting the width of traces as a function of their length, keeping adjacent traces separated by the proper distance, and so on. As he works, the designer is able to call up cookbook design elements from a large on-line reference library and, if these meet his needs, plug them into the current design at specified locations. These design elements are parameterized so that they will work in a variety of situations; the adjustment of parameters for a given context is handled automatically. In addition to the predefined circuit-designer's cookbook (probably distributed on a video disk), the system allows the designer to build up his own personal data base of elements from past designs.

From time to time the designer will want to check his work and see how fast the circuit will run under various test conditions. Simple continuity tests can be run by placing a "probe" at some point on the screen; everything connected to this point changes color in an obvious way. For more complex tests, the user would apply test signals and voltages to certain points in the circuit, then would pass the design to a simulator. Depending on the complexity of the simulator, this task might be done quickly on the local machine, or it might be passed over the network to a very large machine that specializes in simulations but knows nothing about user interfaces. When the designer is satisfied that the circuit is correct, a few keystrokes are sufficient to transmit the design to the automatic mask-making and chip-fabrication facility.

In addition to the cookbook and the simulator, the Engineer's Workbench provides a number of other tools: a desk calculator for numerical problems, a MACSYMA-like desk calculator for symbolic mathematics, and an extensive on-line reference library of publications and handbooks on circuit design. If the design task is large enough to involve several people, the system provides a series of interlocks on the data base similar to those used in large programming projects. These interlocks prevent two people from modifying the same subsection of the circuit at once and systematically record any modifications that are made to a module's specifications.

If consultation with a colleague is needed, a few keystrokes are sufficient to find the other user, wherever he may be working, and to link up the screens of the two users' workstations. The first designer can now describe his problem over a voice link, while pointing out features of the chip layout on the screen. If the colleague is not available at the time, the same combination of voice, pictures, text, and moving pointers can be sent as mail to be read later. The ability to communicate with pictures as well as voice and text is important in many situations, but it is especially critical for engineering tasks.

2.4 The Executive's Workbench

An executive in a large corporation must keep in touch with operations around the world. Most of the corporation's communication is handled electronically by workbenches that can send and receive voice, data, and facsimile transmissions around a building or around the world. Incoming messages are received by the executive's workbench; some are filed until the executive chooses to look at them, others are forwarded to an assistant automatically, and some cause the executive to be notified immediately. If the executive is away from his office, messages can be forwarded to the workbench nearest to him or (via packet radio) to the executive's pocket terminal.

The executive's workbench hosts a number of "decision support systems" that monitor short- and long-term planning, production schedules, international economic fluctuations, and manpower needs. Based on the information from one of these systems, the executive decides that some important work is behind schedule, and he must have a meeting with several of his managers to discuss the problem. His secretary makes a request through her workbench to the managers' workbenches, which maintain their daily schedules. A mutually satisfactory time and place are determined automatically. (Jim has a meeting at noon; George doesn't like to meet before lunch; the conference room is tied up until 2:30.) At the meeting, more information is called up from the workbenches and a decision is made to alter a schedule. The workbench identifies the ramifications of the change on other schedules and sends messages to all of the people affected.

These scenarios are only a few of many that can be imagined. Similar scripts could be written for architects, illustrators, doctors, librarians—anyone who must deal with complex, specialized information. As we analyzed our own requirements for a new environment at CMU, we realized that elements from all the scenarios above would be desirable. We use our computing facilities for programming, document production, design, and communication, and all these activities should be supported.

3. SPICE

In the summer of 1979, a number of us in the Department of Computer Science of Carnegie-Mellon University met to consider the future of our research computing facilities. At a time when we wanted to increase our research productivity, we were faced with the mounting problems of dealing with a diverse set of timesharing computers. Instead of building more sophisticated tools to support our work, we were spending more and more time just maintaining our current ones.

Fortunately, there were several examples of success with personal computing environments in computer science research. Two of the earliest and most important experiments were the Alto/Ethernet environment at Xerox Palo Alto Research Center [Thacker et al. 1979] and the Lisp Machine project at MIT's Artificial Intelligence Laboratory [Greenblatt et al. 1984]. On the basis of the experiences of MIT and Xerox, and on our own analysis, we decided to go ahead with a long-range plan to establish a personal computing environment to replace our timesharing environment by 1985. We named our environment *Spice*, for Scientific Personal Integrated Computing Environment.

Spice differs from other experiments in personal computing in several ways:

• *Capability.* Because we wish to use personal computers as the primary computational resource for people who are used to having access to large computers, we are depending on very powerful hardware and very sophisticated software in Spice. The cost of such a facility is justified by the already high level of capitalization of our researchers and the increased productivity that should result from its use.

• *Language independence.* Spice is not designed around any single programming language; we want users to be able to implement and use a variety of languages. This goal forces Spice to avoid language biases and provide a uniform means for systems written in different languages to communicate.

• *Protection.* We believe the protection of programs and data is just as important in a personal computer as in a timesharing computer. Spice supports access control to files, controls on interprocess communication, and isolates processes by putting each in its own virtual address space.

• *Portability.* The design and construction of personal computers is not part of the Spice project. In order to take advantage of the computers that will appear in the coming years, we are attempting to make Spice easily portable to any computer that can support our notion of a minimal "virtual machine."

• *Integration.* The most interesting—and difficult—part of Spice will be building the application software that makes the scenarios from the previous section practical realities. We intend to build a uniform environment that can support the efficient development and use of these applications.

The full development of Spice will take several years, and it is too early to describe in detail the structure of Spice or the range of its applications. However, in this section we will describe some of the current directions that the project is taking.

3.1   Hardware Specification

It is important to know the hardware capabilities needed for the ultimate Spice environment. This allows the programmer to pace the computational demands of his software as he develops it on slower, prototype systems. For us, this specification is also important as a goal to set before computer manufacturers on whom we will depend for our hardware.

3.1.1   The personal computers
We expect to support several types of personal computers in order to satisfy people with a range of computational needs, but the minimal "Spice machine," needed to meet normal requirements, should look about like this:

• *Processor.* The processor should be microcodable, and typical instruction sets for Pascal or Lisp should execute at about one million (macro-) instructions per second. The microstore should allow for multiple resident instruction sets.[2]

• *Memory.* The computer should provide a virtual address space of 2^{32} bytes per process, with at least 2^{20} bytes of primary memory. The virtual address space should be smoothly addressable and the hardware should have demand paging capability. Each computer should have local secondary (disk) storage of about 100 megabytes, suitable for paging the virtual address space and for caching copies of files from a central file server.

• *I/O.* Each computer should have a high-resolution ($1,000 \times 1,000$ pixels) bit-mapped raster display, a good keyboard, and a pointing device for the display. Color or gray-scale capabilities in the display are desirable. The computer should have provision for audio input and output, and optional video input. It should be easy to attach experimental devices to the computers.

• *Cost.* The computer should be inexpensive enough to justify it as a capital expenditure for a single researcher; about \$20,000 would seem reasonable as a 1985 price in an environment such as ours.

---

[2] The provision of a writable microstore is admittedly an optimization, but we believe it is such an important optimization as to be a fundamental requirement in a practical Spice machine. We believe the microstore is the key that will allow inexpensive hardware to efficiently support multiple languages and the underlying Spice virtual machine.

We believe these specifications can easily be met by 1985. In 1981 we are seeing the delivery of commercial personal computers with about one quarter the performance at twice the price, and the competition has barely started.

3.1.2 The network The network should provide for high-bandwidth communication (10 megabits/second) and be adaptable to a wide range of computers and I/O devices. We believe that compatibility with a wide range of hardware is more important than the choice of a specific network technology, and therefore we encourage the establishment of a network standard.

We expect the network to connect the personal machines to a wide range of peripheral devices and non-personal computers. By attaching our present timesharing computers, for instance, we hope to smooth the migration to the new environment, and those people remaining on the old systems can have access to new resources as they appear. Gateways to other local and non-local networks (such as the ARPANET) will keep our community in touch with other communities in our university and around the world.

3.2 File Storage

Spice expects to have access to a large, (logically) central file storage facility on the network which will act as a reliable repository for most long-term information. The design of this facility is a research project in its own right, even though it has close ties with Spice [Accetta et al. 1980]. A central facility has several advantages over keeping long-term files locally on the personal computers:

1. The location and distribution of information around the community becomes easier, and archiving facilities can be centralized.

2. A user's files are independent of the computer he happens to be using, making it easier for him to move to a different computer either to take advantage of a more powerful processor or to deal with a failure in his usual computer.

3. A large central facility can provide for very large data bases and files too large to hold on an individual machine.

To minimize network traffic and improve response, the local storage of the personal computers will be used as a cache for frequently used data from the central facility.

3.3 The Spice Virtual Machine

Each personal machine will host an operating system kernel that we have named *Accent* [Rashid and Robertson 1981]. Accent, in a combination of hardware, software, and microcode (depending on the individual computer) provides the environment that supports Spice. Some of its features include a very powerful interprocess communication mechanism, transparent access to network facilities and resources, multiprogramming, and independent virtual memory for each process. In a sense, each machine becomes a small timesharing system, supporting many large tasks at once. It is characteristic of our design that we do not believe the nature of the system changes simply because all the tasks are devoted to the needs of a single person. Indeed, we believe that all the mechanisms that have arisen in timeshared systems are needed in some form in a personal computing environment.

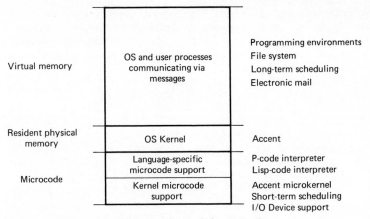

Virtual memory	OS and user processes communicating via messages	Programming environments File system Long-term scheduling Electronic mail
Resident physical memory	OS Kernel	Accent
Microcode	Language-specific microcode support	P-code interpreter Lisp-code interpreter
	Kernel microcode support	Accent microkernel Short-term scheduling I/O Device support

Figure 2. Software/firmware layers in the Spice computer.

3.4   The User Interface

A major goal of Spice—and a major piece of research—is to provide a uniform style of interaction between the computer and user and between individual programs. Such a facility is important for two reasons:

1. A uniform style across applications is a great help to a user approaching an unfamiliar program—he can bring much of his "intuition" from other programs.
2. A uniform style allows programs to share the user interface software. Thus, a programmer need not "reinvent the wheel" in every program.

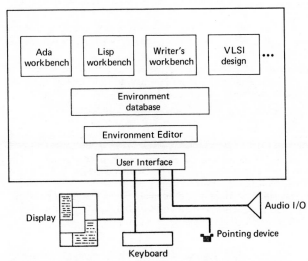

Figure 3. Structure of the Spice user interface.

Spice addresses this issue at two levels. First, we are implementing a rich set of facilities to support the use of the display and other user interface hardware. These facilities will be accessible via the message system and hence will be available to applications written in any language, both locally and over the network. Second, we are designing a high-level model of interaction that will separate the producer and consumer of information. We introduce the notion of an abstract "environment" that contains diverse structured information and that can be queried by programs that want various kinds of information, such as the file to use, or the time of day, or the default directory. A user will provide information to programs by modifying its environment through a set of tools: menu-selection protocols, command-line parsers, voice-recognition programs, intelligent "user assistants," etc. The programs needing the information are ignorant of how the information was provided, and thus they can be portable to many environments with quite different styles of interaction with users.

3.5   Applications

On top of the system and user-interface facilities we intend to evolve a number of the kind of application-specific environments alluded to in the scenarios above. (Of particular importance to us are the programming environments.) There are other research projects at CMU that directly address these problems, and we intend that Spice will be an environment in which these projects can be developed further.

ACKNOWLEDGMENTS

Spice is a cooperative effort of a large number of researchers who have made a common investment in designing and building a computing advanced environment to support their research. Without this shared vision and common effort, a system of the complexity of Spice could not be constructed. The following people have contributed in many ways to the vision of Spice presented in this paper: Peter Hibbard, Eugene Ball, Mario Barbacci, Joe Newcomer, Allen Newell, Rick Rashid, George Robertson, Dan Siewiorek, Bob Sproull, Guy Steele, Howard Wactlar, and Bill Wulf.

This research was sponsored in part by the Defense Advanced Research Projects Agency (DOD), ARPA Order No. 3597, monitored by the Air Force Avionics Laboratory under Contract F33615-78-C-1551.

The views and conclusions contained in this document are those of the authors and should not be interpreted as representing the official policies, either expressed or implied, of the Defense Advanced Research Projects Agency or the US Government.

REFERENCES

[Accetta et al. 1980] M. Accetta, G. Robertson, M. Satyanarayanan, M. Thompson.*The design of a network-based central file system*, Carnegie-Mellon University, Computer Science Department, Technical Report, August 1980.

[Dolotta et al. 1978] T.A. Dolotta, R.C. Haight, J.R. Mashey. The Programmer's Workbench. *The Bell System Technical Journal*, 57:6 (July-August 1978), 2177-2200; reprinted in *Interactive Programming Environments*

[Fraser 1978] A.G. Fraser. Circuit design aids. *The Bell System Technical Journal*, 57:6 (July-August 1978), 2233-2250.

[Greenblatt et al. 1984] R. Greenblatt, T. Knight, J. Holloway, D. Moon, D. Weinreb. The Lisp machine. In *Interactive Programming Environments*.

[Kernighan et al. 1978] B.W. Kernighan, M.E. Lesk, J.F. Ossanna. Document preparation. *The Bell System Technical Journal*, 57:6 (July-August 1978), 2115-2136.

[Knuth 1979] D.E. Knuth. *TEX and METAFONT: new directions in typesetting*. American Mathematical Society and Digital Press, 1979.

[Macdonald et al. 1980] N.H. Macdonald, L.T. Rase, S.A. Keenan. *Writer's Workbench: computer programs for text editing and assessment*. Bell Laboratories Technical Report, 1980.

[McWilliams and Widdoes 1978] T. McWilliams, L.C. Widdoes. SCALD: Structured, Computer-Aided Logic Design. *Proceedings of the Fifteenth Design Automation Conference*, June 1978, 271-277.

[Rashid and Robertson 1981] R.F. Rashid, G.G. Robertson. Accent: A communication oriented network operating system kernel. *Eighth Symposium on Operating Systems Principles*, Association for Computing Machinery, November 1981.

[Reid and Walker 1980] B.K. Ried, J.H. Walker. *Scribe Introductory User's Manual*. Unilogic, Ltd., Pittsburgh, Pennsylvania, 1980.

[Teitelman 1977] W. Teitelman. A display-oriented programmer's assistant. CSL 77-3, XEROX PARC, 1977; reprinted in *Interactive Programming Environments*; see also *Proceedings of the Fifth International Joint Conference on Artificial Intelligence*, Cambridge, Massachusetts, August 1977, 905-915.

[Thacker et al. 1979] C. Thacker, E. McCreight, B. Lampson, R. Sproull, D. Boggs. *Alto: a personal computer*. Xerox Palo Alto Research Center Technical Report CSL-79-11, August 1979.

28 From Interactive to Intelligent Programming Environments

DAVID R. BARSTOW

Schlumberger-Doll Research
Ridgefield, Connecticut

HOWARD E. SHROBE

Massachusetts Institute of Technology
Cambridge, Massachusetts

There has already been considerable experience in the development of advanced programming environments which has taught us many lessons and has allowed us to begin to think of programming in a new way. We review those lessons which have been learned in the construction of LISP based programming environments: in particular the importance of taking advantage of naturally occurring structures where possible. We also suggest that there are many other natural structures whose use could lead to even richer environments; however, exploiting these structures will require more research in Artificial Intelligence as well as in more traditional areas of Computer Science.

1. INTERACTIVE PROGRAMMING ENVIRONMENTS

The environment in which a programmer performs his/her task has many distinct facets. The physical environment, the presence or absence of other people, the personalities of the other members of the work group, the directives handed down from whatever powers exist over him/her, the programming methodologies that the programmer has learned, the reference manuals for the programming language and computer system, all have an impact on the programmer and his/her ability to program effectively. The importance of these factors must not be under-emphasized [Weinberg 1971]. Nonetheless, when we use the term "programming environment" we have something more specific in mind, namely a set of computerized tools which ease the difficulty of communication between the human programmer and his/her computer system. Even in these terms the line is fuzzy at best. In any event, the idea of a programming environment is clearly an evolving one; what we today consider to be a programming environment will probably be considered primitive and limited by future standards.

The tools which are normally associated with programming environments have been motivated by a multiplicity of requirements. Producing good software is an extremely complex task involving many distinct activities. Activities which on the surface would seem simple have turned out to be difficult. For example, despite many years of active research it is still fair to say that there is no completely successful or generally applicable method of specifying what a program is supposed to do. Nor are there systematic techniques for translating a set of requirements into code or for isolating and correcting bugs once the program has been coded. Modern software systems are often developed in an evolutionary process in which new capabilities are added incrementally. Yet the area of "programming through progressive enrichment" [Sandewall 1979a] is also in great need of tools, methodology, and theory.

1.1 Historical Perspective

In the broadest sense, programming environments are the result of attempting to use the computer to alleviate any (or all) of the above problems in the development and maintenance of software. There has been an historical trend in the development of software management tools. The earliest tools were intended to make it possible to interact with a computer at all and were built as long as three decades ago. Before such tools were developed (non-computerized) programming environments consisted primarily of pencil, coding forms, a description of the machine's order code and of the buttons on the console.

It is fair to say that the earliest software management tools mainly took advantage of the raw power of the computer to handle large volumes of data rapidly. In general these tools performed mechanical tasks which had previously been done manually, but with a qualitative improvement in speed. The most obvious examples of this were assemblers, soon followed by compilers for the first high level programming languages. To aid in the debugging process, symbolic debuggers were developed. To help manage the computational resources available to a programmer, operating systems and file systems were developed. To assist in the production and modification of the program text, editors were developed. At about the same time as the earliest text editors, interactive languages were introduced. Many of these advances took place as part of the introduction and commercialization of interactive time-shared computer utilities.

1.2 Modern Programming Environments

A common feature of these earlier tools is that they did not embody a viewpoint on how program construction should (or does) proceed. In contrast, modern environments (to one extent or another) are constructed with a style of work in mind, taking advantage of what are believed to be naturally occurring structures of the software development process. Most modern environments can be classified into one of three types, based on the programming tasks considered and on the approach taken. (As with all such classifications, it is overly simplistic and the boundaries are fuzzy, but we feel it important to recognize that different attempts to build environments have often been motivated by very different sets of concerns.)

• *Environments concerned with the entire life cycle of a program or system.* These environments have generally focused on managing the development of large systems built by many programmers, helping to ensure consistency as modules are developed or modified and to ensure that the system's development proceeds in a reasonable fashion. Among the common tools in this type of environment are data bases that describe the current state of the system, specification languages, and version maintenance systems. CADES is an example of such an environment [Pearson 1979]. (Such systems assume that a software system may be decomposed into separate modules with distinct boundaries and with clear and specifiable interfaces between them. They also generally assume that each individual programmer knows about only a part of the whole system. Finally, they assume that a system's specifications are clearly understood before coding begins.)

• *Environments concerned primarily with the coding phase and whose tools are relatively independent from each other.* These environments are generally oriented toward the support of several compiled languages (and sometimes several dialects of these languages on one or more host systems). Among the common tools provided are compilers, symbolic debuggers, and text editors. Unix exemplifies this kind of environment [Dolotta and Mashey 1976]. (Here the system is built around the assumption that a software system is constructed from a large number of reasonably small modules which communicate via a well-defined convention using "pipes". Finally the system assumes the use of a programmable command language to connect all of these together).

• *Environments which regard coding, debugging, testing and maintenance as a single process of program development through incremental enrichment.* The tools of such environments are integrated into a relatively coherent whole. These environments are generally oriented toward interactive languages. Among the common tools provided are interpreters, debuggers, and language-oriented editors. LISP environments, such as INTERLISP and the MIT LISP Machine, are examples of this category [Teitelman 1977] [Weinreb and Moon 1981]. (These systems have been built to support programming by progressive enrichment. They assume that the program is partitioned into small units of behavior represented by LISP functions and that these units will be tested, debugged, and modified frequently. They further assume that the code is represented as s-expressions and that this s-expression format is a convenient representation for editing).

Programming environments often embody assumptions not only about the technical nature of the software construction process, but also about the social nature of the process as well. Indeed, large software system construction takes place in an extremely divergent set of managerial and social settings making tools appropriate for one context inappropriate in another.

At one extreme is the research setting, in particular, the Artificial Intelligence research setting where at most a few programmers collaborate in the production of a single integrated program which may be hundreds of pages of code in a high level language (usually LISP). In this context, the program exists as an experiment, a test of an idea. None of the code is intended for production use, nor are elegance, or performance to tight efficiency standards important criteria. The programmers themselves are highly educated. Environments intended for this context put a premium on fluidity and ease of modification.

At the other extreme are the large commercial software houses where we find large numbers of people working on a common project. Often this project consists of large numbers of relatively small programs, with perhaps a common data base linking them together. The coders typically are not as highly educated as those in academic settings, nor is their primary goal to test an experimental idea. Instead there is more emphasis on producing accurate, high performance code which can be maintained by someone other than the author(s). Environments intended for such a context place a premium not on fluidity, but rather on structuring and managing program modifications and on coordinating or managing the efforts of so many people.

1.3   Lisp Environments

Given this wide range of starting assumptions about the context and methodology of the programming process, it is not surprising that tools from two different environments which provide nominally the same service may, in fact, be quite different. An editor which is geared to the research environment might facilitate the examination and modification of code from any of a huge number of files. A similar editor for the production software environment might intentionally prevent such activity, or at the least it may place a major focus on documenting the modification.

Rather than superficially surveying the myriad of possible combinations of tools, methodologies and social contexts, we will instead present a view of how the tools of one particular type of environment fit together. We will concentrate on the type of environment with which we are most familiar, that intended for experimental software development in the Artificial Intelligence community using Lisp dialects like INTERLISP, MacLisp and Lisp Machine Lisp.

Lisp programming as practiced in the major research centers always involves the interleaving of coding, execution, testing and debugging (specification and documentation are of lesser importance and in some cases impossible due to the fact that the task to be performed is only poorly understood). It is inappropriate in this context to think of distinct "coding phases" and "maintenance phases". What makes this style of "programming by progressive enrichment" possible is an integrated bundle of tools including a language interpreter, trace and breakpoint package, symbolic debugger and backtracer, symbolic single stepper, and an editor which understands the structure of the source code. Notice that we did not mention a compiler. Although all high quality LISP's have sophisticated compilers (and these compilers are also included in the "bag of tools"), the role reserved for the compiler is simply to make the code run faster. The glue which holds the system together is the interpreter; one grows accustomed to thinking of program execution in terms of direct interpretation of the source (even when working with compiled code).

Lisp programs are written as collections of "functions" which are typically quite small (usually no larger than one screenful of text, often smaller). All code is written in a fully parenthesized syntax; the first item within parentheses indicates what function is to be applied, the other items are the arguments to the function (of course each of these may consist of a function applied to arguments nested within parentheses, and so on). Each unit consisting of an opening parenthesis, function, arguments, and closing parenthesis is called an s-expression. This simple structure leads to enormous power. Since there is only a single action performed by the interpreter (namely applying a function to its arguments) it becomes conceptually straightforward to implement many features such as single-stepping, tracing, and symbolic debugging. Second, the simple s-expression syntax of the language leads naturally to a logical way of displaying code on a page (or a screen).

Lisp editors are designed to allow one to easily move though the structure of nested s-expressions. In the Lisp Machine for example, the code is displayed on a high resolution screen in a prettyprinted format. Single keystroke commands move up or down one level of parenthesis nesting, others move forward or backward over an s-expression or delete an s-expression. Yet other single keystroke commands will jump to the code defining a particular function; a pointing device called a "mouse" can be used to indicate this name if it appears on the screen. Blinkers are used to indicate matching opening and closing parentheses, making it difficult to accidently nest the code incorrectly. Yet another single keystroke command will automatically indent to that place on the next line which is appropriate for this level of s-expression nesting. If one wishes to edit the source of a function which has only been loaded in compiled form, the system automatically fetches it from the file system. Finally, a single keystroke command will enter the new definition into the environment (in either compiled or uncompiled form). This whole editor is itself just a LISP program which can be called from other parts of the system and which can be extended and tailored by the user community to special needs.

Once one has written some code (usually after one has written only a small amount of code) he/she will want to test and debug it. Suppose that there is an error in the code; this will cause an error handling breakpoint to be entered. In this context the user will be "talking to" the interpreter but in the environment obtaining at the time of the error. One can now interactively inspect the value of any variable or move through the stack of function calls leading up to the error, examining what functions had been called, what variable bindings were made at each step. S-expressions can be evaluated in any of these contexts allowing the programmer to ask "What if the code had been written this other way?" At any point in this process the editor can be invoked to inspect or modify any relevant function definitions. Sometimes backing up once the error occurs is inadequate since the function which caused the error has already completed by the time the error manifests itself. In these cases individual functions can be traced or the code can be single stepped, executing each s-expression in turn, proceeding under user control. The error handling facilities and the editor are accessible at any of these stages as well. These facilities can also be used to run a partially developed program. Whenever a part of the program which has not yet been completed is reached an error handling break point is reached. The user can return a value from this break point and the program will continue from this point using this value as if it had been the result returned by the function. Thus, the user can simulate unwritten code, allowing him/her to concentrate on the functioning of that part which has been written until he/she is satisfied with it.

In the most advanced of these systems the above facilities are only a starting point. The use of high resolution displays and pointing devices enhance these capabilities considerably. In all of these cases, however, what makes the interaction smooth is that the system understands the structure of the program and the data upon which it is operating.

It is worth taking note of the particular features of the LISP language which made it possible to develop highly integrated environments very early in the history of the language. The first of these features is the extreme semantic simplicity of the interpreter, the second is the syntactic simplicity of the language and its direct correspondence to linked list data structures.

As we have already mentioned, the Lisp interpreter is quite monotheistic. Its only action is the evaluation of an s-expression by applying a function (the first item of the s-expression) to its arguments (the other items of the s-expression). Since the only way to package code is by defining a function, there is a natural way to trace, single step or cause break points.

The simplicity of program structure in Lisp and the fact that s-expressions are stored internally as linked lists (and that LISP is intended for manipulating linked lists) is the second source of the power of the LISP environments. This ability to treat the code as a data structure allows one to implement trace facilities, for example, just by "wrapping" more code around the original function definition. This extra code can make various checks, print messages, etc. (It can even call the original code). This process of "wrapping" extra code around a function is used for a several purposes and has been given the name of "advising" [Teitelman 1977]. This mechanism, rather than the "doing of violence" to the code suffices for almost all desirable features.

The simplicity of program structure and in particular its print representation makes the job of building a structure-oriented editor much easier than would be the case for syntactically more complex languages. Indeed, this simplicity has led to two distinct approaches to structure-oriented editing of Lisp. One of these (INTERLISP) works on the linked-list representation, generating a print form (or a prettyprinted form as needed). The other approach (LispMachine, Emacs [Stallman 1980a]) works on the print form, incrementally prettyprinting it and generating the linked-list form as needed. Those languages whose syntax definitions run to several pages would find either of these approaches considerably more difficult.

There are several characteristics of the LISP environments which make them particularly well suited to their use in research program development. It is worthwhile to state these features explicitly so that one can consider whether these features might also apply to other programming contexts. The following seem to us to be the key elements:

• *They are highly interactive.* They support and encourage frequent and rapid interaction between the programmer and the computer system. This interaction may take several forms, ranging from display-oriented text editors to interpretive systems, to interactive debuggers for compiled code.

• *They support the incremental development of a program.* "Incremental" should be taken in a fairly general sense. Throughout its lifetime a program goes through several stages with frequent changes. Initially it may exist as a loose mental description of what someone believes he/she wants the program to do. This may then evolve into some kind of more formal specification (or it may not), which in turn may evolve into a design and ultimately into code. At any of these stages the program may also evolve into something either more general or more limited than what was originally intended or expected. This description applies regardless of what methodology a programmer is employing. For example, both "stepwise refinement" and "progressive enrichment" involve some initial description which is then elaborated upon in one way or another. What is unique to the use of an environment is that this process all takes place within the computer, using its resources to help.

• *They include a variety of different tools that the programmer can use for different purposes.* Some of the more standard tools include editors, compilers, debuggers, macro preprocessors, and loaders. Less common are tools like data and control flow analyzers, spelling correctors, configuration controllers, and facilities for remembering previous interactions with the system.

• *The tools provide a coherent and unified whole which is often more than the sum of the individual tools.*   For example, debuggers often access the symbol table produced by a compiler; an editor may keep a data base of changes for later use by an incremental compiler. In some cases (INTERLISP being an excellent example), the tools are highly interconnected, so that many tools take advantage of facilities provided by other tools.

• *They have been tuned carefully to fit naturally into their users' paradigms.*   Natural and frequent operations and commands are often more easily specified than infrequent or obscure ones. Display devices and high quality graphics are often used to enhance the programmer's view of what is happening. Pointing devices (e.g., light pen, mouse) are often more convenient to use than keyboards.

• *The entire runtime environment is accessible to normal programs.*   The process stack, runtime support routines, etc. all exist as explicit data structures and functions which can be called. Thus, the user can easily write extensions to the programming environment or tailor its features to his/her special needs. Many of the features of the current LISP environments have been provided by normal users who were writing programs to meet particular needs; these needs turned out be fairly general and the tools were then incorporated into the system.

The nature of programming is subtly but radically changed by this flexibility. One no longer uses a set of tools to create a program; instead one is part of a community of "system extenders" who achieve their goals by adding to and tailoring a rich programming environment. In such a framework programs are not coded, they are evolved.

• *It is never necessary for the user to think of his code as anything other than the source.*   LISP environments allow direct interpretation of source code as well as execution of compiled code. The two can be mixed in any way the user finds convenient. When debugging or making rapid changes to a section of code the user can work with the source; once a part of a program is stable it can be compiled. If bugs turn up in a compiled program, the source can be substituted to allow the user to debug the program in terms of its source level expression, rather than in terms of its machine language representation. Such flexibility is in principle possible in a completely compiled language, but it is harder to achieve.

In summary, these characteristics lead to the ultimate goal of a programming environment (which is to increase the ability of the programmer to communicate with the computer) by taking advantage of as many naturally occurring structures as is possible.

1.4   Lessons That Have Been Learned

Up to this point, we have tried to be relatively factual. But we believe that there are several important lessons that can be learned from these environments. Although these lessons are based primarily on LISP environments, we believe that they are also applicable outside of LISP. We state these as opinions, because there is clearly room for disagreement. But we feel it important to make them explicit in the hope that future workers will indeed be able to learn from past experiences. The first set of lessons is concerned primarily with the programmer's perception of the environment:

• *It is important to be able to "run" an incomplete program.* Such a program may be incomplete because it is too abstract for conventional techniques to compile it into efficient machine code, or it may be incomplete because it doesn't handle every case required in its specifications. But even when incomplete in these or other ways, it can be extremely valuable to a programmer to be able to try it out, because it enables him/her to focus on a relatively small part of the problem at a given time.

• *The user should be able to view the program from many different natural viewpoints, most of which are "structural" in nature.* For example, there are times when a programmer may want to view a program as a parse tree (when editing), a document (when reading), a control flow graph (when debugging) and a visual image (when looking at it on a screen). The importance of structure is that there are many inconveniences of a programming language that disappear when the need to view it only as a sequence of characters is removed. For example, in an editor for PASCAL, there is clearly no need for forward declarations; they can be supplied perfectly well by a machine when the program's text is passed off to a compiler.

• *Intercommunication among tools is extremely important.* As noted earlier, the most advanced LISP environments seem to be characterized by tools that interact frequently. For example, during a relatively short period the programmer may switch between an editor, interpreter, debugger, and compiler, and each of these, to a degree, must know about each of the others. To do this well is clearly quite difficult and there are many unsolved problems in this area.

• *The programmer should not be required to know the details of the particular language definition used in the current implementation, even though he/she should know the programming language well.* This is extremely important for structure-oriented editors: the commands available to the programmer should be designed around his/her view of the language, not the machine's view of the language. For example, most syntax definitions define a parameter list recursively (a parameter list is a parameter followed by a comma and a parameter list). Imagine the problems which would be caused by an implementation of an editor which made the user follow this definition literally. To get to the third argument he/she would have to first get to the parameter list which is the rest of the given parameter list, then get the rest of that list and then get the first parameter of that parameter list. How much easier it would be to just get the third parameter, leaving the details of what that means to the editor.

Depending on the techniques that are developed for describing the "user's view" of a language, a possible corollary of this lesson is that there does not exist a language-independent generator of language-dependent programming environments (or if one could exist it would not be similar to or as straightforward as the table-driven parser generators used in compiler compilers).

• *The environment's interface must be highly tuned to be as natural as possible for the human programmer.* For example, in an experimental display-oriented editor built on top of INTERLISP's editor, the cursor motion caused by the "right arrow" key actually involves four special cases, depending on the current location in the list structure and what the user sees on the screen. This may seem overly complicated, yet without those special cases, the response to the key feels very unnatural.

The second set of lessons concerns the methodology for developing programming environments:

• *Human interface problems can often be solved by hardware rather than software.* For example, the problem of where to put the cursor when the current edit location is a subexpression of another expression can be solved quite easily if the display device has some way of highlighting part of the screen: highlight the entire subexpression and position the cursor at the operator. As another example, a pointing device such as a "mouse" or a lightpen can be very useful when a programmer wishes to switch between contexts or to make edits which change the syntactic structure of the current expression.

• *When designing environments we should ignore efficiency issues and hardware limitations; when an environment is being used by "real" programmers, efficiency is critical.* Unless we are willing to experiment with potentially inefficient environments, we will forever be limited by today's technology. For example, an INTERLISP programmer pays a fairly high overhead (in terms of time and space) for using such an advanced environment (INTERLISP consumes 150K words out of the 256K words typically available); yet INTERLISP also showed what an advanced environment could be like. The LISP Machine environment consumes even more resources (the initial environment is as large as 1 million words); however, since the LISP Machine environment is designed around newer hardware with an extremely large address space (the address space is 16 million words) these resources are available and the environment performs with adequate efficiency.

As the hardware revolution continues the relative cost of a programming environment will doubtlessly continue to decrease. However, it is important to keep efficiency issues in mind, since the original point of a programming environment is to make the programmer more efficient.

• *The process of developing programming environments is highly experimental.* We have no hope of abstractly defining the "ideal" programming environment, which can then be implemented. Our best strategy, in fact our only viable one, is to continue to develop environments, experiment with them to identify those aspects which are either helpful or useless, and to incorporate these lessons into the next experiment.

2. INTELLIGENT PROGRAMMING ENVIRONMENTS

Interactive programming environments represent a major step forward in the evolution of programming. The next quantum leap will come when programming environments achieve a degree of intelligence. Let us consider briefly what it would be like to use an intelligent programming environment.

2.1 What It Would Be Like

First, interaction between the user and the environment would be almost exclusively in domain-specific or high-level computer science terms. The user would probably never see the "program" which results from the interaction. There would be no need to learn FORTRAN, LISP, or any other computer-oriented language. Rather, the user (probably a domain expert and not a "programmer") would describe his/her problem in whatever terms were natural and convenient. There would be a dialogue of sorts, as the user and environment discuss the problem, eventually agreeing on some high-level description of the problem and an outline of an initial solution.

The next phase might involve experimenting with the solution and alternatives to it. This would probably not require a completely engineered implementation, and would allow the user to get some rapid feedback on some of the assumptions underlying the solution.

Once the user is satisfied with the solution, a fully engineered implementation could be built. This would require fairly little support from the user, except perhaps for comments on efficiency trade-offs that the system is considering. The result of this phase would be not only the target code, but also a data base describing the design decisions that were made during the implementation effort. In effect, this "documentation" would be a complete description linking the domain specific problem description to the low level code.

Later maintenance would not be done at the code level, but rather at the domain level, either in terms of the original problem specification or in terms of the design decisions made during implementation.

In summary, the principal characteristic of an intelligent programming environment is the level of interaction between the environment and the user: primarily domain specific and very high level computer science terms.

2.2 How to Get There

The development of environments such as this clearly require a great deal of research. Two particular directions seem crucial.

2.2.1 Structures to identify and exploit
One critical aspect of interactive programming environments is that they take advantage of different kinds of structure that occur in the programming process, using that structure as an organizational device. The most common structure is some variant of a parse tree. One major direction for future work involves the identification and use of other kinds of structures.

• *Control and data flow.* One very important kind of structure involves control flow and data flow. When a user tries to understand the way a program executes, the control and data flow are more important than the syntactic structure. (Of course, modern programming languages often have syntactic primitives designed to make this easier). While some tools for describing control and data flow exist [Teitelman 1977], much remains to be done. In fact, it is not even clear that the best ways to talk about control and data flow have yet been discovered.

• *Purposive connections.* Another important kind of structure may be termed "purposive connections". Many parts of a program exist so that requirements of some other part are satisfied. Still others exist to meet the overall specifications of the program. There are common patterns of such connections which can be analyzed and catalogued. When the programmer wants to change the structure of his/her system this information can often be put to use to help maintain a consistent and working program. Initial work along these lines has been done in the Programmer's Apprentice project [Rich and Shrobe 1978] [Waters 1979].

• *Programming techniques.* Programmers rarely develop programs from first principles; rather they apply a great deal of knowledge that they have learned, both formally and through practice. It would be of great assistance to a programmer if this kind of knowledge could be structured and made available in a programming environment. Some programming techniques have already been codified into a machine-usable form [Barstow 1979a] [Green and Barstow 1978], but much more must be codified and techniques for making the knowledge simultaneously available to both programmer and environment must be developed.

• *Decision structures.* In the course of developing a program, a programmer makes a large number of design decisions. If these decisions can be recorded explicitly, together with the motivations for making them, it would be much easier for the program to be understood and modified. PECOS and LIBRA [Kant and Barstow 1981] were able to do this for certain moderately-sized symbolic programs: PECOS's knowledge base included descriptions of what decisions were required while LIBRA's abilities at efficiency analysis were used to make these choices.

• *Specification.* The specification of a program involves much more structure than simply a textual description. There are generally inputs and outputs, together with some description of the relationship between them. For real-world programs, such a specification can get quite complex; if the natural structures involved in such specifications can be identified and made explicit it should be of considerable value to the programmer. Abstract datatype specification techniques represent a step in this direction [Musser 1980].

• *Specification development.* Even before a program's specifications can be described, the specification itself must be developed. It seems likely that future programming environments will include tools to assist the user in specification development. While some Artificial Intelligence systems have been built to aid in the interactive development of program specifications (e.g. the PSI system [Green 1977]), this research is still in its infancy.

Note that, in arriving at this step, we have come full circle. Specification development is simply programming where the target language is a specification language rather than a conventional procedural language. But this circle has also brought about a major advancement: programs are now being specified in terms much closer to those of the application domain. A few experimental systems which allow such programming in application domain terms have already been built (e.g. ΦNIX [Barstow et al. 1982]) and this characteristic should be one of the major goals of future experimentation with programming environments.

2.2.2   Techniques for implementing programming environments   In order to develop programming environments along the lines just suggested, it will also be important to develop new implementation techniques. Two categories of techniques seem especially important.

• *Techniques for tool integration.* As noted earlier, many advanced programming environments are characterized by a high degree of tool integration. However, it seems clear that much remains to be learned about the best ways to achieve such integration without sacrificing the modularity that seems so important for large software systems. For example, INTERLISP tools are highly integrated, yet the result is a rather monolithic system which is difficult to modify except along lines foreseen by the initial developers. For example, the fact that the initial I/O device was a line-oriented teletype is so deeply ingrained within INTERLISP that it was extremely difficult to develop a display-oriented editor. It is even more difficult to utilize the display to its maximum advantage. On the other hand, communication between the editor and interpreter of MacLisp/EMACS is done through text files, which to some extent defeats any attempts to achieve tool integration.

• *Human engineering.* Another very important area for development involves the physical interface between the programmer and his/her environment. It seems clear that displays and pointing devices have a strong role to play, but we certainly don't yet know the best way to exploit this newly developed technology. An important related area involves modeling the programmer's view of the developing program. As noted earlier, the appropriate response to a programmer's command seems to depend both on the machine's view of things and on the programmer's view of things. Thus, in order to engineer the environment appropriately we must develop machine-usable models of the programmer's view of things.

2.3 Implications for Software Engineering

The existence of intelligent programming environments would clearly have a major impact on software engineering. There are two areas of special significance.

• *Rapid prototyping.* The need for rapid feedback on specifications is widely recognized. Intelligent programming environments address this need directly, since experimentation with the problem description and solution outline are the primary activities of the first two phases of interaction.

• *Maintenance.* Measurements of time spent in programming activities generally show maintenance to be the dominant activity. The primary difficulty in maintenance is the need to understand the relationship between the code and the specification. The data base of design decisions produced by an intelligent programming environment contains exactly the information needed for this understanding. When coupled with the capability to interact in domain-specific terms, this should considerably reduce the effort required for maintenance and documentation.

2.4 Changing the Nature of Programming

As programming environments grow in intelligence, the distinction between program and environment may vanish. In essence, our current model of programming is that we produce programs that are later run on some target machine. But we may have to change that model: perhaps the basic task of future programmers will be to modify a program and its development environment, never fully separating the two. Winograd and Sandewall have discussed this possibility [Winograd 1979] [Sandewall 1979a]. As we have mentioned earlier the LISP based programming environments which have been developed around the LISP Machine and INTERLISP already have taken on many of these characteristics.

ACKNOWLEDGMENTS

This paper represents the ideas of many people other than the authors. These include both the implementors and the users (the distinction being quite fuzzy) of INTERLISP, MacLisp and the LISP Machine. We gratefully acknowledge their contribution both to our thinking and to our pleasure in programming. Special thanks are due to Erik Sandewall and Alan Perlis who worked with us for several months in the planning of the Schlumberger Workshop on Programming Environments and whose ideas and understandings are reflected (poorly we fear) in this paper.

REFERENCES

[Barstow 1979a] D.R. Barstow. *Knowledge-based Program Construction.* New York: Elsevier North-Holland, 1979.

[Barstow et al. 1982] D. Barstow, R. Duffey, S. Smoliar, S. Vestal. An automatic programming system to support an experimental science. *Sixth International Conference on Software Engineering,* Tokyo, Japan, September 1982.

[Dolotta and Mashey 1976] T.A. Dolotta, J.R. Mashey. An Introduction to the Programmer's Workbench. *Proceedings of the Second International Conference on Software Engineering*, San Francisco, California, October 1976, 164-168; [*Editors' note*: see also [Dolotta et al. 1978]]

[Green 1977] C.C. Green. A summary of the PSI program synthesis system. *Proceedings of the Fifth International Joint Conference on Artificial Intelligence*, Cambridge, Massachusetts, August 1977, 380-381.

[Green and Barstow 1978] C.C. Green, D.R. Barstow. On program synthesis knowledge. *Artificial Intelligence*, 10:3 (November 1978), 241-279.

[Kant and Barstow 1981] E. Kant, D.R. Barstow. The refinement paradigm: the interaction of coding and efficiency knowledge in program synthesis. *IEEE Transactions on Software Engineering*, SE-7:5 (September 1981), 458-471; reprinted in *Interactive Programming Environments*.

[Musser 1980] D.R. Musser. Abstract data type specification in the AFFIRM system. *IEEE Transactions on Software Engineering* 6:1 (January 1980), 24-32.

[Pearson 1979] D.J. Pearson. The use and abuse of a software engineering system. *Proceedings of the National Computer Conference*, AFIPS Proceedings (June 1979), 1029-1035.

[Rich and Shrobe 1978] C. Rich, H. Shrobe. Initial report on a LISP programmer's apprentice. *IEEE Transactions on Software Engineering*, 4:6, November 1978, 456-467; reprinted in *Interactive Programming Environments*.

[Sandewall 1979a] E. Sandewall. *Self-description and reproduction in distributed programming systems*. Informatics Laboratory, Linköping University, report number LITH-MAT-R-79-22, August 1979.

[Stallman 1980a] R.M. Stallman. *EMACS Manual for ITS Users*. Massachusetts Institute of Technology, Artificial Intelligence Laboratory, Memo 554, 1980.

[Teitelman 1977] W. Teitelman. A display-oriented programmer's assistant. CSL 77-3, XEROX PARC, 1977; reprinted in *Interactive Programming Environments*; see also *Proceedings of the Fifth International Joint Conference on Artificial Intelligence*, Cambridge, Massachusetts, August 1977, 905-915.

[Waters 1979] R.C. Waters, A method for analyzing loop programs. *IEEE Transactions on Software Engineering*, SE-5:3 (September 1979).

[Weinberg 1971] G.M. Weinberg. *The Psychology of Computer Programming*. Van Nostrand Reinhold, New York, 1971.

[Weinreb and Moon 1981] D. Weinreb, D. Moon. *The Lisp Machine Manual*. Massachusetts Institute of Technology, Artificial Intelligence Laboratory, 1981.

[Winograd 1979] T. Winograd Beyond programming languages. *Communications of the ACM* 22:7 (August 1979), 391-401; reprinted in *Interactive Programming Environments*.

Bibliography

[ADA Environment Workshop 1979] *Proceedings of the ADA Environment Workshop*, DoD High Order Language Working Group, San Diego, November 1979.

[ADA Phase II Reports 1980] *Dod Common High Order Language ADA Design - Phase II Reports and Analyses*, microfiche.ref. ADA-88-1-M, January 1980.

[ADA Preliminary Manual 1979] Preliminary ADA Reference Manual, *ACM SIGPLAN Notices, Part A*, June 1979.

[ADA Reference Manual 1980] Department of Defense, *Reference Manual for the ADA Programming Language*. July 1980.

[APLSF 1976] *APLSF Programmer's Reference Manual*. Digital Equipment Corporation, Maynard, Massachusetts, DEC-10-LPLSA-A-D, 1976.

[Abrahams et al. 1966] P.W. Abrahams et al. The LISP 2 programming language and system. In *Proceedings of the 1966 Fall Joint Computer Conference*, San Francisco, 661-677.

[Accetta et al. 1980] M. Accetta, G. Robertson, M. Satyanarayanan, M. Thompson *The design of a network-based central file system*, Carnegie-Mellon University, Computer Science Department, Technical Report, August 1980.

[Aho et al. 1974] A.V. Aho, J.E. Hopcroft, J.D. Ullman, *The Design and Analysis of Computer Algorithms*, Addison-Wesley, 1974.

[Aiello et al. 1976] L. Aiello et al. Recursive data types in LISP: A case study in type driven programming. *Proceedings of the Second International Symposium on Programming*, Institut de programmation, Paris, 1976.

[Alberga et al. 1981] C.N. Alberga, A.L. Brown, G.B. Leeman, M. Mikelsons, M.N. Wegman. A program development tool. *Conference Record of the Eighth Annual Symposium on Principles of Programming Languages*, Williamsburg, Virginia, January, 1981, 92-104.

[Allen 1978] Allen, J. *The Anatomy of LISP*. McGraw-Hill, 1978.

[Allshouse et al. 1979] R.A. Allshouse, D.T. McClellan, G.E. Prine, C.P. Rolla. CSDP as an ADA environment. *Proceedings of the ADA Environment Workshop*, DoD High Order Language Working Group, San Diego, November 1979, 113-125.

[Althoff 1981] J. Althoff. Building data structures in the Smalltalk-80 system. *Byte*. (August 1981), 230–278.

[Ambler 1977] A.L. Ambler, D.I. Good, J.C. Browne, W.F. Burger, R.M. Cohen, C.G. Hoch, R.E. Wells. Gypsy: A language for specification and implementation of verifiable programs. *Proceeding of the ACM Conference on Language Design for Reliable Software, SIGPLAN Notices*, 12:3 (March 1977).

[Anderson 1979] O.T. Anderson. *The design and implementation of a display-oriented editor writing system*. Undergraduate thesis, Massachusetts Institute of Technology Physics Department, January 1979.

[Archer et al. 1980] J. Archer, R. Conway, A. Shore, L. Silver. *The CORE user interface*. Cornell University, Department of Computer Science, Tech. Report No. TR80-437, September 1980.

[Ash et al. 1977] W. Ash et al. *Intelligent on-line assistant and tutor system*. Bolt, Beranek and Newman, Report No. 3607, Cambridge, Massachusetts, 1977.

[Ashcroft and Wadge 1977] E.A. Ashcroft, W.W. Wadge. Lucid, a non-procedural language with iteration. *Communications of the ACM* 20:7 (July 1977), 519-526.

[Backus 1959] J.W. Backus. The syntax and semantics of the proposed international algebraic language of the Zurich ACM-GAMM conference. In *Proceedings of the International Conference on Information Processing*, UNESCO, 1959, 125-132.

[Baker 1975] F.T. Baker. Structured programming in a production programming environment. *Proceedings of the International Conference on Reliable Software*, 1975, 172-185.

[Baker 1978] H.G. Baker. List processing in real time on a serial computer. *Communications of the ACM*, 19:4 (April 1978), 280-294.

[Balzer 1969] R.M. Balzer. EXDAMS - EXtendable Debugging And Monitoring System. *Proceedings of the Spring Joint Computer Conference*, AFIPS Proceedings Vol. 34 (1969), 567-580.

[Balzer 1973] R.M. Balzer. Automatic programming. University of Southern California, Information Sciences Institute, 1973.

[Balzer 1974] R.M. Balzer. Language-independent programmer's interface. University of Southern California, Information Sciences Institute, ISI/RR-73-15, March 1974.

[Balzer 1981] R.M. Balzer. Transformational implementation: an example. *IEEE Transactions on Software Engineering*, SE-7:1 (January 1981).

[Balzer and Goldman 1979] R.M. Balzer, N. Goldman. Principles of good software specification and their implications for specification languages. *Proceedings of the IEEE Conference on Specification of Reliable Software*, Cambridge, Massachusetts, April 1979.

[Barnett 1975] J. Barnett. Module linkage and communication in large systems. In D.R. Reddy (ed.) *Speech Recognition*. 1975, 500-520.

[Barstow 1977] D.R. Barstow. *Automatic construction of algorithms and data structures using a knowledge base of programming rules*. Stanford University, Stanford Artificial Intelligence Laboratory, Memo AIM-308, November 1977.

[Barstow 1979a] D.R. Barstow. *Knowledge-based Program Construction* New York: Elsevier North-Holland, 1979.

[Barstow 1979b] D.R. Barstow. An experiment in knowledge-based automatic programming. *Artificial Intelligence* 12:2 (August 1979), 73-119.

[Barstow 1981] D.R. Barstow. The roles of knowledge and deduction in algorithm design. In D. Michie and Y'H. Pao (eds.) *Machine Intelligence 10*, J. Wiley (Halsted Press), 1982.

[Barstow and Kant 1976] D.R. Barstow, E. Kant. Observations on the interaction between coding and efficiency knowledge in the PSI program synthesis system. *Proceedings of the Second International Conference on Software Engineering*, San Francisco, California, October 1976, 19-31.

[Barstow et al. 1982] D. Barstow, R. Duffey, S. Smoliar, S. Vestal. An automatic programming system to support an experimental science. *Sixth International Conference on Software Engineering*, Tokyo, Japan, September 1982.

[Bauer 1976] F.L. Bauer. Programming as an evolutionary process. *Proceedings of the Second International Conference on Software Engineering*, San Francisco, California, October 1976.

[Bauer et al. 1978] F.L. Bauer, M. Broy, H. Partsch, P. Pepper, H. Wossner. Systematics of transformation rules. Technische Universität München, December 1978.

[Belady 1978] L.A. Belady. Large software systems. IBM Watson Research Center, Research Report RC6966, Yorktown Heights, January 1978.

[Bell 1978] *The Bell System Technical Journal*, 57:6 (July-August 1978), Part 2, 1971-1990.

[Berry 1975] D. Berry. Structured documentation. *SIGPLAN Newsletter* (November 1975).

[Bianchi and Wood 1976] M.H. Bianchi, J.L. Wood. A user's viewpoint on the programmer's workbench. *Proceedings of the Second International Conference on Software Engineering*, San Francisco, California, October 1976, 193-199.

[Birtwistle et al. 1973] G. Birtwistle, O.-J. Dahl, B. Myhrhaug, K. Nygaard. *Simula Begin*. Auerbach, Philadelphia, 1973.

[Bishop 1977] P.B. Bishop. *Computer systems with a very large address space and garbage collection*. Massachusetts Institute of Technology, Laboratory for Computer Science, TR-178, May 1977.

[Bobrow 1972] D.G. Bobrow. Requirements for advanced programming systems for list processing. *Communications of the ACM*, 15:7 (July 1982), 618–627.

[Bobrow and Murphy 1967] D.G. Bobrow, D.L. Murphy. The structure of a LISP system using two level storage. *Communications of the ACM*, 10:3 (March 1967), 155-159.

[Bobrow and Raphael 1974] D.G. Bobrow, B. Raphael. New programming languages for AI research. *ACM Computing Surveys* 6:3 (September 1974).

[Bobrow and Wegbreit 1973] D.G. Bobrow, B. Wegbreit. A model and stack implementation for multiple environments. *Communications of the ACM*, 16:10 (October 1973), 591-603.

[Bobrow and Winograd 1977a] D.G. Bobrow, T. Winograd and the KRL Research Group. Experience with KRL-0: One cycle of a knowledge representation language. *Proceedings of the Fifth International Joint Conference on Artificial Intelligence*, Cambridge, Massachusetts, August 1977, 213-222.

[Bobrow and Winograd 1977b] D.G. Bobrow, T. Winograd. An overview of KRL, a knowledge representation language. *Cognitive Science* 1:1 (January 1977), 3-46.

[Boehm 1980] B.W. Boehm. Developing small-scale application software products: Some experimental results. In S.H. Lavington (ed). *Information Processing 80*, North-Holland, 1980, 321-326.

[Borning and Ingalls 1982a] A. Borning, D. Ingalls. A type declaration and inference system for Smalltalk. *Proceedings of the Ninth Annual ACM Principles of Programming Languages Symposium*, Albuquerque, New Mexico, January 1982.

[Borning and Ingalls 1982b] A. Borning, D. Ingalls. Multiple inheritance in Smalltalk-80. *Proceedings of the National Conference on Artificial Intelligence*, Pittsburgh, Pennsylvania, August 1982.

[Bourne 1978a] S.R. Bourne. The UNIX shell. *The Bell System Technical Journal*, 57:6 (July-August 1978), Part 2, 1971-1990.

[Bourne 1978b] S.R. Bourne. An Introduction to the UNIX shell. *The Bell System Technical Journal*, 57:6 (October 1978), 2797-2822.

[Boyer and Moore 1979] R.S. Boyer, J.S. Moore. *A Computational Logic*. Academic Press, New York, 1979.

[Boyle] J.M. Boyle. An introduction to the transformation-assisted multiple program realization (TAMPR) system. Argonne National Laboratory, Applied Mathematics Division (undated).

[Boyle 1978] J.M. Boyle. Extending reliability: Transformational tailoring of abstract mathematical software. *ACM-SIGNUM Conference on Programming Environments for Development of Numerical Software*, October 1978.

[Brachman 1977] R. Brachman. What's in a concept: Structural foundations for semantic networks. *International Journal of Man-Machine Studies*, 9 (1977), 127-152.

[Brinch-Hansen 1973] P. Brinch-Hansen. *Operating System Principles*. Prentice-Hall, 1973.

[Brinch-Hansen 1976] P. Brinch-Hansen. The Solo operating system. *Software Practice and Experience*, 6:2 (1976), 141-206.

[Brotsky 1981] D.C. Brotsky. *Program understanding through cliche recognition*. Massachusetts Institute of Technology, Masters thesis proposal, August 1981.

[Burke 1978] J. Burke. *Connections*. Little Brown, Boston, 1978.

[Burroughs 1969] *Burroughs B6500 information processing systems reference manual*. Burroughs Corporation, Detroit, Michigan, 1969.

[Burstall and Darlington 1977] R.M. Burstall, J. Darlington. A transformation system for developing recursive programs. *Journal of the ACM* 24:1 (January 1977).

[Burstall and Goguen 1977] R.M. Burstall, J.A. Goguen. Putting specifications together. *Proceedings of the Fifth International Joint Conference on Artificial Intelligence*, Cambridge, Massachusetts, August 1977.

[Burstall et al. 1971] R.M. Burstall, R.J. Popplestone et al. *Programming in POP-2*. University Press, Edinburgh, Scotland, 1971.

[Burton 1980] R.R. Burton. Interlisp-D display facilities. In *Papers on Interlisp-D*, Xerox Palo Alto Research Center, Report No. SSL-80-4, Palo Alto, Calif. 1980, 33-46.

[Burton et al. 1980] R.R. Burton et al. Interlisp-D: overview and status. In *Papers on Interlisp-D*, Xerox Palo Alto Research Center, Report No. SSL-80-4, Palo Alto, Calif. 1980, 1-10.

[Buxton] J.N. Buxton. A note on system construction systems. (to be published).

[Buxton 1979] J.N. Buxton. *STONEMAN Material*. September 1979.

[Buxton 1980] *DoD Requirements for ADA Programming Support Environments, STONEMAN*. DoD High Order Language Working Group, February 1980.

[Buxton and Stenning 1979a] J.N. Buxton, V. Stenning. *STONEMAN Informal Draft*. August 1979.

[Buxton and Stenning 1979b] J.N. Buxton, V. Stenning. *STONEMAN Draft*. December 1979.

[Caine and Gordon 1975] S.H. Caine, E.K. Gordon. PDL—a tool for software design. *Proceedings of the National Computer Conference*, AFIPS Proceedings Vol. 44 (1975), 271-276.

[Carlson 1980] W.E. Carlson. ADA: a standard programming language for defense systems. *SIGNAL*, March 1980.

[Cattell 1978] R.G.G. Cattell. *Formalization and automatic derivation of code generators.* Carnegie-Mellon University, Department of Computer Science, Tech. Rept. CMU-CS-78-115, April 1978.

[Cecil et al. 1977] Cecil, Moll, Rinde. *TRIX AC: a set of general purpose text editing commands.* Lawrence Livermore Lab UCID 30040, March 1977.

[Charniak 1972] E. Charniak. *Toward a model of children's story comprehension.* Massachusetts Institute of Technology, MIT-AI-266, 1972.

[Charniak et al. 1980] E. Charniak, C. Riesbeck, D. McDermott. *Artificial Intelligence Programming.* Lawrence Erlbaum Associates, Hillsdale, N.J., 1980.

[Cheatham 1979] T.E. Cheatham Jr. Program development systems. Harvard University, Center for Research in Computing Technology, January 1979.

[Cheatham 1981] T.E. Cheatham, Jr. An overview of the Harvard program development system. In H.Hunke (ed.) *Software Engineering Environments*, North-Holland, 1981, 253-266.

[Cheatham et al. 1979a] T.E. Cheatham, Jr., G.H. Holloway, J.A. Townley. Symbolic evaluation and the analysis of programs. *IEEE Transactions on Software Engineering*, SE-5:4, July 1979.

[Cheatham et al. 1979b] T.E. Cheatham, Jr., J.A. Townley, G.H. Holloway. A system for program refinement. *Proceedings of the Fourth International Conference on Software Engineering*, Munich, Germany, September 1979, 53-63; reprinted in *Interactive Programming Environments*.

[Ciccarelli 1978] E. Ciccarelli. *An introduction to the EMACS editor.* Massachusetts Institute of Technology, Artificial Intelligence Laboratory, AI Memo 447, January 1978 [*Editors' note*: see also [Stallman 1981]].

[Codasyl 1976] Codasyl End User Facility Task Group. A progress report on the activities of the Codasyl End User Facility Task Group. *FDT Bulletin*, issued by ACM-SIGMOD, 8:1, 1976.

[Cohen 1975] P. Cohen. Semantic networks and the generation of context. *Advance Papers of the Fourth International Joint Conference on Artificial Intelligence*, Tbilisi, U.S.S.R. September 1975, 134-142.

[Conrad 1976a] W.R. Conrad. *PROBE User's Guide.* Harvard University, Center for Research in Computing Technology, June 1976.

[Conrad 1976b] W.R. Conrad. *Rewrite User's Guide.* Harvard University, Center for Research in Computing Technology, August 1976.

[Conrad 1976c] W.R. Conrad. COST User's Guide. Harvard University, Center for Research in Computing Technology, November 1976.

[Constable and O'Donnell 1978] R. Constable, M.J. O'Donnell. *A Programming Logic.* Winthrop, 1978.

[Conway 1963] M.E. Conway. Design of a separable transition-diagram compiler. *Communications of the ACM*, 6 (1963), 396-408.

[Conway 1978] R. Conway. *Primer on Disciplined Programming Using PL/CS.* Winthrop, 1978.

[Conway and Constable 1976] R. Conway, R. Constable. *PL/CS—A disciplined subset of PL/I.* Cornell University, Department of Computer Science, Technical Report 76-293, 1976.

[Conway and Gries 1979] R. Conway, D. Gries. *An introduction to programming—a structured approach using PL/I and PL/C.* Winthrop, 1979.

[Cooprider 1979] L.W. Cooprider. *The representation of families of software systems.* Carnegie-Mellon University, Computer Science Department, doctoral dissertation, April 1979.

[Corbato et al. 1965] F.J. Corbato et al. Introduction and overview of the multics system. *Proceedings of the Fall Joint Computer Conference*, Las Vegas, 1965, 185-197.

[Dahl and Hoare 1972] O.-J. Dahl, C.A.R. Hoare. Hierarchical program structures. In O.-J. Dahl, E.W. Dijkstra, C.A.R. Hoare. *Structured programming.* Academic Press, 1972.

[Dahl and Nygaard 1966] O.-J. Dahl, K. Nygaard. SIMULA - An ALGOL-based simulation language. *Communications of the ACM*, 9:9 (September 1966), 671-678.

[Dahl et al. 1970] O.-J. Dahl, B. Myrhaug, K. Nygaard. *Common Base Language*. Norwegian Computing Center Publication S-22, Oslo, 1970.

[Dahl et al. 1972] O.-J. Dahl, E.W. Dijkstra, C.A.R. Hoare. *Structured programming*. Academic Press, 1972.

[Darlington and Burstall 1976] J. Darlington, R.M. Burstall. A system which automatically improves programs. *Acta Informatica*, 6, 1976.

[Davies 1973] D. Davies et al. *Popler 1.5 Reference Manual*. University of Edinburgh, Scotland, 1973.

[Davis 1977] R. Davis. Generalized procedure calling and content directed invocation. *Proceedings of the Symposium on Artificial Intelligence and Programming Languages*, Rochester, New York, August 1977 (published as *SIGPLAN Notices*, 12:8 and *SIGART Newsletter*, 64).

[Davis 1978] R. Davis. Knowledge about representations as a basis for system construction and maintenance. In F. Hayes-Roth, D.A. Waterman (eds.) *Pattern Directed Inference Systems*, Academic Press, 1978.

[DeRemer and Kron 1976] F. DeRemer, H. Kron. Programming-in-the-large versus programming-in-the-small. *IEEE Transactions on Software Engineering*, June 1976.

[Demers et al. 1981] A. Demers, T. Reps, T. Teitelbaum. Incremental evaluation for attribute grammars with application to syntax-directed editors. *Conference Record of the Eighth ACM Symposium on Principles of Programming Languages*, January 1981.

[Deutsch 1973a] L.P. Deutsch. A LISP machine with very compact programs. *International Joint Conference on Artificial Intelligence*, Stanford, California, August 1973, 697-703.

[Deutsch 1973b] L.P. Deutsch. *An interactive program verifier*. University of California, doctoral dissertaion, Berkeley, California, June 1973.

[Deutsch 1981] P. Deutsch. Building control structures in the Smalltalk-80 system. *Byte*. (August 1981), 322–346.

[Dickover et al. 1977] M.E. Dickover, C.L. McGowan, D.T. Ross. Software design using SADT. *Proceedings of the ACM National Conference*, 1977.

[Dijkstra 1976] E.W. Dijkstra. *A Discipline of Programming*. Prentice-Hall, 1976.

[Dijkstra 1977] E.W. Dijkstra. On the interplay between mathematics and programming. E. W. Dijkstra note EWD641, 1977.

[Dijkstra et al. 1975] E.W. Dijkstra et al. On the fly garbage collection: An exercise in cooperation. E. W. Dijkstra note EWD496, June 1975.

[Dippe 1981] M.D. Dippe. Exception-handling in PLAIN. University of California, Laboratory of Medical Information Science, Technical Report #52, San Francisco, 1981.

[Dolotta and Mashey 1976] T.A. Dolotta, J.R. Mashey. An Introduction to the Programmer's Workbench. *Proceedings of the Second International Conference on Software Engineering*, San Francisco, California, October 1976, 164-168; [*Editors' note*: see also [Dolotta et al. 1978]]

[Dolotta and Mashey 1980] T.A. Dolotta, J.R. Mashey. Using a Command Language as the Primary Programming Tool. *Command Language Directions: Proceedings of the 79 IFIP Working Conference on Command Languages*, (D. Beech, ed.) North-Holland, 1980.

[Dolotta et al. 1976] T.A. Dolotta, J.S. Licwinko, R.E. Menninger, W.D. Roome. The LEAP load and test driver. *Proceedings of the Second International Conference on Software Engineering*, San Francisco, California, October 1976, 182-86.

[Dolotta et al. 1978] T.A. Dolotta, R.C. Haight, J.R. Mashey. The Programmer's Workbench. *The Bell System Technical Journal*, 57:6 (July-August 1978), 2177-2200; reprinted in *Interactive Programming Environments*.

[Donzeau-Gouge et al.] V. Donzeau-Gouge, G. Huet, G. Kahn, B. Lang. *The MENTOR User's Manual*. Available from INRIA, Rocquencourt, France.

[Donzeau-Gouge et al. 1975] V. Donzeau-Gouge, G. Huet, G. Kahn, B. Lang, J.J. Levy. A structure oriented program editor: a first step towards computer assisted programming. *International Computing Symposium*, Antibes, France, 1975; also IRIA, Rapport Laboria 114, Avril 1975.

[Donzeau-Gouge et al. 1979] V. Donzeau-Gouge, G. Huet, G. Kahn, B. Lang. Introduction au systeme MENTOR et a ses applications. *Actes des Journees Francophones sur la Certification du Logiciel*, Geneve, Janvier 1979.

[Donzeau-Gouge et al. 1981] V. Donzeau-Gouge, G. Huet, G. Kahn, B. Lang. *The MENTOR Program Manipulation System*, (in preparation).

[Donzeau-Gouge et al. 1984] V. Donzeau-Gouge, G. Huet, G. Kahn, B. Lang. Programming environments based on structure editors: the MENTOR experience. In *Interactive Programming Environments*.

[Druffel 1979] L.E. Druffel. ADA: How will it affect course offerings? *Interface*, I(1979).

[ECL 1974] *ECL Programmer's Manual*. Harvard University, Center for Research in Computing Technology, TR-23-74, December 1974.

[Earley 1974] J. Earley. High level operations in automatic programming. *SIGPLAN notices* 9:4 (1974), 34-42.

[Ellis and Nutt 1980] C.A. Ellis, G.J. Nutt. Computer science and office information systems. *ACM Computing Surveys*, 12:1 (March 1980), 27-60.

[Elzer 1979] P.F. Elzer. *Some observations concerning existing software environments*. Donier Systems GMBH Report, May 1979.

[Engelbart 1971] D.C. Engelbart, Private communication, Stanford Research Institute, Menlo Park, California, 1971.

[Engelbart and English 1968] D.C. Engelbart, W.K. English. A research center for augmenting human intellect. *Proceedings of the Fall Joint Computer Conference*, AFIPS Proceedings Vol. 33, San Francisco, December 1968. 395-410.

[English et al. 1967] W.K. English, D.C. Engelbart, M.L. Berman. Display selection techniques for text manipulation. *IEEE Transactions on Human Factor in Electronics*, HFE-8:1 (March 1967).

[Enslow 1979] P.H. Enslow, Jr. *Portability of large COBOL programs: the COBOL programmer's workbench*. Georgia Institute of Technology, Sept. 1979.

[Falkoff and Iverson 1973] A.D. Falkoff, K.E. Iverson. The design of APL. *IBM Journal of Research and Development*, 1973, 324-334.

[Feiler and Medina-Mora 1981] P. Feiler, R. Medina-Mora. An incremental programming environment. *Proceedings of the Fifth International Conference on Software Engineering*. San Diego, California, March 1981. [*Editors' note*: see also [Medina-Mora and Feiler 1981]]

[Feustal 1972] E.A. Feustel. The Rice Research Computer - a tagged architecture. *Proceedings of the Spring Joint Computer Conference*, 1972, 369-379.

[Fikes and Hendrix 1977] R. Fikes, G. Hendrix. A network-based knowledge representation and its natural deduction system. *Proceedings of the Fifth International Joint Conference on Artificial Intelligence*, Cambridge, Massachusetts, August 1977, 235-246.

[Finseth 1980] C.A. Finseth. *Theory and practice of text editors, or, a cookbook for an EMACS*. Massachusetts Institute of Technology, L.C.S. Technical Memo TM-165, May 1980.

[Fisher 1978] D.A. Fisher. Dod's Common Programming Language Effort. *Computer*, March 1978, 25-33.

[Fisher 1979] D.A. Fisher, Private communication. 1979.

[Fisher and Standish 1979] D.A. Fisher, T.A. Standish. *Initial thoughts on the pebbleman process*. IDA Paper P-1392, June 1979.

[Fisher and Wetherall 1977] D.A. Fisher, P. Wetherall. *DoD Requirements for High Order Computer Programming Languages, Revised IRONMAN*. DoD High Order Language Working Group, July 1977.

[Floyd 1967] R.W. Floyd. Assigning meaning to programs. In J.T. Schwartz (ed.) *Mathematical Aspects of Computer Science*, American Mathematical Society, Providence Rhode Island, 19 (1967), 19-32.

[Floyd 1971] R.W. Floyd. Toward interactive design of correct programs. *International Federation of Information Processing*, 1971.

[Fraser 1977] C.W. Fraser. *Automatic generation of code generators*. Yale University, Department of Computer Science, doctoral dissertation, 1977.

[Fraser 1978] A.G. Fraser. Circuit design aids. *The Bell System Technical Journal*, 57:6 (July-August 1978), 2233-2250.

[Friedman 1974] D. Friedman. *The Little LISPer*. SRA Publications, Menlo Park, California, 1974.

[Galley and Pfister 1975] S.W. Galley, G. Pfister. *The MDL Language.* Massachusetts Institute of Technology, Project MAC Programming Technology Division, Sept 1975.

[George 1968] J.E. George. *Calgen—an interactive picture calculus generation system.* Stanford University, Computer Science Department, Report 114, 1968.

[Geschke and Mitchell 1975] C.M. Geschke, J.G. Mitchell. On the problem of uniform references to data structures. *IEEE Transactions on Software Engineering,* June 1975, 207-219.

[Geschke et al. 1977] C.M. Geschke, J.H. Morris, Jr., E.H. Satterthwaite. Early experience with Mesa. *Communications of the ACM,* 20:8 (August 1977), 540-552.

[Gibbons 1976] Gibbons, G. Letter in ACM Forum. *Communications of the ACM,* 19:2 (1976), 105-106.

[Glasser 1978] A.L. Glasser. The evolution of a source code control system. In S. Jackson, J. Lockett (eds.). *Proceedings of the Software Quality and Assurance Workshop,* ACM, (1978), 122-125; also in *SICSOFT,* 3:5 (November 1978), 121-125.

[Goldberg 1983] A. Goldberg. *Smalltalk-80: The Interactive Programming Environment,* Addison-Wesley, 1983.

[Goldberg and Kay 1976] A. Goldberg, A. Kay. *SMALLTALK-72 Instruction Manual.* Learning Research Group, Xerox Palo Alto Research Center, 1976.

[Goldberg and Robson 1983] A. Goldberg, D. Robson. *Smalltalk-80: The Language and Its Implementation,* Addison-Wesley, 1983.

[Goldberg et al. 1982] A. Goldberg et al. *Smalltalk: Dreams and Schemes.* (in preparation).

[Goldsmith 1974] C. Goldsmith. The design of a procedureless programming language. *SIGPLAN Notices* 9:4 (1974), 13-24.

[Goldstein 1973] I.P. Goldstein. Pretty-printing, converting list to linear structure. Massachusetts Institute of Technology, MIT-AI-279, 1973.

[Goldstein and Roberts 1977] I.P. Goldstein, R.B. Roberts. A knowledge-based scheduling program. *Proceedings of the Fifth International Joint Conference on Artificial Intelligence,* Cambridge, Massachusetts, August 1977, 257-263; also MIT AI-MEMO 405 (February 1977).

[Good 1978] D.I. Good et al. Report on the language Gypsy—Version 2.0 University of Texas at Austin, Certifiable Minicomputer Project, Report ICSCA-CMP-10, 1978.

[Goodenough 1975] J. Goodenough. Exception handling: issues and a proposed notation. *Communications of the ACM* 18:12 (December 1975), 683-696.

[Gordon et al. 1977] M. Gordon, R. Milner, C. Wadsworth. *Edinburgh LCF.* Edinburgh University, Computer Science Department, Report CSR-11-77, 1977.

[Green 1977] C.C. Green. A summary of the PSI program synthesis system. *Proceedings of the Fifth International Joint Conference on Artificial Intelligence,* Cambridge, Massachusetts, August 1977, 380-381.

[Green and Barstow 1978] C.C. Green, D.R. Barstow. On program synthesis knowledge. *Artificial Intelligence,* 10:3 (November 1978), 241-279.

[Green et al. 1979] C.C. Green, R.P. Gabriel, E. Kant, B. Kedzierski, B. McCune, J. Phillips, S. Tappel, S. Westford. Results in knowledge-based program synthesis. *Proceedings of the Sixth International Joint Conference on Artificial Intelligence,* Tokyo, Japan, August 1979, 342-344.

[Greenberg 1979] B.S. Greenberg. Multics Emacs: an experiment in computer interaction. *Proceedings of the Fourth Honeywell International Software Conference,* Bloomington, Minnesota, April 1979.

[Greenberg 1980a] B.S. Greenberg. *Multics Emacs Extension Writers' Guide,* Honeywell Information Systems, Publication #CJ52, Waltham, Massachusetts, 1980.

[Greenberg 1980b] B.S. Greenberg. Prose and CONS (Multics Emacs: a commercial text processing system in Lisp). *Proceedings of the 1980 Lisp Conference,* Stanford, California, August 1980.

[Greenberg and Kissel 1979] B.S. Greenberg, K. Kissel. *Multics Emacs Text Editor User's Guide.* Honeywell Information Systems, Publication #CH27, Waltham, Massachusetts, 1979.

[Greenblatt et al. 1984] R. Greenblatt, T. Knight, J. Holloway, D. Moon, D. Weinreb. The Lisp machine. In *Interactive Programming Environments.*

[Griss 1976] M. Griss. The definition and use of data-structures in REDUCE. *Proceed-*

ings of the ACM Symposium on Symbolic and Algebraic Computation, (R.D. Jenks, ed.), 1976, 53-59.

[Guibas and Wyatt 1978] L.J. Guibas, D.K. Wyatt. Compilation and delayed evaluation in APL. *Proceedings of Fifth ACM Conference on the Principles of Programming Languages,* 1978.

[Guttag 1977] J. Guttag. Abstract data types and the development of data structures. *Communications of the ACM,* 20:6 (June 1977).

[Gutz et al. 1981] S. Gutz, A.I. Wasserman, M.J. Spier. Personal development systems for the professional programmer. *Computer,* 14:4 (April 1981), 45-53.

[Habermann 1979] A.N. Habermann. An overview of the Gandalf project. *Computer Science Research Review 1978-79,* Carnegie-Mellon University, 1979.

[Hall et al. 1980] D.E. Hall, D.K. Scherrer, J.S. Sventek. A virtual operating system. *Communications of the ACM,* 23:9 (September 1980), 495-502.

[Hansen 1969] W.J. Hansen. Compact list representation: definition, garbage collection and system implementation. *Communications of the Association for Computing Machinery,* September 1969, 499-507.

[Hansen 1971a] W.J. Hansen. *Creation of hierarchic text with a computer display.* Argonne National Laboratory ANL-7818, Argonne, Illinois, 1971; also Stanford University, Computer Science Department, doctoral dissertation, June 1971.

[Hansen 1971b] W.J. Hansen. Graphic editing of structured text. In R.D. Parslow, R.E. Green (eds.) *Advanced Computer Graphics.* Plenum Press, London, 1971.

[Hansen 1971c] W.J. Hansen. *Emily user's manual.* Argonne National Laboratory, Argonne, Illinois. 1971.

[Hantler and King 1976] S.L. Hantler, J.C. King. An introduction to proving the correctness of programs. *ACM Computing Surveys,* 8:3 (September 1976).

[Haraldson 1975] A. Haraldson. *LISP - details.* Uppsala University, Computer Sciences Department, 1975.

[Hayes 1974] P. Hayes. Some problems and non-problems in representation theory. *AISB conference,* 1974, 63-79.

[Hayes 1977] P. Hayes. In defence of logic. *Proceedings of the Fifth International Joint Conference on Artificial Intelligence,* Cambridge, Massachusetts, August 1977, 559-565.

[Hearn 1968] A. Hearn. *REDUCE User's Manual.* Stanford University, Stanford Artificial Intelligence Laboratory, Memo 50, 1968.

[Helliwell 1970] R.P. Helliwell. *The Stanford University Drawing System (SUDS),* developed about 1970; Extensive modifications were later made by J. Holloway.

[Hendrix 1975] Hendrix, G.G. Expanding the utility of semantic networks through partitioning. *Advance Papers of the Fourth International Joint Conference on Artificial Intelligence,* Tbilisi, U.S.S.R. September 1975, 115-121.

[Henneman 1964] W. Henneman. An auxiliary language for more natural expression. In E.C. Berkely, D.G. Bobrow (eds.) *The programming language LISP, its operation and applications.* MIT Press, Cambridge, Massachusetts, 1964.

[Hewitt 1972] C. Hewitt. *Description and theoretical analysis (using schemata) of PLANNER: a language for proving theorems and manipulating models in a robot.* Massachusetts Institute of Technology, MIT-AI-TR-258, April 1972; see also C. Hewitt. *PLANNER: A language for manipulating models and proving theorems in a robot,* Massachusetts Institute of Technology, memo 168.

[Hewitt and Smith 1975] C. Hewitt, B. Smith. Towards a programming apprentice. *IEEE Transactions on Software Engineering,* SE-1:2 (March 1975), 26-45.

[Hewitt et al. 1973] C. Hewitt, P. Bishop, R. Steiger. A universal modular actor formalism for artificial intelligence. *Proceedings of the Third International Joint Conference on Artificial Intelligence,* Stanford, California, August 1973, 235-245.

[Hoare 1969] C.A.R. Hoare. An axiomatic basis for computer programming. *Communications of the ACM,* 12:10 (October 1969), 576-580,583.

[Hoare 1971] C.A.R. Hoare. Proof of a program: Find. *Communications of the ACM,* 14:1 (January 1971), 39-45.

[Hoare 1972] C.A.R. Hoare. Proof of correctness of data representations. *Acta Informatica* 1:4 (1972), 271-281.

[Hoare 1973] C.A.R. Hoare. *Recursive data structures.* Stanford University, Computer Science Department, STAN-CS-73-400, 1973.

[Hoare 1978] C.A.R. Hoare. Communicating sequential processes. *Communications of the ACM*, 21:8 (August 1978), 666-677.

[Hodgson and Porter 1980] L.I. Hodgson, M. Porter. BIDOPS: a bi-directional programming system. Department of Computing Science, University of New England, Armidale, N.S.W., Australia, 1980.

[Holbaek-Hanssen et al. 1975] E. Holbaek-Hanssen, P. Handlykken, K. Nygaard. *System description and the Delta language*. Delta project report #4, Norwegian Computing Center Publication #523, September 1975.

[Holloway 1976] G.H. Holloway. *User's guide to the expression analyzer and query facility*. Harvard University, Center for Research in Computing Technology, May 1976.

[Holloway et al. 1978] G.H. Holloway, W.R. Bush, G.H. Mealy. Abstract model of MSG— first phase of an experiment in software development. Harvard University, Center for Research in Computing Technology, TR-25-78, October 1978.

[Holt 1971] A. Holt. Introduction to occurrence systems. In Jacks (ed.), *Associative Information Techniques*. Elsevier, 1971, 175-203.

[Huet et al. 1977] G. Huet, G. Kahn, P. Maurice. *Environment de Programmation Pascal*. Manuel D'Utillisation sous SIRIS 7/8, IRIA, November 1977; [*Editors' note*: see also [Donzeau-Gouge et al]]

[Humby 1973] E. Humby. *Programs from Decision Tables*. McDonald/Elsevier, 1973.

[Ichbiah et al. 1979] J.D. Ichbiah et al. Rationale for the Design of the ADA Programming Language. *ACM SIGPLAN Notices, Part B*, June 1979.

[Ichbiah et al. 1980] J.D. Ichbiah et al. *Reference Manual for the ADA Programming Language*. Advanced Research Projects Agency, U.S. Department of Defense, Arlington, Virginia, 1980.

[Igarashi et al. 1973] S. Igarashi, R. London, D. Luckham. *Automatic program verification I: a logical basis and its implementation*. Stanford Artificial Intelligence Memo 200, May 1973.

[Ingalls 1978] Dan Ingalls. The Smalltalk-76 programming system, design and implementation. *Conference Record of the Fifth Annual ACM Symposium on Principles of Programming Languages*, January 1978, 9-17.

[Ivie 1977] E.L. Ivie. Programmers Workbench—a machine for software development. *Communications of the ACM*, 20:10 (October 1977), 746-753. [*Editors' note*: see also [Dolotta et al. 1978]]

[J. Feldman 1979] J.A. Feldman. High level programming for distributed computing. *Communications of the ACM*, 1979.

[Jackson 1975] M.A. Jackson. *Principles of Program Design*. Academic Press, London, 1975.

[Jensen and Wirth 1977] K. Jensen, N. Wirth. Pascal User Manual and report. *Springer Verlag Lecture Notes in Computer Science*, 18, 1977.

[Johnson and Lesk 1978] S.C. Johnson, M.E. Lesk. Language development tools. *The Bell System Technical Journal*, 57:6 (July-August 1978), Part 2, 2155-2176.

[Johnson and Ritchie 1978] S.C. Johnson, D.M. Ritchie. Portability of C programs and the UNIX system. *The Bell System Technical Journal*, 57:6 (July-August 1978), 2021-2048.

[Joy 1977] B. Joy. *Ex Reference Manual*. Department of Electrical Engineering and Computer Science, University of California, Berkeley 1977.

[Kahn 1978] G. Kahn. Normalisation et documentation des programmes. Note technique, IRIA, Mai 1978.

[Kanerva 1973] P. Kanerva. *TVGUID: A User's Guide to TEC/DATAMEDIA TV-Edit*. Stanford University, Institute for Mathematical Studies in the Social Sciences, 1973 (online document).

[Kant 1979a] E. Kant. A knowledge-based approach to using efficiency estimation in program synthesis. *Proceedings of the Sixth Internation Joint Conference on Artificial Intelligence*, Tokyo, Japan, August 1979, 457-462.

[Kant 1979b] E. Kant. *Efficiency considerations in program synthesis: a knowledge-based approach*. Stanford University, Computer Science Department, Tech. Rept. STAN-CS-79-755, September 1979.

[Kant and Barstow 1981] E. Kant, D.R. Barstow. The refinement paradigm: the interaction of coding and efficiency knowledge in program synthesis. *IEEE Transactions on Software Engineering*, SE-7:5 (September 1981), 458-471; reprinted in *Interactive Programming Environments*.

[Kay 1974] A. Kay. *SMALLTALK, a communication medium for children of all ages.* Learning Research Group, Xerox Palo Alto Research Center, 1974.

[Kay and Goldberg 1976] A. Kay, A. Goldberg. *Personal dynamic media.* Learning Research Group, Xerox Palo Alto Research Center, 1976; excerpts published in *IEEE Computer Magazine*, March 1977, 31-41.

[Kernighan and Mashey 1981] B.W. Kernighan, J.R. Mashey. The UNIX Programming Environment. *Computer*, 14:4 (April 1981), 12-24; reprinted in *Interactive Programming Environments.*

[Kernighan and Plauger 1976] B.W. Kernighan, P.J. Plauger. *Software Tools.* Addison-Wesley, Reading, Massachusetts, 1976.

[Kernighan and Ritchie 1978] B.W. Kernighan, D.M. Ritchie. *The C Programming Language.* Prentice-Hall, Englewood Cliffs, New Jersey, 1978.

[Kernighan et al. 1978] B.W. Kernighan, M.E. Lesk, J.F. Ossanna. Document preparation. *The Bell System Technical Journal*, 57:6 (July-August 1978), 2115-2136.

[Kersten and Wasserman 1981] M.L. Kersten, A.I. Wasserman. The architecture of the PLAIN data base handler. *Software—Practice and Experience*, 11 (1981), 175-186.

[Kersten et al. 1981] M.L. Kersten, A.I. Wasserman, R.P. van de Riet. Troll—a database interface and testing tool (in preparation) 1981.

[King 1969] J.C. King. *A program verifier.* Carnegie-Mellon University, Computer Science Department, doctoral dissertation, 1969.

[King 1971] J.C. King. Proving programs to be correct. *IEEE Transactions on Computers*, 20:11 (November 1971).

[King 1976] J.C. King. Symbolic execution and program testing. *Communications of the ACM*, 19:7 (July 1976).

[Kiscki and Nagel 1976] E. Kiscki, H.-H. Nagel. *Pascal for the DECsystem 10.* Institut für Informatik der Universität Hamburg, Mitteilung NR. 37, IFI-HH-M-37/76, November 1976.

[Knuth] D.E. Knuth. Bit manipulation (draft of section 7.1 of *The Art of Computer Programming*).

[Knuth 1968a] D.E. Knuth. *The Art of Computer Programming, Vols. 1-3.* Addison-Wesley, Reading, Massachusetts, 1968,1969,1973.

[Knuth 1968b] D.E. Knuth. Semantics of context-free languages. *Mathematical System Theory Journal*, 1968, 127-145.

[Knuth 1979] D.E. Knuth. *TEX and METAFONT: new directions in typesetting.* American Mathematical Society and Digital Press, 1979.

[Kowalski 1975] R. Kowalski. Predicate calculus as a programming language. *International Federation of Information Processing*, 1975.

[Krasner 1983] G. Krasner (ed.) *Smalltalk-80: Bits of History, Words of Advice*, Addison-Wesley, 1983.

[Kurtz 1978] T.E. Kurtz. BASIC. *SIGPLAN Notices*, August 1978.

[LIS 1976] *The system implementation language LIS.* CII-Honeywell-Bull, Document 4549 EL/EN, Louveciennes, France, 1976.

[Lamport 1975] L. Lamport. On the fly garbage collection: once more with rigor. Massachusetts Computer Associates CA-7508-1611, Cambridge Massachusetts, August 1975.

[Lampson and Pier 1980] B.W. Lampson, K.A. Pier. A processor for a high-performance personal computer. *Seventh International Symposium on Computer Architecture*, La Baule, France, May 1980.

[Lampson et al. 1974] B.W. Lampson, J.G. Mitchell, E.H. Satterthwaite. On the transfer of control between processes. *Proceedings of Programming Symposium*, Paris, April 1974, *Springer Verlag Lecture notes in Computer Science*, 19 (1974), 181-203.

[Lampson et al. 1977] B.W. Lampson, J.J. Horning, R.L. London, J.G. Mitchell, G.J. Popek. Report on the programming language EUCLID. *SIGPLAN Notices*, 12:2 (February 1977).

[Lauer and Campbell 1975] P.E. Lauer, R.H. Campbell. A description of path expressions by Petri nets. *Second ACM Symposium on Principles of Programming Languages*, 1975, 95-105.

[Leavenworth and Sammet 1974] B. Leavenworth, J. Sammet. An overview of nonprocedural languages. *SIGPLAN Notices* 9:4 (1974), 1-12.

[Lesser 1975] V. Lesser. Parallel processing in speech understanding systems: a survey of design problems. In D.R. Reddy (ed.) *Speech Recognition*. 1975, 481-499.

[Leveson and Wasserman 1981] N. Leveson, A.I. Wasserman. A methodology for information system design based on formal specifications (submitted for publication) 1981.

[Levesque 1977] H. Levesque. *A procedural approach to semantic networks*. University of Toronto, Department of Computer Science, TR-105, 1977.

[Levin et al. 1965] M. Levin et al. *The Lisp 1.5 Programmer's Manual*. Massachusetts Institute of Technology, 1965.

[Lewis and Porges 1979] J.W. Lewis, D.F. Porges. *ALBE/P: a language-based editor for Pascal*. Yale University, Department of Computer Science, 1979.

[Liskov and Zilles 1974] B. Liskov, S. Zilles. Programming with abstract data types. *Proceedings of the ACM SIGPLAN Conference on Very High Level Languages, SIGPLAN Notices*, 9:4 (April 1974).

[Liskov and Zilles 1975] B. Liskov, S. Zilles. Specification techniques for data abstraction. *IEEE Transactions on Software Engineering*, SE-1:1 (March 1975).

[Liskov et al. 1977] B. Liskov et al. Abstraction mechanisms in CLU. *Communications of the ACM*, 20:8 (August 1977), 564-576.

[Liskov et al. 1978] B. Liskov et al. *CLU Reference Manual*. Massachusetts Institute of Technology, Laboratory for Computer Science, Computation Structures Group Memo 161, July 1978.

[Loveman 1977] D. Loveman. Program improvement by source-to-source transformation. *Journal of the ACM*, 24:1 (January 1977).

[Low 1978] J.R. Low. Automatic data structure selection: an example and overview. *Communications of the ACM*, 21:5 (May 1978).

[Lycklama 1978] H. Lycklama. UNIX on a Microprocessor. *The Bell System Technical Journal*, 57:6 (1978), 2087-2101.

[MUMPS 1976] *Introduction to MUMPS-11 Language*. Digital Equipment Corporation, Maynard, Massachusetts, DEC-11-MMLTA-C-D, 1976.

[Macdonald et al. 1980] N.H. Macdonald, L.T. Rase, S.A. Keenan. *Writer's Workbench: computer programs for text editing and assessment*. Bell Laboratories Technical Report, 1980.

[Macsyma 1974] *MACSYMA Reference Manual*. Massachusetts Institute of Technology, Mathlab Group, Project MAC, Cambridge, Massachusetts, September 1974.

[Manna and Waldinger 1979] Z. Manna, R. Waldinger. Synthesis: dreams = > programs. *IEEE Transactions on Software Engineering*, SE-5:4 (July 1979).

[Mashey 1976] J.R. Mashey. Using a command language as a high-level programming language. *Proceedings of the Second International Conference on Software Engineering*, San Francisco, California, October 1976, 169-176.

[Mashey and Smith 1976] J.R. Mashey, D.W. Smith. Documentation tools and techniques. *Proceedings of the Second International Conference on Software Engineering*, San Francisco, California, October 1976, 177-181.

[Masinter 1980] L.M. Masinter. *Global program analysis in an interactive environment*. Xerox Palo Alto Research Center, Report SSL-80-1, January 1980.

[McCarthy 1978] J. McCarthy. The history of LISP. *Sigplan Notices*, 13:8 (August 1978), 217-223.

[McCarthy et al. 1962] J. McCarthy, P. Abrahams, D. Edwards, T. Hart, M. Levin. *LISP 1.5 Programmer's Manual*, MIT Press, Cambridge, Massachusetts, 1962.

[McCarthy et al. 1967] J. McCarthy, D. Brian, G. Feldman, J. Allen. THOR—a display based time sharing system. *Proceedings of the Spring Joint Computer Conference*, AFIP Proceedings Vol. 30 (1967), 623-633.

[McCauley and Drongowski 1979] E.J. McCauley, P.J. Drongowski. KSOS—the design of a secure operating system. *Proceedings of the National Computer Conference*, AFIPS Proceedings (June 1979), 345-353.

[McCauley et al. 1979] E.J. McCauley, G.L. Barksdale, J. Holden. Software development using a development support machine. *Proceedings of the ADA Environment Workshop*, DoD High Order Language Working Group, San Diego, November 1979, 1-9.

[McDermott 1974] D.V. McDermott. *Assimilation of new information by a natural language-understanding system*. Massachusetts Institute of Technology, Artificial Intelligence Laboratory, AI-TR-291, February 1974.

[McDermott and Sussman 1972] D.V. McDermott, G.J. Sussman. *The CONNIVER Reference Manual*. Massachusetts Institute of Technology, Artificial Intelligence Laboratory Memo 259, May 1972.

[McDonald 1974] D. McDonald. The LISP indexer. Massachusetts Institute of Technology, Artificial Intelligence Laboratory, May 1974.

[McWilliams and Widdoes 1978] T. McWilliams, L.C. Widdoes. SCALD: Structured, Computer-Aided Logic Design. *Proceedings of the Fifteenth Design Automation Conference*, June 1978, 271-277.

[Mealy 1978] G.H. Mealy. Notions. In R.T. Yeh (ed.) *Current Trends in Programming Methodology*. Prentice-Hall, 1978.

[Medina-Mora and Feiler 1981] R. Medina-Mora, P. Feiler. An incremental programming environment. *IEEE Transactions on Software Engineering*. SE-7:5 (September 1981), 472-482.

[Melese 1980] B. Melese. *Manipulation des programmes Pascal au niveau concepts du langage*. Universite d'Orsay, These de 3eme cycle, Juin 1980.

[Metcalfe and Boggs 1976] R.M. Metcalfe, D.R. Boggs. Ethernet: distributed packet switching for local computer networks. *Communications of the Association for Computing Machinery*, 19:7 (July 1976), 395-404.

[Mikellsons and Wegman 1980] M. Mikellsons, M.N. Wegman. PDE1L: the PL1L program development environment principles of operation. IBM Watson Research Center, Research Report RC8513, Yorktown Heights, November 1980.

[Miller 1968] R.B. Miller. Response times in man-computer conversational transactions. *Proceedings of the Fall Joint Computer Conference*, AFIPS Proceedings Vol. 33 (1968), 267-277.

[Miller 1978] R. Miller. UNIX—a portable operating system? *Operating Systems Review*, 12:3 (July 1978), 32-37.

[Mitchell 1970] J.G. Mitchell. *The design and construction of flexible and efficient interactive programming systems*, Department of Computer Science, Carnegie-Mellon University, Pittsburgh, Pennsylvania, 1970.

[Mitchell and Wegbreit 1977] J.G. Mitchell, B. Wegbreit. Schemes: a high level data structuring concept. Xerox Palo Alto Research Center, CSL-77-1, January 1977.

[Moon 1974] D. Moon. *MACLISP Reference Manual*. Massachusetts Institute of Technology, Project MAC, 1974.

[Morcos-Oury 1979] E. Morcos-Oury. Etude des effets de bord des appels de procedure et de fonctions dans le langage PASCAL. Universite Paris XI, These de 3eme cycle, Octobre 1979.

[Morgan 1970] H.L. Morgan. Event sequenced programming. Cornell University, Department of Operations Research, Tech report 119, July 1970.

[Morgenstern 1976] M. Morgenstern. *Automated design and optimization of management information system software*. Massachusetts Institute of Technology, Laboratory for Computer Science, doctoral dissertation, September 1976.

[Moriconi 1978] M.S. Moriconi. A designer/verifier's assistant. SRI International, Computer Science Laboratory, Technical Report CSL-80, October 1978.

[Morris and Wegbreit 1976] J.H. Morris, B. Wegbreit. Subgoal induction. Xerox Palo Alto Research Center, CSL-75-6, July 1976.

[Moses 1970] J. Moses. The function of FUNCTION in LISP. Massachusetts Institute of Technology, Project MAC, Memo MAC-M-248, June 1970.

[Mosses 1979] P. Mosses. *SIS - semantics implementation system. Reference Manual and User Guide*. Report DAIMI MD-30, Computer Science Department, Aarhus University, August 1979.

[Musser 1980] D.R. Musser. Abstract data type specification in the AFFIRM system. *IEEE Transactions on Software Engineering* 6:1 (January 1980), 24-32.

[Naur 1969] P. Naur. Programming by action clusters. *Behandling Informations-tidskrift for Nordisk*, 9:3, 1969.

[Nordström 1970] M. Nordström et al. *LISP F1-a FORTRAN implementation of LISP 1.5*, Computer Sciences Department, Uppsala University, Sweden, 1970.

[Nordström 1976] M. Nordström. A method for defining formal semantics of programming languages applied to Simula. Uppsala University, doctoral dissertation, 1976.

[Nordström and Tholerus 1974] M. Nordström, T. Tholerus. *A parsing technique applied to the programming language REDUCE*, Computer Sciences Department, Uppsala University, Sweden, 1974.

[Neuhold 1978] E.J. Neuhold (ed.) *Formal Description of Programming Languages*. North-Holland, 1978.

[O'Neill 1977] J.T. O'Neill (ed.) *MUMPS language standard.* ANSI Standard X11.1, American National Standards Institute, 1977.

[PL/I 1976] *OS PL/I Checkout Compiler, CMS Users Guide.* IBM, SC33-0047/2, 1976.

[Papert 1971] S. Papert. *Teaching children to be mathematicians vs. teaching about mathematics.* Massachusetts Institute of Technology, Artificial Intelligence Laboratory, Memo 249, 1971.

[Parnas 1972] D.L. Parnas. A technique for software module specification with examples. *Communications of the ACM*, 15:5, May 1972.

[Parnas 1975] D.L. Parnas. *On the design and development of program families.* Fachbereich Informatik, Technische Hochschule, Darmstadt, July 1975.

[Pearson 1979] D.J. Pearson. The use and abuse of a software engineering system. *Proceedings of the National Computer Conference*, AFIPS Proceedings (June 1979), 1029-1035.

[Pebbleman 1978] *DoD requirements for the programming environment for the common high order language, PEBBLEMAN.* July 1978.

[Pebbleman 1979] *DoD requirements for the programming environment for the common high order language, PEBBLEMAN revised.* January 1979.

[Pinc and Schweppe 1973] J.H. Pinc, E.J. Schweppe. A Fortran language anticipation and prompting system. *Proceedings of the ACM National Conference*, Atlanta, Georgia, 1973.

[Ploedereder 1979] E.O.J. Ploedereder. Pragmatic techniques for program analysis and verification. *Proceedings of the Fourth International Conference on Software Engineering*, Munich, Germany, September 1979.

[Popek 1979] G.J. Popek et al. UCLA secure UNIX. *Proceedings of the National Computer Conference*, AFIPS Proceedings (June 1979), 355-364.

[Pratt 1973] V. Pratt. Top down operator precedence. *ACM Symposium on the Principles of Programming Languages*, Association for Computing Machinery, 1973.

[Pratt 1977] V. Pratt. The competence/performance dichotomy in programming. *Fourth ACM Symposium on The Principles of Programming Languages*, Association for Computing Machinery, 1977, 194-200.

[Putz 1983] S. Putz. Managing the evolution of Smalltalk. In G. Krasner (ed.) *Smalltalk-80: Bits of History, Words of Advice,* Addison-Wesley, 1983.

[Rashid and Robertson 1981] R.F. Rashid, G.G. Robertson. Accent: A communication oriented network operating system kernel. *Eighth Symposium on Operating Systems Principles,* Association for Computing Machinery, November 1981.

[Reid and Walker 1980] B.K. Reid, J.H. Walker. *Scribe Introductory User's Manual.* Unilogic, Ltd., Pittsburgh, Pennsylvania, 1980.

[Reiger 1976] C. Reiger. The commonsense algorithm as a basis for computer models of human memory, inference, belief and contextual language comprehension. in R. Schank, B. Nash-Webber (eds.) *Theoretical Issues in Natural Language Processing,* 1976, 180-195.

[Reps 1981] T. Reps. *Optimal-time incremental semantic analysis for syntax-directed editors.* Cornell University, Department of Computer Science, Tech. Report No. 81-453, March 1981.

[Reynolds 1970] J.C. Reynolds. GEDANKEN—a simple typeless language based on the principle of completeness and the reference concept. *Communications of the ACM*, 13:5, May 1970, 308-319.

[Rich 1977] C. Rich. *Plan recognition in a programmer's apprentice.* Massachusetts Institute of Technology, Artificial Intelligence Laboratory, Working Paper 147, May 1977.

[Rich 1980] C. Rich. *Inspection methods in programming.* Massachusetts Institute of Technology, Artificial Intelligence Laboratory, MIT/AI/TR-604, August 1981.

[Rich 1981] C. Rich. A formal representation for plans in the Programmer's Apprentice. *Proceedings of the Seventh International Joint Conference on Artificial Intelligence,* Vancouver, August 1981.

[Rich and Shrobe 1976] C. Rich, H.E. Shrobe. *Initial report on a LISP programmer's apprentice.* Massachusetts Institute of Technology, Artificial Intelligence Laboratory, Technical Report 354, December 1976.

[Rich and Shrobe 1978] C. Rich, H. Shrobe. Initial report on a LISP programmer's apprentice. *IEEE Transactions on Software Engineering*, 4:6, November 1978, 456-467; reprinted in *Interactive Programming Environments.*

[Riddle et al. 1978] W.E. Riddle, J.C. Wileden, J.H. Sayler, A.R. Segal, A.M. Staveley. Behavior modelling during software design. *IEEE Transactions on Software Engineering*, SE-4:4, July 1978.

[Ridsdale 1971] B. Ridsdale. The visual display unit for data collection and retrieval. In R.D. Parslow, R.E. Green (eds.) *Advanced Computer Graphics*. Plenum Press, London, 1971.

[Risenberg 1980] M. Risenberg. Software costs can be tamed, developers told. *Computerworld*, Jan. 29, 1980, 1-8.

[Ritchie 1978] D.M. Ritchie. UNIX time-sharing system: a retrospective. *The Bell System Technical Journal*, 57:6 (July-August 1978), 1947-1969.

[Ritchie 1979] D.M. Ritchie. The evolution of the UNIX time-sharing system. *Proceedings of the Symposium on Language Design and Programming Methodology*, Sydney, Australia, 1979.

[Ritchie and Thompson 1974] D.M. Ritchie, K. Thompson. The UNIX Time-Sharing System. *Communications of the ACM*, 17:7 (July 1974), 365-375.

[Ritchie and Thompson 1978] D.M. Ritchie, K. Thompson. The UNIX Time-Sharing System. *The Bell System Technical Journal*, 57:6 (July-August 1978), 1905-1929.

[Ritchie et al. 1978] D.M. Ritchie, S.C. Johnson, M.E. Lesk, B.W. Kernighan. The C programming language. *The Bell System Technical Journal*, 57:6 (July-August 1978), 1991-2019.

[Robinson and Krzysiak 1980] R.A. Robinson, E.A. Krzysiak. An integrated support software network using NSW technology. *Proceedings of the National Computer Conference*, AFIPS Proceedings (1980), 671-676.

[Rochkind 1975] M.J. Rochkind. The source code control system. *IEEE Transactions on Software Engineering*, SE-1:4 (December 1975), 364-370.

[Rosenschein and Katz 1977] S.J. Rosenschein, S.M. Katz. Selection of representations for data structures. *Proceedings of the Symposium on Artificial Intelligence and Programming Languages*, Rochester, New York, August 1977, 147-154 (published as *SIGPLAN Notices*, 12:8 and *SIGART Newsletter*, 64).

[Roubine and Robinson 1978] O. Roubine, L. Robinson. *SPECIAL Reference Manual*. Technical Report CSG-45, SRI International, Menlo Park, California 1978.

[Rovner 1976] P.D. Rovner. *Automatic representation selection for associative data structures*. Tech. Rept. TR10, The Unviersity of Rochester, Computer Science Department, September, 1976.

[Rowe 1976] L.A. Rowe. *A formalization of modelling structures and the generation of efficient implementation structures*. University of California at Irvine, Computer Science Department, doctoral dissertation, June 1976.

[Rulifson et al. 1971] J. Rulifson, R. Waldinger, J. Derksen. A language for writing problem-solving programs. *International Federation of Information Processing*, 1971.

[Rulifson et al. 1972] J.F. Rulifson et al. *QA4, a procedural calculus for intuitive reasoning*, Stanford Research Institute, Menlo Park, California, 1972.

[Rychener 1977] M. Rychener. Production systems: a case for simplicity in AI control structures. Draft of paper submitted to ACM National Conference, 1977.

[S. Feldman 1979] S.I. Feldman. MAKE—a program for maintaining computer programs. *UNIX Programmer's Manual*, 9 (April 1979), 225-265.

[Sacerdoti 1977] E. Sacerdoti. The non-linear nature of plans. *Advance Papers of the Fourth International Joint Conference on Artificial Intelligence*, Tbilisi, U.S.S.R. September 1975, 206-214.

[Sacerdoti et al. 1976] E. Sacerdoti. *QLISP: a language for the interactive development of complex systems*. Stanford Research Institute, Menlo Park, California, 1976.

[Sandewall 1968] E. Sandewall. LISP A: a LISP-like system for incremental computing. *Proceedings of the Spring Joint Computer Conference*, AFIP Proceedings Vol. 32 (1968), 375-384.

[Sandewall 1975] E. Sandewall. Ideas about management of LISP data bases. *Advance Papers of the Fourth International Joint Conference on Artificial Intelligence*, Tbilisi, U.S.S.R. September 1975, 585-592.

[Sandewall 1977] E. Sandewall. Some observations on conceptual programming E.W. Elcock and In D. Michie and (eds.) *Machine Intelligence 8*, John Wiley & Sons, N.Y, 1977.

[Sandewall 1978] E. Sandewall. Programming in the interactive environment: the LISP experience. *Communications of the ACM*, 10:1 (March 1978), 35-71; reprinted in *Interactive Programming Environments*.

[Sandewall 1979a] E. Sandewall. *Self-description and reproduction in distributed programming systems.* Informatics Laboratory, Linköping University, report number LITH-MAT-R-79-22, August 1979.

[Sandewall 1979b] E. Sandewall. *Why superroutines are different from subroutines.* Software Systems Research Center, Linköping University, report number LITH-MAT-R-79-28, November 1979.

[Sandewall 1979c] E. Sandewall. A description language and pilot-system executive for information-transport systems. *Proceedings of the Conference on Very Large Data Bases*, Rio de Janeiro, 1979.

[Sandewall et al. 1979a] E. Sandewall et al. Linköping Office Information System - an overview of facilities and design. *Data*, Copenhagen, January-February 1979.

[Sandewall et al. 1979b] E. Sandewall, E. Jungert, G. Lönnemark, K. Sunnerud, O. Wigertz. A tool for design and development of medical data processing systems. *Proceedings of Medical Informatics*, Berlin, September 1979.

[Sandewall et al. 1980a] E. Sandewall et al. Provisions for flexibility in the Linköping Office Information System. *Proceedings of the National Computer Conference*, AFIPS Proceedings (1980).

[Sandewall et al. 1980b] E. Sandewall, H. Sörensen, C. Strömberg, A system of communicating residential environments. *Proceedings of the LISP Conference*, Stanford, California, 1980.

[Schwartz 1975] J.T. Schwartz. *On programming: an interim report on the SETL project, revised.* New York University, Computer Science Department, Courant Institute of Mathematical Sciences, June 1975.

[Seybold 1978] P.B. Seybold. TYMSHARE's AUGMENT: Heralding a New Era. *The Seybold Report on Word Processing*, 1:9 (October 1978), Seybold Publications, Inc., Media, Pennsylvania.

[Shaw 1979] M. Shaw. A formal system for specifying and verifying program performance. Carnegie-Mellon University, Department of Computer Science, Tech. Rept. CMU-CS-79-129, June 1979.

[Shaw and Wulf 1980] M. Shaw, W.A. Wulf. Toward relaxing assumptions in languages and their implementations. *SIGPLAN Notices*, 15:3 (March 1980).

[Shaw et al. 1977] M. Shaw, W.A. Wulf, R.L. London. Abstraction and verification in Alphard: defining and specifying iteration and generators. *Communications of the ACM*, 20:8 (August 1977), 553-563.

[Shortliffe 1973] E.H. Shortliffe. An artificial intelligence program to advise physicians regarding anti-microbial therapy. *Computers and Biomedical Research*, 6 (1973), 544-560.

[Shortliffe 1976] E.H. Shortliffe. *Computer-Based Medical Consultations.* American Elsevier, New York, 1976.

[Shrobe 1978] H.E. Shrobe. Plan verification in a programmer's apprentice. Massachusetts Institute of Technology, Artificial Intelligence Laboratory, Working Paper 158, January 1978.

[Shrobe 1979] H.E. Shrobe. *Dependency directed reasoning for complex program understanding.* Massachusetts Institute of Technology, Artificial Intelligence Laboratory, Tech. Rept. 503, April 1979.

[Skinner] G. Skinner. *Ged User Documentation.* Cornell University, Department of Computer Science.

[Smith 1969] L.B. Smith. *The use of man-machine interaction in data-fitting problems.* Stanford Linear Accelerator Center, Report 96, Stanford, California, 1969.

[Smith 1970] D.C. Smith. *MLISP.* Stanford Artificial Intelligence Laboratory, Stanford, California, 1970.

[Snow 1978] C.R. Snow. The Software Tools Project. *Software—Practice and Experience*, 8:5 (September-October 1978).

[Snowdon 1971] R.A. Snowdon. PEARL: An interactive system for the preparation and validation of structured programs. Computing Laboratory, University of Newcastle Upon Tyne, November 1971.

[Spitzen et al. 1978] J.M. Spitzen, K.N. Levitt, L. Robinson. An example of hierarchical design and proof. *Communications of the ACM*, 21:12, (December 1978).

[Sproull and Thomas 1974] R.F. Sproull, E.L. Thomas. A network graphics protocol. *Computer Graphics, SIGGRAPH Quarterly*, Fall 1974.

[Stallman 1980a] R.M. Stallman. *EMACS Manual for ITS Users*. Massachusetts Institute of Technology, Artificial Intelligence Laboratory, Memo 554, 1980.

[Stallman 1980b] R.M. Stallman. *EMACS Manual for TWENEX Users*. Massachusetts Institute of Technology, Artificial Intelligence Laboratory, Memo 555, 1980.

[Stallman 1981] R.M. Stallman. *EMACS: The Extensible, Customizable Display Editor*. Massachusetts Institute of Technology, Artificial Intelligence Laboratory, Memo 519a, 1981; reprinted in *Interactive Programming Environments*.

[Standish 1978] T.A. Standish (ed.) *Proceedings Irvine Workshop on Alternatives for the Environment, Certification and Control of the DoD Common High Order Language*, June 1978.

[Standish et al. 1976] T.A. Standish, D. Harriman, D. Kibler, J. Neighbors. *The Irvine program transformation catalogue*. Computer Science Department, University of California at Irvine, January 1976.

[Steele 1975] G.L. Steele. Multiprocessing compactifying garbage collection. *Communications of the ACM*, 18:9 (September 1975), 495-508.

[Steele 1976a] G.L. Steele. *LAMBDA, the ultimate imperative*. Massachusetts Institute of Technology, Artificial Intelligence Laboratory, Memo 353, Feb 1976.

[Steele 1976b] G.L. Steele. *LAMBDA, the ultimate declarative*. Massachusetts Institute of Technology, Artificial Intelligence Laboratory, Memo 379, November 1976.

[Steele 1977] G.L. Steele. *Fast arithmetic in MACLISP*. Massachusetts Institute of Technology, Artificial Intelligence Laboratory, Memo 421, September 1977.

[Steelman 1978] *DoD Requirements for High Order Computer Programming Languages, STEELMAN*. DoD High Order Language Working Group, June 1978.

[Stockenberg and Taffs 1979] J.E. Stockenberg, D. Taffs. Software test bed support under PWB/UNIX. *Proceedings of the ADA Environment Workshop*, DoD High Order Language Working Group, San Diego, November 1979, 10-26.

[Stonebraker et al. 1976] M. Stonebraker, E. Wong, P. Kreps, G.D. Held. The design and implementation of INGRES. *ACM Transactions on Database Systems*, 1 (1976), 189-222.

[Stoneman 1979] *Preliminary STONEMAN*. DoD High Order Language Working Group, November 1979.

[Sussman 1973] G. Sussman. *A computational model of skill acquisition*. Massachusetts Institute of Technology, Artificial Intelligence Laboratory, MIT-AI-297, 1973.

[Sussman and McDermott 1972] G.J. Sussman, D. McDermott. From PLANNER to CONNIVER—a genetic approach. *Proceedings of the Fall Joint Computer Conference*, AFIPS Proceedings (1972).

[Sussman et al. 1970] G.J. Sussman, T. Winograd, E. Charniak. *Micro-Planner Reference Manual*. Massachusetts Institute of Technology, Artificial Intelligence Laboratory, Memo 203, July 1970.

[Suzuki 1976] N. Suzuki. *Automatic verification of programs with complex data structures*. Stanford Artificial Intelligence Laboratory Memo AIM-279, Stanford, California, February 1976.

[Suzuki 1981] N. Suzuki. Inferring types in Smalltalk. *Proceedings of the Eighth Annual ACM Principles of Programming Languages Symposium*, Williamsburg, Virginia, January, 1981.

[Swinehart 1974] D.C. Swinehart. *Copilot: a multiple process approach to interactive programming systems*. Stanford Artificial Intelligence Laboratory Memo AIM-230, Stanford University, July 1974.

[TECO] *TECO Programmer's Reference Manual*. Digital Equipment Corporation, Maynard, Massachusetts, DEC-10-ETEE-D (revised from time to time); see also *PDP-6 Time Sharing TECO*. Stanford University, Stanford Artificial Intelligence Laboratory, Operating Note 34, 1967; see also P.R. Samson. *PDP-6 TECO*. Massachusetts Institute of Technology, Artificial Intelligence Laboratory, AI Memo 81, July 1965.

[Tanenbaum 1978] A.S. Tanenbaum. Implications of structured programming for machine architecture. *Communications of the ACM*, 21 (1978), 237-246.

[Tanenbaum et al. 1980] A.S. Tanenbaum, J. W. Stevenson, H. van Staveren. *Description of an experimental machine architecture for use with block-structured languages*. Informatica Rapport IR-54, Wiskundig Seminarium, Vrije Universiteit, Amsterdam, 1980.

[Teichroew and Hershey 1977] D. Teichroew, E.A. Hershey III. PSL/PSA: a computer-aided technique for structured documentation and analysis of information processing systems. *IEEE Transactions on Software Engineering*, SE-3:1 (January 1977), 42-48.

[Teitelbaum 1976] T. Teitelbaum. A formal syntax for PL/CS. Cornell University, Department of Computer Science, Technical Report 76-281, 1976.

[Teitelbaum 1979] T. Teitelbaum. *The Cornell Program Synthesizer: a microcomputer implementation of PL/CS*. Cornell University, Department of Computer Science, Tech. Report No. TR79-370, June 1979.

[Teitelbaum 1980] T. Teitelbaum. *The Cornell Program Synthesizer: a tutorial introduction*. Cornell University, Department of Computer Science, Tech. Report No. TR79-381, July 1979, revised January 1980.

[Teitelbaum and Reps 1980] T. Teitelbaum, T. Reps. The Cornell Program Synthesizer: a syntax-directed programming environment. *Communications of the ACM*, 24:9 (September 1981), 563-573.

[Teitelman 1969] W. Teitelman. Toward a programming laboratory. *International Joint Conference on Artificial Intelligence*, Washington, May 1969, 1-8.

[Teitelman 1972a] W. Teitelman. Do What I Mean. *Computers and Automation*, April 1972.

[Teitelman 1972b] W. Teitelman. Automated programmering—the programmer's assistant. *Proceedings of the Fall Joint Computer Conference*, AFIPS Proceedings (1972), 917-922; reprinted in *Interactive Programming Environments*.

[Teitelman 1973] W. Teitelman. CLISP—Conversational Lisp. *Proceedings of the Third International Joint Conference on Artificial Intelligence*, Stanford, California, August 1973, 686-690.

[Teitelman 1977] W. Teitelman. A display-oriented programmer's assistant. CSL 77-3, XEROX PARC, 1977; reprinted in *Interactive Programming Environments*; see also *Proceedings of the Fifth International Joint Conference on Artificial Intelligence*, Cambridge, Massachusetts, August 1977, 905-915.

[Teitelman 1978] W. Teitelman. *INTERLISP Reference Manual*. Xerox Palo Alto Research Center, Palo Alto, California, December 1978.

[Teitelman et al. 1971] W. Teitelman, D.G. Bobrow, A.K. Hartley, D.L. Murphy. *BBN-LISP TENEX Reference Manual*. BBN Report, July 1971.

[Tennent 1976] R.D. Tennent. The denotational semantics of programming languages. *Communications of the ACM*, 19:8 (August 1976), 437-453.

[Tennent 1977] R.D. Tennent. Language design methods based on semantic principles. *Acta Informatica*, 8 (1977), 97-112.

[Thacker et al. 1979] C. Thacker, E. McCreight, B. Lampson, R. Sproull, D. Boggs. *Alto: a personal computer*. Xerox Palo Alto Research Center Technical Report CSL-79-11, August 1979.

[Tholerus 1975] T. Tholerus. *REC - a recursive programming language with visible control stack*. Computer Sciences Department, Uppsala University, 1975.

[Thompson 1968] K. Thompson. QED text editor. Bell Telephone Laboratories, Murray Hill, New Jersey, 1968.

[Thompson 1975] K. Thompson. The UNIX command language. In *Structured programming - Infotech state of the art report*. Infotech International Ltd., Berkshire, England, March 1975, 375-384.

[Tichy 1979] W.F. Tichy. Software development based on module interconnection. *Proceedings of the Fourth International Conference on Software Engineering*, Munich, Germany, September 1979.

[Tinman 1976] *DoD Requirements for High Order Computer Programming Languages, TINMAN*. DoD High Order Language Working Group, June 1976.

[Tompa and Ramirez 1980] F. Tompa, R. Ramirez. *An aid for the selection of efficient storage structures*. University of Waterloo, Department of Computer Science, Tech. Rept. CS-80-46, October, 1980.

[Townley 1978] J.A. Townley. Program analysis techniques for software reliability. *Proceedings of the ACM Workshop on Reliable Software*, Bonn University, September 1978.

[Tsichritzis and Klug 1978] D. Tsichritzis, A. Klug (eds.) The ANSI/X3/SPARC DBMS Framework Report of the Study Group on Database Management Systems. *Information Systems*, 3 (1978), 173-192.

[UK MoD ADA Study 1979] *United Kingdom MoD ADA Support System Study.* System Designers Ltd.,/Software Sciences Ltd., 1979.

[Van De Riet 1977] R.P. Van De Riet. Basis- an interactive system for the introductory course in informatics. *International Federation of Information Processing,* 1977.

[Wasserman] A.I. Wasserman. USE: a methodology for the design and development of interactive information systems. In H.-J. Schneider (ed.) *Formal Models and Practical Tools for Information System Design,* North Holland, 31-50.

[Wasserman 1974] A.I. Wasserman. Online programming systems and languages: a history and appraisal. Laboratory of Medical Information Science, University of California, San Francisco, Technical Report #6, 1974.

[Wasserman 1979] A.I. Wasserman. The data management facilities of PLAIN. *Proceedings of the ACM SIGMOD Conference,* Boston, Massachusetts, 1979, 60-70.

[Wasserman 1980] A.I. Wasserman. The design of PLAIN—support for systematic programming. *Proceedings of the National Computer Conference,* AFIPS Proceedings Vol. 49 (1980), 731-740.

[Wasserman and Booster 1981] A.I. Wasserman, T.W. Booster. *String handling and pattern matching in PLAIN.* Laboratory of Medical Information Science, University of California, San Francisco, Technical Report #50, 1981.

[Wasserman and Sherertz 1976] A.I. Wasserman, D.D. Sherertz. A balanced view of MUMPS. *Proceedings of the ACM SIGPLAN/SIGMINI Symposium on Programming Systems in the Small Processor Environment, ACM SIGPLAN Notices,* 11:4 (April 1976), 16-26.

[Wasserman and Shewmake 1981] A.I. Wasserman, D.T. Shewmake. Automating the development and evolution of user dialogue in an interactive information system. In L. Methlie (ed.) *Evolutionary Information Systems.* North Holland, 1981.

[Wasserman et al. 1981] A.I. Wasserman et al. Revised report on the programming language PLAIN. *ACM SIGPLAN Notices,* 16:5 (1981).

[Waters 1976] R.C. Waters. A system for understanding mathematical Fortran programs. Massachusetts Institute of Technology, MIT/AIM-368, August 1976.

[Waters 1978] R.C. Waters. *Automatic analysis of the logical structure of programs.* Massachusetts Institute of Technology, MIT/AI/TR-492, December 1978.

[Waters 1979] R.C. Waters. A method for analyzing loop programs. *IEEE Transactions on Software Engineering,* SE-5:3 (September 1979).

[Wegbreit 1974] B. Wegbreit. The treatment of data types in EL1. *Communications of the ACM,* 17:5 (May 1974), 251-264.

[Wegbreit 1976] B. Wegbreit. Goal-directed program transformation. *IEEE Transactions on Software Engineering,* SE-2:2 (March 1976); also in *Third Annual Symposium on Principles of Programming Languages, ACM SIGPLAN/SIGACT,* January 1976.

[Wegbreit et al. 1972] B. Wegbreit et al. *ECL Programmer's Manual.* Harvard University, 1972.

[Wegner 1980] P. Wegner. The ADA language and environment. *Proceedings of Electro/ 80,* Western Periodicals Co., North Hollywood, California, May 1980.

[Weiher 1967] W. Weiher. Preliminary description of EDIT2. Stanford Artificial Intelligence Laboratory, Operating Note 5, Stanford, California, 1967.

[Weinberg 1971] G.M. Weinberg. *The Psychology of Computer Programming.* Van Nostrand Reinhold, New York, 1971.

[Weinreb 1979] D.L. Weinreb. A real-time display-oriented editor for the LISP Machine. Massachusetts Institute of Technology, Department of Electrical Engineering and Computer Science, undergraduate thesis, January 1979.

[Weinreb and Moon 1981] D. Weinreb, D. Moon. *The Lisp Machine Manual.* Massachusetts Institute of Technology, Artificial Intelligence Laboratory, 1981.

[Weissman 1967] C. Weissman. *LISP 1.5 primer.* Dickenson Publishing Co., Belmont, California, 1967.

[Weizenbaum 1972] On the impact of the computer in society. *Science,* 176 (1972), 609-614.

[Weyer 1982] S. Weyer. *Searching for information in a dynamic book.* Xerox Palo Alto Research Center, Report No. SCG-82-1, Palo Alto, California, February 1982.

[Whitaker 1977] W.A. Whitaker, The U.S. Department of Defense common high order language effort. *SIGPLAN Notices,* February 1977.

[Wilcox 1976] T.R. Wilcox, A.M. Davis, M.H. Tindall. The design and implementation of a table driven, interactive diagnostic programming system. *Communications of the ACM* 19:11 (November 1976), 609-616.

[Winograd 1971] T. Winograd. *Procedures as a representation for data in a computer program for understanding natural language.* Massachusetts Institute of Technology, Artificial Intelligence Laboratory, doctoral dissertation, 1971.

[Winograd 1972] T. Winograd. *Understanding Natural Language.* Academic Press, 1972.

[Winograd 1973] T. Winograd. Breaking the complexity barrier (again). *Proceedings of the ACM SIGIR-SIGPLAN Interface Meeting*, November 1973; reprinted in *Interactive Programming Environments.*

[Winograd 1974] T. Winograd. *Five lectures on artificial intelligence.* Computer Science Department, Stanford University, STAN-CS-459, 1974.

[Winograd 1979] T. Winograd Beyond programming languages. *Communications of the ACM* 22:7 (August 1979), 391-401; reprinted in *Interactive Programming Environments.*

[Winston 1977] P. Winston. *Artificial Intelligence.* Addison-Wesley, 1977.

[Winston and Horn 1981] P.H. Winston, B.K. Horn. *LISP.* Addison-Wesley, 1981.

[Wirth 1971a] N. Wirth. Program development by stepwise refinement. *Communications of the ACM*, 14:4 (April 1971).

[Wirth 1971b] N. Wirth. The programming language PASCAL. *Acta Informatica*, 1 (1971), 25-68.

[Wirth 1977] N. Wirth. Modula: a language for modular multiprogramming. *Software— Practice and Engineering*, 7 (1977).

[Wolf and Woods 1980] J. Wolf, W.A. Woods. The HWIM speech understanding system. in *Trends in Speech Recognition*, Prentice-Hall, Englewood Cliffs, New Jersey, 1980.

[Woods 1970] W. Woods. Transition network grammars for natural language analysis. *Communications of the ACM*, 13:10 (October 1970), 591-606.

[Woods 1975] W. Woods, What's in a link? In D. Bobrow, A. Collins (eds.) *Representation and Understanding*, Academic Press, 1975.

[Woodward 1979] J.P.L. Woodward. Applications for multilevel secure operating systems. *Proceedings of the National Computer Conference*, AFIPS Proceedings (June 1979), 319-328.

[Wulf 1974] W.A. Wulf. *ALPHARD: toward a language to support structured programs.* Carnegie-Mellon University, Computer Science Department, April 1974.

[Wulf 1977] W.A. Wulf. Some thoughts on the next generation of programming languages. In A.K. Jones (ed.) *Perspectives on Computer Science*, Academic Press, 1977.

[Wulf et al. 1976a] W.A. Wulf, R.L. London, M. Shaw. *Abstraction and verification in Alphard: an introduction to language and methodology.* Carnegie-Mellon University, Department of Computer Science, 1976.

[Wulf et al. 1976b] W.A. Wulf, R.L. London, M. Shaw. An introduction to the construction and verification of Alphard programs. *IEEE Transactions on Software Engineering*, SE-2:4 (December 1976).

[Wylbur 1968] *Wylbur Reference Manual.* Stanford University Computation Center, Campus Facility Users Manual, Appendix E, Stanford, California, 1968.

[Yourdon and Constantine 1978] E. Yourdon, L.L. Constantine. *Structured Design*, Yourdon Press, New York, 1978.

[Zelkowitz 1971] M. Zelkowitz. *Reversible execution as a diagnostic tool.* Cornell University, Department of Computer Science, doctoral dissertation, January 1971.

Index

ABOUT THE EDITORS

DAVID R. BARSTOW, of Schlumberger-Doll Research, has written
for a number of books and professional journals and is
internationally recognized as a leader in artificial intelligence
and automatic programming. From 1977 to 1980 he was on the
faculty at Yale University and was a consultant for both the
General Electric Company and Systems Control, Inc. before
joining Schlumberger-Doll Research in 1980. A Phi Beta Kappa
graduate of Carleton College, he received his Ph.D. with
distinction in Computer Science from Stanford University.

HOWARD E. SHROBE, of MIT, is a leading authority in artificial
intelligence. After receiving his B.S. in mathematics from Yale
in 1968, he worked for both the General Electric Company and
Honeywell as a systems engineer. Together with MIT's Charles
Rich and Richard Waters, he started the Programmer's
Apprentice Project, which uses artificial intelligence in
programming environments. Currently, he is a principal
research scientist at the Artificial Intelligence Laboratory at
MIT where he received his masters and Ph.D. degrees. He is
also a member of the technical staff of Symbolics, Inc.

ERIK SANDEWALL, of Linköping University, was educated at
Sweden's Uppsala University where he received his doctorate in
1969. He has taught at Uppsala and MIT, and, since 1975, has
been Assistant Professor of Computer Science at Linköping
University in Sweden. Among his present research interests are
office information systems, application modelling, and
programming environments viewed as one particular kind of
office information system.